EMPIRES
IN WORLD HISTORY

EMPIRES

IN WORLD HISTORY

POWER AND THE POLITICS OF DIFFERENCE

JANE BURBANK AND FREDERICK COOPER

PRINCETON UNIVERSITY PRESS *Princeton and Oxford*

Published by Princeton University Press, 41 William Street, Princeton, New Jersey 08540
In the United Kingdom: Princeton University Press, 6 Oxford Street, Woodstock,
Oxfordshire OX20 1TW

Library of Congress Cataloging-in-Publication Data
Burbank, Jane.
   Empires in world history : power and the politics of difference / Jane Burbank and
Frederick Cooper.
        p. cm.
   Includes bibliographical references and index.
   ISBN 978-0-691-12708-8 (hardcover : alk. paper) 1. World history. 2. World politics.
3. Imperialism—History. 4. Colonization—History. 5. Colonies—History.
6. Power (Social sciences)—History. 7. Difference (Philosophy)—Political aspects—
History. I. Cooper, Frederick, 1947– II. Title.
   D32.B94 2010
   909—dc22   2009036785

British Library Cataloging-in-Publication Data is available

This book has been composed in Bembo
Printed on acid-free paper. ∞
press.princeton.edu
Printed in the United States of America

10 9 8 7 6 5 4 3 2 1

CONTENTS

LIST OF ILLUSTRATIONS

FIGURES

PREFACE

This book began with a series of conversations, with each other—one of us a specialist on British and French colonial empires in Africa and the other a historian of Russian and Soviet empires—with our graduate students when we offered a course titled "Empires and Political Imagination" at the University of Michigan and later at New York University, with colleagues whose expertise covered parts of the world we did not ourselves know well, with participants in numerous conferences and seminars over the last ten years in North America, Eurasia, Africa, and Australia, and with NYU undergraduates when we developed a course on empires for first-year students. Our book reflects this genesis.

Our goal in teaching and in writing has been to make a complex story clear to students at all stages and to readers with an interest in history while challenging scholars' representations of the past. We want to widen perspectives on the political history of the world without relying on the usual—and we think misleading—shorthands and signposts: a transition from empire to nation-state, a distinction between premodern and modern states, a focus on Europe and the west as uniquely powerful agents of change, for good or for evil. The form of this book—both a narrative and an interpretive essay—follows from its multiple goals. Many debates among historians and political theorists lie in the background, most of them still ongoing, and both of us have plunged into these controversies in other contexts. In this book we paint a big picture without arguing over every brushstroke. We do not footnote the many works that have been critical to our study; instead, we provide guides to further reading with each chapter.

This book is about some empires, not all. We have concentrated broadly on Eurasia—from its Pacific to Atlantic edges—with attention to overseas empires in the Americas and Africa, plus some forays elsewhere. One could make different and fully justifiable choices as to which empires to write about, but our Eurasian focus offers both a wide range of imperial types and a story of dense and long-term interaction. We hope the questions we pose will be useful in analyzing other empires and other arenas. This is a book about politics with attention to political economy; it is not an economic history of the world—a subject others have addressed very well. Nor is it a book about imperialism as a singular kind of domination. We explore instead the multiplicity of ways that different empires worked, and look at both the extent and limits of their efforts across time and in a variety of contexts.

A word about terminology. In a book that covers over two thousand years of history, we need to refer to territory now included in a familiar country but where political boundaries have shifted many times. We sometimes describe a historical event taking place in "the territory now known as Spain" or "the space we now call Europe," but this can turn tiresome. We try to make clear shifting relationships between political authority and territory, but in many contexts we use current place-names as a shorthand. It is also a simplification to treat states of any kind as actors and decision makers—as in "France decided to . . ."—but we sometimes take that shortcut, avoiding a long discussion of who within France acted in such a way and who thought differently, except when such distinctions are important to our argument. We have employed contemporary and simplified English-language equivalents for most names and places.

The more significant shortcuts are intrinsic to the project itself. Every few paragraphs in this book covers a field of inquiry graduate students would study for two years before turning to their thesis projects. Our training and research over several decades address a small fraction of the areas and times we consider here. Not having several lifetimes to work on this book, we adopted four strategies. First, we consulted works of compelling synthesis written by specialists in each field—books that pull together the history of an empire over many years or discuss a broad subject—as well as Cambridge and Oxford and other collective histories. Second, we incorporated insights and findings from recent publications on particular empires and their contexts. Third, we participated in conferences on empires and colonialism, where experts debated the latest research.

A partial list of our hosts includes the Social Science Research Council, the School of American Research, Duke University, Harvard University, UCLA, the University of Texas, the University of Wisconsin–Milwaukee, the Netherlands Institute for War Documentation, the Centre d'Etudes et de Recherche International, the Ecole des Hautes Etudes en Science Sociales, Humboldt University, the German Historical Institute in Moscow, the Central European University, the Open Society Institute, the Russian Academy of Sciences, and Bogazici University, as well as Columbia University and New York University (many times over). We presented portions of our work and received valuable comments at the University of Ottawa, Sydney University, Griffiths University in Brisbane, Hobart University in Tasmania, the University of Otago, and the Ecole Normale Supérieure in Paris.

Fourth—and most important—we have relied on our colleagues. Fred Cooper's thoughts on colonial questions benefited greatly from an earlier collaboration with Ann Stoler; Jane Burbank's imperial perspective on Russia owes much to joint projects with David Ransel, Mark von Hagen, and Anatolyi Remnev. We began our joint work on this topic at the University of Michigan, where an exceptionally dynamic academic community helped us get going. Our interest in extending our study to earlier periods and new spaces, such as the Ottoman Empire, took off when Fatma Müge Göçek sent us to Istanbul. The International Institute at Michigan and its director, David Cohen, sponsored the first seminar on the history of empires that we offered in 1999–2000. We note with pride that several students in that seminar have gone on to do distinguished work on empires and are now professors at universities in several areas of the world.

Teaching about empires to a large class of undergraduates after we moved to NYU inspired us to begin writing a book on the subject. We showed early drafts of our manuscript to our new colleagues, who briefed us on current trends in their fields, saved us from embarrassing errors, and pointed us in fruitful directions. We would like to thank in particular Zvi Ben-Dor Benite, Lauren Benton, Joy Connolly, Nicole Eustace, Karen Kupperman, David Ludden, Leslie Peirce, Joanna Waley-Cohen, and Larry Wolff. Students in the graduate seminar on empires at NYU provided numerous insights and, as we inflicted drafts on them, attentive readings. Our undergraduates gave us useful and provocative feedback, and our teaching assistants helped us gauge what worked and what did not. Karen Weber assiduously chased down references, quotations, and figures.

Over several years, colleagues from many universities provided astute readings of all or large parts of various drafts of the manuscript. We appreciate the comments of all who volunteered them, but especially the heroic assistance of those who took on the thickest piles of paper—Jeremy Adelman, Matthew Connelly, Pieter Judson, Beatrice Manz, Mark Mazower, Leslie Peirce, David Ringrose, Kathy Ringrose, Alessandro Stanziani, and Willard Sunderland. Brigitta van Rheinberg has been both an encouraging editor and a stern disciplinarian as we cut our manuscript down to a size that somebody could lift. Dimitri Karetnikov and Clara Platter guided us through the intricacies of putting together an appropriately illustrated book. Shane Kelly created maps of most of the world over two thousand years with skill and patience.

At a critical midpoint in our writing, we benefited from a month of reflection and discussion at the Rockefeller Foundation's Bellagio Center on Lake Como, where Romans had once sojourned. In the final weeks of a project we had lived with for ten years, we enjoyed the hospitality of the brand-new Institut d'Etudes Avancées de Nantes, in a region of France that has fought for and against empires and experienced the profits and destruction of imperial projects for centuries. Our thanks, then, to all who made this book possible.

Nantes, June 2009

EMPIRES
IN WORLD HISTORY

IMPERIAL TRAJECTORIES

We live in a world of nearly two hundred states. Each flaunts symbols of sovereignty—its flag, its seat in the United Nations—and each claims to represent a people. These states, big and small, are in principle equal members of a global community, bound together by international law. Yet the world of nation-states we take for granted is scarcely sixty years old.

Throughout history, most people have lived in political units that did not pretend to represent a single people. Making state conform with nation is a recent phenomenon, neither fully carried out nor universally desired. In the 1990s the world witnessed attempts by political leaders to turn the state into an expression of "their" nationality: in Yugoslavia—a country put together after World War I on terrain wrested out from the Ottoman and Habsburg empires—and in Rwanda, a former Belgian colony. These efforts to create homogeneous nations led to the slaughter of hundreds of thousands of people who had lived side by side. In the Middle East, Sunnis, Shi'ites, Kurds, Palestinians, Jews, and many others have fought over state authority and state boundaries for more than eighty years since the end of the Ottoman empire. Even as people struggled for and welcomed the breakups of empires over the course of the twentieth century, conflicts over what a nation is and who belongs within it flared around the world.

In the 1960s, France, Great Britain, and other former colonial powers—whose empires had once embraced nearly a third of the world's population—became more national after shedding most of their overseas parts, only to cede some of their prerogatives to the European Economic Community and later to the European Union. The breakup of the Soviet Union and its communist empire led to other shifts in sovereignty. Some new states declared themselves multinational—the Russian Federation—while others—Uzbekistan, Turkmenistan—strove to produce homogeneous nations out of their diverse peoples. In central Europe, leaders of several post-Soviet states—the Czech Republic, Hungary, Poland, and others—turned

1

in another direction and joined the European Union, giving up some of their reconstituted authority for the perceived advantages of belonging to a larger political unit.

These conflicts and ambiguities about sovereignty around the globe suggest that historical trajectories are more complicated than a movement toward nation-states. Empires—self-consciously maintaining the diversity of people they conquered and incorporated—have played a long and critical part in human history. For much of the last two millennia, empires and their rivalries, in regions or around the world, created contexts in which people formed connections—as ethnic or religious communities, in networks of migrants, settlers, slaves, and commercial agents. Despite efforts in words and wars to put national unity at the center of political imagination, imperial politics, imperial practices, and imperial cultures have shaped the world we live in.

This book does not follow the conventional narrative that leads inexorably from empire to nation-state. We focus instead on how different empires emerged, competed, and forged governing strategies, political ideas, and human affiliations over a long sweep of time—from ancient Rome and China to the present. We look at repertoires of imperial power—at the different strategies empires chose as they incorporated diverse peoples into the polity while sustaining or making distinctions among them.

Empires, of course, hardly represented a spontaneous embrace of diversity. Violence and day-to-day coercion were fundamental to how empires were built and how they operated. But as successful empires turned their conquests into profit, they had to manage their unlike populations, in the process producing a variety of ways to both exploit and rule. Empires mobilized and controlled their human resources differently, including or excluding, rewarding or exploiting, sharing out power or concentrating it. Empires enabled—and tried to control—connections and contacts. In some circumstances, people saw something to be gained from incorporation into a large and powerful state. More generally, empire was the political reality with which they lived. People labored in enterprises sustaining imperial economies, participated in networks nurtured by imperial contacts, and sought power, fulfillment, or simply survival in settings configured by imperial rule and by imperial rivalries. In some situations, people found ways to escape, undermine, or destroy imperial control; in others, they sought to build their own empires or to take the place of their imperial rulers. Empires compelled political controversies, innovations, conflicts, and aspirations well into the twentieth century. Even today, empire as a form, if not as a name, is still invoked as a political possibility.

Empire was a remarkably durable form of state. The Ottoman empire endured six hundred years; for over two thousand years a succession of Chinese dynasties claimed the mantle of imperial predecessors. The Roman empire exercised power for six hundred years in the western Mediterranean area, and its eastern offshoot, the Byzantine empire, lasted another millennium. Rome was evoked as a model of splendor and order into the twentieth century and beyond. Russia has for centuries sustained imperial ways of ruling over distinctive populations. By comparison, the nation-state appears as a blip on the historical horizon, a state form that emerged recently from under imperial skies and whose hold on the world's political imagination may well prove partial or transitory.

The endurance of empire challenges the notion that the nation-state is natural, necessary, and inevitable, and points us instead toward exploring the wide range of ways in which people over time, and for better or worse, have thought about politics and organized their states. Investigating the history of empires does not imply praising or condemning them. Instead, understanding possibilities as they appeared to people in their own times reveals the imperatives and actions that changed the past, created our present, and perhaps will shape the future.

Imperial Repertoires

This book does not look at all empires in all times and places. It focuses on a set of empires whose histories were distinctive, influential, and, in many cases, entwined. Empires were not all alike; they created, adopted, and transmitted various repertoires of rule. Our chapters describe the ranges of ruling strategies that were imaginable and feasible in specific historical situations, the conflicts that emerged in different power structures, and the contentious relationships among empires that emerged at particular moments and over time drove world history.

An imperial repertoire was neither a bag of tricks dipped into at random nor a preset formula for rule. Faced with challenges day by day, empires improvised; they also had their habits. What leaders could imagine and what they could carry off were shaped by past practices and constrained by context— both by other empires with their overlapping goals and by people in places empire-builders coveted. People on contested territories could resist, deflect, or twist in their own favor the encroachment of a more powerful polity. Recognizing imperial repertoires as flexible, constrained by geography and history but open to innovation, enables us to avoid the false dichotomies of continuity or change, contingency or determinism, and to look instead for actions and conditions that pushed elements into and out of empires' strategies.

Our argument is not that every significant state was an empire, but that for most of human history empires and their interactions shaped the context in which people gauged their political possibilities, pursued their ambitions, and envisioned their societies. States large and small, rebels and loyalists and people who cared little for politics—all had to take empires, their ways of rule, and their competitions into account. Whether this imperial framework has come to an end is a question we address in the final chapter.

We begin with Rome and China in the third century BCE, not because they were the first empires—their great predecessors include Egyptians, Assyrians, Persians, Alexander the Great's enormous conquests, and more ancient dynasties in China—but because these two empires became long-lasting reference points for later empire-builders. Rome and China both attained a huge physical size, integrated commerce and production into economies of world scale (the world that each of them created), devised institutions that sustained state power for centuries, developed compelling cultural frameworks to explain and promote their success, and assured, for long periods, acquiescence to imperial power. Their principal strategies—China's reliance on a class of loyal, trained officials, Rome's empowerment, at least in theory, of its citizens—had lasting and profound effects on how people imagine their states and their place in them.

We next consider empires that tried to move into Rome's place—resilient Byzantium, the dynamic but fissionable Islamic caliphates, and the short-lived Carolingians. These rivals built their empires on religious foundations; their histories display the possibilities and limits of militant monotheism as an arm of state power. The drive to convert or kill the unfaithful and to spread the true faith mobilized warriors for both Christianity and Islam, but also provoked splits inside empires over whose religious mantle was the true one and whose claim to power was god-given.

In the thirteenth century, under Chinggis Khan and his successors, Mongols put together the largest land empire of all time, based on a radically different principle—a pragmatic approach to religious and cultural difference. Mongol khans had the technological advantages of nomadic societies—above all, a mobile, largely self-sufficient, and hardy military—but it was thanks to their capacious notions of an imperial society that they rapidly made use of the skills and resources of the diverse peoples they conquered. Mongols' repertoire of rule combined intimidating violence with the protection of different religions and cultures and the politics of personal loyalty.

The Mongols are critical to our study for two reasons. First, their ways of rule influenced politics across a huge continent—in China, as well as in the later Russian, Mughal, and Ottoman empires. Second, at a time when no state on the western edge of Eurasia (today's Europe) could command loyalty and resources on a large scale, Mongols protected trade routes from the Black Sea to the Pacific and enabled cross-continental transmission of knowledge, goods, and statecraft. Other empires—in the region of today's Iran, in southern India or Africa, and elsewhere—are not described in any detail here, although they, too, promoted connections and change, long before Europeans appeared on the great-power scene.

It was the wealth and commercial vitality of Asia that eventually drew people from what is now thought of as Europe into what was for them a new sphere of trade, transport, and possibility. The empires of Spain, Portugal, France, the Netherlands, and Great Britain do not enter our account in the familiar guise of "the expansion of Europe." In the fifteenth and sixteenth centuries Europe was unimaginable as a political entity, and in any case, geographical regions are not political actors. We focus instead on the reconfiguration of relations among empires at this time, a dynamic process whose consequences became evident only much later.

"European" maritime extensions were the product of three conditions: the high-value goods produced and exchanged in the Chinese imperial sphere; the obstacle posed by the Ottoman empire's dominance of the eastern Mediterranean and land routes east; and the inability of rulers in western Eurasia to rebuild Roman-style unity on a terrain contested by rival monarchs and dynasts, lords with powerful followings, and cities defending their rights. It was this global configuration of power and resources that brought European navigators to Asia and, later, thanks to Columbus's accidental discovery, to the Americas.

These new connections eventually reconfigured the global economy and world politics. But they were a long way from producing a unipolar, European-dominated world. Portuguese and Dutch maritime power depended on using force to constrain competitors' commercial activity while ensuring that producers and local authorities in southeast Asia, where the riches in spices and textiles came from, had a stake in new long-distance trade. The fortified commercial enclave became a key element of Europeans' repertoire of power. After Columbus's "discovery," his royal sponsors were able to make a "Spanish" empire by consolidating power on two continents and supplying the silver—produced with the coerced labor of indigenous Americans—that lubricated commerce in western Europe, across southeast Asia, and within the wealthy, commercially dynamic Chinese empire.

In the Americas, settlers from Europe, slaves brought from Africa, and their imperial masters produced new forms of imperial politics. Keeping subordinated people—indigenous or otherwise—from striking out on their own or casting their lot with rival empires was no simple task. Rulers of empires had to induce distant elites to cooperate, and they had to provide people—at home, overseas, and in between—with a sense of place within an unequal but incorporative polity. Such efforts did not always produce assimilation, conformity, or even resigned acceptance; tensions and violent conflict among imperial rulers, overseas settlers, indigenous communities, and forced migrants appear throughout our study.

Empire, in Europe or elsewhere, was more than a matter of economic exploitation. As early as the sixteenth century, a few European missionaries and jurists were making distinctions between legitimate and illegitimate forms of imperial power, condemning Europeans' assaults on indigenous societies and questioning an empire's right to take land and labor from conquered peoples.

It was only in the nineteenth century that some European states, fortified by their imperial conquests, gained a clear technological and material edge over their neighbors and in other regions of the world. This "western" moment of imperial domination was never complete or stable. Opposition to slavery and to the excesses and brutality of rulers and settlers brought before an engaged public the question of whether colonies were places where humans could be exploited at will or parts of an inclusive, albeit inequitable, polity. Moreover, the empires of China, Russia, the Ottomans, and Habsburgs were not imperial has-beens, as the conventional story reads. They took initiatives to counter economic and cultural challenges, and played crucial roles in the conflicts and connections that animated world politics. Our chapters take up the trajectories of these empires, with their traditions, tensions, and competitions with each other.

We examine as well the strikingly different ways in which imperial expansion across land—not just seas—produced distinct configurations of politics and society. In the eighteenth and nineteenth centuries, the United States and Russia extended their rule across continents. Russia's repertoire of rule—inherited from a mix of imperial predecessors and rivals—relied on bringing ever more people under the emperor's care—and of course exploitation—while maintaining distinctions among incorporated groups. American revolutionaries invoked a different imperial politics, turning ideas of popular sovereignty against their British masters, then constructing an "Empire of Liberty" in Thomas Jefferson's words. The United States, expanding as Americans conquered indigenous peoples or acquired parts of others' empires, created a template for turning new territories into states, excluded Indians and slaves from the polity, and managed to stay together after a bitter civil war fought over the issue of governing different territories differently. In the late nineteenth century the young empire extended its power overseas—without developing a generally accepted idea of the United States as a ruler of colonies.

Britain, France, Germany, and other European countries were less reticent about colonial rule, and they applied it with vigor to new acquisitions in Africa and Asia in the late nineteenth century. These powers, however, found by the early twentieth century that actually governing African and Asian colonies was more difficult than military conquest. The very claim to be bringing "civilization" and economic "progress" to supposedly backward areas opened up colonial powers to questioning from inside, from rival empires, and from indigenous elites over what, if any, forms of colonialism were politically and morally defensible.

Empires, in the nineteenth and twentieth centuries, as in the sixteenth, existed in relation to each other. Different organizations of power—colonies, protectorates, dominions, territories forced into a dominant culture, semi-autonomous national regions—were combined in different ways within empires. Empires drew on human and material resources beyond the reach of any national polity, seeking control over both contiguous and distant lands and peoples.

In the twentieth century it was rivalry among empires—made all the more acute by Japan's entry into the empire game and China's temporary lapse out—that dragged imperial powers and their subjects around the world into two world wars. The devastating consequences of this interempire conflict, as well as the volatile notions of sovereignty nourished within and among empires, set the stage for the dissolution of colonial empires from the 1940s through the 1960s. But the dismantling of this kind of empire left in place the question of how powers like the United States, the USSR, and China would adapt their repertoires of power to changing conditions.

What drove these major transformations in world politics? It used to be argued that empires gave way to nation-states as ideas about rights, nations, and popular sovereignty emerged in the west. But there are several problems with this proposition. First, empires lasted well beyond the eighteenth century, when notions of popular sovereignty and natural rights captured political imagination in some parts of the world. Furthermore, if we assume that the origins of these concepts were "national," we miss a crucial dynamic of political change. In British North America, the French Caribbean, Spanish South America, and elsewhere, struggles for political voice, rights, and citizenship took place *within* empires before they became revolutions *against* them. The results of these contests were not consistently national. Relationships between democracy, nation, and empire were still debated in the middle of the twentieth century.

Other studies of world history attribute major shifts to the "rise of the state" in the "early modern period," two terms tied to the notion of a single path toward a normal and universal kind of sovereignty—the "western" kind. Scholars have advanced different dates for the birth of this "modern" state system—1648 and the Treaty of Westphalia, the eighteenth century with its innovations in western political theory, the American and French revolutions. But expanding our outlook over space and back in time and focusing on empires allows us to see that states have institutionalized power for over two millennia in different parts of the world. A story of European state development and other people's "responses" would misrepresent the long-term dynamics of state power in both Europe and the rest of the world.

To the extent that states became more powerful in England and France in the late seventeenth and eighteenth centuries, these transformations were a consequence of empire, rather than the other way around. As powers trying to control large spaces, empires channeled widely produced resources into state institutions that concentrated revenue and military force. War among empires in the eighteenth, nineteenth, and twentieth centuries set the stage for revolutionary movements that challenged Europe's empire-states.

In other words, this study of empire breaks with the special claims of nation, modernity, and Europe to explain the course of history. The book is an interpretive essay, based on analyses of selected imperial settings. It suggests how imperial power—and contests over and within it—have for thousands of years configured societies and states, inspired ambition and imagination, and opened up and closed down political possibilities.

Empire as a Type of State

What, then, is an empire, and how do we distinguish empire from other political entities? Empires are large political units, expansionist or with a memory of power extended over space, polities that maintain distinction and hierarchy as they incorporate new people. The nation-state, in contrast, is based on the idea of a single people in a single territory constituting itself as a unique political community. The nation-state proclaims the commonality of its people—even if the reality is more complicated—while the empire-state declares the non-equivalence of multiple populations. Both kinds of states are incorporative—they insist that people be ruled by their institutions—but the nation-state tends to homogenize those inside its borders and exclude those who do not belong, while the empire reaches outward and draws, usually coercively, peoples whose difference is made explicit under its rule. The concept of empire presumes that different peoples within the polity will be governed differently.

The point of making such distinctions is not to put things into neatly defined boxes, but the opposite: to look at ranges of political possibilities and tensions and conflicts among them. People frequently tried to turn the polity in which they lived into something else—to claim autonomy from an overbearing emperor in the name of a people or to extend one people's power over others to make an empire. Where "nations" did become meaningful units of power, they still had to share space with empires and to meet challenges posed by them. Would a state that depended on the human and material resources of one people and one territory be able to survive in relation to powers whose boundaries were more expansive? Even today, people in Pacific islands (New Caledonia, in relation to France) or Caribbean ones (Puerto Rico, in relation to the United States) and elsewhere weigh the advantages or disadvantages of disassociating themselves from larger units. As long as diversity and political ambition exist, empire-building is always a temptation, and because empires perpetuate difference along with incorporation there is always the possibility of their coming apart. For these reasons, empire is a useful concept with which to think about world history.

At times, makers of new states consciously built empires of their own, as did revolutionaries against Britain in eighteenth-century North America. At other times, newly independent states pursued a national route, as in decolonized Africa in the late twentieth century, and soon discovered their vulnerability vis-à-vis larger-scale polities. Empires themselves sometimes tried to create nations—preferably on another empire's territory, as British, French, Russian, and Austro-Hungarian leaders did on Ottoman lands in the nineteenth century. There was and is no single path from empire to nation—or the other way around. Both ways of organizing state power present challenges and opportunities to the politically ambitious, and both empires and nation-states could be transformed into something more like the other.

What other political forms can be distinguished from empire? Small-scale groups more or less culturally homogeneous, often organized around divisions of tasks by gender, age, status, or kinship, are frequently considered the antithesis of empire. Some scholars shun the term "tribe" as condescending, but others use it to describe a social group that can be flexible, interactive, and politically creative. In this sense, a tribe may develop as people extend power over others and give themselves a name and sometimes a mission. On the Eurasian steppe, tribes united into huge confederations, and these at times made empires. The Mongol empires of the thirteenth century arose from the politics of tribal formation and confederation.

The fact that tribes, peoples, and nations have made empires points to a fundamental political dynamic, one that helps explain why empires cannot be confined to a particular place or era but emerged and reemerged over thousands of years and on all continents. In conditions of wide access to resources and simple technology, small advantages—larger family size, better access to irrigation or trade routes, good luck, ambitious and skillful rulers—can lead to domination of one group over another, setting in motion the creation of tribal dynasties and kingships. The only way for a would-be king or tribal leader to become more powerful is to expand—taking animals, money, slaves, land, or other forms of wealth from outside his realm rather than from insiders whose support he needs. Once this externalization of sources of wealth begins, outsiders may see advantages in submitting to a powerful and effective conqueror. Emboldened kings or tribal leaders can then use their new subordinates to collect resources in a regular—not a raiding—way and to facilitate the incorporation of new peoples, territories, and trade routes without imposing uniformity in culture or administration. Tribes and kingdoms provided materials and incentives for making empires.

To tribes and kingdoms—polities distinct from empires but with the potential of becoming them—we can add city-states. The ancient Greek city-state gave some later societies models and vocabulary for politics—the city as "polis," a unit of political inclusion and participation—as well as the idea of civic virtue, in which membership implies certain rights and duties. But like the tribe, the city-state was not a uniform, static, or isolated entity. Greek democracy was for free men only, excluding women and slaves. City-states had hinterlands, took part in trade along land and sea routes, and fought against other polities and with each other. City-states that prospered as nodal points in commercial networks or controlled connections as did the Venetians and the Genoese, could become tempting targets for empires, might try to coexist with empires or even turn themselves, as Rome did, into empires.

The political logic of enrichment through expansion has produced empires around the globe as a major form of power. Pharaohs of Egypt, Assyrians, Guptas of south Asia, the Han Chinese, Turkic and other peoples of central Asia, Persians, Malians and Songhai of western Africa, Zulu of southern Africa, Mayans in central America, Incas in South America, Byzantines, and Carolingians in southeast and northern Europe, and the Muslim caliphates all used the flexible strategy of subordinating others to make empires—large, expansionist polities that are both incorporative and differentiated.

Today the most frequently invoked alternative to an empire is the nation-state. The ideology of the nation-state presumes that a "people" asserted and won its right to self-rule. This idea, however, may be the product of a different history—of a state that through institutional and cultural initiatives convinced its members to think of themselves as a single people. Whether its roots are considered "ethnic," "civic," or some combination of the two, the nation-state builds on and produces commonality as well as a strong, often vigorously policed, distinction between those included in and those excluded from the nation.

If nations have been prominent in political imagination in many areas since the eighteenth century, the nation-state was not the only alternative to empire, then or in more recent times. Federation was another possibility—a layered form of sovereignty in which some powers rest in separate political units while others are located at the center, as in Switzerland. Confederation takes this idea one step further by recognizing the distinct personality of each federated unit. As we shall see in chapter 13, as recently as the 1950s influential leaders in French West Africa argued that a confederation in which France and its former colonies would be equal participants was preferable to the breakup of empire into independent nation-states. Canada, New Zealand, and Australia, and later South Africa, became self-governing over the nineteenth and twentieth centuries but remained associated with the "British Commonwealth." In the twenty-first century, confederation in different forms still attracts political attention in Europe, Africa, Eurasia, and elsewhere, suggesting the advantages of distributing governmental functions and aspects of sovereignty over different levels of political organization.

Tribes, kingdoms, city-states, federations, and confederations, like nation-states, have no defendable claim to be "natural" units of political affinity or action; they came and went, sometimes transformed themselves into empires, sometimes were absorbed into empires, disappearing and emerging as empires fought with each other. No single type of state bears a fixed relationship to democracy as a governing principle. From the Roman Republic of the third century BCE to twentieth-century France, we encounter empires without emperors, governed in different ways, called by different names. Dictators, monarchs, presidents, parliaments, and central committees have ruled empires. Tyranny was—and is—a possibility in nationally homogeneous polities, as well as in empires.

What is significant about empires in history was their ability to set the context in which political transformations took place. The enticements of subordination and enrichment kept empires in motion, in tension or conflict with each other and with other kinds of states. Memories of empires past, rejection and fear of empires, and aspirations to make new complex polities inspired and constrained leaders and followers, the ambitious, the indifferent, and the compelled.

Themes

If empire—as a form of state—was persistent over time, empire—as a way of rule—was not uniform. This study focuses on the different ways empires turned conquest into governing and on how empires balanced incorporation of people into the polity with sustaining distinctions among them. As we trace trajectories of empires in this book, we consider the following five themes.

Difference within Empires

Our chapters focus on how empires employed the politics of difference. We use this term more broadly and more neutrally than today's multiculturalists who call for recognition of distinct communities and their presumed values. A claim based on cultural authenticity is only one way to make difference an element of politics. The politics of difference, in some empires, could mean recognizing the multiplicity of peoples and their varied customs as an ordinary fact of life; in others it meant drawing a strict boundary between undifferentiated insiders and "barbarian" outsiders.

Recent studies of nineteenth- and twentieth-century colonial empires have emphasized that empire-builders—explorers, missionaries, and scientists, as well as political and military leaders—strove to make "we/they," "self/other" distinctions between colonizing and colonized populations. From this perspective, maintaining or creating difference, including racialized difference, was not natural; it took work. Colonial states, especially in the nineteenth and twentieth centuries, exerted great effort to segregate space, provide people from the metropole with a home away from home, prevent colonial agents from "going native," and regulate sexual relations between different populations.

If we break out of nineteenth- and twentieth-century reference points and out of European colonial frameworks, social difference takes on other meanings—for both subjects and states. Distinction does not everywhere imply a binary split into colonized and colonizer, black and white. An empire could be an assemblage of peoples, practicing their religions and administering justice in their own ways, all subordinated to an imperial sovereign. For many empires, loyalty, not likeness, was the goal; recognition of difference—particularly of local leaders who could manage "their" people—could enhance maintenance of order, collection of taxes or tribute, and military recruitment. Empires could profit from skills and connections developed by distinct communities. Difference could be a fact and an opportunity, not an obsession.

The extremes of this spectrum between homogenization and the recognition of difference were never fully and durably enacted, but they allow us to think about the consequences of each strategy and of mixes of the two. By way of introduction, we look briefly at two examples.

Over its long existence, the Roman empire tended toward homogenization, based on a distinctive culture that developed as Rome expanded. Rome drew on the prestige of Greek achievements and on practices from conquered regions around the Mediterranean to produce identifiably Roman styles in urban design, arts, and literature. The institutions of Roman empire—citizenship, legal rights, political participation—proved attractive to elites across the huge empire. The notion of a single, superior imperial civilization open in principle to those who could learn its ways was intrinsic to the Roman way of rule. Incorporation through likeness left barbarians, slaves, and others out.

Rome's initial practice of taking other people's gods into the imperial pantheon was later compromised by the spread of monotheistic Christianity, especially when it became a state religion in the fourth century CE. This more restrictive and homogenizing Roman model endured long after the empire fell. Rome imagined as a Christian civilization whose light could shine around the world became a reference point for later empires—Byzantine, Carolingian, Spanish, Portuguese, and others. Islamic empires that tried to take Rome's place also struggled to make a unified religious community, founded on the worship of one god.

The Mongols' imperial strategies offer a strong contrast to this homogenizing strategy. From early times, the steppe empires of inner Asia were not built around a fixed capital or a central cultural or religious conception but founded on a superior person, the Great Khan. The leaders of the far-reaching Mongol empires of the thirteenth century learned their statecraft from both Eurasian and Chinese sources. Mongol empires sheltered Buddhism, Confucianism, Christianity, Daoism, and Islam; Mongol rulers employed Muslim administrators across Eurasia and fostered arts and sciences produced by Arab, Persian, and Chinese civilizations. Empire in the Mongol style, where diversity was treated as both normal and useful, inflected repertoires of power across Eurasia and on its edges.

All empires were to some degree reliant on both incorporation and differentiation. Empires could mix, match, and transform their ways of rule. Roman-style centralization and homogeneity—missions to civilize and exploit the backward—were tempting to some Russian and Ottoman modernizers in the nineteenth century, when western European empires seemed to be outpacing eastern ones. But transformations—wished for or unconsciously adopted—were more likely to be partial and could go in both directions. In Russia, reformers found that attempts to impose uniformity ran up against the vested and competing interests of local intermediaries with a stake in the imperial edifice. And nineteenth-century British officials—who could hardly admit to using Mongol techniques—sometimes acted like the other kind of empire, concentrating firepower, terrorizing populations, and then moving on, leaving in place a thin administration that compromised with local leaders, extracted revenue, and was cautious—and miserly—about spreading British education and culture.

Imperial Intermediaries

Rulers of empire sent out agents—governors, generals, tax collectors—to take charge of territories they incorporated. Could they send enough of these people—at sufficiently low cost—to govern every village or district in a widely dispersed realm? Rarely. Most often, imperial rulers needed the skills, knowledge, and authority of people from a conquered society—elites who could gain from cooperation or people who had earlier been marginal and could see advantages in serving the victorious power. Another kind of intermediary was a person from the homeland. What Romans referred to as "colonies" and the English in the seventeenth century called "plantations" took people from an empire's core to new lands. Transplanted groups, dependent on linkages to home, were expected to act in the imperial interest.

Co-opting indigenous elites and sending settlers were strategies that relied on intermediaries' own social connections to ensure their cooperation. Another tactic was just the opposite: putting slaves or other people detached from their communities of origin—and dependent for their welfare and survival solely on their imperial masters—in positions of authority. This strategy was used effectively by the Ottomans, whose highest administrators and commanders had been extracted from their families as boys and brought up in the sultan's household. In this case, dependence and difference were entwined: it was usually Christian boys who were converted into the sultan's officials.

Imperial agents, wherever they were from, required incentives as well as discipline. Empires unintentionally created subversive possibilities for intermediaries, who could circumvent imperial purposes by establishing alternative networks or allegiances, attaching themselves to other empires, or rebelling, as did some European settlers in the Americas in the eighteenth and nineteenth centuries. Because empires preserved distinction, they augmented centrifugal possibilities: discontented intermediaries could find institutional or cultural supports for their actions. What successful empires produced, usually, was neither consistent loyalty nor constant resistance: they produced contingent accommodation.

By focusing on intermediaries, we emphasize a kind of political relationship that is often downplayed or ignored today—vertical connections between rulers, their agents, and their subjects. We tend to think of nations in horizontal terms—all citizens are equivalent. Or we describe societies as stratified—nobles, elites, commoners, masses, subalterns, workers, peasants, colonizers, colonized. The study of empires goes beyond the categories of equal individuals or layered groups and draws attention to people pushing and tugging on relationships with those above and below them, changing but only sometimes breaking the lines of authority and power.

Imperial Intersections: Imitation, Conflict, Transformation

Empires did not act alone. Relationships *among* empires were critical to their politics and to their subjects' possibilities. At times, elites in Rome and China thought of themselves as having no rivals; they had difficulties on their borders, but these were provoked, in their view, by uncivilized inferiors, not equivalent powers. But some of these outsiders—for example, Goths in west Eurasia and Xiongnu nomads in the east—enhanced their own capacities by raiding, bargaining, or serving their powerful settled neighbors. Imperial edges—on land or sea—offered opportunities to rivals. Intersections between nomadic and settled peoples were formative for empires, as each drew on the other's technological and administrative skills. Distance from an imperial center could allow fledgling empires to take off. In Arabia, crossed by trade routes but far from imperial controls, Muslim leaders in the seventh century had a chance to consolidate their followers and expand, mostly across territory that had once been Roman.

The intersection of empires provoked competition, imitation, and innovation—and both war and peace. Fragmentation of empires had lasting consequences for the future. For centuries after Rome's hold gave way, ambitious rulers aspired to put together an empire on a Roman scale; aspirants included Charlemagne, Charles V, Suleiman the Magnificent, Napoleon, and Hitler. In Europe, no would-be emperor ever won the contest to replace Rome. The most powerful constraint on making a new unipolar power was other empires: the British and Russian empires were crucial to defeating, over a century apart, the imperial plans of Napoleon and Hitler.

Rivalry among a small number of empires, each with resources beyond any one nation, drove the history of the twentieth century—initiating the two world wars that widened and transformed, yet again, the competition among great powers. Japan's imperial conquests in southeast Asia opened a wedge in Europe's colonial empires, allowing former imperial intermediaries to make bids or wars for their own states, but imperial competition reemerged in cold, hot, and economic wars that continue to this day. From Rome and China to the present, the intersections of empires and their efforts to exercise power over distance, over different peoples, and over other states have had transforming consequences for politics, knowledge, and lives.

Imperial Imaginaries

Imperial leaders, at any time or place, could imagine only so many ways to run a state. For many rulers or would-be rulers, imperial context and experience were formative. In some empires, religious ideas provided a moral foundation for power but also provoked contestation. Both the Byzantines and the Islamic caliphates faced challenges from groups whose principles derived from shared religious values. Catholicism served as both legitimation and irritant to Spanish empire; Bartolomé de las Casas's denunciation of Spanish violence against Indians in the Americas in the sixteenth century called on Christians to live up to their purported principles. "Civilizing missions" declared by European empires in the nineteenth century existed in tension with racial theories. The missionary and the mine owner did not necessarily see empire in the same terms.

The question of political imagination is thus central to our study. Attention to the imperial context helps us understand the kinds of social relations and institutions that were conceivable or plausible in specific situations. For instance, when a revolution opened up the language of "the citizen" and "the nation" in France in 1789, this produced both a debate in Paris and a revolution in the Caribbean over whether these concepts applied on islands where slavery and racial oppression had reigned. Imperial experience could inspire political creativity, as when people who grew up in the Russian empire designed the world's first communist state as a federation of national republics. The variety and dynamic of political ideas in the past—when empires both opened up political imagination and constrained it—caution us not to take today's political structures so much for granted that we blind ourselves to a fuller array of alternatives.

Repertoires of Power

Emperors stood atop pyramids of authority, sometimes trying to build upon rather than crush their subordinates' claims to a territory or a group of people. Within a single empire, some parts might be ruled directly from the center, while in others local elites retained partial sovereignty. Emperors and other imperial governors and their subordinates could try to adjust these arrangements. The fact that empires could redefine their allocations of power and privilege made them ambiguous kinds of states, capable of adapting to new circumstances. Political flexibility could give empires long lives.

We emphasize repertoires of imperial power, not typologies. Empire was a variable political form, and we accent the multiple ways in which incorporation and difference were conjugated. Empires' durability depended to a large extent on their ability to combine and shift strategies, from consolidating territory to planting enclaves, from loose supervision of intermediaries to tight, top-down control, from frank assertion of imperial authority to denial of acting like an empire. Unitary kingdoms, city-states, tribes, and nation-states were less able to respond as flexibly to a changing world.

The pragmatic, interactive, accommodating capacity of empires makes us skeptical of arguments that assume a fundamental redefinition of sovereignty, usually dated to the seventeenth century, when Europeans are said to have created a new system of potentially national and separate states. Whatever political theorists wrote (and elites and emperors wanted to believe), political power at that time and after, and well beyond Europe's confines, continued to be distributed in complex and changing ways. The world did not then—and still does not—consist of billiard-ball states, with impermeable sovereignty, bouncing off each other.

The history of empires allows us instead to envision sovereignty as shared out, layered, overlapping. Catherine the Great of Russia was at once and officially an empress, an autocrat, a tsaritsa, a lord, a grand princess, a commander, and a "possessor" of her various lands and peoples. Napoleon left kings or princes in place in some areas he conquered while ruling others more directly with his famous prefects. Private corporations with charters from European powers exercised functions of state from the late sixteenth (the Dutch East India Company, the British Levant and East India companies) to the end of the nineteenth century (the British East Africa Company). In the nineteenth and twentieth centuries Britain, France, and other powers proclaimed "protectorates" over some areas—Morocco, Tunisia, parts of coastal east Africa, and parts of Vietnam—under the fiction that the local ruler, while remaining sovereign, had voluntarily ceded some of his powers to the protecting empire.

The kind of sovereignty regime and the particular structures of power could make a difference to how states emerged out of colonial empires. That Morocco and Tunisia exited the French empire with less violence than did Algeria had much to do with the formers' status as protectorates and the latter's as an integral part of the French Republic. The possibility and sometimes the reality of layered sovereignty were long-lasting within European empires. And in other areas of imperial transformation—such as the Russian Federation formed in 1991—nested and manipulable sovereignty continues to the present.

The Dynamics of Empire

Although distinguishing empires with chronological labels—"modern," "premodern," or "ancient"—is tautological and unrevealing, empires did change over time and in space. Empires' capacities and strategies altered as competition drove innovations in ideas and technology and as conflicts challenged or enhanced imperial might.

A few key shifts in these repertoires underpin the arguments of this book. The alliance between monotheism and empire—in fourth-century Rome and seventh-century Arabia—was a transformation of enormous importance, setting forth a restrictive idea of legitimacy—one empire, one emperor, one god. Both Christianity and Islam were shaped by their imperial origins. Christianity emerged inside a powerful empire and in tension with it, setting limits on the kinds of power early Christian leaders could claim. In some later circumstances, clerics reinforced imperial unity; in others popes contested the power of kings. Islam developed on the edge of previous empires. Its leaders had the space to develop a religious community and then to build a specifically Islamic form of power. In both cases, claims to speak for one god were repeatedly contested, producing schisms within empires as well as jihads and crusades between them. Competitions for universal empire founded on religious community continued in the formerly Roman sphere for over a millennium—and in transmuted forms have emerged again in the enlarged world of the twenty-first century.

Across the Eurasian landmass, political transformation was driven by nomads' capacity for making empires or making deals with them. Nomads upped the military ante in early times when they introduced the armed and mounted warrior as the weapon of choice. The most dramatic and influential of nomads' political interventions came from the Mongols in the thirteenth century. Through their conquests, the Mongols transmitted administrative practices, including religious pluralism, as well as military organization and communications technology. Mongol statecraft was amalgamated into China's imperial tradition; Russian princes earned their way to power as clients of Mongol khans.

The Ottoman empire appears at the center of our story, as an empire that managed to blend Turkic, Byzantine, Arab, Mongol, and Persian traditions into durable, flexible, and transforming power. The Ottomans defeated the long-lived Byzantine empire in 1453, consolidated control at the vital junction of trade routes connecting Europe, the Indian Ocean, and the Eurasian landmass, and incorporated land and people from the outskirts of Vienna to eastern Anatolia and over much of the Arabian peninsula and north Africa. This brought the Ottoman empire close to the scale of the Roman empire and into such a dominant position that rulers in western Europe were impelled to sponsor voyages around Africa to reach Asia with its riches. From these conflicts and challenges among empires, new maritime connections emerged.

If the "discovery" of the Americas was an imperial accident, it had a transformative impact. The New World and the Old and the oceans themselves became spaces on which the long-term competition of empires continued. The overseas thrust of European empire was disruptive in different ways to the world of empires. China and the Ottomans long remained too strong for European powers to do more than nibble at their edges. For centuries after Europeans reached their shores, societies in Asia retained their cultural integrity; rulers made advantageous deals with newcomers; commercial elites prospered and innovated. But internal strife eventually opened up exploitable cracks to outsiders.

The subjection of New World empires—the Aztecs and Incas notably—happened faster, and was more thoroughgoing. In the Americas, colonization led first to demographic decline and then vast relocations of peoples, as European settlement and the forced migration of enslaved Africans to parts of the Americas produced new kinds of societies.

As empires continued their destructive intrusions in the Americas and their rivalries with each other, the extent and effects of transcontinental connections were growing. The mining of silver by indigenous Americans under Spanish rule in what is now Peru and Mexico, and then the production of sugar by enslaved Africans under several empires in the Caribbean, began to transform the world economy. Food crops—maize, potatoes, tomatoes, rice—traveled across oceans. Empires tried to keep such activities under their control—with only partial and temporary success.

The most decisive economic breakthrough occurred around 1800 in Great Britain. Important as domestic reforms were to the agricultural and industrial revolutions in Britain, imperial resources—especially low-price sugar—and imperial enterprises—financial institutions, shipbuilding, armies and navies—were also essential factors. Trade had long been only partially a matter of markets; it depended on imperial might, on protecting vital lands and trade routes from other empires, pirates, and freebooters.

By 1800, Britain's economic advantages were such that it could survive the loss of part (not the most valuable) of its empire—in North America—deepen its involvement in India, retain its colonies in the West Indies, fight off Napoleon's ambitions for European dominance, and pursue its interests elsewhere under the name of "free trade," using or threatening to use naval power to preserve British interests. Britain came to the fore during a period—short by imperial standards—when European empires appeared to dominate the world. Its repertoire of empire was shifting—but so was that of other powers. As some European rivals began to catch up with Britain's industrial economy, the interempire competition for resources led to a preemptive rush for colonial acquisitions and initiated a new phase of violence and war.

But the extension of empires over the world also transformed the space in which political ideas propagated and new ones developed. Since the sixteenth-century critiques of Spanish abuses of Indians, empires had been sites of debates over political legitimacy and sovereign power. In the late eighteenth century, the relationship of person, nation, and empire came under scrutiny. The antislavery movement in Britain targeted what had been the most lucrative dimension of empire and asserted that enslaved Africans should be treated as imperial subjects, not as exploitable objects.

The French revolution opened up the question of whether rights in a nation applied in colonies—perhaps going as far as to require that slaves be freed and made French citizens. French officials, for pragmatic as well as principled reasons, came out on both sides of the question in the 1790s. The status of "subjects" in the empire was periodically debated until 1946, when a new constitution declared all subjects to have the "qualities" of the French citizen—a change that exacerbated rather than relieved uncertainty over whether "France" was a society of equals or of non-equivalents.

That such debates continued unresolved for so long should make us reflect on conventional representations of processes that produced a "modern" world. It is not accurate to argue that western European empires suddenly stopped acting like empires, began to think like nation-states, set out to collect colonies to supply the nation with glory and lucre, then faced the disjuncture between their espousal of national self-determination and their denial of it to others. Much as the idea of a nation governing itself became part of European political thinking, an "epoch" of empire did not give way to a new nationalized sovereignty regime or to generalized acceptance of the nation-state in the nineteenth century.

The language of nationally based community founded on shared history, language, or customs was used by some to argue for making new empires—the German one, for example—but implementing these ideas was not easy where populations were mixed and where already existing empires commanded major resources. The Ottomans, Austria-Hungary, and Russia, with their multiethnic, multiconfessional empires, struggled to find ways to make national community work for themselves, while competing with each other and other empires. The national question combined explosively with imperial rivalry to provoke a series of bloody conflicts—war in the Crimea in the 1850s, repeated wars in the Balkans, the Boxer Rebellion in China, and even more murderous conflagrations in the twentieth century, when Germany and Japan launched their drives for their own kinds of empires.

The volatile politics of imperial rivalry on a global scale raised the question of whether the "colonial" empires of the nineteenth and twentieth centuries were a new kind of polity, distinct from the empires of the past. Some Europeans argued that their empires were a superior sort; others, like Lenin, saw them as a product—also unique—of capitalism. Some scholars today argue that the possibility of popular sovereignty at home—and Enlightenment ideas more generally—led European political thinkers and rulers to draw a sharper line than ever before between people who were inside the polity and outsiders who were considered unqualified to participate in governing themselves. But, as we noted above, Europeans still had to find intermediaries to do much of the work of running an empire, and they had to provide publics at home with an acceptable view of the state they lived in. The new technologies of war and communications did not necessarily penetrate to the level of village or commune. Claims to be bringing uplift and progress to Africa and Asia led to criticism both at home and abroad: why were colonial empires doing so little to fulfill their mission and why did land-grabbing, forced labor, and a great deal of violence persist?

Whatever was new or old about European colonialism in the nineteenth century, it was, from a historical perspective, short-lived: compare roughly seventy years of colonial rule over Africa to the Ottoman empire's six-hundred-year life span. Far from consolidating a world order based on the distinction between European nation and non-European dependence, the assertive imperialism of the late nineteenth and twentieth centuries gave rise to questions about the legitimacy and viability of colonialism and to more conflicts among new and old empires.

During World War II the long contest among rivals to control Europe's destiny played itself out on a global scale and provoked another shift in the world of empires. Japan's conquests of European colonies in southeast Asia proved especially devastating—to the eventual winners of this war among empires as well as to the losers. Germany, defeated as an empire, flourished as a nation-state. So too did Japan. France, Britain, and other colonial powers tried to revive their empires with new economic and political arrangements, only to find themselves faced at mid-century with both revolts and unbearable costs. The price of including African and Asian people in empires that were expected to provide services to their citizens proved too high. After shedding most of their colonies, European states took steps toward confederation with each other, opening up complex renegotiations of sovereignty that continue today.

The postwar reconfiguration brought to the fore two powers with histories of imperial expansion: the USSR and the United States. The Soviet Union combined the strategy of recognizing diverse "nationalities" with a one-party state to spread a communist web over its many national groups and to ignite challenges to capitalist empire elsewhere. The United States strove with Protestant abandon to extend its idea of democracy in a manner reminiscent of Rome and practiced free-trade imperialism, combining market power with military might. Americans expected the world to speak their language, want their political system, and love their culture, and, just when they seemed to be triumphant, ran into trouble, especially in areas Romans, Byzantines, and Ottomans had once governed. Meanwhile, China, its boundaries close to those attained by the Qing emperors, its strong system of officialdom intact, mobilizes its huge population, controls its elites with a tight rein, contends with restless populations of Tibetans and Muslims, sends—without proselytizing—its entrepreneurs, specialists, and laborers abroad, and commands vital resources around the world. China, Russia, and the United States do not consider themselves to be empires, but imperial pathways made them what they are.

A focus on empires, their repertoires of rule, and their intersecting trajectories thus revises conventional chronologies and categories and helps us see how, when, and where world history took new directions. Ambitious leaders, middling agents, and the weak had to position themselves in relation to powers that commanded supranational resources. The networks developed by empires dragged people across oceans into slavery, drew settlers and itinerants into new relationships, fostered diasporas, provided intellectual sources of international law, and provoked challenges to power.

We are left with questions about our own time. Has the normality of empire come to an end? Is the only alternative the nation-state with its capacity for violence in the cause of homogeneous community? Or are there other alternatives that can recognize diverse types of political association without insisting on uniformity or hierarchy? An attentive reading of the history of empires brings us face-to-face with extremes of violence and hubris, but also reminds us that sovereignty can be shared, layered, and transformed. The past is not a single path leading to a predetermined future.

IMPERIAL RULE
IN ROME AND CHINA

2

In the third century BCE, two empires were taking shape at distant edges of Eurasia. Rome and China eventually stretched over enormous spaces, incorporated far-flung populations, created effective ways to rule them, and fostered ideas about government that have lived to our times. Empires were not invented by the Romans or the Chinese. Along the Nile, Egyptians had lived in empires from the third millennium BCE. Empires had come and gone in Mesopotamia, India, Africa, and Asia for many hundreds of years. At the very time when Romans were putting their small city into republican order and warring states fought each other in China, Alexander the Great subdued peoples and kingdoms from the eastern Mediterranean into central Asia and the Indies. But Alexander's empire depended on the presence of his army and perished with him after twelve glorious years, while Rome and China managed to sustain control over enormous territories for centuries. What made these two empires so enduring and so influential in the political history of the world?

Part of the answer is that both Rome and China produced effective solutions to the fundamental problem of how to govern and exploit diverse populations. Some of their strategies resemble each other; others defined distinct repertoires of rule. Roman and Chinese empire-builders faced different economic possibilities and hazards, worked with different political antecedents, and transformed the spaces they claimed and conquered in different ways. In this chapter, we will emphasize their administrative institutions, their legitimizing strategies, and their relations with outsiders.

The World Made by Rome

In Roman times historians looked back at their past with deep curiosity about what had made the empire so powerful and successful. For Polybius, a Greek scholar living in Rome after having been taken hostage in 167

BCE, the problem was to explain "under what kind of constitution it came about that nearly the whole world fell under the power of Rome in somewhat less than fifty-three years—an event certainly without precedent" (*The Histories*). Romans recognized the importance of Rome's Mediterranean location. Proximity to the sea, good communications to Greece and north Africa with their ports and hinterlands, a temperate climate, agrarian potential—these were among Rome's spatial assets. But other peoples had tried or were trying to make this space their own. Why was it Rome—and not another city-state—that created a polity around all sides of the sea, uniting most of Europe and the entire north African coast with the lands of ancient empires in the Middle East?

A Republic Built on War and Law

The starting point was conquest, as with most empires. But sustaining and expanding control depended not just on violence but on the ongoing linkage of human and economic resources to central power. Creative political organization enabled Rome to provide for a huge and spread-out army, to give people incentives for cooperation with the imperial center, and to propagate a persuasive culture based on military prowess, rule-based order, divinely sanctioned authority, and the virtues of civic life. Romans' political and cultural innovations—their citizenship, their law, for a time their republic, and later its memory—drew old and new elites into government and army. Rome absorbed cultural achievements of earlier empires into its civilization, accommodated local religions and laws while extending the sway of Roman gods, and offered an attractive Roman way—Roman roads, Roman architecture, Roman writing, Roman festivals. Romans created an imperial vocabulary, institutions, and practices that would be called upon by empire-makers, critics, and defenders for the next two thousand years.

Let's begin with war and with the political initiatives that propelled Rome into empire. The legends of Rome's founders—Trojan sailor/soldiers led by their wandering demigod Aeneas—and of the Romans' first king, Romulus—abandoned as a baby to die, nursed to life by a wolf—extolled hardiness, valor, daring, fidelity, and combat as primary virtues. Romulus was said to have killed his own brother, and conflict within the political elite would be an ordinary part of Roman life.

Around 500 BCE, the Romans replaced their king with a republic—a political innovation of enormous consequence. Most of the enormous territory that we know as the Roman empire was acquired from the second century BCE to the first century CE. During most of this time, Rome was ruled by elected representatives of its people, reminding us that there is no incompatibility between empire and republican government. In periods of declared emergency, the republic was led by dictators but it was only in 27 BCE, when Augustus took the title of emperor, that elected leadership gave way to one man's lifetime rule.

Romans did not move into the place of an earlier empire, as Alexander had done when he defeated his Persian enemy. Instead Romans created their imperial space by conquering and incorporating tribes, cities, and kingdoms in Italy, and later moving on beyond their core area. The centuries of conquest included near defeats, inspired loyalty, and embedded military values deeply in the institutions and spirit of the empire.

The first territory conquered by the Romans was the area we know today as Italy. With its spine of mountains, grain-producing plains, and port cities, this was a landscape of potential wealth. The peninsula was populated by Gauls from across the Alps in the north; Etruscans at the western top of the peninsula; Latins, including Romans, Sabines, and Samnites, in the middle, and colonies of Greeks and Carthaginians at the base of the "boot" and on the islands of Sicily, Sardinia, and Corsica.

In the fourth century BCE, the Romans fought both sophisticated Etruscans and marauding Gauls. According to the Roman historian Livy, after a victory over the Etruscans—regarded by the Romans as more cultivated than themselves—the Romans planned to leave their city and make the old Etruscan capital, Veii, their new home. But in 387, when the Gauls burned most of Rome, the military leader Camillus pleaded with the Romans to stay in Rome where their gods were located and not to provide their "barbarian" enemies with an image of retreat. The destruction of the city was turned into an appeal for homeland loyalty.

As Romans took over more places and people, they adjusted their institutions to the tasks of ruling an imperial capital city and distant places. A king, who was both a political and a military leader, could not be at two locations at once; instead Romans installed two consuls, also known as chief magistrates, each elected to hold office for one year. The source of the magistrates' authority was election by Rome's soldier-citizens. By creating a body of citizens whose decisions were the source of law, Romans took sovereignty out of royal or celestial hands and located it in themselves.

This radical move from kingship to republic was accompanied by measures designed to prevent a return to one-man rule. Personal authority in the republic was constrained by a strict term limit on magistracies, by the electoral power of the people's assemblies, and by the authority of the senate—a council of serving or former magistrates and other men of high office. Underlying these institutions and giving them force was a commitment

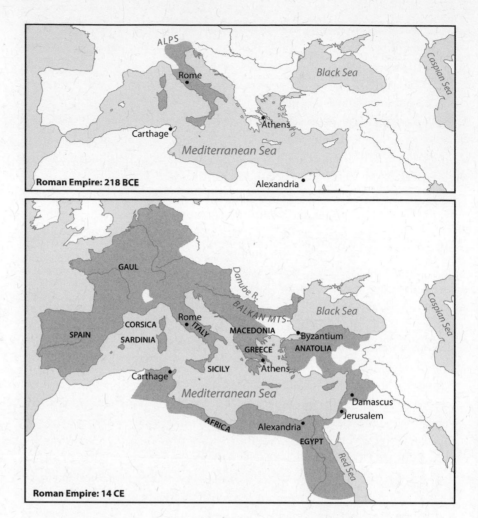

Map 2.1
Expansion and
contraction of
Rome.

to legal procedures for defining and enforcing rules and for changing them. The historian Livy described Rome as "a free nation, governed by annually elected officers of state and subject not to the caprice of individual men, but to the overriding authority of the law" (*History of Rome*).

Where did this law come from? Throughout the republic in practice and in principle during later Roman history, the source of law was the Roman people. Although magistrates, including the consuls, were lawmakers by virtue of their ability to issue binding commands and to make decisions in judicial matters, the approval of assemblies of citizens was essential to making a magistrate's proposal into a law. The assemblies could also conduct criminal trials. The Roman commitment to legal authority and procedures was compatible with hierarchies of status, wealth, and military rank. Slaves and women were not citizens and not participants in Roman sovereignty.

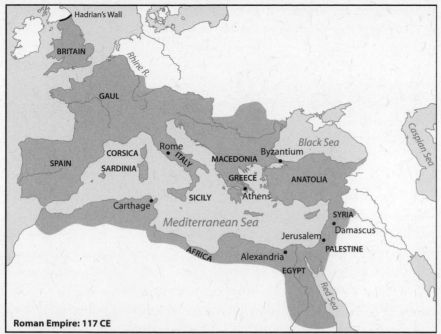

Roman Empire: 117 CE

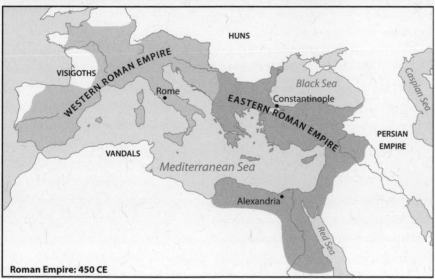

Roman Empire: 450 CE

Only certain categories of people could vote, and not all citizens could be chosen as magistrates and consuls. Republican Rome did not break the powers of the richest families but contained and exploited their competition through institutionalized procedures. The magistrates were elected by assemblies, based on units of the army, and richer taxpayers had more electoral clout than others.

Rome's republic managed to combine respect for hierarchy, openness to talent, and the principle of popular sovereignty. The republic's multiple institutions allowed ambitious newcomers—often military heroes—as well as men of established wealth, pedigree, or service to shape policy in their interests. The general principle that law was made by the people and their elected representatives proved both inspiring and manipulable, and perhaps therefore enduring.

Institutions for Empire

The word "imperial" has a history. In Rome, *imperium* first referred to the king's power to impose execution or beatings, to draft citizens into armies, and to command armies on campaigns. That power was transferred to the consuls under the republic, underlining the tight connection in Roman governance between military and civil matters. Imperium meant the power to condemn people to death or to make them fight. In the Roman republic, obsessed with limiting individuals' powers, imperium was not absolute. Consuls' rights as commanders in chief of armies existed only outside Rome itself. Over time, Roman citizens, or categories of them, acquired the right not to be condemned to corporal punishment or death. Romans not only exercised imperial power; they thought about its meaning, analyzed its underlying concepts, justified and transformed its use.

Making empire had its consequences. In 241 BCE, when consuls were leading Roman armies against their neighbors, the office of *praetor* was created to expand military and judicial command over new areas and to deal with legal matters between Romans and conquered peoples. Later, as Romans expanded their control well beyond Italy, they sent praetors, with troops, to take charge of unruly regions. In the early republic, citizens had voted in gatherings based on army units, or "centuries," and in assemblies based on their membership in Roman "tribes." As the empire grew, the assembly of tribes (*comitia tributa*) became a more prominent locus of popular power. It elected officers called tribunes, conducted trials, and had powers to intervene with magistrates in cases involving "plebs"—commoners. The gradual shifts in institutions of popular sovereignty enabled both old ("patrician") and new families who profited from the expansion of Rome's economic base to have voices in politics and to merge into a class of "good men," or *nobilitas*. The assembly of tribes also provided Rome with an institution that could be used to incorporate outsiders who had not been part of the republic.

Innovations in government created by the Romans echo in our political vocabulary. Patrician, plebian, and noble—these concepts configured ways of thinking about status; senates and committees are still with us. In many countries, magistrates fulfill legal functions and courts are referred to as tribunals. Consuls carry on diplomatic relations. This is not to say that Rome established institutions for all time or all places, but rather to suggest the long trajectories of political forms and ideas—imitated, transformed, and reinterpreted in different contexts.

To govern outside their capital, Romans developed strategies that would enter the repertoires of later empire-builders. One of these was the enlargement of the sphere of Roman rights. The closest towns in Italy were simply annexed; free males became Roman citizens, and elites could become Roman nobles. The extension of citizenship beyond Rome was an innovation of enormous consequence, but at first even within the Latin core area, cities and their populations were doled out different sets of rights. In some cases, the population was required, as were Roman citizens, to serve as soldiers but were not allowed a voice in politics. As the Romans conquered more distant, non-Latin areas of Italy, they made treaties with leaders of defeated cities, giving them some internal autonomy in return for subordination to Rome in fiscal and military matters.

Romans also extended their realm by founding what they called colonies. Other powers in the Mediterranean, such as Rome's enemy, Carthage, had settled people in areas distant from their place of origin. The Romans tweaked this imperial practice by establishing colonies with their own citizenship regimes and with military functions. Here citizenship was fungible: settlers sent out from Rome and other Latin cities gave up their rights in Rome to become citizens of the new colonies. Colonies were typically established in areas that needed defense. For individual soldier-agriculturalists and their families, assignment to a colony could be both an opportunity—to become a more important person in a much smaller city than Rome—and a loss—leaving Rome for a frontier outpost. People sent out to establish colonies brought their language, expectations, and experience of Roman ways with them.

By the time the Romans completed their conquest of Italy, they had produced three different ways of attaching land and people to their empire: (1) annexation, limited citizenship, and eventual assimilation for nearby Latins, (2) limited self-government for some non-Latin cities and tribes, and (3) colonies of Latins displaced to frontier regions.

Later empires would use these strategies to expand and govern, but of particular import for Rome's future was that its citizenship came to be desired by non-Romans, and was preferable to substantive autonomy in allied cities or colonies. From 91 to 88 BCE, Rome's Italian allies rebelled against their lack of full Roman rights and fought Rome to attain them. After much debate, the senate made the momentous decision to grant citizenship to all Latins. Extending citizenship became both a reward for service and a means to enlarge the realm of loyalty. Later soldiers from outside Rome could earn citizenship by serving in the army for twenty-five years; victorious generals granted citizenship to individuals far away from Rome.

The Latins' push for Roman citizenship came after Rome's spectacular success at extending power beyond the peninsula. To defeat their most powerful rival, the Carthaginians with their colonies in Sicily and their capital on the north African coast (today's Tunisia), Romans learned to fight at sea. In their first war with Carthage (264 to 241 BCE), the Romans lost many naval battles but ultimately won and occupied Sicily, Sardinia, and Corsica. It took until 204 BCE for Rome to defeat Carthage for good and take over its colonies in Africa and Spain. Rome went on from there, conquering Macedonia, Greece, and Anatolia to the east, and Gaul and much of England to the northwest in the first century CE. In three centuries, the Romans spread their empire over the whole of the Mediterranean and its European and near Asian hinterlands.

With their move overseas, Romans produced another institution—the province ruled by a military commander with the powers of a magistrate. Praetors were appointed for Sardinia, Sicily, Spain, Africa (the area around Carthage), and Macedonia between 227 and 146 BCE. The Roman system of administration has been called "government without bureaucracy." Power rested almost everywhere in the hands of a single authority—a praetor or a consul—along with a few assistants, mostly friends, family, or other people personally connected to him, as well as a few minor officials of low ranks, including slaves.

Government, from Rome's perspective, was mostly about collecting taxes, either as money or produce, mobilizing soldiers, and sustaining the infrastructure—roads, aqueducts—that kept the empire together. In the overseas areas, the link between military and citizenship that defined Rome so strongly was altered. The task of governors outside Italy was to collect taxes that would pay for the Roman army, not to muster soldier-citizens. In the provinces, local practices were mostly left in place, while elites could be granted the coveted privilege of Roman citizenship. This minimalist approach to administration nourished a fundamental division between Romans, including assimilated elites with their shared political and cultural practices, and non-Romans whose institutions and lifeways were multiple and different from each other.

Romans found a way to express this distinction in law. In outlying areas, Romans, as in Rome itself, could have their legal matters decided under Roman law. Non-Romans, for most ordinary matters, could consult their own authorities—a practice that today would be called legal pluralism. But what happened when a Roman and a non-Roman had a business matter to resolve? This question led Romans to produce theories that distinguished the civil laws of different nations—laws that were understood to be different for different peoples—from the law of all nations (a single set of rules) to be applied to foreigners in the Roman empire by the praetor or to disputes between Romans and non-Romans.

For Romans, expansion produced its own motive, by rewarding soldiers with plunder and commanders with slaves, glory, and more plunder. In the subordinated regions, governors and their minuscule staffs had to rely on local leaders to collect taxes, whether in money, kind, or soldiers. Collaboration with local elites, like colonization and enslavement, drew people into new networks and gradually produced cultural spaces for the incorporative activities at which Romans excelled.

The Empire Gets an Emperor

By the second century BCE, the tasks of imperial government began to overwhelm the republic's minimalist institutions. Rome's judicial bodies could not provide sufficient recourse, particularly with regard to the charges of corruption that the much enlarged empire produced. Romans stretched the rules of their republic as generals were granted special powers, more resources, and longer terms in their commands, sometimes to keep them out of the capital.

Struggles over power in republican Rome took a violent turn about 133 BCE when the tribune Tiberius Gracchus was assassinated by senators. The entrenched association of political with military command made the much expanded republic vulnerable to wars between rival leaders. Some old families in the senate tried to defend the institutions of the republic against the ambitions of individual consuls. When Julius Caesar emerged victorious from imperial conquests and battles with his rivals, he was accused of wanting to make himself a king. Caesar had decked himself out in regalia from the Roman past, cumulated offices and powers, allowed the opening of temples for his cult, and adopted an heir, Octavian. All this signaled that Caesar regarded the empire as his to rule and to pass on. Senators assassinated Caesar in 44 BCE, shortly after he had taken up the ominous new office of "dictator for life."

It was Octavian, Caesar's adopted son, who managed to make himself Rome's first emperor, the possessor of overarching, superior, lifelong, and legal authority. After Caesar's death, Octavian shed his pre-adoption name "Gaius Octavius," took on the military rank "Imperator," embellished this with references to his deified father, and created a new empowering identity as "Imperator Caesar Divi Filius." In 27 BCE, the senate granted Octavian an array of new powers along with yet another title, "Augustus," an honorific previously applied to gods, suggesting their capacity to "augment," to make something better. Octavian was made *princeps*, or First Citizen, and the republic was replaced by what the Romans came to call the "principate," a new kind of government with power vested in a single leader.

Just as the republic had been a work in progress for about five hundred years, the principate too evolved over time. Augustus lived for forty-one years as emperor; this medical good fortune helped consolidate the principate. His adopted son Tiberius succeeded him in 14 CE. During this time of relative peace and prosperity, the institutions of governance, war, finance, and culture were adjusted to both the emperor's superior powers and the demands of ruling the enormous polity. After the violent conflicts and wars that had plagued the republic, Romans were drawn to the prospect of order; they appear to have accepted the transformation of older institutions into a more concentrated form of power. In Augustus's time, the emperor possessed *imperium maius*, meaning "power greater than that of the man who should govern any province he should enter." This conception of the emperor as the ruler of other rulers, an adaption of the Assyrian and biblical king of kings, would persist for centuries.

Augustus was granted the final say in all matters of public business; he could halt legal actions against any Roman citizen; and he could bring laws to a vote by the Roman people. In a further erosion of republican sovereignty, Augustus's successor, Tiberius, took the electoral powers of the popular assemblies and gave them to the senate. The emperor could make war or peace; he was the head of the senate and the administration of Rome; and he enjoyed a personal exemption from the constraints of all other laws. These functions and others were formally conferred upon the emperor by law in 14 CE. Romans, following legal procedures, had taken the critical step of transferring power to a supreme ruler. This potential of republican empire, like the concept of emergency powers, would be remembered, feared, and repeated well into the twentieth century.

Augustus accumulated an enormous fortune from plunder, gifts, taxes, and revenues from his personal estates and from provinces under imperial control. This immense wealth enabled the emperor to bail out the Roman treasury from his own. The huge territories that belonged to the emperor were called his *patrimonium*. The connection of this concept to that of father (pater) was of course not accidental. It indicated that the emperor was both the head of his own household and the father of all Romans—like the legendary Aeneas—and also signaled the importance of other fathers to the polity. We will encounter the association of empire, fatherhood, and household—what social scientists, looking back to Rome, call patrimonialism—again.

There was no absolute divide between the emperor's resources and those of the Roman state. Under Augustus's successors, an office called the *fiscus*—or "money bag"—was charged with administering both the emperor's personal lands and the provinces assigned to his direct governance. In the beginning, the people who collected taxes on these areas were mostly slaves or new freedmen. Over time aristocrats entered the emperor's personal staff, eroding further the authority of the magistrates in the senate and enhancing the significance of service in the emperor's court.

The other locus of the emperor's power was the military, although this was always a double-edged sword. Augustus kept the link between citizenship and military service—for the most part, the standing army was to be composed of citizens—but moved troops, with their generals, out of Italy and to the border zones. A new elite corps—the Praetorian guard—protected the emperor. Augustus also created a standing navy. To enhance his personal control, Augustus appointed men of equestrian rank who had not been elected as magistrates to high command in the military and the provinces, bypassing both senators' prerogatives and popular voting.

These changes had long-term, unintended consequences. Sending Roman legions to the borders spread Roman ways far over the empire, in addition to diminishing, for a time, violence in the capital. The Praetorian guard could take its turn at playing the politics of rivalry for the emperorship. The manipulation of equestrian and other orders kept the principle of social ranks in place, but it also drew new men into the imperial elites. In principle, the emperor as the sole, lifelong military commander controlled the whole, but this principle was often turned on its head.

By Augustus's time it was expected that a son or adopted son of the emperor would succeed him. But this did not end the matter, for these sons could fight each other, and military prowess remained a

Figure 2.1
Roman emperor
Caesar Augustus
(27 BCE–14 CE),
statue from
30 BCE.
Spencer Arnold,
GettyImages.

core value. In theory, the senate appointed emperors; in practice the senate or senators murdered some of them. The Praetorian guard also assassinated and declared emperors. In the third century CE—a time of economic difficulties and internal strife for Romans—military success decided power struggles over who would be emperor. The incorporation of ambitious men from the provinces into the imperial army and into honorable ranks meant that people from outside Rome—such as Septimius Severus—could become emperor. The openness of the system, its multiple legitimating institutions, the ethos of military glory—these were a recipe for regicide. There were twenty-six Roman emperors between the years 235 and 285 CE, and only one of these died naturally in the office.

An Imperial Economy

The frequent, bloody, and scandalous struggles over who would be emperor make it clear that—unlike the case of Alexander the Great—it was not the person of the emperor that held the empire together or determined its fate. Instead, a large-scale, differentiated, and productive economy, extensive networks of material and personal connections, and successful ideological outreach attracted and compelled subjects' loyalty.

The economy of Rome was not a thought-out system but a hodgepodge of practices. As with other sedentary societies before the advent of machine production, the wealth of the system depended on agriculture, precious metals and other natural resources, and the ability to treat, transport, and exchange these goods. Both small farms and large estates were run by men with their own patrimonial authority over land, slaves, free laborers, and families. As new territories were added, new resources could be taxed, distributed, or both. For some of the conquered, defeat by Romans meant enslavement, but for some of the victors, more slaves meant greater capacity to work and manage estates. The allocation of lands in distant provinces to senators gave them a stake in maintaining commercial linkages.

Taxation was key to the whole operation. The Romans taxed land, persons, inheritances, slave owning, imports, and exports. The famous Roman censuses were taken with tax collecting as a goal. The people in charge of collecting taxes were sometimes officials, sometimes "tax farmers"—individuals who contracted to collect taxes in an area. Rome—and, as we shall see, China—came up with mechanisms to count, tax, extract, and distribute over two thousand years ago.

Feeding the army and the city of Rome were large-scale operations. In the second century CE, the number of men in arms grew to about 400,000. One Egyptian source recorded a soldier's daily ration as about two pounds of bread, a pound and a half of meat, a quart of wine, and about half a cup of oil. Then there was Rome. Feeding Rome alone required 200,000 tons of wheat a year. In Augustus's time, the city had a population of about a million—edging out the Chinese capital Chang'an (unknown to the Romans) as the most populous city on earth. Perhaps a quarter of the inhabitants of Rome were citizens; the rest were dependents, slaves, and foreigners.

Functionally, the empire was a huge economic space, fostered by peace, security, and political unity. The whole was essential to the well-being of its parts. Africa, Sicily, Sardinia, and Egypt provided grain for Rome; Gaul, the Danube, and the Balkans fed the army; and Italy, Spain, the south of Gaul, and Anatolia—all commercially active areas—paid their taxes in money, which was used to compensate soldiers and officials (see map 2.1). The system was kept going by imperial officials, but also by merchants, ship commanders, and other purveyors who transported products—food, luxury goods, primary materials, arms—across seas and overland to purchasers or official suppliers.

The large and integrated economic space had a profound effect on how people lived. Local elites ran the slave plantations that produced much of the empire's grain, and made fortunes—large and small—out of their imperial connections. Daily life even in distant places and even for the humble was made more comfortable than before Roman rule; olive oil and wine were shipped around the Mediterranean and influenced what much later became known as Turkish, Greek, Italian, French, and Spanish cuisines. Peasants lived in houses with tiled roofs—more waterproof and less flammable than thatch—and ordinary households used high-quality pottery. The poor were undernourished by our standards, but overall starvation was unusual. Roman authorities stocked grain reserves for emergencies.

In the third century CE, rapid and murderous turnovers in emperors, external assaults by a variety of foes—Goths and other "barbarian" tribes, pirates, the Persian empire—and stress on soldiers' remuneration as inflation reduced their salaries undermined Rome's security. Rome's periphery shrank under assaults of tribes who had become savvy in Roman ways and were ready to sell their "protection" to besieged populations. But it took a very long time—hundreds of years—for the imperial system to become unhinged from the framework established in the late republic and the first two centuries of the principate.

A Seductive Culture

The Roman empire offered people of social standing, both in and outside the capital, an opportunity to participate in a civilization that celebrated its divine origins, earthly grandeur, and superior way of life. For many centuries, the empire was able to absorb and integrate earlier cultures into a synthetic Roman way.

Cities were not, of course, a Roman invention, but Romans transformed them and spread an adaptable model around the empire. The rectangular city plan, with cross streets and space set aside for public works, had been a Greek specialty. Romans modeled their urban centers on Greek cities in southern Italy, adding new features, such as the triumphal arch. Marble was cut in enormous quantities for Roman buildings; the use of concrete allowed construction of vaults and domes, adorned with elaborate decoration. Roman improvements included water and sewage systems, public baths, sports facilities, and huge amphitheaters for civic spectacles, adapting Greek models to accommodate larger publics. The city of Pompeii had five large bathing centers for its twenty thousand inhabitants when it was covered in ashes by the explosion of Mount Vesuvius in 79 CE.

Law was part of this Roman civilization, both a means of governance and a support for the social order. For most of the empire's history, law was not recorded in a uniform way. It was only in the sixth century—and in Constantinople, the eastern Roman capital (chapter 3)—that the emperor Justinian sponsored the collection of laws in a single code. What was Roman about Roman law from republican times, and what became a powerful historical precedent, was professional interpretation, operating in a polity where the manner of making law was itself an ongoing and legitimate political concern. Rulers had issued laws in much earlier times; the Babylonian king Hammurabi who ruled from 1792 to 1750 BCE had a law code inscribed in stone. The Greeks had laws and theories of the state and the good, but they did not create a legal profession. From the mid–second century BCE, just as the republic was expanding most aggressively in space and institutions, jurists appeared in Rome, drawing up legal documents, advising magistrates, litigants, and judges, and passing on their learning to their students.

Prominent Romans argued that law was founded on reason and that humans, as reasoning creatures, should therefore participate in and follow it. Romans made the practical point that law was expressed in the rules of a particular state. When Roman consuls and emperors justified their wars as responses to aggression or violation of agreements, they assumed that there were rules of interstate conduct as well. Law had the potential of becoming universally valid. Cicero insisted that "an oath to an enemy nation must be honored, but not a promise of ransom to a pirate, who is not a lawful enemy, but . . . the common enemy of all the world, and with a pirate there is no common basis for either faith or words."

Coming under the developed rules of Roman law was part of the attraction of citizenship to imperial elites, as was the right to be judged by a Roman court. Commoners in many areas of the empire knew at least some of the rules of Roman law, but their chances of getting official adjudication of their complaints were far lower than those of the powerful.

The public life of empire was shaped by learning and art. Emperors lavished spectacular buildings upon Rome, and local elites vied with each other's displays of civic art and architecture in imperial cities. Romans' admiration for earlier civilizations meant that the cultural achievements of Greeks, Persians, and Egyptians could be emulated, incorporated, and built upon. Scholars, artists, and scientists from all over the empire found places inside Roman culture and left their mark upon it.

The language of learning and creativity at the time of Roman expansion was initially Greek. Even as Latin surged beyond rhetoric to become a language of poetry, love, and sex, the Roman cultural ideal was learning in both Greek and Latin. A Greek word, *paideia*, described this right kind of education: one that prepared youth for a life of knowledge and sensitivity to beauty, and taught the social skills to attain calm nobility and civic virtue. Athens became a beloved and satisfyingly archaic symbol of the universal values expressed in the Roman idea of "*humanitas*." Both a judgment and a mission, humanitas meant "civilized behavior," expressed in learning and in relationships to others, in limits on how power was to be used, in the goal of enabling even conquered people to realize what was conceived of as their human potential. The opposite of humanitas was barbarism; barbarians were uneducated people who did not live in cities (at least not Roman cities), were poorly dressed and badly behaved, and could not be trusted to understand Roman laws.

> *"True law is reason, right and natural, commanding people to fulfill their obligations and prohibiting and deterring them from doing wrong. Its validity is universal; it is immutable and eternal. . . . There will not be one law at Rome, one at Athens, or one now and one later, but all nations will be subject all the time to this one changeless and everlasting law."*
>
> —Cicero, On the Laws

Humanitas had an open-ended quality. In theory, and in practice, barbarians could become Romans, if they played by Rome's rules and lived up to Rome's idea of civilization. Humanitas could also disguise the violence of Roman empire—pillage, enslavement, looting, killing, destruction. But other vital elements of humanitas were a capacity for self-criticism, concerns about degeneration, and an openness to political debate. Both the inclusion of civilized critics and the exclusion of those who did not see the virtues of the Roman way created a widely shared elite culture—a world of imagined and real connections to the empire and its ideals.

Religion

The capacity of Roman conquerors to absorb, inflect, but not fully homogenize is evident in their response to other people's faiths. In the beginning, the Romans themselves were polytheists—believers in many gods—as were most of their imperial subjects, except for Jews and, later, Christians. Having many gods made it easy for Romans to add on deities. The gods of ancient civilizations such as Isis of Egypt or Baal of Syria came to be worshiped in Italy, sometimes with new names. As Romans came into contact with Greeks, Zeus morphed into Jupiter, Athena into Minerva. Augustus built a temple that associated himself with Mars, the Avenger, as well as others that honored his deified father, Julius Caesar, and Venus, the goddess-mother of Aeneas.

Conquering an area, then bringing its gods to Rome, the "temple of the whole world," was an ordinary Roman practice. Organizing an imperial cult was a status symbol for new cities in Gaul and other provinces. Some gods were troublesome. In 187 BCE, the senate abolished the cult of Bacchus, the god of fertility and wine, whose enthusiasts lured respectable people away from their households to party in his name.

Gods and humans were imagined to be in close, sometimes carnal, contact. Their proximity combined with Rome's universalistic aspirations inspired some to wish for a man-god, who would bring salvation to all of humanity. The birth of Jesus of Nazareth was prefigured in this fashion, but the same kinds of hopes could be directed elsewhere. Augustus, who brought a generation of peace to Romans worn out by civil wars, was a plausible and appreciated savior.

Monotheism, more than messiahs, created problems for Rome's inclusive religious regime. Jews, who believed their single god to be the only one, came under Roman rule as the empire expanded eastward. Romans allowed Jews to practice their religion, but conflicts between Jews and Roman authorities led to a revolt in Palestine in 66–74 CE. The Jewish temple in Jerusalem was destroyed, and many Jews moved further to the west, bringing their religious practices to north Africa, Spain, and southern Europe. Proselytizing Christianity also disrupted Rome's religious heterogeneity, but Christians' universalistic claims and their penchant for organization mirrored Rome's own qualities and played a critical role in the transformation of culture and politics in the empire's last centuries.

The New Politics of the Late Empire

By the year 212 CE, Roman governing practices, civilizational ideas, and material culture had transformed societies from the British Isles to north Africa, from the Rhine to Syria and Egypt. Most people in this area knew no other world than the Roman one. That world would last for two more centuries as a unified political order—and for millennia, in political imagination—but, for historians looking back on it, some weaknesses in the system are apparent.

For one thing, the empire had ceased to extend its territory, which meant the ability to distribute new resources was drying up. For another, Rome's very success made it the target of assaults by tribes along its borders and by peoples migrating into southeast Europe from the Eurasian steppe. Many were led by warriors who wanted to settle inside the empire and to share in its largesse. Meanwhile, troops stationed for long periods in areas far from Rome offered support for rival commanders seeking power and even the emperorship. Emperors went back to being military commanders out of necessity and tried to govern from frontier cities far from Rome. But it was essential for Rome to control land and sea routes; agriculture and commercial production had become specialized and dependent on efficient and secure transport. Over the long term, the empire built on a tight linkage between military force and legitimate power would slowly be torn apart on this same principle.

People living in third-century Rome would not have seen their polity as doomed; Roman leaders continued to make innovations in their political arrangements, some with far-reaching consequences for future empires. The most dramatic—at least in hindsight—of these was the extension of Roman citizenship to all male, non-slave inhabitants of the Roman world in the year 212 CE.

Citizenship, as we have seen, had been central to Roman politics from republican days, a means to draw loyal servitors into the empire's regime of rights, a status so advantageous that Latins had fought for the privilege of becoming Romans in the first century BCE. The institution of citizenship was also connected to the most basic mechanisms of imperial rule—military service, law, and, providing for them both, taxes. The emperor Caracalla's enlargement of citizenship in 212 CE has been interpreted as a measure of necessity: if all free males in the empire were made citizens, they could be called to serve in the army, to submit compensation if they did not serve, and to pay inheritance taxes imposed on citizens. But Caracalla's declaration focused on religious cohesion: with citizenship, the worship of Roman gods would be extended throughout the empire. An incorporating and unifying impulse was at the core of the new policy. Through military service, taxation, legal protections, and common deities, tens of millions of people—free males with their families—would be connected more directly to the empire's projects and to a Roman way of life.

But common gods and citizenship were not enough to hold the empire together, and they were unacceptable to some. Christians, like Jews, were monotheists, and by the third century Christianity had spread to many parts of the empire. The religion had taken shape under Roman rule, and its focus on otherworldly rewards and punishment was an accommodation to Rome's overwhelming power on earth. But during Rome's hard times, many people, distressed by ongoing wars, barbarian inroads, and supply failures, turned to Christianity with its promises of solace and salvation. Emperors responded at first by scapegoating Christians as the source of the empire's problems, outlawing them as rebels against Rome and its gods. Persecution created martyrs, and the sect continued to grow and to attract even highborn Romans.

In 311, Galerius—one of four rulers of the empire at a time of divided imperial authority—shifted course. The ailing emperor decreed the end of official persecution of Christians, asking them to pray for the emperors and for the common good. A year later on the eve of battle for the emperorship, Constantine Augustus dreamt that he should display the cross and that this would determine the outcome of his campaign against a rival. After his victory, Constantine made Christianity one of the empire's legalized religions.

There was still a problem: Christians did not tolerate other gods, animal sacrifices, or temples that honored other gods. But monotheism, for emperors, was also a temptation. Christians' universalistic claims and the networks of clerical command they had developed over centuries of strife and persecution could be harnessed to Rome's worldly ambitions. Constantine took his opportunity to align sacred and secular universalism under a single god as he attempted to reunite the divided empire. Over the next century Christianity was established as the state religion. Other religions were declared superstitions; other priests were demoted and taxed; other temples were torn down; other gods were disfigured and dethroned. By the end of the fourth century in much of the empire to be Roman meant to be Christian, and belonging to another religion was a civil offense, punishable by Roman law.

Constantine's conversion marks a hardening of Roman politics at a time when the empire was suffering major losses and assaults from various tribes. The earlier expansion of citizenship had managed to bring people of many religions under Roman law, but connecting the state to a single, monotheistic religion narrowed possibilities for inclusion in the polity even as it defined a universalizing vision of imperial culture.

"An effective Goth wants to be like a Roman; only a poor Roman would want to be a Goth."

—Theodoric, Ostrogoth king

The end of Roman empire is not easy to define, because when the victorious Constantine moved the capital to Byzantium and renamed it Constantinople in 324, an eastern Roman empire was begun out of the old (chapter 3). Well before the capture of Rome by the Visigoth leader Alaric in 410, Romans were losing the ability to hold their polity together. Romans had tried to protect their borders at low cost by making alliances with largely Germanic-speaking tribes in frontier areas. Tribal people's service to Roman authority and participation in imperial culture shows that "barbarians" were not the uncivilized outsiders that the term implied; they wanted "in" on Rome's empire. But as future empires would also learn, the effort to co-opt diverse forces into an imperial system worked only as long as the center was perceived as necessary to the interests of people on peripheries or as long as the empire's leaders had the power to compel the transfer of taxes and goods. Rome did not so much fall, as disaggregate itself, as emperors split up the realm, and barbarian warriors took the lead both as military servitors of Rome and as conquerors of formerly Roman spaces.

The gradual waning of the western empire left multiple but much weaker powers on its territories, all of them shaped in fundamental ways by their Roman past. Some barbarians served as Rome's last military leaders; others took over the protection of local communities when Roman defenses failed. As the empire decomposed, provincial populations retained many Roman institutions, while hybrid nobilities of Roman and tribal origins tried to sustain social standing and to control their much reduced resources. The Roman peace was gone, along with the taxation regime and the vast, integrated economy that had distributed money, skills, people, and products throughout the empire. Sanitation systems, tiled roofs, and hard-fired pottery disappeared for centuries in northern and central Europe; literacy declined; poorly fed cattle shrank in size. The air in Italy turned cleaner as mines ceased to operate.

The imperial project based on conquest and the projection of a single civilization over the Mediterranean and its hinterlands fell on many swords. The very success of the enterprise had made it ripe for attack by outsiders who stopped expansion and reduced imperial resources; the connection between military command and political leadership was a formula for civil wars; the turn toward Christianity as the sole state religion undermined the empire's capacity for syncretic absorption of different peoples.

But many Roman inventions outlived the formal empire and were given new meanings centuries later. Humanitas—the idea that civilization was both a human capacity and the distinguishing possession of insiders with the right to rule barbarians—this, too, like arches, amphitheaters, and gridded cities, left its traces on the landscape that had been Rome and on many later empires. The ideal, if not the practice, of rule through law and representative political bodies also lived on. Latin, which had once tied diverse elites to Roman culture and politics, inflected speech across Europe and transmuted into Romance languages—Italian, French, Spanish, and Portuguese. The institution of citizenship—based in duties and rights, and extendable beyond a people or a city—would be periodically revived and reinterpreted as a means of political inclusion.

Constantine's empire in Byzantium brought a Latin and Roman-based political structure to a primarily Greek-speaking—but in fact enormously diverse—area on the eastern Mediterranean; the eastern empire survived for another thousand years. Rome's collapse left in place a powerful imperial imaginary linked to Christianity, the inspiration for new conquests and new civilizing missions. On all sides of the Mediterranean, Romans had created a space for empire, one that attracted the conflicting ambitions of Byzantines, Islamic caliphs, Carolingians, and later powers.

China: A Different Space for Empire

As Rome was transforming itself from a city-state to a republican empire, on the other side of the Eurasian landmass a victorious monarch succeeded in uniting core territories of central China under one man's rule. After centuries of competition, intrigue, and all-out warfare against neighboring rivals, the Qin king made himself emperor in 221 BCE. Qin control succumbed to internal conflict and external assault only fifteen years later, but imperial power was restored by Liu Bang, the founder of the Han dynasty. These two founding rulers left their mark on our political vocabulary: Qin (pronounced chin) morphed into China in many languages; Han became an ethnic label for those defined as the major people of the empire. Han rulers consolidated the Qin's territorial, administrative, and ideological achievements, and over the next four centuries developed an imperial political culture that outlived dynastic failures, periods of disintegration, civil wars, and even revolution. The notion of China as a political unit rightly governed by a single central leadership has been shared by rulers, would-be rulers, state-minded elites, and ordinary people for over two thousand years.

The most obvious characteristic of Chinese empire is its huge landmass, but as with Rome, it was the politics of empire that produced this spatial "fact." Unlike Rome's space, woven around the Mediterranean and its hinterlands, the Chinese polity was not defined by obvious natural contours. The great rivers flowing from west to east supplied, potentially, the ingredients—water and soil—for productive farming, but making the Yellow River or the Yangzi into secure, life-sustaining resources required diking and other kinds of organized management. The northern plains could support both agriculture and animal herding; the central regions were populated by farmers who grew wheat and, to the south, rice. Connecting even the core territories was not easy. No waterways ran north and south, and hilly terrain made land transport costly and difficult. The relatively undifferentiated but fertile central area offered rewards to those who managed to spread their power over peasants who labored on the land, but it was also promising terrain for challengers who could rebel against their lords or try to rule the whole themselves.

Early Romans had expanded the power of their city-state from an area peripheral to the great empires of the eastern Mediterranean. Although Romans benefited from the inspiration of Greek civilization and from statecraft selectively borrowed from other Mediterranean port cities, they enjoyed a relatively blank slate for designing what turned out to be a highly innovative imperial politics. The Qin had access to a different past and present, and learned from both. For one thing, earlier empires had already come and gone in northern and central China since at least 1750 BCE, leaving residues of administrative practices and political expectations. The Qin ruled one of several kingdoms that competed for the space and remembered power of empires past. Keys to Qin success were their conscious adaptation of strategies designed to enhance central control and their rigorous, brutal efforts to prevent fragmentation from happening again.

The critical factor for sustaining empire in the central areas was controlling elite intermediaries who could use local resources to make themselves into warlords and challengers. The Qin solution to this perennial imperial problem was militarized centralism and the elimination of nobility as a claim to state power. The Qin's successors, the Han, were forced to make compromises with regional families, with predictable centrifugal consequences in the long run. The exigencies of imperial politics in a space where underlings could provide for themselves drove this oscillation between harsh centralization and risky devolution of power.

Another challenge came from the north and west where nomadic and settled peoples intersected, generating revenue, tactics, and trouble for the empire. Nomads controlled and fostered long-distance trade (see chapter 4); through their commercial connections, Chinese products could be transported across deserts, steppe, and mountains to central Asia and beyond. Nomads had provided the earliest Chinese states with means to make war and empire—chariots, metal technologies (bronze and iron), and horse-based armies. Of the nomads' inventions, cavalry—used effectively against Chinese infantry—was the most crucial to contests among the warring states. Once the state of Zhao adopted armed and mounted archers as its core troops, other kingdoms had to follow suit.

In the wars between competing kingdoms, the Qin enjoyed an advantage related to their location. The Qin's base was west and north of the intersection of the Yellow and Wei rivers, near spaces contested by nomadic peoples. The walls built by the Qin marked this competition in a physical but not static way. Barriers of tamped earth and stone marked Qin advances

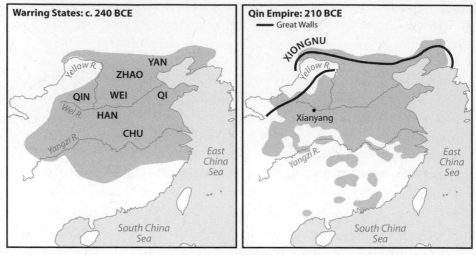

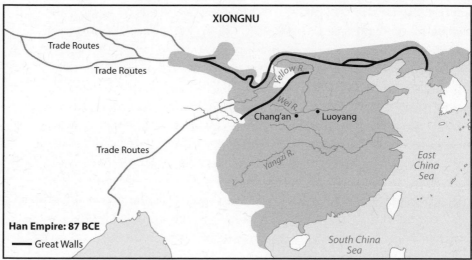

Map 2.2
Consolidation, expansion, and contraction of Chinese empire.

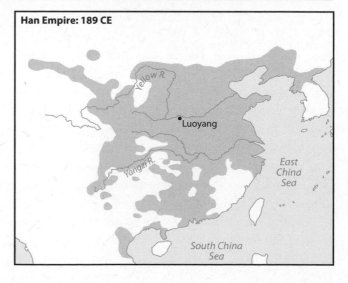

into undefined territory, protected pastures for Qin horses, and enabled an inverted kind of trench warfare against nomadic challengers. Once an extension into the nomads' areas had been achieved, walls fitted out with watchtowers sheltered the inside population from raids by people who had been displaced. Build and move on was the principle of the wall, not setting up a fixed border for all time.

Nomadic societies were themselves hardly static. Around 209 BCE, on the steppe to the north and west, Modun, a ruthless outcast, patricide, and brilliant tactician, united nomadic clans into a huge confederation—the Xiongnu empire—that ultimately extended from Manchuria across Mongolia to the Altai highlands and into central Asia. Chinese empire and Xiongnu empire were entangled from the start, and their interactions in war and in diplomacy shaped China's statecraft and ideology in fundamental ways.

China's imperial geography was starkly different from Rome's. Once the imperial capital was established in Rome, "roads"—on land or sea—connected diverse regions and their products to a fixed central point. The integrated Mediterranean economy and the privileges and properties granted to Rome's servitors meant that elites stayed rich by keeping the whole together and had nothing to gain from going their own way. For China, the central agrarian area with its relatively undifferentiated but sustaining resources offered lords and peasants the means to rebel against central or local authorities or both. On the other hand and as counterintuitive as this may seem, the unstable frontier regions to the west and north with their mixed economies and long-distance connections were a vital source for Chinese empire. Outsiders along the edges generated political and military innovations, enhanced material and cultural connections to other world areas, and, as it sometimes turned out, provided new blood and dynamism to regenerate imperial dynasties.

A Tool Kit for Empire

The struggles between warring kings took place on a terrain where earlier great empires—the Shang (1750–1027 BCE), the Zhou (1027–770 BCE)—had left their imprints. After the Zhou dynasty lost control over much of its realm in the eighth century BCE, memories of their glory inspired five centuries of combat, as kings attempted to regain supreme authority. The Qin's victory in 221 BCE was based on this dynasty's selective transformation of both ancient ways and tactics used by their rivals into a formidable war machine.

A key element of the Qin's eventual victory was their ability to take the services and loyalty of peasants away from regional elites. The Zhou dynasty had relied on devolving power to subordinate kings and princes, who then, in a pattern that would haunt imperial leaders ever after, could accumulate sufficient resources to escape from their sovereign's control or challenge it. During the warring states period, competitors developed ways to surmount this problem. The Chu state based in the southern region ruled conquered territories through centrally appointed officials, who replaced local royals and collected statistics on people and resources. The Jin state, after losing many of its aristocrats in a battle with the Qin in 645 BCE, offered land grants to populations outside its fortified city. This strategy became a fundament of Chinese empire: the state allocated land to peasants, who in turn paid taxes and served in the military. This bargain with incorporated outsiders did not include citizenship as it did in Rome; it instead created a world of farmers who owed their most crucial resource—land—and their service to the state.

The wars among competing states spread military technology and statecraft across what we think of now as Chinese space. Chariot warfare was developed into a deadly art. The Qin state got its start in the ninth century BCE as a horse-raising dependency of another kingdom. In the fifth century, the ruler of the Wei state rationalized the land grant regime by establishing a standardized land allotment for each household, undertook massive irrigation projects, and set up reserve granaries to protect farmers from price fluctuations. A century later, the Qin turned the tables on the Wei kingdom by attracting its counselors and co-opting its reforms.

The Qin advisor Shang Yang, who had spent time at the Wei court, tightened up the Qin's hold on resources and loyalty by giving peasants legal rights to their land, including the right to buy and sell it. Each plot of land was laid out on a grid defined by irrigation ditches and pathways and linked to a term of service and an amount of taxation. As the Qin expanded, they applied this system of irrigation and regular plots to new areas, creating the fertile terrain that fed their war machine and, ultimately, their imperial state. The system was fine-tuned with annual reports, forecasts, statistical data on supplies, the occupations and capacities (age, health, work, sex) of the population, account keeping, standardized coinage and measures, and performance evaluations. This apparatus of intensive surveillance and social control—practices often associated with "modern" or "western" governance—was perfected by the Qin in the third century BCE.

Shang Yang's reforms enforced a political system based on three pillars—the sovereign, his law, and a regulated society. The ruler was the source of all law, and society's task was to follow this law and enforce it. Codified law—law as a list of crimes and punishments—and the idea of the ruler's lawmaking role were not new with the Qin, but Shang Yang took earlier legalism in a typically militaristic direction. Suspicious of the disruptive potential of empowered officials and contemplative scholars, he proposed that the people themselves could become the enforcers of law through systems of self-surveillance, shored up by rewards for denunciations and harsh penalties for both crime and not reporting it. One correlate of this strategy was that knowledge of the laws had to be widespread, so that no official would dare to subvert law on his own.

The purpose of this top-down, popularly enforced regulatory state was agricultural production and warfare. The regime was deeply suspicious of intermediaries—regional nobles, its own officials, cultural specialists. Rewards for military accomplishments were determined according to a system of twenty ranks. The standardized land plot facilitated aligning military units with the households that supported them. All social status was made dependent on military performance, and rank could be used—legally—to have punishments for crimes reduced. These interlocking systems were designed to make merit, not lineage or lo-

> *"If the country is strong and carries out war, then the poison is shipped to the enemy. The state will have no rituals, music, or parasitic officials and it will inevitably be strong."*
>
> —*Book of Lord Shang*

Figure 2.2
Terra cotta soldiers with horses from the mausoleum of the first Qin emperor. Imperial workshops created an army of thousands of soldiers, with horses and chariots, to accompany the emperor into the afterlife. The statues are housed in the Museum of the Terra Cotta Warriors, opened in 1979, near Xian City, China. Christian Kober, GettyImages.

cal authority, the basis for material and other rewards. Shang Yang fell victim to his own exigencies—and to the impossibility of abolishing the personal element of power. He was executed in 338 BCE after insisting that a tutor of the royal family be punished according to the laws.

To augment the peasant infantry, the Qin ruler established crack military units, modeled after those of a rival kingdom. In the third century BCE, the Qin adopted a policy of attacking people, rather than simply absorbing conquered territories. The goal was to destroy a rival's possibility of ever fighting back. The result was enormous bloodshed. In 260 BCE, Qin armies killed, it is asserted, four hundred thousand soldiers of their main competitor, the Zhao. After an interlude of losses inflicted by rivals allied against them, the Qin completed their imperial conquest by defeating all six remaining states in seven years. In 221, the Qin goals, as set out by an advisor, of "vanquishing various states, completing an empire, and uniting the world" were attained.

Military Centralism in Power

The first Qin emperor, named Zheng, was born in 259 BCE. Scholars of the subsequent Han dynasty cast doubts on the legitimacy of the emperor's birth and the status of his biological father. His mother was described as the concubine of a rich merchant, who gave her already pregnant to his client, the Qin king. This anti-myth of origins suggested the ambiguous place of merchants in the imperial order and conveniently undercut the earlier dynasty in favor of the Han. But when Zheng ruled, he refashioned himself beyond reach of calumny. He called himself "august emperor" (*huangdi*), referring to the highest god (*di*) of the ancient Shang empire and to the attribute *huang*—shining, celestial. This claim added divine sanction to the traditional claim of the ruler to be the source of order and law. The emperor traveled to the sacred high mountains of his realm, where he conducted sacrifices, left accounts of his deeds, and proclaimed his authority over the earth—"wherever sun and moon shine."

If the Qin empire were to last, the emperor's claim to universal power had to be recognized throughout his enlarged realm. The empire was divided into command areas, and further into counties; these were administered by officials appointed from the center and subject to recall at any time. Three different officials—a governor, a military commander, and an imperial inspector—supervised each commandery. Qin governance by centrally appointed officials contrasts with Rome's empowerment of local elites and senators to exploit distant territories on their own.

Accounting and communication were facilitated by the creation of a simplified script that was used across areas where people spoke many languages and recorded them differently. The Qin issued a new imperial currency, used uniform weights and measures, and even standardized the width of axles—so that carts would travel in the same ruts along the empire's roads. These were extended and improved through the massive use of convict or other compulsory labor. The Qin road network radiated out from their capital at Xianyang as far as inner Mongolia and through the eastern provinces. Canals were constructed to enhance the river connections.

> *"Anciently, the people everywhere had their own local customs. They differed in what they found beneficial and in their likes and dislikes. . . . This is why the sage-kings created laws and regulations, with which to straighten and correct the hearts of the people. . . . The purpose of all laws, statutes, and ordinances is to teach and lead the people, rid them of dissoluteness and depravity, . . . and turn them toward goodness."*
>
> —from a letter circulated in 227 by the governor of a Qin commandery

The point of this integration was to collect revenue, service, and information. Travel and transport on Qin roads was controlled through checkpoints, passports, and fees. The lifeblood of the empire was taxation, assessed unequally on different groups. Merchants paid a higher poll tax than did peasants. Slave owners paid two times the rate for free people on each slave. Peasants owed both a harvest tax, adjusted to the size of their allotment, and a head tax. Males owed labor, depending on their age and status, as well as military service. A requirement that households with more than one adult male paid taxes at a higher rate enforced the nuclear family as the unit of production.

These systems demanded the services of an extensive civil service. But the emperor's officials and advisors had to be controlled, as did their sources of information. Particularly unnerving was the multiplicity of precedents that could be gleaned from China's long history, including such irritants as the Zhou model of dependent vassal kings. The Qin response was to gather up the great books of the past, lock them up in an imperial library, and allow access only under government supervision. A similar tactic was used to control regional elites. The emperor required powerful families to move to his capital, Xianyang, where he could keep an eye on them. There former local rulers were provided with palaces and given the opportunity to develop a genteel culture, but many still schemed about regaining their past glories.

The triumphant Qin rapidly created the conditions of their defeat. Gigantic projects—canals, walls, roads—strained the empire's resources. The Qin could not turn off their war machine, and after 221, they continued to expand both in the watery and fragmented south and against the Xiongnu. But the mobilization of huge armies (500,000 to attack in the south) and enormous gangs of forced labor (700,000 prisoners to build the first emperor's tomb) were probably less devastating than the extremes of discipline used against elite subordinates. After the death of the first emperor, civil war broke out, and prominent families, former royals, and opportunists all joined the fray. In

202 BCE, after eight years of warfare, Liu Bang, a commoner, former barfly, and prodigal son, declared victory over the empire the Qin had created.

Making China Work

Liu Bang took a negative lesson from the Qin's alienation of elite subordinates. He was quick to credit his military leaders for their part in his victory, and as Gaozu, the first Han emperor, he took a less centralized approach to administration. Gaozu reinstated subordinate kingdoms in the eastern half of his empire, while keeping the Qin's command organization in the western regions. Kings, as holders of the highest noble rank, were required to render homage to the emperor annually and to report on tax collection and revenues, some of which they were entitled to retain. In the command areas—later known as provinces—the Han established a second tier of nobles who were entitled to collect taxes and to transfer some of them to the center. The key to the Han's longer-lived dynasty was sustaining multiple lines of authority, avoiding too much centralization or too much diffusion of power to intermediaries. Still, two centuries later, the tendency toward farming out power would have its own destructive effects.

The Han emperor moved the capital, first to Luoyang in the south where his family had roots, and later to Chang'an, not far from the old Qin capital, which had been burned to the ground. Leaving his family's place of origin for the Qin's west-central space enhanced the emperor's all-encompassing and unlocalized status. In an initiative that dismissed all talk of his disgraceful past—and insulted his father to boot—Gaozu claimed that his real parent was a dragon god. This origin was subsequently incorporated into the cult of the emperor as the "son of heaven."

The emperor's legitimacy rested not just on his heavenly origins but on his place in a fixed and moral social order. Under the Han dynasty, ideas attributed to the philosopher Confucius (Kong zi) were recorded, systematized, and propagated as a code of conduct. During his lifetime (551–479 BCE), Confucius had been preoccupied with the decline of the Zhou dynasty. He extolled the virtues of a society based on each person's performance of his given role. "Let the ruler be a ruler and the subject a subject; let the father be a father and the son a son": this saying put imperial and patriarchal power in the same frame and gave a social dimension to the Qin's system of ranks. A man should bear himself with integrity and righteousness, be loyal, considerate, and altruistic, respect tradition, and practice good manners at all times. These values, like those of *humanitas* for Romans, provided a framework for elite education and ideal behavior.

The Chinese emperor's divine mandate could accommodate more ideological possibilities than the Confucian story of ordered ranks and virtuous civilization might suggest. Various contemplative tendencies could coexist with state cults connecting the emperor to gods of the earth and sky. Some advisors and emperors were inclined to accept the natural way (*dao*) of the universe; others opened up new searches for harmony and order. In religious matters, Chinese empire sustained for a longer time than Rome a flexible and adaptive capacity. Buddhism reached China during the Han dynasty, and images of Buddha, like those of other divinities, could be integrated into local and imperial rituals.

The Qin had developed law into a sharp tool of rule. Death, mutilation, and hard labor were the only punishments. During the Han dynasty some mutilations were abolished and replaced by corporal punishment. Two kinds of action could mitigate a sentence: amnesties—usually issued to a whole class of people on the occasion of a happy imperial event—or redemption—meaning that a person could buy himself out of punishment. Both mitigations linked people to their rulers, while official codes emphasized the law-bound nature of authority.

For the Han, unlike the Romans, a large and intricately organized body of officials was critical to imperial power. The tradition of learned advisors offered rewards and pitfalls both to ambitious councillors and to the emperor, who benefited from multiple sources of advice but could also succumb to flattery and intrigue. The capital city, with its dominating and off-bounds imperial palace, teemed with officials and their staffs and servants. Officials served on a scale of ranks—eighteen in 23 BCE—with a sliding scale of remuneration. The Grand Tutor, three grand ministers (of finance, of works, and the commander in chief of the military), and nine lesser ministers, as well as a powerful secretariat, could influence, guide, or obstruct the emperor's will. So, too, could the emperor's family, including the emperor's mother, whose powers were enhanced by the seclusion of the imperial court. These competing networks diversified the information, goals, and capacities of the centralized administration.

Government by officials was invigorated by meritocratic selection. The emperor recruited not from an aristocracy but from the sons of landowners, and in 124 BCE he created an imperial academy—some call it a university—to train them in techniques of rule, record keeping, and Confucian ideals. By 1 CE a hundred men a year were passing examinations by scholars and entering the bureaucracy. Young men from the provinces, usually nominated by officials, were brought to the capital to study and be evaluated. Candidates were placed in service throughout the empire; the most highly appreciated served in the capital.

Education as a path to higher rank and fortune brought in new blood and ideas, provided a significant degree of upward mobility, and attached provincial elites and wealthy families to the imperial center. It also produced its own corruptions that emperors at times tried to remedy—privileged access to learning, favoritism in examinations and placement, cliques of officials who had gone through the system together, and a tendency toward formulaic approaches to administration. Most important, for provincial and local elites, the rewards of officialdom countered temptations to transform intermediary positions into challenges to the emperor's command—a problem that bedeviled Rome's successors.

Respect for rank and office was not a recipe for social stasis; it provided a ladder for both advances and declines. Ambitious families extended their reach and protected themselves by making connections inside and outside officialdom. People of low rank—peasants infrequently, merchants more often—could make their way into positions of power by mobilizing resources and using them to influence officials. The calumny about the Qin emperor's ignoble origins highlighted the role that a great merchant had played in the founding of that dynasty, while making clear the proper order of things. Merchants should serve the state, never the other way around.

The commercial life of cities was both a target for administrative control and a source of energy for the system as a whole. In Qin and Han cities, markets were laid out on grids, surveyed by officials from a centrally located government tower, and rigidly separated from imperial palaces and parks. Quality control and taxation required inspection and accounting. Prices, according to Qin law, had to be written on tags attached to each item up for sale. In the Han capital Chang'an, commerce and manufacturing took place in two gigantic walled-in market areas, the ancient equivalent of shopping malls. Inspired by their ruler's collections of exotic gifts, Han subjects could, for a price, enjoy cosmetics and foods produced beyond imperial borders.

Those borders had long been a source of both innovation and danger. The actions of nomadic peoples continued to push Chinese rulers to come up with ways to deal with peoples whom they could not absorb. The Xiongnu nomads who had consolidated their empire in the western regions during the energetic expansion of the Qin state were one major threat.

"I and the chanyu are the parents of the people. Problems that emerged in the past from the misdeeds of our subordinates should not ruin our brotherly happiness. . . . I and the chanyu should cast aside the trivial problems of the past and together follow the great way."

—Emperor Wen, 162 BCE

Relations with the Xiongnu, who well understood the vulnerabilities and resources of Chinese leaders, took two basic forms. One was war—war that the Chinese military often lost to mobile, self-supplied cavalry, organized in decimal units, led adroitly by the Xiongnu's supreme leader, the *chanyu*, protected by his crack imperial guard. The other strategy was making a deal—paying the Xiongnu for peace. Qin and Han emperors tried both approaches. Arguments for battle appealed to ambitious military men and to counselors fed up with

Xiongnu raids and desertions to the nomads. But after 200 BCE when an aggressive war against the Xiongnu ended with the Han emperor encircled and forced to sue for peace, marriage alliance became the principal arrangement.

The policy had four elements: transfers of Chinese products desired by the nomads; a Han princess given in marriage to the chanyu; the ranking of Han and Xiongnu as equal states; and the establishment of the Great Wall as a boundary between the two. In 162 BC a treaty assigned the chanyu rule over the "archers" north of the Great Wall and the Han emperor dominion over the settled people to the south.

The division of the world into two equivalent but distinct empires gave rise to reflection about what made Chinese empire different from the nomadic one. Scholars created an image of Chinese people as the opposite of their challengers: settled not mobile; eaters of grain, not meat; wearers of cloth, not fur. But even if later Chinese historians reified Chinese and "barbarians" as eternally in conflict with each other, in reality the intersection of Han and Xiongnu commands often took the form of interempire diplomacy. The recognition that the nomads had their own social order and that the best way to control it was to deal with its leaders as political authorities became a fundamental element of Chinese imperial strategy.

But diplomacy was not enough for either empire, and each had to worry about internal fragmentation and defections to the other side. Both the chanyu and the emperor sought allies among the other's subordinated peoples—a tactic we will see time and again. Han armies under Emperor Wu, seeking to outflank the Xiongnu, campaigned into central Asia, conquering Ferghana in 101 BC. Competition between the Xiongnu and the Han continued for another century, but when the Xiongnu began to fragment, leaders of their subordinated peoples renegotiated their relationships with the Han and received official honors for their submission. Xiongnu nobles confirmed their loyalty through tribute presented to the Han emperor. The nomads' tribute of horses and armor and their dispatch of hostages to the Chinese court were rewarded with lavish gifts of silk, gold, rice, and money, demonstrating the superiority of Han power.

The Dangers of Success

Han efforts to control their western borders drove the empire's rulers into fundamental reconfiguration of their army, with long-term and unintended consequences. The empire turned away from universal military service, finally abolishing it in 32 CE. Peasant infantries were no match for the nomads on the borders, and during the last century BCE the empire began to use peasants' fees to employ professional soldiers, usually nomadic peoples who had submitted to the emperor and could effectively counter other nomads on the frontier. But allowing peasants to buy off service stretched their resources and sent many into debt and servitude, enhancing the powers of local elites who could mobilize debtors or recalcitrant recruits for their own purposes. An impressive revolt of strong families against an over-centralizing emperor in the opening decades of the first century CE had shown that peasants could transfer their loyalty to regional elites. The Han responded by moving former nomadic peoples inside the empire to counter or prevent local rebellion. The outsourcing of both external and internal defense to tribal chieftains coincided with the relocation of the revived Han dynasty eastward and the rebuilding of a capital in Luoyang.

Over two centuries, Han strategies had successfully undermined Xiongnu unity, but the defeat of chanyu sovereignty had, in the long run, devastating consequences for the Han. When Xiongnu rewards dried up, nomadic frontier troops went back to raiding settled populations. Peasants responded by retreating eastward, and the Han government, unable to force resettlement of the western borderlands, focused its defensive efforts on the capital. The empire slid down the slippery slope of decentralization by giving provincial governors control over their officials, including military ones, and the power to recruit. The result was warlordism in the much reduced center and loss of control over the frontier units. The empire produced by military centralism had disconnected its peasants, swallowed its nomads, and armed its intermediaries against itself.

Rome and China, Insiders and Outsiders

The Han lost control in the worst-case scenario for Chinese empire—under assault from insubordinate lords at a time when the dynasty's nomadic supporters and allies were also divided and dangerous. But four centuries later, the empire was put back together, first by the Sui and later by the Tang, a mixed Turkic-Chinese dynasty that regalvanized the polity with nomadic military skills, Buddhism, and long-distance trade. The pattern of disaggregation and reconstitution of Chinese empire resumed after the Tang and continued into the twentieth century. We will take up the story of Chinese empire in chapter 7. Here we turn to a question of imperial history. Why was Chinese empire repeatedly put back together in roughly the same area, while Rome—as a state—never revived?

First, let's look at some similarities. Both empires emerged at about the same time—from the third cen-

Chinese Dynasties
(a partial listing)
Qin, 221–206 BCE
Han, 206 BCE–220 CE
Imperial collapse, 220–589
Sui, 589–618
Tang, 618–907
Fragmentation, 907–60
Song, 960–1279
Yuan, 1279–1368
Ming, 1368–1644
Qing, 1644–1911

Figure 2.3
A Roman arch and
a Chinese wall

Roman arch of Trajan at
Thamugadi (Timgad), Algeria.
Photograph from late 1880s.
Library of Congress.

Great Wall of China.
Photograph by Langdon
Warner, 1923–24. Special
Collections, Fine Arts Library,
Harvard College Library.

tury BCE to the third century CE, on opposite sides of the great Eurasian landmass. Chinese products, exchanged along transcontinental land routes, reached the Mediterranean, but neither empire knew much of the other and each imagined itself to rule a whole world. Both Rome and China were founded on military might and agrarian production and relied on rigorous taxation to link the two. Both empires built roads—China's were probably twice as long as Rome's—to connect their huge spaces; both made learning an attribute of their elites; both cultivated genteel behavior and nurtured scholarship; both used censuses; both could direct their taxes to support enormous armies and the imperial court. Both empires managed huge populations—about fifty or sixty million people—and both lasted, as states, for centuries. Their repertoires of power were enduring—often in memory and sometimes in practice. What distinguished these powerful and influential empires from each other?

Political geography made a difference. Qin and Han leaders built upon ideas of rule articulated across a large space as far back as the second millennium BCE, elaborated by Zhou kings, and honed during wars between descendant states. Rome's militant republicanism had no direct political ancestor. Romans drew inspiration from distant powers in the eastern Mediterranean—Greece, Persia, and Egypt—but they were dealt a freer hand when it came to creating imperial institutions.

Through conquest, taxation, and sheltered commerce, Rome made the Mediterranean into a single world, but this integrated economic system centered on the sea was also vulnerable. When emperors and their armies moved away from Rome, the system began to fragment. Without the empire's connecting structures, the differentiated economy declined and the center was not worth retaking. Constantine's move to the east was a relocation to a more promising imperial space (see chapter 3), while roads, commerce, artisanal production, and urban life to the west declined.

Chinese empire over the centuries did break up into fragments, but sooner or later a conqueror would manage to put them back together. China was not centered on a single city on a single sea, where commerce and taxation linked a diversified economy. When Chinese emperors found it helpful or necessary, they moved the capital to another site. The empire kept itself in motion in other ways: resettling dangerous subordinates in a different place was a strategy for controlling the emperor's worst threat—regional power. Interactions with nomadic and other peoples at moving frontiers pushed Chinese leaders into long-distance exploration, military improvements, and political innovation.

The fixing of Romans to Rome and the spatial flexibility of Chinese empire had consequences for the way each state was run. Roman political institutions developed in a city where citizen-soldiers had votes and power.

The republic's daring political innovation of popular sovereignty was connected to its manageable city space, and the radical idea of granting citizenship to defeated outsiders allowed the empire to expand outward while not—for a very long time—disrupting the capital's command. Although the offices and duties of various institutions—the senate, the magistrates, the consuls, the popular assemblies—were altered over time, a commitment to preserving citizens' rights and legal process was preserved, at least in principle.

Chinese rulers also were committed to rule by law, but operated from different assumptions about it. The emperor did not ask the populace to approve his legislation; instead he fulfilled his duty to society by issuing correct regulations and appropriate punishments for violations. Chinese law at this formative time was a set of rules, emanating from the emperor. From this perspective—in contrast to Rome's multiplicity of legal sites—there was no reason to establish a separate judiciary; law was part of administration. Wise officials might interpret the law, but their advice was addressed to the emperor, not debated and manipulated in a more or less public forum. In the Chinese provinces, governors, county leaders, and their assistants processed judicial matters; this important task was kept out of the hands of local nobles.

As we suggested in chapter 1, all empires had to keep their intermediaries both subordinate and loyal. Rome and China came up with distinct ways to do this and their managerial strategies are another part of the answer for why China revived and Rome did not. For China, the key institution was rule by officials. The empire had been created out of conflicts between rival kings, and the main threat to Chinese empire from the start was that subordinated royals or other regional powers could tear the polity apart again or seize command. Against this possibility, Qin and Han leaders created their system of centralized officialdom extending to the countryside. Recruitment, education, and examinations mobilized talent from localities, drawing the best and the brightest into the imperial administration. The rewards for imperial elites could be enormous—in resources, prestige, and a cultured way of life—and perhaps this is why Chinese empire remained a political ideal worth fighting for in the long interludes between successful dynasties.

Rome managed its intermediaries indirectly. From the very beginning, military excellence was one route to advancement even to the highest ranks, but local elites could also stay put, participate in public imperial cults, pay their taxes, and have their lifeways enhanced by Rome's cultural and commercial connections. The empire rewarded its elites with land, slaves, legal status, and comforts. Great senatorial families and others acquired an interest in their provincial properties, where they could live in Roman ways as part of the privileged citizenry. Here, though, is another clue to the empire's gradual disappearance. Unlike China, where elites had the skills to become imperial officials and the motivation to re-create empire, in late Roman times local aristocrats lacked both of these. As the rewards and discipline of empire dried up, regional elites applied their cultural capital—including notions of law and sovereignty—locally, sustaining Roman ideas but not the empire itself. China began when local lords seized political initiative to build an empire; Rome ended when local lords chose to go their own ways.

In conclusion, we turn to two other themes—political imagination and the politics of difference. Both empires respected knowledge and deployed it, in overlapping but different ways. Roman intellectuals could praise Rome's glories, create heroic myths of origins, and redefine its civilization to suit the times. They could also bemoan their countrymen's corruption and decline, thereby keeping purportedly Roman virtues and political principles in play. Chinese scholars extolled the virtues of earlier rulers—or cast doubts upon them—to inform and glorify the present dynasty. Rome's calendar incorporated its former emperors into the names of months, presumably honoring them for all time. Chinese eras began afresh with each new emperor; the year was known by his name and numbered by his length of rule. This practice and others pointed to the primacy of the emperor in the present and the future.

What difference did these propaganda efforts and ruling habits make to the political conceptions of subjects? In both cases, for the vast majority of the population, whether slave or free, the empire was a given, and politics was oriented toward more immediate powers—owners, tribal leaders, landlords, military commanders. Still, both empires projected ways of belonging that could be accessed and interpreted by people of different statuses; these political creations set their mark on the world.

Roman citizenship was a major invention. The concept, perhaps adapted from Greek city-states, was institutionalized in the republic and sustained through the empire's expansion. Both the Romans' decision to extend citizenship beyond their city and Caracalla's extension of citizenship to all free adult males in the empire in 212 BC had profound impacts on how rights and sovereignty could be imagined. Imperial citizenship had multiple meanings—a legal status with obligations and protections, a source of pride and honor, a sense of cultural superiority, a personal bond with state power and with other citizens even over a huge space. The polity could exist in the persons of its members, not just in the group of servitors around the emperor or his rivals for power. How this bond with the state and other citizens would be activated, what it could express and produce, and what it meant for empires—these were questions that would be worked, reworked, opened, and never really closed from the time of Roman empire to the present.

That Roman citizenship was coveted meant that not everyone had it. But the Romans' strong notion of the superiority of their way of life was accompanied by a belief that all peoples, however barbarous their origins, if properly educated, could ultimately become part of *humanitas*. Still, there was only one kind of humanity that qualified as civilization—the Roman one.

Chinese emperors, ministers, and military men also believed in the superiority of their civilization and also were confronted by outsiders who lived differently. But the Chinese way of dealing with nomadic others corresponded to China's great creation—government by officials. Selected leaders with "barbarian" origins could, as individuals, become the emperor's subordinates and advisors, acquiring the virtues associated with good governance. As collectivities, China's outsiders could be recognized and dealt with through pragmatic alliances, tributary relations, and military emulation. Some scholars rewrote these interactions into stark oppositions between Han and barbarian, but even these accounts acknowledged that barbarians had their way too.

Both Roman and Chinese leaders endeavored to keep their diverse populations loyal and productive. First by extending citizenship and later with their adoption of Christianity, Romans promoted the notion of a singular, superior political community based on shared rights and culture. Chinese leaders, situated at the cusp of settled and nomadic peoples, did not demand this uniformity or offer anyone the potentially disruptive rights of citizens. But Chinese empire accommodated and exploited inputs from outsiders, and the empire's diplomacy paid heed to the reality of alien powers and the respect due to them. Rome and China two thousand years ago expressed two variants on the politics of difference. Their approaches to questions of political belonging and of how to treat people from outside a core culture made lasting impacts on the trajectories of imperial power.

AFTER ROME

Empire, Christianity, and Islam

R ome shaped the geography of later polities; memories of Rome galvanized empire-builders over the next millennium. Across a vast space, elites had engaged Roman culture and politics; the Latin language, Christianity, and ideas of civic activism were available to ambitious leaders. This chapter explores empires that tried to take Rome's place. We consider themes that run through this book—the emergence of new competitors on the fringes of empires; the emulation of earlier empires in imperial imaginaries; the synthesis and transformation of prior practices; the problem of finding intermediaries and keeping them loyal; and the recurrence of imperial fragmentation. We explore a major innovation in the history of empires: the linkage of imperial power to monotheism, in its Christian and Islamic variants, and the implications of a potentially all-embracing religion for empires' politics of difference.

The Roman empire in the late fourth century was not the polity that had absorbed the gods of conquered people. It had become a Christian realm. Monotheism was a tool of empire, but it also presented a danger that proved all too real: schism. The claim of an emperor to be the singular earthly spokesman for a singular divinity gave rise to challenges: might not someone else be the true representative of the divine? Might not the problems of the empire—from plague to loss of a battle—be a sign that the emperor had betrayed the faith? Christianity and Islam, both "religions of the book" and built on a shared heritage, inspired contests over imperial authority.

Empires, as we have seen, can be adaptable to cultural and linguistic differences among people they encountered. Monotheism did not necessarily imply conflict with nonbelievers. Muslims, Jews, and Christians in the Mediterranean world and beyond could trade and otherwise peacefully interact with others. But the combination of empire and monotheism carried a lethal possibility—rival expansionist efforts, based on visions of all-embracing, mutually exclusive civilizations. Would such conceptions be softened by the realities of governing a complex polity? The exercise of imperial power by Christians and Muslims brought questions of tolerance and exclusion to the fore.

Looking at Christian and Islamic polities as empires, we see entwined histories and structural similarities. States that asserted unity under a single god were vulnerable to both the grandeur and the volatility of their rulers' claims.

From Rome to Constantinople

If ever a city was the focal point of imperial space, it was Rome, the Eternal City. Yet in 324 CE Emperor Constantine created a second capital in the city of Byzantium. First named New Rome, it soon became known after its founder as Constantinople. The center of imperial authority shifted to a Greek-speaking region, although Byzantium itself, like many trading centers of the empire, had a diverse population. The language of government remained Latin. Byzantium was positioned at an advantageous crossroads, joining the eastern Mediterranean, the Black Sea, and trans-Asian trade routes. Perhaps the emperor wanted to enhance his autonomy from leading Roman families. When Constantine inaugurated his new capital in 330, he decorated a column with figures from Greek mythology and from Christian narratives, linking classical traditions to the new state religion.

Religion and Power in the Eastern Roman Empire

Constantine's empire was still Roman, but in the late fifth century it split into eastern and western parts with separate rulers. Some later emperors tried to put it back together, but without success. The western part, including Rome itself, was taken over by Ostrogoths at the end of the fifth century. There, imperial authority gave way to fragmented political power, the breakdown of economic and cultural linkages, and military conflict. The eastern empire became known as "Byzantine" only after its fall. From the beginning, the court culture of the eastern empire reflected not only its Latin heritage and Greek location but the influence of other polities that had been jostling each other for centuries, particularly the Sassanian empire in Persia.

The glory days of Byzantium came in the sixth century, during the reign (527–565) of Justinian and his queen, Theodora. Justinian defeated

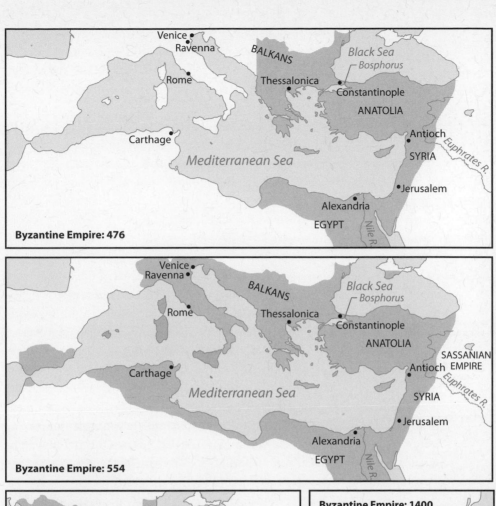

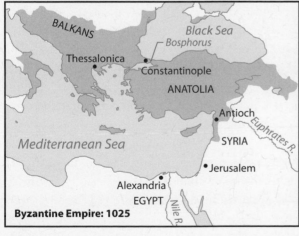

Map 3.1
Expansion and contraction
of the Byzantine empire.

Empire, Christianity, and Islam

> *"Every community governed by laws and customs uses partly its own law, partly laws common to all mankind. The law which a people makes for its own government belongs exclusively to that state and is called the civil law, as being the law of the particular state. But the law which natural reason appoints for all mankind obtains equally among all nations, because all nations make use of it. The people of Rome, then, are governed partly by their own laws, and partly by the laws which are common to all mankind."*
>
> —Justinian's code, prologue

the Ostrogoths in Italy and restored Roman rule in its new Byzantine form. Byzantine armies reconquered north Africa from the Vandals, and they maintained a standoff—sometimes through war, sometimes by making peace—with the Sassanian empire. Justinian's Roman conception of a law-bound empire was expressed in the *corpus juris civilis*, a codification of Roman law published in 534. The Justinian code was an adaptation as well as a restatement of Roman law, influenced by Christianity and representative of an emperor's will; it reaffirmed the state's obligation to offer its subjects trials before a judge and specified the content of the law. But Justinian's success made things harder for his successors: the cost of his wars left the empire in financial difficulty and its extended frontiers vulnerable.

The population of the eastern Roman empire was extremely diverse; the major language groups included Greek, Latin, Slavic, Coptic, Arabic, and Berber. Cities—from Alexandria to Antioch to Thessalonica—were cosmopolitan; seventy-two languages were supposedly spoken in Constantinople. Armenians, Greeks, Jews, and Latins had an accepted place in the empire's commercial life. Like Rome, the eastern empire was a network of urban centers, including some nine hundred cities with characteristic institutions: bath, school, church. Greek was the liturgical language, Latin the administrative one, but no effort was made to impose either on the population in general. The countryside provided the agricultural surplus to sustain the web of cities but remained diverse in peoples and languages, linked to but not fully part of imperial culture.

The singular figure of the emperor who provided order and protection for the differentiated polity was complemented by devotion to a singular divinity, whose appeal was not limited to local cults and ancestors and whose worship provided a common moral basis for interactions across wide spaces. Emperor Theodosius completed the transition to Christianity begun earlier. He banned pagan ceremonies in 392, closed temples, and destroyed idols. Allied to the state, the Christian church became wealthy: it owned land, collected donations from the rich, and benefited from a state subsidy. Some of this revenue was turned into help for the poor, but much went into churches and works of art. The vast church of Hagia Sophia in Constantinople, built during the reign of Justinian and Theodora, linked scale and refinement in extraordinary display. Justinian sent craftsmen to adorn buildings across the empire; the striking mosaics of Ravenna's churches (on the Adriatic coast of Italy) are one famous example. Monasteries, endowed

Figure 3.1
Justinian I,
Byzantine
emperor, and his
retinue, c. 547 AD.
From a mosaic
in the church
of San Vitale,
Ravenna, Italy.
Bridgeman
Art Library,
GettyImages.

by the rich, shaped an ecclesiastical culture and through their connections tied the Christian world together.

Was Christianity a unifying force for empire? Linking a proselytizing religion of apparently universal appeal, buttressed by scriptural authority, to institutions of state offered the prospect of true world empire—one god, one empire, one emperor. But Christianity would be a unifying force only if divergent interpretations—and there were many—of church doctrine were either tolerated or suppressed. Furthermore, the multiplicity of religions in the Byzantines' spaces required attention. Over time, the Byzantines developed several approaches to religion: the empire was hostile to polytheism; relatively tolerant of the monotheistic Jews; willing, after the rise of Islam, to trade with Muslim partners even in the midst of war; and in general pragmatic about the involvement of Christians with non-Christians in commercial networks. The empire was much less tolerant of difference within Christianity. As early as 325, Constantine tried to get squabbling bishops to reach a consensus on doctrine, but doctrinal disputes proved bitter and divisive, especially when dissenters risked being labeled heretics.

The patriarch in Constantinople was known as the "patriarch of the whole world" (*oikoumene* in Greek). Other patriarchates were set up in Alexandria, Antioch, and Jerusalem, with bishoprics in other cities. Whereas the church in Rome tried to soldier on as an independent institution after the Ostrogoth conquest, Christianity in the eastern Mediterranean was tightly linked to the Byzantine empire. The emperor in Constantinople represented himself as God's sole regent on earth; he appointed the Christian patriarch and presided over church councils. Both ruling and ecclesiastic authorities were often divided by doctrinal controversies, notably one over the place of icons in worship. Still, the eastern church became a distinct entity. It declared its separation from the Rome-based church several times, and the split of 1054 turned out to be definitive. After 800, when Charlemagne was crowned emperor by the pope in Rome, two alternative kinds of church-empire relations, with two imperial descent lines from Rome, were set into uneasy relation to each other.

The close association of church and empire in Byzantium—as well as conflict with Islamic polities—redefined empire as a community of belief in a way that Rome had not done before. This kind of Christian empire slowly shaped a commonwealth of peoples, linked by history and religious culture, subject to varying degrees of political control from the center. The influence of the church spread beyond the empire itself, where distance from Constantinople gave religious leaders more room to maneuver. By the ninth century, church leaders—unlike their western counterparts who insisted on using Latin—were propagating Christianity in Slavic languages. The eastern church eventually gave birth to a number of variations on orthodox Christianity: Greek, Russian, Armenian, and Coptic orthodoxies that long survived the Byzantine empire. In the western part of Europe, Roman Christianity evolved into the Catholic church, claiming to be universal, but defined de facto by the extent and limits of papal authority. The Byzantines' version of Christian orthodoxy proved innovative and adaptable to the politics of empire, creating ties—organizational and ideological—across a huge space.

The Byzantine empire maintained Roman core institutions—the army, perhaps 650,000 men in the late fourth century, and the much smaller class of officials, some 30,000–40,000 men. Most important, the Byzantines continued the taxation practices of the Romans. Paying bureaucrats and soldiers through taxation distinguished the Byzantine empire from the polities that emerged from the breakup of the western empire, where kings relied on local lords to supply men and materiel. Constantinople retained the capacity to build aqueducts and roads and to provide stable coinage for over seven hundred years; the empire-state was present in the daily practices and imaginations of people across a wide space.

The Byzantine emperor—as we shall see in other durable empires—was able to control resources that gave him a certain distance from the imperial aristocrats or local elites that made up society. Adapting court practices from Persia and elsewhere in the region, the Byzantines used eunuchs as advisors, subordinate officials, servants, and especially as the people who controlled access to the emperor. With no dynastic ambitions and not bound by the gender roles of either males or females, eunuchs were, as Kathryn Ringrose puts it, "the perfect servants."

The ability to concentrate forces for battles to extend or protect territory and to awe its subject population was essential in this widely extended empire. With its capital on the well-defended Bosphorus and in possession of a wide range of resources and the means to redistribute them, the Byzantine empire was better able to maintain itself in the face of raiders, pirates, covetous insiders, migrating peoples, and imperial aggressors than was Rome to the west. The Byzantines revolutionized naval warfare by outfitting their vessels with flame-throwers that spewed burning naphtha over the sea, terrifying their enemies.

Byzantium, like Rome before it, supplemented its full-time soldiers with fighters from border areas—with the so-called barbarians (Goths, Huns, Scythians, Slavs, later Turks) against whom the empire defined itself. Like the nomads on the Chinese borders, these troops had much to gain from cooperating with a large and well-organized imperial system, but had no particular loyalty to it. In the seventh century, under assault by Arab forces, the Byzantines reorganized their provincial administration and military. Dividing territory into districts called "themata" under a military commander, the empire provided land for soldiers to use, with the expectation that the soldiers' descendants would also serve and use land in the theme. Pay could therefore be reduced while loyalty to the military unit was maintained. The reform, a strategy partway between the tax-funded army inherited from Rome and reliance on aristocrats with their retainers as in most of post-Roman western Europe, had its risks for an empire centered on the court and its cities. Themata could become dispersed centers of power, and soldiers could think of resources as their own. By the eleventh century, magnates were acquiring rights to revenue from peasants that the state earlier had exercised more directly, and the system came to resemble more closely that of the post-Roman west. Both the alien fighting force and the land grant system were useful but dangerous elements of many imperial repertoires.

Routine administration depended on cities running their own affairs through municipal councils, to whom the imperial government assigned required tasks—repairing buildings and aqueducts, policing the city, cleaning streets, maintaining markets, and housing soldiers. Locals were watched over by the Roman system of prefects—administrators and judges responsible directly to the emperor, each covering a specific territory. Rituals of power displayed imperial authority, providing nobles and imperial servants with status-confirming roles, even if we cannot know how much these demonstrations actually awed the populace. Byzantine rule depended on a three-way balancing of the emperor's ability to reward and punish, the bureaucracy's capacity to apply predictable regulations, and local elites' interest in interactions that imperial protection permitted. When the Byzantine empire was challenged by costly wars and loss of territory, its urban culture became more difficult to sustain and the multiple vernacular cultures within its boundaries became stronger.

Like Rome, Constantinople did not have a clear or fixed system of imperial succession. The death of an emperor meant competition between factions of the elite for military support and popular acclamation. Emperors had to ensure the loyalty of the military against other potential leaders—at the cost of considerable revenue. Different groups tried to recruit their own "barbarians" against others. Some Byzantine emperors came from the edges of empire and, usually through military prowess, worked their way up the political hierarchy.

Administering such a huge empire put substantial burdens on a mostly agricultural economy. While the large slave plantation—with much of its labor derived from outside the polity—had been a mainstay of the western Roman empire, the eastern empire was more dependent on the *colonus*, the tenant farmer. *Coloni* were tied to farms and could be punished for running away. Their status was hereditary. The consequence of landowners' right to extract rent from tenant farmers—enabling lords to pay their tenants' taxes—was the consolidation by the eighth century of a landed aristocracy.

Imperial Connections: Opportunities and Vulnerabilities

The Byzantine economy drew revenue from diverse regions of considerable fertility—the olive and wine areas along the Mediterranean, the Nile valley, the Balkans, the upper Euphrates valley, the upland regions of Syria—as well as from cities, with their artisans and merchants. Imperial rule both protected and drew its strength and coherence from linkages among urban and agricultural regions. The Byzantines adopted flexible tactics based on taxing commerce and letting others—such as Venetians—do much of the work of exchange and transport.

Interconnection also brought vulnerability. An outbreak of plague in the 540s, for instance, spread across Egypt, as far west as Spain and as far east as Persia. Commercial agents—as in other empires—both made use of imperial protections and cut across them, producing profits, tensions, and at times conflict. Venetian merchants, active all around the eastern Mediterranean, were happy to cooperate with imperial powers who would protect sea and land routes and provide a reasonably stable currency. Shortly after 1100, Venetians were granted their own waterfront quarter in Constantinople. Only later, as Byzantine power waned in the thirteenth century, would Venice become a rival and threat to Byzantium's territorial integrity. By then, the Byzantine empire had not only survived for centuries but also prevented the kind of economic decline that ensued after the "fall" of Rome. The evidence of archaeology—stone houses in Byzantine cities, prosperous monasteries, well-diffused coinage, and remnants of a rich trade in olive oil and wine—reveals the economic advantages of Byzantium's multiribbed imperial umbrella.

Succession struggles and civil conflicts produced cycles of consolidation and dissipation of power. These stresses made Byzantium vulnerable to forces along its edges. The wars between Persia and Byzantium weakened both parties enough to offer opportunities to a new empire expanding in the seventh century, the Islamic caliphate. The Byzantine empire lost its provinces in Syria and Egypt—vital for grain, taxes, and connections—but repulsed a major attack on Constantinople in 678—and repeated assaults later on (map 3.1). Had the strategic center not held out, speculates Judith Herrin, the Islamic empires "would have spread Islam throughout the Balkans, into Italy and the West during the seventh century, at a time when political fragmentation reduced the possibility of organized defense."

The Byzantine empire emerged from these conflicts much reduced in size, and empires—dependent on the center's ability to redistribute resources to supporters—often run into trouble when they contract. After losing some of the church's major patriarchates as well as economic assets to caliphates, the empire found it difficult to collect land taxes. It became harder for the Byzantines to defend their reduced terrain and maintain their prestige.

Yet the empire seemed to have more than one life. It recovered in the ninth century, later lost outlying territory, and again revived resplendently under Basil II between 990 and 1025—advancing in the Balkans and east of the Black Sea, containing Islamic encroachment from Syria, and keeping territory in southern Italy despite Muslim invasions from Sicily. Basil made his deals with local potentates, Christian and Muslim, at the edges of his power, and got his taxes collected. His biggest threats came not from communities he conquered but from other empires—especially Islamic ones— and his own generals, who both maintained and at times tried to usurp his power. Weakened by succession troubles after Basil's death, subsequent emperors could not carry off the combination of shock, awe, and deal-making that Basil effected, and the empire shrank back once again.

In 1071, the Turkic-speaking Seljuks inflicted a harsh defeat on the Byzantines and set off a round of panic and internecine conflict within the empire's military elite. The Seljuk empire propelled the occupation of much of Anatolia by Turkic-speakers. Its control of the Holy Land after 1077 prodded knights, kings, and popes in western Europe to launch a series of crusades to take it back for Christendom. The government of Constantinople was more interested in getting help against the Seljuks than in the crusade itself, and relations with crusaders passing through were far from easy. The worst moment came in 1204 when crusaders sacked Constantinople and established a Latin kingdom there, pushing Byzantine rulers into Anatolia. The slaughter of Christians by other Christians, the looting of churches, and the appointment of a Latin patriarch began a sixty-year period of Latin domination over Constantinople.

The Byzantine empire did not simply disappear into a world of crusading Christians, militant Muslims, and Mediterranean commercial networks. The Byzantines left their marks—administrative practices, religious and artistic culture—on later empires, most visibly on the Ottomans (chapter 5) and on Russia (chapter 7). The empire was eventually reduced to little more than a city-state (map 3.1), but it endured until 1453, when a new imperial power led by the Ottomans seized the capital on the Bosphorus. That makes a run of over 1,100 years for the empire of Constantinople—not bad for a polity often regarded as an overcomplicated archaism. Byzantium's diversity, administrative flexibility, and grand ritual presence had transformed earlier traditions into a loose-fitting, impressive, sometimes frayed, but long-lasting imperial robe. Without the durability and adaptability of this empire on the eastern Mediterranean, world history would have taken a different course.

Clash of Empires? Islam in the Mediterranean World

In the past as today, many who preached about a "clash of civilizations" between Christians and Muslims were trying to create divisions, not describe them. Islamic and Christian religions drew on common cultural materials, and both were shaped at the intersection of the Mediterranean Sea and its adjacent landmasses, extending into Europe, Africa, and southwest Asia. The clashes were real enough, but they had more to do with similarity than difference, with overlapping ideas, resources, and territorial ambitions.

Whereas Christianity developed *within* the Roman empire and proclaimed that Caesar should be given his due—long before capturing the imagination of the emperor himself—Islam took root at the edge of empires, close enough to absorb their traditions, distant enough to be able to constitute a political community of the faithful. Its key texts—the Quran,

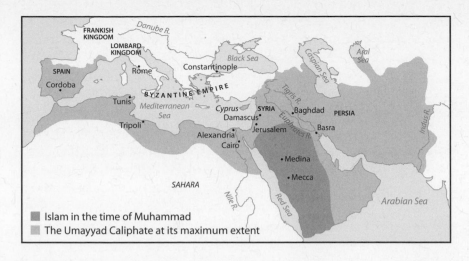

Map 3.2
Expansion of
Islamic caliphates.

The legend on the map reads:

■ Islam in the time of Muhammad
■ The Umayyad Caliphate at its maximum extent

the Hadiths, the Sharia—were written down as Muhammad turned the community into an empire; they retrospectively defined a polity whose purpose was rule under God's law. Christianity and empire were woven together only in the fourth century after Christ—and in Byzantium. Even there, emperor and patriarch remained distinct, while in the west pope and kings were long in tension with one another. But Islam's connection to empire-building and its capacity to spread both faith and power were present from the start.

The kinship-based societies of western Arabia lived on trade routes that crossed the desert, connected to the Roman and later Byzantine empires and across the Arabian Sea and Indian Ocean to south and southeast Asia. Mecca was both a node in a trading network and a center of religious cults. Even polytheistic communities of the area were familiar with Judaism and Christianity, and some regarded Abraham (Ibrahim in Arabic), Moses (Musa), and Jesus (Isa) as their own prophets. The first Islamic polity developed in a space close enough to centers of Roman/Byzantine and Sassanian power to learn their techniques of rule and incorporation. The surrounds of Mecca could not support a dense population—it was a marginal area for pastoralism and poor for agriculture—and the birthplace of the new polity provided few of the geographical or social conditions for becoming a durable imperial center, at least if one were thinking territorially in Roman style. But in Arabia, as in other places where tribal organization and long-distance commerce intersected, a different imaginary of empire could take shape—one where capitals could move around and fragmented populations could be united around a ruler's person and political vision.

Muhammad lived from 570 to 632, a time when Byzantine power was faltering. It was not unusual in the region of Mecca for people to allege

> *"I have been sent to the human race in its entirety."*
>
> —Muhammad, Hadith (saying of the Prophet)

that spirits spoke to them, but Muhammad claimed to speak with the one God (Arabic = Allah), who called for the submission of all people and declared Muhammad to be his Messenger. Building on the prophetic traditions of Jewish and Christian scriptures, Muhammad's followers held that they had received through him a true revelation, unmediated and unedited by any human institution. They called themselves Muslims, those who submitted to God. Local leaders forced Muhammad and his followers out of Mecca, and their flight to Medina, known as the *hijra*, became a symbol of Islamic unity. The new community, the *umma*, was united by belief in a single god and reverence for his prophet. What was the relationship of these pioneers to political authority?

Expansion, Community, and Islamic Authority

At first glance, the umma—in which the boundaries of political and religious community coincide—was the antithesis of an empire's perpetuation of difference among its populations. Indeed, early Muslims aspired to a high degree of homogeneity and equality within the collectivity, a reaction to the feuding of tribes and the tyranny of clan leaders that had forced the exodus from Mecca. Islam, like other monotheistic religions, appealed to many in a world that was becoming more interconnected and that local gods could not unite. Although early Muslims were not concerned with proselytizing as were the early Christians, Islam offered an overarching, appealing moral framework. A single set of practices, the five pillars, marked the universe of faith: affirmation of a single God and Muhammad, his Messenger; prayer five times a day; fasting during the month of Ramadan; alms-giving; and pilgrimage to Mecca at least once in a lifetime. The world was divided into *dar al-Islam*, the world of peace ruled by Islam, and *dar al-harb*, the world of war outside. From the start, the polity Muhammad built was based on the notion of a single religious community, something that the Roman/Byzantine empire developed only slowly. But as the umma extended itself, the singular community became more complex and fissionable. Its rulers faced the opportunities and dilemmas of empire.

A body of Islamic law—the Sharia—and religious doctrine, based on the Quran and interpretations of the Prophet's texts and sayings, emerged gradually to fill out the minimal requirements of belonging. As a scholar of early Islamic politics puts it, the Muslim community by the time of Muhammad's death had "acquired the main characteristics of a state." One's thoughts and deeds were no longer just a matter of responsibility to one's kinsmen but to an organized polity. Islam was first propagated among neighboring Arab tribes—culturally similar to each other but politically distinct. Tribal members who were attracted to the faith, who became clients of Muslim leaders, or who were captured by the Muslim armies could be incorporated into a body of common belief, regulated by law. The incorporative community could act in ways that other Arab tribes could not, in political as well as religious terms.

Just as the Roman empire was not simply a projection of the city of Rome, the expansion of an Islamic polity was not simply a projection of Mecca and Medina. Institutions and conceptions evolved as the budding empire extended its reach. The Muslim ideal of the unity of political and religious communities led quickly to controversies over the nature of authority between Muhammad's direct descendants and his early followers, between visions of religious purity and the practicalities of expansion, and between rival factions who claimed the same universal mandate.

Islam's expansion was remarkably swift. Outside the area near Medina, it looked a lot like an imperial conquest: the work of a small, well-led, relatively well-paid army with a core of disciplined soldiers and allies from Arab tribes. From Arabia, the conquest moved, still in Muhammad's lifetime, into areas where a largely Arab population lived under Byzantine rule. The Byzantine empire in Syria had already been weakened by war with the Sassanid empire of Persia. By 636, four years after the Prophet's death, the Byzantines were forced to retreat from Syria; the Muslims made good use of Byzantine bureaucracy in setting up their own administration there. The next year Muslim forces defeated the Sassanians in battle. Egypt came under attack in 641, western Persia a decade later. For all the expansion at the expense of the Byzantine empire, Arab advances fell short of Constantinople. But by the early eighth century Arabs had reached what is now Spain to the west and India to the east—a much more rapid extension of empire than that of Rome.

As with Rome, the making of an imperial polity required leaders to come to grips with the diversity of the people being conquered. Muhammad's successors decided shortly after his death that Arabs should not settle the countryside they conquered but concentrate in towns where they could maintain their coherence, be ready for military action, and live off taxation, which was higher for non-Muslims (Jews, Christians, Zoroastrians, and others) than for Muslims. Leaders did not depend on the ambitions of local elites to become "Muslim" the way Gauls or others could become "Roman"; instead Muslim authorities acknowledged the presence of distinct religious communities—called *dhimma*—who would pay the tax demanded of non-Muslims. Jews and Christians, as people of the book, had higher status than polytheists.

But Islam was attractive as a religion, and Muslims had something to offer as patrons. Many individuals joined the conquerors—often as clients of

Muslim leaders. Conversion and clientage produced an expanding Muslim population, initially largely Arab but no longer the same Arabs who had initiated the conquest.

The rapid growth of a Muslim superpower produced conflict at the center. With Muhammad's death in 632, succession became an issue between those who could claim descent from the Prophet (via his daughters, since he had no sons) and the core of followers who had made the pilgrimage with him to Medina. The mantle of succession went first to Abu Bakr, an early follower and father of one of Muhammad's wives. He was called caliph (Arabic = khalifa), meaning successor. A long controversy ensued over the nature of the caliph and over his roles as both leader of the faith and ruler of a people.

Two tensions—over succession and powers of the caliph—were quickly confounded. The third caliph, Uthman (ruled 644–56), was criticized for turning the caliphate into an ordinary kingship. He was assassinated and succeeded by Ali, the husband of Muhammad's daughter. The refusal of some community leaders to recognize Ali led to a civil war lasting until 661. Ali was assassinated, and the followers of Abu Bakr took power. The claim of Ali's son Husayn—asserting his direct descent from the Prophet—to the caliphate led to another civil war in 680. Husayn, too, was assassinated. Muawiyah, whose long reign lasted from 661 to 680, established a principle of dynastic succession, and the Umayyad caliphate came into being.

During these formative years, religious figures, the *ulama*, began to claim authority to interpret religious texts and traditions for themselves, cutting into the caliph's religious command and rewriting Islamic history in ways that divided religious and political power. As the Umayyads' power coalesced, the followers of Ali formed a rival faction, the Shi'ites. Their interpretation of Islam was different from the Sunni faith of the Umayyads, who had prevailed in the struggle for the caliphate. The Shi'ites' claim was based on descent, the Sunnis' on loyalty and community. Shi'ite opposition made clear that neither the monotheistic nature of Islam nor the resources of a growing empire ensured a single vision of what an Islamic polity should be. Some adherents of these rival traditions are still fighting today.

Damascus, in what had been Roman Syria, became the home of Umayyad power after 661; Mecca remained a spiritual center. The most durable part of the Umayyad conquest proved to be its western extremity, Spain, reached in 711 by Arab armies that had followed the tracks of Roman empire across north Africa. A mix of Arabs and Muslim converts from Berber communities settled there. The converts, with few social ties, became loyal supporters of the Umayyad caliphate. Conquering much of the Iberian peninsula—a varied landscape shaped by settlements of Phoenicians, Celts, Jews, and others and waves of conquest by Romans and Visigoths—the caliphate built its base in the southern city of Cordoba. It did not seek to eliminate or assimilate the Christian and Jewish populations. The sweep of Islamic empire across the southern Mediterranean was interrupted by a Berber rebellion in 741, which was put down with difficulty, and then by conflict within the caliphate itself. The Umayyads stayed on in Spain, despite losing the earlier core of the empire in Syria around 750. Other Muslim dynasties, of Berber origin, later took power in Spain—Almoravids in 1086, Almohads in 1147—and it was only in the thirteenth century that Christian kings began to push back Muslim rulers. The last bastion of Islamic rule in Iberia lasted until 1492.

There was no mass migratory movement of Arabs across north Africa. The Berbers in north Africa stayed linguistically distinct and only slowly converted to Islam. The existence of distinct religious groups was taken for granted across the Umayyad empire. In Syria, Greek remained for some time the language of routine administration.

But was the Umayyad dynasty living up to its religious mandate? Conquest produced tendencies counter to the egalitarian, communitarian ideals of the early umma: the use of clients and slaves in subordinate roles, differentiation between Meccan and non-Meccan Arabs, then between Arabs and non-Arabs, incorporation of Byzantine and Persian areas with their more hierarchical traditions of imperial government. Shi'ites denied the legitimacy of the caliph's succession, and they were not the only dissenters and rebels. The expansion of the caliphate made the question of its authority more acute: was the caliph becoming more an emperor and less a protector of true Islam? The egalitarian principles of Islam could be invoked against the hierarchical tendencies of the caliphate.

A powerful rebel movement developed in the mid-eighth century, drawing support in what is now Iraq, Iran, and Afghanistan and questioning both the legitimacy and the practices of the caliphate. The Abbasids, taking their name from a relative of Muhammad, drove the Umayyads from Damascus in 750 and founded a new dynasty. Despite Shi'ite elements in the rebellion, the Abbasids reverted to the Sunni line and sought to maintain their own chain of command and hierarchy. The Abbasids controlled a large empire that loosely covered the former Roman territories of north Africa and the eastern Mediterranean and former Sassanian territories in Iraq and parts of Persia. Claiming to restore the unity of the Prophet's house, the Abbasid dynasty lasted, nominally at least, from 750 to 1258. It established Baghdad as its capital, a planned city designed to symbolize Abbasid power. One hundred thousand workers reportedly helped build it. This empire, like others, could re-center itself. Baghdad gave a focus to a new world power, universalistic in its aspirations, unified in its structure, splendid in its artistic and cultural efflorescence.

The Abbasid caliphate suffered from difficulties typical of empires unable to bind their provinces into a single economic system, as Rome had done.

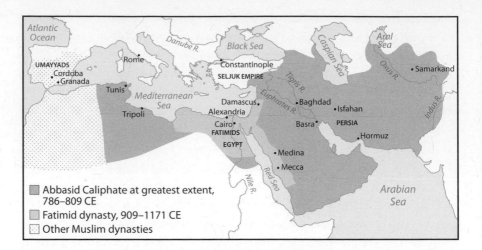

Map 3.3
The Abbasid
caliphate.

(Map legend)
Abbasid Caliphate at greatest extent, 786–809 CE
Fatimid dynasty, 909–1171 CE
Other Muslim dynasties

(Map labels) Atlantic Ocean · UMAYYADS · Cordoba · Granada · Rome · Danube R. · Black Sea · Constantinople · SELJUK EMPIRE · Caspian Sea · Aral Sea · Samarkand · Oxus R. · Tunis · Mediterranean Sea · Damascus · Tigris R. · Baghdad · Isfahan · Euphrates R. · Tripoli · Alexandria · Basra · PERSIA · Cairo · FATIMIDS · Hormuz · EGYPT · Medina · Mecca · Nile R. · Red Sea · Indus R. · Arabian Sea

The edges of the empire could integrate themselves into economic circuits that the center did not control. This in some places led to the establishment of new dynasties, notably the Fatimids (named after Fatima, the Prophet's daughter) in Egypt in the tenth century, who espoused a form of Shi'ism. Even closer to the Iraqi core of the caliphate, sectarian and dynastic conflict produced breakaway Islamic states that acknowledged the overlordship of the Abbasids by invoking the name of the caliph in Friday prayers, but in effect constituted localized kingdoms.

The spread of Islam beyond Arabic-speaking areas eventually proved as much a problem as a triumph. Persia, where the Sassanian dynasty had weakened, was conquered by Muslims but never assimilated to Arab culture. There, Shi'ism eventually gained a prominent place. Many Turkic-speaking peoples also converted to Islam, and by the eleventh century Seljuk Turks were beginning to develop imperial ambitions of their own.

In the face of conflict as well as ambition, caliphs needed institutional mechanisms to maintain power. They built a formal structure of government, dividing the state into provinces, with governors and military authorities, and setting up courts to enforce Islamic law. Like the Byzantines, they devised a system of tax collection, with receipts divided between provinces and the center, and they used revenue to pay (or buy) soldiers and officials. They made less formal arrangements with tribes who had contributed to conquests or takeovers.

In their quest for intermediaries to help govern the empire, the Muslims turned to outsiders, not only as allied groups but as individuals who could be detached from their communities of origin. People from the fringes or outside the umma counterbalanced the ruler's own kinsmen and tribesmen for whom loyalty could turn to treason all too easily. Personal clients (Arabic = *mawali*) were crucial to the caliph, an entourage directly beholden to him that could distribute rewards or inflict terror on his behalf. High officials and generals were sometimes slaves, captured or purchased at a young age, brought up in the palace, converted to Islam, and stripped of all ties except those to the caliph. Some offices were held by eunuchs, who could have no dynastic ambitions of their own. Similar strategies had been used earlier by the Byzantines and Persians.

In this way, the once tightly knit umma, now an expanding empire, came to depend increasingly on non-Arab soldiers—Persians, Kurds, and especially slaves from Eurasia who spoke Turkic languages. Such slaves offered the mystique and skills of Eurasian peoples—they were fearless soldiers and excellent horsemen. Whereas a western European king relied on vassalage—a relationship with a noble who could bring his own followers into service—the caliph depended on making people without social standing or kinsmen into the dependent instruments through which he exercised power over subjects. Aristocracies based on powerful, locally rooted families were notably absent from Islamic polities.

At the top of the system was the mutual dependency of caliph and his top official, the vizier, a relationship charged with emotion. Narratives in Arabic literature describe the close tie between the most powerful Abbasid caliph, Harun al-Rashid (786–809), and his vizier, from the Barmakid family of the distant Oxus valley who had earlier recruited supporters for the Abbasid revolution. Harun eventually came to fear his friend and vizier and had him and his family executed. We see here the intensity and fragility of the personal but unequal relationship of emperor and intermediary. This story was often told as a morality tale: a warning to an overmighty vizier, to the community against the self-interested foreigner who comes between caliph and people, and to the caliph that personal power can lead to blindness toward one's subordinates and irresponsibility toward one's people.

That different Islamic rulers could extend their power over others and that leading subordinates could break out of their roles made for a volatile politics of empire. Abbasid caliphs could become dependent on their Turkish soldiers, who in the ninth century imposed their choice for vizier and in 869 killed a caliph. As we have seen, local kingdoms only vaguely acknowledging the religious authority of the Abbasid caliph sprang up, keeping tax revenue to themselves. The rich province of Egypt came under the rule of a different dynasty, the Fatimids. And for a time after 945, a Shi'ite dynasty, the Buyyids, controlled Iraq itself, leaving the caliph the head of the Sunni community alone. A stronger shock came from the Muslim, Turkic-speaking Seljuks, who captured Baghdad in 1055, gave their leader the title of sultan, and left the Abbasid caliph with essentially no temporal power. It was a much decimated Abbasid caliphate that was dealt the final blow in 1258 by another rapidly expanding empire. The Mongols from the steppes of inner Asia sacked Baghdad once again, slaughtered much of its population, installed their own kind of rule, and moved on to further conquests (chapter 4).

The other caliphates faced similar threats within the world of Islam. Near the end of the twelfth century, Salah al-Din, of Kurdish origin and a military commander for a Syrian ruler, challenged the Fatimids in Egypt, defeated them and took a Shi'ite stronghold back into the Sunni camp. Upon his patron's death, Salah al-Din seized power for himself and became the dominant force in Egypt, Syria, and western Arabia, including Mecca and Medina. He successfully fought back European crusaders in Jerusalem.

But in turn, Salah al-Din's imperial project was weakened after his death by succession disputes, during which military slaves, largely of Turkic origin, decided to dispense with their patrons. Known as mamluks, the slave servitors and soldiers took power in 1250. Mamluks, in addition to their earlier victories against the crusaders, were also responsible for stopping one of the greatest military conquests in history—the Mongols who sacked Baghdad and were advancing on Egypt (chapter 4). In 1260, the Mongols were finally stopped by the Mamluk army. Mamluks retained control of Egypt (and beyond it for a time) until the Ottomans defeated them in 1517 (chapter 5).

Beyond Empire in the Islamic World

What began as a single community worshiping a single god building a single empire turned into multiple centers of imperial power. In each of these centers, leaders seeking intermediaries directly beholden to them contended with the ambitions of those intermediaries to seize the state for themselves. The high points of imperial power—the Umayyads in Damascus and Cordoba, the Abbasids in Baghdad, the Fatimids in Cairo—brought together resources that made possible lavish flowerings of art and science. But it was the combination of a universalistic vision of religious community with the concentration of resources under imperial command that gave Islam an influence geographically broader and more long-lasting than that of the individual empires.

For several centuries, the Islamic world was the most dynamic and creative heir to Hellenic, Roman, and Persian cultures. Economic historians describe the space of Islam as urban islands linked by trade routes, lubricated by precious metals and a wide range of commodities. Crops like sugar, rice, and cotton were introduced to former Roman areas via these connections. So many slaves were imported into Iraq to cultivate sugar and cotton that a slave revolt occurred in the ninth century. The caliphates' coinage became standard across a wide space and was used beyond territories they controlled. Muslim Spain flourished economically under Umayyad rule, producing wheat, sugar, and fruits.

The Umayyad conquest profoundly shaped art and architecture in Spain, particularly in Andalusia. In Abbasid Baghdad under Caliph Harun al-Rashid, Islamic literature, art, medicine, and science flourished. Much of what "the west" knows of Greek philosophy and literature came from Arabic translations, later retranslated into Latin. The meeting of Arabic and Persian cultures produced new literary genres and philosophical works. As a center of urban life and culture, only Constantinople could rival Baghdad, Cairo, and Cordoba.

Meanwhile, diasporic Islamic communities, often pioneered by merchants and anchored by scholars, spread into central and southeast Asia and China. In some cases, including southeast Asia, monarchs deeply involved in long-distance trade converted to Islam and created durable Muslim poli-

Figure 3.2
Mosque of Ibn Tulun, Cairo, Egypt. The mosque was built on orders of the Abbasid governor of the region in the 870s. Roger Viollet, 1904, GettyImages.

Empire, Christianity, and Islam   79

ties. In central Asian cities, Persian and Arab scholars shaped a cosmopolitan, Islamic urban culture in an area subject to the assaults of other empire-builders, some of whom came from polytheistic traditions (chapter 4). Arabic offered a language for worship and learning shared across space and political divisions; the Quran and the sayings of the Prophet were studied intensively. The Muslim community of the Prophet's time was a reference point for scholars, a model of good governance to which the caliphate was supposed to measure up.

Islamic law offered Muslims, wherever they were and under whoever's rule they found themselves, a means to regulate their societies and to interact with others, but just what constituted an Islamic order remained subject to interpretation and debate. The boundaries of even the Abbasid empire at its height thus represented only a portion of the influence of Islam and only a part of the political forms Islamic scholars and Muslim rulers could imagine.

Different concepts of the umma were in play: the original idea of an all-embracing community, egalitarian within itself and seeking to absorb or combat outsiders; imperial visions that recognized non-Muslim communities within a much expanded space and employed converts, clients, and slaves in Islamic governance; and a network, extending beyond political authority, linked by texts, scholarly communication, pilgrimage, and commerce among Muslims. "Islam" no more defined a singular and unchanging political organization than did Christianity in the post-Roman world.

Muhammad's religious community thus spread widely, while the idea of a caliphate as a specifically Islamic form of empire—and disagreements over it—inspired Umayyads, Abbasids, Fatimids, and others as they extended their Muslim domains from the heartlands of Arabia, Syria, and Iraq across north Africa and Spain and to central Asia and India. The multiplicity of these claims to Islamic empire led to conflict and interrupted expansion. But, as we will see in later chapters, the practices of Muslim rule were flexible and the ideal of Muslim community remained strong.

A New Rome, Again? Charlemagne's Catholic Empire

In 800, Charles, king of the Franks, traveled to Rome, where the pope crowned him "Emperor and Augustus." A king crowned by a church, Charles gestured toward the glory of Rome at a time when another Christian emperor sat on the well-established Byzantine throne, and while Harun al-Rashid ruled his caliphate from Baghdad. Of the three imperial formations, Charlemagne's was built on the least propitious foundations—the relatively limited economic possibilities and the institutional hodgepodge of what later became known as continental Europe. His empire was also the shortest

Figure 3.3

Coronation of Emperor Charlemagne by Pope Leo III in St. Peter's Cathedral, Rome, in 800. From a French manuscript, *Chroniques de France*, 1375–79, in Bibliothèque Municipale, Castres, France. Bridgeman Art Library, GettyImages.

lived, and its story takes us back to the processes that make empires in the first place and also lead to their demise.

Charlemagne's imperial enterprise took shape after four hundred years of fragmentations and recombinations of political power on what had been Roman space. The collapse of Rome had led to the decay of the infra-structure that state authority and fiscal resources had supported—aqueducts, roads, urban amenities. The western part of the former empire became more rural; local lords attracted armed followers to themselves; landlords extracted surplus production from peasants by a variety of coercive means. The quality of consumer goods enjoyed earlier by much of the Roman empire's popu-lation declined; artisans had smaller markets. Local and regional exchange did continue—and some aristocrats could make themselves rich—but the pattern of economic activity was highly uneven and elite accumulation of resources uncertain.

Roman empire did have long-lasting effects: the spread of a common language, Latin, among elites and the emergence of what became the Romance languages, and the expansion of Christianity. Networks of monasteries and hierarchies of ecclesiastical officials developed across a wide area, with a pope in Rome. Perhaps most important was the memory of empire and the possibility of reconstituting Rome. Aristocrats could aspire to become kings and kings could aspire to build empires—if they did not prevent each other from doing so.

Kingdoms were held together not by ties of similarity but by vertical connections between unequals—king to lord, lord to vassal, vassal to peasant. Without an overarching political power like that of Byzantium, Christianity did not provide a unifying framework or a sure support for royals. The pope was one of many players in the game of political expansion, hemmed in by the shifting powers over formerly Roman territory—the Ostrogoth conquerors, the Byzantine reconquerors, the Lombard kingdom that installed itself north of Rome once the Byzantine reunification had spent its force.

In the eighth century imperial potential came closest to being realized among people known as the Franks. Many centuries later, French and German nationalists tried to annex the history of the Franks to their separate claims to nationhood, both claiming descent from the great Frankish king—Charlemagne for the French and Karl der Grosse for the Germans. Franks were a Germanic-speaking people, but the westernmost among them, living in what is now France, picked up the Latin of the late Roman empire and produced a language that evolved into French. Eastern Franks retained their Germanic language. Under dynamic leaders like Clovis, founder of the Merovingian dynasty, the Frankish elite partly converted to Christianity and expanded its area of control. But despite their pretensions to grandeur, the Merovingians faltered with each succession, dividing territory among heirs. Only after 714 did the king's leading general and minister, Charles Martel, put together a more unified and effective military machine and expand Frankish control over more territories and peoples. Just as the first Arab Muslim polities developed on the edge of the great empires, the Franks benefited from being relatively far away from Christian Byzantium as they consolidated power.

Charles Martel did, however, run up against Islamic empire. In 732, he defeated a raiding party of Muslims from Umayyad Spain near the city of Poitiers. We need not accept the claim that he saved Christian western Europe from Islam—Europe as such did not exist, and the Muslim presence had another 750 years to go in Spain—but the incident did much to boost Charles Martel's stature. His son Pippin was made king of the Franks. It was

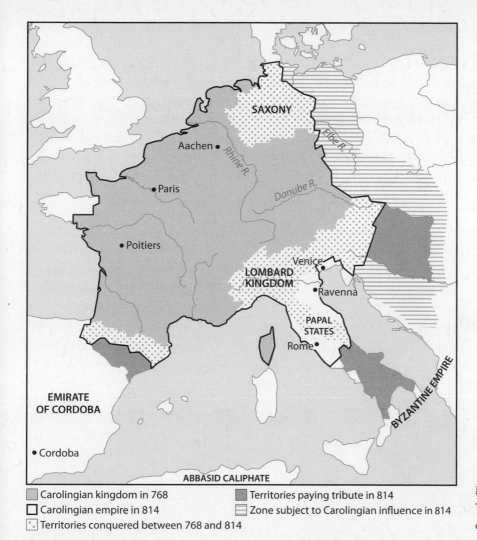

Carolingian kingdom in 768
Carolingian empire in 814
Territories conquered between 768 and 814
Territories paying tribute in 814
Zone subject to Carolingian influence in 814

Map 3.4
The Carolingian empire, c. 814.

Pippin's son Charles who, after becoming king in 768, gave the kingdom the name of empire and did his best to make it stick.

Military conquest was as usual at the core of Charlemagne's achievement, including the incorporation of kingdoms of substantial size. His ascent depended on the acquisition and distribution of the spoils of war. Pushing out in all directions from the Frankish core in the Rhineland, defeating Lombards, Saxons, Bavarians, and others, he wove together regions that had once been tied to Rome.

Charlemagne's system of imperial connections was not Roman. His empire had no fixed capital but instead was ruled from palaces at key points, among which he moved with his large retinue, making himself impressively visible to accept the homage of lords who had pledged to serve him. Power was vertically organized: it was Charlemagne's ability to command nobles, with their retinues and revenues, that made him strong. As cavalry became increasingly important to warfare, the wealth of the armed man—who supplied his own horse and armor—became the key to the power of a king or emperor.

Charlemagne created other channels of command to spy on and influence his intermediaries. Some 250 "counts" were appointed to supervise tax collection, announce decrees, call up warriors, and administer a district. In addition, Charlemagne relied on two sets of officials—royal vassals and royal envoys—who were directly responsible to him. This system recognized the advantages of using men who knew local languages and were part of local hierarchies as administrators in a diverse realm. At the same time, Carolingian government contained checks and balances to avoid the danger facing all empires—that imperial intermediaries would take off on their own. All free persons were required to take an oath of loyalty to the emperor. But direct relationship to the emperor was only one dimension of the political system: everyone owed allegiance to someone else. Multiple hierarchies of allegiances made the empire hang together and created the risk that if it fell apart, each piece might challenge the rest.

"He [Charlemagne] cherished the Church of St. Peter the Apostle at Rome above all other holy and sacred places, and heaped its treasury with a vast wealth of gold, silver, and precious stones. He sent great and countless gifts to the popes; and throughout his whole reign the wish that he had nearest at heart was to re-establish the ancient authority of the city of Rome under his care and by his influence, and to defend and protect the Church of St. Peter, and to beautify and enrich it out of his own store above all other churches."

—Einhard, chronicler of Charlemagne

Charlemagne aspired to provide religious and ideological coherence to his diverse empire. Fortunately for him, the pope needed him just as much as he needed the pope. Hemmed in by a Lombard kingdom that did not fully respect his authority, challenged by the Byzantines, and threatened by corruption scandals within the church, Pope Leo III benefited from Charlemagne's defeat of the Lombards and the protection he bestowed on the papacy. Both parties could imagine that the ceremonial bestowal of the title of emperor would tie worldly and religious authority together in mutually helpful ways. In the year after his coronation, Charlemagne spent five months in Rome, underscoring his ties to the Eternal City.

The imperial title and the Roman connection brought together religious and political power at the top. Under Charlemagne, each county had not just a count but also a bishop. Bishops—in fact if not in theory—were appointed by the emperor. Abbeys were founded throughout the realm, richly endowed with land and peasants. Bestowing an abbey upon a loyal knight gave him a significant income and the empire another stitch in the fabric that held it together. Charlemagne's empire contained over six hundred monasteries. In this sense, Charlemagne was saying, as one scholar puts it, "We have no Romans or Germans here, nor is there a place for Franks, Bavarians, or Aquitanians. This is a Christian empire, which is Roman and cannot be anything else." But of course bishops, like other religious authorities, could be unruly, and ecclesiastical institutions could accumulate and use resources for their own ends.

Economically, the Carolingian empire differed from Rome in two ways. First, its geographic center of gravity was no longer the Mediterranean but the Rhine, in northern Europe, where France, Belgium, and Germany converge today. The empire built on the area's robust grain production, enhancing both the concentration of wealth and the lines of exchange radiating outward from the region. A unified monetary system facilitated commercial connections. The Carolingians could by no means match the wealth of the Roman empire at its height, but the decline in sea and land connections from about 300 to 700 was at least partially reversed. With commercial relations to northern peoples (Danes, Anglo-Saxons), through Lombards to Venice, through the Balkans to Byzantium, and via Persians and others across Eurasia, the Carolingians were connected to multiple economic circuits. Not least of the empire's resources was a trade in people of the region—captives taken in Charlemagne's wars of expansion—who entered well-established slave-trade routes through Venice and other southern ports to the Muslim world, where slaves were in demand for political and household purposes as well as agricultural work.

Second, the large plantations—latifundia—worked by slaves that had been a part of the Roman system had in large part given way to manors worked by people in a variety of dependent relations. These included slavery, but more frequently farmers were tied to the land as serfs and tenants. As in other growing empires, the redistribution of booty was critical to Charlemagne's power at first, but as success made frontiers more distant and campaigns more difficult, internal accumulation of wealth became more consequential. The emperor acquired, through conquest, gift, and inheritance, vast lands with numerous peasants. Charlemagne employed taxation and tolls, not as effectively as Rome had, but with a similar goal of regularizing revenue collection.

Charlemagne's legal initiatives accommodated and recorded the diverse customs of different peoples, while attempting to make some laws apply throughout the empire. An array of authorities—local customs, imperial decrees, and Christian canon—made law a flexible tool of imperial rule.

Appropriately for an empire dependent on a manorial economy and on keeping dispersed nobles loyal—on creating a reliable aristocracy without Rome's resources—Carolingian law was attentive to defining subjects' statuses and to regulating their relationships. Nobles and clergy were on top; at the bottom were slaves, serfs, tenants, and other dependent cultivators. In between was a significant—but probably shrinking—category of small-scale "free" peasants, heavily burdened by the "census," a payment somewhere between a tax and land rent, as well as by demands for military service.

The emperor remained at the apex of different kinds of vertical relationships, and if he could play them off against each other state authority remained strong. But he could only go so far, his successors even less. On European terrain, aristocratic privilege proved more durable than imperial power.

Carolingians and Byzantines made intermittent efforts at reconciliation. In Charlemagne's time churchmen acknowledged the unity of Christendom and debated—without agreeing—what Christianity meant. Charlemagne entered into marriage negotiations with the Byzantine regent (later empress) Irene over the marriage of his daughter to her son. Some years after this effort failed, Charlemagne was negotiating to marry Irene himself, when her top officials, apparently fearing that this alliance would undermine their position in the court, staged a coup d'état. It was only in the eleventh century that the religious split between eastern and western empires became so wide that political reconciliation became almost unimaginable. The sacking of Constantinople in 1204 by crusaders sealed the division between Catholics and Orthodox Christians.

Charlemagne and his Abbasid counterpart, the caliph Harun al-Rashid, made a brief effort to recognize the reality of the other's power. Initiating an exchange of regal gifts, Harun al-Rashid gave Charlemagne an elephant, which the Carolingian emperor took with him on expeditions and military campaigns. Charlemagne did not have anything so splendid to offer in return, but he did send the caliph horses, hounds, and fabrics. This was as close as Byzantine, Islamic, and Carolingian rulers came to acknowledging that they were part of a world of empires, interacting with and setting limits on each other, despite the claims of each to represent God's rule on earth.

Crowned king of the Franks in 768, Charlemagne died an emperor in 814. His successful extension of power was recognized by Byzantines and Muslims, who began to refer to people we now call Europeans as "Franks." Charlemagne had been an institutional and ideological innovator. His references to Rome concealed his reconfiguring of empire into a web of palaces, counties, bishoprics, and monasteries. His administrative system, like that of the Chinese emperor, relied on multiple channels of information, but the basic structure of the empire—unlike that of Rome or China—was aristocratic, the noble with his land and peasants providing support and fealty to the emperor.

Charlemagne had intended to follow family tradition by dividing his vastly expanded realm among his sons, but the untimely deaths of two of them left the whole realm in the hands of Louis the Pious. Upon Louis's death, the empire was split into three regions. The Carolingian empire endured in recognizable form until the 880s when it fell to enemies to the north, east, and southeast, as well as to the divisive greed of its warrior aristocrats. But its entrenchment of a Catholic, aristocratic system on a politically volatile space left long-lasting traces on the area that afterward would be identified as Europe.

A portion of the former empire was later reunited via another arrangement between the pope and a secular ruler. Otto, a German king, was declared Holy Roman Emperor in 962. The de facto control of multiple Germanic kings over their lands and the weakness of the papacy made Otto's domain less than a formal empire, and its claims to being holy and Roman were weak as well. Aristocracies and various local rulers—margraves, counts, and dukes—loomed even larger in the Holy Roman Empire than in the Carolingian one. From 1438, princely electors consistently chose someone from the Habsburg dynasty to be emperor, the most dynamic of whom, from 1520, was Charles V (chapter 5). Charles, however, was the last Holy Roman Emperor to be crowned by a pope. The empire persisted as a loose confederation—of up to three hundred principalities—cooperating against the Ottomans but with little unity beyond that. Yet another empire would finally, in 1806, be its undoing—that of Napoleon (chapter 8).

Europe was a relatively impoverished space for empire, once bereft of secure attachments to the economic assets of the Mediterranean or other distant sites. Political authority was fragile and fissionable, encumbered by the fixing of revenues to agricultural terrains, the absence of sufficient resources to keep all eyes on the same imperial prize, the tension between a church that could alone legitimate the title of emperor, the kings and princes who sought monarchical power for themselves. In these conditions, incorporating different polities and groups into some sort of overarching entity that would command authority and achieve accommodation was difficult. But the fact that German-speaking kings, far from Italy, wanted to call themselves emperors and Roman reminds us of the durable memory of the Roman empire, of the diffusion of Latin and other cultural connections, and of the importance to elites of imagining their place in a universe larger than the linguistic or cultural communities they came from.

Jihads and Crusades in a World of Empires

It is tempting to pause for a rueful moment over the elephant that Harun al-Rashid gave to Charlemagne and the unsuccessful attempts to forge a marriage alliance between the Carolingian and Byzantine emperors. The gift and marital negotiations were efforts to stabilize relations among empires. Their failure points to the fact that empires were in competition, searching for advantages against each other, while power brokers within them might try to use or to prevent alliances that would affect their own fortunes. The expansion of monotheistic religions added a new dimension to this older structural situation. Christianity and Islam offered at the same time a cultural basis for imperial unity, a dangerous potential for internal schism, and new grounds for wars between empires.

The concept of jihad in Islam has been controversial for centuries, from at least the eighth to the twenty-first. Does it mean an obligation upon the Muslim to propagate the faith? An inner struggle for personal perfection? Or does it imply that anyone who resists the faith can be coerced, killed, or enslaved? Such questions were debated by Islamic jurists, but they were also embroiled in the mix of self-interest, pragmatism, and idealism of imperial politics. The idea of military victory as divine confirmation had been an important buttress for the Roman empire. But the fervor of the community that Muhammad built, followed by the rapidity of his successes in Syria, Iraq, and Egypt, gave rise to a more general principle—holy war, or jihad. The holy warrior personally took up the defense and expansion of the umma; no aristocrats stood between him and the community. But the early caliphates soon ran up against the disappointing fact that much of the Byzantine empire was unconquerable. Then there were the internal divisions among Muslims. It was not so clear against whom one should wage jihad and with whom one should try to coexist.

Crusade is also an ambiguous notion. It, unlike jihad, was not a word used at the time. The armies of knights from western Europe who went to Jerusalem—the first such army captured that site in 1099—were called pilgrimages or expeditions and grew out of a widespread pilgrimage tradition in early Christianity. The crusades addressed—albeit some time after the fact—the losses to Muslims of Christian holy lands, not just sacred places but constituent parts of what had been a pan-Mediterranean universe in which Christianity had grown up. Crusader ideology implied a universal view of humanity—that Christianity could and should be adopted by everyone, and that those who did not convert could be killed. Beyond this, crusades were as much caught up with political conflict and personal ambition as jihads. Living in a world that was politically fragmented but sharing belief in Christianity and hierarchy, the early crusaders, as Thomas Bisson writes, were "men in search of lordly reputation."

The key role of Frankish knights in the crusades reflected the spatial diffusion of Christianity that had occurred under the Carolingians—churchmen had spread ideas of pilgrimage and penitence. Crusading allowed this knightly class (particularly younger sons) the chance to escape obligations, prove themselves, impress superiors, dispense patronage, and find—away from the limitations nearer to home—places to raid, establish new domains, and justify a place of honor within the terms of medieval Christianity. Popes saw in the crusades a way toward their own imperial expansion, in the face not only of Islam but of the Byzantine church and of tensions and conflicts with Catholic aristocrats and kings.

The divisions within the Muslim world, in their turn, generated instability in the holy land and elsewhere. The takeover of Jerusalem by a faction of Islamic but non-Arab Seljuks was the precipitating factor for the first crusade, starting in 1096. Following Pope Urban II's call to rescue holy sites of Christianity, the crusades were part popular movement, part organized expedition.

The early crusaders, living—as did most armies of the era—off the land, did considerable violence and looting all along the way. Byzantium had an ambivalent relationship to the crusades, having sought western Christians' help against the Seljuks with the idea of protecting Constantinople rather than capturing Jerusalem. Turnover—and usurpation—of the Byzantine throne meant that Byzantine support for Christian armies was inconsistent. The sacking by crusaders of Constantinople in 1204 and the displacement for some decades of the Byzantine emperor into Anatolia created long-lasting bitterness.

Crusades established "Latin kingdoms" along their routes, including those of Jerusalem in 1099 and Constantinople in 1204. Knights, their families, and others settled in cites along crusaders' routes, spreading Catholic culture and western European languages in the Balkans and eastern Mediterranean. This process created new connections but not a fully integrated Christendom.

The kingdoms founded by crusading armies had an unruly history—a seesaw of power between Islamic rulers in conflict with each other and crusader kings and Byzantine elites whose support was variable. Leaders of Latin kingdoms—like the Islamic rulers they fought—could think of their actions in religious terms and use religious war to build their reputations. The idea that holy war could produce holy peace—a world community living in harmony enforced by Christian authority—became a justification for empire, looking back to the precedent of Rome. But the usual outcome was more war and less peace.

The crusades that emerged out of a divided Christianity did not destroy Muslim power or bring Byzantium under the wing of the papacy, but they did make an impact on Muslim and Byzantine perceptions of their enemies. Assaults on cities by ambitious lords were nothing new to the region, but the behavior of the victorious armies shocked Arabs and Orthodox Christians. In Jerusalem the crusading armies slaughtered Jews on the street and burned them alive in their

> *"At least they [the Muslims] did not rape our women, reduce our inhabitants to poverty, didn't strip them and make them walk naked through the streets, didn't cause them to perish by hunger and fire. . . . But that's how we were treated by these Christian people who cross themselves in the name of the Lord and share our religion."*
>
> —Christian chronicler of the crusades

synagogue, massacred thousands of worshipers in the Al-Aqsa mosque, and attacked Greek Orthodox, Armenian, Coptic, and other eastern Christian churches. A century later in Constantinople, crusaders slaughtered Orthodox priests, burned great libraries, desecrated Hagia Sophia and other Orthodox churches, and carted off and melted down Byzantium's treasures. To both Byzantine and Muslim elites, the barbarous behavior of the "Franks" or "Latins" went beyond the ordinary experience of conflict.

The crusader kingdom of Jerusalem was overrun by the Muslim armies of Salah al-Din in 1187; the last remnants of the region's Latin kingdoms were finished off by the Mamluks a century later. By then, this region—torn up by religious division and earthly ambition—had encountered a new imperial dynamic. Mongols—Eurasian people who brought with them new modes of warfare and new imperial practices including a healthy dose of confessional indifference (see chapter 4)—captured Baghdad in 1258. They had previously reached the outskirts of Vienna. They were only stopped by the Mamluks of Egypt in 1260. The future of Christian and Islamic empires looked in doubt.

Conclusion

By the thirteenth century CE, universalistic religion had not produced a universal empire. The three imperial systems considered in this chapter sought to harness monotheism to solve problems inherent in the structure of empire: how to capture the imaginations of people across a broad and differentiated space and how to keep intermediaries in line. Rome had given people from Britain to Egypt good reason to participate in imperial institutions of government and to think of themselves as Roman. Rome's coming apart left its would-be successors different resources to work with.

Monotheistic religion quickly proved to be a two-edged sword, providing a moral framework transcending locality but opening the door to schisms based on equally universalistic claims to religious legitimacy. The three kinds of empire faced schisms—Catholic/Orthodox, Sunni/Shi'ite—and tensions over the relationship of politics and religion—popes/kings, caliphs/ulama, emperors/patriarchs.

Two extremes of approaches to intermediaries (clients and slaves versus aristocrats) are evident in the Islamic and Carolingian empires, with Byzantium in between. Charlemagne probably had little choice, since a politics of lordship had become entrenched in the nearly four hundred years since the coming apart of the Roman empire. He had to co-opt aristocrats, with their armed followers and subordinated peasants, into his chain of command. The best he could do was to rely on multiple chains of vertical authority: from emperor to counts, vassals, envoys, and bishops, each with his subordinates.

Islamic rulers did not have to contend with an entrenched aristocratic culture. They could use Byzantine (Roman) precedents for imperial tax collecting—and early on in Syria, even Byzantine tax collectors. Both Umayyads and Abbasids took pains to avoid creating an aristocracy, relying instead on slaves and clients to be their intermediaries, from high to low ranks. They could make their deals with regional potentates, but it was the relative autonomy of the caliph and his household that put these empires in a strong position to handle challenges.

Both poles of this continuum of imperial government were capable of fostering rapid expansion—one by bringing in groups of followers of intermediate lords, the other by bringing in individuals detached from social connections—but Charlemagne's version proved much less durable, coming apart as readily as it had been put together. The household model had its vulnerabilities, too: when intermediaries developed a sense of corporate identification, they might come to think that they could run things on their own, as mamluks in Egypt eventually did. All the empires—including the Byzantine—had problems with succession, but the centrally paid office-holders and armies were better able to preserve cross-generational continuity than was the aristocratic system of the Carolingians.

Clashing monotheisms, it would seem, took empire toward a sharp distinction between people who were included in the polity and others—nonbelievers—who were out. Jihad and crusade certainly entered imperial repertoires as ideologies of mobilization in the cause of a religiously homogeneous imperial community. Yet actually running an empire had its own imperatives, and a polarized politics of difference was impossible to sustain. Empires had to come to grips with the diversity and mobility that characterized the spaces of the former Roman empire. Byzantine and Islamic empires ruled over Jews, Christians, Muslims, and others; these groups—as communities as much as individuals—offered useful networks to imperial leaders. If Charlemagne's world was less religiously diverse than Justinian's or Harun's, it was certainly linguistically varied—including people who would later be considered French, German, and Italian.

If neither Christian nor Islamic empires could create a polity that was both uniform and universal, they did weave webs of connection across and beyond their domains. The Carolingians spread Christianity, sponsored monasteries, and helped build an ecclesiastical hierarchy that long outlasted their empire. Charlemagne's conquests and later the crusades sent knights across vast spaces, and some warriors took root in places from Saxony to Jerusalem, creating what Robert Bartlett calls an "aristocratic diaspora." They brought with them a culture of class distinction and practices of extracting revenue from peasants and building armed retinues. Byzantium gave birth to orthodox churches in many areas of Eurasia and influenced the trajectory of Russian empire (chapter 7). Islam was propagated at first by conquest, later spreading along trade routes beyond conquered territory, but it would not have gone so far without the political successes of the Islamic empires.

Managing a politics of difference in expanding and contending empires was no easy task, and the fate of rulers was highly uneven. History is littered with failed imperial endeavors, and the very scale of successful empires limited the opportunities for new ones. This is why empires often got their start at the edges of established empires or when interempire conflicts created openings for political initiative. Both Muslims and Christians tried to use the threat of the other to forge mighty powers, but crusading knights and contending caliphates did more to reveal Christian and Muslim disunity than to overcome it. Universal Christendom and a worldwide Islamic umma remained in the realms of aspiration and violence.

Several roads led out from Rome: some to dead ends, others to unanticipated crossroads. In subsequent chapters we will follow empires that started out from other places; some of these—the Seljuk Turks of the eleventh century and the Mongols of the thirteenth—came into the eastern Mediterranean arena and altered the course of empire history. We will see more instances of the mixing and layering of imperial experience. Here we have focused on the impact of a momentous innovation—the linking of empire to universalizing monotheism. The idea of one god both added moral passion to questions of inclusion and exclusion and raised the stakes of an emperor's claim to sovereign power. But even leaders who ruled in the name of a single god had to confront the mixity of the peoples they sought to govern. In some cases, they put these differences to work for their own purposes. Both fervor and pragmatism shaped the politics of Christian and Islamic empires as they tried to re-create Rome's universe on new foundations.

EURASIAN CONNECTIONS

The Mongol Empires

4

In the middle of the thirteenth century, a vast and devastating conquest transformed the world of empires. In 1206, an assembly of tribal leaders in Mongolia proclaimed Chinggis Khan their sovereign. By 1241, Mongol troops had devastated Kiev, defeated Poland, conquered Hungary, and, under the fearsome Khan Batu, were advancing on Vienna. Thirty-five years later, Chinggis's grandson Khubilai Khan captured the Song dynasty's capital in China. Cities, kingdoms, and empires fell or surrendered to this apparently invincible force, which for the first and possibly last time united Eurasia from China to the Black Sea under the rule of a single family.

Vienna was spared only because Batu learned of the death of Great Khan Ogodei, Chinggis's successor, and returned to Mongolia to select a new leader. Baghdad was not so lucky. In 1258, Mongols under Chinggis's grandson Hulegu sacked the city and killed the caliph. The Byzantine ruler of Trebizond on the Black Sea got the lesson and, like the Seljuk Turks, agreed to subordinate himself and his domain to the Mongol emperor. Overwhelmed by the Mongols' war machine, surviving rulers were soon sending ambassadors to the courts of Mongol khans, and in a few decades the sheltering sky of Mongol empire offered safety and rewards to merchants, clerics, scholars, artisans, and officials.

The empires established by Mongols were not long-lived, at least when compared to Rome or Byzantium. What makes Mongols count in world history are the connections they made across Eurasia and the imperial technologies they adapted, transformed, and passed on to later polities. In this chapter we will look at the origins of Mongol might, the astonishing career of Chinggis Khan, Mongol repertoires of power, the trajectories of Mongol khanates, and the impact of Mongol empires on world politics and culture.

Eurasian Paths to Power

The Romans created their Mediterranean empire over four centuries; Chinggis Khan and his direct descendants made a much larger Eurasian empire in seven decades. What kind of society could master the challenge of long-distance war and transform Eurasia with its scattered peoples into a web of material and cultural exchange? It may seem paradoxical that a nomadic people could rule over rich cities and long-established civilizations in China and central Asia, but the economy of pastoral nomadism and the political practices of earlier Eurasian empires gave the Mongols a well-stocked tool kit for empire.

We have already encountered Eurasian nomads and considered their impact on the formation, institutions, and vulnerabilities of Chinese empire (chapter 2). The Xiongnu who terrorized Han rulers into treaties and tribute payments were only one of many nomadic peoples who circled around China, penetrated its defenses, and demanded lucrative deals. At the other end of the silk route, the Romans were also forced to pay off mobile enemies—the "barbarians" who had journeyed west—or to hire them as mercenaries. In the fifth century CE, Attila, the great leader of the Huns, controlled a huge area from the Black Sea well into central and northern Europe. He allied himself with Romans, Goths, or both and collected a lavish tribute from the Byzantine emperor. Fortunately for the city of Rome, Attila cut short his invasion of Italy in 452. When he died a year later he was honored by his followers as having "terrorized both empires of the Roman world."

Xiongnu and Huns, and later Turks and Mongols, emerged from a historically productive territory, the great stretch of steppe, forest, and tundra reaching across Finland through Siberia and northern central Asia and further to today's China. Beginning with the first millennium BCE this area was the site of political tension and innovation, as nomads pushed into milder regions and as agriculturalists tried to settle on nomads' spaces. Arriving on the scene after other nomadic empires had come and gone, Mongols had the advantage of learning from predecessors, adopting their tactics, and adding some of their own.

Organized mobility was crucial to life on the Eurasian steppe—a rolling plain, interrupted by high mountains and streams, with extreme variations in temperature, from minus 40 degrees Fahrenheit in winter to over 100 in summer. Pastoral nomads became adept at distributing scarce resources to widely dispersed populations and at moving about with animals that fed on the steppe's product—grass—and provided their herders with food, clothing, shelter, transportation, and exchangeable goods.

The most important of the nomads' animals were horses and sheep, but cattle, goats, and camels could be part of the system. The short, hardy, Przhevalski horse—named for its nineteenth-century Russian "discoverer"—could dig for grass under snow and run for up to sixty miles a day. Horses were milked and used for transportation; dead horses provided meat and skins for leather. In a pinch, nomads drank blood directly from a horse's veins—a tactic that played into the nomads' perennially bad press. Mare's milk was fermented to make an alcoholic beverage—*kumis*. Sheep provided nomads with meat, skins for clothing, and wool to insulate their portable homes (the buildings we know as yurts). Because steppe grass was not fast-growing enough to support all these animals year-round in a single place, steppe nomads migrated seasonally, often traveling one hundred miles between summer and winter pastures.

Long-distance herding allowed nomads to supply themselves with most basics, but the Eurasian borderlands offered enticing products: grain to supplement nomads' diets, metals to enhance their weapons, and luxuries—like tea and silk—to use or trade. Nomadic empires acquired some settled people's technologies for themselves—the smelting of iron was a specialty—and held artisans and craftsmen in high esteem. Controlling and sheltering trade along the silk route to China and elsewhere was another way to gain access to valuable commodities. For millennia in Eurasia nomadic and sedentary peoples interacted—through trade, diplomacy, marriage, some sharing of space, and more or less intense raiding and warfare. When push came to shove, the nomads' formidable military skills gave them a sharp edge over their neighbors.

Although nomads are remembered for their superior horsemanship, it was their management of people that created a distinctive style of Eurasian empire. The basic unit of steppe society was the family. To survive, a family of nomads needed not only its own animals but also links to other people that could be sustained over a wide area. Over time successfully allied families could constitute themselves as a tribe. A Eurasian tribe was supposedly composed of people descended from a single ancestor, but in fact tribes were open to joiners of various kinds. The practice of "sworn brotherhood"—*anda*—allowed men to enter another tribe by becoming a "brother" of a powerful man. Or a person could decide to forsake his own lineage and become another person's follower—his *noker*. Exogamy—marrying outside the kinship group—created other alliances. Such marriages could mean carrying off women from other tribes or taking foreign princesses as wives.

These practices opened up allegiances far beyond those of blood. Whole tribes could become subordinated to others because they wanted protection or because they had been defeated. Allegiance could be firmed up through sworn brotherhood, loyal service, and marriage. Pragmatic alliances among tribal leaders could grow into powerful and wide-reaching super-tribal confederacies. These associations offered nomads ways to protect routes and pastures, to conduct campaigns of extortion and plunder against external powers, or to conquer them. But who would command super-tribal confederacies and mobilize them to gain and distribute resources? Who, in other words, could become an emperor on the steppe?

Well before the Mongols became an imperial power, Turkic peoples in Inner Eurasia had created their word for supreme ruler. The Turkic empires (552–734 CE) that spread from China into central Asia were ruled by a khaqan. Subsequent Eurasian powers—the Uighurs in Mongolia, the Khazars in the Caucasus, the Bulgars on the Volga River—adopted variants of this title, including khan. The khan's rule was envisioned as a mandate from Tengri, the chief god of the sky and the nomads who lived under it.

But heavenly favor, as we have seen, is open to multiple interpretations, especially when it comes to choosing an emperor. The Romans had used different approaches: election, descent, adoption, assassination, and civil war. Islamic polities fought over Muhammad's heritage. The Mongols, following their steppe predecessors, combined warriorhood and lineage. Their system was described by Joseph Fletcher, referring to Irish practices, as tanistry. When a chief died, the circle of contenders included both sons and brothers who had to fight and negotiate a way to the top. The system did not foster brotherly love—fratricide was a feature—but it was based on a reasonable assumption. The member of the chief's extended family best qualified for war and diplomacy should lead, not a son who happened to be firstborn.

At the highest level of power, competitions to become khan could involve both combat and deals with potential allies and subordinates. When the result was more or less clear, a great council—a *kuriltai*—was held to proclaim the new leader. This institution—the assembly of tribal leaders to produce a major and binding decision—is still used in Afghanistan and other Eurasian political spaces. The conflicts that took place after a khan's death were not a succession crisis but rather a normal, rigorous procedure for choosing the best man. A khan had to belong to a chiefly family, win the run-up competition, and be chosen by other great leaders.

Charisma was demanded and produced by this system. The special qualities of the khan and his lineage were interpreted as signs of heavenly fortune, *qut* in Turkic. Like other Eurasian nomads, Mongols believed that the world was full of spirits humans could address, appeal to, and appease. These beliefs easily accommodated other religions. Christians—including sects who had lost doctrinal struggles under the Byzantines—and Buddhists were protected by nomadic rulers. Mongols worshiped Tengri as an overarching, superior deity; they thought of high places as sacred for their proximity to heaven. The Mongols' spiritual helpers were shamans—humans with special powers to contact spirits and secure their assistance. A skillful leader might rely on a shaman, but he also might access the gods himself. In contrast to the contemporary empires of the Mediterranean, steppe rulers were not constrained by institutionalized churches, the disruptions of schism, or the exclusions of monotheism.

Eurasian peoples were experienced in making, raiding, challenging, and dividing empires. China, which fragmented and reunited several times after the fall of the Han dynasty (chapter 2), remained a major attraction for competing nomadic and semi-settled groups. Turkic khanates controlled the profitable silk route off and on while the Sui (581–617) and Tang (618–907) dynasties were trying to reunify and manage the Chinese empire. After the breakup of the khanates in the eighth century CE set Turkic groups in motion westward toward Byzantium and other imperial possibilities (chapter 3), one confederacy, the Uighurs, took up the challenge of both helping the Tang defeat their enemies and extorting huge amounts of silk as a reward.

The Song dynasty, founded in 960, oversaw the development, expansion, and reorientation of China's economy; exports through port cities and flourishing trade with southeast Asia more than offset the transcontinental trade routes. Under the Song, China's population exploded to over one hundred million. But the Song, too, were compelled to rely on or fight another nomadic empire—the Khitans, whose avid protection of the silk route is recorded in many foreign names for China—Kitai in Russian, Cathay for Europeans. The Khitans added a postal system (the *yam*) and the *ordos*—the movable armed camp of a ruler—to the Eurasian repertoire of rule.

The Khitans and later the Jurchens were Manchurian peoples who managed to wrestle large regions away from the Song and to found dynasties of their own in northern China—the Liao (916–1121) and the Jin (1115–1234). The Mongols also came from forested areas of Manchuria, from where they moved west into what later became known as Mongolia, then under Khitan control. It was here that Chinggis Khan's ancestors established themselves as a nomadic tribe, with their own totemic animal ancestors—a blue wolf and a doe—and their sacred mountain, Burqan Qaldun. But most important to what came later was the accumulated political experience of these and other Eurasian peoples.

What counted most for conquest was, of course, the army. Both Khitans and Jurchens used institutions created much earlier, such as the Xiongnu's organization of their army in a decimal system and the personal guard of the ruler (chapter 2). Warriors fought in units of 10 men; these groups were combined in 100s, 1000s, and 10,000s. Chinggis Khan fine-tuned the decimal-based units by breaking apart tribal contingents and redistributing warriors among separate units. Each soldier was responsible for all the soldiers in his group; when one failed all were punished.

Training was provided by life on the steppe—riding horses from a very early age, hunting as a favored sport, obedience to the clan or unit leader. Mongol horsemen used short stirrups, enabling speed and mobility. Warriors could ride forward and shoot backward, a favorite subject for artists after the conquest. Other tactics included the fake retreat, drawing the

Figure 4.1
Mongol warriors on horseback, illustrated in a Persian manuscript from the 1430s of Rashid al-Din's *Universal History*, c. 1310. Bibliothèque nationale de France, Manuscrits orientaux.

enemy into disorganized pursuit and eventual slaughter, bogus camps, and mannequins on horseback. The Mongols' basic and formidable weapon was the double-arched compound bow, made of layers of sinew and bone on a wooden frame, but they added new arms in the course of their conquests—armored cavalry with lances, Chinese artillery, and gunpowder.

There were no more than a few hundred thousand Mongols in the early thirteenth century, but at the end of Chinggis Khan's life about 130,000 were in his army—between a third and a quarter of the size of the Roman army at its peak. This modest population controlled about half of the world's horses in the thirteenth century. Nomadic life meant that the whole society could be mobilized for war; women followed campaigns with supplies and sometimes fought with men. Going home was not a goal—the point of war was plundering, sharing out the booty, and moving on to get more. The Mongols took their provisions with them and deposited them in advance of battle. They knew where to find water. When caught away from their supply lines, they had their survival foods, including horse blood. All this meant that when Chinggis Khan put together his army he commanded a terrifying force.

Making Empires, Mongol-Style

In this book so far we have emphasized imperial institutions, imaginaries, and repertoires of power more than emperors. Chinggis Khan merits a detour, for his life story illustrates basic elements of Eurasian political practice as well as the critical role of the leader in a personalized, patrimonial system. Chinggis created his mystique as he made his way to power. Overcoming apparently insurmountable obstacles was evidence of Chinggis's "good fortune" and became part of his legend and cult.

Around 1167 a male child, Temujin, was born into a chiefly but not powerful family in Mongolia. Temujin's father had made himself an anda (sworn brother) of Togrul, leader of the powerful Kerait confederacy; Temujin's mother had been kidnaped from yet another clan. At a very young age, Temujin was engaged to a girl, Borte, from his mother's tribe. None of this was unusual or particularly promising. Temujin's fate took a perilous turn when, after a Tatar tribesman killed Temujin's father, the family was deserted by his father's clan. Temujin, his mother, and her other children were left to forage on their own.

In these inauspicious circumstances, Temujin displayed a forceful personality that brought him friends, enemies, and victims. With one of his brothers, Temujin murdered a third brother in a fight. In 1180, Temujin was captured and nearly killed by a clan formerly allied with his father's. After

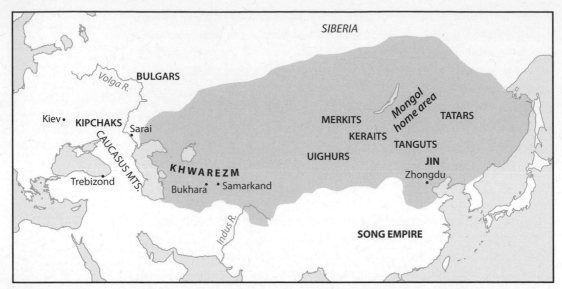

Map 4.1
Mongol empire:
1227.

this new disaster, Temujin used Borte's dowry as an offering and subordinated himself to his father's sworn brother, Togrul. Service to Togrul, an accomplished steppe leader, and life with the Turkic-speaking Keraits who sheltered both Christians and Buddhists gave Temujin new resources. He acquired his own loyal followers, nokers who left their tribes to follow him, and his own anda—his childhood friend Jamuqa, a man of high status, with his subordinates. These alliances came in handy when Borte was abducted by the Merkit tribe. Temujin, his allies Togrul and Jamuqa, and their followers defeated the Merkits, retrieved Borte, and exacted brutal revenge. Temujin acquired status as a chief.

By about 1190, Temujin was elected a khan by several clan leaders, who promised to obey him in war and peace and to give him the booty of their conquests to distribute. Temujin began to refashion his predecessors' institutions: he augmented his personal guard with artisans and cooks, as well as his closest commanders. Temujin and his former anda, Jamuqa, became rival chiefs on the steppe, each commanding about thirty thousand warriors. After a loss to Jamuqa in 1187, Temujin fled toward northern China. He used his warriors to assist the Jin dynasty and his patron, Togrul. The Jin emperor made Togrul "overall khan" and enhanced Temujin's status. For Temujin, subordination to the Jin provided exposure to the Jurchens' practices and to China with its alluring riches.

Returning to the steppe as a great leader, Temujin resumed the task of getting rid of rivals or incorporating them into his command. He outmaneuvered his former comrade Jamuqa and defeated his childhood enemies. But when Temujin. turned against Togrul, his former superior and overall khan, he was forced into another of his retreats, back to Manchuria. Temujin ultimately defeated Togrul, who died in battle, and killed his anda Jamuqa. In a horrifying display of ultimate power, Temujin also had his shaman executed.

Temujin became Chinggis Khan at a great kuriltai of steppe leaders in 1206. The name Chinggis, like the Romans' honorific Augustus, was the creation of a triumphant individual, distinguishing himself from earlier overall khans. Temujin chose a title that referred to the divine counterpart of the sky-god Tengri; Chinggis were spirits that ruled the earth. Chinggis Khan was the lord of the world.

Figure 4.2
Kuriltai at which Temujin is proclaimed Chinggis Khan, illustrated in a Persian manuscript from the 1430s of Rashid al-Din's *Universal History*, c. 1310. Bridgeman Art Library, GettyImages.

Throughout this long odyssey, Chinggis had practiced the arts of nomadic politics and pushed beyond their limits. He had risen from grubbing for roots with his outcast mother to become an emperor by exploiting familiar institutions—sworn brotherhood, pledged subordination, exogamous marriage, the obligations of revenge, service, and reward—in a series of astute alliances and ruthless assaults. He broke rules when he was strong enough to do so, and he made the severance of clan ties a primary tactic. In fierce enforcement of personal, not blood-defined, loyalty, he executed or threatened with execution many of his closest male relatives. After slaughtering rebellious subordinates, he took remnant families under his protection. Displaying his warrior charisma, Chinggis boasted that he wore "the same clothing and . . . [ate] the same food as the cowherds and horseherders" and that he cared "for my soldiers as if they were my brothers." The politics of personal loyalty, based on plentiful reward for ruthless service, now demanded that Chinggis go further.

The most obvious target was China, with its grain, linen and cotton, bronze and copper, mirrors, gold, satin, rice wine, and the ultimate luxury commodity, silk. In the thirteenth century, the Chinese empire was enticing, divided, and vulnerable. The Song emperors, whose rule had fostered trade, urbanization, innovations in science, engineering (gunpowder), arts, and cultural production (such as movable type), commanded the southern region, while the Jin dynasty ruled in the north. But in a tactic that distinguished him from earlier steppe leaders, Chinggis turned his attention first to problematic spots in his core area and to powers along trade routes, especially the lucrative silk road.

Chinggis sent his son Jochi to subdue tribes in Siberia, while he drove out the tribes who had assisted Jamuqa. Some groups saw the writing on the wall: the Uighur Turks submitted voluntarily. Their alphabet gave the Mongols a means to record their conquests and Chinggis's regulations. Chinggis then set out in 1209 against the Tangut empire located between the Mongol core and Chinese lands. The Tangut leader surrendered in 1210, and sent a huge tribute to seal the peace. He refused to send troops to join the Mongol army; this turned out to be a terrible mistake. With his core area united, Chinggis declared war on the Jin dynasty and after a prolonged campaign captured the Jin capital, Zhongdu, near today's Beijing, in 1215. The result was more tribute, as well as a Jin bride for Chinggis. Chinggis was coming full circle, conquering powers that had earlier sheltered him.

After this momentous success in northern China, Chinggis shifted course and began to move west, defeating challengers and acquiring subordinates, including Muslims who welcomed the Mongols' indifference to other people's religions. Having conquered the powers of inner Asia, Chinggis made a diplomatic overture to a rich ruler located in the area of today's Iran, the shah of Khwarezm. Part of his proposal, according to the Iranian historian and Mongol administrator Rashid al-Din, declared, "We should undertake to assist and support each other in times of need and to ensure the security of the caravan routes from disastrous incidents in order that merchants, on whose flourishing trade the welfare of the world depends, may move freely hither and thither." Unfortunately for the shah of Khwarezm and his subjects, this message was not treated with the seriousness it deserved. Chinggis's envoys and merchants were executed.

In response, Chinggis mustered a huge army of soldiers from his areas of conquest and descended upon central Asia in 1219. Cities were destroyed with terrible violence, unless their leaders submitted to Mongol rule. Men were systematically executed; women and children were enslaved. Artisans, whose skills were revered, were sent to serve Mongol courts. Clergy, too, with their useful access to spirits, were allowed to live, making anti-Mongol holy wars unlikely.

In 1221 Chinggis extended his campaign across today's Iran and Afghanistan to the Indus River. Some Mongol troops continued into the Caucasus, the Ukraine, and up the Volga. These forces traveled about 12,500 miles in four years, inflicted defeats on Georgians, Kipchak Turks in the Ukraine, Rus' princes in the Kiev area, and Bulgars of the Volga region. But Chinggis was sensitive to limits and the dangers of encirclement. He refrained from going on into India and headed back toward Mongolia, for what turned out to be his final campaign.

By this time Chinggis had made himself emperor of the earth, and he did not want to leave it. He consulted Daoist monks, who told him that he could prolong his life if he gave up his pleasures—the hunt, licentious behavior, and drunkenness. Chinggis had not lived a life of luxury, but he did drink a lot—a favorite Mongol leisure activity—and he had numerous sexual partners. While Chinggis's senior wife, Borte, remained the most powerful woman in his household, he acquired many other wives and concubines through war and diplomacy. Some of these women he presented to his sons and favorite warriors. Mongol trophy wives could become, like Borte, powerful actors in their new homes. The Mongols' practice of multiple marriages outside their own group, combined with their victorious wars, meant that their descendants are widespread in the world today.

Chinggis's life ended during a campaign of revenge. In 1226, he set out against his old enemies, the Tanguts, who had earlier refused to supply him with soldiers. The next year Chinggis died—exactly how is still a controversy—and Mongol forces killed in his honor the entire population of the Tangut city Zhongxing. Chinggis's body was transported in secret back to Mongolia. He was buried near Burqan Qaldun, the mountain he had worshiped on his way to power. The grave was disguised, and the region around it became a forbidden, sacred space.

Chinggis had made the most of ideologies, institutions, and statecraft developed earlier in Eurasia. His sacred aura proven by overcoming hardship and defeating his rivals, the steppe commander enjoyed the benefits of organized, mobile, self-sufficient armies; dynastic outreach expanded through incorporative marriage strategies; profits, beauty, and security delivered by protected merchants, artisans, and clergy; script to record income, distributions, and decrees; revenue from multiple sources (trade, tribute, war, and taxation)—in short, the attributes of statehood minus the disruptive exclusions of monotheism. From an institutional perspective, thirteenth-century Eurasia offered ingredients for empire missing at this time in Europe. Still, it took an individual to weave—or force—tribes, cities, confederacies, and other empires into a single polity, under the rule of the Great Khan.

Pax Mongolica

How could violent conquest lead to a "Mongol peace," as some historians have described the late thirteenth century, when the "flourishing trade" Chinggis proposed to the shah of Khwarezm indeed took place across Eurasia? Then, as later, the expansion of economic connections was forged by force; markets do not become "global" on their own. But for survivors of the Mongols' initial devastations, the conquest enabled commercial and cultural expansion (as had the Romans' extension of their space) and opened up new political possibilities and imaginaries, both on the steppe and around its borders. For the Mongol rulers, their officials, and other subordinates, peace allowed syntheses of repertoires of rule that would have long-lasting influence on later empires.

But first, there had to be a peace. After Chinggis's death, transcontinental empire depended on Mongol leaders coming to stable terms with each other. Well aware of the explosive potential of tanistry, Chinggis had declared his third son, Ogodei, his successor and insisted that his other sons support this choice in writing. In 1229, after an interlude of jockeying for power, Chinggis's prominent descendants and officials gathered in a huge kuriltai to confirm Ogodei as Great Khan. Members of Chinggis's family—sons, surviving brothers, and at least one daughter—were given a territory, an *ulus*, to rule; the Great Khan exercised his coordinating authority over the whole.

The realist tradition of Eurasian politics allotted the eldest son the pastures farthest from those of his father. In Chinggis's time, this meant "as far west as the Mongol hoof had trodden"—a fateful designation for the peoples of eastern Europe. The steppes west of the Volga became part of the ulus allotted to Chinggis's oldest son, Jochi, and inherited by Jochi's son Batu. Chinggis's second son received lands in central Asia. The youngest son,

Tolui, received the heartland area of Mongolia. Great Khan Ogodei began constructing walls and palaces for a new Mongol capital at Qara Qorum, a place Chinggis—with his good fortune—had visited. An uneasy, punctuated unity among Chinggis's closest descendants lasted into the middle of the thirteenth century, time enough for the empire to take on a truly transcontinental shape.

The second stage of Mongol expansion was carried out with the combination of terror and diplomacy used in the first conquests. To the east, Mongols continued their campaign against the Jin dynasty, completing the conquest of northern China in 1234. Part of Tibet was annexed around 1250, after Mongols cultivated ties with ambitious Buddhist Lamas. The campaign to conquer southern China under the Song dynasty presented the greatest challenge, but after extensive preparation aided by Chinese advisors, Chinggis's grandson Khubilai Khan finally defeated the Song in 1279 and founded the next dynasty, the Yuan. After repeated attempts to conquer Japan failed, the Mongols reached their limits at the Pacific.

On the other side of the world, the boundary on ambition was not so clear. In 1236, Chinggis's grandson Batu led his Mongol army west of the Urals. In five years, these forces pushed as far as Ukraine, Poland, and Hungary. As we have seen, the Mongol steamroller stopped when Batu returned to Mongolia after Great Khan Ogodei's death. Later Batu established himself in the steppe region of his ulus with its grasslands and connections to the Black Sea, the Caspian, the Volga, and transcontinental trade. He named his realm the Kipchak Khanate, recalling the Turkic-speaking Kipchaks who had controlled this area but were now subject to the Mongols' formidable power. The khanate subsequently became known as the Golden Horde (chapter 7).

In between China and the Golden Horde, Mongols fortified their controls over the two other regions allotted to Chinggis's successors. Mongke, elected Great Khan in 1251, ordered his brother Hulegu to complete Chinggis's conquest of southwest Asia. Hulegu defeated the Shi'ite Ismailis and then turned on the Abbasids (chapter 3). He besieged Baghdad, conquered it, and killed the caliph along with an alleged two hundred thousand city residents. Hulegu's armies were finally stopped as he advanced toward Egypt by the troops of the Mamluk sultan. Hulegu established himself as the first dynast of the Il-Khans, based in Iraq and Iran. The fourth ulus—of Chagatai, Chinggis's second son—extended east from the Aral Sea, encompassing the trade route cities of Khwarezm and linking the three other Mongol realms—the Il-Khans, the Golden Horde, and Yuan China—with each other.

One source of the Mongol peace, then, was more war—war that drew most of Eurasia in under one or other of the Chinggisid rulers. But another was diplomacy. Wise rulers, like those of the Armenians, and would-be rulers, such as Rus' princes near Moscow, learned that submission to the Mon-

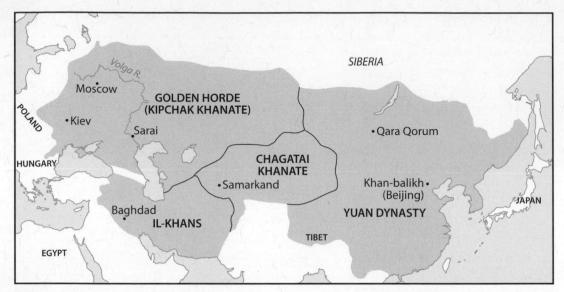

Map 4.2
Mongol empires: 1294.

gol khans could bring protection and, for some, great wealth (chapter 7). As for the inner circle, the Mongol imperial family was able to divide control over its realm and rule for over four decades. Each choice of a Great Khan was preceded by a period of a few years when the Chinggisids maneuvered and schemed against each other, practicing tanistry on the largest scale, but the principle of the ulus offered a way out from total war.

Four Chinggisid dynasties emerged from the conquests: the Golden Horde, under the descendants of Jochi, with its capital in Sarai on the Volga; the neighboring Chagatai khanate, roughly in today's Uzbekistan; the Il-Khans in Persia, under the descendants of Hulegu; and the Yuan dynasty in China, headed from 1260 to 1294 by the well-remembered Khubilai. The sons of Ogodei, the first Great Khan after Chinggis, failed in the succession struggles and eventually lost all their territories. The more successful descendants of Chinggis's son Tolui (Hulegu and Khubilai) ended up with two of the four large khanates.

By 1260, we can speak about Mongol empires in the plural. When Great Khan Mongke died in 1259, Khubilai, who was in China, did not wait for a kuriltai but simply had himself proclaimed sovereign by his troops. Khubilai made his own capital at a place he called "city of the khan" or Khan-balikh—later Beijing. In each of the khanates, Mongol rulers drew strength from Eurasian political principles while continuing to adopt management strategies from the conquered. The Mongol way of rule, rather than a single formal empire, fostered connections between east and west, transformed culture, demographics, statecraft, and commerce, and provoked new aspirations in the widening world.

The Mongol Way

Great Khan Ogodei is reported to have said, "The empire was created on horseback, but it cannot be governed on horseback." The saying was undoubtedly an import from Chinese advisors, who had a longer experience of the problem. As the Mongols' task changed from conquering to ruling, they relied on local intermediaries and developed ways to control them. Mongol sovereignty in the khanates was distinguished by its adaptability to local circumstances, including religion, artistic expression, science, and comforts, but also by tenacious adherence to particular elements in the Eurasian repertoire of power.

In China, the khan had to be remade into an emperor. By reuniting north and south and adding on Tibet, the Mongols' conquests gave China the largest dimensions it had yet known. Khubilai, who had recruited Chinese advisors early on, quickly seized upon the powerful and self-obfuscating imperial tradition to emphasize his status as a universal ruler. Whereas earlier dynasties had taken names with a geographical reference, the name Yuan meant "origin of the cosmos." It diverted attention from the awkward fact that the Mongols were not from a Chinese area. Khubilai had his emperorship proclaimed by edict in 1272. This impressive decree gave scholarly Chinese bureaucrats grounds to claim that the Yuan had inherited the Mandate of Heaven legitimately and would bring it glory.

The Mongols preserved or transformed as needed the institution of the khan and his command in all their conquest areas. A second expandable technology of rule was registration—essential to taxing their populations effectively. Before the conquest, Uighur counselors had provided Mongols with a writing system and secretarial expertise. In China, Great Khan Mongke ordered in 1252 the largest census ever taken; censuses were compiled in the Kipchak Khanate, including the lands of the Rus' princes. The decimal system that organized the Mongol armies was applied to the counted populations and used to conscript soldiers. In the Rus' lands, officials were given titles such as leaders of "hundreds" and of "ten thousands." The Mongols used a variety of taxes—on people, on trade, on herds—and, informed by their transcontinental experts, they adjusted their collection mechanisms in different parts of the empire. In areas ruled by the Il-Khans, the poll tax was progressive, about seven times higher for the rich than the poor.

The Mongols' approach to exacting resources was pragmatic—they could cancel taxes to help out one group, augment them to punish another—but in almost all cases they needed intermediaries from conquered areas who could carry out their orders, collect revenues or goods, and deliver them. For nomadic leaders, the risk posed by local authorities was clear—they could break away from subordination and into overlordship. The Mongols had a strategic response to the double-edged sword of indirect rule: military ranks were mostly reserved for Mongols, while officialdom was open to civilians, and servitors of both kinds were harnessed to higher authorities through personal ties. These systems of separation and dependence allowed Mongols to use knowledgeable people from different areas but avoid relinquishing too much power to them.

The Mongol way of managing intermediaries included moving them around the empire, while fine-tuning their administrative practices to the demands of particular areas. After Chinggis's first devastating assaults in today's Iran, Persians, Uighurs, Mongol subtribal leaders, and Jews were deployed as high officials in the region. But later, under the Il-Khans, most administration was back in the hands of old Persian families. In China, the Mongols were more cautious about relying on Chinese intermediaries with their well-developed administrative tradition. The Yuan rulers left low-level officials in charge of the vital task of tax collection in local areas, while engaging foreigners—Muslims from central Asia and the Middle East, Uighurs, and members of Mongol subtribes—as top administrators. Keeping the highest posts for non-Chinese may have pushed Chinese elites into arts and literature, both of which thrived under Yuan rule. In a strike against officialdom and for personal loyalty, the examination system for entry into the Chinese civil service was suspended from 1238 to 1315.

At the highest level of politics, the Mongol empires remained true to Eurasian dynastic principle. The emperor—the khan—had to be a Chinggisid, a descendant of Chinggis's own family. But people who served the dynasty were not bound by this rule. The apparatus of government was open to individuals of various origins and religions who might compete with each other—as military leaders had done—to be the most useful to their rulers.

During their conquests Mongol leaders appeared indifferent to religion, certainly in comparison with Byzantine, Islamic, and Carolingian imperial rulers. What some Europeans much later interpreted as Mongol "tolerance" of multiple religions derived from conditions quite unlike monotheistic postulates—the Eurasians' interest in spiritual advisors, the multiplicity of faiths on the territories Mongols conquered, and the pragmatic politics of alliance through exogamous marriage. Chinggis, for example, in one of his post-victory settlements arranged for his son Tolui to marry a niece of the Ong (Overall) Khan. This woman, Sorhokhtani, belonged to a Christian group known as Nestorians, losers in one of the Byzantines' confessional quarrels. She became the mother of the Great Khans Mongke and Khubilai, as well as of Hulegu, the conqueror of Iran. Mongol leaders cultivated contacts with religious leaders, brought them to their courts, and did not tax church revenues. Under the Il-Khans in the early years of Mongol rule, Buddhists, Christians of several varieties, Jews, and Muslims all flourished.

Over time, many Mongols converted—to different religions. Il-Khan Oljeitu (1304–16) was probably a Shamanist, a Buddhist, a Christian, and a Sunni and a Shi'i Muslim at different times in his life. Mongols cultivated Tibetan Buddhist authorities and protected Buddhists in China; Great Khan Khubilai became a Buddhist. The better-known Mongol conversion was to Islam. After Hulegu destroyed the Abbasid caliphate in 1258, there did not seem to be much hope for Islam in this area. But within a generation Mongol rulers in Persia had become Muslims, as did many of their followers. This choice set the stage for a great flowering of Islamic culture under the Il-Khans and their successors.

Law was part of the Mongol way of rule. Early in his rise to power, Chinggis adopted regulatory practices from literate servitors and captives; he required an adopted son to record in a "Blue Book" the lands and peoples he assigned to his subordinates. Chinggis's orders were also supposed to be written down and preserved. No text of the law code known as Chinggis's Great Yasa survives, but as we have noted with the Romans, law can play a role in governance in several ways—as a set of rules, as a way of making judgments, as the concern of courts and jurists. Mongol khans both issued laws and enabled the making of lawful judgments.

Histories of Mongol rule written by contemporaries describe the khan as a dispenser of justice, guided by the advice of counselors, including Muslim, Jewish, and Christian authorities. Many legal judgments in Mongol lands were delivered directly by religious or tribal authorities, who were expected to resolve conflicts within their subordinated groups. Mongols' willingness to devolve authority to punish crimes that did not concern the state directly was expressed—negatively—in China: the Yuan dynasty, unlike earlier ones, did not produce a penal code. Mongols' treaty-making practices and their willingness to negotiate terms of subordination, surrender, and exchange were also aspects of a legal culture based on declared loyalty, backed up by contractual arrangements.

The Mongol way was also the great trade route that connected khans, officials, merchants, travelers, and their exchange partners across Eurasia. Rapid communications made the silk route into a media highway. The yam system set up by Great Khan Ogodei in 1234 was a series of way stations, situated every twenty-five or thirty miles, the distance that horses with their loads could conveniently travel in a day. These posts were provisioned with horses and supplies for authorized users—diplomatic envoys, couriers carrying imperial orders, and merchants. Travelers carried a medallion inscribed in Mongolian to prove that their transit had official sanction. This *paisa* (a Chinese word) was the ancestor of our passport systems. The yam combined functions: merchants could be controlled and taxed, while official messengers could change horses and continue on and cover perhaps two hundred miles a day. The Mongols had transformed a courier service operated earlier in northern China by the Khitans into a transcontinental network of control, taxation, and exchange.

The Mongol connection stretched from the Pacific to the Mediterranean and the Baltic and enabled an enormous transfer of knowledge, ideas, and techniques across long distances. Buddhists in Persia, Muslim advisors in China, and the far-flung missions of various Christians were part of a great remixing of peoples and religions in the thirteenth and fourteenth centuries. But even where people stayed put, diets and cuisine, medical and geographic knowledge, and artistic and architectural environments were transformed by contacts and travel across the continent. If Mongol elites ate meat broth with fermented mare's milk at their great kuriltai in 1246, a century later Yuan rulers in China could dine on wheat breads and pasta, chickpeas, walnuts, almonds, pistachios, eggplant, honey, and syrups. Their old standby, mutton, could be seasoned with spices, marinated, roasted, and served on a bed of hummus! The cuisine we associate with the Middle East had traveled to Asia, along with cooks. Sharing recipes was a two-way street. Rice, a staple in China, became a desired food of the Persian elite during the reign of the Il-Khan Ghazan.

The Mongol way established access to an array of medical systems—Chinese, Korean, Tibetan, Muslim, Nestorian Christian, and others. The Il-Khans' Chinese physicians advocated acupuncture, the application of herbal pastes and mercury, and used pulse-taking for diagnosis. Again, connections worked both ways: Ibn-Sina's (Avicenna) *Canon on Medicine*, produced in central Asia in the early eleventh century, was listed in the Yuan imperial library's catalog for 1273. This knowledge did not help, however, when disease transited the steppe, most devastatingly in the mid-fourteenth century, a time of great plagues in China and black death in Europe. What travelers brought with them, then and now, was not always benign.

Avid for knowledge of earth and sky, Mongols financed mapmaking and astronomy. The Yuan dynasty sponsored a geographical academy, staffed by Muslim cartographers. These fourteenth-century specialists knew the shape of Africa and the Mediterranean more accurately than Europeans knew Asia's contours. The Il-Khans triggered a building boom in the second half of the thirteenth century, when they refitted their cities with domes decorated with glazed tile mosaics, synthesizing Persian, Chinese, and Turkic motifs and skills. Manuscript illustration and calligraphy also flourished under the Il-Khans, who admired the Persian courtly epic and engaged Chinese painters to decorate histories and tales. Carpet-making, an art form with practical uses invented by nomads, was elaborated and spread across Asia. The key to this explosion of artistic production was wealth, patronage, and the mixing of artistic traditions, as Mongol rulers attracted the greatest artists, artisans, and scholars to their courts.

The foundation for this cultural explosion was the economic expansion nurtured by the Mongol peace. Mongol investment in commercial activities, maintenance of a high-speed transit and communications system across Eurasia, protection of merchants and artisans, and practices of dispute resolution all expanded the horizons of possibility and imagination for long-distance trade. Mongols displayed none of the ambivalence toward merchants found in China. On the contrary, the Mongol regulatory regime included institutions that facilitated long-distance trade and local productivity, among them a form of partnership between the state and individual entrepreneurs. Venetian and Genoese merchants as well as officials in Black Sea ports profited from the Mongols' pro-merchant, cosmopolitan, rights-granting practices, linking Eurasian commerce to the eastern Mediterranean.

The Mongols' protection of religious institutions, their inclusion of different cultural regimes and distinctive social groups within their polities, and their fostering of trade and cultural exchange allowed scholars at the time to think that a whole world was finally available for study. Rashid al-Din wrote in his *Collected Chronicles* completed around 1310 that only under Mongol rule was it finally possible to make "a general account of the history of the inhabitants of the world and different human species." His goal was to examine the manuscripts and wisdom of each people—the biblical prophets, Muhammad, the caliphates, Mongols, Turks, Chinese, Jews, Indians, and Franks—and to collect these in something "unprecedented—an assemblage of all the branches of history."

Rashid al-Din's idea of humanity was composite. The world was made up of different peoples, each with its own knowledge and beliefs, its own scholars and sources—an assemblage, not a ladder or a staircase. This imperial imagination—a vision of a connected, differentiated, and therefore rich world—linked ambitious people like Rashid al-Din to other knowledge specialists. What held the whole together was the protection and patronage of Mongol khans.

Meltdown and Reprise

Mongol connections transferred technologies that reshaped the political, economic, and cultural frame of the world long after the Mongol empires themselves vanished. But as a coordinated system under recognizable dynastic control, the Mongols' huge empire lasted only a few decades. Breakdown was related to what had made the empire so aggressive in the first place. Mongol power depended on distributing resources to warriors and followers; the system required expansion. Shifts of allegiance had been essential to Chinggis's success; they could also tear his empire apart. The creation of separate uluses may have staved off the end, but as the Mongol leaders settled down in their areas, they lost both tactical advantages over their rivals and motives for unity among themselves. War between Mongol khanates became as promising as war at the edges of nomadic empire.

The most settled of the four khanates succumbed first. The Il-Khans, who ruled from 1256 to 1335, were caught between two effective Eurasian-style military powers—the Mamluks (chapter 3) based in Egypt and the Mongols of the Golden Horde (chapter 7). The Mamluks and Golden Horde made peace with each other in the interests of a lucrative trade through the Black Sea and Constantinople to Egypt; the Il-Khans, now a Muslim power, allied with various "Franks" but without much effect. The last ruler, Abu Sa'id, even made up with the Mamluks. But in 1335, the dynasty failed on its own principles. Despite many wives, Abu Sa'id left no direct male heir; more fatally, in the usual power struggle after his death, no one candidate from the extended imperial family emerged a clear winner. The territory he had controlled fragmented for forty years. Many Mongols who lived there merged into the Turkic-speaking, Muslim tribes of the area.

The Yuan dynasty lasted thirty years longer. Here Mongol descendants of the conqueror Khubilai faced a different geography of power. Khubilai had put northern, central, and southern regions of China together under one emperor; the problem as for the Qin and the Han (chapter 2) was how to keep it that way. Threats to Yuan control came from different directions—Mongol warlords in the north, peasant and Buddhist rebels in the south. The last Yuan ruler, Toghon Temur, was chased out of Beijing by a Chinese renegade who established the next, non-Mongol dynasty, the Ming (chapter 7).

The two khanates situated in the middle of Eurasia and farthest from its contested edges had more durable futures, each in its own way. The Kipchak Khanate (the Golden Horde) had spread its wings under Batu, Chinggis's grandson, over an ideal terrain for horse raising and trade and not far from an agricultural space—the future Russia—where an array of princes competed for power and understood the potential of subordinated sovereignty (chapter 7). It was also close enough to major trade routes in all directions. The khanate's capitals on the Volga—Sarai and later new Sarai—became immensely rich. Batu's brother Berke, khan from 1257 to 1267, was a personal convert to Islam, and later under Uzbek Khan (1313–41), the Horde became a Muslim power. The Horde broke up according to the principle that had put it together—the capacity of ambitious leaders to break with their overlord, form new coalitions, and ally themselves with outsiders, such as the Ottoman Turks (chapter 5), to attack the Horde and its wealth. Beginning in 1438, the Golden Horde disaggregated into separate khanates along the Volga and in the steppes north of the Black Sea; these khanates in turn were gradually—and mostly violently—incorporated into other empires over the next 350 years.

Chagatai's ulus in central Asia split into two parts—Transoxiana and Mughalistan—by the late thirteenth century and eventually dissolved into loose confederations of tribal and military units, each with tenuous connections to urban and agricultural regions. This area, where traditions of pastoralism and rough-and-ready alliances were well preserved, produced the last great Mongol conqueror. At the end of the fourteenth century, Tamerlane (Temur, in Turkic)—a Mongol by descent, a Muslim at birth, a Turkic-speaker—repeated Chinggis's feats of fighting his way to the heights of command and conquering, ruthlessly, much of Eurasia, if only for a short time.

Tamerlane played the field of rival authorities with consummate skill—allying with men from other tribes, with former enemies, and with aggressors from outside the ulus to defeat the leader of his own tribe, as well as all his earlier rivals and patrons. By 1380, Tamerlane personally controlled the ulus of Chagatai and possessed a fabulously appointed capital at Samarkand. He went on to subjugate, with impressive violence, the whole of Persia and Afghanistan, the Caucasus, territories of the Golden Horde, and northern India. His troops captured Baghdad in 1393, looted Sarai in 1396, and sacked Delhi in 1398. In 1402, Tamerlane defeated the Ottomans (chapter 5) in Anatolia, ending the career of the great conqueror Bayezid. Henry III of Castile, Charles VI of France, and Henry IV of England congratulated Ta-

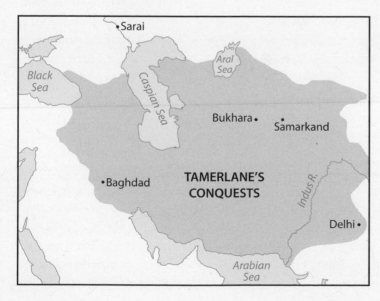

Map 4.3
Tamerlane's
conquests.

merlane on this victory. Tamerlane set out to conquer China, but died on the way in 1405.

Tamerlane took care to link himself to Chinggis's memory, evoking a difficult and deprived youth, retreats from near defeat, and direct contacts with the divine. But Tamerlane was not from the Chinggisid line and could be seen as breaking with the strong dynastic tradition the Mongols had entrenched. To address this problem, Tamerlane put a nominal Chinggisid at the head of the ulus of Chagatai; he also took a wife who was a Chinggisid and could provide him with royal sons. This effort succeeded in producing many claimants to the Chinggisid lineage throughout central and south Asia. One of Tamerlane's Chinggisid descendents, Babur, founded the Mughal empire in India in 1525.

Royal blood alone could not hold Tamerlane's empire together. Tamerlane willed his command to one of his grandsons, but the realm immediately broke into first four and then many regions, where rivals competed for fifteen years of bitter war. Like Chinggis, Tamerlane had surrounded himself with army commanders from many tribes and areas; like Chinggis, he had used the rewards of conquest to keep his war machine going. Tamerlane enhanced the Mongols' strategy of dual governance—local administrators and Mongol military commanders—by systematically relocating tribal leaders away from their home territories, combining troops from different regions into mixed forces under new leaders, and keeping personal control over the appointment of both civilian and military authorities.

This ultra-personalization of authority, based on breaking up local networks, worked well for Tamerlane, but it also undercut any subsequent leader's ability to mobilize and reward followers. The region reverted to the fluid politics of shifting alliances and rivalries among multiple chiefs; Afghanistan has posed management problems for empires to this day. What remained strong after Tamerlane was the mystique of a personal empire, led by a single, all-powerful ruler. This concept of sovereignty was transmitted through memories of both Tamerlane's devastating violence and the subsequent order he was able to impose.

Why Mongols Matter

The possibility of a wide-ranging, enriching imperial peace conquered and protected by a single mighty sovereign was one of the Mongols' contributions to political imagination in central Asia and its adjacent spaces. That the Great Khan was a royal conqueror from afar, not a local son, corresponded to the experience of the widely dispersed populations of the steppe, desert, and mountainous regions. Once victory had been gained, Mongol rulers allowed people to continue their religious practices and relied on local authorities to do most of the work of governance. Sophisticated administrators filled offices in the nodal points of khanates; they could serve different leaders when Mongol control faltered. The adoption of Islam by some Mongol khans facilitated a symbiosis of Chinggisid rulership and Persian-influenced, urban-centered artistic and literary culture. The skills and designs of craftsmen and architects were carried into other areas as power leaked out of the khanates.

Although the Mongol empires fragmented quickly, the unification of Eurasia left its imprint on later polities. The Mongols' protection of religious institutions, their governing practices based on recognized difference, with no fixed center or core population; the cultivation of personalized loyalty as the sovereign's means of control; the fluid politics of contingent allegiance, pragmatic subordination, and treaty making—this repertoire remained in play long after Chinggis's empire disintegrated.

The world around Eurasia was transformed as well. As we shall see, some inheritors of Mongol experience overcame the problem of durability that the great conquerors had not solved and through a synthesis of Mongol and other traditions built or rebuilt large and long-lasting empires—Ottoman, Russian, and Chinese. In India, the Muslim Mughals, Tamerlane's descendants, governed a multitude of peoples for over 250 years, enhancing commercial connections without imposing their religion on the diverse population. Trade and communications fostered by Mongol supervision opened up new vistas to rulers, merchants, and explorers. After studying Marco Polo's account of his transcontinental travels two centuries earlier, in 1492 Christopher Columbus began his voyage to the land of the Great Khan.

BEYOND THE MEDITERRANEAN

Ottoman and Spanish Empires

A lthough Mongols built a bigger empire than the Romans had, and in a shorter time, the khans did not create institutions that could keep the whole space together for very long. The Ottomans did exactly this, blending Eurasian practices with the imperial creations of the eastern Mediterranean and its hinterlands. At the western end of the same sea, a breakthrough of a different kind allowed rulers to patch together a composite empire from elements that today are part of Austria, Germany, Belgium, the Netherlands, France, Italy—and Central and South America. The Habsburg dynasty could not overcome the tendency toward division within Europe, but the Americas offered promising terrain and a way around Ottoman power. The Ottomans and the Habsburgs produced new sorts of empire, and as they did so opened up new questions about the relationship of imperial rulers to subject peoples and to the intermediaries in between. This chapter looks at two empires, extending power in different ways, in conflict with each other.

Our protagonists include two great architects of empire, Suleiman the Magnificent, the Ottoman sultan from 1520 to 1566, and Charles V, ruler of multiple domains in Europe and the Americas from 1516 and Holy Roman Emperor from 1520 to 1556. The competition between these rulers was intensified by their different faiths and their conflicting claims to places once ruled by Rome. Both leaders were inspired by prophetic visions that their dynasties would rule all of the known world. For the Ottomans, conquest of Constantinople—the second Rome—in 1453 and Suleiman's extensions of the realm seemed to fulfill a destiny going back to Alexander the Great. For the Habsburgs, the defeat of the last Muslim caliph of Granada in 1492 and the unification of Spanish kingdoms with the Holy Roman Empire were steps toward universal Christian empire.

If Charles V aspired to build a new Rome, his power emerged from the volatile politics left in Rome's wake. On the common ground of Christianity, many lords and kings continued for centuries to assert conflicting

5

Figure 5.1

Charles V, oil painting by Dutch artist
Bernard van Orley, first half of the six-
teenth century. Musée du Louvre, Paris.
Bridgeman Art Library, GettyImages.

Suleiman I as a young man, from an
ink and gold leaf drawing of 1579,
in Topkapi Palace Museum. Nakkas
Osman, GettyImages.

powers. Suleiman's possibilities grew out of a more mixed imperial landscape. Taking over Byzantine territories and going beyond them, the Ottomans drew on multiple imperial pasts—Mongol, Turkic, Persian, Arab, and
Roman. The Ottoman polity was more inclusive than the monotheistic
Mediterranean empires, more durable than the Mongol khanates. Blocked
by the Ottomans and constrained by nobles within their realm, Spanish
monarchs looked in a different direction—overseas—for new sources of
imperial strength. Chapter 6 takes up this process of imperial extension, ex-
amining the maritime empires of Spain, Portugal, the Netherlands, England,
and France as endeavors whose effects went far beyond the goals of their
initial architects.

Chapter 5

Our focus in this chapter is on two ways of organizing imperial power. In the Ottoman case, the emperor ruled through subalterns incorporated into his household, people deliberately recruited from outside Ottoman society. In Habsburg Spain, emperors drew their military force from magnates who had their own followers to contribute to the imperial endeavor—or potentially to be used against it. The relative autonomy of Ottoman rulership from the powers of landed aristocracies gave sultans great flexibility in dealing with the populations of the empire. The Ottomans incorporated leaders of diverse cultural groups into administrative roles and extended protection (and claims) over subjects of different religions. Spanish rule, on the other hand, was notably intolerant of religious difference.

Empires do not grow out of whole peoples who set out to dominate other whole peoples. The Ottoman empire was not specifically Turkish, the Habsburg not specifically Spanish. In both cases society was reshaped by the process of empire-building.

"These emperors Charles and Suleiman possessed as much as did the Romans . . . each worked to become the king and lord of the world; but we see that because of our sins Suleiman succeeded better than Charles at satisfying his wants and managing his intrigues. Both of them had about the same age but different fortunes; both gave themselves over equally to war, but the Turks succeeded better at fulfilling their projects than did the Spanish; they devoted themselves more fully to the order and discipline of war, they were better advised, they used their money more effectively."

—Lopez de Comara, chronicler of the conquistador Cortes, 1540s

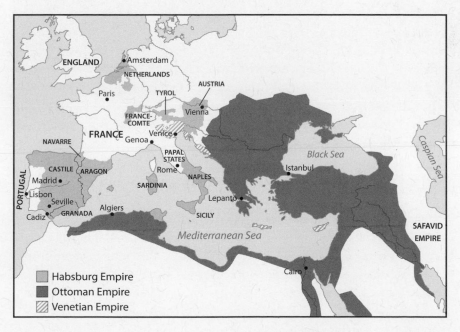

Map 5.1
Habsburg and Ottoman empires, sixteenth century.

Composite Monarchy and the Origins of the "Spanish" Empire

"Spain" was not a propitious place to launch an empire. It was cut by mountains into regions that tended to go their own way culturally and politically. The last Islamic ruler was ejected from Granada only in 1492. The elegant paintings by Velasquez of emperors who led Spain in its imperial glory display the blue eyes, blond hair, and jutting chins of the Habsburgs, whose roots were not in Iberia but in north-central Europe. The Spanish empire did not spring from a strong and united territory; nor was its leadership particularly Spanish.

In the late fifteenth century, the area the Romans had called Hispania was divided into the kingdoms of Castile, Aragon, Portugal, Granada, and Navarre. What united their leaders, except for Granada's Muslim king, was the Catholic religion and shared beliefs in the rules of monarchical politics. Descent was the crucial concept for the transmission of political authority—subject to the usual qualifiers of rebellion and fratricide—and new kings inherited not just land but a panoply of hierarchical relationships, extending through local lords down to peasants. The king's "jurisdiction" was in effect a contractual arrangement that recognized the rights of subordinate magnates. Charles V continually made the rounds of his empire to shore up these ties.

Lords possessed armed retainers and peasants on their land—hence both power and revenue. Lords might together swear fealty to a king who offered protection or the strength to subordinate new populations, but lords also sought to prevent a king from acquiring too many personal followers or too many lands of his own. Kings thus had to keep unruly lords, with their rights in property and in people, within the fold. Royal sovereignty was built on layers of dependence—from king to magnates to lesser lords and eventually to soldiers and peasants. When royal families made strategic marriages and combined families—not necessarily speaking the same language—and lands—not necessarily contiguous—they created what J. H. Elliott terms a "composite monarchy."

From Reconquest to Habsburg Empire

The marriage in 1469 of Ferdinand, heir to the throne of Aragon, king of Sicily and Sardinia, and claimant to the throne of Naples, to Isabella, heiress of Castile, produced a union of two adjacent but separate kingdoms. This was unfortunate for the kings of France and Portugal, who also wanted to ally with Isabella and who went to war over Ferdinand's "conquest." Castile—with six times the population of Aragon—was indeed the prize, but the wedding did not fuse the monarchies into a unitary polity. The marriage contract specified that on her death Isabella would pass her Castilian proprietorship to her descendants, not to her husband.

Still, the timing of this marriage alliance was good and the royal couple particularly astute. They presided when Granada was finally defeated. Their effort drew on soldiers from Castile and Aragon, but also on the connections its rulers, particularly Ferdinand, had across Catholic Europe: the army included Swiss mercenaries and used Italian-made cannons maintained by German technicians. The fight against Muslim rulers—later dubbed the "Reconquest"—inspired a sense of commonality among Catholics, and after Ferdinand and Isabella's triumphal entry into Granada cemented the legitimacy of the united crowns. In 1494 the pope declared Ferdinand and Isabella to be "Catholic kings," melding the principles of dynastic power with Christianity.

Along with victory came a drive to rid the polity of non-Catholic elements. Some 200,000 Jews, forced to choose between conversion and expulsion, left Spain. Many ended up in the Ottoman empire, which made more room for religious diversity. The Muslims of Granada were initially allowed to keep their faith, but after 1502 they were ordered to convert or leave the region. Occasional rebellions and endemic warfare with the Ottomans put the loyalty of Muslim converts in question; they were deported, first from Granada and finally, in 1609, from all the kingdoms of Spain. The loss of approximately 300,000 people did little to help the economic growth of the region. Anxious about the sincerity of forced converts and heresy more generally, the Spanish monarchy, with papal authorization, developed the institution of the Inquisition, policing the orthodoxy of belief and behavior. It was only in 1834 that the Inquisition was definitively abolished.

Large landowners were the mainstay of the Iberian economy, but towns in Castile and Aragon also possessed large amounts of land and a form of subordinate sovereignty. Citizenship had lost the empire-wide significance of Roman times. It was now focused on local institutions: citizens had to be accepted by established members of a town, from which they received both rights and obligations. The autonomy of nobles and municipalities stood between the monarch and his subjects. Hence the importance, already evident in the forces mobilized for the Reconquest, of looking for human and material resources beyond Castile and Aragon.

Maritime routes and commercial connections had been part of the Mediterranean world for centuries, pioneered by Phoenicians and Greeks, developed by the Romans, and more recently dynamized by people from such city-states as Genoa. Genoese were among the principal bankers for Castile and Aragon; Genoa's fleet helped fight the Ottomans in the Mediterranean; and Genoa contributed Spain's most famous sailor, Christopher Columbus. Castile and Aragon raised credit from bankers in other Italian cities, as well as in German ones.

But the Ottomans' growing command over the eastern Mediterranean and then, in the sixteenth century, their expansion westward across northern Africa limited opportunities on this sea. The kingdoms of Spain also took account of their neighbors and rivals in Portugal, whose growing interest in looking overseas had to be matched (chapter 6). In the 1480s, the forces of Castile and Aragon ventured into the nearby Atlantic, to the Canary Islands. The colony eventually produced sugar and other tradeworthy crops. The colonizers of these islands were not uniquely Spanish but included Portuguese, Italians, Catalans, Basques, and Jews. Slaves from Africa soon became the mainstay of agricultural labor. Colonizers described the conquered inhabitants of the islands with some of the pejoratives later applied to indigenous peoples in the Americas—pagan, naked, barbarous.

When Queen Isabella died in 1504, her daughter Juana, who had married Archduke Philip of Habsburg, inherited her title. The widowed King Ferdinand married the niece of the French king. After years of dynastic confusion, the son of Juana and Philip was proclaimed king of Castile in 1516. Four years later, he became ruler of the Holy Roman Empire, and hence the Emperor Charles V. At the time he became king, the sixteen-year-old Charles was in Belgium, a site of Habsburg power. He had little previous connection to Spain. His closest advisors and military leaders were from the Netherlands, Burgundy, and Italy. His female relatives Mary of Hungary and Juana of Portugal acted as regents of the Netherlands and Spain during much of his reign. Charles's paternal inheritance from the Habsburg side was a rich one, and within a few years his titles included king of Castile, king of Aragon, duke of Burgundy, and count of Barcelona, as well as Holy Roman Emperor (chapter 3). Charles married the daughter of the ruler of Portugal. Of his unusually long reign—forty years—about sixteen were spent in Spain.

The composite monarchy was thus supported by a web of dynastic and material linkages. The Italian and Netherlands domains were vital to the empire of Charles V, but neither was integrated into a unitary polity. The emperor drew on financiers in both regions, on soldiers and sailors from throughout his domains, and on mercenaries beyond. Within Europe, Charles's empire was not militarily aggressive, for the politics of marriage and inheritance had already brought together large and rich—but not contiguous—territories. The emperor's task was to maintain control of these areas, fending off local elites who wanted to run their own shows and alliances of monarchs trying to check the potentially all-engulfing power of the Habsburgs or, notably in the case of the king of France, mount an empire-building effort of their own.

Maintaining imperial authority became more complicated when some parts of the domain in Germany began to convert to Protestantism (Luther posted his famous theses in 1517). Conversion challenged the unifying principle of Catholic monarchy and threatened the integrity of the Holy Roman Empire. Catholic France was nonetheless able to build an alliance of sorts with German Protestants, Danes, and Italian princes threatened by the Habsburgs and even with the Ottoman empire. The Habsburgs sought alliances with England and—to harass the Ottomans—with Persia. Such trans-religious cooperation was pragmatic and inconsistent, but it was part of the politics of European empires, each composite or heterogeneous, each seeking domination over a continental space or to prevent someone else from doing so. Within Habsburg domains, the religious question became mixed up with efforts of regional elites to attain autonomy, notably when much of the Dutch elite converted to Protestantism in the mid-sixteenth century. The Dutch rebellion became a sinkhole for the emperor's riches. The fissionable quality of European society made composite empire harder to sustain than to patch together.

The costly wars and the difficulties of extracting revenue from subordinate polities within Europe put Charles V and his successor, Philip II, at a disadvantage in their competition with their greatest rival, the Ottoman empire. The Ottomans, taking over north African territory previously ruled by Roman, Byzantine, and Islamic empires, installed relatively loose forms of overrule, allied with local potentates, and reached as far west as Algeria by 1519. Moving north from the Balkans, the Ottoman army was at the gates of Vienna in 1529. The best the Habsburgs could do was to prevent the Ottomans from going beyond Hungary and from invading Spain itself. The Habsburgs managed to keep the Ottoman fleet (but not corsairs connected to the Ottomans) in the eastern part of the Mediterranean and to reach some fragile truces in the 1580s. Defending multiple flanks of their patchwork empire, the Habsburgs could not expand east from Vienna or south into north Africa.

The breakthrough that finally brought new resources, new territory, and new people into the Habsburg empire occurred overseas—the unintended consequence of Ferdinand and Isabella's sponsorship of a sea voyage to China that ended up in the Americas. The Crown was slow to see the usefulness of the Caribbean islands Columbus had sailed into, but in the 1520s the silver and gold of the Aztec and Inca empires raised the stakes of overseas ventures. By the 1550s, when American silver mines came into their own, it was clear that Spain had latched onto something lucrative.

But even with a modest beginning, the monarchy was in a better position to control overseas resources than domestic ones. For Spanish empire-makers, the key task, extending into the nineteenth century, was to devise institutions that would keep diverse parts of the empire dependent on the imperial center. In this process, they not only built an overseas empire but created Spain itself.

Empire in Europe and the Americas

Columbus's discoveries provoked rival powers to assert their claims on what now seemed a much larger world. In 1494 the Spanish and the Portuguese, with the help of the pope, agreed to divide their regions of influence along a line that ran around the earth's sphere. Portugal's share included Asia, Africa, and what became Brazil, where its ventures were concentrated, and the Spanish gained the Caribbean and much of southern and central America (map 6.1). The vision of space was universalistic—a Catholic world—but its political management had to be negotiated and divided among Catholic monarchs.

On their own, neither the Catholic church nor Catholic monarchs could give much substance to this global vision. Spanish imperial expansion was dependent on individual adventurers who raised capital and military forces to plant the flag of the king. With a few hundred men, Hernando Cortes attacked the Aztecs in 1519; Francisco Pizarro conquered the Incas in 1531–33. The man who first circumnavigated the globe in 1519–22 in the name of Spain was Portuguese, Ferdinand Magellan, who had failed earlier to get the backing of the Portuguese Crown. Adventurers were drawn to the Caribbean by the prospect of pillage, conquistadors to the mainland by reports of gold and silver. Later more regular forms of settlement and extraction would be developed.

For Charles V—and even more so his successor, Philip II—the goal was ensuring that the benefits of these ventures helped the monarchy. The gold and silver shipped back to Spain, especially after 1550, were vitally needed to preserve the empire in Europe, where wars and revolts were driving the Habsburgs into debt to bankers in Germany, Italy, and the Netherlands. The New World's metals and other products became elements in wider networks of finance and commerce. Silver and gold from the Americas were fundamental to European trade with Asia, since European powers generally had little of interest to sell to Chinese or Indian merchants, from whom the Europeans were buying spices, textiles, and other products.

From 1500 to 1800 about 80 percent of the world's silver was mined in Spanish America (Japan was the other major producer). What the Habsburgs had to do was ensure that all goods—sugar as well as silver—coming into Europe and all exports to the Americas passed through Spanish ports. The minting of silver coins was carefully controlled, and their imperially regulated purity helped make the Spanish peso the most important global currency in an era of expanding commerce. The Crown insisted on a monopolistic structure of trade. All merchant vessels had to pass through the port of Cadiz; later the monopoly was transferred to Seville. Officials in these Castilian towns could keep close watch on the trade and enforce collection of revenue.

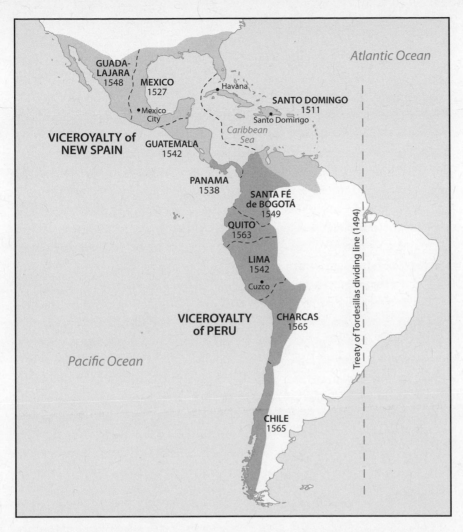

Map 5.2
Habsburg
viceroyalties and
audiencias in the
Americas.

In the Americas, as settlement replaced pillage and barter and as European expansion reached beyond the conquered centers of older empires, the Crown devised ways to incorporate spread-out lands and peoples. Veterans of subdivided authority within Europe, Spanish rulers parceled out territory using two levels of administration—viceroyalties and audiencias. In the colonies, the Crown was freed from some of the constraints it faced in Europe: it did not have to respect entrenched magnates with their people and lands or towns with their civic structures. The New World was considered Castilian territory, and the emperor appointed only Castilians to positions in the region's administration. But opportunities for monarchical authority in the Americas were not unlimited. The Crown faced the challenges of maintaining control over long distances and over settler, indigenous, slave, and mixed populations, as well as managing the disruptive potential of local administrators, indigenous intermediaries, merchant oligarchies, and an ecclesiastical apparatus.

Settlers came slowly at first. Perhaps 120,000 Spaniards reached the Americas by 1570, somewhat over 400,000 by 1650. Here, too, the Crown tried to exercise control, and at the end of the sixteenth century decreed that only subjects of the "Spanish kingdoms" would be allowed to board ship to the Americas. The plural makes clear that Spain was not a unitary state, but an amalgam that was Spanish and that now extended to the Americas.

Why would ambitious people who had set themselves up in a new world submit to royal control? Settlers' attachment to empire was conditional, in Spanish America as elsewhere. But there were good reasons in the sixteenth century to seek political connection rather than autonomy. Other empires were a threat; settlers needed strong defenders. Moreover, the world market was far from a self-regulating mechanism, and long-distance trade was as much a military venture as a commercial one. As more actors entered the picture—making it more "market-like"—some of them took to seizing goods by force. Piracy enhanced traders' need for protection. The annual convoy of silver-bearing vessels from the Americas to Spain was in part the provision of security, in part a royal attempt to control trade. Empire also offered civilizational and spiritual connections to Christians living among conquered people. With settler populations spread out over large spaces across the ocean, Spain offered something more profound and universalistic than the cultures of town or region. In short, much was to be gained by putting up with the monarchy's monopolistic trading practices and administrative authority. Empire made sense—at least to settlers; what it meant for indigenous people and slaves will be considered in the next chapter.

The empire became an administrative and legal structure and a set of ties of commerce and sentiment. Administering this growing overseas venture as well as the Holy Roman Empire and the various polities of Habsburg Europe was a daunting task, made more difficult by restiveness in the Netherlands and Protestant challenges in German-speaking areas. In 1556, two years before his death, Charles V decided to abdicate and to divide his realm. His brother Ferdinand got the old Habsburg lands in central Europe. This branch of the Habsburg empire was later rent by religious wars and lost considerable territory to Protestant monarchs, but eventually it adapted a more cosmopolitan mode of existence and lasted until 1918 (chapter 11). The rest of Charles V's domains went to his son Philip; these included Castile, Aragon, Milan, Naples, Sicily, the Netherlands—and the Americas.

Philip II, unlike his father, was mostly resident in Spain. He did not call himself emperor. In 1554, shortly before his accession to the throne, he married Mary Tudor, who became queen of England on the death of her father, Henry VIII. Until Mary's premature death in 1558 Philip could call himself king of England, although he did not rule it and under the marriage agreement could not pass on the title. The twists and turns of dynastic succession and intrigue within England next put Elizabeth on the throne—she became Philip's enemy. A dynastic crisis in Portugal brought an important part of Europe and substantial overseas colonies (chapter 6) into Philip's branch of the Habsburg domains in 1580, but he and his successors ruled these separately, not as integral parts of Spain, until 1640. The Philippines were conquered during Philip's reign. A single dynasty now ruled Portugal, Spain, parts of what are now Italy and the Netherlands, port cities in the Atlantic, Pacific, and Indian oceans, and American lands from Brazil to Mexico—bringing what contemporaries called "the four corners of the world" under Catholic monarchy. Not only the monarchy, but missionaries, traders, officials, and adventurers now acted in globe-spanning networks, ruling, trading with, and converting a great variety of peoples—and coming up against the limits of their own capacity to impose their visions on others.

Philip had a lot to defend. Against the Ottomans in the Mediterranean his navy won, with help from his allies, a big battle at Lepanto in 1571, but this defeat did not dent Ottoman power for long. Philip faced uprisings at home, in Aragon in the 1580s and 1590s (his successors would face others in Catalonia), and, beginning in 1566, rebellions in the Netherlands that would go on for eighty years. This revolt of Protestants against Catholics—involving a militant populace as well as an autonomy-minded elite—threatened both the system of composite monarchy and Spain's access to grain, timber, and other commodities from northern Europe. Opposition in the Netherlands simmered and at times erupted over decades, and although it did not always block commerce, it was always costly.

Philip's most spectacular attempt to remake the European map was his effort to eliminate a Protestant contestant that was beginning to make itself felt on the waves—England. History would have looked different if the Armada of 1588 had been successful, and it came close. But it failed against the English fleet. Meanwhile, Philip consolidated Castilian domination of the American empire by controlling both governors and settlers. His most serious problem was paying for it all, particularly the battles with England and the defense of the Netherlands. The silver of the Americas was crucial to his finances, but by the 1590s labor shortages in the Americas (following large losses of population) as well as the settlers' increasing tendency to do business with each other or to bypass Spanish efforts at monopolizing trade were reducing royal revenues. In 1596, Spain stopped paying its bankers (not the first such episode), eventually working out a deal that left it saddled with debt payments.

"Spain kept the cow and the rest of Europe drank the milk."

—Samuel Pufendorf, seventeenth-century jurist and philosopher

In 1598 Philip II died, leaving in place a vast transoceanic empire. More than the trading, enclave empires of Portugal and later the Netherlands (chapter 6), it integrated extra-European territories and non-European peoples under a monarchy based in Europe and intent on maintaining its central position. But in Europe itself, this empire had little room to maneuver.

Neither Charles nor Philip could tear down the rights of provincial elites in Europe, seize the resources in land and people those rights entailed, or overcome the vagaries of inheritance arrangements, marriages, or rebellion in a composite monarchy. Both rulers remained tied into networks of European exchange that they could not fully control—Dutch and Genoese financiers, Swiss soldiers, and the papacy. Territorial authority was most effectively consolidated in the Americas, the Philippines, and Spain, less so in Philip's other European domains. The Crown was the element that linked all these parts.

We will explore the extent and the limitations of imperial power overseas in the next chapter. Here we have seen how flexible dynastic arrangements and access to finance, manpower, and other resources from different parts of Europe made possible rapid political aggrandizement, within Europe and beyond, and also brought on the challenge of managing and paying for such a wide-ranging land and sea empire. What Charles V and his successors could not do was make good on their initial promise—to bring together the former western Roman empire under a single Catholic monarch. They accomplished something else: they made a new set of long-distance connections, redefined how Europeans imagined their world, from Chile to the Philippines, and put Spain at the center of that imaginary.

Making the Ottoman Empire

The Ottomans emerged at the crossroads of empire. They were not an "eastern" power that clashed with "the west," but a political formation that melded strategies adapted from earlier empires and their challengers on the connected continents of Europe, Asia, and Africa.

In geographic terms, the Ottomans enjoyed an edge, or even two. Until the Habsburgs made something of their overseas ventures, the Ottomans operated in a richer, more varied environment. The lands and waters of the eastern Mediterranean with their linkages to central Asia, Egypt, and India offered a wide range of political experiences, social practices, and sources of wealth. From these materials, the Ottomans created a huge land and sea empire. This empire was both territorial—a vast landmass—and nodal—based on ports and centers of commerce on long- and short-distance trade routes. Holding it together required skills developed on the Ottomans' long road to power.

Recombinant Eurasian Pathways

The Ottomans were the most successful of many Turkic-speaking groups who jostled each other in Anatolia during the shaky final centuries of Byzantine rule. As we have seen, disruptions in inner Asia had for several centuries sent waves of Turkic nomads into central Asia and out to its edges (chapter 4). Migrations of pastoralists into Anatolia intensified after one group of Turkic-speakers, the Seljuks, captured Baghdad in 1055 and other groups moved on. Ambitious tribal leaders had plenty of opportunity to make, unmake, and switch alliances, to serve promising overlords, and to try to displace them in a political landscape repeatedly resculpted by crusaders, Byzantine emperors, provincial rulers, Venetian merchants and naval forces, Arab caliphs, and Mongol khans, as well as rebels against and subordinates of all of the above.

Osman, the founder of the Osmanli dynasty, began his journey to fortune and fame as a raider, warrior, and tribal leader in Bithynia, a landlocked Byzantine province south of the Sea of Marmara. Not so central as to be a major concern for the Byzantines, yet studded with towns and villages, the area offered distinct possibilities to aspiring chiefs. By the mid-1320s, Osman had defeated a small Byzantine army and occupied several Byzantine fortresses. In 1326, Osman's son Orhan captured the city of Bursa, which became the first Ottoman capital. Taking sides in a Byzantine power struggle, Orhan backed the winner, married his daughter, and received territory in Gallipoli. Turks from Anatolia began to cross over into Thrace. By the time of Orhan's death in 1362, he controlled cities and coastal areas in both Asia and Europe—in western Anatolia and along the Dardanelles and the northern Aegean.

In making their empire, Osman and his descendants drew on the civic culture of Greek and Latin cities; institutions produced by Christian, Muslim, Jewish, and other religious groups; Byzantine vassalage; and military and administrative practices from Arab empires. From Eurasian predecessors, the Ottomans took the ideal of the superior leader, the khaqan or khan, with his good fortune, heavenly blessings, and lawgiving powers; exogamous and strategic marriage; and the fluid politics of alliance and subordination. But the last act of making an empire was precarious. After Osman's great-grandson Bayezid had made the Byzantine emperor Manuel II and the Serbian prince Stephen Lazarevic his vassals, defeated the Bulgarian tsar, soundly trounced crusaders united against him, and advanced deep into Anatolia toward the Euphrates, he ran up against another Eurasian conqueror. Tamerlane, a Turkic-speaker, Muslim, and master rebuilder of Mongol empire (see chapter 4), detached Bayezid's subordinated tribal leaders with their followers from his armies and captured Bayezid. He died as a prisoner in 1402.

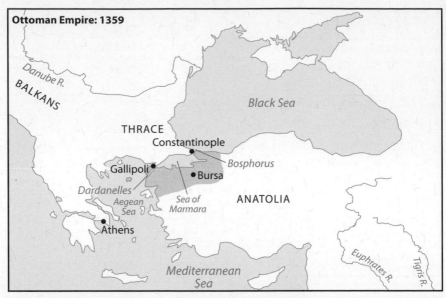

Ottoman Empire: 1359

Danube R.

BALKANS

Black Sea

THRACE

Constantinople

Gallipoli

Bosphorus

Dardanelles

Bursa

Aegean
Sea

Sea of
Marmara

ANATOLIA

Athens

Euphrates R.

Tigris R.

Mediterranean
Sea

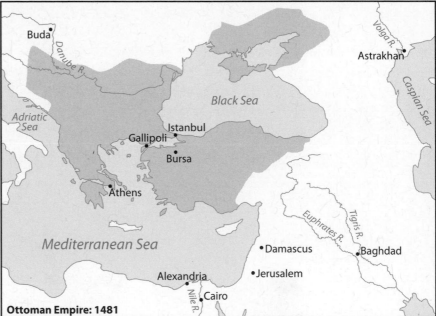

Buda

Danube R.

Volga R.

Astrakhan

Adriatic
Sea

Black Sea

Caspian Sea

Istanbul

Gallipoli

Bursa

Athens

Euphrates R.

Tigris R.

Mediterranean Sea

Damascus

Baghdad

Jerusalem

Alexandria

Nile R.

Cairo

Ottoman Empire: 1481

Map 5.3
Expansion
of the Ottoman
domains.

An Empire by Land and Sea

It was perhaps the slow and uneven course of empire-building that gave a succession of Ottoman rulers and advisors the chance to reflect upon experience, to absorb tactics from others, and to take new initiatives that, once power was secured, allowed the Ottoman empire to last until 1922. Over the half century after Bayezid's defeat, his descendants reconquered

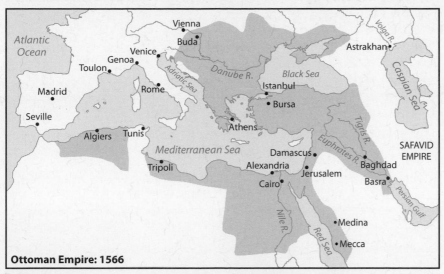

Ottoman Empire: 1566

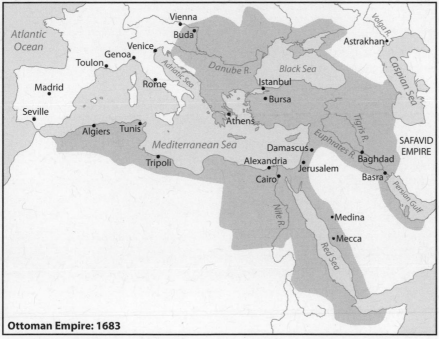

Ottoman Empire: 1683

lost territories and put together a larger and more resilient empire. Tactics used on the way included strategic marriages—to Princess Mara of Serbia in 1435, for example—as well as the suppression of revolts led by renegade holy men and other upstarts. Imperial control was at its most vulnerable in four conditions—when rival sons competed for power, when enemies and rebellious vassals attacked simultaneously from two sides of the empire, when the Ottoman navy competed against the more technologically advanced Venetians, and when the Ottoman sultan's own special troops, the Janissaries, decided to take things into their own hands. Ottoman leaders developed strategies to deal with all these threats.

A must for Ottoman empire-builders was making the imperial city of their world their own. The Ottoman conquest of Constantinople took place by land and sea, making effective use of Greek sailors, Serbian soldiers, a Hungarian cannon builder, and others. The Ottomans had improved their seafaring skills and technology by taking over Italian trading cities—and their experts and artisans—on the Aegean littoral and islands. They built ships at Gallipoli from where they could command the Dardanelles and established two fortresses on the Bosphorus. Before Sultan Mehmet II began his army's march toward Constantinople in 1453, the Byzantine capital was already cut off on both sides by Ottoman ships. When the Byzantines tried to protect their capital with their famous floating chain, the Ottomans loaded their boats onto carts, wheeled them around the hills north of the city, and put them back in the harbor inside the chain. At the same time, the army broke through the city walls. The Roman empire of the east—after over 1,100 years—came to an end.

The Ottomans thus succeeded in putting land and sea together in a polity that in time enfolded Anatolia, the Balkans, Thrace, and areas along the eastern Mediterranean, the Black Sea, and the Aegean into a single imperial space. Once they had cleared the Black Sea of hostile pirates, Ottoman rulers could settle into regulated exploitation of both territories and trade.

With command of the Bosphorus, the Ottomans made sure that diverse trading groups could carry on and pay their due. Anatolia attracted merchants from around the Mediterranean; their presence encouraged farmers to grow cotton and other crops for export. Overland trade routes from Asia passed through the Black Sea, where Venetians, Genoese, and others extended the link to the Mediterranean. Greek merchants traveled the entire Mediterranean; many were Ottoman subjects. The Indian Ocean trade routes, largely in the hands of Gujarati, Arab, and other Muslim merchants, as well as Armenian and Jewish traders, were connected to those of the Persian Gulf and Red Sea. Egypt, connecting Red Sea, Nile, and Mediterranean, was a crucial node in Eurasian exchange, and from 1517 it was an Ottoman province. From there, Ottoman power was extended westward along the north African coast to Algiers, not far from Spain, displacing or incorporating tribes, colonies, kingdoms, emirates, and rival empires. The Ottomans' formidable location, with its control of connections between Europe, central Asia, north Africa, and India, pushed European navigators to sail around the southern tip of Africa, but these long-distance efforts by no means eclipsed the sea and land routes.

Keeping these far-flung networks functioning required both military might—to control ports and command cities—and law—to protect the people who carried out trade. Ties of religion and kinship—among Jews, Armenians, Greeks, and others—offered mechanisms for transmitting information and credit, as well as trust, across great distances, over long stretches of time, and where the interface with other groups was uncertain. The Ottoman empire allowed religiously defined communities to settle most legal issues themselves and to exercise their own forms of leadership—as long as they acknowledged the sultan's suzerainty, paid their taxes, and kept the peace. Recognition of diasporas and their benefits enabled merchants to connect nodal points of trade, transport, and culture. Meanwhile, Anatolia, the Balkans, Syria, and the Nile valley provided agricultural resources and revenue, which helped pay for the administrative apparatus. The hallmark of Ottoman empire was not spreading a homogeneous culture among local elites but putting diversity to work for the polity.

The Ottomans' inclusionary economy contrasts with the attempted monopolies that western European empires tried to enforce, of which the silver convoys between Spanish America and Seville are an example. The danger of the Ottomans' diversified approach and their multiple networks was that components might find the imperial center unnecessary to their activities or that they could make better deals with other powers. Defections and wars for control beset the Ottomans from the east and west and the middle. The Habsburgs, as we have seen, fought numerous times to attain ports and territories around the Mediterranean; the Venetians were off-again, on-again Ottoman allies and foes. To the east, the Ottomans' main enemy, for a time, was the Safavid empire (1502–1722) in Iran, an area of silk production and overland connection. The Ottomans' religious tolerance did not apply to the Safavids, who were Muslim but Shi'ite (chapter 3). As in western Europe, divisions within the supposedly universal religious community, in this case the house of Islam, both set empires at each other's throats and constrained their ambitions. With or without religious motives, across the Ottomans' huge space, rebels of various kinds—pirates, princes of border areas, bandits—wanted part of the action for themselves.

Both the wealth of the Ottomans' land and sea connections and the need to defend them kept the Ottomans focused on the world they had made. The Ottoman state had no particular reason to push very hard in the growing competition for trade across the Atlantic or around the Cape of Good Hope in the sixteenth and seventeenth centuries; it had a good thing going where it was.

Sexual Politics of Succession

Securing the dynasty took luck and innovation. Mongol-Turkic style imperial succession was marvelous for generating an effective coalition builder and warrior-leader, terrible for holding an empire together. Osman's immediate successor lived for thirty-eight years after his father, a great stroke of luck for launching an empire. The first rule of Ottoman succession was exclusionary, sacral, and familiarly Eurasian: only a member of the dynasty could take the dead sultan's place and any one of the sultan's sons was eligible to succeed him. But Ottoman succession differed from Mongol practices in an important respect. Royal brothers did not divide up the realm among themselves and choose a Great Khan as an overlord; instead each contender fought for the whole. At several critical moments on the way to empire, an Ottoman leader's death produced an enormous power struggle among rival sons, wars in which Byzantine, Balkan and Anatolian leaders, and later Safavids were only too willing to take sides in their own interests.

One dynastic technology that emerged from wars among brothers, with their armies of subordinates and allies, was fratricide. Murad I set the pattern by killing all of his brothers after his accession to the throne in 1362. When Mehmet II's father, Murad II, died in 1451, he left two sons from two different mothers. Immediately upon becoming sultan, Mehmet II ordered the execution of the other son, an infant. In the sixteenth century, a dead sultan's funeral procession—staged only after the new sultan had taken the throne—could be followed by the small coffins of child princes. Law was produced to justify dynastic fratricide in the name of the "good order of the world."

Who were these princes? In the early centuries of empire-building Ottoman sultans and princes married into elite families in areas they coveted, often to non-Ottomans, including Greeks and other Christians, with the goals of forging alliances and creating networks of family subordinates. But these political marriages only rarely produced children. When the Serbian princess Mara, the widow of Sultan Murad II, was being considered as a wife for the Byzantine emperor Constantine XI, a diplomat informed concerned parties that Mara "did not sleep with" the sultan. After Murad's time, this kind of marriage had served its purpose, and the Ottomans dispensed with it in favor of sultanic concubinage.

Replacing wives with concubines to generate the sultan's heirs braided Muslim family law and Turkic-Mongol exogamy into a new kind of dynastic security regime, very different from the interfamily politics of western European royalty. In Islamic law of the period, a man could, depending on his resources, have up to four wives and any number of slave concubines. Children from his marriages were legitimate, but so too, if the master wished, were his children with concubines. Legitimation of a slave's child brought privileges for the mother, and upon the master's death, she became free. In the sultan's case, his sons by concubines could advance—with good luck and under a mother's guidance—to the throne.

Another tweaking of Islamic rules further constrained the sultan's sex life. Once a sultan's consort gave birth to a potential heir, she was not allowed to share the sultan's bed again but would accompany her child, a prince and a candidate for both sultanate and murder, out to the provinces, where the boy would be given a governorship. Competition to become the next sultan took place on a somewhat level playing field—no son would be born of a wife, and each had a different slave mother.

These mothers learned their skills in another Ottoman institution— the imperial harem. Like Chinese forbidden cities, the sultan's palace was a quasi-sacred place organized by layers of security and seclusion: an outer courtyard open to the public, an inner courtyard for reception of officials and embassies, a first harem where boys selected for imperial service were trained by their eunuch guards, and finally the sultan's family harem, also guarded by eunuchs. Women living in the harem, and in particular the sultan's mother—the *valide sultan*—and the favorite concubine—the *haseki sultan*—were at the center of Ottoman power. The valide sultan defended the interests of her son from birth, intrigued for his advancement and survival, advised him, and on occasion set conditions during a succession struggle.

Ottoman succession practices strengthened sultanic control. Reproduction through concubinage brought new blood—usually from formerly Christian captives—into the otherwise monogenetic dynastic line, and it engaged the powers of senior women in the Ottoman variant of tanistry. At the same time, sultanic concubinage was an answer to a typical imperial problem—controlling subordinates. Astute marriages had helped Ottomans in their years of conquest and expansion, but once the empire took on its enormous shape, alliances with still powerful families within it could have dangerous consequences. By shutting off the dynasty from in-laws, the sultans eliminated a whole array of contenders for power.

Marriage came back into the picture where the sultan's daughters were concerned, once again reinforcing his control over elites. Beginning in the mid-fifteenth century, princesses (born of slaves) and harem concubines were married to the sultan's most powerful servitors. Viziers and other powerful and possibly threatening men thus "married up" and into the royal household, but in a highly dependent way. A husband of a harem woman was required to divorce any earlier wives and became a *damad*, a sultan's son-in-law. His children would not be royals.

The Ottoman's dynastic reproductive regime avoided the pitfalls—and the seemingly unending warfare and great opera material—of monarchical marriage in western European style. But even sultanic rules were made to be broken—by the sultan, especially if the sultan was Suleiman I and the woman was Aleksandra Lisowska, also known as Roxelana or Hurrem. Hurrem was a Christian from western Ukraine, then part of the Polish empire.

She was captured by Tatars and presented to Suleiman, probably at the time of his accession in 1520. In the line of duty Suleiman had already produced a son with another concubine, but he fell in love with Hurrem. After the birth of their first child in 1521, he scandalized the harem by renouncing all other sexual partners and marrying off the other concubines to servitors and favorites. Suleiman fathered at least six children by Hurrem in ten years. Again breaking the rules, he married her around 1534.

Like other powerful harem women, Hurrem served as the sultan's informant, diplomat, and propagandist. She carried on a personal correspondence with the Polish king Sigismund I and with the sister of the Safavid monarch in the interests of peace between the empires. Following the injunctions of Islam to perform pious deeds, Hurrem used revenue from lands and taxes assigned to her to finance building projects, including a famous public bath and mosque complex in Istanbul. Here, too, an older Mongol-Turkic tradition—of the powerful first wife and mother of the khan—came to life in the synthetic Ottoman context.

Slaves of the Sultan

The concubines of the imperial harem were not the only slaves serving in the empire's high places; leaders of armies, admirals of the navy, governors of provinces, heads of treasury and taxation bureaucracies, and members of the imperial council were also *kul*—the sultan's personal slaves. During their centuries of empire-building, Ottomans incorporated the most basic element of slavery—the detachment of a person from his or her social milieu—into a technique of rule.

Slavery was widespread in the Ottomans' core area. Because Islamic law forbade enslavement of Muslims or of the protected Christians living in Muslim lands, Muslim rulers were constrained to acquire slaves from outside their domains. Slaves, many of them "Slavic," had long been exported from north of the Black Sea to the Mediterranean, north Africa, and central Asia; victorious armies in these areas also enslaved defeated groups. Slaves were made to work in various ways—as laborers, domestics, and soldiers. Both Abbasids and Seljuks used slave troops in their armies; the Mamluks who stopped the Mongol advance in the thirteenth century were themselves slave soldiers, whose name came from the Abbasid term for military slaves (chapter 3). The Ottomans, who defeated the Mamluks in 1517, elaborated new methods for recruiting both soldiers and high officials.

Raiding for slaves was an active business along the Ottomans' moving borders, notably in the Caucasus. But as incorporation of territory into the empire dried up this source, the Ottomans bent Islamic prohibitions and turned to their own population for recruits into the sultan's service. Their

Figure 5.2

Devshirme: recruitment of children for the sultan's service. An Ottoman officer (seated, with tall hat) supervises the recording of information about the children, who are shown holding bags with their belongings. Townspeople look on, and the background suggests a Christian village in the Balkans. From *Suleymanname: The Illustrated History of Suleiman the Magnificent*, Topkapi Palace Museum. Bridgeman Art Library.

Ottoman and Spanish Empires

systematic levy of boys from mostly Christian subjects was known from the fourteenth to the eighteenth centuries as the *devshirme* or "collection." Communities were required to provide a certain number of boys, as young as eight years old, to the sultan's recruitment officer. Only sons were not "collected," for otherwise their fathers would not have the resources to pay their taxes. Turks were not recruited for a different reason: their Muslim, unenslaved families might try to claim relationships with the sultan to gain privileges, such as tax exemptions. The point of drafting Christians was to bring into the sultan's service boys who were outsiders to the palace, just as the sultan's reproduction with slave concubines prevented alliances with powerful Ottoman families.

The processing of devshirme recruits was a highly regulated affair. Boys were assembled, registered, marched to Istanbul, circumcised, and then subjected to a fate-determining selection. Most boys began years of training to become Janissaries—members of the imperial guard. Perhaps modeled on the Mamluk slave soldiers, the Janissaries were recruited from the Christian Balkans. A smaller group of boys, chosen to serve in the sultan's household and government, disappeared into the palace where they were supervised by eunuch guardians; required to keep silent in public; and educated in Islamic teachings and law, the Ottoman language, and crafts and sports of the ruling elite. Some rose to become the sultan's highest servants—governors, diplomats, ministers, and even the grand vizier, the highest-ranked administrator of the realm.

For boys taken into the palace, the collection offered a channel of upward mobility, fulfilling the dreams of many a Christian peasant family. For the sultan, making an administrative and military elite from dependent outsiders was an innovative solution to the problem of sustaining imperial power. Each great minister or advisor was the sultan's creation and could be dismissed and replaced by him. Suleiman I had eight different grand viziers. Execution of such powerful men was as frequent a practice as royal fratricide. Both focused the minds of survivors.

The practice of royal concubinage and the selection of top advisors from "collected" and converted Christian boys meant that the sultan ruled through a household of his own making. Liberated from linkages to noble families, advised by officials dependent on his will, the sultan exercised an extreme form of patrimonialism over his personal slaves and through them over the empire.

Consolidating a Service Elite

There were two weak points in this system of dependent, unfree officials. One was that the imperial guard—a problem in other empires as well—had to be armed, militant, and nearby. In battle, the Janissaries surrounded the sultan in the center of the field, ensuring his survival; back in the palace, the Janissaries also protected the sultan, but they could turn against him. In 1622, Sultan Osman II was assassinated by his Janissaries after he had offended them in multiple ways—too harsh a punishment regime, insistence on continuing a war with Poland against the Janissaries' wishes, refusal to execute advisors accused of corruption, and, allegedly, a plan to replace the Janissaries with a different kind of armed force.

The second weak point in the system was created by a typical imperial scenario, one we have observed on the western Mediterranean and in China. The Ottomans needed to collect enough revenue and soldiers to defend their empire without allowing potentially rebellious and always greedy nobles to entrench themselves in the provinces. In the early centuries of Ottoman expansion, sultans had dealt with powerful families by moving them away from their home territories and making them overlords in distant areas. But the problem of controlling local lords repeated itself as the empire grew toward its greatest size in the late sixteenth century. At the same time, defending the empire became even more expensive, as innovations in military strategy and technology—particularly mobile artillery and new ship design—required funds to retool the Ottomans' army and navy.

The Ottomans came up with several responses to the problem of getting resources and still keeping imperial elites loyal, effective, and not too secure in their areas. A first principle derived from the theory that all land was the sultan's to distribute or regulate at will. Building on the Byzantines' land-for-armed-service system (chapter 3), the Ottomans granted military servitors authority to collect taxes and fees from a district as well as plots of land (*timar*) for their own use. By the late sixteenth century, this system was being converted into tax farms, the sale of which provided income to palace officials in Istanbul. Tax farming could not create new resources, but it gave elites a good reason to seek the patronage of the sultan.

A second principle was the impermanence of officeholding. The sultan could replace officials at will, rewarding loyal service, punishing incompetents. Appointments could also be used to make rebels part of the system. A testimony to the attractions of Ottoman officialdom was that powerful bandits tried to bargain their way into the state's bureaucracy, petitioning the sultan to make them officeholders and the rightful collectors of men and money.

In part because their empire was so large, Ottoman rulers could not have a single way of ruling or controlling their intermediaries. Personalized

> *"This slave petitions that if he is appointed to the post of the beylerbey of Aleppo he will undertake to go with 5,000 men to the campaign called for the coming spring. Likewise, if by the favor of the sultan he is given, with the aforementioned province, a vezirate, then he promises to take 10,000 men to the campaign."*
>
> —from Canboladoglu Ali Pasha, 1606

authority facilitated flexibility, compromise, and pragmatism. In border regions that were hard to defend, the Ottomans acknowledged local rulers with their titles and command. This was the case with Kurdistan, where sultans never were able to tie tribal chiefs into the palace regime of rule. In more central areas, the displacement of powerful clans to distant places, the recruitment of outsiders to the highest posts, the appointment of governors-general (both princes and the sultan's high-ranking slaves), and the manipulation and redrawing of provincial boundaries all worked against the entrenchment of regional strongmen. But over time, families worked connections to power to their own benefit, and Ottoman rulers responded by integrating local elites into the Ottoman governing class, putting notables in charge of lucrative state functions. Co-optation into officialdom prevented consolidation of linkages outside the state. The system's most effective tool was its largesse: it paid to be an officeholder.

Protecting a Multiconfessional Polity

For ordinary people, direct contact with the sultan's government was an unusual event apart from paying taxes and supplying recruits. What other functions might the empire have served for the vast majority of subjects who were not drawn into serving the state?

The Ottomans called their empire the "well-protected domains," underscoring the sultan's responsibility to defend his subjects. One kind of protection was defense against aggression—from outside the polity and from bandits within. Ottoman law offered another kind of shelter to the empire's diverse subjects. In family and religious matters, Christians of various rites, Jews, and other non-Muslim subjects were under the legal authority of their own communities' leaders. What linked these groups and their different legal practices to the sultan's overarching authority was a personal and official tie. Chief rabbis, metropolitans of the Greek Orthodox church, and leaders of Armenian Orthodoxy and of other Christian groups held their offices as recipients of sultanic warrants. In return for their service to the sultan they were exempted from taxation and received rights to various revenues and resources. The protection and use of clergy of different faiths, a practice of Mongol and other empires in the region, became part of the Ottoman regime.

The primacy of Islam among the religions of the empire developed during centuries of expansion and conflict—often with other Muslim leaders. The Anatolian territory where the Ottomans first emerged was spattered with Christian and Islamic communities that followed a variety of teachings and spiritual leaders. Pragmatic relationships with conquered or allied rulers, including Christian warlords, and selective adaptations from different traditions, rather than commitment to militant Islam, helped Osman, Orhan, and their descendants extend their empire. As the Ottomans added their own imprint to the Islamic-Iranian administrative culture developed earlier by the Abbasids, Seljuks, and Il-Khans, they continued to draw powerful Christians from the Byzantine cities and Balkan nobility into their elite. Triumphant Ottoman warriors did not require that Christian captives convert to Islam or be killed. They took a more practical approach—demanding ransoms for captives, sometimes manumitting slaves who converted to Islam, sending defeated Christian nobles to distant areas as provincial governors. Besides, conversion to Islam was happening without compulsion as people responded to the possibilities opened up by the Ottomans' successful empire project.

The rule of Bayezid I (1389–1402), who named his sons Jesus, Moses, Solomon, Muhammad, and Joseph, could be considered a high point of Christian-Muslim harmony. In Bayezid's capital, Bursa, it was possible to debate the proposition of a Muslim preacher that Jesus and Muhammad were prophets of equal merit. But this syncretic religious culture was put to a difficult test in 1416 when ecumenical sentiments were expressed by the Anatolian dervish Borkluje Mustafa during a major rebellion against the Ottoman rule. Borkluje Mustafa advocated the equality of Christians and Muslims and the communal sharing of property. He defeated two Ottoman armies before being put down ruthlessly by Mehmet I's vizier Bayezid Pasha, who is said to have "killed everyone in his path without sparing a soul, young or old, men and women." From the 1430s on, a new emphasis was put on Islam as the religion of the dynasty and the Ottoman elite.

After years of wars against the Safavids, who claimed the leadership of Islam for their Shi'ite dynasty with its capital in Iran, Sultan Selim I (1512–20) ended Safavid rule in Anatolia in 1516. He continued on to fight the Mamluks, whose sultan was killed in battle. With Selim's victories, the Ottomans acquired vast new territories in Egypt, Syria, Lebanon, Palestine, and the Arabian peninsula, including the holy cities of Jerusalem, Medina, and Mecca. The Ottoman sultan could now style himself the guardian of Islam and the superior of all other Muslim monarchs. This claim was directed not at Christians but against the Ottomans' Muslim rivals—the Safavids and others who claimed divine inspiration or authority.

As was the case for Christian leaders in western Europe, making the emperor the defender of a faith could cut two ways. Over the next centuries, the cult of Islamic fighters for the true faith (*gazi* warriors) and contestation over Islamic leadership could be turned against the Ottomans by upstarts, ambitious subordinates, and other challengers, most relentlessly by the Shi'ite Safavids. But the sultan's authority was also enhanced in many areas by his oversight and guidance in Islamic matters, including the supervision of Islamic justice.

Islamic law (Sharia) was not a single body of legislation but a tradition of competing schools of interpretation, based on the Quran and the sayings of the Prophet. The Ottomans adopted the Hanafi school of Sunni law—dominant in Anatolia under the Seljuks—and established a system of colleges to train judges in this tradition. These judges were charged with deciding legal matters for most Muslims. But Sharia law was inadequate for many imperial tasks, particularly because it treated major social violations as civil matters between parties. The Ottomans employed a second kind of law—*kanun*—to fulfill the sultan's role of protection, as well as to regulate taxation and property matters.

Ottoman kanun distinguished between taxpaying subjects (the majority) and the sultan's servitors, *askari,* who received a salary from the state or from lands assigned to them. Askari were not to be judged by the regular courts but by sultanic officials. The sultan's servants, who included cavalrymen, the sultan's male and female slaves, judges, professors, and muftis, plus their families, were subject to his legal power to inflict corporal or capital punishment. This division of the population into taxpayers and servitors with different rights contrasts strongly with the Roman ideal of an inclusive taxpaying citizenry.

Ottoman law was a system of legal regimes—secular, Islamic, other religious laws and customary practices—all authorized by a central, overarching power. Codifications reflected this heterogeneity. The Law Book of 1499 recorded tax obligations throughout the empire, based on collections of decrees, local legal registers, fatwas, and other regulations. People of different faiths were able to resolve minor legal matters in ways determined by their own religious authorities. The universal aspect of Ottoman law was that most subjects had access to it at some kind of court, but not all cases and not all people came under the sort of unitary code that Justinian had issued in the Roman/Byzantine empire.

The principle of recognized difference was of great importance for the empire's capacity to govern huge territories inhabited by non-Muslims, to absorb diasporic minorities, and to play against the religious intolerance of other empires. In the Balkans and in Hungary, Ottoman law offered rights to Greek, Serbian, and Protestant Christians that would have been inconceivable under the Catholic Habsburgs or Polish rulers. Not just Muslims but Jews expelled from Spain during the Inquisition could find new homes and the protection of legal status in the Ottoman empire. Sultans used divisions within Christendom for their own purposes; Suleiman cooperated with the Catholic king of France on military ventures and his successors traded and negotiated with the Protestant queen Elizabeth of England to undermine the Habsburgs.

The notion that different people should be judged according to their own laws was applied by Ottomans to foreigners living in the empire. The model for this practice was the treatment of Galata—the cosmopolitan quarter of Istanbul where the Genoese had a colony. Sultan Mehmet II's decree of 1453 allowed the Genoese to adjudicate their internal matters. This kind of agreement was extended to various powers who had colonies of merchants scattered about the Ottoman domains. "Extraterritoriality" in legal matters was rooted in Ottoman—and before that Byzantine—practice. In exchange for their protection of Europeans—Franks, as Ottomans called them—Ottomans insisted that sovereigns elsewhere allow Ottoman merchants to settle in protected ways. With the so-called capitulations—the granting of rights to "foreign" legal process—and their insistence on protections for merchants and diplomats, the Ottomans transmitted earlier principles of Eurasian diplomacy into Europeans' international practices.

Conclusion: A Tale of Two Empires

Charles V, Holy Roman Emperor, king of Castile and Aragon (1516–56), and Suleiman I, Ottoman sultan, the "Law-Giver," and king (Kaysar, Caesar) of kings (1520–66), both aspired to regain the grandeur and the scale of the Roman empire. For Charles, the linkage to Rome's Christian past was obvious, although his relations with the pope were far from easy. But Suleiman's claim to succeed Roman power was just as logical. The Ottomans had defeated and replaced the Byzantines who led the eastern Roman empire, conquered a great deal of Rome's Mediterranean space, and taken over as protectors of Christians in the Balkans. As Cortes was conquering the Aztecs, the Ottomans were expanding into Syria, Palestine, Egypt, and Arabia. By the mid-sixteenth century, the Ottomans were ruling a third of Europe and half the shores of the Mediterranean. Moreover, Islam was the latest of the three monotheistic religions, a successor to both Judaism and Christianity, and the Ottomans, unlike most previous Islamic and Christian rulers, had found a way to recognize—in law and administration—these confessions and most of their variants without compromising the primacy of the imperial center. What could be more imperial—overarching and universal—than an inclusive polity under the sultan's protection, especially when compared with the exclusionary ideology of the Spanish Inquisition?

Christianity was meanwhile tearing itself apart in Europe: religious wars in France, particularly acute in the 1560s and 1570s, the Eighty Years' War in the Netherlands, conflict in England and Scotland. Despite gestures of unity against the supposed threat of Islam, the toxic mix of religious exclusivity and imperial ambition split Europe's claimants to power into eastern and western Christians, Protestants and Catholics, with enormous bloodshed. A few political thinkers, such as Jean Bodin in the 1570s, imagined that a monarchical, territorial state could rise above magnate power and sectarian strife, but the reality of composite empires and their enemies was otherwise.

The rivalry between Ottoman and Spanish empires was fought out over decades in wars on land and sea. Charles never could dislodge the Ottomans from Algeria or stop the attacks on Spanish ships in the western Mediterranean by corsairs who at times allied with the Ottomans. On the other end of Habsburg domains, the Ottomans reached the outskirts of Vienna. Charles and his brother Ferdinand, the Habsburg king of Austria, and Suleiman fought bitterly over Hungary, and in 1547 Ferdinand had to give up his claim to become king of Hungary and pay tribute to the Ottomans for his right to rule some Hungarian territories. Based on this treaty, which referred to Charles as the "King of Spain"—not emperor—Suleiman could claim that he was the "Caesar of the Romans."

But Suleiman had his eastern edge problems, too, namely the Safavids with their claims to Islamic supremacy. The unruly borderlands between the two Islamic powers defied Ottoman control. At mid-century, Charles V attempted to ally with Suleiman's enemy, the Safavid shah; Suleiman in turn assisted the French king (from the late 1520s into the 1550s) and German Protestant princes. The Ottomans sent a naval expedition to help France fight the Habsburgs in 1543; the fleet wintered over at Toulon, provisioned by the French at Suleiman's request. Charles and Philip II feared that Spain might be subject to attack. Charles's abdication in 1556 did not change this contestation over Rome's former empire in the west. Suleiman died on a final campaign in Hungary in 1566; his armies triumphed there nonetheless. That the two great empires pulled back from all-out confrontation in the 1570s reflected both challenges and opportunities—the Ottomans' need to put down rebels and consolidate their gains in Arabic-speaking regions, the Habsburgs' profitable venture in the Americas, their conflict with France, and the difficulty of holding together the rambunctious states in their European domain.

The Ottomans' paramount if shifting position in southeastern Europe and the Mediterranean should not surprise us. Suleiman had a standing army of nearly ninety thousand in the 1520s, the cavalrymen supported by their land grants, and at its core the Janissaries, the sultan's personal guard. Charles V and other western European rulers had to raise armies via local magnates or mercenaries, at great cost. At the end of Suleiman's reign, the Ottoman empire stretched from Buda to Mecca, from Algiers to Basra. It was an empire of enormous resources, mobilized through a system of rule that attracted, disciplined, and contained potential upstarts. Against this self sustaining polylith, the Spanish, with their fractious subordinates and their debts to merchants outside their realm, had an uphill battle.

The Spanish response to the Ottomans' geostrategic advantages, as well as the unruliness of their own domains, was expansion overseas. They had some success with oceangoing trade, but defending control in Europe meant that money did not stay in Spain. Under Suleiman, the Ottomans also tried to expand their reach, sending a fleet to the Mughals in India in 1541. But they could not dislodge the Portuguese with their superior ships from the Indian Ocean trade routes. Neither Charles nor Suleiman, nor the most prescient of their advisors, could predict the long-range consequences of overseas trade and empire. What they did know was the extent of each other's power and they learned the limits of their own.

Let us look back at these two empires and what they had accomplished. Charles V and his immediate successors forged an empire that became far more "Spanish" than it was at first. Constrained by the volatility of sovereignty in Europe, they tied European Spain and its American offshoots together through deference to a shared monarch, religious affinity, the state's coercive and administrative capabilities, and protection against other empires. Spanish became the hegemonic language throughout this space and Castilians appointed by the king exercised more authority in the Americas than they could in Charles's European domains; Catholicism was enforced as a shared religion. An uneasy interaction between one church and one dynasty, as well as between monarchy and landed magnates, signaled a new universalism, based on a single, Christian, European civilization extended to new continents as well as uncertainty over who would control this process. For the Ottomans, the fundamental principle of universal empire was pragmatic inclusivity under sultanic rule, the protection of subjects' already existing religious and customary practices, a subtle melding of Islamic and imperial law, and a bureaucracy detached—ideally—from any permanent family power.

These different strategies invite us to consider two contrasting ways of organizing imperial power. "Ideal types," as Max Weber called them, do not reveal the messy workings of actual political systems, but they help us think about broader problems that rulers faced and multiple—but limited—solutions to them. We will contrast a system of class hierarchy and a system of patrimonial rule, keeping in mind that actual polities draw on both principles.

In the class hierarchy model, commoners, including the poor, have ties to each other from shared experience. Aristocrats depend on mutual recognition of each other's status and on a social and legal system that supports their privileges—access to land, to arms, and to the king's court, and deference from those beneath them. Class hierarchy implies strong ties within classes and weaker ties between them. For the would-be king or the would-be emperor, the extent to which nobles have privileges as a class is both useful and a problem: useful for pulling together men and money needed to rule, for keeping external rivals at bay and the people on the bottom at work and in order; a problem because aristocrats might act together to check the power of the king.

In the patrimonial model, power extends from family and household. The king is a father to his people, providing protection and expecting deference. He seeks direct, vertical ties with supporters, who in turn have personal ties with their own dependents. A patrimonial ruler tries to minimize his various dependents' ties with each other. If the class model emphasizes horizontal ties, the patrimonial model depends on vertical ones. The patrimonial ruler most fears that his subordinates will take their dependents off in another direction—to join a rival ruler or to replicate the patrimonial system under a new king. He must provide resources that would not be available from smaller political units or rival ones. His strategy is to ensure that these chains of vertical linkages converge on himself, while at the same time he builds up his household by acquiring direct dependents with no other social ties, vertical or horizontal.

The empires of Charles and Suleiman had elements of both class and patrimonial systems, but Charles's empire in Europe worked closer to the class hierarchy model, Suleiman's to the patrimonial one. Charles depended on a relatively homogeneous regime of religion and law to maintain a stable class hierarchy in which his superior position was recognized. But he did not fully control either the material or the ideological basis of his power. He had to work with the self-conscious civic orders of towns, with arms-bearing magnates backed up by their followers, and a church that was both jealous of its authority and challenged by splits within Christianity. In contrast, the Ottoman sultan worked through controlled connections to different and separate religious, legal, and cultural groups.

"The entire monarchy of the Turk is governed by one lord, the others are his servants; and, dividing his kingdom into sanjaks, he sends there different administrators, and shifts and changes them as he chooses. But the king of France is placed in the midst of an ancient body of lords, acknowledged by their own subjects, and beloved by them; they have their own prerogatives, nor can the king take these away except at his peril."

—Machiavelli, *The Prince*, chapter 4

The form that Spanish empire took in Europe and its American territories goes back to Rome—and to the way its western regions came apart. Despite the synthetic, absorptive process by which Roman power came into being, the late empire produced a singular Roman culture identifiable throughout its domains, uneven in its penetration of the daily lives of ordinary people, but highly persuasive to elites. Among the rewards for those who chose the Roman way were superior status in the provinces and social mobility within the empire's institutional structure. As the center lost control over resources and disaggregated, aristocracies became more local, clinging to land and peasants for survival, and more ambient, looking for protection through alliances with other magnates or from promising superiors. This volatile landscape of violence and contingent loyalty lasted for centuries.

Would-be emperors in the former western Roman empire thus had to turn to patrimonial strategies if they wished to break through the limits set on power by horizontal affinities, a daunting task. That many Spanish magnates controlled substantial land revenues and numerous armed men—and that other potential supporters of the Habsburgs had similar resources—made cutting through class hierarchy extremely difficult. Both magnates and local communities tried to maintain aristocratic principles over patrimonial ones by limiting the extent to which emperors could put "their" men in positions of authority.

On the Atlantic edge of Europe, empire-building at a distance seemed more attractive. The Americas were a place where a monarch and a Castilian elite could get around magnate power. The system of viceroyalties and audiencias—and royal appointments to these positions—was an attempt to do overseas what could not be done at home, to rule an empire in a more patrimonial manner, by means similar to those used by Mongol khans or Ottoman sultans. That still left the question of how effective the institutions Christian Europeans created would be. Could they exercise durable authority over the indigenous and immigrant peoples of the Americas?

The Ottomans created their empire in a different space. They started out in Anatolia, and from the beginning kept local lords from remaining local by moving them around. The cultural configuration of their empire, especially after the defeat of the Byzantines, was variegated: the Ottomans ruled over trading outposts, ancient cities, landed warlords, diasporas of traveling merchants. The key to tying this together was not to make it uniform but to let unlike communities run their affairs in unlike ways under the supervision of officials tied vertically and as firmly as possible to the sultan. The crucial institution was literally patrimonial—the sultan's household, based on similar structures in the Turkic, Mongol, Persian, and Arab worlds but with important variations. Sultanic reproduction through slave concubines and recruitment of the sultan's highest advisors and his bodyguard from outside the Turkish-speaking, Muslim population were bulwarks against aristocracy. By externalizing the source of high command and even part of the sultanic bloodline, the Ottomans prevented the creation of a social stratum that could claim autonomous status and resources.

Ottoman patrimonialism also worked by recognizing hierarchy within the various unlike communities of the empire, with their own laws, beliefs, languages, and leaders. Islam was not necessarily more conducive to this kind of orchestrated tolerance than was Christianity—jihads and crusades have much in common—and divisions among Muslims both inside and outside the empire challenged the sultan's claim to be God's shadow on earth. But the Ottomans did not have to deal with institutionalized religious power along the lines of the papacy. Building on Eurasian models of pragmatic rule and occupying Byzantium's multicultural space, the sultan could both take the caliph's place and shelter other people's religions.

Neither the Spanish of Charles's times nor the Ottomans of Suleiman's could avoid all the perils of ruling empires, but they did break out of the limits in which Mediterranean-based empire-builders had found themselves since Rome began to lose its grip. One emperor spread and consolidated power over lands and seas around the eastern Mediterranean, the other began to look across the ocean. Both efforts shaped for centuries, in different directions, the geography of power.

OCEANIC ECONOMIES
AND COLONIAL SOCIETIES

Europe, Asia, and the Americas

6

The men who sailed forth from western Europe across the seas in the fifteenth and sixteenth centuries did not set out to create "merchant empires" or "western colonialism." They sought wealth outside the confines of a continent where large-scale ambitions were constrained by tensions between lords and monarchs, religious conflicts, and the Ottomans' lock on the eastern Mediterranean.

The ambitions of maritime voyagers were shaped by the world of power and exchange they knew. Linkages across Eurasia created and sustained by Mongols, Arabs, Jews, and others inspired Columbus when he set out for the enticing empire of the Great Khan. He brought with him an interpreter to communicate with the court of China—a Jew, converted to Christianity, who spoke Arabic. When Columbus and his crew arrived instead on an island in the Caribbean, the first words spoken by a "European" explorer to an "American" people were in the language of Islam.

If the perspectives of men like Columbus reflected the world order of their times, the consequences of the voyagers' actions were out of proportion to their intentions. Competing for access to Asian commercial networks, European powers established militarized entrepots at key points in commercial networks and slowly began to extend political authority and settlement. A new continent was accidentally discovered and new forms of colonization devised. Transatlantic commerce grew eightfold between 1510 and 1550 and another threefold by 1610.

In Asia, the growing European presence from the end of the fifteenth century entailed less the "opening" of the region to long-distance trade than the intrusion into preexisting economic systems in the Indian Ocean and southeast Asia of a new kind of militarized commerce, pushed by Portuguese and later Dutch, British, and French traders, companies, and state actors. The fortified entrepots and—in some areas—larger settlements established by Europeans in Asia in the sixteenth and seventeenth centuries were precarious endeavors when compared to the consolidation of the Mughals' hold over much of India in the sixteenth century, the Ming's extensive empire in China, or the Manchus' reconstruction of China in the seventeenth century. We can better understand the innovations and limits of European maritime empire-building by looking at political and economic actions as they developed in their own time—with different consequences in the Americas, Africa, and Asia—than by projecting backward the apparent dominance of European powers in the nineteenth century into a single story of "European expansion."

The sixteenth century, some historians claim, was "the most warlike" in European history. Although the violence of local lords against each other was less endemic than earlier, conflict among a small number of players, defending or asserting imperial dominance, was exacerbated by religious tension between Christians and Muslims, Catholics and Protestants. Competition among European empires promoted a triple dynamic: an attempt to keep economic resources within the imperial fold, the development of military strength through innovations in technology and state control over human and fiscal resources, and the deployment of those resources over space—eventually across all the world's oceans.

Maritime empires were the result of strenuous attempts to channel long-distance commerce—to impede others' connections while extending one's own. The key to this endeavor was armed merchant shipping and the establishment, maintained by force, of a range of institutions in Africa, Asia, and the Americas: the enclave trading colony that brought key intersections in economic networks under imperial control; the plantation colony, where a small number of colonizers exploited land and mines with local or imported labor; and the settlement of European migrants who displaced or decimated indigenous people or forcefully incorporated them into a new kind of social order, the colonial situation.

In this chapter we emphasize major changes in how empires, developing out of Europe, interacted and conflicted with each other as they moved beyond the Mediterranean region and across the seas. We explore repertoires of imperial power, including the combinations and sequences of enclave, plantation, and settlement strategies of empire-builders. And we point to the limits of the power of the maritime empires: their destructive conflicts with each other, their internal weaknesses—particularly in keeping intermediaries under control—and the strength and adaptability of the polities and networks in Asia and Africa.

Trading enclaves and networks, plantations and mines, and agricultural settlements were sites of encounter of European newcomers with indigenous people and with slaves moved from one part of an ocean-spanning system to another. The part of the world with the least prior immersion in long-distance connections, the Americas, experienced the most devastating effects of colonization—demographically, politically, and culturally. But even there empire-builders could not efface earlier forms of economic and social organization or escape the need for intermediaries—European and/ or indigenous—to maintain control over disparate territories.

Administrators, priests, and other European agents of empire did not confront indigenous peoples living in timeless cultural authenticity but rather people experienced in social interactions and politics, including those of empire. The patterns that emerged from these confrontations reflected not just imposed authority but also the initiative of indigenous people to make use of new possibilities without giving up everything that had been theirs.

One might call the European empire-builders of the late fifteenth and sixteenth centuries the Mongols of the sea—their advantage was in mobility, the ability to concentrate resources, and military technology adapted to a particular situation. They moved in where they could and avoided areas where the barriers were high. They did not have the Mongols' capacity for pragmatic interaction with the people they encountered. Strong ideas of religious and ethnic distinction emerged overseas, but so did mixture across such lines as well as debates over how far difference justified exploitation and denigration within empires trying to establish legitimate rule.

This chapter relates several intersecting and overlapping histories—of coercion, commerce, and conversion, of empires pushing outward and facing their limits, of the cumulative, and often unintended, effects of attempts to exercise power at great distances and in multiple spaces.

A Polycentric World of Trade?

The Indian Ocean and the seas of southeast Asia were long plied by merchants of diverse origins: Indians from Gujarat (western India), Arabs from the Hadramaut (southern Arabia), Jews, Armenians, Chinese, Malays. Entrepot cities—Hormuz, Melaka, Manila—provided bases for merchant communities, each with its own quarter within the city and with links to other ethnically organized trading networks. These entrepots were sometimes part of small polities—similar to the city-states of Italy or the Hanseatic league along the Baltic—but some were under the authority of imperial rulers like the Mughals, who encouraged but did not directly participate in trade. The spread of Islam into southeast Asia provided a framework of law and common understanding, fostering the growth of sultanates along trade routes in the Malay peninsula and the Indonesian archipelago—not that these states were immune from conflict with each other or their neighbors. Kingdoms of considerable size took root on the mainland, in Burma and Thailand no-

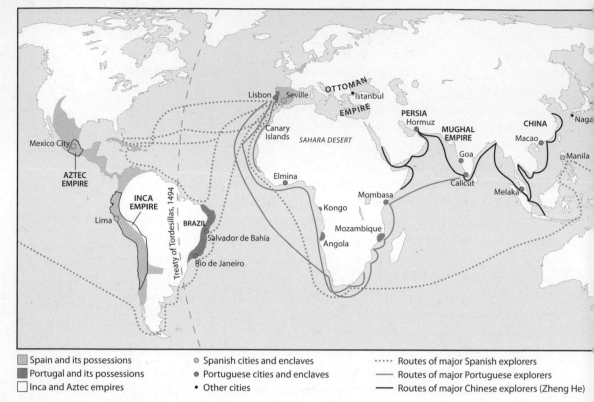

Map 6.1
Spanish and Portuguese exploration and conquest
in the late fifteenth and early sixteenth centuries.

tably, and they profited from the expansion of commerce without seeking to
dominate it. The period *before* the arrival of Europeans in the Indian Ocean
and China Sea was the great era of "free trade" within the region.

Well ensconced by the fifteenth century in the Black Sea, the eastern
Mediterranean, and Arabia, the Ottomans controlled the major bottlenecks
connecting southeast Asia and Europe. They stood to gain from the growth
of trade in pepper and spices, as well as silk and porcelain from China and
cloth from India. Europe, by comparison, did not have much to offer. It was
an American commodity, silver, the demand for which was enhanced by the
vitality of Asian trade and the need for a stable medium of exchange (paper
currency had long been in use in China), that enabled Europeans to pay for
more imports in the sixteenth century.

The biggest imperial actor in Asia was ambivalent about overseas trade.
The Ming empire focused on its tax base—an enormous peasantry—and
engaged in extensive commerce overland across Eurasia, worried about nomadic populations along its northern and western frontiers, and sought to

subdue or intimidate nearby states. The great admiral Zheng He—an imperial eunuch—voyaged as far as east Africa between 1405 and 1433, even before the Portuguese reached that region—a trip that was part exploration, part commerce, and part a demonstration of power. But the government put an end to such expeditions and banned Chinese participation in overseas commerce for a time, keeping a close eye on foreigners or anyone else trading across the sea. Why the Ming drew back from maritime expansion is something of a puzzle, but it highlights the importance of both spatial and political contexts. European explorers of the fifteenth century departed from the edges of a fragmented continent; their rulers sought alternative sources of revenue and authority outside local and regional power structures. Chinese rulers did not need to leapfrog overseas or to spend the state's resources on a navy.

But if sponsoring long-distance trade was not an ambition of the Chinese empire after Zheng He, it was the project of many Chinese individuals and families. Chinese merchants were active in southeast Asia; some settled in places like Manila or Melaka precisely because China's government was wary of their becoming an autonomous, affluent group closer to home. Even without state investment in overseas trade, the Chinese economy—with its coveted exports of silk, porcelain, and tea—was a major factor in the maritime commerce of southeast Asia.

The critical issue for western Europeans was not getting commodities from the east to Europe—land routes flourished and sea routes were not necessarily cheaper. The issue was control. Europe's increasing involvement in long-distance maritime commerce was a quintessentially political story—about establishing and protecting one's own linkages and interfering with, or destroying, those of others.

Monarchs, Merchants, and European Maritime Empires

From Rome across Eurasia to China, we have seen the importance to rulers and would-be rulers of acquiring external resources to strengthen themselves vis-à-vis their own societies. We now look at two ways in which social tension at home translated into economic initiatives abroad: one sponsored in the fifteenth century by the Portuguese monarch as he attempted to distance himself from his own nobility and keep control of the territories, networks, and revenues generated overseas; the other, about a century later, initiated by a merchant company and a wealthy, trade-minded Dutch elite rather than by a monarchy. Both Portugal in the fifteenth and sixteenth centuries and the Netherlands in the seventeenth were small states with limited power—compared to Habsburg Spain, let alone the Ottomans or China—

and small populations. Necessity drove them outward; their pioneering role in establishing long-distance commercial networks brought them rapid success. Sustaining this new form of empire would be the difficulty.

Historians now put Dom Pedro alongside his more famous brother Prince Henry the Navigator as architects of early maritime exploration, trade, and conquest in the name of Portugal. The point is the same: the monarchy's need for external sources of wealth and power. Henry himself never got farther than north Africa, where he led a military expedition in 1415. Portuguese explorers made good use of other people's knowledge. Their caravel combined the northern European square-rigged vessel with the lateen sails of the Mediterranean ship, making it both fast and maneuverable. The magnetic compass was a Chinese contribution; the astrolabe had been perfected by Arab navigators. Knowledge of navigation and geography came to Portugal from Italian mariners, whose connections to Eurasian trading systems had been made possible by the Mongol peace (chapter 4).

The west African expeditions began in 1434 and reached Cape Verde (in today's Senegal) in 1444. African spices were an early focus, only later overshadowed by the Asian spice trade. From the 1440s, the sale of slaves was bringing in revenue, but the big item was gold, mined by Africans some distance from the coast. Maritime connections enabled the Portuguese to bypass the Muslim-controlled gold trade across the Sahara, and by the 1480s trading "castles" along the west African coast had become key entrepots of the trade. This region imported slaves, which the Portuguese supplied from further east and south along the African coast. The Portuguese also installed small colonies in islands on the eastern side of the Atlantic: Madeira, the Canaries (until the Spanish took them away), the Azores, and later Sao Thomé, Principe, and Fernando Po.

The Portuguese Crown set up two institutions, the Casa da Guiné and the Casa da Mina, through which the slave trade of Africa was required to pass. The system depended on indigenous rulers doing business with the Portuguese enclaves; the attraction for local leaders was profit and arms useful in regional conflicts. In the central African kingdom of Kongo, the conversion of the king by Portuguese Catholic missionaries added a cultural dimension to the connection between an indigenous polity and a European maritime network.

In the island colonies, sugar cultivation began on a small scale, rapidly escaped Portuguese control, and eventually transformed the world economy. Sugarcane had an earlier interempire history, passing through Persia and Mesopotamia to Egypt, introduced by Muslims into the Mediterranean world and into Spain in the tenth century. A breakthrough occurred with two imperial projects—the seizure of areas better suited than Spain to the crop and the systematization of slave acquisition. The latter became increas-

Figure 6.1

Bartering along the African coast in Guinea, c. 1690, a pen and
ink drawing by Rutger van Langerfeld. State Museum in Berlin.
Bildarchiv Preussischer Kulturbesitz, ArtResource.

ingly the focus of Portuguese Atlantic trade from its African entrepots, especially after sugar began to be cultivated in the Spanish Caribbean and Portuguese Brazil. Beginning in 1595 the Spanish government gave Portuguese
merchants the *asiento*, the contract to supply its New World colonies with
slaves. With the growth of slave trading from the well-fortified Portuguese
bases in Angola in the seventeenth century, the linkage between increasingly
militaristic kingdoms in Africa and the plantation complex of the Americas
was strengthened—at a tremendous cost in violence throughout a large part
of west and central Africa.

From the start, the real prize lay further east—in other people's trading
systems. The Portuguese explorer Vasco da Gama sailed in 1497 around Africa to India. There he encountered the Indian Ocean merchant networks
run by Gujaratis, Arabs, Malays, Chinese, and others that were moving African products (ivory) and Asian commodities (spices) to Europe and China,
as well as to other locations within south and southeast Asia. What the Por-

tuguese fleet could do was concentrate power—ships with cannons—to inflict damage and terror upon the population of a promising location, build a fort, and begin to buy produce brought from inland. Innovations in artillery and fortress design were part of what made an enclave empire possible, but continued success also depended on at least a fraction of local people acquiring an interest in the Portuguese connection.

The *feitoria* or factory, the fortified trading post, was the heart of the trading enclave, from Elmina in west Africa to Mozambique and Mombasa in east Africa, Hormuz in the Persian Gulf, Goa in western India, Melaka in the Malayan peninsula, and Macao in China. Like the Spanish monarchy, Portuguese rulers were able to develop state institutions in overseas colonies in ways they could not at home. A powerful viceroy surrounded by military, judicial, and ecclesiastical leaders governed the Estado da India, the network of trading enclaves and forces from southeast Africa to the coast of China. In Lisbon the Casa da India kept a monopoly over imports from Asia.

This type of empire depended not only on the factories in strategic points but on making itself necessary to people who were already producing and marketing valued goods. In fact, intra-Asian trade remained much larger than Asian trade with Europe. The armed ships and fortified enclaves of the Portuguese constituted a kind of protection racket, and Indian Ocean traders of many origins paid their dues and took what they could from the system. The practice was reminiscent of the tribute extracted by many groups living along trade routes in Eurasia and elsewhere, but Portuguese kings evoked a novel theory based on their interpretations of papal bulls to justify their operations: Portugal was "sovereign of the seas," with the right to declare monopolies, levy duties, issue passports, and enforce its authority through judicial processes. This global assertiveness masked the narrower range of practical possibility. Portugal could concentrate power on key points in the system but had to tread lightly elsewhere. Even in Portugal's sixteenth-century heyday, other Asian empires—the Mughals, Aceh, empires in Burma, and Thailand—had more powerful militaries and were growing more rapidly. But as long as Portuguese commerce provided goods useful to others—including guns, and eventually New World silver—multiple imperial endeavors could coexist.

The Portuguese empire's future depended on fending off private interlopers and rival empires and keeping enclaves in line. Entrepots remained vulnerable to local rulers—the Safavids' takeover of Hormuz in 1622 and Japan's expulsion of the Portuguese community in 1638 are cases in point. Nevertheless, as the first European power to push itself into the already developed networks of Asia, Portugal had its moment of success. The king's desire for resources independent of his metropolitan magnates was met: half of King John III's revenue in the 1520s came from overseas trade. For a time, Lisbon was a central point in the spice trade from Asia and Africa to Europe.

Lacking capital to finance numerous trading voyages, the Crown granted royal monopolies where it could and tried to keep traders of all origins tied to the "casa" system and its enclaves. But the enclaves themselves depended on officials—many of them the younger sons of Portuguese nobles—and on soldiers and sailors, most of whom were not Portuguese at all, often recruited locally. The intermediary problem proved severe: administrators could turn enclave colonies into personal fiefs and trade on their own. Portuguese in the colonies intermarried with local people, adapted to local customs, and began to shape a "Portuguese" society that was less and less bound to Portugal. Such arrangements enabled a small kingdom in Europe to manage a vast empire and to persist in some areas for centuries, but they also made it harder for the monarchy in Lisbon to keep revenue and control to itself. Without the officeholding system of China or the household of the Ottomans, Portuguese empire relied on a patrimonial strategy (chapter 5): offices and commands allotted by the king, elites in the colonial enclaves making themselves the centers of patronage.

Some scholars see the enclave empire as particularly Portuguese in contrast to the settlement orientation of the Spanish. It is true that the number of Portuguese in Asia was tiny, perhaps ten thousand administrators and soldiers in the seventeenth century. Portugal had few settlers to send out. But the seaborne empire did not stay at sea: the repertoire of Portuguese empire expanded as opportunities opened. Colonists set themselves up on large farms in the Zambeze Valley in Mozambique (map 6.1) and in Ceylon (map 6.2). Portuguese moved into the hinterland of their Indian entrepots. The biggest exception to enclave, seaborne empire was very big indeed—Brazil. Here Portuguese newcomers encountered a much less dense population than that of southeast Asia; the diseases they brought with them lowered population even further. Indigenous political power was not an obstacle, and Brazil was also much closer to Portugal than was Asia. Portuguese linkages across the Atlantic brought the deciding, human factor: slave labor. Northeastern Brazil became the first great sugar plantation colony of the Americas. From the 1690s, the gold of Minas Gerais in central Brazil created a new boom and a further demand for African slaves. By the mid-eighteenth century over a million Africans had been forcefully moved to Brazil.

Here we see the dynamics of empire: Portugal, with its enclaves in Africa and resources and experience gained from coercion and commerce across oceans and continents, seized by conquest a large territory in the Americas, then profited from the linkages of African labor, American land, and European markets. The actual capture of slaves occurred, from a European point of view, offstage, in wars and raids conducted by African polities.

But supervision of slaves in the plantation colony, protection against revolt, and containment of runaway communities that slaves created in hinterland zones demanded an alert and active military. Built around the subordination of an entire category of people, the plantation complex differed from both the enclave empire and the territory of settlement.

Brazil, particularly the sugar-producing zone in its northeast, was for nearly three centuries the world's biggest buyer of slaves. Portugal—and later the Netherlands, France, and England—tried initially to keep the purchasing and transportation of slaves, plantation production, and the supply of sugar inside their empires by favoring traders with ties to the monarchy, offering royal charters to chosen companies, and imposing tariffs. But the usual threats to an empire's control of commerce soon emerged: interlopers and untied traders moving into parts of the business, armed attacks by other empires, growing autonomy of increasingly affluent settlers in the colonies vis-à-vis the state in Europe. In Brazil's case, the last factor was striking. Brazil-based traders, owing allegiance to Portugal but acting independently of its government, began to forge direct connections to Africa. The wealthy colony started to overshadow the Europe-based monarchy that had spawned it.

Territorial empire in Brazil, while it suffered from competition from sugar plantations in the Caribbean and later attacks from the Dutch, was more defensible than the nodes and networks of Portugal's seaborne empire. Armed commerce is not cheap; patronage is not an efficient way to run a globe-spanning operation; and other empires were following in Portugal's footsteps.

Portugal was also caught up in interempire politics within Europe. It had benefited from a treaty with Spain, brokered by the pope in 1494, that divided the two Catholic powers' zones of interest (chapter 5). But when the Crown of Portugal passed to the Habsburgs (1580–1640), Portugal was stuck with Spain's enemies—England (the failed Armada of 1588 sailed from Lisbon) and the Habsburg province of the Netherlands, which rebelled against Philip II. The wars drained revenue and disrupted commerce.

By the 1590s, most of the Netherlands were in effect independent, although it took about sixty years for the break to be mutually accepted (chapter 5). Dutch elites began to develop a new kind of empire that clashed directly with Portuguese interests.

Dutch cities, especially Antwerp and Amsterdam, had become economic centers under Habsburg rule. Banking, textile manufacturing, and the convergence of trading networks linking north and south Europe, England and the continent, and the Baltic/North Sea regions led to the accumulation of capital and commercial skill. Even as wealth from the Americas was passing through Spain, much of it ended up in the Netherlands. In 1581, the elites of different Dutch cities declared independence from Spain and formed the United Provinces. They found themselves a monarch—William of Orange—to preside over the whole but kept most power in the hands of the provincial assemblies and an assembly of the United Provinces. While all European powers experienced tensions between central rulers and aristocracies or provincial elites, the Netherlands leaned strongly to the side of diffusing power to interlocking familial and provincial clusters, in contrast to France, with its increasingly strong monarchy in the sixteenth century, or to Spain, where royal authority looked overseas to distance itself from aristocratic power.

In each province, a small number of magnates used kinship, marriage alliances, and clientage to keep resources in their hands. Ambitious and commercially minded, these families devised ways to pool resources for long-distance sea voyages, culminating in the formation of the Dutch East India Company, the VOC (Vereenigde Oost-Indische Companie), in 1602. The VOC was a joint stock company managed by the Heeren 17 (the 17 Directors), who represented stockholders from six different cities. The VOC, not the state of the Netherlands, made an empire, and it did so by combining the joint stock company's capacity to accumulate capital with the mechanism of armed, coercive commerce pioneered by the Portuguese.

The VOC *had* to play the empire game, for the Dutch conflict with Spain, and hence after 1580 with Portugal, closed the Lisbon spice market to Dutch traders. Sending its own armed merchant fleet to the spice islands, the VOC had to deal carefully with indigenous producers at the far end of the trading system. The company was more bellicose in the middle, attacking ships and entrepots of the Portuguese merchant empire. After establishing a base in the small town of Jayakarta, renamed Batavia (now Jakarta), on the island of Java in 1619, the VOC's breakthrough came in 1641 when it captured Melaka—a key entrepot of the southeast Asian trade—from the Portuguese.

The Indonesian archipelago at this time was divided into many kingdoms or sultanates, most of which had been Muslim for a century or more, and had developed links through Indian, Chinese, and Malay traders to commercial circuits across much of southeast Asia and to China. The VOC offered local rulers long-distance commercial connections and, as one historian puts it, "muscle and money they could use to achieve their ambitions in their own corner of Indonesia." Batavia began to overshadow its neighbors; the town grew from 8,000 people in 1624 to 130,000 in 1670. The VOC was increasingly able to pressure local rulers to grant it monopolies of key export items, to make their people grow more pepper and other spices, and to supply labor for the company. In some instances, the VOC destroyed productive trees and massacred entire communities for refusing to

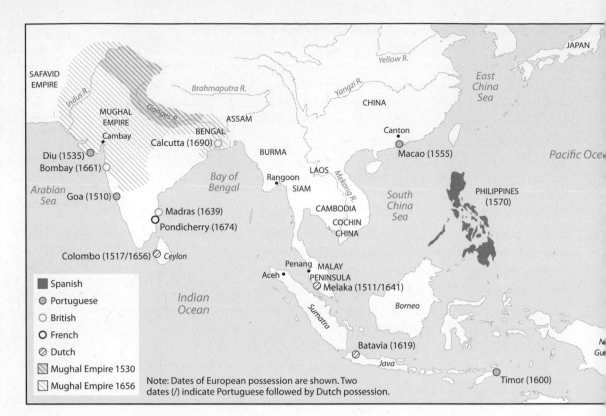

Map 6.2
South and southeast Asia, sixteenth
and seventeenth centuries.

cooperate with its monopolistic practices. In the 1620s, the VOC established
a monopoly of the nutmeg trade in much of the region; in the 1650s it did
likewise with cloves. By the eighteenth century the VOC was also growing
crops on its own estates, using slave labor. The system depended both on the
VOC's monopoly of the European connection and on networks of Chinese,
Malay, Indian, and Javanese traders within the region.

   With its headquarters in Batavia and major posts in Bengal, Ceylon,
Melaka, Thailand, China, and Taiwan, and a supply base for long voyages on
the Cape of Good Hope (southern Africa), the VOC ran a more dynamic
operation than did the Portuguese entrepot traders. Unlike the kings of
Portugal or Spain, the VOC did not have to worry about fending off aristocrats. Its corporate organization was innovative. The Dutch state gave the
company a charter and legitimized its exercise of functions usually associated with sovereignty—the use of force to capture entrepots and later to
extend territorial control, the governing and policing of those territories,
and negotiation with foreign sovereigns. As it exercised these functions, the

VOC began to look more and more like a state while remaining a profit-making enterprise.

By 1669, the VOC was the richest corporation in the world and an impressive military force in southeast Asia, owning 150 merchant ships and 40 war vessels, employing 50,000 civilians and 10,000 soldiers. The company's fabulous wealth, garnered in the East Indies, fed the flourishing social and artistic life of seventeenth-century Amsterdam. The VOC fought local kingdoms on Java and Sumatra—disunited despite having been for the most part converted to Islam—and put down attempts to retake Batavia. It superintended an increasingly differentiated society in its entrepots, where substantial intermarriage between Dutch men and local women produced mixed people, some of whom used paternal connections to make their way in this rough world of competitive commerce.

M. Postlethwayt on the reasons for the VOC's success: "its being absolute, and invested with a kind of sovereignty and dominion, . . . [it] makes peace and war at pleasure, and by its own authority; administers justice to all; . . . settles colonies, builds fortifications, levies troops, maintains numerous armies and garrisons, fits out fleets, and coins money."

—entry in *Universal Dictionary of Trade and Commerce of 1751*

The VOC system, like any empire, needed to keep its agents and intermediaries—Dutch or indigenous—tied to the apex of the system. The distances between the Netherlands and Batavia and among the entrepots within southeast Asia made this problem particularly acute. Initially, the threat was agents who could use their knowledge of the networks connecting the VOC to indigenous merchants and producers to bypass the company and keep profits to themselves. Later, when the British East India Company became established in Bengal, the danger was defection—that agents and intermediaries, Dutch or otherwise, might deliver their goods and connections to a rival if that rival paid them more.

A second weakness emerged from what had been a strength—the flexibility of the VOC's financing and governance. As a private corporation the VOC did not have the depth of military resources available to states—especially to states bigger and more centralized than the Netherlands. And its strategy of enforcing monopolies meant high military expenditures for the VOC as well as low prices for export crops and high import prices for peasants and other producers in the parts of southeast Asia the company controlled. Conflict with England, carried out from the Caribbean to the China Sea, took its toll. The VOC could not pass the cost of better protection and more aggressive challenges onto taxpayers. And private investors, unlike states, had an exit option if things went badly: they could try to make their fortune in another place or via another network.

In the eighteenth century, as competition heated up, the VOC lacked the capacity of the British to deploy a more varied repertoire of imperial strategies and resources (discussed later in this chapter). Dutch decline began by the 1720s as the British used trade regulation and naval power to keep much of the Atlantic trade and the North Sea/Baltic route in British hands. The VOC lost ships and markets during the Anglo-Dutch wars of the 1780s. In 1798 the VOC went bankrupt. Eventually Java, Sumatra, and other areas dominated by the VOC became colonies of the Dutch state.

The Portuguese and the Dutch, lacking the size and internal coherence of the Chinese and Ottoman empires, had played the best cards they had: mobility, mastery of sailing technology, access to capital, and the ability to concentrate forces on key points of long-distance commerce. The Portuguese empire of networks and nodes was vulnerable to a Dutch corporation with more flexibility and resources, and the VOC in turn reached the limit of what a company could do against competition from powerful states—but not before these empires pioneered the restructuring of political and economic relationships in much of southeast Asia and parts of the Atlantic. The overseas ventures of the Portuguese and Dutch had given birth to a colonial situation.

Land, Society, and Morality in the Making of an Overseas Empire: Spain in the Americas

We have already looked at the "Spanish empire" as a composite monarchy based in Europe (chapter 5). Now we shift the focus overseas to examine an imperial project that began as a quest for a new sea route to Asia but ended ashore in the Americas, in a period overlapping Portuguese and Dutch maritime ventures. The Spanish Crown neither ran nor financed overseas commerce, but it did try to ensure that its fruits passed through Cadiz or Seville and that the monarchy got its cut. Although the Crown administered the overseas territories as viceroyalties of Castile and encouraged people from "the kingdoms of Spain" to settle the Americas, its interests in incorporation of indigenous people into a Catholic monarchy did not always coincide with the desires of conquistadors and settlers to exploit indigenous people as they saw fit.

Columbus, on his second voyage to the Caribbean, brought 1,500 colonists, conditioned by wars against Islam and the conquest of the Canary Islands to see conquered peoples as infidels or inferiors. The early colonists pillaged local resources; disease dealt the next blow to the islands' people. The Spanish government soon attempted to regularize settlement patterns and to move toward agricultural production. Governors tried to make indigenous chiefs supply labor, but with populations decimated they sought a workforce on neighboring islands. After experimenting with different crops, the Spanish began to pursue sugar around 1515. Sugar took off some years later when the land of the Caribbean was joined to the labor of Africans. Meanwhile, colonization was driven by a quest for more immediately attainable wealth—gold and silver.

The conquest of the American mainland is often told as a tale of European masculine valor: the defeat by about 600 Spaniards of the Aztec empire (1519–21) and later (1531–33) the equally improbable conquest of the Incas by no more than 200 conquistadors. Both conquests were facilitated by high-quality weapons, horses, and mobility. Disease, brought by the Spaniards, is also seen as a cause of the defeat of indigenous empires; smallpox hit the Aztec capital just before Cortes' final siege.

The "steel and germs" explanation for the rapidity of conquest has not convinced all specialists. The newcomers' technological advantages were insufficient and in any case only temporary; differential mortality was a long-term process, not something that happened at the moment of outsiders' assault. Thinking about the endemic vulnerabilities of empires helps us understand the situation. The Aztecs and the Incas were themselves imperial formations of relatively recent origin, with highly concentrated power and wealth at the center and often violent relations with not entirely assimilated people at the edges of their empires. When the Europeans arrived, indigenous people were not sure whether the newcomers were enemies, gods, or evil spirits—or potentially useful allies against an oppressive power. These uncertainties made it harder for their rulers, who had no way of knowing what was in store for them, to respond effectively. Cortes and Pizarro recruited allies among disaffected peoples, thereby making their armies as large as the Aztec and Inca forces they fought against. The battle against the Aztecs was hard-fought, with Spaniards suffering reverses, despite their indigenous allies and the hesitations of the Aztec emperor Moctezuma.

The conquest of the Inca empire—more centralized than that of the Aztecs—was also facilitated by turning those excluded under Inca power into indigenous allies. Surprise, trickery, mobility, and daring enabled the European invaders and their allies to kill the Inca (the emperor), desecrate the symbols of his power, and grab massive quantities of gold and silver. Subduing Inca society as a whole was a much longer process.

If demographic collapse was not a cause of Aztec or Inca defeat, it was an effect. The more mobile Spaniards had a wider range of immunities than did the indigenous peoples of the Americas. In some estimates, the population of Mexico fell from 25 to 2.65 million in the half century after the conquest,

Two Spanish views of motives for conquest:

From the letter of Bernard Diaz, a soldier in Cortes' army fighting the Aztecs, on his goals: *"to serve God and His Majesty, to give light to those in darkness, and also to get rich."*

From a comment of Pizarro, conqueror of the Incas, to a priest who raised the question of his religious duty in propagating faith in Peru: *"I have not come here for such reasons. I have come to take away their gold."*

that of Peru from 9 to 1.3 million, but others argue that the baseline figures are hypothetical and the impact of disease not so easy to measure. That extensive suffering followed conquest is not in dispute.

The conquerors set out to destroy the top of Aztec and Inca society and to exploit the people on the bottom, but they needed to be careful in the middle. The centralization of the Aztec and Inca polities was an advantage to the conquerors, delivering into Spanish hands a population already familiar with hierarchical relationships. Collecting tribute—a huge burden on a declining population—and rounding up labor, particularly for gold and silver mines, required indigenous intermediaries. Men who had acted as intermediaries between the Inca ruler and local communities often played a similar role for the Spanish, as caciques who took their cut of tribute but often tried to moderate the exactions on their people. Indian communities in the Andes were eventually required under the *mita* system to send men in rotation to work under harsh conditions in the silver mines: one out of seven adult males would go each year. Having adapted the Inca patrimonial hierarchy to colonial top-down authority, the Spanish did little to fulfill the Inca's role in redistribution to his people.

Some Inca royals cooperated for a time but chafed at Spanish arrogance and desecration of sacred symbols. In 1536–37, Manco Inca was able to mobilize up to fifty thousand men against the Spanish and lay siege to the ancient capital, losing out as parts of his alliance defected. Rebellions and plots continued into the 1570s.

The largely male invaders, starting in Mexico with Cortes' troops themselves, intermarried—or at least reproduced—to a significant degree with daughters of native elites, beginning a process of *mestizaje* (mixing). The famous chronicler of the Inca empire and the Spanish conquests, Garcilaso de la Vega, was the son of a conquistador and an Inca princess; he proudly proclaimed his mestizo origins. But colonized society was disarticulated society. The elite, concentrated in centers of state power, existed alongside indigenous communities that experienced colonization mainly as the labor and tribute demanded of them. These groups were largely unassimilated and impoverished. Another kind of mixed population was formed by people dislocated from their social positions by war, disease, and exploitation. African slaves were a group apart, but Spanish settlers formed unions with many Africans, whether by marriage, rape, or something in between, producing other mixtures. Spanish authorities and the church tried to maintain an administrative structure, the República de los Indios, to keep Indians separated from settlers, but in reality social categories were both fragmented and overlapping.

The lowland, less settled populations of Central and South America were in some ways harder to conquer than the Inca highlands. Raiding parties,

Figure 6.2

"Las Castas" (the races). Anonymous eighteenth-century painting, from a series showing different combinations of Spanish, Indian, and African parents and their offspring—a frequently painted theme in the art of Spanish America. Panels shown: the child of a castizo (son of an Indian and a Spaniard) and a Spanish woman is Spanish; the child of a Spanish man and a black (Moorish) woman is a mulatto; the child of a chino (child of a black man and a Spanish woman) with an Indian woman is a salta atras; the child of a salta atras and a mulatta is a lobo. Museo Nacional del Virreinato, Tepoltzotlan, Mexico. Schalkwijk, ArtResource.

traders, missionaries, and land-grabbing settlers were agents of slow and uneven transformation, from today's Chile to California. Resistance and rebellions were frequent. Once Indians had horses, they could fight back more effectively. They also could use Spanish cultural resources—such as bringing court cases over abuses—in their defense. In a few places, southern Chile for instance, the invaders were unable to impose their will into the 1590s. Elsewhere, Spanish leaders learned to lower expectations of tribute and labor, to leave considerable autonomy to communities, and to keep looking for intermediaries who would work with them. The Spanish had to adapt to the low population density they had helped to bring about.

Lining up the people needed to exercise authority over a spread-out population at an affordable price was no easy task. One solution, intended to be provisional, was the *encomienda* system. Based on European notions of a lord's authority over dependent people, the encomienda was in effect a grant in Indians. The king gave a client the right to collect tribute and demand labor from indigenous people on a given—often quite large—piece of land, while obliging the *encomendero*, as such a royal follower was called, to defend the Crown and instruct the people in the Christian faith. Parceling out land and people in this way broke up indigenous political units and fostered dependence on the encomendero. In practice, encomenderos needed the cooperation of the heads of kinship groups or local chiefs to collect tribute or labor, and they had little choice but to bargain with such men. Encomenderos also maneuvered to put their own interests ahead of those of royal officials and the faraway king. Royal attempts in 1542 to make the encomienda non-hereditary could not be turned into reality.

By granting a combination of rights and duties to Spanish settlers in Mexico and other parts of conquered regions, the monarchy was getting from its own emigrants some of the intermediaries empires need to do their work and at the same time incorporating the people of the Americas into a political hierarchy. Encomiendas evolved in different directions across Spanish America, in some cases into a landed class presiding over dependent laborers and peasants, in others into mixed and unequal communities of indigenous, Spanish, and mestizo populations, under varying degrees of state surveillance. Indians on encomiendas, indigenous communities that retained a degree of integrity, high-status elites who kept a close connection to Spain, slaves in lowland plantations, peasants in highland communities, and individualistic cattle keepers on the frontiers did not constitute a common Hispanic culture but a fragmented society with uneven attachments to an imperial order and to Christianity.

As we have seen (chapter 5), the financing of the entire enterprise—building ships, equipping armies, capitalizing trading ventures—depended largely on capital from outside Spain. The combination of externally raised capital, the monarchy's debts from defending its European territories, and dependence on sources beyond Spain for the consumer goods that settlers in the New World wanted meant that much of the vast earnings from the gold and silver mines passed through the Iberian peninsula to the Netherlands and Germany. The Crown's share—the so-called royal fifth of gold and silver exported from the Americas—was by the 1550s quite considerable and used to defend the European and overseas realms, but capital formation within Spain was modest, and efforts to improve the structure of the domestic economy were even more so. As the war to keep the Netherlands within the Habsburg fold intensified, the silver of Peru and Mexico was not enough to keep Spain out of bankruptcy in 1596.

There was wide agreement in the sixteenth century that the conquerors were creating a Catholic empire, but there were different ideas about what that meant. Missionaries began a long campaign to propagate the faith with efforts to combat idolatry and sacrifice. Sacred spaces of indigenous societies were systematically destroyed. The linkage of indigenous religion to the authority of Inca, Maya, or Aztec rulers meant that conquest undercut the coherence of religious practices. Along the edges of Spanish expansion in the Americas, mission stations were sites of religious transformation, but they were also agricultural outposts, where clerics tried to mold a Christian, productive, obedient peasantry—protecting Indians on their lands, perhaps, from the worst excesses of encomenderos as well as from the appeals and dangers of Indians as yet unsubdued.

The monarchy—as usual trying to obtain tighter control in the Americas than it could at home—attempted to oversee the appointment of clergy and keep tabs on their activities, but the church-mission system and the administrative hierarchy were never congruent. The state exempted Indians from the Inquisition after 1571 but encouraged other institutions aimed at enforcing as well as propagating the faith among indigenous peoples: the Provisor of Natives, Tribunal of the Faith of Indians, Natives' Courts. African rituals among slaves were also the targets of repressive efforts by church and state.

Conversion did not necessarily produce the passive Christian Indian that the missionaries sought. Local religious practices proved more durable than royal cults like those of the Inca. Interaction did not so much produce a generalized syncretism of Catholic and indigenous religious practices as a highly uneven geography of religious belief and practice. Polytheistic Indians could incorporate elements of Christianity, such as saint cults, into their practices. Limited as mission education was, it provided some Indians with skills that could be used not only to try to make their way into the church hierarchy but also to transcribe chants in the Nahuatl language in Roman letters or rework Peruvian chronicles into a language that mixed Spanish and Quechua. Some people of indigenous origin became learned Catholic theologians. Within the coercive colonial situation, religious conversion could foster adaptation to a Spanish-dominated cultural system or the preservation of memories and collective rituals that belied the inevitability and normality of Spanish domination.

The Spanish Crown laid out the institutions and rules of a state more effectively in the Americas than in Europe. It created a territorial administration, divided into viceroyalties and in turn into *audiencias* (see map 5.2). It kept these offices in the hands of Castilians beholden in theory to the king. Its many laws and decrees, bearing the king's seal, made their way across the Atlantic and down the hierarchy. Jurists in Spain, much influenced by Roman law now imbued with Christian purpose, interpreted such laws and institutions in relation to the concept of imperium (chapter 2). Indians were incorporated into the symbolic and institutional structures of empire and could try—with limited success—to use them to hold off abusive tax or labor collection. The threat of rebellion lurked in the background—and at times burst forth. This, too, made officials conscious of the limits of their domination.

The colonial world was slowly reshaped by the increasing presence of settlers from the kingdoms of Spain. Between 1500 and 1650, 437,000 Spaniards went to the New World, as did 100,000 Portuguese, far more than went to Asian outposts of those empires. The slave trade also reshaped the demography of the Americas: by 1560, the number of Africans in Spanish America exceeded the number of Spanish, and the Brazilian slave trade was even more large-scale. Slaves went to many parts of Iberian America but were concentrated in a few plantation areas, such as the Caribbean islands and northeastern Brazil. Different fragments of colonial society drew on different memories—of Africa, of indigenous empires, of Spain.

The exploitation of conquered indigenous people was questioned shortly after it began, as priests persuaded Queen Isabella to stop the enslavement of Indians in the islands. The most sustained and widely heard attack on Spain's treatment of the Indians came between the 1510s and 1560s from a Dominican friar, Bartolomé de las Casas. He presumed that colonies and metropole together constituted a single polity, a moral space. His argument hinged both on the hypocrisy of a Catholic monarchy that proclaimed a duty to save the souls of Indians while abusing their bodies and on a stance of empathy toward Indians. Las Casas made much of Indians' civilizational attainments, particularly of their empires. His argument did not apply to Africans, who in his eyes had not achieved the same, and it did not imply that all subjects of the king were equivalent. But Las Casas did not see colonies as starkly divided between those who were true members and people who served those members. He envisioned an empire of subjects—of human

Figure 6.3

"Cruelty of the Spanish," by Theodore de Bry, illustrating Bartolomé
de las Casas's "Account of the First Voyages and Discoveries Made by
the Spaniards," 1613. One of a series of illustrations of Spanish abuses
of Indians. Snark, ArtResource.

beings who had different and unequal relationships to the monarch and to
Christian civilization.

The laws of 1542—drawing on earlier papal proclamations against the
enslavement of Indians and responding in part to the controversy provoked
by Las Casas—were intended to limit the ways in which encomenderos
exploited indigenous labor. Never enforced, these royal decrees were the
homage vice paid to virtue. By the next century, Las Casas's sympathetic account of Indian religion resonated less and less in Spanish America as both
state and church consolidated their authority and more settlers and mesti-
zos moved into and remade what had been indigenous communities. But
Las Casas's indictment of abuse of Indians remained all too relevant. It was
evoked by critics of empire in other European contexts (Las Casas's work
was translated into English in 1583) as well as in Spain.

No decision had been made in Madrid or Seville to occupy or exploit
"the Americas." The conquistadors had raised their own troops, and not too
many of them. For sailors, settlers, and officials overseas, the empire offered
opportunities. For the monarchy, empire provided a means to build insti-

tutions of state overseas that could not be put in place at home. But over time, the incorporation of millions of new people—Asian, African, American—into an empire opened debates over whether such people could be treated as an inferior category, available for exploitation, and whether they were part of an imperial society, built on hierarchy, monarchy, and Christian universalism.

Companies, Planters, Settlers, and the State: The Making of the British Empire

It is only by reading history backward that the story of the British empire appears as the inevitable triumph of a British way of making empire or doing capitalism. In the sixteenth century, the British Crown had little desire to devote resources to overseas ventures. Merchants were getting goods into and out of England across spaces that others controlled—via Venice, the eastern Mediterranean, and central Asia, for instance. The efforts of publicists like Hakluyt and Purchas to popularize trade and proselytizing did not resonate very far. The notion of "British" meant little before the Union with Scotland in 1707 and the word "empire" in the sixteenth and seventeenth centuries referred to England being "entire of itself," independent of any superior authority.

But empire-building, once others were doing it, was a game that had to be played and had to be won—at the risk of losing control over supply routes. That England would do well at this was not clear for a long time: in 1588 the Spanish Armada came close to defeating the British navy. A century later the British monarchy was in such trouble—divided between Protestant and Catholic factions—that the Dutch were able to intervene successfully on the side of the Protestant claimant to the throne, William of Orange. And Catholic France remained a serious rival: it was the most populous monarchy in Europe, and its kings exercised strong patrimonial power over a large territory, secured by allotting (or selling) offices to regional aristocrats and aspiring elites. A menace across the Channel, France was also looking to establish colonies of trade and settlement in North America, plantation colonies in the Caribbean, and outposts in India.

Actors with diverse intentions made the British empire. English pirates raided Portuguese and Spanish vessels, sometimes with the acquiescence of the Crown, always out for themselves. Traders ventured forth on their own but could only get so far without running into restrictive policies of other empires. To examine Britain's imperial trajectory, we will look at contiguous empire in the British isles, the role of private companies, colonies of settlement, and plantation colonies.

The incorporation of the Scottish kingdom (a process culminating in 1707) entailed giving Scottish elites a stake in the British system. Rebellious lower classes in Scotland made Scottish lords all the more willing to cooperate with the British monarchy. The process might not have worked so well had the empire overseas not offered many Scots—and not just the upper classes—roles and profits superior to those they enjoyed at home. For a time, King James I of England/James VI of Scotland considered styling himself "emperor of the whole island of Britain," but he could not unify English and Scottish law, English and Scottish churches, or English and Scottish versions of their own histories—or admit the plurality of his realm. So he contented himself with being a king of two kingdoms, three with the addition of Wales.

Wales was a lower-key version of the Scottish pattern, but Catholic Ireland was different, forced to become a more fully subordinated polity. English—Protestant—magnates founded what they called "plantations" in Ireland, bringing Protestant settlers from England, Wales, or Scotland to become tenants on these large parcels. The government and Protestant elite argued that these plantations would not only enhance agricultural production beyond the capacities of the backward Irish but civilize them as Roman colonization had civilized the Britons. One scheme from 1585 entailed 35 English landlords and 20,000 settlers; as many as 100,000 people moved across the Irish Sea by 1641. Plantations, as the word was used here, recalls the "colonies" of the Roman empire: the implanting of people from one place in another, ignoring or subordinating the claims of people who might see such space as their own.

In Ireland, British elites worked out a politics of difference and subordination. Putting English or Scottish settlers on the land implied that Ireland's Catholics had no genuine rights or attachment to land, like the "nomads" that so many empires scorned. Meanwhile, Catholicism in Ireland—"popery" as it was called—met with harsh discrimination. "Otherness" to Britain began across the Irish Sea, and while English institutions were to some extent replicated in Ireland, the influential ones—the Irish Parliament notably—were reserved for Protestants. Irish Catholics became part of a British empire, an available source of labor at times, a font of disorder at others. The government feared Irish rebels might conspire with Catholic France, and only in the nineteenth century were Irish soldiers officially allowed in the British army, although many had in fact served earlier. They eventually became a mainstay of British military power in India.

Chartered companies provided a second mode of colonization. What was considered in the nineteenth century the jewel in the British Crown, India, did not belong to the Crown until 1858. India was colonized by a private company, the British East India Company (EIC). Founded in 1599, it followed in the footsteps of the Levant Company (1581), which had moved into the eastern Mediterranean trade after it became clear that Spain and Portugal could not dominate commerce in the Mediterranean region. The Levant Company and English officials negotiated commercial agreements with the Ottoman empire and willingly supplied the Ottomans with tin and lead for use in artillery. This was not quite the Protestant-Muslim alliance against the Catholic Habsburgs that the queen and the sultan briefly discussed, but it was certainly a commercial venture with overtones of interempire connection. In 1600 the EIC was granted a charter by Queen Elizabeth I, giving it a monopoly on English trade east of the Cape of Good Hope. Its initial 125 shareholders set out to compete with the Dutch VOC, and while they could not match their power and networks in southeast Asia, they did well in India.

There they encountered another empire, much more populous than even the Ottoman. The Mughals, descendants of Tamerlane's last Mongol empire, had imposed a layer of Islamic authority and Persian-influenced elite culture over a religiously diverse, but primarily Hindu, population. Following Mongol patterns, Mughal emperors left both indigenous religious leaders and local potentates considerable scope. The subcontinent had experienced many layers of empire-building before the Mughals, and particularly in the south older patterns persisted. The possibility of serving imperial rulers had made the fortunes and extended the long-distance connections of certain families. The Mughal empire was still in formation when Europeans first appeared in the Indian Ocean; it had taken over Gujarat, in western India, in the early 1570s, Bengal a few years later (see map 6.2).

The Mughals were above all a land empire, and given the large and well-connected population over which they presided, this source of revenue was quite ample. They provided roads, credit and banking facilities, and security over a large area. For the most part, the Mughal emperors were content to let enterprising traders, such as Gujaratis, run their operations, just as the Ottoman sultans of this era were content to see commercial activities in the hands of Armenians, Greeks, Jews, and other non-Muslim merchants. But such groups and individuals could shift allegiances when a new protector appeared on the scene.

The EIC—with its direct links to an important European market—had something to offer Mughal emperors and regional leaders, and Indian elites' contingent accommodation was indispensable to the company's operations. For over a century, the company did not challenge Mughal sovereignty. The EIC's early, modest success came from its connections to Indian producers and traders and to Indian sources of credit. Its most important exports from India included silk, indigo, saltpeter, and tea, as well as cotton textiles—one of the great successes of Indian industrial production of the era. The EIC benefited from a monopoly on English trade to India—sanctioned by the British government at first, maintained by buying out rivals later on—and it tried to get exclusive rights to trade at its key ports from the Mughal emperor.

At the end of the seventeenth century, the EIC was still primarily a trading company—and an increasingly successful model of the joint stock company and of long-distance enterprise. From their fortified posts at Calcutta, Madras, and Bombay, EIC agents were aware that the Mughal empire was losing its grip on its own subordinate polities. The EIC chose its allies among those polities, kept providing the Mughal emperor with revenue, and made its deals.

Indians served the company directly as scribes and accountants, and indirectly through their own commercial networks within India and beyond—to Africa, Arabia, Persia, Russia, China, and southeast Asia. Although Indian elites bought English products, England—and Europe generally—had less to offer to Asia than Asia to Europe, so American silver, as elsewhere in Asia, completed the commercial circle. The EIC's main worry was that someone—especially the French—would cut in on this arrangement, as the EIC had cut in on the Dutch.

For the "company men," the EIC's insertion of itself into Asian trading networks proved very lucrative, and large profits were repatriated. Scots were prominent among EIC agents, and their success helped reconcile many Scottish families to the benefits of British empire. The men who ran the company's operations did not try to make India "British" as the conquistadors and viceroys made parts of the Americas Spanish. It was only in the late eighteenth century, as company practices gradually came to resemble the coercive, administrative, and financial processes exercised by empires elsewhere, that the EIC's policies toward indigenous populations would become an issue for the king and parliament in England (chapter 8).

The company model of empire—with government charters defining monopolies and legitimizing private exercise of governmental functions but with capital markets footing much of the bill—was used by the British in other parts of the world. The Royal Africa Company (established 1663) developed an infrastructure of oceangoing ships, "factories" in Africa, and finance that supplied slaves to British colonies in the Caribbean. But the success of private interlopers in expanding trade and driving down prices led the Crown to conclude that the interests of the plantation system as a whole would be better served by allowing competition in supplying slaves.

The Virginia Company (1606) provided the capital and initiative to launch another type of colonization—settlement in North America. Many of its well-born investors thought of themselves as creating a "commonwealth" in the New World—a virtuous political community, reflecting more the values of republican Rome than the greed and corruption of the later Roman empire. That such a model could be implemented under the limitations of the royal charter and amidst the deprivation and conflict of Virginia's early years was not evident. Initially, the Crown had granted the company a limited *dominium*—the right to possess territory—rather than *imperium*—the right to rule, a notion that English jurists took from Roman law. Only with time, experience, and confrontation with indigenous peoples would the law and practice of settlement evolve toward imperium.

The British monarchy, then, did not so much initiate the settlement of North America as try to control a process animated by companies, individuals, and dissenting religious organizations. But the role of the state was formative in two respects. First, the Crown's involvement provided a legal argument against Spanish assertions that the pope's dispositions of the 1490s had given the Spanish monarch possession of all land along the western Atlantic. British jurists denied that such land had been the pope's to give away, and claimed that only *effective* possession by a civilized state created imperium, an argument that both built on and encouraged the exercise of power over people and land in North America. Second, the diplomatic and military forces of the state were potentially available to give substance to such claims. The wars between England and France (sometimes allied with Spain) throughout the eighteenth century were in part fought about and on these overseas "possessions."

The North American "plantations," dependent as they were on private finance, were slow to develop and vulnerable. They were very slow to show anything like a profit. In the case of Virginia this only came after the company's demise in 1625, and thanks to tobacco, indentured servitude, and slavery—of dubious connection to the idea of "commonwealth" of the colony's founders. But migration to British North America was steady and on a larger scale than that from Spain to Spanish America. Some eighty years after the initial voyages, about 250,000 people of European origin were living in British North America, compared to 150,000—spread over a vastly larger area—at a similar period after the early voyages from Spain. Spain went much further, however, in recognizing the place of indigenous populations *within* the Spanish empire.

Unlike the dramatic assault of conquistadors on the Aztec and Inca empires, the process of colonization in North America, where Indian societies were more decentralized, was more "infiltration" than "invasion," as one historian puts it. The early settlers were of two minds about the societies they were encountering. The Virginia settlers could recognize in Powhatan, leader of the large and powerful Indian confederation called by the same name, an emperor who insisted that many communities acknowledge his superior authority. Other Indians were seen, like the Irish, as nomads not

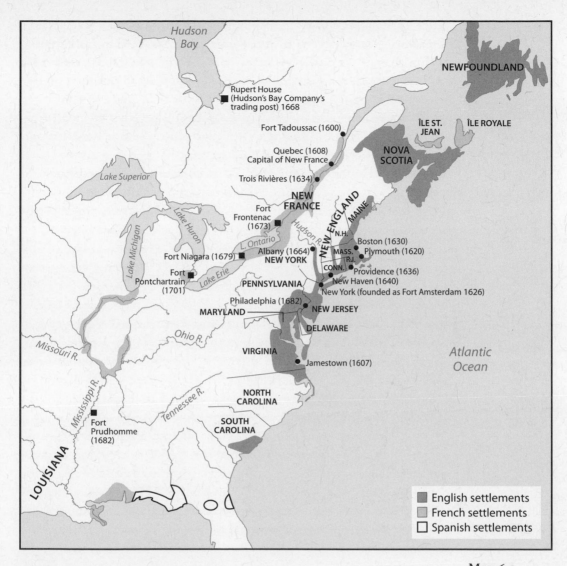

Map 6.3
Settling
North America,
seventeenth
century.

Within the map:

Hudson Bay

NEWFOUNDLAND

Rupert House
(Hudson's Bay Company's
trading post) 1668

Fort Tadoussac (1600)

ÎLE ST. JEAN

ÎLE ROYALE

Quebec (1608)
Capital of New France

NOVA SCOTIA

Trois Rivières (1634)

Lake Superior

NEW FRANCE

NEW ENGLAND

MAINE

Fort
Frontenac
(1673)

Lake Huron

Hudson R.

L. Ontario

N.H.

Fort Niagara (1679)

Lake Michigan

Albany (1664)

Boston (1630)

MASS.

Plymouth (1620)

NEW YORK

R.I.

Lake Erie

CONN.

Providence (1636)

Fort
Pontchartrain
(1701)

New Haven (1640)

PENNSYLVANIA

New York (founded as Fort Amsterdam 1626)

Philadelphia (1682)

NEW JERSEY

MARYLAND

DELAWARE

Ohio R.

Missouri R.

VIRGINIA

Jamestown (1607)

Atlantic
Ocean

Mississippi R.

Tennessee R.

NORTH
CAROLINA

Fort
Prudhomme
(1682)

SOUTH
CAROLINA

LOUISIANA

■ English settlements
▒ French settlements
□ Spanish settlements

truly settled on the land, described by some settlers as "a hidious and disolate wildernes, full of wild beasts and wild men"—and hence up for grabs by those whose fences and farms demonstrated possession.

But in practice, settlers for many years needed Indians as trading partners and lacked the strength to push them away. Some Indian communities regarded their relationship with settlers as reciprocal rather than subordinate. Indians sometimes invoked, albeit without much success, the authority of the English king against settler abuses. Colonial governments came to accept that land had to be purchased from Indians, but under conditions whereby different conceptions of land and pressure from colonists made the market less than "free." The colonists had to adapt to new physical and social geographies and economic possibilities, from slave-based rice and tobacco plantations of South Carolina and Virginia, to grain farming and fishing in the northeast, to the inland fur trade. Without tacit understandings and trade relations with Indian farmers, trappers, and hunters, the fledgling settlements might not have taken root.

By the time the mainland colonies were getting a toehold, Britain was acquiring islands in the Caribbean, the prize being Jamaica, obtained from the Spanish in 1655. Initially bases for harassing the Spanish and other rivals, the islands were transformed by the advent of sugar cultivation and the massive importation of African slaves. If in 1650 most settlers on both continent and islands were white, by 1700 the white-black ratio was 7.5–1 on the mainland, 1–3.6 in the West Indies. The plantation islands were a very different kind of colony—a topic to which we will return.

What kind of state could preside over this matrix of settlers, sugar planters, companies, traders, Indians, slaves, and pirates, of Englishmen, Scots, Welsh, and Irish, living in long-cherished parishes or new homes? It was a state that had developed considerable means of exercising power—precisely because it had to do so over large spaces and against serious rivals. And because of its complex makeup, the state faced not just the usual empire problem of governing different people differently but also the task of governing people who thought they were the same but lived in different places.

Empire gave the British polity both the means and the necessity to strengthen itself into what John Brewer calls a "fiscal-military" state, focused on war and on the protection of sea routes, with a high level of taxation and strong banking institutions adapted to financing large-scale expenditures, both public and private. In the eighteenth century, between 75 and 85 percent of annual government expenditures went to the military or debt service to pay off past wars. Britain developed a fiscal administration and a judiciary capable of enforcing laws, particularly those concerning property.

The fiscal-military state neither needed nor desired to participate as directly in overseas trade as did the Portuguese monarchy, and it was not so entwined with the EIC as the Netherlands were with the VOC. Instead, the state combined its support for trade and settlement—military, legal, diplomatic—with the regulatory authority of Parliament to ensure that diverse elements of the imperial economy would connect through Britain itself. The Navigation Acts of the 1650s and 1660s forbade the importation into Britain of Asian, African, or American goods in foreign ships, so that British firms would dominate the re-export business and connect the growing Atlantic economy with trade across the Baltic and North Sea regions to the European continent. Within Britain, the state moved away from monopolies and toward allowing competition. The state thus inserted itself into global commercial circuits, enhancing linkages of domestic and overseas economies and strengthening its own fiscal well-being. The Dutch state lacked the coercive and regulatory power to do likewise, and this helps explain why the connections between state and company in the Netherlands did not produce a similar expansion of imperial authority.

Like the Spanish monarchy in the Americas, the English government was anxious to establish an institutional apparatus that was both the sign and substance of state power—governors, courts, and a Board of Trade and Plantations to oversee transatlantic trade. Kings asserted royal prerogative over colonial administration, as if colonies were part of the king's composite monarchy of diverse dominions.

Such a state had much to offer to merchants and settlers, but it also regulated and taxed them. And the question of how much sovereignty would rest in the hands of which people was posed not just in London but in parts of the empire. Out of the "English" revolutions of the 1640s and 1680s, the propertied classes carved themselves spaces of significant power—in a Parliament that checked royal will, in local government run by propertied electors, and in a judicial system that put subjects before a jury of their peers. The charters and interpretations emerging in these years became a virtual English "constitution"—not one document but many, underpinned by belief in fundamental and shared law. This law was increasingly seen as emanating from the body politic itself, not as being given by the king.

The growing population of settlers abroad saw no reason why the "rights of Englishmen" should not apply to them: they took with them across the sea assumptions about the security of property and participation in governance. London both wanted and contested the civic engagement of overseas settlers. It insisted that colonies pay the costs of their own administration—including the salaries of administrators from Great Britain—but raising revenue gave the colonies experience in government. When Britain demanded more from its empire, colonists' sense of their place within the layers of sovereignty was affronted. In the 1680s, the king tried to tighten control over North American as well as West Indian colonies, installing governors with fewer links to local landowners. He thereby provoked colonial support for the Glorious Revolution of 1688–89 back at home. When Parliament kept insisting on its right to set taxes, settlers tried to claim that they were subjects of the king, not of Parliament, citing royal charters and their lack of parliamentary representation. Even as Britain was defining itself through its empire, issues of rights and political participation across this uneven space were producing tensions that would one day explode.

The place of slaves in empire was, for a time, all too clear. That of Indians was less obvious. There was no British equivalent of the República de los Indios, whatever the latter's shortcomings. Indians were still unsubdued—and valuable trading partners—along the edges of the mainland colonies;

within them, Indians could claim the protection of the king. When French and Spanish empires were active on the North American continent, Indian polities were sought as valuable allies and could play empires off against each other. Britain's defeat of its rivals in the mid-eighteenth century would make things harder for Indians, American independence even more so, a topic we take up in chapters 8 and 9.

Great Britain allowed more room for autonomy of colonies than did seventeenth-century France, and Britain's domestic and imperial economies interacted more dynamically than those of France, Portugal, or Spain. By the end of the seventeenth century, the British had developed a range of different ways of interacting with, governing, and exploiting indigenous populations, settlers, and slaves. And, without intending to do so, British leaders had created an empire-wide sphere in which they could be challenged.

The Slave Trade, Slavery, and Empire

For Britain, France, and in parts of the Portuguese and Spanish empires, it was slavery that made empire pay and empire that made slavery possible. Northeastern Brazil pioneered the sugar plantation on a massive scale, but Britain and France became increasingly dynamic participants in the sugar economy. Total imports of people to the Americas from Africa had been below 1,000 per year in 1500, but passed 10,000 per year in 1600 and stayed over 60,000 for most of the 1700s. The slave trade eclipsed all other forms of transatlantic migration: in the sixteenth century, about 25 percent of people who crossed the ocean were slaves, in the seventeenth century 60 percent, in the eighteenth century over 75 percent. The British Caribbean, especially Jamaica, was a prime destination, as were the islands of the French Caribbean, Saint Domingue most notoriously. Because mortality was horrendous, the planters' appetite for slaves was never-ending. In the case of Britain, the sugar colonies made the entire Atlantic enterprise work. The growing number of laborers devoted to cane created a demand for provisions that stimulated the food-exporting economy of New England in the late seventeenth century. Meanwhile, sugar mixed with tea from China and India began to provide a significant portion of the calories of industrial workers in England, whose products went to North America and the Caribbean, as well as to markets beyond the empire, including Africa.

Because empire was a mobile political form, it created demands for labor where no potential laborers lived or wanted to go. Enslavement is a process of displacement—of alienating a person from his or her social roots. Alienation and displacement made slaves useful as soldiers and high officials, as well as ordinary servants, in some empires that we have examined and as units of labor in others, from Greece and Rome onward and in a variety of circumstances in Africa and Asia as well. But the linkages formed by imperial expansion—particularly into the ecologically rich and demographically fragile regions of the American tropics—took slavery to an unprecedented scale. Imperial power was crucial to the creation of slave labor systems as well as to their maintenance; organized force was needed to deter or defeat slave rebellions and to protect land, slaves, processing machinery, and ships from other empires or pirates. The sugar islands of the Caribbean were subject to all these threats.

In chapter 8 we will consider the relationship of empire and slavery to capitalist development. Here we explore the implications of the empire-slavery nexus beyond the border of the maritime empires—in Africa. Slavery and the slave trade existed in Africa prior to the fifteenth and sixteenth centuries, but not on the scale they reached once the transatlantic connection developed. For social and geographic reasons, what Albert Hirschman calls the "exit option" was relatively open to people in much of Africa. Some places offered the resources to sustain prosperous societies, but around them were regions with resources adequate for survival, and kinship structures in Africa made mobility a collective process. A would-be king who tried to extract too much from his own people ran into the danger that subjects would flee or use their united strength to resist subordination. Power depended on controlling and exploiting people external to one's own society and on attracting followers detached from their own group or coercing outsiders into service.

We arrive at a tragic intertwining of histories. Europeans were determined to put their new lands to work, and labor had to come from somewhere else. In parts of Africa, kings could gain resources (guns, metals, cloth and other goods with redistributive potential) by seizing someone else's human assets. Raiding slaves from another polity and selling them to an outside buyer externalized the problem of supervision as well as recruitment. Over time, the overseas outlet for captives gave advantages to the most militarized of African states—Asante, Dahomey, Oyo, Benin—and produced more efficient slave-trading mechanisms. Militarization of some kingdoms put neighbors that did not follow suit in jeopardy. The chance to sell war captives propelled a vast system of slave catching and slave marketing. The African slave trade depended on acts of coercion initially committed in Africa, outside the Atlantic imperial system, but it was driven by that system's appetite for labor, by its transoceanic trading mechanisms, and by the capacity of empire-states to build regimes capable of disciplining a huge labor force, uprooted and brought into colonial societies.

Connections, Territories, Empires

The world became more interconnected in the sixteenth century, but not because anyone set out to make it that way. Under Portuguese, Spanish, Dutch, French, and British auspices, state power was used not just to gain access to new goods and new lands of settlement but to prevent others from doing so. None of the imperial regimes could maintain the monopolies they sought, but the fact that they tried put pressure on others to build overseas empires, too. Nor could any empire—or European empires in general, if one wants to impose a retrospective unity on them—actually make the world its frame of reference. The Ottoman and Chinese empires were too powerful to become enmeshed in a European web; the interior of Africa was inaccessible. European maritime empires depended on links to commercial networks, in Africa as well as Asia, that Europeans did not control or even know very much about. The world in the eighteenth century was still multipolar.

We should be careful about making the sixteenth century into an avatar of "globalization." Instead, thinking about a history of *connections* allows us to focus on the changes specific to this time. From the perspective of empire, we will first review reconfigurations of power and commerce around the world, then look at changes and limits on changes in the nature of sovereignty.

In the western part of the former Roman empire, the quest to revive imperial hegemony led each aspiring power to compete for resources within Europe and beyond the seas. European empires interacted, sometimes violently, with a wide range of polities across the world, but they did so in the context of their rivalry with each other. Not all empires were in this game. The Ottoman and Chinese empires could opt out and continue, for a long time, to prosper.

Competing empires had to devise new repertoires of power. Innovations in shipbuilding, navigation, and armament were crucial tools. Trading enclaves, company monopolies, plantations, and colonies of settlement became staples of overseas empires. European empire-builders could be extremely destructive—with effects beyond their intentions. Even so, indigenous people sometimes made their compromises, played off invading empires against each other, took trading opportunities to gain new tools and crops, and at times found something in the invaders' religious institutions and social practices to meld with their own.

The world did become more connected in this period. The operations of empires extended ties, visible in the length of trade routes (Amsterdam to Batavia, for example) and tightened market relations such that mining silver on one continent become critical to the money system on another.

Expanded imperial circuits also presented opportunities to trading communities (Greeks, Armenians, Jews, Arabs, Gujaratis) who operated along the lines and in the interstices of power. Trade networks did more than carry commodities around the world. They carried genes—of people, crops, and animals, not to mention diseases, from plague to syphilis and smallpox. Commercial connections also carried ideas and social practices. Not only Christianity but also Islam, which had earlier crossed the Indian Ocean, moved faster with the growth of exchange. The annual pilgrimage of Muslims to Mecca as well as networks of scholars continued to move people across spaces. Despite the monopolistic goals and practices of maritime empires, they could not control the circuits or the practices they fostered, and where networks overlapped, they were not woven into a single pattern of cultural and material connections.

One might in retrospect say that it was precisely the vulnerability of western European empires—their deadly competition—that drove them to improve their military and administrative capacities, and that the Ottoman and Chinese in the long run suffered from their earlier success. No one in the early eighteenth century knew that. What they did know was that they lived in a world of empires, and each—from China to Portugal—was striving to build and maintain power with the material and imaginative means at its disposal.

In these circumstances, empires, as always, had to work with intermediaries, and they had to play the politics of difference, to juggle incorporation and differentiation. In Asia, European empires were obliged, whether they liked it or not, to interact with a variety of local powers, from Mughal emperors to local traders, producers, and creditors. That they sometimes destroyed entire communities—as the Dutch did in trying to secure a monopoly of spices—did not necessarily make the system more effective. The costs of coercion were high. The intended and unintended destructiveness of colonization in the Americas confronted Spanish rulers with a labor deficit, but empire space offered solutions to such self-created problems, too—the importation of yet another kind of labor force, African slaves in this instance, from one continent to another.

Had any aspiring power—from Portugal to England to the Mughals—tried to play by the rules of "free" markets, thinking they could avoid the cost and burdens of running an empire, they would promptly have been marginalized or eliminated from the scene. Telling a story of "economic development" or "the rise of the west" cannot, therefore, get us very far.

Nor do theories of "sovereignty" that treat the state abstractly, without focusing on how states, as they actually existed, constrained each other into mobilizing the resources of diverse populations and territories. Some scholars distinguish neatly between a premodern politics that is not about territory but personal allegiance to a monarch (perhaps through a hierarchy of lords and magnates) from one in which the polity is defined as a bounded territory. The period we are discussing in this chapter is a prime candidate for such a transition. But rather than divide the world into epochs we should recognize that alternative concepts of territoriality and sovereign power coexisted and were debated and struggled over. We should not mistake a political actor's claim to territory or a political thinker's assertion of a territorial principle for a definition of an era or for a characterization of a transition in political practices.

The most dramatic changes from the sixteenth to the eighteenth century were not in the depth of rulers' control over a given territory but in the extent of space over which power was exercised. In the Americas, the kings of Portugal and Spain built an apparatus of direct monarchical control over territory and trade that they could not erect at home. The fiscal-military state that developed in England by the early eighteenth century was both motivated and enabled by the state's ventures overseas. English rivalries with Spanish, Dutch, and French empires from the Atlantic to the Indian Ocean meant that a great deal of what the state had to do (witness the Navigation Acts) was to ensure that England would be at the center of dispersed economic processes, from sea routes all over the world to sugar plantations in the Americas to trading outposts in India. The French state, under Louis XIV, came as close as any to producing a tightly bound regime at home, thanks in part to the relatively compact area—now called the "hexagon"—that the monarchy tried to rule. Yet France, too, was acting like an empire among empires, had its overseas adventures and conflicts, was playing dynastic politics with its neighbors and was dependent on patrimonial relations with regional elites, and hence less absolute than the designation "absolutist monarchy" suggests.

European states had to reconfigure themselves in the context of global empire, but one can easily exaggerate the extent of change within Europe itself. The Treaty of Westphalia (1648) is often heralded as the beginning of a new regime, signaling the acceptance by major European powers of the principle of territorial sovereignty, mutually recognized, of each state. But the treaty was less innovative and less far-reaching. At Westphalia, European powers (the Holy Roman Emperor, the princes of that realm, the kings of France and Sweden) attempted to end a prolonged period of religious and dynastic conflict—known as the Thirty Years' War in Germany or the Eighty Years' War between Habsburg Spain and the Netherlands. The Dutch got their independence—but they were already inventing a different kind of sovereignty in the East Indies. The treaty recognized the sovereignty of some three hundred princes on territories under the Holy Roman Empire, but the empire remained an overarching political entity, somewhere between a confederation and an empire for another 158 years. Sweden and France were assigned new territories, not necessarily speaking the same language or with any loyalty to a state.

The signatories to the treaty were neither very national nor neatly bounded; they pursued and were subjected to imperial ambitions for the next three centuries. A variety of different and nonequivalent forms of state persisted long after 1648: strong monarchies like those of France and Spain, a Dutch merchant republic, a Polish aristocratic republic, a Swiss confederation, Italian merchant republics. Europe kept its popes, emperors, kings, dukes, counts, bishops, city administrations, and landholding lords. Emperors interacted with each other and fought over or passed around component parts of their domains as they had before. France was generally England's rival, but sometimes its ally against the United Provinces. Dutch support helped one faction to oust another in an English civil war in 1688–89. A new dynastic combination emerged in 1700 (despite British attempts to prevent it), when Bourbons, springing from the lineage of the kings of France, became the kings of Spain.

The Treaty of Westphalia was supposed to promote religious tolerance among Catholics, Lutherans, and Calvinists and limit the ability of princes, by their own conversion, to try to change the religious affiliations of "their" territories. But religious strife did not cease and the territorial principle of sovereignty was neither new in 1648 nor respected afterward. The layered sovereignty of emperor over king over prince was still a viable European option in the nineteenth century and new forms of layered sovereignty, as we shall see, were invented in the twentieth. The idea of "Westphalian sovereignty"—a world of bounded and unitary states interacting with other equivalent states—has more to do with 1948 than 1648 (chapter 13).

The interactions among unequal, composite, and unstable empires did push innovations in diplomacy and law. As we have seen (chapter 5), the Ottomans had offered communities of foreigners the right to be governed by their own rules and had insisted on protection of ambassadors and embassies in other countries. As the VOC and EIC squared off against each other, Hugo Grotius produced his treatise, "Freedom of the Seas" (1609), borrowing from maritime traditions—the sea as an open highway—of the Indian Ocean. But the sea was less free in the seventeenth century than it had been in the fifteenth. Meanwhile, faced with the capacity of Mughal sovereigns to obstruct or enhance their commercial operations, Europeans broke canon law rules against making treaties with non-Christian powers and recognized the legitimacy of their negotiating partners. These innovations in what would later become known as "international law" took place at the interfaces between empires and their various legal traditions—Roman, Christian, Ottoman, Muslim, Mughal. Diplomacy and law were not focused on regulating relationships among equivalent states but gave legitimacy and order to a highly unequal world.

If empire always implied governing different people differently, the empires of the Americas brought out explicit debates about what a politics of difference should be. Catholic empire, Las Casas insisted, included indigenous Americans, whose civilizational status deserved recognition even as they were the objects of conversion. American colonists relied on a politics of sameness—insisting that their geographical displacement did not diminish their rights as Englishmen. Neither argument gave much thought to slaves except as units of labor, but most empires gave lip service, at least, to a minimal code of conduct for slave owners if they wanted to be considered respectable members of the social order. The institutions of empire gave some subordinated peoples a small opportunity to demand protection from the Crown against local authorities and landowners, hardly enough to save them from the greed and brutality of elites. But not all imperial elites thought that conquered or enslaved people were there to be humiliated and exploited at will; the relationship of incorporation and differentiation was not necessarily going to remain the same.

The extension of empires around the world from the fifteenth to the seventeenth centuries was not a single-minded conquest by a securely organized Europe but rather a multifaceted transformation. Societies and polities were disrupted, reconfigured, and created as rulers extended power across space, sought intermediaries, and manipulated hierarchies. Along the way, a few people, like Bartolomé de las Casas, paused to ask, what have we wrought?

BEYOND THE STEPPE

Empire-Building in Russia and China

A s rulers in Europe reached around their neighbors' territories, over local aristocracies, and outside the continent for resources, two empires—one youthful, one ancient—sought to extend command over the great spaces of Eurasia. From Moscow—a spreading center of imperial power since the fifteenth century—Russian explorers traveled east beyond the Volga and eventually ran up against another empire that was also on the move—in the opposite direction. China, reunited in the seventeenth century by the Qing dynasty, pushed west and north into Siberia. Between the two empires were Mongol and other nomadic tribes, who competed with each other for grazing routes, trade monopolies with sedentary neighbors, and super-tribal leadership (chapter 4).

7

On land, as at sea, imperial competitions transfigured the geography and politics of empire. While Spain and Britain contested imperial control of oceans, Russia under the Romanovs and China under the Qing swallowed up their nomadic challengers and closed up the space for empire-making in the center of Eurasia. This chapter looks at Russian empire, from the ninth century through the reign of Peter the Great, and at China after the fall of the Yuan dynasty and into the eighteenth century. We will focus on how Russian and Chinese rulers mixed new strategies into their repertoires of rule, how they managed their intermediaries, and how each turned difference into an imperial asset. We conclude with the encounter of three empires—Mongol, Chinese, Russian—with each other in central Eurasia and the highlands of Tibet.

Russia's Eurasian Empire

The Rus' Way

Compared with China, Russia was an upstart state and an improbable one. A Russian polity took shape during the fourteenth and fifteenth centuries in an area without a name that no great power cared very much about. Just as an off-center position near the Mediterranean had sheltered Roman expansion, distance from the principal sites of world politics benefited Russia's princely clans as they maneuvered for small-scale advantages in woodlands between the Dnieper and Volga rivers. On their way to power, ambitious princes were able to draw on strategies used by several empires. By combining elements of Turkic, Byzantine, and Mongol statecraft, Russia's leaders were able to jump-start an empire on a space of forests, marshes, and scattered, roving population.

Russia got its name and some attributes of its imperial culture from warrior princes who founded a state in Kiev in the ninth century. While the Vikings were busy raiding Europe's seacoasts, Rus' boatmen took an easterly way to fortune. Circumventing warring states and competing lords in central Europe, the Rus' pioneered new routes from the Baltic ports down the Volga to the Black Sea and Byzantium and back up the Dnieper River. On their expeditions, the Rus' encountered Turkic peoples, with technologies useful to an aggressive and mobile clan. The payoff came when the Rus' reached the Byzantine empire—with its wealth, markets, and access to trans-Eurasian commerce.

The forested regions traversed by the Rus' provided them with exportable commodities—amber, furs, honey, wax, lumber, and pitch—and exportable people—Slavs, who had been captured or purchased and sold as slaves since ancient times. By 900, the Rus' had grown rich on raiding, trading, and controlling transport. In Kiev, their capital, Rus' princes turned themselves into a Eurasian-style ruling dynasty, distinct from the Slavic peasants in the surrounding area and the artisans who flocked to the prosperous city on the Dnieper River.

The Rus' princes became known as the Riurikids, the sons of Riurik. Their founding legend, recorded by Christian chroniclers centuries later, explained how outsiders became rulers: "Riurik and his brothers were invited by the Slavic tribes to rule their land and to bring peace among them." The great leader from a distant place who is able to make and keep the peace became an enduring element of imperial imagination in the area. Like Turkic khaqans (chapter 4), Rus' princes practiced lateral succession—from brother to brother—but, in theory, they mitigated fratricidal struggles by giving each brother a principality to rule while waiting in line for Kiev, the jewel in their crown. Each prince had his armed followers. With these gangs of dependent protectors, the princes rotated—with considerable violence against each other—among the principalities.

As the Rus' settled into ruling Kiev, they turned to a familiar strategy to consolidate their power—establishing a state religion. At first, the Rus', who like the Slavs around them were polytheists, incorporated and synthesized

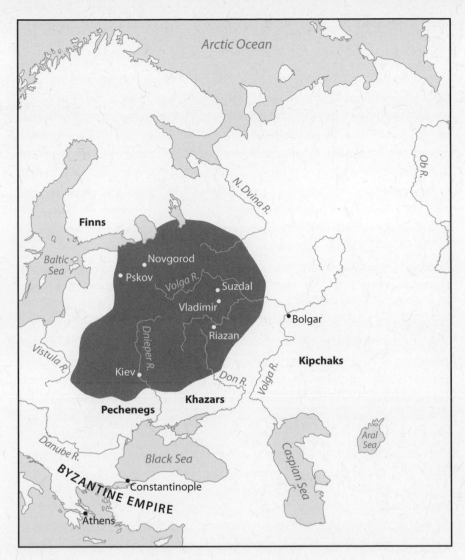

Map 7.1
Kievan Rus'
c. 1015.

various deities, much as the early Romans had done. The greatest of the Rus' leaders, Vladimir (980–1015), set up an ample pantheon of Norse, Finnish, Slavic, and Iranian gods on a hill in Kiev. Perhaps influenced by contacts in Constantinople, Vladimir later turned toward monotheism and had to make a choice. Byzantium, with its spectacular rituals and architecture, set a shining example of imperial power enhanced by eastern Christianity. Judaism, the faith adopted by Khazar nomads north of the Black Sea, and Islam were also candidates, as was the Latin Christianity of Italian merchants.

Russian chronicles tell the story of Vladimir's decision. Judaism was rejected as the religion of a defeated people who had lost their state; Islam was eliminated because of its prohibition on alcohol. The chronicle says "drink is the joy of the Russian people." Monogamous Christianity posed another problem, for Vladimir had more than one wife and many concubines. Reasons of state must have prevailed, for Vladimir gave them up when he converted to eastern Christianity and promptly married the sister of the Byzantine emperor. Or perhaps alcohol trumped sex.

Vladimir welcomed Byzantine clergy, who baptized the people of Kiev in the Dnieper River in 988. A metropolitan was sent from Constantinople to manage church affairs. Byzantine clerics brought with them scriptures translated into Slavic and recorded in an alphabet (Cyrillic) invented for this purpose. In the ninth century, the eastern church had rejected the Roman-style insistence that only some languages—Latin, principally—were worthy of expressing God's word. The choice for a multilingual Christianity fit nicely with Byzantium's imperial ambitions (chapter 3) and later proved useful to the Rus'. Still, as had happened with the Romans, Vladimir's choice did not mean that everyone turned Christian right away. The Slavic population continued to worship their local gods, sometimes rebelled against forced conversion, and produced a variety of synthetic religious practices over many centuries.

Christianity in the Byzantine style transformed the city of Kiev and the cultural repertoire of its rulers. The construction projects of the Rus' princes drew architects, icon painters, blacksmiths, stone cutters, potters, goldsmiths, silversmiths, and tile makers to Kiev. Other towns to the north—Novgorod, Suzdal, Vladimir—built churches and developed distinctive icon-painting styles. Clergy in the Rùs' lands produced saints' lives, chronicles, and sermons—some translated from the Greek, others created by local churchmen.

But religion was not enough to sustain empire-building by the Rus'. First, the rotation system provoked ongoing succession struggles. Rus' princes allied with nomads and raiders from the steppe regions in their efforts to leapfrog over relatives or supersede them. Second, when Constantinople began to falter—sacked by crusaders in 1204—Kiev's economy based on connecting nodes of commerce shrank. Fissures in the dynasty combined with economic downturn meant that when Mongols began their devastating campaigns across Eurasia and into the Riurikids' terrain, the princes were no match for the newcomers. One by one the principalities were defeated; Kiev was besieged and conquered in 1240.

Clients of the Khan

The Mongol conquest marks the end of Kiev's claim to superior authority in the Rus' lands and the beginning of a new imperial dynamic. After the Mongol leader Batu, grandson of Chinggis, took his armies home in 1242 to participate in the selection of a Great Khan (chapter 4), surviving

Riurikids moved back into the principalities and went on warring with their neighbors. Among the strongest of the princes was Alexander Nevskii, leader of the northern cities of Novgorod and Pskov. He drove back Sweden's attempt to take over the trade routes to the Baltic in 1240 and an invasion by Teutonic knights in 1242.

And then, their succession issues settled, the Mongols struck back, this time with a political arrangement that eventually enhanced the Riurikids' statecraft. After Great Khan Ogodei's death, Batu had been allocated his father Jochi's ulus, renamed the Kipchak Khanate and later the Golden Horde (chapter 4). Ruled by Mongols from about 1243 to late fourteenth century, the khanate wielded power over Kiev, Vladimir, the future Moscow, and the Volga and Dnieper routes. Sarai, Batu's capital on the Volga, was well placed to serve the Mongols' interests in controlling trade routes. But the forested areas on the western reaches of the khanate were not that attractive to the Mongols, who relied on delegated officials, often assisted by local authorities, to rule and exploit these regions. Mongol overlordship gave the Riurikids a second chance. Based in their small towns, the princes competed with each other to gain the khan's favor, to collect taxes for him, and to become, as in Kievan times, the Grand Prince over all the rest.

The Mongol khans facilitated the Riurikids' return to rulership with Eurasian-style cachet. The prince of each area journeyed to Sarai to be confirmed in authority over his realm. In return for a pledge of loyalty and gifts of furs, livestock, slaves, and silver, the khan issued a patent of authority called a *iarlyk*. The first iarlyk was granted in 1243 to Prince Iaroslav Vsevolodovich from the town of Vladimir. Subordination before the khan was not a matter of choice; princes who did not perform the proper rituals of subservience were executed. Mongols and Rus' were both committed to dynastic leadership—the Mongol khans were all Chinggisids, the Rus' princes Riurikids. When Riurikids had conflicts among themselves, they called on the khan for arbitration. Once in the khan's service, the princely tax collectors could keep something for themselves. The best deal could be made by marrying into the khan's family.

After the Mongol conquests, the eastern Christian clergy learned quickly where the better part of valor lay. An Orthodox bishop was set up in Sarai. Like the Riurikid princes, Orthodox clergy in the ulus received their authority from the Mongols, enjoyed their protection, and profited from their exemption of churches from taxation. During the thirteenth and fourteenth centuries, Christian priests prayed for the well-being of the khans, and church leaders traveled to Sarai to assist the khans and their families. As Kiev faded in importance, the Orthodox hierarchy in the former Rus' lands relocated, first to Vladimir, then in the early fourteenth century to Moscow.

As empire-builders, princes in the Moscow region worked at the intersection of three imperial pathways. From their ancestors—the Rus'—came the prince's legitimacy as a royal dynasty. From the Byzantines, they acquired a handy version of eastern Christianity, recorded in a Slavic script. And from their Mongol sovereigns, they learned by direct experience how to manage and live off dispersed populations. Moscow emerged as its leaders made choices from these traditions and transformed them, creating a synthetic, resilient, and self-adjusting imperial politics.

Moscow Rules

The Moscow princes are often called Daniilovichi after their most prominent ancestor, Daniil, Alexander Nevskii's son, made prince of Moscow by the Mongol khan in 1263. In 1318, Daniil's son, Iurii, also a loyal servitor of the Mongols and nicknamed Dolgorukii—"Long Arm"—for his formidable tax-collecting skills, was appointed Grand Prince of Vladimir. The family lands of the Daniilovichi were centered on Moscow, with its riverside fortress (*kremlin*). After decades of competitions for superior power among various Riurikids and Mongols, often allied with each other, the Daniilovichi were the most successful of the Riurikids at holding onto their lands, extending their rule over the other principalities, and making their way toward empire.

The first and most essential ingredient of princely survival was keeping the good graces of the Mongol khans by buying them off, fulfilling ritual functions, and contributing troops to campaigns. Second, the Daniilovichi had to have something to tax, and in their area of modest resources and thin population, this meant expansion from their Moscow base, bringing more land, rivers, people, and connections to the north and later down the Volga under their control. Third, the Daniilovichi were good at marriage politics. They managed to marry sons up into the khanate and, at the same time, married their daughters to the sons of rival princes, a patriarchal variant on Mongol exogamy that drew other Riurikids into the orbit of the Daniilovichis' patrimonial command. Finally, the Muscovite princes were lucky in the game of dynastic reproduction. They lived long, which was good for shoring up family power, but they did not produce many sons.

Major Rulers and Their Reigns in Kiev and Muscovy

Grand Prince Vladimir
  (980–1015)
Grand Prince Iaroslav
  (1019–54)
Grand Prince Vladimir
  Monomakh (1113–25)
Alexander Nevskii, Prince of
  Vladimir (1252–1263)
Iurii Daniilovich "Long Arm,"
  Grand Prince of Vladimir
  (1318–22)
Ivan I "Money Bag," Grand
  Prince of Vladimir
  (1327–41)

Grand Princes of Moscow

Dmitri Donskoi (1359–89)
Vasilii I (1389–1425)
Vasilii II (1425–62)
Ivan III "the Great"
  (1462–1505)
Vasilii III (1505–33)
Ivan IV "the Terrible"
  (1533–84)

This meant that the Daniilovichi could break the habit of splitting up their territories among their progeny—the process that had so fragmented the Kievan elite.

With its lock on trade to the east, the Kipchak Khanate was a major target of ambitious empire-makers; this vulnerability played into the prospects of the Muscovites. Especially after Tamerlane razed Sarai in 1395 (chapter 4), the Moscow Grand Princes began to keep taxes for themselves and to demand tribute from their own subordinates. By the mid-fifteenth century, the Kipchak Khanate had split in four—the khanates of Kazan, Astrakhan, Crimea, and the remnant Kipchaks. After 1462, the Kipchak khan did not appoint Moscow's Grand Prince.

Over the next two centuries, while Portuguese, Spanish, Dutch, and British agents were establishing enclaves and settlements across oceans, the Moscow princes expanded their control of peoples and resources over land in all directions, creating a multiethnic and multiconfessional empire. Tribes living in the core area were Finns, Slavs, and mostly pagan before their incorporation into Muscovy. The top of the social hierarchy was mixed in origins, because Mongol families had entered Muscovite service.

Conquest of Novgorod and its hinterlands in 1478 brought more Finnish groups under Moscow's rule. Russians had to contend with other expansionist powers—Livonians, Swedes, and Poles—for this northern region and access to the Baltic. The death of Grand Prince Vitovt of Lithuania in 1430 gave the Muscovites, who had earlier married into the prince's family, a chance to expand to the west. They began a long and difficult drive to incorporate Slavic populations and territories ruled by Lithuania, which, with its Polish partner, continued to obstruct Moscow's way. Ukraine was annexed in the mid-seventeenth century through an agreement with the Cossacks of the area. Westward expansion brought Roman Catholics under Moscow's rule. To the south, where the Black Sea with its connections was the ultimate goal, Ottoman power set limits on Russian growth.

The most promising direction for the Muscovites was east. Russian military men, adventurers, and merchants moved across Siberia in search of furs, compelling native peoples to submit to Moscow's sovereignty, pay tribute, and support troops and fortresses. To the southeast, along the Volga and into central Asia, the goal was controlling trade routes. In the areas claimed by fractious Mongol khanates, Moscow could begin to turn the tables on its former sovereign.

The Grand Prince tried to absorb the Kazan khanate on the Volga by putting his own candidate on the Tatar throne, but when the attempt failed and the khan sought allies against Moscow, Ivan IV (the Terrible) attacked. With the conquest of Kazan in 1552, Muscovy became an even more diverse polity. The elite of the Kazan khanate was Tatar and Muslim, and the

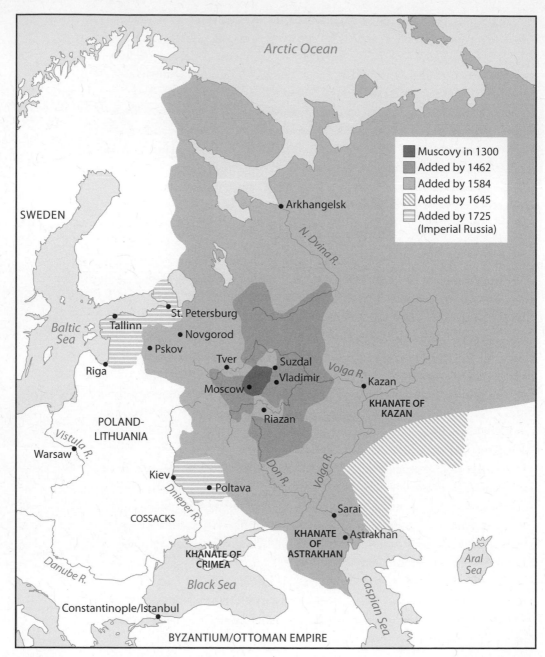

Map 7.2
Expansion
of Russia.

people spoke Turkic, Finno-Ugric, and other languages. Some were Muslims, some pantheists, few were Christians. Ivan continued his successful reversal of steppe politics, making Moscow's candidate the khan of Astrakhan and later annexing it. Moscow now claimed for itself the critical connection between the Volga and the steppe routes to Asia—the place where the Kipchak Khanate had once prospered.

Conquest, tribute, taxation of the agricultural population, and control of trade gave Muscovite princes the makings of an empire, but could they keep control for more than a few generations? Neither of their models—the Mongols with their tanistry and the Riurikids with lateral succession—offered a solution to the violent strife among contenders for power that usually broke up a Eurasian dynasty's domain. Related to this was a more general imperial problem—how to keep elites loyal to the dynastic sovereign. Over time, Russians produced highly effective ways to attach their intermediaries to the ruler.

The Muscovite princes made a crucial innovation by extending the practice of marriage alliances to elites drawn into their expanding polity. New clans were headed by boyars; clans were arranged in a pecking order that determined assignments to offices. A council of boyars collectively advised the ruler. The Grand Princes married women from subordinate clans rather than foreigners; this practice grafted whole families onto the dynasty and gave them a vital interest in it. Only a Daniilovich could be Grand Prince, and the weakest link in this marriage regime was the family's low fertility. What had been an asset in the rotational game became a disadvantage if the Grand Prince produced no son, or a weak-minded or short-lived one—contingencies that could and did put the empire at great risk.

A second tactic was crudely material. As the Kipchak khans had done before them, the Grand Princes declared themselves the masters of all the land of the expanding realm, but they handed out large parts of it to their elites, both old and new, on the condition of loyalty and service. Two patrimonial principles—the ruler's ultimate ownership of all resources and the conditional land grant—underlay Russian government for most of its history. As personal dependents of the Grand Prince, elites who received land and people on it to exploit for their own families were unlikely to form a united aristocracy. In ceremonies, boyars touched their foreheads to the floor before the Grand Prince and called themselves his "slaves." A slave of this kind could become rich through the Grand Prince's allocations as the empire expanded.

If marriage and land grants kept elites attached to Moscow, what did the Grand Princes offer commoners besides defense and exactions? Gradually Orthodox Christianity was turned into an ideology of empire, offering spiritual and ritual connections between the court and commoners. As the khanates weakened and especially after the fall of Constantinople to the Ottomans in 1453, Orthodox clerics turned to Muscovy to bulk up the church. In 1448, a bishop from Riazan was chosen the metropolitan of Moscow without bothering to get the approval of the patriarch in Constantinople. The Orthodox clergy naturally wanted the Muscovites to treat them as well as the Mongols had.

Once Moscow princes seemed to have the upper hand over their former masters, clerics influenced by Byzantium's example tried to make the church a power behind the Moscow throne. This move required transforming imperial symbolism from a Eurasian to a Christian mode and providing Moscow with a more usable past. Churchmen created a satisfying genealogy for Russia's rulers, claiming that the Muscovite Grand Princes received their authority from the Byzantine emperors and that they were descendants of Augustus Caesar. The khans' overlordship, so critical to Moscow's ascent, was turned into the "Tatar yoke."

"Alas, my tears flow greatly, for the holy churches received such favor from these faithless pagans. As for you, Orthodox princes and boyars, strive to show beneficence to the holy churches, lest on the day of judgment you be shamed by these barbarians."

—a fifteenth-century chronicler

In 1547 Ivan IV, who in his minority had ruled as Grand Prince, took the new title tsar or Caesar, tying himself to the Roman past. Charlemagne had made the same connection with his coronation in 800 CE, as did Ivan's contemporaries Charles V and Suleiman, as well as the German kaisers in the nineteenth century. Russian tsars would later add the appellation "autocrat" to their titles, from the Byzantine word for complete ruler. The tsar's crown was renamed the hat of Monomakh, after the Byzantine emperor Constantine Monomachus. In fact, the crown was made in central Asia and had nothing to do with Byzantium—except in the effective disinformation campaign carried out by Moscow clerics.

Moscow's leaders negotiated the transformation of the metropolitan of Moscow into the patriarch of Russia's own eastern Orthodox church in 1589. In the same year, after convening a kuriltai-like "Council of the Land," the tsar issued a new law code setting forth the right of every subject to appeal to the tsar for protection of honor and well-being. The khan had turned into both Caesar and God's servant; the tsar offered his subjects an image of Christian community led by the autocrat and guided by the church.

Consolidating Patrimonial Empire

The three pillars of the Muscovite state were clan politics centered on the tsar, the land grant system, and the church with its unifying ideology. The maintenance of patrimonial discipline over the tsar's elite servitors was crucial to Moscow's imperial trajectory. As we have seen, nobles scattered about western Europe effectively checked the aspirations of kings and emperors at this time, while the Ottomans arranged their high command to prevent a nobility from taking shape and power. Moscow took a different course and managed to produce a nobility that was both dependent on the autocrat and engaged with the imperial project.

Because the land grant was key to keeping elite servitors loyal, expansion was the lubricant and fuel of Moscow's imperial mechanism. New regions and their resources, often more enriching than those of the center, supported the tsar, his family, and his servitors, as well as the clergy. But growth also produced vulnerabilities. Extension brought Muscovy up against other powers with imperial ambitions—Sweden, Poland-Lithuania, the Ottoman empire, China, and Mongol and other tribal confederacies on the steppe. Even successful conquest meant drawing in people of many different cultures, some of whom could play Moscow off against other empires.

In the late sixteenth century, Moscow's distinctive patrimonial regime almost collapsed after a crisis set in motion by the tsar himself. Ivan IV, whose nickname "the Terrible" (*groznyi*) meant awe-inspiring, divided the realm into two parts—one to be run by the boyars and the church and one by his own loyalists. This tactic, as well as Ivan's short-lived placement of a Chinggisid khan on the throne in his place, his rejection of the moral guidance of the Orthodox church, and his ruthless persecution of his enemies, were Mongol-style attempts to assert his personal supremacy and break the powers of the clergy and the boyars. Ivan's worst failure as a ruler concerned his immediate family. In a fit of rage, it is thought, he killed one of his sons and left only a single weak-minded heir, known as Fedor the Bellringer. When Fedor died in 1598, the Riurikid dynasty was finished.

By this time, the system had self-preserving elements built in, including the Moscow princes' marriage policy. The boyars chose one of their number to be tsar—Boris Godunov, who had married Fedor's sister. But Boris was not himself a Riurikid and thus lacked dynastic legitimacy. Fedor's death opened up a huge power struggle among Russian elites—both those who had suffered under Ivan and those who had cast their lot with him—as well as outside powers—Poles and Swedes who coveted Russian lands and the wealth accumulated by the tsars. During the "Time of Troubles" (1584–1613), the ideology of royal descent turned out to be a powerful mobilizing force. Two different men claimed to be Ivan's son, Dmitrii, using the charisma of the dynasty as they reached for the throne. After years of destructive warfare, the boyars chose a new tsar, settling on Mikhail Romanov, aged only sixteen and from a relatively minor clan. Both of these characteristics inclined the other families to agree on him.

Russian Tsars and Dynasties, 1547 to 1725

Riurikids (Daniilovichi)

Ivan IV (Grand Prince, 1533–47, tsar 1547–84)
Fedor Ivanovich "the Bellringer" (1584–98)

1584–1613: Time of Troubles

Boris Godunov, regent and then boyar tsar; civil war, pretenders, Swedish and Polish invasions

Romanovs

Mikhail Romanov (1613–45)
Aleksei Mikhailovich (1645–76)
Fedor III (1676–82)
Peter I and Ivan V (1682–89)
Peter I (1689–1725)

The new imperial dynasty lasted in principle, but probably not genetically (thanks to the conjugal difficulties of Catherine the Great), until 1917.

In the half century after the Time of Troubles, the young Romanov dynasty accommodated Russia's noble clans with new laws on labor. Both tsars and nobles had been plagued by their inability to keep people working on "their" lands, because peasants were prone to pick up and leave for the expanding territories of the empire, where someone else would be happy to put them to work. Responding to nobles' complaints, the state first restricted and in 1649 abolished altogether peasants' right to leave a landed estate. This reallocation of rights expressed the deal struck between the tsar and his kind of nobility—serfs for loyalty.

Limiting peasants' mobility gave nobles good reasons to support the tsar, but what about high-ranking churchmen—the other intermediaries of Russian empire? The tsars had benefited enormously from Orthodoxy's harmonizing ideology, its rituals of accommodation, and its missionary efforts while not having to deal with the institutionalized authority of a pope in Rome. But from the times of Mongol protectorship the church had possessed its own landed estates, its own peasant agriculturalists, its own courts, and, after 1589, its sometimes self-important patriarch. During the reign of Alexei Mikhailovich (1645–76), the second Romanov tsar, the Orthodox church was weakened by a schism in its ranks. Alexei initially supported the domineering patriarch Nikon, who wanted to "purify" Russian Orthodoxy by taking it back to its Greek roots, aligning Russian practices with those of the high clergy in Kiev, and conveniently facilitating Moscow's expansion in Ukraine. In Russia, however, the campaign to get rid of home-style rites provoked rebellions against Nikon and in favor of the "old belief." In a master stroke of personal power, Tsar Alexei dismissed the unpopular patriarch but kept his reforms. The tsar's authority was enhanced, the divided church's diminished, the clerics disciplined.

Adding Europe to the Mix

In the conventional narrative of Russian history, Peter the Great plays the role of the great westernizer—the tsar who acquired western technology and started Russia on a whole new path toward Europeanness. Accordingly, Russia's next centuries are explained by the country's "backwardness" and its slow pace in "catching up" with Europe. One problem with this perspective is that the "Europe" Russia was supposedly catching up to was a place of many states, societies, and cultures, not a self-conscious whole. A more worldly perspective, including empires around the globe with their multiple and interactive pasts, allows us to see Peter with his advisors, officials, and subordinates continuing along their prior imperial pathway, applying the pragmatic, absorptive, mixing, and evolving practices of Russian governance.

Figure 7.1

Peter the Great portrayed at the Battle of Poltava (1709). Peter is crowned by an angel at the moment of his great victory over the army of Charles XII of Sweden. Portrait in the Tretyakov Gallery, Moscow. GettyImages.

Peter the Great, a son of Tsar Alexei Mikhailovich, survived a murderous struggle between the clans of his father's two wives. In 1696, at the age of twenty-four, he became the sole tsar, having earlier shared the office with his half brother. As a boy, Peter had lived in the foreigners' area of Moscow, and he became an enthusiast of "western" technology, especially boat building, sailing, mathematics, and military strategy. He made two trips to Europe as tsar; during one he disguised himself as a simple worker so that he could be an apprentice shipbuilder in Holland. Peter's military ambitions inspired many of his reforms, including annual conscription of one recruit from every twenty families. After initial reversals and decades of combat, Peter achieved his major goals—defeating the Swedes and securing Russia's ports on the Baltic. Returning from a successful battle against Russia's other major foe, the Ottomans, Peter had a Roman-style arch built in Moscow, decorated with Julius Caesar's motto—"I came, I saw, I conquered."

Many of Peter's innovations—replacing the boyar duma with a "senate," having this senate (not the church) proclaim him "emperor" in 1721, founding the Academy of Science, issuing Russia's first newspaper, using a "Table of Ranks" to classify state service, reorganizing the administration into "colleges"—manifest his attraction to practices he observed in various European states. But there was nothing novel or particularly Russian about trying to acquire the military and cultural resources of rival powers. What was Russian was the way Peter carried out his quest. His capacity to command gigantic and disruptive actions—constructing an entirely new capital, named in honor of his own saint, uprooting nobles who were required to build residences there, shaving off of beards, organizing mixed-sex dance parties—derived from the long-term buildup of imperial power, and in particular from successful disciplining of imperial elites.

Peter did not attempt to make his multiconfessional empire Christian in ways that European rulers had tried. Like Ivan IV, Peter flaunted his supreme authority over both churchmen and high-ranking nobles. He discontinued the practice of having the tsar lead the patriarch's horse across Red Square on Palm Sunday—a ceremonial sign of the tsar's submission to God's will. With his boon companions, Peter concocted outrageous rituals—an "order of Judas," a mock prince-pope, masquerade weddings, obscene parodies of religious sacraments—designed, apparently, to show clerics and would-be aristocrats that he could ride roughshod over their expectations of consultative authority.

The emperor backed up personal humiliation with administrative reform, creating an office to manage church properties and collect taxes on them. In 1721, Peter issued a charter of rules for the clergy and replaced the patriarch with a council, the Holy Synod. The church did not fight back. Clerics, like secular officials, recognized the emperor's personal power to protect, reward, and punish. On the other hand, Peter's spectacular mocking of Orthodox practices made him a subject of popular critique; was the strange tsar the Antichrist? Peter's public breach with Orthodox ceremony continued to produce sectarians and self-proclaiming true tsars for the rest of the imperial period.

Many of Peter's cultural initiatives—particularly his demand for educated servitors—proved highly attractive. European architects reshaped domestic and urban spaces; theaters, academies, museums, and the study of foreign languages transformed amusements and scholarship. European idioms—from various periods—were interspersed with or overlaid on earlier Eurasian motifs, producing what is to this day a spectacular and baffling stylistic mix. Russian elites cultivated "western" attitudes as links to a wider world of civilization, enhancing their position vis-à-vis subordinate populations in the empire.

But there were limits to how far Peter could go against the nobility's idea of patrimonial power. Peter tried to establish the emperor's freedom to name his own successor. He also outlawed dividing up a noble's land grant among all sons, a reform modeled on English primogeniture and directed against the old Kievan/Mongol/Muscovite patterns of giving each descendant something to live on. After Peter's death, the nobility sabotaged both innovations. For the rest of the eighteenth century, the highest families of the nobility, through consultation, assassination, and conspiracy, managed to rally around the future emperor or empress who would do them the most good and to get rid of or obstruct emperors who tried too hard to rein them in. Expansion of the empire made it easier for Russian families to keep dividing their estates among their children.

By the time of his death in 1725, Peter with the help of his chastened elites had absorbed, manipulated, or rejected elements of Kievan, Mongol, Byzantine, and western European practices and transformed them into a strong imperial system recognizable as a great and threatening power by other states. As a principle, patrimony won over class (see the conclusion to chapter 5). Nobles were allocated land and labor in reward for loyal service; they did not try to rid themselves of the autocracy but instead strove to be close to the emperor or be connected to the highest offices of state. A strong residue of Mongol-style statecraft inflected the relations of the emperor with his servitors; high officials, nobles, and clergy all depended on chains of personal command for their positions.

Official ideology mixed secular with theocratic claims. The emperor was a lawgiver, who allocated rights and goods to subjects. The Orthodox church was run by the emperor's rules. Nobles could make their personalized blends of Orthodoxy with "western" culture, hire French tutors for their children, read foreign books, and consider themselves civilized. Despite the primacy of Orthodoxy as the official religion, the various populations of the empire worshiped in many ways. None of this seemed bizarre or problematic for people who lived in an empire whose outstanding characteristic was not its difference from "Europe" but the effective and pragmatic melding of multiple imperial cultures.

China: Punctuated Evolution of Imperial Statecraft

For all its relative youth and perhaps because of its absorptive qualities, the Russian empire managed from the mid-fifteenth century to spread intermittently outward from Muscovite territories and retain political coherence under the rule of two dynasties—the Riurikids and their successors, the Romanovs. The much older Chinese empire did not sustain its territorial

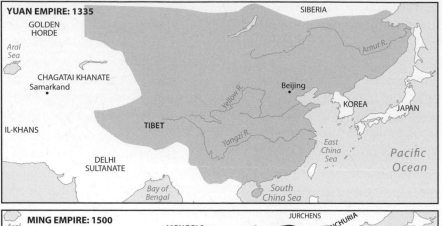

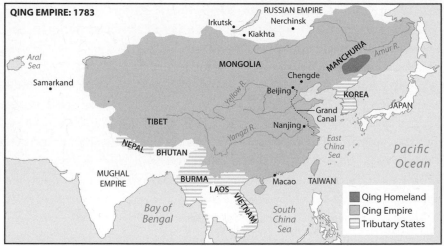

Map 7.3
Yuan, Ming, and
Qing empires.

hold or dynastic continuity so consistently. What kept Chinese empire in play as the state shattered, relocated, and reformed and as the capital moved about was a powerful imperial tradition and self-conscious, sophisticated statecraft. As dynasties rose and fell, their successors, advised by trained officials, successfully claimed the Mandate of Heaven.

Sustaining the Chinese imperial trajectory required adjustments, innovation, and often the illusion of continuity. One perspective on China's history claims that non-Han rulers were promptly "sinified"—absorbed into institutions and norms established in a "Chinese" past. This thesis of ethnicized homogeneity contrasts strongly with Russia's self-representation as a multipeopled place. But the trajectory of Chinese empire was in fact interactive with non-Han peoples, attentive to cultural difference, and, in part because of this, dynamic. In this section, after a brief consideration of Yuan and Ming rule, we focus on the seventeenth through the nineteenth centuries, when a dynasty created in avid proximity to China seized the imperial throne and forged an effective variant of the politics of difference. The Qing (Manchu) emperors expanded China's space farther than had any of their predecessors and turned cultural divides inside the enlarged empire into a technology of imperial rule.

Dynastic Successors: Yuan and Ming

As we have seen (chapter 4), Chinggis Khan's grandson Khubilai conquered northern China, then defeated the Song dynasty in the south, moved the capital north and renamed it Beijing, and founded a new ruling dynasty, the Yuan (1279–1368). The communications networks fostered by the Yuan, their appreciation of applied technologies, and their encouragement of commerce gave a push to entrepreneurial activities as well as to improvements in the production of cotton and silk. Taking over areas formerly ruled by Tanguts on the west, the Jin to the north, and the Song in the south, the Yuan reunited the empire and vastly extended its reach.

The Yuan mixed Chinese and Mongol ways by retaining strong markers of social status but re-ranking them according to the empire's new priorities. Mongol warriors held the highest social rank, followed by Muslims from western and central Asia who served as tax collectors and administrators, then northern Chinese, with longer experience of Mongol rule, then Chinese from the Song area in the south. At the same time, the Yuan tried to systematize governance by dividing the entire realm into provinces, governed by officials and military commanders appointed by the center.

Like earlier dynasties, the Yuan had to deal with nomads on their borders. The problem was no longer buying off powerful predators—since Mongol warriors now protected China from the inside—but rewarding nomadic tribes who kept the Yuan supplied with horses. The emperors took on a new role—making ad hoc grants of grain, money, and animals to tribal leaders who could use these resources to assist—and control—their subordinate peoples. This patrimonial tactic—a kind of reverse tribute system—made exterior nomadic groups into supplicants of the emperor and kept them conveniently dependent and at a distance.

The Yuan took up what turned into a long-term Chinese imperial project—control over Tibet. In this physically difficult—for Mongols—terrain,

Figure 7.2
Kazakh envoys offering tribute of horses to the Qianlong emperor (1736–95). The tribute system initiated in ancient China was used by later dynasties. This hanging scroll is the work of the Jesuit Castiglione, who arrived in China in 1715 and was appointed to the post of court painter in Beijing. Musée des Arts Asiatiques-Guimet, Paris. ArtResource.

the Yuan applied their policy of sheltering religions strategically. Before his final defeat of the Song, Khubilai Khan had taken Phags-pa, a Tibetan lama, under his wing. Phags-pa declared Khubilai a universal Buddhist ruler and provided him with a script for recording the Mongolian language. In 1270, Khubilai invested Phags-pa as imperial preceptor in Tibet, supporting his client's religious authority in return for political subordination and, of course, taxes. As a technology of imperial rule, the "lama-patron" system had its downside, opening up struggles among Buddhist factions, aspiring Mongols (many of them Buddhists), and later emperors.

For the Yuan dynasty, more direct threats were Mongol-style infighting among princes of the ruling clan and poor management of China's agrarian resources. Fragmentation at the top and overtaxation of peasants weakened Yuan capacity to master the basic challenge of Chinese empire—holding the polity together in a productive area where intermediary authorities had the resources to hive off from the center or try to conquer it. In the 1350s, Yuan power was challenged by peasant revolts, Buddhist conspiracies, and ambitious rebels. A charismatic Chinese peasant, born poor, raised as a Buddhist novice, and later advised by discontented scholars, joined in the fray. After seventeen years of campaigning, in which he first united then defeated in battle or killed his rivals, Chu Yuan-chang founded a new dynasty, the Ming ("brilliant") and took the reign title Hongwu ("vastly martial"). He ruled from 1368 to 1398.

Hongwu's consolidation of power sent some Yuan warrior elites with their followers back to Mongolia, where they reestablished the earlier pattern of tributary relations with China's new leaders. The Ming emperor

played the "barbarian" card against the defeated Yuan, attributing their exploitative and divisive last years to their Mongol origins. Hongwu moved the capital once again, south to Nanjing on the Yangzi River, cut off the Mongol-controlled transcontinental trade, and replaced convenient paper money with silver. The Ming revived the examination system that the Yuan had largely abandoned.

But the anti-foreigner strategy of the Ming was neither thorough nor lasting. The capital was moved back to Beijing during the rule of the emperor Yongle (1403–24). Yongle enhanced Khubilai's capital, creating the splendid Forbidden City within it. After a brief reaction against Yuan economic practices, the Ming resumed the promotion of technological innovations and commerce—with a greater focus on connecting interior regions. Concerned to augment grain production and delivery, they poured resources into building and maintaining the Grand Canal between Beijing and the region south of the Yellow River. As we have seen (chapter 6), the Ming initially supported naval expeditions around the China Sea, across the Indian Ocean to the Persian Gulf, Arabia, and Africa.

Unlike territorially constrained European leaders, the Ming did not follow up their long-distance voyages with overseas colonization or enclaves—they had no need for this. They expanded their control to the south and the west, using the familiar method of subordinating native chiefs, with their peoples, while Chinese peasants gradually moved into pacified areas. The Ming profited from connections with already established Chinese merchant communities in southeast Asia as well as from rents paid by the Portuguese in Macao, without having to take on the costs of direct rule or combating pirates. Expansion into Vietnam and enforcement of the lama-patron system in Tibet, both begun by the Yuan, remained part of the Ming imperial project.

For two and a half centuries, the Ming presided over a fabulously wealthy and creative civilization that gave much of the world its tableware ("china"), its beverage (tea), and its luxury textile (silk). What Europeans had to exchange for Chinese products was mostly silver, a product of their empire-building in the Americas. For the Ming, as for the Song, Tang, and earlier dynasties, the main task of empire was managing the internal economic and social space, as well as the demands and disruptions posed by nomadic confederations around its edges.

While emphasizing their Chinese origins, the Ming relied on a mé-lange of ruling practices that had been forged by earlier emperors, advisors, and military leaders. The Ming retained provincial structures used by the Yuan and reaffirmed the traditions of rule by officials and through imperial law. Extensive literacy and advanced print technology assisted the imperial agenda. The state sponsored publication of central and provincial gazettes; officials sent to distant regions produced ethnographies of "natives." The Ming bureaucracy grew into the biggest on earth.

Chinese families could aspire to have their sons advance into the highest bureaucratic ranks, but there were other respectable ways to thrive. Large landlords became rich producing food and raw materials for the integrated internal market; merchants enjoyed a high living standard in cities and towns. The imperial administration ran its own manufacturing operations. Ming porcelain embodied China's cultural compound: the blue-on-white designs used imported cobalt applied to patterns derived from central Asia and India; new production processes—a kind of assembly-line organization—enabled workers to produce china in huge quantities for both internal and external markets. The Ming retained the Yuan's religious pluralism. Muslims, Jews, and Christians could worship their god in their own ways. Mosques, Buddhist and Daoist temples, and shrines to Confucius were part of the cultural landscape.

The successful economic integration of a huge space under the Ming produced changes in lifeways that recall the effects of Rome's Mediterranean empire. As in Rome, the poor participated marginally in the expansion of well-being, but to elites, the empire offered both prosperity and refinement. The lively urban culture fostered by the Yuan morphed under the Ming into a dynamic mix of learning and creativity. Boys studied for years to acquire the skills to take the state examinations. Artists produced new genres, including novels and musical theater. The elite lived in comfortable houses with elegant interior design, savored refined cuisine, and discussed paintings and poetry. Women of genteel families participated in the cultivation of letters and arts. It was expected that female courtesans would be accomplished in poetry and music. Many industries produced for the cultural market—block printing for books, papers, and inks. The quality of urban life in Ming China dazzled visitors from Europe. Across the world, Ming tastes and products—lacquered screens, painted papers, brocades, and of course porcelain—set standards for luxury and attracted merchants to the richest empire of its time.

Ming Missteps and the Making of the Manchus

As with Rome, the most visible problems had to do with the edges of the empire, where wealth attracted raiders. The long Pacific coast—where Chinese commerce flourished through linkages to southeast Asia, the islands offshore, and far overseas—was subject to assault by well-equipped Japanese forces, miscellaneous pirates, and fugitives from Chinese, Japanese, and Portuguese control. At the nomadic interface to the west and the north, contentious tribes had to be incorporated or placated or both. Like earlier dynasties (chapter 2), the Ming had to muster the resources to pay armies to fight, pay outsiders not to fight, or pay outsiders to help fight internal and external foes. Carrying this off depended, as before, on taxation and management of the tax collectors.

The Ming confronted an enormous management challenge—commanding the loyalty and some of the production of a significant part of the world's population. The sheer size of the bureaucracy and the court increased the burden on farmers' and others' revenues. Other intractable pressures came from climate change—lower temperatures during the "little ice age"—epidemics (perhaps the result of increased contact with outsiders), and floods that overwhelmed the gigantic waterworks. All these could make the countryside restless and unreliable. But none of this would seem to doom the world's richest power, with its well-educated managers and sophisticated urbanites.

The weak spot in the system was the emperor and his relations with his officials. From the late sixteenth century, fissures appeared inside the Ming elite. The emperor Wanli (1573–1620) took the mystique of imperial aloofness to an extreme by isolating himself inside the Forbidden City. Worse, he stopped consulting ministers and scholars and depended on palace eunuchs to be his conduit to the bureaucracy. The eunuchs seized this opportunity to insert themselves into the power hierarchy, demanding fees for their services and taking over revenues and revenue collection from officials and provincial lords. Scholars fought back at this break with the tradition of ruling through trained officials. The Donglin Society called for a return to Confucian virtues, but this movement of critique was crushed by a clique of eunuchs in the early seventeenth century. Arrests, murders, and suicides of eminent officials discredited the court and indirectly the dynasty. The episode underlines a key to sustaining imperial power: the emperor's inter-mediaries must serve more than their immediate interests. Chinese scholars understood this; the court eunuchs did not.

The fatal blow to the dynasty came from people at its edges who even more than in the past had much to covet and to gain from China. From the start, the Ming had worried about a familiar danger—Mongol tribes north and west of the Great Wall—and tried to deal with it. Expansion north into the area we now call Manchuria and control over the various Jurchen tribes there seemed to offer the prospect of exploiting old Mongol-Jurchen rivalries as well as firming up connections to the Ming's Korean allies. Em-ploying what Chinese called a "loose rein" strategy, the Yongle emperor in the early fifteenth century sent troops into Manchuria to subordinate tribal leaders and incorporate Jurchens into commanderies and garrisons. Jurchen tribal chiefs were given Ming titles as leaders of these military subunits.

The loose rein strategy left room for Jurchen and other tribes to jockey for trading mandates and tributary relationships with the Ming. As the Ming economy grew, these commercial opportunities and protection payments fed new super-tribal confederacies, just what the Ming most needed to avoid. In the late sixteenth century, Nurhaci, a brilliant strategist from a Jur-chen tribe, adroitly exploited the accidental death of his father and grandfa-ther during a Ming campaign. In recompense, he took over the trading and tribute permits of several Ming subordinates.

Nurhaci soon monopolized all trade between Jurchens and the Ming and drew Mongol, Jurchen, and other tribes into his orbit. Well beyond Manchuria, he enhanced his command through marriage alliances, treaties, and military might. In 1616 Nurhaci founded his own empire. He gave it the name "Jin," recalling the earlier Jurchen dynasty that had ruled northern China before the Yuan (chapter 4). The Ming woke up too late to Nurhaci's threat; in 1619, he defeated a Ming army of over one hundred thousand and seized several Chinese border cities.

Nurhaci's choice of a name for his empire pointed not to his family's lin-eage but to a mix of earlier traditions. That his tribe's language was different from the Jurchens' was no obstacle to borrowing an early dynasty's gran-deur. Ethnicity was not fixed in terms we recognize today; what counted was superior overlordship and nobility. In addition to the dynastic name Jin, Nurhaci also enjoyed the title khan, acquired in 1606 as he extended his control in Mongolia, later enhanced with various adjectives—"wise," "reverend," "enlightened," and so forth. Both "Jin" and "khan" brought with them imperial glory and signaled the unification of Jurchens and Mongols under Nurhaci's command.

In the most critical of imperial institutions—the army—Nurhaci recon-figured the commanderies and garrisons set up by the Ming in Manchuria into an institution called the "banners." The organization of Jurchen troops with their families into separate units, each with its own distinctive flag, broke up earlier lineage groups and provided the emperor with spoke-like connections to his several armies. Banner commanders were members of Nurhaci's advisory council. The system, which recalls Chinggis Khan's and Tamerlane's efforts to fracture established loyalties, was yet another synthesis of earlier imperial practices. In nomadic fashion, the banners included soldiers' families, but each soldier was also assigned a tract of land to be cultivated for his support. This new war machine provided Hong Taiji, the second Jin khan, with the means to conquer Korea (1638), further expanding the Jin's young empire.

Hong Taiji had been chosen khan after the usual demanding competition following his father's death. Unlike the rest of Nurhaci's children, Hong Taiji was literate. Learning from Chinese advisors who had aided his advance, Hong Taiji established a bureaucracy modeled on the Chinese administration, created two new sets of banners—one for Chinese soldiers and their families and another for Mongols—and set up the Department for Mongol Affairs (1634). He took Nurhaci's denominating tactics one step further, renaming the Jurchens and the dynasty. From 1635, all Jurchens were to be known as Manchus. In 1636, after receiving the imperial seal of the Yuan emperors from the widow of a defeated Mongol khan, Hong Taiji renamed the ruling dynasty once again: the name Qing (pure, clear) obliterated the Jurchens' past as subordinates of the Ming. The Qing were now imperial sovereigns over Manchus, Mongols, Koreans—an open-ended list. Nurhaci and Hong Taiji had taken up China's loose rein and created an ethnicity—Manchu—a dynasty—Qing—and an empire.

Crumbling Ming control opened the pathway to the center of the Chinese imperial world. In 1644, after a Chinese rebel captured Beijing and the disconsolate Ming emperor committed suicide, a general loyal to the Ming invited the Qing to send troops to help him retake the capital. At the time, the Qing emperor was Hong Taiji's ninth son, a five-year-old boy, ruling under the regency of his uncle Dorgon. Dorgon saw his chance, and Manchu, Mongol, and Chinese banners under Qing command rode into China, regained the capital, abandoned their Ming allies, and did not leave.

Claiming the Mandate of Heaven for themselves, the Qing took up the familiar task of reuniting China. The banners proved their worth over the next half century, as the Qing defeated forces led by anti-Ming rebels and pro-Ming loyalists and went on to conquer Taiwan, much of Mongolia and Tibet, and parts of central Asia. By the end of the eighteenth century, the Qing had doubled the territory they took over from the Ming, making China second only to Russia in size. The empire's population grew robustly—although the actual rate is a matter of controversy—reaching 420 million in 1850. The dynasty lasted 267 years.

Manchu Rules

The Qing synthesized yet another variation on China's imperial tradition. The key elements of government—the lawmaking emperor and his extensive bureaucracy—were transformed by highlighting ethnic distinctions between Han and Manchu. The Qing put difference to work for empire, enhancing the emperor's role as protector of all the empire's peoples.

The first task after cleaning up resistance to the seizure of the throne was to prevent the usual problem of Eurasian-style empires—their breakup into subunits led by the emperor's progeny or other nobles. The War of Three Feudatories (1673–81) was a shakedown critical to the empire's survival. The leaders of the three areas were Chinese military leaders who had assisted the Manchu conquerors and been rewarded with huge domains. These lords wanted to keep their lands as their personal realms—in which case China might have disintegrated into kingdoms as in western Europe—but the young emperor Kangxi (1661–1722) would have none of this. After the dirty work of military reconquest was done, the regions claimed by these insubordinates were abolished.

The key to preventing future fragmentation was the banner system, lacing military might, military organization, and ethnic difference into the social structure and the governance of the Qing empire. Manchu bannermen were sent to serve in garrisons and towns, where they lived in settlements distinct from those of the Han Chinese, and received grain, weapons, and subsidies for personal expenses and upkeep of their horses. At the same time, bannermen were required to maintain their ties with Beijing; only Manchu bannermen lived in Beijing's inner city. Moving Manchus into the centers of Chinese cities displaced Chinese inhabitants, and these transformations of urban life made the new order explicit, tangible, and tough.

The Qing's regime of ethnic separation, called "Manchu apartheid" by Frederic Wakeman, was not directed against the Chinese majority; it addressed a specific problem faced by earlier Chinese rulers, as well as by Ottoman and other empires founded on the military might of warrior confederacies. How could armies that had lived on raiding and trading from outside the borders be turned into non-predatory and reliable troops inside the empire? The Qing answer was nomadic, bureaucratic, and ethnic. By organizing military men into units that were moved about the empire and maintained by imperial grants, the Qing kept their troops mobile, yet tied to the emperor and his court. Manchu bannermen were expected to cultivate their fighting skills from youth and to make a life of military prowess, but they now served a huge empire's purposes—not just conquest, but settlement, defense, and policing.

If ethnic separation was more about controlling Manchus than Chinese, it also became part of the Qing's imperial system. The Manchu banners and Manchu army were paralleled by the Green Standard army of Chinese. Manchu military men and Han governors provided two systems of information and connection to the emperor and could spy on each other. Here we see another version of Tamerlane's dualistic government. Parallel hierarchies, based on the principle of ethnic separation, concentrated power in the emperor.

At the top levels of the bureaucracy, the Qing made room for both Han and Manchus by creating a system of parallel ranks: a Manchu presiding officer and a Han one, a Manchu second in command, and a Han second in command. Preserving the examination system in these conditions required a kind of affirmative action program—preparation courses and favoritism in grading—to help Manchus compete with the better-educated Han. Since there were many more Han competitors than Manchu ones, the system privileged Manchus in proportion to their numbers, but still kept the best-educated Han at the top rungs of imperial service. The exam system was not the only way to power. Success in battle could be rewarded with top positions in official ranks, and this also benefited Manchus.

The Emperor's Universe

Using ethnic criteria in these situations was not a violation of equality—Qing society was based on rank and difference—but a way to draw in different peoples under the emperor's rule and to use and control ambitious members of each group inside the imperial administration. The Ming, Yuan, and earlier dynasties had established precedents for mixing "outsiders" into China—subordinating chieftains who were expected to manage "their" people, using non-Chinese administrators in Han areas, advancing promising individuals from the borderlands into the bureaucracy. Ming officials had teetered between a dichotomous notion of *min*—Chinese subjects—and *man*—outsiders—and a more Roman-style idea that the outsiders would want and could acquire Chinese ways. Theories of civilizational hierarchy—with the Chinese at the top, of course—described various groups of primitive foreigners, but the Ming did not hesitate to use and reward individual leaders from non-Chinese groups.

Rewarding outsiders was one thing, being ruled by them another. The Qing worked out a tactically brilliant solution to this challenge. First, they played on the politics of difference and established their own Manchu way. Second, the Qing turned the notion of distinctive cultures to their ideological advantage by cultivating the emperor as the protector of all of China's diverse populations. Hong Taiji's descendants gave the Chinese emperor the qualities of a universal khan, who ruled a world of peoples. The "family" united under the emperor's guidance combined the Confucianist principle of paternal authority with an insistent recognition of differences among the family members.

Despite this appeal to family values, the Qing did not continue the Ming practice of passing the throne to the eldest son. Like Peter the Great of Russia who in 1722 abolished earlier succession rules, the Kangxi emperor assumed the right to choose the most capable heir on his own. He may have hoped to protect the hard-won empire from the vagaries of heredity (the usual Chinese way) and the dangers of all-out Eurasian-style tanistry. Both models were rejected in favor of the super-paternalism of the emperor, free to name his own successor; this kept Qing princes alert and courtiers connected to the fount of power. Patrimonialism intersected with officialdom as well: the councils and ministries around the emperor served at his whim. Qing emperors devoted a great deal of their time to personal communication with subordinates, writing letters, and reading and commenting on reports.

As befit the multiethnic composition of the empire, Qing pronouncements were recorded in at least two languages—Manchu and Chinese—commonly three, and sometimes four, including Mongolian, Tibetan, and Uighur, a Turkic language written in Arabic script used by many central Asian Muslims. In addition to publishing the *Secret History of the Mongols* (1662) and other materials in Mongolian, the Qing sponsored publications of Tibetan poetry and religious texts. The Kangxi emperor was literate in Manchu, Mongolian, and Chinese; the Qianlong emperor (1736–95) knew Tibetan as well.

In their early decades, Qing emperors and other Manchus were both attracted to and wary of Chinese culture—novels, poetry, and the like. In 1654, the Shunzi emperor seemed to backtrack on his support of Chinese, writing: "Reflecting on the study of Chinese writing, I think it may lead to entering into Chinese customs and the gradual loss of our old Manchu usages." But this position did not hold. Manchus and the Chinese in the top levels of the government had to communicate efficiently with each other and the emperor. In 1725, knowledge of Chinese was made mandatory for all top government officials. By 1800 the court had lost the fight to preserve Manchu as the spoken language of the bannerman and Manchu was used less and less in the cultured world of Beijing. But these gradual shifts did not signal the end of ethnic apartheid, since bannermen began to speak a kind of Manchu-inflected Chinese that still set them apart.

Language was one marker of difference in the empire, but hairstyles, dress, and body sculpting were other means whereby unlikeness could be manifested, enforced, exploited, or undermined. In the early post-conquest days, the Manchus had tried a policy of uniformity. The regent Dorgon commanded all Chinese men to adopt Manchu hairstyles—shaved forehead and hair braided in the back in a single "queue." (This gave rise to an ironic comment—"Keep your hair and lose your head" or "Lose your hair and keep your head.") Dorgon also tried to enforce Manchu-style dress. Manchu high-collared jackets fastened at the shoulder were to replace flowing Ming robes with unwarriorly long sleeves. This policy was largely successful over the long haul, but it did not apply to everyone. When the Manchus conquered new territories to the west where many Muslims lived, Muslims were excused from Manchu hairstyles.

For women, hair counted too, of course, and so did feet. Consistent with the active role of women in nomadic societies, Manchu women did not bind their feet. When the Qing assumed control of China, they tried to outlaw foot binding for everyone. But the Chinese population did not accept this rule. For Han families, stunted feet remained a sign of female beauty and well-being. The Qing abandoned their policy in 1668, and foot binding became a cultural marker: Han women did it; Manchus did not. This sign of difference was undermined by the formidable force of fashion. Manchu women came up with pedestal shoes that lifted their unstylishly big but natural feet off the ground and under their robes, forcing them to walk in the tottering way of Han women with bound feet.

Manchu women had distinctive legal rights as well, probably another carryover from the nomads' gender regime. The ultra-patriarchal Han discouraged widows from remarrying, while Manchus encouraged young widows to form new families. By legalizing both norms, the Qing enabled a differentiated fertility regime that helped Manchus produce more children. Later, in the eighteenth century, when inroads were being made into the regime of ethnic separation, the norm of chaste widowhood came to be applied to both Han and Manchu women.

Like the Muscovites, the Qing used marriage to shore up their rule, but in the Qing case, the goal was to prevent minority Manchus from mixing with and vanishing into the Han majority. Manchu women were forbidden to marry Han men, although Manchu men could take Han women as second wives and concubines. Unmarried Manchu bannerwomen, and not Han ones, had to present themselves as possible "elegant females" to the procurers for the imperial palace. Selected girls had to serve there; after five years they might be married off to Manchu elites, become imperial concubines, or be sent home where they could marry only with permission from the banner captain. This restrictive marriage regime signaled the Qing's turn away from Mongol-style exogamy, at least for the Manchu banners.

Like the Yuan and the Ming, the Qing respected and fostered the arts, and gave them their own militaristic imprint. The Qing emperors cultivated hunting as a ritual sport; representations of great hunting expeditions, military campaigns, and imperial inspection tours were portrayed in scroll paintings. Official histories recounted and embellished the one-family story as well as the emperor's heroic and farsighted leadership. Commemorative temples, an outdoor museum of distinctive palaces at Chengde, colossal stone memorials inscribed in multiple scripts, grand portraits of the regime's outstanding commanders, and compilations of the emperor's own military writings all cultivated the mystique of imperial success at war, expansion, and subsequent inclusion of diverse peoples.

Confucianism offered a paternalistic moral theory, useful to the politics of drawing different populations into an imperial family headed by the emperor. The Kangxi emperor worked to integrate the Han cultural corpus into his official pronouncements, issuing sixteen Sacred Maxims in 1670. These were intended to sum up Confucian moral values: hierarchical submission, generosity, obedience, thrift, and hard work.

"The Lord of Heaven is Heaven itself. . . . In the empire we have a temple for honoring Heaven and sacrificing to him. . . . We Manchus have our own particular rites for honoring Heaven; the Mongols, Chinese, Russians, and Europeans also have their own particular rites for honoring Heaven. . . . Everyone has his way of doing it."

—**Yongzheng emperor, 1727**

The Qing continued the multiconfessional policies of the Yuan and the Ming, allowing Muslims, Buddhists, Daoists, and Christians to practice their religions and build temples, as long as they did not impede the Qing's agendas. The Kangxi emperor welcomed Jesuit advisors and employed them as mapmakers, translators, and medical experts, but did not recognize the pope's claim to authority over Christians in China. The Qing attitude toward religions matched their imperial disposition: different faiths could be protected by the Qing emperor, but not by an outside power. They played this tactical game in reverse in Tibet, by reviving the lama-patron relationship with the Dalai Lama to advance Qing interests in the region.

As for themselves, the Qing never declared an official Manchu religion, but they meshed shamanist practices that they brought with them from Manchuria with rituals linking divine fortune to their demonstrated military prowess. Like Mongol rulers, the Qing were eclectic in their own religious tastes. The Yongzheng emperor (1723–35) was an ardent Buddhist, who consulted with religious specialists of several schools. Daoism was also practiced by the emperors.

Qing legal practice also combined difference and universal rule as underlying principles. The emperor's law was not the same for all. Bannermen did not have to submit to civil authorities for some violations; scholars of certain ranks were exempt from corporal punishment; and various peoples on the borderlands came under special jurisdictions. What was universal about Qing law was that every subject was protected, ultimately, by the emperor and his rules and decisions, as in Russia. Like the Ottoman sultan, the Qing emperor was supposed, in theory, to be the decider of all death penalties. Foreigners on Qing territory were also covered by Qing law, a premise that became a point of contention with outsiders. British, French, and American merchants dealing in the busy ports along the Chinese coast expected that their rowdy sailors would get special treatment (as they would have in Istanbul). But no, the emperor was willing to cut off all foreign trade if a culprit were not turned over to his justice.

As prosecutions involving foreigners revealed, notions of law and jurisprudence developed in European empires conflicted with founding elements of the Qing judicial system. Qing judges were appointed by the emperor; lawyers were absent from court proceedings; and court officials interpreted the law. Also shocking to westerners—although this was not unique to China—was that people could buy off their sentences. Whatever outsiders thought, the reality of the Chinese law was that it covered all subjects and the emperor was its source.

Over time, the Qing regime of ethnic difference and universal emperorship produced unintended effects. As we have seen, Manchu women might strive to look more like the fashionable Chinese and Manchu bannermen could find many aspects of a "Chinese" culture more attractive than a life in the saddle. Complaints about bannermen going soft—walking around in slippers, forgetting how to prepare arrows, decking themselves out in silks and sables, spending too much time at theaters and operas or worse—began soon after the conquest. In the other direction, ambitious Chinese men could try to enter the privileged Manchu banners—putting an ever bigger burden on the state budget. Although in theory Han generals organized supplies and Manchu ones commanded troops in battle, conditions in the field made Manchus take on organizational tasks and let Han generals become military leaders. At the top of the system, Han and Manchu leaders sat together in the emperor's Grand Council.

These crossover tendencies were not produced by defects in the system of ethnic distinction, but by the ways that humans operated in it. The Qing's representational consolidation of peoples into distinct groups and their symbolic unification of the populations of the empire into a multicultural family not only lasted until the end of their dynasty but also provided both a target and a tool to nationalists and empire-builders who succeeded them.

Closing Up the Space of Empire

By the end of the seventeenth century, the Qing were running into the other great cross-continental thrust—of Russian armies, explorers, and diplomats who also strove to subdue Turkic and Mongol nomads and to consolidate their hold on Eurasia. This interempire clash over space happened much later than in Europe, where emperors and their subordinates had been competing for the same terrain since Roman times, and earlier than in the Americas, where the territorial borders between empires were not stitched together until well into the nineteenth century (chapter 9).

The major figure in this contest for continental empire for the Qing was the Kangxi emperor. Like his contemporary Peter the Great, the Kangxi emperor ruled first as a child, dominated by his regents. His father had died of smallpox, and the son who survived the malady seemed a good choice to powers at court. (The Qing developed a vaccination against smallpox, a technology that inspired later European efforts.) At the age of sixteen, the young emperor arrested his chief regent, rid himself of problematic officials, and took command. As we have seen, he successfully defeated the three feudatories, forestalling fragmentation of the realm.

For the rest of his life, the Kangxi emperor campaigned to extend the empire in most possible directions. To the east, he sent a naval expedition to Taiwan, ruled by a rebel Chinese family who had harried coastal cities. In 1683, Taiwan was integrated into China's provincial system. The Qing did

Figure 7.3
Kangxi emperor (1661–1722). The emperor in informal dress, painted on a hanging silk scroll by court artists. Palace Museum, Beijing.

not go farther overseas or try at this point to extend formal control along the southeast Asian littoral. Instead they taxed foreign imports, allowed the Portuguese to maintain and pay for their entrepot in Macao, supported commerce along the Pacific coast, and set up customs offices at port cities to control French, Danish, British, Dutch, and eventually American merchants and their companies (chapters 6 and 10).

To the north and west, the Qing encountered two seemingly more formidable rivals—the Russians and the Zunghars, led by Galdan (1671–97), the last of the Mongol super khans. The Kangxi emperor took a dramatic initiative toward the Russian empire. From the early seventeenth century, Russians had sought trading rights in China; they had also moved into the Amur River region where they had a fortress and fought a few battles with the Qing. In this sparsely populated region, both Russians and Qing had problems with deserters from their regimes of tribute collection. After a few mishaps and insults as each empire claimed superiority over the other, the rivals realized that they would do better by cooperating: each side's deserters would be sent back and both empires could gain from long-distance trade. In 1689, with the help of the Qing's Jesuit advisors and Mongolian translators, Russian and Qing delegations signed a treaty at Nerchinsk, drew up a boundary, and agreed that people would owe tribute to the power on their side of the line. A preliminary border was marked out in Russian, Chinese, Manchu, Mongol, and Latin. Both Russians and Qing drew up maps to define their conquests. This might be seen as the Eurasian equivalent of the pope's division of the Americas between two Catholic empires.

The treaty of Nerchinsk secured the north enough to allow the Qing to move against Galdan and the Zunghars. Like earlier tribal leaders, Galdan had attempted to monopolize trading mandates at the Chinese border. He was a former lama and close to religious hierarchs in Tibet. When Galdan challenged Qing patronage of the Dalai Lama, a familiar and deathly ballet of negotiations, interventions, subverted loyalties, double dealings, and efforts to detach followers ensued.

The Qing attacked Galdan in 1690, with the help of rival Mongol tribal leaders. Galdan likewise exploited fissures among the Qing's subordinates and kept Qing armies occupied for seven years, until his death, probably by poison, in 1697. The Kangxi emperor celebrated the "final elimination of the Mongol menace" in Beijing. After much effort he extracted Galdan's remains from one of his Zunghar competitors, crushed the khan's bones, and scattered them to the winds.

The defeat of Galdan opened the way for the Qing to strengthen their hold over Turkic and Mongol groups in what later became Xinjiang province and to continue their interventions in Tibet. Zunghar Mongols nonetheless continued to annoy the Qing and escape from their control. When the Zunghar chief Galdan Tseren (1727–45) tried the classic tactic of seeking support from the Qing's rival, the Russian empire, the border agreements of the two powers came into play. The principles of Nerchinsk were firmed up by the Kiakhta treaty, signed in 1727, and the frontier marked with boundary stones. The Russians were to control the nomads of Siberia and Manchuria, and the Chinese were in charge of the Khalka Mongols on their side of a 2,600-mile-long border. The two empires would not shelter the other's enemies or assist refugees fleeing across the line.

Only in 1757, after a Zunghar leader drew other Mongol groups into rebellion against the Qing, did the Qianlong emperor (1736–95) order a wholesale massacre of the Zunghars as a people. This exception to the Qing policy of formal subordination and calculated deals with defeated leaders corresponded to a new territorial reality: the Qing were no longer dependent on Mongol or other allies on their western frontiers. The nomads in the middle of Eurasia had been swallowed by two empires.

Mongol, Russian, and Qing competitors all relied on tactics developed in Eurasia, at intersections between nomadic and settled peoples, with their empires or imperial aspirations. The Russians and the Qing, each interacting with European empires by land or sea and each intent on managing their Mongols, settled their differences through negotiation. By the seventeenth century, the Zunghars, who depended on the traditional resources of Eurasian nomads—the politics of pragmatic alliance and the self-supporting mobility of mounted warriors—had lost the technological advantages Mongols had enjoyed four hundred years before. Russia and China with their complex economies and external connections had more to offer willing subordinates; both powers eventually attained the military might to enforce their particular refinements of Eurasian universal empire upon the nomads.

The two victorious empires survived civil wars, dynastic failure, and external assaults, each time reviving elements of their earlier imperial ways. Like other successful empires, they managed to control different and often distant populations and at the same time tie subordinates tightly into the imperial project. Rebels wanted to seize these empires, not destroy them. Keys to the success of the young Russian empire and the old Chinese one were their creative mixes of ruling practices, their distinctive solutions to the intermediary problem, and their exploitation of difference to enhance imperial power.

For the Russians, the core institution was the dependent nobility, tied to the ruler by clan and marriage politics, the land grant system, and the emperor's favor. Entry into this group was not ethnically determined: Tatars were there from the formative years; Germans, Poles, and many others would join later. The acceptance of difference as a normal fact of imperial

Table 7.1
Russian, Qing, and Zunghar Leaders: A Century of Imperial Encounter in Eurasia

Russian emperors	Qing emperors	Zunghar khans

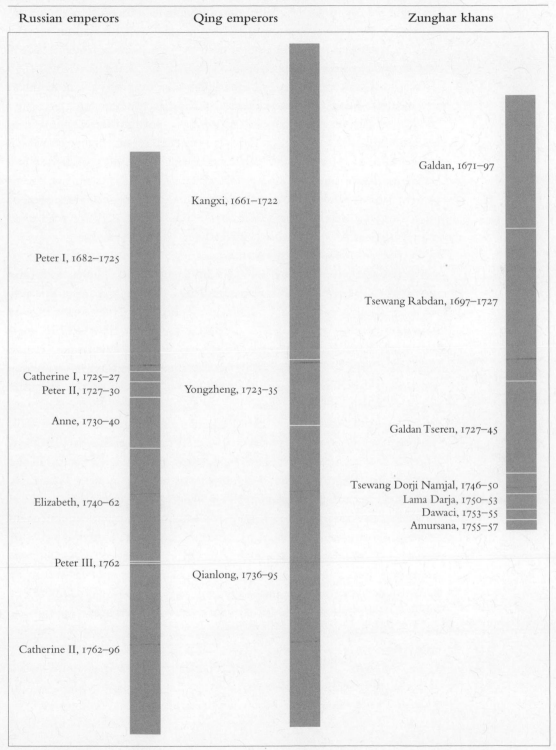

Galdan, 1671–97

Kangxi, 1661–1722

Peter I, 1682–1725

Tsewang Rabdan, 1697–1727

Catherine I, 1725–27
Peter II, 1727–30

Yongzheng, 1723–35

Anne, 1730–40

Galdan Tseren, 1727–45

Elizabeth, 1740–62

Tsewang Dorji Namjal, 1746–50
Lama Darja, 1750–53
Dawaci, 1753–55
Amursana, 1755–57

Peter III, 1762

Qianlong, 1736–95

Catherine II, 1762–96

life enhanced the flexibility of patrimonial governance. As long as there were new lands to distribute, the imperial elite could absorb new people, who, like the old ones, would be controlled through their personal ties to the sovereign. This was a creative adaptation of khan-style patrimonialism to Russia's territorial opportunities, without the threats to sovereignty posed by European aristocracies.

For the Qing, the blend was different—reliant on officials rather than noble landlords and on statecraft articulated and refined over centuries. The ideal of an ancient Chinese cultural order did not prevent Manchu conquerors from latching onto Chinese institutions or Han bureaucrats from helping their new rulers. One Eurasian element was the practiced manipulation of military and civilian chains of command and, as with the Russians, the cultivation of personal ties to the emperor as the ultimate source of power, disgrace, life, and death. With the banner system, the Qing sharpened the tool of difference—creating distinctively ethnicized units and separating, to some degree, Manchus from Han.

Accommodation to difference, not its eradication, was a hallmark of the two regimes. Both imperial systems developed flexible ideologies that differed fundamentally from the unifying religious projects of Catholic and Protestant empires. Russian rulers promoted Orthodoxy, but kept it under their control, expanded early into Muslim territory, and did not try to make everyone Christian (see chapter 9). For the Qing, the Mandate of Heaven was sufficient divine legitimation; the emperors changed their own faiths, protected diverse religious institutions inside the empire, and put external religious leaders under their ardent protection.

Both systems created myths that disguised their Eurasian origins. Russians did not acknowledge their Mongol past, especially when the steppe turned into a zone that they were conquering. Chinese rulers, even those who asserted their own distinctiveness, represented political tradition as much more continuous than it had been. Nonetheless, both empires had woven Eurasian threads into imperial statecraft. Each had an emperor who, like a universal khan, ruled over different groups, made the law, relied on educated bureaucrats, granted titles and privileges to loyal servitors, took them away at will, dealt pragmatically with outsiders, and regarded distinctive peoples as the building blocks of his superior command.

EMPIRE, NATION, AND CITIZENSHIP IN A REVOLUTIONARY AGE

8

We argued in chapter 6 that there was no revolution in sovereignty in seventeenth-century Europe: the relationship of ruler, people, and territory remained ambiguous and fluctuating. In the eighteenth century, there was a revolution in *ideas* of sovereignty. Thinking about the relationship of revolution and empire is difficult because we like our revolutions to be very revolutionary. Our textbooks tell us that an "epoch" of kings and emperors gave way to an "epoch" of nation-states and popular sovereignty. But the new ideas of sovereignty were important precisely because they differed from actually existing institutions and practices, within Europe as much as in its overseas empires. They were arguments; they fostered debate. Within Europe itself, monarchical and aristocratic privileges remained in tension with "the people's" claim to rights and voice for the entire nineteenth century. During the century after France's revolution of 1789 announced the principle of republican government, the state was republican for about a third of the time; for most of it, France was governed by men who called themselves king or emperor. The question of which people were sovereign remained unresolved into the mid-twentieth century.

The eighteenth century's new arsenal of political ideas made it possible to *imagine* a non-empire: a single people sovereign over a single territory. From the start, the working out of such an imaginary took place not in nationally defined polities within Europe but in a much bigger and uncertain space. Empire was the stage, not the victim, of eighteenth- and early nineteenth-century revolutions.

But the nature of political alternatives within—and against—empires shifted in fundamental ways. In cities like London and Paris, flush with wealth—derived in part from overseas trade and lucrative sugar colonies—merchants, artisans, and elements of the lesser nobility developed a new interactive politics that broke the pattern of vertical relationships cultivated by monarchical regimes and challenged the idea that "rights" came from on high and were passed down to particular individuals or collectivities. Instead, political thinkers in England and France and elsewhere argued that sovereignty was vested in a "people," that the ruler's authority stemmed from these people, and that he had to respond to their will through institutions designed to express it. People had rights stemming from their belonging to a polity, and those rights constrained a ruler's choices.

In the context of empire, ideas of natural rights and social contract opened up a new question: who constituted the people? Would citizenship be "national"—focused on a people who represented themselves as a single linguistic, cultural, and territorial community—or would it be "imperial," embracing diverse peoples who constituted the population of a state? Or could participation in state institutions create a national community, at least in parts of the empire? Would people who had emigrated to dependent territories overseas have their own representative institutions or participate in central ones? Neither extreme position—total assimilation of all people in the empire to the status of citizen nor complete reduction of colonized populations to rightless, exploitable objects serving a nation to which they did not belong—gained unqualified acceptance. Just what rights and what degree of belonging adhered to people of different origins and living in different parts of an empire remained a burning question.

In this chapter, we look at a series of interconnected revolutions. The revolutionary spiral began in interempire conflict: the Seven Years' War of 1756–63, considered by some to be the first world war. With Prussia and Hanover allying with Britain and Austria, Russia (initially), Sweden, Saxony, Portugal, and Spain allying with France, the war was fought in the Americas and India, over the seas, and in Europe. The war's cost forced its winner, Britain, to tighten control and extract more resources from its overseas components, leading to rising anger and mobilization among elites in the thirteen colonies of North America as well as to tighter territorial control in India. Loss of colonies and war debt pushed France to tighten the screws at home and enhanced French dependence on its most lucrative remaining colony, Saint Domingue; these were both significant steps toward a revolutionary situation. Spain, like Britain, saw the need for "reform" to regularize and deepen its control over American colonies, and it, too, upset its relationship with imperial intermediaries on whom it depended. The revolutionary dynamic in France ended in another vigorous form of empire-building, by Napoleon, whose conquest of Spain precipitated a struggle between elites located in Europe and Spanish America that in turn fostered other revolutionary mobilizations. Had diplomats in 1756 been more cautious about getting into an interempire war, the revolutions in the British, French, and Spanish empires might well not have taken place, at least not at the time and in the form they did.

In France, revolution resulted in the death of the monarch, but not of the empire. The question of whether the rights of man and of the citizen would extend to different categories of people in the empire became inescapable. In British North America, the revolution took thirteen colonies out of the monarchy and out of the British empire, but it did not take away empire's power to shape politics. American patriots proclaimed an "Empire of Liberty"—although they did not mean for all people in the empire to enjoy its liberty (chapter 9). If "national" visions of the state were the consequence more than the cause of revolutions in Spanish America, such ideas did not discourage some ambitious leaders from proclaiming their own empires or erase the acute tensions over hierarchy and cultural difference produced in the imperial past. Brazil's road out of the Portuguese empire was to declare itself an empire in its own right—under a branch of the same royal family that ruled in Lisbon.

It was a process, not a given outcome, that made the age revolutionary. New ideas, new possibilities, and new struggles came to the fore, and empires still faced the old problems of acting in relation to other empires and recruiting elites to do the daily work of government throughout their diverse spaces. Once we get away from a nation-centered view of history and the assumption that history moves inexorably toward correspondence of one "people" with one state, we can focus on longstanding debates over what democracy, citizenship, and nationality actually meant and when, where, and to whom these notions applied—within empires, in interempire rivalries, in mobilizations against empires.

We need to consider other forms of revolution, not just those celebrated on Independence or Bastille Day, not the purposeful creations of their makers: the industrial and agricultural revolutions of the eighteenth and nineteenth centuries, the explosive development of capitalism. To some political thinkers and activists, imperialism grew out of capitalism, but as we have seen, empire as a political form was not new in a capitalist age. The questions of how empire shaped capitalism and how capitalism shaped empire inspire another look at the interactions between economic and political processes. Our story up to the eighteenth century has shown European states both expanding and trying to constrain long-distance connections; profiting from the productive and commercial initiatives of other people, especially in Asia; working around empires, notably the Ottoman and Chinese, that were too powerful for them to assault directly; and failing to penetrate inland in most of Africa and southeast Asia. Did capitalist development in Europe, especially in Great Britain, and the wealth and technological improvements it produced provoke a parting of the ways between Europe and the rest of world, including the Chinese, Russian, and Ottoman empires? Did this economic transformation take the story of interempire influence and competition in a new direction?

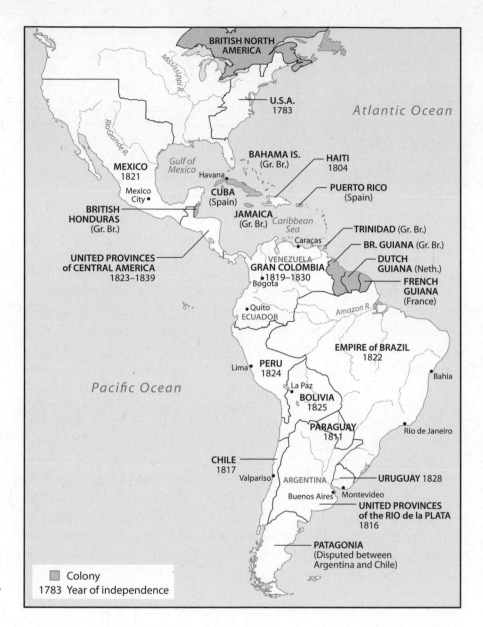

Map 8.1
Empire and independence in the Americas, 1783 to 1839.

Labels on map:

BRITISH NORTH AMERICA

U.S.A. 1783

Atlantic Ocean

Mississippi R.

Rio Grande R.

BAHAMA IS. (Gr. Br.)

HAITI 1804

MEXICO 1821

Gulf of Mexico

Havana

PUERTO RICO (Spain)

Mexico City

CUBA (Spain)

BRITISH HONDURAS (Gr. Br.)

JAMAICA (Gr. Br.)

Caribbean Sea

TRINIDAD (Gr. Br.)

BR. GUIANA (Gr. Br.)

DUTCH GUIANA (Neth.)

Caracas

UNITED PROVINCES of CENTRAL AMERICA 1823–1839

VENEZUELA

GRAN COLOMBIA 1819–1830

Bogota

FRENCH GUIANA (France)

Quito

ECUADOR

Amazon R.

EMPIRE of BRAZIL 1822

Lima

PERU 1824

Bahia

La Paz

BOLIVIA 1825

Pacific Ocean

PARAGUAY 1811

Rio de Janeiro

CHILE 1817

Valpariso

ARGENTINA

URUGUAY 1828

Buenos Aires

Montevideo

UNITED PROVINCES of the RIO de la PLATA 1816

PATAGONIA (Disputed between Argentina and Chile)

Legend:
Colony
1783 Year of independence

Capitalism cannot be understood simply as market exchange or even as a system of production based on wage labor. Capitalism was also a work of the imagination. Just as a complex and conflict-ridden history lay beneath the surface of representations of the "nation" as the natural unit of politics, capitalist development was both a historical process that gave rise to new markets in goods and labor and an ideological process that made such markets appear "natural." As empires collided and competed in the eighteenth and nineteenth centuries, questions about which forms of political and eco-

222 Chapter 8

nomic behavior were normal and legitimate became acute. We will argue in chapter 10 that making wage labor into a norm of British society depended on marking it off from other forms of labor—notably slavery—and that this process of distinguishing one kind of work from the other took place in the space of British empire.

We argue in this chapter that the concept of a French "citizen" who had rights and obligations toward a state was worked out in the space of French empire. The political ideas that acquired such apparent force in the American and French revolutions provided tools for different sides in long-running struggles over who had what rights and in what place. The age of revolution provided no definitive answer to these questions. In the pages that follow, we look at the ambiguous but ongoing place of empire in revolutions of the late eighteenth and early nineteenth centuries and at political movements that defined themselves both within and against imperial regimes.

The Franco-Haitian Revolution

Almost all of the immense body of scholarship on the French revolution is so focused on a national France that the revolution in the colonies all but disappears. Yet when the revolution began in 1789, Saint Domingue—producer of half the western world's sugar and coffee—was of enormous importance to the French economy and its propertied elite. Revolution rapidly became a question of empire.

Nation and Revolution in Imperial Europe

Scholars today regard the French revolution not as the work of a collective actor—be it the "bourgeoisie" or the "popular classes"—but as a dynamic process, pushed on by the interaction of multiple actors with different interests and desires. A strong monarchy had developed state institutions and patrimonial ties to elites across France, more intensively than in much of eighteenth-century Europe. But aristocrats chafed at royal power, non-noble property owners at the privileges of the aristocracy, and peasants at the dues and services they owed to landowners. The older, hierarchical, patriarchal conception of French society and the sponsorship of royal and aristocratic patrons corresponded less and less with the increasing self-confidence of urban professionals or of elite women who saw themselves as consumers and active participants in spaces of sociability (such as cafés, salons, and political meetings). Magazines, newspapers, books, and scandal sheets proliferated and spread ideas of Enlightenment thinkers among the literate population and those to whom these texts were read aloud. As the context for political debate widened, the concept of "citizen" came to the fore.

The French old regime had gone further than other European states to distinguish a body of citizens from "foreigners," but its administrators conceived of the citizen as a subject of state sovereignty, not its source. The political activists of the late eighteenth century developed a different vision. They drew on older ideas of the politically engaged citizen, citing precedents from Greek cities, the Roman republic, and Renaissance city-states. As in the past, the politicized ideal of citizenship was not all-inclusive, for it implied the ability and the will to be active in civic affairs. At certain moments, the Parisian "crowd" propelled political leaders in radical directions; at others it was elite reformers who pushed ideas to their limits.

The revolutionary moment in France was precipitated not only by internal changes in political consciousness and organization but also by the stresses of interempire conflict. France lost the war of 1756–63 and with it its Canadian colonies and all but a few outposts of its south Asian ones, but kept the horrifically lucrative sugar islands, notably Saint Domingue. Winners and losers were left with enormous debts, and if Britain could try to extract more from its colonies—with consequences its leaders did not predict—France had to turn inward.

As demands for more taxes went down the French hierarchy, resistance pushed upward. Vulnerable and needing cooperation, Louis XVI in 1789 called a consultative meeting of the Estates General, something that increasingly powerful kings had dispensed with since 1614. The representatives of the three "estates" into which French society was organized—clergy, nobility, and commoners—refused the old terms under which the Estates General had met and turned the meeting into a National Constituent Assembly. Here the claim was heard that the people, not the king, were sovereign.

On July 14, 1789, a crowd stormed and destroyed the Bastille, while in rural areas many peasants refused to pay dues to landowners and sacked manors. The assembly was becoming the de facto government; it abolished the nobility and reformed the system of rural dues. In August, it passed the Declaration of Rights of Man and of the Citizen, which declared, "The principle of all sovereignty resides essentially in the nation. No body or individual may exercise any authority which does not proceed directly from the nation." It stressed equality before law and representative government. But what was the French nation?

The revolution soon ran into the non-national nature of European politics. Austria (where Queen Marie Antoinette was from) and Prussia threatened to invade France in 1791. This threat galvanized people's sense of "la patrie en danger" and led to efforts to assemble a voluntary army of citizens. But the national idea was not sufficiently strong. By 1793, compulsion was added to the spirit of citizenship in recruiting soldiers; systematic conscription followed. Threats from abroad and radicalization of the revolutionary regime at home (including the execution of the king and queen) were part of a volatile mix that gave rise to waves of terror and counterterror and then to a more conservative turn. Meanwhile, France had been declared a nation and a republic, and the constitution and a plethora of revolutionary writings enshrined an ideology of republicanism that has been both invoked and violated ever since. Power resided in the people through their elected representatives; the state was one and indivisible; liberty, equality, and fraternity were its core principles.

This was a bold assertion of a new kind of sovereignty, but the boundaries of equal citizenry were contested from the start. Women were considered citizens, but not "active" ones—they did not get the vote until 1944. Whether the republican ideal implied social and economic, as well as political, equivalence was debated. Many property owners feared that too much political participation by the propertyless would threaten not only their own interests but social order. Fear of chaos was the cover behind which a more authoritarian government crept into post-revolutionary politics; in 1797 the new executive authority, the Directory, refused to accept defeat in an election. Tension escalated until a palace coup in 1799 brought in General Napoleon Bonaparte. In a startling reversal of revolutionary vocabulary, he declared himself emperor in 1804.

Citizenship and the Politics of Difference in the French Empire

Let us now look at what is usually left out of the story. One cannot draw a sharp line around European France. Neither Enlightenment philosophy nor revolutionary practice provided a clear idea of who constituted the French people or what the relationship of European France to France overseas should be. Some political thinkers, insisting that they were applying reason to society, developed classifications of human populations that explained why African and Asian peoples could not participate in civic life. Others refused to recognize particularity among people and assumed that their own ideas of the universal should apply to all. Still others used their enlightened reason to provide a more nuanced view of human difference.

For Denis Diderot, espousing universal values implied recognizing the integrity of different cultures. From his perspective, European assertions of the right to colonize others were illegitimate—a sign of the moral bankruptcy of European states. The Abbé Grégoire opposed colonization as currently practiced. He detested slavery, but not converting and "civilizing" other people. In 1788, leading Enlightenment figures founded the Société des Amis des Noirs to plead the cause of slaves in the French empire. While they did not agree on the significance of cultural difference, these theorists and activists embraced the fundamental equality of all humans and denied that people in the colonies could be enslaved or exploited at will. Most abolitionists favored gradual emancipation, weaning the imperial economy from its degrading practices without entailing social upheaval.

But the metropole's intellectuals were not the only parties interested in the relationship of colonies to the revolution. White planters in Saint Domingue translated citizenship doctrine into claims for a measure of self-rule. Their delegations to Paris lobbied for colonial assemblies to have the power to regulate matters of property and social status within the colony, insisting that colonies that mixed slaves and free, African and European, could not be ruled by the same principles that governed European France. But the revolutionary assemblies in Paris also heard from *gens de couleur*, property-owning, slave-owning inhabitants of Caribbean islands, usually born of French fathers and enslaved or ex-slave mothers. In Saint Domingue, they were a substantial group, owning one-third of the colony's plantations and a quarter of the slaves—and many of them did not lack for money, education, or connections to Paris. Citizenship, they insisted, should not be restricted by color. The Paris assemblies temporized.

Everyone involved, including the Paris revolutionaries, had to rethink positions when slaves entered the fray in August 1791. Two-thirds of the slaves of Saint Domingue were African born, and the revolt emerged from networks shaped by African religious affinities as well as knowledge of events in Paris. Rebels burned plantations and assassinated planters across an entire region of the island. The Saint Domingue revolution soon turned into multiple, simultaneous struggles: between royalists and patriots, between whites and gens de couleur, between slaves and slave owners. Subsets of each category sometimes allied with others, often switching allegiances. Political action was not defined by membership in a social category.

The revolutionary state feared losing a valuable colony to royalist counterrevolution or to the rival empires of England or Spain. The gens de couleur now seemed to leaders of the French Republic to be a necessary ally. In March 1792, the government in Paris agreed to declare all free people to be French citizens with equal political rights. In 1794, one of their number, Jean-Baptiste Belley, took a seat in the French National Constituent Assembly as a delegate from Saint Domingue. The door to imperial citizenship was now ajar.

It opened further as the French government found it could not control the multisided conflict without enlisting slave support. In 1793, the republican commissioner in Saint Domingue decided to free the slaves and declare them citizens. Paris—where the revolutionary dynamic had also entered a more radical phase—ratified his edict and the next year extended it to other

Figure 8.1
Portrait of Jean-Baptiste Belley, by Anne-Louis Girodet de Roussy Trioson, 1797. A man of color, elected to represent Saint Domingue in the French legislature, Belley leans on the bust of the Abbé Raynal, a leading (white) advocate of the rights of slaves, while looking toward a distant future. Musée National du Chateau de Versailles. Bridgeman Art Library, GettyImages.

colonies. The 1795 constitution declared the colonies an "integral part" of France. France became, for a time, an empire of citizens.

That slaves were needed to fortify the military was hardly new in the history of empires—Islamic empires and others had used this tactic. And slave-fighters had been deployed earlier in imperial competitions in the Caribbean. But the practicalities now corresponded to a principle that was indeed new—citizenship. Unlike the personal dependence of the fighting slave upon the master, the participation of the ex-slaves of Saint Domingue in the French military was linked to their new status.

The Saint Domingue revolution was thus a movement for freedom within empire before it was a movement against empire. The most revered leader of slaves, Toussaint L'Ouverture, embodied the ambiguities of the situation. A literate and skilled freed slave, he joined the slave revolt early on and rapidly rose to leadership. He contemplated for a time allying with the Spanish, but when France, not Spain, moved toward abolishing slavery, he went over to the French side, becoming an officer of the republic and by

1797 the de facto ruler of French Saint Domingue, fighting against royalists and rival empires and in defense of ex-slaves' newly claimed liberty. In 1801, still proclaiming his loyalty to France, Toussaint wrote a new constitution for Saint Domingue.

Neither French leaders nor Toussaint wanted to see sugar production end and they did not have an alternative to the watchful eyes of landowners and officials, at least, they thought, until ex-slaves had acquired the self-discipline of the "free" worker. Not all ex-slaves agreed; there were revolts within the revolution over issues of labor and of autonomy, as well as a daily struggle as ex-slaves sought control over their working lives and insisted that the state regard them—in officials' records of names, marriages, and deaths, for instance—in the same way as white citizens.

If the actions of Saint Domingue's people forced the Paris revolutionaries to keep rethinking what they meant by citizenship, the dynamics of empire in Europe had an enormous effect on the colonies. When Napoleon came to power he reversed the stumbling moves toward inclusive, empire-wide citizenship. In the overseas empire, Napoleon was a thoroughgoing restorationist, reflecting his personal connections to old regime settlers in the Caribbean (including but not limited to the slave-owning family of his first wife, Josephine). He wanted not only to restore the pre-revolutionary special status of colonies but to reinstate slavery as well. In 1802, he sent an army to Saint Domingue to do just that. He dissembled about his purpose enough to induce Toussaint, still acting within the framework of imperial citizenship, to surrender. Toussaint was sent off to prison in France, where he soon died. It was the Napoleonic version of empire—not a national or republican one—that ended Toussaint's vision of emancipation within France.

Other generals of slave origin continued the fight. The ex-slave armies combined with the devastation of yellow fever on Napoleon's army proved too much for the great emperor. In 1803, he gave up. The next year, the victors proclaimed the Republic of Haiti.

A struggle for freedom and citizenship within a revolutionary empire thus ended up with Haiti taking itself out of the empire. France's other sugar colonies, Guadeloupe and Martinique, where rebellions had been contained, had to endure forty-four more years of slavery until another revolutionary situation in European France, combined with another round of revolts in the plantation colonies, definitively turned the remaining slaves of the French empire into citizens.

Haiti's independence posed a new problem to the world's empires. Was Haiti in the vanguard of emancipation and decolonization? Or was it a symbol of the dangers of losing control over African slaves? Not only France but other imperial states had strong reasons to keep Haiti a pariah and not a vanguard. Only in 1825 did France give Haiti conditional recognition as a sovereign state, and then only after Haiti agreed to pay compensation for France's supposed losses. Full recognition finally came in 1838. The United States recognized Haiti in 1862, in the midst of its own civil war.

When in 1938, C.L.R. James, born in what had been the British slave colony of Trinidad, wrote his famous history of the Saint Domingue revolution, *The Black Jacobins*, he tried to put Haiti back in the vanguard of liberation and use its example to argue for the end of colonialism around the world. In 1946, an African political leader elected to serve in the French legislature in Paris, Léopold Senghor, invoked the moment 150 years earlier when France recognized the citizenship of black slaves. He was trying to persuade other deputies to return to the promise of revolutionary France and make all subjects in the colonies into citizens, with the same rights as those of European France. The Franco-Haitian revolution of 1789–1804 brought before the world questions about the relationship of citizenship and freedom—within and beyond empires—issues that are still debated today.

Napoleon

Napoleon now lies in his opulent tomb in Paris, a few kilometers from the Arc de Triomphe, his monument to himself and the glorious battles by which he conquered most of Europe. The French nation, as it has come to be, has appropriated the Napoleonic legend for itself. But Napoleon's history sits uneasily within a retrospective assertion of a French nation-state. Napoleon's conquests—at their peak embracing about 40 percent of Europe's population—are well-known, so let us concentrate on two questions: Did his empire represent a new, post-revolutionary notion of empire politics, less aristocratic and hierarchical, more centralized and bureaucratic? How French was the French empire under Napoleon?

The case for a new kind of empire rests on Napoleon's apparent interest in turning the rationalism of the Enlightenment into a logically planned, integrated, centralized system of administration, staffed by people chosen for competence and allegiance to the state, irrespective of social status. Science—including geography, cartography, statistics, and ethnography—would guide state officials and shape the population's conceptions of itself. The state's role in defining and superintending society through a single legal regime was embodied in the Napoleonic code. The code was more systematic than Justinian's compendium of the sixth century (chapter 3); it set out both public and private law, to be applied in a uniform and disinterested—and above all predictable—manner by judicial institutions. Taxation was high, but thanks

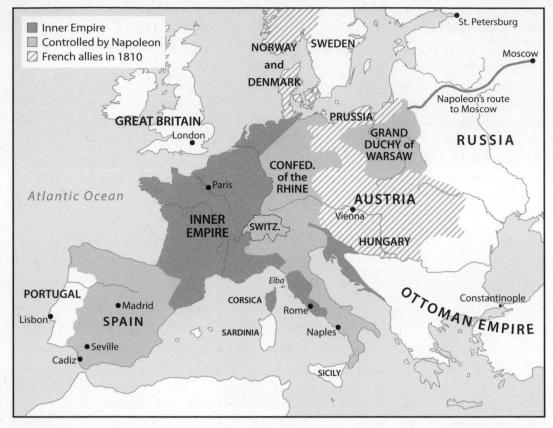

Map 8.2
Napoleonic empire in Europe.

to the systematic registration of land, its basis was transparent. A direct relation of citizen to sovereign was to replace the entrenched privileges of nobles and clergy, the arbitrary corruption of pre-revolutionary monarchy, and deference to local elites and local traditions. Napoleon abolished the one symbolic rival—long since voided of power—to his claims to overarching imperial authority in Europe: the Holy Roman Empire. Napoleon was of course a dictator and not a democrat, but in this argument, his imperial regime embodies the ideals of a French citizenry united behind its leader and rationalized bureaucracy—two products of revolution and Enlightenment, extended across Europe onto Russia's lands.

The case for reversion to an older mode of empire, on the other hand, starts with the symbolism of state power that Napoleon invoked, none more striking than his taking the title of emperor, his public display of thrones and robes and crowns, and his prevailing upon the pope to conduct the coronation—even with the twist Napoleon gave the ceremony by taking the crown from the pope's hands and placing it on his own head. All of this deliberately and obviously echoed the coronation of Charlemagne one thousand years earlier, just as Napoleon's triumphal arches claimed the heritage of Rome.

The revolution's break with aristocratic government was compromised in two more fundamental ways. First was Napoleon's allocation of noble titles and *dotations* (property given to people who served the regime, heritable in the male line) to many of his generals and leading supporters, including a considerable number of people who had held titles under the old regime as well as to elites in some conquered territories, creating (or re-creating) what one scholar calls an "imperial nobility." Second was his use in conquered areas of another classic strategy of emperors: ruling different places differently. If that meant in some contexts—northern Italy, for example—incorporating new territory into the basic administrative structure of France and imposing standardized laws and practices of bureaucracy, it meant in others—the

Figure 8.2
Napoleon on his imperial throne, Jean-Auguste-Dominique Ingres, 1806. Musée de l'Armée, Paris. Bridgeman Art Library, GettyImages.

Duchy of Warsaw, for instance—co-opting rather than displacing the local aristocracy. Such strategies went against the notions of equality that the revolution had promoted. And the Napoleonic code was a patriarchal one, reinforcing male authority within the households of citizens.

An imperial perspective lets us avoid the false dichotomy between continuity and change. Napoleon faced challenges common to all empires, balancing the need to co-opt defeated kings and princes against systematic top-down authority, finding a workable strategy somewhere between creating a homogenized elite and ruling each part of the empire separately. Other emperors across the world had tried to use officials distanced in one way or another from the society they were administering; the Chinese had pioneered a carefully recruited and educated bureaucracy long before the Enlightenment. Napoleon assimilated new ideas of government into classic imperial strategies.

Michael Broers argues that Napoleon conceived of an "inner empire"—present-day France except for the Vendée, the Netherlands, countries around the Rhine, Switzerland, much of northern Italy—in which a civilizing, centralizing, bureaucratizing model of rule was most strictly imposed. Then came an "outer empire" in which local aristocracies played a much stronger role and the Napoleonic reforms—particularly in regard to the privileges of nobles—were attenuated. Napoleon installed his relatives (brothers Joseph in Naples and Spain, Louis in the Netherlands, Jerome in Westphalia, brother-in-law Joachim Murat in Berg) as monarchs. In the Confederation of the Rhine, sixteen princes were nominally in charge of specific territories, loosely consolidated and interlaced with Napoleon's own officials. He was in effect federating smaller kingdoms or duchies into larger units, all under the umbrella of the Napoleonic empire.

The multiple channels of authority—of which prefects, on the Roman model, were the main but not the only means of passing information up and orders down—served a structure in which the emperor was, as in the past, the king of kings. Among Napoleon's potential allies, submonarchs, or enemies were the Habsburgs—with their own claims to empire. The Habsburg rulers sometimes fought Napoleon, sometimes—recognizing his superior power—allied with him. A Habsburg princess became Napoleon's empress after he divorced Josephine. Habsburg claims to imperial status became hollow with Napoleon's military dominance. But for the Austrian elite, Napoleon was an emperor one could live with or under, preferable to other empires on their flanks, Ottoman and Russian.

The crux of the Napoleonic machine was the sustenance of the army. The revolutionary ideal—a citizen army serving the nation—had been compromised even before Napoleon assumed power. People fought for their country because they had to. Napoleon (like Peter I in Russia a century earlier) systematized conscription. Doing so entailed the penetration of state power—military and administrative—to the village level, for it was from rural areas that most conscripts had to come. In addition to an administration under a prefect in each territorial division, Napoleon posted his gendarmerie, a militarized police force.

Conscription was applied not just to the pre-Napoleonic boundaries of France but to conquered territories as well. Resistance to conscription was higher in the mountainous villages of central France than in non-French-speaking areas such as the Rhine, parts of Italy, and Westphalia. By and large, the apparatus of state wore down defiance, producing an army that was more imperial than French. Only a third of the immense army that attacked Russia in 1812 was from "France."

This brings us to the second question: how French was the empire? The language of administration was French, and many—but not all—of the prefects and military authorities installed in non-French-speaking areas were from France. Gradually local elites were recruited into the roles defined by French occupants of these positions. Some authors speak of a French "cultural imperialism" imposed on places like Italy, where Napoleonic officials thought people backward and in need of civilizing influences—the French law code, competent civil servants, and a scientific attitude—to be wielded against priests and reactionary aristocrats. Yet much of "France" was being "civilized" at the same time as regions that spoke Italian, German, or Polish. Parts of western France, the Vendée, were ruled lightly because the region was considered obstreperous and dangerous, while Poland was also ruled lightly—in order to co-opt its nobility.

Elites in some conquered territories found good reason to follow a course taken in many empires going back to Rome—contingent accommodation. The rationalizing side of Napoleonic administration appealed for a time at least to certain liberal, commercially minded people, who embraced its anti-aristocratic, anticlerical side. But Napoleon strongly identified stable social order with landownership—although not with royalists and feudal lords—and landed elites had their reasons to prefer peace under Napoleon to war against him. Many liberals who had welcomed Napoleon became disillusioned with his system; some resisted French rule on national grounds. Spain comes perhaps the closest to widespread guerilla warfare against an invader, but even there, mobilization was directed in part against Spanish elites who were oppressing peasants. The fighters in different provinces of Spain could not act together in a sustained and coherent fashion, and parts of the "Spanish" campaign against Napoleon were led by British generals.

Napoleon's empire is sometimes seen as continental rather than overseas—but only because his overseas ventures did not succeed. Napoleon's only major defeat by what became a national liberation movement occurred at the hands of Saint Domingue's ragtag armies of slaves, ex-slaves, and free people of color, with help from France's imperial enemies, American merchants, and tropical microbes. Napoleon's other, earlier, overseas venture, the conquest of Egypt in 1798, proved short-lived. British intervention helped restore this territory to the Ottoman empire. In Egypt, Napoleon had sought both to push his imperial genealogy back to the pharaohs and to bring science and rational rule to a part of the "backward" Ottoman empire. He had also hoped to build on Saint Domingue and Louisiana to forge an imperial expanse across the Caribbean and Gulf of Mexico. In neither Egypt nor Saint Domingue was the outcome his to determine. In 1803 Napoleon was reputed to say, "Damn sugar, damn coffee, damn colonies!" as he sold off Louisiana to the United States for cash to finance his other imperial dreams.

Overextension is a conventional and unsatisfying explanation for Napoleon's defeats; in the history of empires no clear line separates overextension from extension. Napoleon tried to harness the resources of central Europe—with considerable success—but Russia could bring to bear those of Siberia and Ukraine, while Britain had overseas territories, as well as the world's premier navy. Napoleon succumbed not to the welling up of national sentiment against the reactionary power of empire but to other empires, notably the British and the Russian. As Napoleon's army lost its grip after the debacle of his invasion of Russia in 1812, components of his conquest reconstituted themselves as politically viable entities—around monarchic and dynastic figures—in somewhat different forms than before. Polities like Baden and Bavaria had absorbed smaller units around them under Napoleonic overrule and emerged as stronger, more consolidated entities afterward. When the king of Prussia tried to organize the fight against Napoleon in 1813 he appealed not to "Germans" but to "Brandenburgers, Prussians, Silesians, Pomeranians, Lithuanians."

The components of the empire that had come closest to integration into France (northern Italy, the Rhine, the low countries) experienced the most profound effects of Napoleon's empire, including increased professionalization of governing elites. Napoleon's defeat allowed for a degree of federation among polities he had subdued and that reconstituted themselves as allies against him. Elites across Europe who had for a time been swayed by Napoleon's project of regularized administration and legal codification would influence the later course of politics. Post-Napoleonic Europe remained dominated by a small number of strong players: Russia, Austria, Prussia, Great Britain, and—as before—France. The peace negotiated at Vienna in 1815 reinforced this monarchical consolidation. The major winners kept their emperors; France, some twenty-five years after its revolution, went back to having a king.

Napoleon's conquests, his governments, and his defeats had profound effects on the building of states. But state and nation did not coincide in Napoleon's empire, and fighting Napoleon did not bring state and nation together among his enemies. Napoleon was not the last ruler who came close to incorporating the European continent into a vast empire, and although late nineteenth-century empire-builders looked overseas, their actions were still part of the competition between a small number of empire-states centered in Europe. France, after episodes of monarchy, revolution, and a new republic (1848–52), came under a regime that called itself the Second Empire and was headed by a man who called himself Napoleon III (nephew of the original). The Second Empire endured until 1870, and like the first its end came through the actions of another empire, in this case the newly unified German Reich. The rise and fall of both Napoleons left in place a Europe of empire-states, mixing variously the voice of citizens with the power of monarchs, combining contiguous and distant territories and culturally diverse populations (chapter 11).

Capitalism and Revolution in the British Empire

We saw in chapter 6 that "Britain" emerged not as a coherent project of a single people but out of varied initiatives, state and private, that were gradually tied together: composite monarchy in the British isles, and piracy, chartered companies, trading enclaves, plantation colonies, and colonies of settlement overseas. A "fiscal-military" state, linked to strong banking institutions, provided the revenue for a navy that could protect settlements and trade routes and channel a major portion of the world's commerce through British ships and British ports. England had its share of internecine conflict, but the success of Parliament, representing largely landed gentry and aristocracy, in limiting royal power made it possible for the Crown's empire-building to complement rather than contradict the interests of magnates. With the consolidation of government by the "King in Parliament" after the civil war of 1688 and under the pressure of a long series of wars against France—to counter Louis XIV's efforts to dominate Europe and possibly impose Catholic kings on England—Britain developed a government capable of managing diverse ventures abroad and social and economic change at home.

England, Empire, and the Development of a Capitalist Economy

The eighteenth century was for the British empire revolutionary in more ways than one. The nexus of plantation slavery overseas and agricultural and industrial development at home was tightened up during the extraordinary expansion of the sugar economy. Creeping colonization of India by a private company escalated into a process of territorial incorporation in which the Crown took a closer supervisory role. Revolution in the North American colonies revealed both the limits of empire and the extent to which principles of British politics had been diffused across an ocean.

What is the connection between Britain's leading role in the development of capitalism and its imperial power, even taking into account its loss of thirteen North American colonies in the 1780s? Kenneth Pomeranz offers an illuminating comparison of the economies of the Chinese and British empires, the first a great land empire with connections across Eurasia, the second deriving its strength from the sea. Pomeranz argues that in the early eighteenth century the potential for economic growth and industrial development in the two empires—especially in heartland regions—was not notably different. Their agriculture, craft industries, commercial institutions, and financial mechanisms were roughly comparable. The "great divergence" occurred at the end of the eighteenth century.

Capital accumulated through the slave trade and sugar production—considerable as it was—does not explain the different trajectories of these empires. It was the complementarity between metropolitan and imperial resources that pushed Britain's economy ahead. Sugar was grown in the Caribbean; labor came from Africa. Feeding workers in England was not therefore constrained by the limits of land and labor at home. Combined with tea, another imperial product, sugar did much to keep workers in the cotton mills for long hours—without devoting British resources to the potatoes, grain, or sugar beets that would have been alternative sources of calories. Similarly with the cotton that clothed workers: other fibers might have been grown in England, but slave cotton from the southern United States in the early nineteenth century did not demand land in the British isles or labor within metropolitan Britain.

China's imperial system was oriented toward extracting revenue from land; both land and labor were internal to the system. Britain's superior access to coal played an important part in its industrial growth, but the capacity to push opportunity costs in land and labor overseas gave Britain a distinct advantage. Other differences came into play only because of Britain's maritime empire: British use of joint-stock companies, for example, provided no great advantage in domestic manufacturing, but it brought together the large resources needed for transport and fighting capacity to sustain long-distance, coercive operations.

Britain had made itself into a center of redistribution for goods arriving not only from its dependencies in the West Indies, North America, and India but from many parts of the world. By the 1770s, over half of British imports and exports were coming from or going to areas outside Europe. With the growth of industry as well as of financial and commercial institutions, Britain's economic power became increasingly self-perpetuating. It could lose the North American colonies without losing their trade, cling to the valuable sugar islands, and extend the breadth and depth of its reach into Asia. By the end of the eighteenth century, its industries produced commodities that people in the Americas, Africa, and even Asia wanted to buy.

The trajectory of the British economy cannot be attributed only to imperial ventures, including plantation slavery. Were slavery the decisive factor, then Portugal or Spain, the imperial pioneers in this regard, should have taken the lead in industrializing. It was the symbiosis between metropolitan and imperial factors that explains why Britain *used* its empire so productively. With less dynamic domestic economies, such as those of Spain and Portugal, much of the benefit of exporting to colonies went to financial institutions outside imperial territory. Portugal and Spain took a long time to move away from regimes of landowning nobles with dependent peasants, and France's peasants were relatively secure on their land. In Britain's case, landowners in the seventeenth and eighteenth centuries curtailed tenant farmers' and other cultivators' access to land and used more wage labor in agriculture.

In the interpretation of Karl Marx—who had considerable if grudging respect for the material successes brought by capitalism—what distinguished the capitalist system was not just free markets but the separation of the majority of producers from the means of production. The violent extinction of England's small farmers' access to land left the majority with no choice but to sell the one thing they had—their labor—and left land and factory owners with no choice but to buy it. Capitalism was more successful in the long run than household production, serfdom, or slavery—and one could now add communism—because it compelled the owners of the means of production to compete to hire labor and to employ that labor as efficiently as everyone else.

The ability and need of property owners to hire labor was not an automatic effect of markets or coercive power; it depended on juridical and political institutions capable of conveying legitimacy to ownership. Britain, having survived its civil wars and mobilized resources to fight Spanish and French empires, ended up with a solidly institutionalized state system. It struck a balance between the conservative aristocratic privilege of Spain and the monarchical centralism of France. Its merchant class was as avidly entrepreneurial as that of the Netherlands, but it had a stronger state. Britain was in a position to develop a flexible repertoire of power that, for a time, no rival could achieve.

Commercial linkages centered on Great Britain tied together what Edmund Burke called a "mighty and strangely diversified mass": slave-owning sugar producers, New England farmers, Indian nawabs, sailors, fishermen, merchants, peasants, and slaves. The European population of the North American colonies grew between 1700 and 1770 from 250,000 to 2.15 million—over a fourth of the population of Britain itself. Exports from England and Wales to the thirteen colonies tripled between 1735 and 1785—in the midst of political conflict. It was in 1773 that reference was first made to "this vast empire on which the sun never sets." Some English writers saw themselves as the inheritors of the Roman republic. As David Armitage has pointed out, the British state was "neither a solely metropolitan nor an exclusively provincial achievement; it was a shared conception of the British Empire."

Where slaves were numerically predominant, as in the Caribbean, fear of slave revolt—and vulnerability of rich islands to other empires—meant that whites needed the assurance of the empire connection. Settlers in North America, facing substantial indigenous populations, had different and conflicting options with regard to empire. Native peoples could be dangerous, hence a need for the presence of an imperial army; they could be useful trading partners, playing a complementary role within an imperial economy. But indigenous peoples' land was desirable to settlers, pulling imperial authorities into conflicts they did not necessarily want. The British government regarded indigenous peoples within the colonies as subjects of the king and tribes beyond colonial boundaries as under the king's "protection." After the Seven Years' War—in which French and British had vied for alliances with Indian groups and fought those on the opposite side—the British government drew a line west of which colonists were prohibited from settling, hoping to diffuse clashes over land while reserving to the Crown— not local governments—all rights to negotiate with Indians. This provision became a source of settler-government conflict, exacerbated by repeated violations by settlers eager to buy or seize land in fertile interior valleys.

The ideas that made the British empire both British and an empire eventually fostered rebellion against it. British creoles expected that institutions of parliamentary government for men of property would be reproduced wherever in the empire they lived—and that meant assemblies in the individual colonies. To a certain extent their expectations were fulfilled, although colonial assemblies were more ad hoc inventions than mini-parliaments. John Adams even suggested that the capital of Britain could be located in North America. Had American colonists obtained the authority they wanted, they might have turned the British empire into a confederation—each component with its own governing institutions, its own sense of political unity, and, as the efforts of George Washington and others to gain control of inland river valleys made clear, its own imperial ambitions.

Such a solution, however, risked creating what British jurists who knew their Roman law called "imperium in imperio"—an empire within an empire. Colonists, until the eve of the revolution, cherished the British connection but disagreed over its terms, wanting at the very least a measure of provincial government and acknowledgment of their rights. Some colonists claimed, perhaps disingenuously, that the founding charters of their settlements made them subject to the king, but not Parliament. Parliament thought otherwise, and was adamant that it alone had the power to tax, while the regulation of commerce, via the Navigation and other acts, was essential to tying the diverse parts of the empire to Britain itself. The vast debts acquired in the war of 1756–63, in backing up the East India Company's aggressive stance in India, and in conflicts with Native Americans led London both to tighten its own officials' control over administration and to impose higher taxes—including those on its North American subjects. The Sugar and Stamp acts (1764, 1765) that entered the legend of American rebellion were part of this empire-wide fiscal problem. Elites in the Americas—the merchants, law-

Figure 8.3
"Forcing Tea Down America's Throat," by Paul Revere for the *Royal American Magazine*, 1774. British men hold down "Lady Liberty," while the British prime minister pours tea down her throat. Britannia—the symbol of what was truly British—averts her eyes. The cartoon protests British retaliation for the Boston Tea Party of 1773, itself a protest against British policies forcing consumers in New England to buy tea shipped by the British East India Company, a restriction that hurt American merchants. Hulton Archive, GettyImages.

yers, and large landowners who were the vital intermediaries of an imperial regime—were the most directly affected by such measures, and they took the lead in the escalating protests that eventually led to war.

From an imperial perspective, the American revolution was a British civil war. Many residents of the Thirteen Colonies identified strongly enough with their brethren in the British isles or saw enough of a common interest with the empire that they gave the Crown their contingent accommodation. The "loyalists" were an important dimension of the war. Like any effective empire, Britain tried to exploit differentiation to save its dependencies, enticing slaves to desert masters and fight for Britain with freedom as the reward. Slaves also called themselves "loyalists," and after their side lost the war many of them followed the lines of imperial connection to Nova Scotia or Sierra Leone. Britain tried with some success to get Indian allies, as it had against the French in the war of 1756–63, and many rebels came to regard Indians as their enemies. In a wider perspective, the revolution turned into yet another interempire war, for France and Spain entered on the side of the rebels, took some territory in the Caribbean and Florida, diverted British forces into the West Indies, and challenged the British navy sufficiently to make reinforcing and resupplying the army difficult, a significant contribution to the outcome of the war.

On the rebels' side, leaders' desire for unity inspired them to make clear that, despite class differences, white settlers of modest means were part of the American political community. In so doing, they sharpened racial divisions. The patriotic struggle brought together poor and rich whites; the fate of slaves was work (chapter 9).

Coming soon after the victory over their French imperial rival in 1763, defeat at the hands of colonial rebels forced British leaders to come to grips with the limits of empire. The seemingly sure way to enracinate British power across an ocean—to settle British subjects—had fallen afoul of an old problem of empire: that intermediaries could use their ideological and political affinity to the metropole not to sustain that connection but to twist it in new directions.

Empire after Revolution

In the end, British rulers were not willing to sacrifice parliamentary sovereignty to accommodate the demands of creole rebels or to pay the price of continued warfare to bring them back into the imperial fold. But if the loss of North American colonies deprived the British government of tax revenue, Britain continued to trade with Americans, to the profit of commercial interests on both sides of the Atlantic. Having lost an empire of kith and kin, Britain now was left with a less populous, less wealthy version of the settler colony—Canada—plus islands in the Caribbean where most of the inhabitants were slaves, and—via an arrangement with a private company—parts of India. To many in England, it appeared as if holding the remaining empire together would depend less on appeal to a common "Britishness" and more on the direct exercise of power over people regarded as backward or elites seen as tyrannical. But British ability to carry off this harsher control was still constrained by the need to give local elites a stake in the imperial enterprise, by the danger even in the most oppressed slave society of rebellion, and by the conviction of at least some members of the imperial establishment that the political and moral viability of empire depended on recognizing the place of all subjects within the polity.

India was the focus of both more intensive colonization and increasingly difficult questions about what deepening involvement meant to British conceptions of their political institutions. Creeping colonization—a company interested in trade, profiting from preexisting commercial networks in India and southeast Asia and gradually taking on more of the functions of sovereignty—started to move much faster after mid-century. In 1756 the nawab of Bengal nearly threw the East India Company out; this became the occasion for the company to make use of its military capabilities and local allies to win a major victory over local rulers in 1757 at the battle of Plassey. The Seven Years' War, meanwhile, led the British state to contribute large new military resources so that the company and its Indian allies could defeat the French and their Indian allies in the contest for dominance over south Asia. The ante was raised.

Map 8.3
India, 1767 and 1805.

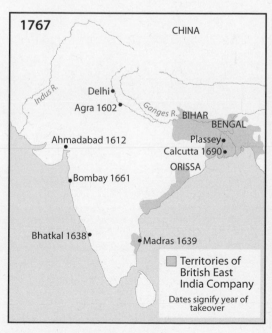

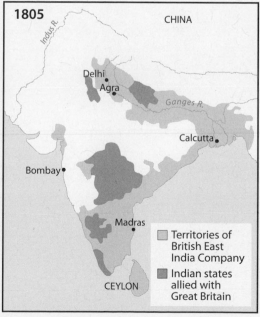

With his own power much diminished and the company strengthened, the Mughal emperor in 1765 ceded to the East Indian Company the *diwani*, the right to administer and collect taxes in Bengal, Bihar, and Orissa. The EIC would now enjoy the revenue produced by some twenty million people in an area of India notable for its productive agriculture—in rice and export crops—its cloth and other industries, and its sophisticated commercial and financial elites. The large majority of people defined as "inhabitants of India" came under the jurisdiction of courts supervised by the company but administering what officials considered to be Islamic or Hindu law. In much of the Indian subcontinent the business of government—the de facto exercise of sovereignty—was from then on a profit-making activity.

The key to success was to pass the costs onto the people being governed. The EIC used locally recruited troops known as sepoys. The political map of India became a patchwork: areas of company rule spreading out from Bengal, regions of continued Mughal rule, and independent principalities. In south-

Figure 8.4
Robert Clive, leader of the British East India Company, receiving the land revenues of Bengal, Bihar, and Orissa, 1765, painted by Benjamin West. British Library, London. HIP, ArtResource.

ern India, for example, the company conspired with the ruler of Hyderabad against the powerful Tippu Sultan of Mysore, fighting a series of wars until Tippu was killed in 1799 and Mysore became an allied state. But company attempts to expand out of Bombay and Madras were constrained by the British government's worries about adding to its war debts of 1756–63, the strength of indigenous polities, and the limits that even cooperating rulers put on company actions. The EIC tried to use Mughal institutions and the legitimacy of the Mughal emperor where they carried weight, and its efforts at tax collection relied on hierarchies of indigenous officials, who got enough of the rewards to cooperate. While the EIC remained what it had originally been—a joint-stock company engaged in commerce—it acted more and more like a state, collecting revenue, making treaties or fighting wars with regional potentates, and exercising juridical authority. Some company men became fabulously wealthy in this semi-monopolistic trade system and the quintessentially non-market process of collecting taxes.

The effects of the EIC's more explicit use of power crept back to England. The British government since the 1770s had been taking more seriously its supervisory role over the company, and India had become part of the imaginary universe of the British elite. Some three hundred publications about India appeared in Britain between 1750 and 1785. The colonizing system lent itself to abuse. Like Las Casas in sixteenth-century Spain, Edmund Burke two centuries later based his campaign against EIC abuses on the assumption that empire constituted a moral sphere in which rulers could be held to account. Burke accused Warren Hastings, governor-general of India since 1773, of condoning cruelty to civilians, extorting money from local rulers, impoverishing the country, and enriching himself.

Hastings was tried before Parliament—a process that went on for seven years. In the end he was acquitted, but Burke's accusation, coming right after the American revolution, opened up a range of questions about what sort of empire Britain was ruling. The government tried to get the EIC to clean up its operating procedures, appointing a new governor-general for the company (none other than Lord Cornwallis, loser of the final battle against American rebels) and insisting that the EIC regularize its tax-collecting methods. The so-called Permanent Settlement of 1793 defined the revenues that zamindars—landlords—had to provide the state and ensured that they would have to extract

"I impeach him in the name of all the Commons of Great Britain, whose national character he has dishonoured. I impeach him in the name of the people of India, whose laws, rights, and liberties he has subverted; whose properties he has destroyed, whose country he has laid waste and desolate. I impeach him in the name, and by virtue, of those eternal laws of justice, which he has violated. I impeach him in the name of human nature itself, which he has cruelly outraged, injured, and oppressed in both sexes, in every age, rank, situation, and condition of life."

—Edmund Burke, attacking Warren Hastings in Parliament, 1788 these payments at the expense of their tenants or risk having their land sold away for debt. Needing intermediaries, British officials helped rigidify hierarchy in Indian society—only to criticize Indian society for being hierarchical. We will return in chapter 10 to the long-term consequences of these strategies.

Burke was not the only well-established figure questioning the way the British empire was governed. Adam Smith was also critical of the East India Company and empire and slavery more generally. For Smith, the development of open, not restricted, markets was in Britain's long-term interest. Unconvinced that the British way of life was the only route to progress, he favored a more empathetic and humble attitude toward non-European societies and a less bellicose one toward other European polities. A movement against slavery and the slave trade developed in the last two decades of the eighteenth century, beginning with petitions to Parliament to abolish British participation in the trade. Challenges like these made clear that whatever happened in the empire was a matter of concern at home, even when it affected people who lived in distant places and with whom the king's English or Scottish subjects had little cultural affinity.

Meanwhile, there were other emperors and empires to fight. The French revolution, the development of radical models of sovereignty with potential appeal to enemies of aristocracy and monarchy within Britain, and the subsequent return of France to empire-building from 1799 to 1815 challenged Britain's imperial achievements. Resources from beyond the British isles and Britain's earlier development of a navy to protect commerce across vast oceanic spaces were critical to containing and ultimately defeating Napoleon's imperial designs.

Britain's victory over Napoleon brought it new assets in the Mediterranean (Malta, greater influence in Egypt) and—at the expense of Napoleon's subordinate partner, the Netherlands—new territories in South Africa, Ceylon, and parts of India, Java, and the Caribbean. Far from softening before the examples of republicanism and citizenship in North America and France, Britain moved to consolidate its authority over the large empire it had managed to retain and to extend.

After a rebellion in Ireland in 1798, the island was incorporated more fully into Britain with the Union Act of 1801. The act abolished Ireland's Protestant-dominated parliament, bringing Irish deputies to London, where they were a minority. Catholics were not allowed to stand for Parliament until the "Catholic Emancipation" of 1828, and even then property requirements for voting kept most Catholics away from the polls. There was poor relief in England—miserly to be sure—but not in Ireland, and Irish who sought this aid in England could be deported home. Ireland was not a colony, not a county, and not an incorporated kingdom; it was not like

Canada or Jamaica. Ireland was a part of an empire that ruled different people differently.

In the late eighteenth century, the Crown had begun to exercise more direct control over the expanding territory acquired by the East India Company. It acquired unchallenged mastery of the seas with Napoleon's defeat. In the early decades of the nineteenth century, Great Britain could afford to balance closer administration of some territories it controlled with the exercise of economic power vis-à-vis formally independent states (chapter 10). British leaders had learned, most strikingly in North America, that direct imperial control had its dangers. In the Caribbean and India, tensions between subordination and incorporation in an empire-state were becoming visible. As the marriage of empire and capitalism was producing an economy of unprecedented dynamism, questions were being raised about destructive practices taking place under Britain's rule.

Empire, Nation, and Political Imagination in Spanish America

Empire—in name and in fact—did not disappear from Europe with the French or North American revolution, and it became an ambition in the newly independent United States. But did the "nation-state" emerge as an alternative? As interpreted by Benedict Anderson, the "creole revolutions" of North and South America were the crucibles of nationalism, reflecting the changing "circuits" along which creoles—Europeans who settled and reproduced in colonies—moved, bypassing the imperial centers of London or Madrid. National imagination was enhanced by the development of newspapers within the respective colonies. Empire no longer framed creoles' political discourse, and the imagined community—Anderson's famous phrase—came to be their colonial territory in the Americas.

But national communities were only one element of political imagination at this time. As we have seen in the revolutions of Saint Domingue and the Thirteen Colonies, political mobilizers used imperial idioms and addressed imperial institutions; secession emerged as a goal only when imperial conflicts proved unresolvable. In South America as well, the "horizontal" affinity that Anderson regards as constituting a nation of equivalent citizens was less salient than the differentiated society colonization had produced. Relations between free and slave, between cosmopolitan elites and parochial peasants, were intrinsic to a vertical social order. Nationalism emerged as an ideology to defend unequal social orders, but only after imperial structures had failed to manage conflicts within the empire form of state.

While the creole revolutions of Spanish America (1809–25), like that of British North America, began as struggles within the framework of empire, that framework was monarchical, not parliamentary. The Spanish monarchy (see chapter 5) had been the focus of transatlantic loyalty. As in North America, attempts to "reform" and consolidate imperial power in Europe led to conflict overseas. The Bourbon dynasty, in power since 1700, no longer fit the pattern of composite monarchy. Facing, like Britain and France, heavy debts from the Seven Years' War, the Bourbons brought Aragon, Catalonia, and other provinces under more direct authority and tightened up financial control. In Spanish America, they intervened more intensely in areas largely populated by Indians, at the expense of tacit understandings between state officials and indigenous elites. Settlers of European and mestizo origin moved into previously Indian lands, producing tensions and, in the 1780s, large-scale rebellions, repressed with great loss of life.

In the 1790s chronic warfare in Europe added to the costs of containing tension in the Americas. The Spanish state had to squeeze more and more out of an empire that could no longer expand. The forward–looking elites of early nineteenth-century Spanish America first sought to loosen the constraints of the mercantilist system by regulating who could enter commerce through guilds in the major entrepots rather than through a single control mechanism dominated by merchants of the Spanish port of Cadiz. Reformers sought to revitalize economic ties through ocean-crossing networks of personal relations, kinship, and credit.

Napoleon provided the immediate impetus to tear apart an already frayed imperial structure. He conquered Spain in 1808 and installed his brother as king. Taking refuge from Napoleonic power in Cadiz, Spanish leaders established a parliament, the Cortes, which tried to maintain a semblance of a Spanish state. Spanish subjects who were located overseas had every reason to fear that their patronage connections and mercantilist trading systems were in jeopardy. The precedents of revolution in France and parliamentary government in Great Britain suggested alternatives to both Spanish monarchy and Napoleonic empire, but elites in Spanish America also feared the danger of a Haitian-style revolution. In most of Spanish America, slaves were not as numerous as in the Caribbean, and slavery was part of a range of hierarchical, labor-managing institutions; populations included mixtures of different peoples, of Indian, African, and European origin and of quite unequal statuses. Creole elites, to a large extent, thought that their familiarity with local practices meant that they could manage hierarchy better than could European Spaniards.

The Cortes became the site of conflict between "Peninsulares" (from the Iberian peninsula) and American delegates over the distribution of seats, over how to count non–white or mixed people from the colonies, over constitutional provisions, and over the control of trade. The poverty and weakness of the monarchy and the Cortes made the issues appear increasingly zero-sum. Peninsulares feared that they might be colonized by their former colonies, by people who were not fully "Spanish." We will encounter similar fears during other moments of imperial reconfiguration, such as France as late as the 1940s when colonial subjects were demanding more political voice in Paris (chapter 13).

For the Spanish of the Americas, European Spain was becoming less useful and more burdensome. The sequence is important: there had been no prior consolidation of "national" sentiment in New Spain, New Granada, or other American territories but instead a more gradual movement from demands for fuller voice within empire to local assertions of autonomy to widespread calls for secession from Spain. The Cadiz legislature tried to hold together the empire by gestures of inclusion, proclaiming in the constitution of 1812 that "The Spanish nation is the union of all Spaniards of both hemispheres." That formulation opened up more questions than it answered. Indians were formally included in that nation, but their participation was not on equal terms; people of African origin were excluded. Moreover, the Cortes was unable to accommodate the economic and political demands of overseas Spaniards without giving up the control the Peninsulares insisted on. When King Ferdinand VII was restored to power in 1814, he reacted to conflict not by compromise but by escalating repression—denying the legitimacy of the liberal constitution of 1812.

As disputes over putting the Spanish empire back together escalated, efforts to exit from empire took root in the Americas. Simon Bolivar emerged as the leading spokesman for a vigorous project of building Spanish-speaking, American nations, following Enlightenment ideals of rationally ordered progress and liberty. Bolivar's vision was also exclusionary. People who did not speak Spanish or share in the elite's values were not to participate fully in the new order.

Within the Americas, Iberian Spain still had its supporters, as well as its military and administrative institutions. The result was civil war: a series of conflicts in different parts of the Americas. Spanish efforts to stop secession, with their inevitable excesses, alienated many people whose support had once kept the empire together. These conflicts brought out the tensions within colonial society, particularly over the highly unequal social structure. As both sides tried to get slaves to fight for them, slavery became untenable on mainland Spanish America. Slavery died, not from the diffusion of liberal principles or slave revolt but from the inability of slave owners and political leaders to contain the effects of involving slaves in their revolutionary conflict. On the mainland, diverse forces mobilized by Bolivar and others fought campaigns into the 1820s.

Where Spain was able to hang in, not surprisingly, was on the plantation islands, Cuba and Puerto Rico. There, the protection of an imperial government was essential to a slave system that had been growing in size and intensity thanks to reduced competition after the liberation of Saint Domingue's slaves (and would get another boost from the abolition of the British slave trade, discussed in chapter 10).

The wearing down of the financially strapped government of imperial Spain and the eventual triumph of creole armies (see map 8.1) produced neither geographic unity—a commonwealth of Spanish-speaking American nations—nor independent republics of equals. The constitutions of Latin American states in the 1820s were hybrid documents, accepting the end of slavery as a fait accompli, making some accommodations to Indians, but trying to protect the new republics from too much democracy and too much cultural plurality. But in the balance of power *among* empires, the emergence of so many independent states out of an old empire had important effects: the new states—exactly as feared by leaders of France, Russia, and the United States—were porous to British capital and commercial influence. Britain's imperial repertoire, as we shall see, now put more emphasis on economic power, with the threat of the British navy in the background.

The pattern in Brazil was different. Brazilian elites had already acquired much of the autonomy Spanish elites in the Americas were seeking at the beginning of the nineteenth century. Brazil seemed on the verge of overshadowing its mother country. With their pioneering sugar economy producing capital that European Portugal could not generate, Brazilians outfitted slave ships that traded directly with Africa. When Napoleon took over Portugal, the king installed himself in Brazil, making it a colony without a metropole. Brazil's economic power—it was the largest importer of slaves in the first half of the nineteenth century—was growing. When, well after Napoleon's defeat, Portugal wanted its monarch back, the royal family split, and many Brazilians thought they had become the imperial center. Dom Pedro's decision to stay in Brazil left Portugal to his relatives and made Brazil independent without a war of secession. In 1822, Dom Pedro took the title of emperor of Brazil— the older empire had produced a second one, an enormous state ruled by a slaveholding oligarchy. This was hardly a social revolution. Brazilian elites, like those of Venezuela, Argentina, and elsewhere, worked hard over the ensuing decades to produce national ideologies able to contain conflicts that emerged during the struggles that had ended up with independence.

Political Possibilities, Political Tensions

The Chinese communist leader Chou En-lai is reputed to have replied to a question about the political significance of the French revolution, "It is too soon to tell." Most commentators have not been so prudent. The French revolution and those in North and South America have been transformed into founding myths in their respective countries and are thought to mark the emergence of citizenship, of national economies, of the very idea of the nation. But in their own time, the revolutions' lessons were inconclusive. The French revolution seemed to promise that the values of liberty it espoused would apply not just to a state located in Europe but to a transcontinental empire, with African-born slaves joining European-born citizens. But subsequently the double fact of Haiti's independence and Napoleon's restoration of slavery in France's other islands excluded—for the time being—the possibility of an empire of citizens.

The patriots who created the United States declared that people who constituted themselves as a political community had the right to determine their collective fate, but this right was denied to slaves and taken away from Indians, against whom wars of conquest were conducted with more vigor than under the eighteenth-century British empire (chapter 9). The revolutions of the Americas began by drawing on ideas of English liberty, French citizenship, or Spanish monarchy to redefine sovereignty and power within imperial polities but ended up producing new states that shared world space with reconfigured empires. The secession of states from the British, French, and Spanish empires did not produce nations of equivalent citizens any more than it produced a world of equivalent nations.

That states like the United States, Colombia, or Haiti emerged in an imperial context and not from a prior, generally accepted, national idea does not diminish their significance or impact on the future. Each in its own way marked out the possibility of a "people" constituting a sovereign nation. The complexity of each struggle—the exclusions built into the attempt to forge political community, the uncertainties over what that community would be—forced people to debate repeatedly what they meant by liberty, by nation, by sovereignty, by people. Popular sovereignty was far from an accepted norm in western Europe, and within empires' spaces overseas it was unclear whether the idea of a rights-bearing individual would be a contagious proposition or one jealously guarded by a select few.

The temptations and habits of empire continued to set the context for different resolutions of this question—in a post-revolutionary France that reinstated the colonial subordination it had briefly abandoned in the 1790s and embarked on a new imperial adventure lasting until 1815, in a United States that freed itself from a king and settled slaves on territory seized from Indians, in South American states that treated indigenous people as non-equivalents, in a British empire that could use a wide repertoire of strategies in different parts of the world. The nation had become an imaginable possibility in world politics. But the leaders of France, Great Britain, Spain, and the United States did not want to limit their political compass to national boundaries. Nor could they prevent ideas of popular sovereignty from spreading across oceans, providing settlers of European origin, slaves, and indigenous peoples with a new language, alongside others, that they could use to make claims against empires.

EMPIRES ACROSS CONTINENTS
The United States and Russia

9

In the eighteenth and nineteenth centuries, American and Russian empires reached west and east around the northern hemisphere, over two continents, and across the Pacific Ocean. Both Russians and Americans were convinced of their "manifest destiny" to rule huge territories, but their strategies for expansion and their ways of ruling developed from different imperial experiences. This chapter explores variants of the politics of difference, adjusted and refined as the two empires extended their command over space and people.

British settlement of North America had brought "freeborn Englishmen" to a new world, but revolutionaries had proven all too free, overthrown their king, and embarked on their own project, an "Empire of Liberty." As the United States expanded westward, regions were incorporated, then transformed from territories into states, each one an equivalent unit of the polity. In theory, the Constitution guaranteed American citizens their natural and equal rights; in practice, citizenship was restricted to certain populations. Slaves, of African origin, were excluded from the start. Americans initially recognized diverse indigenous "nations" within the polity, but eventually extruded them, confining "Indian" peoples to reservations.

On the Eurasian continent, Russian rulers did not break with practices of sovereignty inherited from their mixed Mongol, Byzantine, and European past (chapter 7). The Romanovs accepted as a given the multiplicity of the populations over which they ruled. Their politics of difference allowed them to reward—selectively—elites of incorporated regions, to accommodate under supervision a variety of religions and customary practices, and to parcel out rights and duties pragmatically. The principle of differentiated governance was applied in both old and new parts of the empire. Russia's way of ruling different people differently enabled the emperor and officials to reconfigure the rights of subjects without the bloody civil war over slavery that almost destroyed the younger American empire.

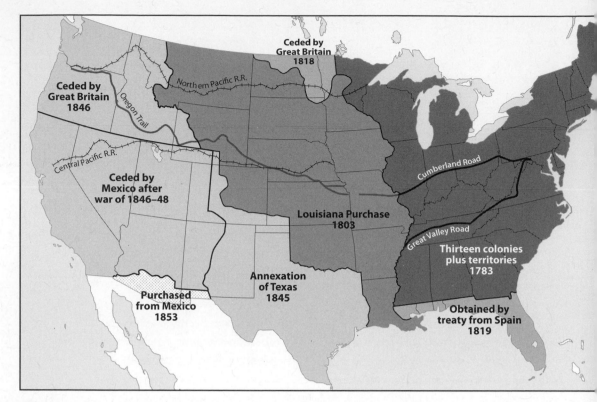

Map 9.1
Expansion
of the United
States.

The map contains the following labels:

Ceded by Great Britain 1818

Ceded by Great Britain 1846

Northern Pacific R.R.

Oregon Trail

Central Pacific R.R.

Ceded by Mexico after war of 1846–48

Cumberland Road

Louisiana Purchase 1803

Great Valley Road

Thirteen colonies plus territories 1783

Annexation of Texas 1845

Purchased from Mexico 1853

Obtained by treaty from Spain 1819

Space and Empire in North America

Trade, Land, Labor, and New World Societies

Let us step back in time. The "new world" was not a blank slate. For two millennia before Europeans arrived on the scene, empires and tribal groups had crisscrossed the Americas, trying to control trade routes, managing settled populations and their production, and adjusting to environmental possibilities. Starting out from coastal colonies and extending inland by sea routes and agricultural settlements, Europeans brought with them technologies (iron and brass), animal species (the horse), and commercial demands (furs) that vastly expanded possibilities for wealth, power, and conflict in the Americas.

Europeans also brought their ways of interpreting the societies they encountered. British colonials called upon a mix of ideologies: the rights of Englishmen, but also the notion of "civilizing" intervention, based on their occupation of Ireland and their disdain for Irish "nomads" in contrast to the agriculturalist and the property owner. Even some admirers of Las Casas's defense of Indians against Spanish oppression thought that North American Indians had failed to master nature, lacked the cultural attainments of Incas or Aztecs, and had a correspondingly weaker claim against English assertions of possession.

But other explorers and settlers observed Indians living in settled villages, under respected chiefs or kings, producing commodities Europeans wanted and buying others that Europeans had for sale. As British settlers moved inland from the Atlantic coast, most land was obtained by purchase—not necessarily under conditions of symmetry between buyer and seller, but nonetheless a de facto acceptance of Indian land rights. A tension between the recognition of Indians as communities with a place in an expanding imperial polity and the claim that they were uncivilized, dangerous, and could be uprooted ran through the first phases of colonial settlement.

When Europeans arrived, the Indian population was much lower than it had been in the past. Milder temperatures from about 900 to 1350 had given way to a less hospitable climate. Indians lived by hunting, gathering, cultivating, and fishing along the coasts and inland waterways of the continent. On the plains, they hunted buffalo and other animals; in the southwest, groups combined hunting with agriculture. Settlements were widely dispersed; language groups had less in common with each other than did the Germanic and Romance languages of Europe or the Turkic languages spread widely across Eurasia. Communities were mostly small scale but sometimes linked into regional confederacies. Unlike the regions where the Aztec and Inca empires had taken shape, North America did not offer its natives the concentrated resources needed to support a very large-scale polity. This constraint on empire-building changed after newcomers with connections to Europe, Africa, and beyond entered the Indians' world.

Map 9.2
Expansion
of Russia.

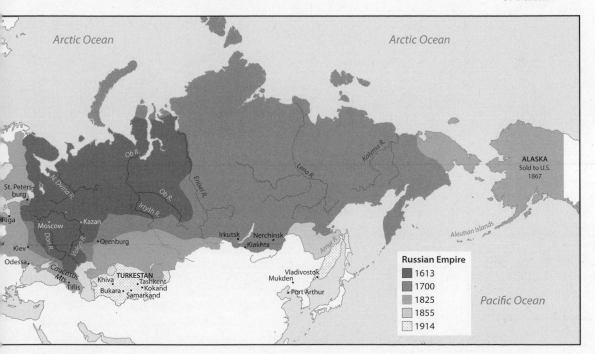

In 1492 there were about two million people living east of the Mississippi. These numbers dropped precipitously because of the diseases that Europeans, beginning with the Spanish, brought with them, weakening the social fabric of many Indian societies. Nonetheless, the European population of North America was very small compared with that of Indians; there were only about 250,000 Europeans on the continent in 1700. But by 1750, the number of Euro-Americans and Afro-Americans east of the Mississippi had reached around 1.25 million, outnumbering the indigenous population.

In sixteenth-century travel accounts Europeans described Indians with a mixture of wonder at their way of life, condescension toward their unmanly failure to domesticate nature, and a sense that these people could be managed and made helpful to the recent arrivals. Empire was part of this encounter, from both sides. Pocahontas's story as told by Europeans and handed down to later generations—that she fell in love with Captain John Smith and saved him from execution by her father, Powhatan, whom Smith referred to as emperor—was a romantic retelling of Powhatan's ritual effort to make Smith into a vassal and hence to incorporate English settlers into his empire. The later version of the tale obscured Powhatan's political power and transformed his kind of patriarchy into a loose sexual order, but nonetheless suggested the dependency of the settlers in their tiny enclaves upon the good will of indigenous people.

Indians seized the new opportunities for trade and made use of the goods that contacts with Europeans offered. Explorers—whether the English in Virginia or the French in what would later be Canada—describe the Indians' eagerness to participate in exchanges. Metals in particular were highly coveted and refashioned into tools, ornaments, and weapons. Gradually, Indians adopted European products as their own—clothing, blankets, hatchets, swords, knives, kettles, guns, and animals. Indians adjusted quickly to the use of guns—and European traders were happy to sell them—although for hunting the bow and arrow remained the most reliable weapon. Indians had something to trade back—forest products, especially beaver pelts in the northern areas, and later, buffalo skins from the plains. As the fur trade propelled Russians first across Siberia and later across the north Pacific to the Aleutians and Alaska, English and French explorers traveled inland from the Atlantic coast, establishing lines of trading posts to the Great Lakes region and beyond.

Imperial linkages slowly transformed the political and economic potential of the Atlantic rim and its hinterlands. Scottish, Irish, and English settlers, driven by economic hardship and religious and political tensions in the British isles, arrived relentlessly. The British sugar islands of the Caribbean used products from New England—fish caught off its shores to feed slave workers and financial services for elites. New commodities found their niche in the British Atlantic system—tobacco in Virginia and rice in South

Carolina. As commercial agent, provisioner, and consumer, North America was folded into the Atlantic slave-trading system (chapter 6).

Slavery was a dynamic element in the shaping of colonial society in North America. Slaves and the slave trade contributed to commercial expansion in cities like New York. Slave labor made possible the development of a plantation economy in the Caribbean and parts of the mainland without reliance on the labor of independent and mobile indigenous people. Let us look briefly at Virginia in the seventeenth century.

The leaders of Virginia saw themselves as patriarchs presiding over women, children, servants, and slaves, holding off—yet interacting with—Indians. Initially, the lives of slaves and the poorer settlers, especially indentured servants, overlapped, and there was considerable mixing, including legal marriage, between white colonials, initially largely male, and female slaves and Indians. As tobacco production and slavery became entrenched, leaders tried to draw lines more sharply, using law to construct a racial order. While women of European origin were regarded as dependents of their husbands and the font of domestic life, women of African descent were defined as laborers, like African males. A 1662 law clarified older practices by making the children of a slave mother slaves, regardless of paternity (a sharp contrast to Islamic law); another law declared that conversion to Christianity did not imply freedom. African slaves were distinguished legally from Indian war captives. In 1691, a law required banishment from the colony of a white man or woman, of any status, who married "a negroe, mulatto or Indian man or woman bond or free." Within the colony, free people of African descent were denied political participation.

Wealthy male landowners had dominated colonial Virginia from the start, but patriarchal authority was now differentiated along racial lines. Slaves were marked by race, not just by status, and the condition was made inheritable, not reversible by conversion, acculturation, or marriage. Colonial leaders took pains to assure white men of modest means that they could found households, participate in the defense of the settlement, and consider themselves part of the polity. With Indians excluded, Africans subordinated, and the courts enlisted to enforce the newly demarcated border among social categories, a new kind of society was being made. It would later be the springboard—Washington, Jefferson, and Madison were all Virginian slave owners—for political mobilization in the American revolution.

In seventeenth-century North America as a whole, the geographical and political contours of a new order were far from clear or permanent. Connections to the wider imperial world had affected political and military relations among Indians. Like Mongol tribes who competed over trade mandates from Chinese authorities, North American Indians fought over the rewards of long-distance commerce. The introduction of the horse, brought

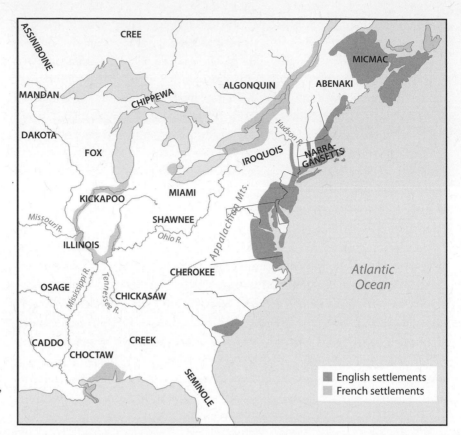

Map 9.3
Settlers and
Native Americans,
seventeenth
century.

The map shows the following labels:

ASSINIBOINE, CREE, MICMAC, MANDAN, CHIPPEWA, ALGONQUIN, ABENAKI, DAKOTA, FOX, IROQUOIS, NARRA-GANSETTS, KICKAPOO, MIAMI, SHAWNEE, ILLINOIS, Ohio R., CHEROKEE, OSAGE, CHICKASAW, CADDO, CREEK, CHOCTAW, SEMINOLE, Missouri R., Mississippi R., Tennessee R., Hudson R., Appalachian Mts., Atlantic Ocean

■ English settlements
■ French settlements

to the hemisphere by the Spanish, transformed Indian economy, warfare, and politics. The Sioux used horse-related skills to become buffalo hunters and move into the Great Plains, displacing other tribes. In the Great Lakes region, Iroquois-speaking peoples attacked Algonquin-speakers to gain control over hunting territory for beavers and to take captives who would replace their wartime and other losses.

Imperial oversight could be a tool for Indians against settlers. In New England, Narragansett and other Indians asserted that they, as subjects of the king of England with whom they had treaties, should not have to submit to the self-interested authority of settlers. For a time the mistreatment of Indians by colonists led royal officials to exercise more direct authority. But the trend was against the Indians as colonists became more entrenched and assertive.

Where Indians were between empires, they had some room to maneuver. The fur-trading zone around the Great Lakes constituted in the late seventeenth and early eighteenth centuries what Richard White calls a "middle ground," where competing Indian polities and rival imperial powers—France and Britain—sought alliances and commercial relationships. The small number of explorers and traders, their dependence on Indians' knowledge of the environment and tribal politics, the absence of European women, and the competition between European empires made social relations in this large region volatile and multisided. European newcomers— missionaries, military men, and fur traders—allied themselves with Indian groups against the Iroquois, tipping the scales against the formerly dominant confederation. In both the Great Lakes area and the Ohio Valley, communities of Indians of diverse origins and people of mixed Euro-Indian descent developed around trading centers. Younger men, able to sell furs and obtain European commodities, challenged the domination of patriarchs.

The French were initially more eager than the British to form alliances with Indian confederations, but their failure to sustain these relationships— especially when a weakening French economy had less and less to offer— contributed to the French defeat in the Seven Years' War of 1756–63. This war—especially the fact that the war had a victor—was disastrous for Indians. The French defeat ended the need for both parties to seek Indian allies and facilitated the increasing infiltration of English settlers inland.

Native Americans discovered both opportunity and dangers in the shifting competition among empires. There was no united front against Euro-Americans; instead, Indians maneuvered well into the eighteenth century in the interstices of imperial rivalries. But Euro-Americans kept coming and they had worldwide connections; the balance of power and influence shifted in their direction.

Natives and Settlers: An American Version

Indians' mixed, adaptable economies came under siege when Europeans arrived. Euro-American farming was a profoundly territorial operation, much more so than the economy of the Eurasian steppe. Settlers plowed the same fields year after year, where Indians had rotated their planted lands. Settlers cut down trees to extend cultivated areas as the soil was depleted; they brought with them domesticated animals that ate up grasses deer and elk had fed on. Both Europeans and Indians overhunted fur-bearing animals to meet the lucrative demands of world markets. These practices profoundly disrupted the ecological balances that Indians had previously both exploited and preserved.

At the end of the Seven Years' War, European inhabitants of the areas won from the French were absorbed as subjects into the British polity even though most were Catholic; Indians in these regions, on the other hand, did not acquire the status of subject but were proclaimed to be under the king's "protection." Indians

"Our fathers had plenty of deer and skins, our plains were full of deer, as also our woods, and of turkeys, and our coves full of fish and fowl. But these English having gotten our land, they with scythes cut down the grass, and with axes fell the trees; their cows and horses eat the grass, and their hogs spoil our clam banks, and we shall all be starved."

—Narragansett leader Miantonomo, recorded in 1642

did not have the same rights to land as anyone else: they had just a claim to use it. West of a line crossing the Appalachian Mountains, adjusted several times, Indians could transfer land only to the government—which reserved to itself the right to allow or disallow settlement and sale to European farmers. Allegedly protecting the Indians against settler encroachment, the 1763 settlement defined Indians outside of a society and polity in which ownership of property and the right to dispose of it were central.

European settlers pushed into the western zone, bought or took land illicitly, and expected the imperial government to protect them. However individualistic and pioneering the settlers moving into the Ohio Valley, they needed state support. British failure to satisfy settlers' expectations contributed to their alienation from their imperial sovereign and their desire for a state that would decisively take their side. Meanwhile, Indians in the Ohio Valley gradually lost not only the basis of their livelihood—land, hunting, and trade—but also their chance to secure a place inside the British empire.

In the southwest region of North America, multiple European empires intersected Indian tribal politics. After 1535, the Viceroyalty of New Spain, from its capital in Mexico City, pressed claims to territory extending from Central America north into today's California, New Mexico, Arizona, and part of Texas. When French explorers moved down the central river systems and west into the plains, the Spanish and the French empires came into direct competition. The Indians of the area (Apaches, Pueblos, Navajos, Comanches, Sioux, and Wichitas among them) made alliances with the Europeans and against each other, shifting partners as opportunities arose. Apaches fought for captives, whom they sold to the Spanish.

Missions and estates established by Spanish colonizers and worked by Indian labor opened up opportunities for mobile tribes around them, a small-scale version of the temptations agrarian empires in Eurasia provided to nomads at their edges. Apaches raided Spanish settlements for livestock and imported goods, and the Spanish tried to settle Apaches down, make deals with them, or capture them as slaves. When, as a result of the Seven Years' War, the French ceded Louisiana—a huge area to the west of the Mississippi—to Spain, the Spanish gradually made peace with some of the Indians, but not all. In one Mexican province, Apaches killed 1,674 people, took 154 captives, forced the abandonment of 116 haciendas and ranches, and stole 68,256 head of livestock between 1771 and 1776.

Over time, the Catholic Spanish managed to settle many of the contentious people they had encountered, with disastrous consequences for Indians. In California, the mission system turned Indians into laborers, converted, disciplined, and deprived of resources. During the heyday of the missions in California (1771–1830) the Indian population in the area between San Diego and San Francisco dropped from 72,000 to 18,000. Mexico's convoluted route to independence from Spain in 1821 resulted in secularization of the missions in 1833, but not the erosion of the power of a landowning elite. Many Indian workers ended up as dependent laborers on the new ranches set up by elites in parts of Mexico, including California.

Why did American Indians gradually lose to intruders on their terrain? The answers involve imbalances in technology, but these in turn were connected to the timing of imperial encounters and the possibilities of a particular space. Eurasian nomads could prosper and at times become leaders of great empires because they were the most effective warriors of their time and because there was something they could live off or seize—the wealth of settled China above all. With these promising ingredients, Xiongnu, Mongols, and others evolved political techniques to coordinate conquest and governance on a huge scale, from at least the second century BCE (chapter 4). In the fifteenth century North American Indians, while skilled in warfare and raiding, had no China to induce them into large-scale cooperation; nor had they developed the technologies and political organization associated with the animal that made Mongol power possible—the horse.

The Europeans came first as nomads of the sea, with their superior weapons. Then, as their numbers swelled, they applied their ideologies and practices of ruling and exploiting territorialized empire. Settlers' intrusive presence on the land undermined Indians' self-sufficiency. Although Indians rapidly adapted horses and new weapons to both prey upon and produce new wealth, Europeans controlled external commerce and defended private property, and they expected government to enforce their claims. Struggles for empire in Europe and the experience of transoceanic mobility and settlement had provided Europeans with political resources that proved devastating to Indian societies.

Why Unite the States?

In 1776, when a gathering of American patriots declared their independence from Great Britain, their grievances concerned oppressive taxation, restrictions on commerce with "all parts of the world," and the Crown's approach to Indians. Indian leaders had petitioned the king's representatives, as royal subjects, for support against settlers' manipulations, and aggrieved colonists claimed that "He [the king] has excited domestic insurrections amongst us, and has endeavored to bring on the inhabitants of our frontiers, the merciless Indian savages, whose known rule of warfare is an undistinguished destruction of all ages, sexes, and conditions."

With the success of the American rebellion, holding together thirteen ex-colonies in which people had diverse interests and unequal relationships became the task of the new leadership. The rebels had empire on the mind.

Jefferson looked toward an "Empire of Liberty." George Washington called for the "formation and establishment of an empire." But putting an empire together did not follow automatically from success at revolution. After the peace was signed in 1783, American leaders feared, with reason, that the states united loosely by the Articles of Confederation (ratified by all only in 1781) had lost cohesion as a polity. Authorities in the states were unable to agree on how to pay the debts incurred in war; they had no money and no credit. A British commentator wrote in 1781 that the Americans would never be "united into one compact Empire, under any species of Government whatever. Their Fate seems to be a DISUNITED PEOPLE, til the end of time."

The urgency of unification followed from the interempire competition at the time. American rebels had fought one empire, been assisted by its enemies, and feared being reabsorbed into one or another imperial sphere. Europe's empires were not only dangerously powerful but dangerously competitive. Proponents of federation were afraid that the imperial wars Europeans had engaged in for centuries would continue in the Americas. Without a framework for united action, they argued, the states would break apart into two or three sections—the slaveholder, plantation-based South, the commercial and settler areas of the North, and middle regions about which no one could be sure. If the ex-colonies became separate countries, they would be swallowed up and mobilized against each other.

The major question for American empire-builders was how to construct a new type of polity that would not ride roughshod over the rights of its component parts, the states, or over what they had declared to be the natural rights of individual citizens. Advocates of uniting the states called for federation, based on equivalence of component units and division of powers between different levels of government. Anti-federalists saw a warning in the history of empires: the concentration of power in the person of the emperor. Centralism could lead to despotism, and too much uniformity— the late Roman kind of empire with one law for all citizens—would be unworkable.

Worry about the weakness of separated states as well as fear of the despotism of consolidated empire shaped terms for what turned out to be, for a time, a successful unification, expressed in the constitution drawn up in 1787, reviewed and ratified the next year. The post-revolutionary settlement created a single polity that both recognized the established authority of component states and offered a forum in which citizens were represented equally. Each state would have two senators in the Senate, while seats in the House of Representatives would be determined by population.

But not all people would be counted or governed the same way. Slaves would not be citizens and would not vote, but states in which slaves lived could count each slave as three-fifths of a person when calculating the number of its representatives (a percentage used in assessing taxes as well). The allocation of representatives would also exclude "Indians not taxed," an expression that presumably distinguished between Indians who still lived in "tribes" and those who had melted into the Euro-American population and were taxed by the states along with everyone else. Exclusion and an arithmetic of partial incorporation were part of American empire from the start.

The name of the new polity, United States of America, implied that it was the immigrants who possessed America, obliterating any prior sovereignty of the continent's indigenous peoples and occluding memories of conquest and dispossession. The label Indian, which might have reminded Europeans of their geographical ignorance in the past, was retained, endowing natives instead of newcomers with foreignness.

Citizens, Indians, and the Making of an American Empire

Like early Romans, enthusiasts of the new American union saw no contradiction between republican government and imperial expansion; the system of divided powers was thought to prevent the trajectory toward dictatorship taken by earlier empires. The founding legislators hit upon a formula that permitted growth of the polity in an incremental and peaceful fashion: new states could be added to the union "on an equal footing with the original states, in all respects whatsoever," proclaimed the Northwest Ordinance of 1787. It was taken for granted that the states would be configured territorially, not by ethnicity, religion, or any social characteristic of the population. This equivalence in the terms of incorporation into the United States—as opposed to recognizing colonies, principalities, dominions, or other differential statuses—distinguished the United States from other composite polities.

But living on the territory of the states did not mean inclusion in the polity or enjoying equal rights. The Naturalization Act of 1790 opened the possibility of becoming a citizen to any "free white person" who had resided in the country for two years, demonstrated good character, and pledged allegiance to the new constitution. Citizenship in the new country would thus be relatively open to European immigrants but closed to Africans and Native Americans. In the following pages we trace the marginalization of indigenous peoples in the first century of the new republic; we then turn to slaves, whose denial of rights seemed unambiguous at the time of the republic's founding but who became the focus of a conflict that nearly destroyed the polity.

Although Indians, including members of the same tribe, fought on both sides in the war of independence—or tried to stay out of it—victory over Great Britain was interpreted by Euro-Americans as giving them dominion over Indian lands. "You are a subdued people," the Iroquois were told. The British betrayed their Indian allies with the Treaty of Paris; the whole of "British" territory south of the Great Lakes was simply handed over to the Americans. John Dickinson of Pennsylvania drew the conclusion that all "the back country with all the forts" was now in the possession of the United States and that the Indians "must now depend upon us for their preservation." He advocated that if Indians did not "immediately cease from their outrages," the republic should use its victorious army to "extirpate them from the land where they were born and now live." Washington asked his generals to attack the Iroquois and "lay waste all the settlements . . . that the country may not be merely overrun but destroyed." Jefferson was convinced that Indians' "ferocious barbarities justified extermination. . . . In war they will kill some of us; we shall destroy all of them."

For a time, the U.S. government asserted that Indians had lost sovereignty and all rights to land. Later, anticipating the violence that acting on this principle would entail, American policy retreated to something like the British formula: Indians had rights of occupation, but not of ownership. This became known as "Indian title." Only the government could acquire land from Indians and redistribute it.

The Indian Trade and Intercourse acts of the 1790s were based on the assumption that Indians were separate peoples, even within the original thirteen states, and that the federal government had the exclusive right to deal with them. Indians remained the only category of people within the United States with whom the government interacted via treaties, a relationship that endured until 1871.

If Indian communities could be seen as corporate bodies outside the normal structures of American politics, Indians still lived on land settlers coveted, especially along the great waterways and valleys—the Mohawk, Ohio, and Mississippi rivers and the Great Lakes. The new government cemented its support among westward-looking citizens by building forts to protect them against Indians, in the process fostering communications and commerce and a sharply divided racial order. The "Empire of Liberty" was developing a different imperial way from that of the British—more responsive to the will of those defined as citizens, less bound to mercantilist regulation of commerce, concerned primarily with white, male, Protestant voters aspiring to occupy a continental space. Indigenous Americans bore an increasing burden of this new style of empire.

Legal documents and the language of paternalism were both deployed to make clear Indians' lack of sovereignty. Under the Treaty of Greenville, drawn up in 1795 between the United States and tribes that had fought with unreliable British help to defend their territory in Ohio, the Indian signatories swore that they "now, and will henceforth, acknowledge the 15

United States of America to be our father." General Anthony Wayne replied: "I now adopt you all, in the name of the President of the Fifteen Great Fires of America as their Children."

For Euro-Americans, Greenville and other treaties made with Indians were about land; these declarations often ratified encroachments that had already occurred. Individuals and states speculated in Indian land before the federal government bought it, and the sale of Indian territory helped fund the government as Euro-Americans moved west. After the United States held off the British empire and its Indian allies in the war of 1812, American leaders had reason to believe their polity could survive external assaults and that they could act as they wished against the Indians. To Andrew Jackson, treaties with Indians were an "absurdity" because Indians were the "subjects of the United States," and a sovereign power did not negotiate with a subject. Treaties were still drawn up with various Indian groups, but legal cover for this great land grab came to matter less and less.

This extrusion of Indians from the body politic was expressed in official terms describing Indian status. In the beginning of the nineteenth century, Indians were officially designated as "resident foreign nations," a legal signal that although Indians indeed resided on the continent, they were not American. Echoing and harshening earlier paternalistic rhetoric, the Supreme Court in 1823 declared Indians "an inferior race of people, without the privileges of citizens, and under the perpetual protection and pupilage of the government." In 1831, Chief Justice John Marshall described Indians as "domestic dependent nations" whose relation to the United States was that of "a ward to his guardian." The formula recognized Indians as distinct peoples, existing within a space over which the United States alone held sovereignty; they could not govern themselves.

Over the first decades of the nineteenth century, Indians were pushed to the margins of the expanding settler populations, but in some areas they were surrounded by settlers who wanted Indian lands. The Louisiana Purchase of 1803 provided a way out: it opened up new areas for settlers but also for "removal" of Indians from the east. Under the Indian Removal Act, passed by Congress in 1830, the president was empowered to make treaties that would extinguish Indians' claims to territory anywhere in the states and to grant them land west of the Mississippi in exchange.

This law was directed at the Cherokees, who had adopted many of the attributes of settler civilization, formed their own government, and written a constitution for themselves. These initiatives would seem to qualify Cherokees as politically mature, able to give their nation a legal structure, but their assertiveness was considered dangerous and their lands inside the boundaries of the state of Georgia were coveted by white Americans. Although the Supreme Court had decided that only the federal government had authority over Indian affairs, the Cherokees were evicted when President Andrew Jackson let stand Georgia's claim to 4.6 million acres of Cherokee land. In 1835, a treaty was signed by Cherokee representatives committing the tribe to leave Georgia. Three years later, 16,000 Cherokees were forcibly marched to Oklahoma. One out of eight died as a consequence of their removal.

When the Indian Appropriations Act of 1851 designated fenced-in land for Indians expelled to Oklahoma, the "reservation" system came into being. The reservation was a particular kind of imperial institution—not the "República de los Indios" in which indigenous peoples were recognized as a distinct, subordinate, but integral component of the Spanish empire and where religious affairs and juridical status were of concern to the king, and not the "colony" that became a key institution of British and French empires in the late nineteenth century, where in the absence of large numbers of settlers, indigenous people lived on land that was in effect theirs and had an inferior, but recognized, place as imperial subjects. The reservation was a zone of exclusion—outside the American "nation," on land that often bore no relation to ancestral territories, isolated from other Native Americans. Indians on reservations allegedly retained tribal identifications, yet were subject to the whims of soldiers, bureaucrats, or settlers who might demand still more land.

Map 9.4
Indian removals
and reservations.

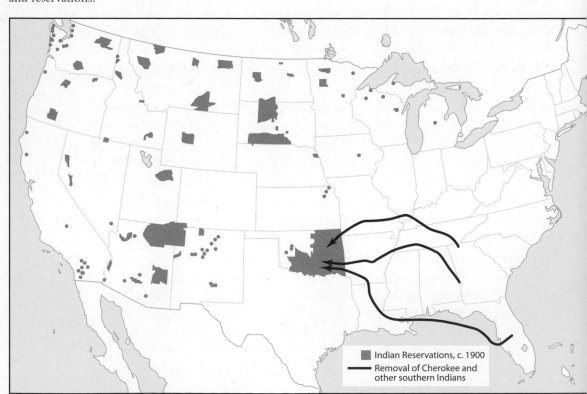

Indian Reservations, c. 1900
Removal of Cherokee and other southern Indians

The Sioux, major suppliers of buffalo pelts to U.S. merchants, were in the way of migrants rushing across the plains to California and its gold. The Horse Creek Treaty of 1851 delimited Sioux territory, but allowed the United States to build roads and military posts and emigrants to pass through it. Annuities of $50,000 were to be paid to each tribe for fifty years. This treaty, like others, was undermined and reinterpreted by both its signing parties and provoked divisions within and among Indian tribes. By the 1860s the Great Plains were the site of vicious warfare—between settlers and Indians, between Indians and other Indians, between the U.S. military and Indians. Despite several stunning military victories, Indians could not defeat the sustained onslaught of military adventurers and determined advocates of settlement.

The expansionist dynamic brought the United States into conflict not only with Native Americans but with another state—Mexico—born of another empire—Spain. Settlers who moved into southwest North America wanted government protections similar to those they received in territories already under U.S. control. In some areas, they took government into their own hands—as in the founding of Texas—and in some instances they generated confrontations over whether slavery should be permitted in areas of settlement. In 1846, conflict along the frontier drew an American army into war with Mexico.

The goal of the American war effort was explicitly territorial. As a senator from Michigan noted in a debate about how far the United States should go into Mexico, "We do not want the people of Mexico, either as citizens or subjects. All we want is a portion of territory which they nominally hold, generally uninhabited, or, where inhabited at all, sparsely so, and with population which will soon recede, or identify itself with ours." But of course there were people on the land, and their relation to the federal government depended on who they were. Citizens of Mexico in the annexed areas acquired American citizenship, in effect a collective naturalization, via the 1848 Treaty of Guadalupe Hidalgo. Indians could only become citizens if they left their tribes. Slaves and their descendants had no citizenship rights at all. A Supreme Court decision of 1857 (the Dred Scott case) hardened slaves' and ex-slaves' exclusion—holding that states could not confer citizenship upon them even if they so chose—and permitted slavery in the territories.

The North American kind of domination over Indians disrupted the complex property regime developed during Spanish expansion. In what is now New Mexico and Colorado, settlers of Spanish and Indian origins had served their patrons as sharecroppers or day laborers on huge land grants, acquiring rights to cultivate portions of the land. But the U.S. Congress refused to ratify an article of the Treaty of Guadalupe Hidalgo that would have recognized these property rights enjoyed under Mexican law. The takeover in the name of freehold land and free labor—as opposed to what American leaders sneered at as "feudalism"—dispossessed Mexican women who had earlier controlled their own property, as well as Indians who lost rights of usage on their patrons' estates.

With the extension of continental empire to the west, the Euro-American "pioneers" marched along the road to full participation in political life and to statehood; Indians were on a path to reservations; blacks were trapped in a tunnel that led only to more slavery in more areas of the country. But the Dred Scott case, at first a sweeping victory for slaveholders, helped provoke a political conflict over slavery that eventually boiled over into civil war.

The Northern victory in the Civil War fortified both the idea of national destiny and the federal government's power to promote it. For Indians, it was another step toward lasting deprivation. The war's end left experienced army officers searching for ways to distinguish themselves; for many that way was west. The expansion of the railroad network, discoveries of gold and other minerals, and the near extinction of the buffalo left indigenous communities only a marginal and demeaning place in the empire of private property and liberty.

A treaty signed by some Sioux in 1868 included annuities, allotments of clothing for thirty years, food rations for four years, the abandonment of forts along the Bozeman Trail, but also confinement to reduced reservations. Indians accused of wrongdoing were to be handed over to American courts, and all children between the ages of six and sixteen were required to attend school. After the Lakotas refused to sell the Black Hills for six million dollars, all Sioux were commanded to report to agencies managed by the U.S. government. The plains exploded into warfare once again, with Sioux, Cheyennes, Arapahoes, Pawnees, and Shoshones fighting with or against the U.S. Army. Sitting Bull with many Sioux followers left for Canada, the "Grandmother's country." He returned in the 1880s but was arrested and killed in 1890. The great Sioux warrior Crazy Horse surrendered on May 7, 1877, only to be murdered four months later.

"We must act with vindictive earnestness against the Sioux . . . even to their extermination, men, women, and children."

—General William Tecumseh Sherman, 1866

In 1871, the U.S. Congress once again revised the legal status of indigenous peoples, declaring that "hereafter no Indian nation or tribe within the territory of the United States shall be acknowledged or recognized as an independent nation, tribe, or power with whom the United States may contract by treaty." Illogical on the surface, this law expressed the fundamental denial that had characterized American policy all along: an Indian "nation or tribe" was neither accepted within the body politic nor recognized as having autonomy or even par-

Figure 9.1
"Cheyennes Going to Their Reservation." Illustration from *Leslie's Monthly Magazine*, 1874. This picture of sad but obedient retreat does not represent the resistance of many Cheyennes to settlers' incursions and the U.S. Army's attacks. Two years after this image appeared, Cheyennes participated in the Battle of Little Bighorn at which General Custer and his army were annihilated. New York Public Library.

tial sovereignty. Agents of the government continued, when convenient, to make "agreements" with obliging tribal leaders if they could be found, but the reservation defined Indians' place outside the political system.

By the 1870s humanitarian groups, many of their members eastern Protestants, engaged in campaigns to assimilate and reform Indians. The Bureau of Indian Affairs expanded rapidly into a full-scale administrative bureaucracy. Missionaries and others established schools for Indian children, cut their hair, and enforced compliance with teachers' notions of discipline. According to a succession of agreements, the United States was required to provide the Indians on reservations with food—a fixed weight of beef, flour, corn, sugar, beans, and coffee every day "until the Indians are able to support themselves." This commitment, like others, was fungible, but the principle was clear enough. The apparent options for Indians were to adopt Christianity, settled agriculture, and American culture or remain minors and outsiders to the nation. They could become Americans only by ceasing to be Indians.

The extrusion of Indians from the polity and the seizure of their lands were repeated in other areas. From the 1820s to the 1850s, natives of Hawaii lost most of their land to American speculators and missionaries, who preached the virtues of white civilization, Christian values, and the law of private property. But what about private property in people? On the eve of the revolution, slavery had been legal in all colonies except Rhode Island. Although American revolutionary leaders were aware of a nascent antislavery movement in England, a proposed clause abolishing slavery was dropped from the Declaration of Independence. For over eighty years, slavery proved compatible with the institutions and ideals of the American republic. But slowly the Constitution's solution to the fundamental question posed by slavery—partial devolution of sovereignty to the states and the cynical counting of slaves for purposes of representation—fell apart.

Connections between empire and slavery were volatile outside and within the United States. Transatlantic imperial networks and competitions not only made slave owners rich but gave rise to antislavery movements across empires. The Haitian revolution of 1791–1804 and the emancipations in the British Caribbean of the 1830s sent mixed messages to slaves, planters, and abolitionists—undermining the normality of slavery and making clear to slave owners what they had to fear (chapters 8 and 10). Within the United States, the formula that had seemed to assure peaceful expansion of the union—the possibility of making states from settled territories—opened up the sore of slavery to political contention at the federal level. Would new states be "slave" or "free"? Slavery required a coercive apparatus to back up planters' authority, and southerners' insistence that the federal government help return slaves who escaped the South made "free states" complicit in the slave system.

The tension between unity and difference in the American polity degenerated into civil war. As southern states seceded and the remainder of the "union" attacked to bring them back, the United States came close to breaking up into at least two federations, organized around different principles. In four years of war, 620,000 people lost their lives.

For the American president, the war was about holding the polity together first and about slavery second. Abraham Lincoln declared that he would "save the Union without freeing any slave" if he could do it. But he could not, even though his administration contemplated ways to expel slaves to colonies in other countries, another sign of the deep reluctance to admit blacks into the citizenry. As it became clear that the Union armies could attract and use slave soldiers and laborers, the president and the Congress moved gradually toward abolition.

Slavery had led to the near dissolution of the union; war to put it back together pushed the leaders of the ultimately victorious side to open the doors of citizenship. Slavery was prohibited throughout the United States by the Thirteenth Amendment ratified in December 1865, after having been rejected by the House of Representatives the year before. That black slaves would fight and die for their freedom had helped bring freedom about. But what kind of freedom? The four million ex-slaves expected the wherewithal to support their independence, while former owners were determined to hold onto their labor force. Some southern states adopted "Black Codes" to force ex-slaves to accept plantation labor on the planters' terms, but these laws were voided by the federal Civil Rights Act of 1866.

The main question as with so much else in the American empire was land. Some antislavery politicians had suggested redistributing the fields of slaveholding rebels—providing "40 acres and a mule" to each ex-slave—but such talk came to naught. While the U.S. government was busy expropriating Indians, it was unwilling to do the same to slave owners whose property was considered private. As General Robert V. Richardson put it in 1865, "The emancipated slaves own nothing, because nothing but freedom has been given them."

Ex-slaves thought they should get something more, and many struggled to get a measure of economic independence and to participate in politics during the brief window when the federal government enforced the laws sufficiently for them to do so. Planters fought back with terror—the Ku Klux Klan—by invoking property law, and by other means, fair and foul. Under the eyes of the federal military, "Reconstruction" governments, with black participation, took office in ex-Confederate states, and some achieved a credible if modest record of reform in an area recently ruled by a planter oligarchy.

But Reconstruction was subject to the faltering will of northern voters, the use of terror and manipulation of racial anxieties by whites in southern states, and the widespread bias in American politics in favor of property owners. When federal enforcement of constitutional and legal positions faltered in the mid-1870s, it became clear that southern elites would gain decisive control over a subordinate labor force. In much of the cotton-growing South, the eventual fate of ex-slaves was to become sharecroppers on lands retained by former slave owners.

If the differentiated treatment of populations—Indians, Mexicans, blacks, plantation owners, loyal and disloyal—was a familiarly imperial way to run a polity, the war was a step toward a more unified, more national United States. During the war, the president and the federal government acquired new powers. A national banking system and standard currency, national taxation, and national conscription were outcomes of the conflict. After the war the states that had rebelled were run as occupied territories under military command. Nowhere was the new power of Washington clearer than in the postwar amendments to the Constitution that outlawed slavery and declared that citizens' rights could not be denied on the basis of "race, color, or previous condition of servitude." For about a decade, the promise of a national citizenry open to blacks as well as whites was a serious one and it remained the focus of hope and claims ever after.

The Fourteenth Amendment, for all its promise of a singular citizenship, still treated "Indians not taxed" differently: they would not be counted toward representation in national government. Only in 1924 did a federal law make it clear that all Indians were in the jurisdiction of the United States and hence citizens.

Women, too, were excluded from the declarations of equality and rights; a draft of the Thirteenth Amendment specifying that "all persons are equal before the law" was rejected on the grounds that it would make women the equals of their husbands. When ex-slaves entered the realm of citizenship, reformers assumed that freedmen would be heads of families, with dependent wives and children. Congress had already asserted its prerogative to supervise marital institutions by passing the Morrill Act for Suppression of Polygamy during the war, directed at Utah territory where many Mormons had settled. After the war, a federally minded jurist complained that Mormons' polygamous families constituted an unacceptable "imperium in imperio." Unlike other empires—including the Russian one—the United States would allow only one regime of marriage: one woman subordinated to her husband, who controlled family property.

"In 1789 the United States was a wilderness lying upon the outskirts of Christendom; she is now the heart of civilization and the focus of energy. The Union forms a gigantic and growing empire which stretches half round the globe, an empire possessing the greatest mass of accumulated wealth, the most perfect means of transportation, and the most delicate yet powerful industrial system which has ever been developed."

—Brooks Adams,
 The New Empire, 1902

After the Civil War, a new rhetoric of the "nation" gradually took hold, replacing that of "union." The United States enveloped much of the North American continent. Railways extended from coast to coast, north to south. Commercial connections, print journalism, telegraph communication, and corporations with a nationwide reach gave substance to the unity the government proclaimed. The United States had no external competitors for its territory, and settlers had won the struggle with North American Indians and with others who did not conform to their ideas of family and power. War, law, and expansion had asserted and enhanced an American imperial way—with its fixation on territory, property ownership, monogamous family life, and female subordination; its confidence in its enlightened and advanced civilization; its firm belief that the American way of life was both superior and based on universalistic values that would be welcomed by all others; and its unacknowledged erasure of the sovereignties of the indigenous people of the continent. The United States was ready to take its place as a major power in a world largely composed of or claimed by other empires.

Russian Rules

As the United States moved west in the eighteenth and nineteenth centuries, the Russian empire continued to expand in three directions. To the west, involvement in Europe's empire wars brought more of the Baltic littoral and parts of Poland and Lithuania into the Romanovs' empire. To the south, Russia warred off and on against the Ottomans, in a long contest for control over Ukraine, the Caucasus, the peoples and territories around the Black Sea, and, as an ultimate goal, Istanbul (which the Russians insisted on calling Constantinople) and unhindered access to the Mediterranean. In the last third of the nineteenth century, Russian forces defeated khanates in central Asia and pushed up against the British empire's ambitions in India and Pakistan. To the east, the Romanovs gradually consolidated their claims over nomadic peoples (see chapter 7) and outposts in Siberia. In the eighteenth century explorers went overseas to found colonies in California and Alaska. Between 1700 and 1900 Russia became an enormous cross-continental empire, the largest in the world (see map 9.2).

Just as the evolution of American strategies toward Indians and slaves transformed and clarified the fundament of republican empire for the United States, Russian leaders' engagement with the many peoples on the lands stretching out from their core area revealed and shaped a long-lasting imperial politics. A first principle of Russian governance was pragmatic recognition of difference. Russian elites were not obsessed with making their acquired subjects conform to a single cultural style or property regime. That Siberian tribes, Cossack hosts, Polish nobles, and central Asian Muslims would have their laws and customs and their religious beliefs was a fact of life, to be put to use in governance where possible. The Russian way of consolidating imperial power was to leave, for the most part, already existing social relations and rules in place and to get local people to carry out many of the state's essential tasks—policing, judging, and collecting.

A second rule was that rules did not have to apply to everyone. The autocracy did not struggle to find a satisfying formula for admitting territories to the polity, as had the Americans. Each new conquest could be assessed, ad-

Figure 9.2
"Chukchis." Chukchis are an indigenous people living in far east Russia,
on the edges of the Arctic Sea. After failing to conquer the Chukchis in the
first half of the eighteenth century, Russians settled into trading with them.
This illustration, which highlights the Chukchis' warm clothes and supplies
of furs, tusks, and whalebone, is from the account by Count Fedor
Petrovich Litke (1797–1882) of his round-the-world voyage in 1826–29,
sponsored by Emperor Nicholas I. New York Public Library.

dressed, delimited, and administered according to its particular requirements
and possibilities. In Muslim regions, the autocracy could decree that civil
disputes and family conflicts would be decided according to Sharia; in other
areas and for other people, local customary practices could be acknowledged
as grounds for legal resolutions. Finland, incorporated in 1809 as a reward
for Russia's short-lived alliance with Napoleon, retained its parliament, its
bureaucracy and judiciary, as well as, for a time, a small army of its own.

A third principle was that the rules could be changed. Unencumbered by
the confining legalism of contractual governance, constitutional principles,
or representative bodies, tsarist officials could adjust the regulations for each
and every area and group at any time. In practice, officials close to the emperor exercised a great deal of personal influence over imperial policy, as
long as they remained within the inner circles of patrimonial power. The
politics of uncertainty kept elites on their toes.

Although many Russian intellectuals became enthusiasts of the theory of "natural rights," the empire was governed on the principle of assigned and alienable rights emanating from the state. These rights were allocated to groups, not to individuals: the right to be married at a certain age, to engage in certain kinds of property transactions, to live in certain areas, to own serfs. For individuals, the imperial regime of rights defined possibilities, set limits, and provided a reference point for aspirations. A peasant might want to "become" a merchant, for example, and there were legal ways to do this. Officials worked reforms, rewards, and punishments through the system of rights as well: deciding whether to grant a collectivity the same, better, or worse rights than those of other groups.

The emperor rewarded and controlled his elite servitors through this rights regime, granting newcomers privileges that they had enjoyed under earlier rulers, taking away rights from misbehavers. To more lowly elements of the population, Russian empire offered other packages of rights and institutions, including lower-level courts where subjects could litigate minor matters, usually according to already existing practices and norms. Drawing "customs" in under the umbrella of imperial law engaged local people in doing the basic tasks of governance themselves. It was a cheap way to keep the peace and to outsource the extraction of tribute and taxes.

The empire was overlaid with multiple maps of difference. Religion—the empire included various kinds of Christians, Muslims, Jews, Buddhists, as well as animists—was one register; ethnicity—observers counted between sixty and eighty "nations" in the eighteenth century—was another. Geographical location, prior sovereignty, tribal allegiances, and occupational categories offered other ways of looking at the population. Russian officials did not begin with the whole but with the parts. The parts, though, were in motion, and a stable alignment of peoples, spaces, and confessions could not be had. Migrations, resettlements, and long-distance contacts continued to mix people up, and most important, it was not in the interests of the governors to draw up eternal territorial boundaries and to fix power forever in tribal, ethnic, or clerical hands. Rights were assigned to groups, but both rights and groups were kept in play by Russia's imperial leaders.

Making Difference Work

As we noted in chapter 7, Russia's position between east and west was a condition created and exploited by the empire's rulers. The gradual absorption of large parts of Ukraine and Poland provides an example of Russia's flexible imperial strategies.

Russia took in Polish and Ukrainian territories bit by bit. In the seventeenth century, Muscovy fought with and outmaneuvered a rival empire—

the Polish-Lithuanian Commonwealth (formed in 1569). Russian diplomats persuaded Cossack leaders in the Dnieper area to ally with Moscow by granting privileges to the Cossack elite and substantial autonomy to the most powerful leader, the Hetman. Clerics from Ukraine traveled to Russia's capital, where they contributed the cachet of their connections to ancient Kiev and their experience in combating Catholicism to the imperial tool kit. But when Hetman Ivan Mazepa, one of the richest men in Europe, allied with the king of Sweden against Peter the Great in 1708, Russia, with its own Cossack allies, crushed Mazepa's forces and forced him to flee. Henceforth emperors controlled the Hetmanate more tightly while continuing to grant loyal Cossack elites the rights of Russian nobles. Elsewhere in the region, and in Estonia and Livonia as well, the tsars left local nobles in charge of administration and justice, guaranteeing them their "previously and legally acquired privileges."

The bulk of Polish territory came under Russian control between 1772 and 1795, as the empires of Prussia, Russia, and Austria divided Poland among themselves in three partitions (more were to come over the next two centuries). Nobles in the Polish-Lithuanian Commonwealth had taken class power, based on land and peasant labor, to an extreme. They elected their own king and required unanimity in their parliament. This diverse empire, populated by Poles, Belarusians, Ukrainians, Germans, Latvians, Armenians, Tatars, Jews (the biggest Jewish population in Europe), and others, was crisscrossed by monotheistic religions with their scrappy politics. Controversies among Christians—Catholics, Orthodox, Lutherans, and Uniates (Christians who accepted the primacy of the pope but followed eastern rites)—opened the door for Russia to position itself as the defender of non-Catholic minorities. But Poland's other neighbors—Prussia and Austria—opposed Russia's active "protection" of the Commonwealth and wanted their share, too. The first partition of 1772 allotted about a third of Poland's population and 30 percent of its territory to the three powers. In 1791, Polish nobles provided a convenient provocation to greedy outsiders when, inspired by news from France, they gave themselves a written constitution—the first formal declaration of representative government in Europe and the second in the world. The result was the second partition and, after a short war of "liberation," the "general, final, and irrevocable" partition of the whole Commonwealth by Russia, Austria, and Prussia in 1795.

As a consequence of the eighteenth-century partitions, Russia acquired a huge territory and over seven million new subjects. Only some of these were Poles, only some of them were Catholic, and only some of them were nobles. Russian imperial administration depended on managing multiple elites. The Baltic Germans of the former Duchy of Kurland were reallocated their former privileged status and their local institutions of self-government. Many of them become high officials in the Russian government with a reputation for unstinting loyalty and exactitude. Polish nobles, too, were given an attractive deal. Although the territories that had been "Polish" became provinces of the empire and the parliament was abolished, loyal Polish elites of noble origin were granted the status of Russian nobles. In 1795, 66 percent of the "Russian" hereditary nobility was of Polish origin. Polish magnates entered the ruling circle of the empresses and emperors, including Prince Czartoryski, Alexander I's foreign minister from 1804 to 1806.

Despite the fact that the three powers that divided up Poland had pledged to eradicate the "Kingdom of Poland" from historical memory, Russian administration of former Polish domains took place in Polish. Polish nobles ran their local administrations, even in Belarusian areas. Russian officials at the imperial center recognized the potential of the venerable educational institutions in the formerly Polish areas and modeled reforms of Russian universities on Polish ones.

For centuries, religion had been at the root of destructive conflict both inside and outside Polish-Lithuanian lands. Russians guaranteed "unrestricted freedom" of religious practice to their new subjects in the area. But this was not an "anything goes" kind of freedom. Imperial rulers sought to control the hierarchy of each faith. Without waiting for the pope's approval, the Catholic church of the area was put under a single bishop in Mogilev. Jews were granted their prior "freedoms" to practice their religion and hold property; their communal institution, the *kahal*, was recognized and assigned the usual administrative and economic tasks. In the 1770s and 1780s, Russian administrators abolished Jews' status as an ethnic group, assigning them civil status as either merchants or townspeople. This arrangement dragged Russian administrators into conflicts among Jews, nobles and peasants, Poles and Ukrainians, as well as Russian merchants, who resented Jewish "privileges."

These tensions were at the core of the attempt in 1804 to regulate areas of settlement for Jews and to clarify their rights and obligations. Jews were subjected, for a time, to a double taxation, but they (unlike Christian townspeople) enjoyed the right, also for a time, to substitute a payment for sending recruits to the army. This and subsequent rulings about Jews' particular rights and duties were not exceptions from a standard code of citizenship but typical resorts to differentiated regulation of a group.

The Orthodox clergy often pushed for a more activist stance, and some elites rhapsodized about building a more fully Orthodox community. The tsars launched intermittent efforts at mass conversion. But a pragmatic acceptance of multiconfessional reality kept Russia's rulers from making Christian unity a principle of state. Even attempts by Orthodox clergy to assert control over Uniates came to little. In Ukrainian areas, the game of regulation and reconversion of various Christians continued; after major interruptions in the Soviet period, it resumed after 1991.

In "Polish" lands as elsewhere, the empire played its cards differently at different times and with different peoples. This was how Russian empire worked—inconsistently, but legally. Some patterns emerge from this apparently ad hoc process. First, elites were recognized, incorporated into the regime of status privilege, and used to rule regions and to assist in running the empire as a whole. Second, Russia did not share the deadly aspiration to religious homogeneity that had destroyed so many lives in western Europe and the Americas. There were ways to manage religious diversity, and the art of empire was in wary supervision that could keep the peace and, if possible, augment the state's authority and coffers.

The Empress and the Law

At the time of the Polish partitions, the Russian emperor was a woman, Catherine the Second and the Great. (For Russia in the eighteenth century, empresses were not exceptions, but the rule.) Catherine's reign was a high point of Russia's synthetic and mutable imperial culture, decked out in western fashions, fine-tuning allocated rights, putting clan politics around the autocrat on extravagant display.

Catherine, a royal from a small Prussian principality, came to the throne by regicide, displacing her husband, Emperor Peter III, who had alienated nobles connected to the court. Peter was ousted in an efficient coup and later killed by one of Catherine's favorites. Under Catherine, the nobility, especially the great magnates, flourished. The conquest of the southern steppes brought them land and serfs; expanded military control cut down on runaways; and the empress—sensitive to the circumstances that had put her on the throne—issued a Charter of the Nobility in 1785. This document exempted nobles from state service and corporal punishment, and gave them rights to travel abroad, maintain private printing presses, and hold their lands as family property. Catherine's much discussed sexual life was another means of shoring up ties to influential nobles. Avoiding the vulnerability of public remarriage, Catherine rewarded her lovers and ex-lovers with high office and enormous land grants. She was secretly married to her true love, advisor, and military commander, Prince Potemkin.

"By the beneficent grace of God, We, Catherine II, Empress and Autocrat of all Russia—of Moscow, Kiev, Vladimir, Novgorod, Tsaritsa of Kazan, Tsaritsa of Astrakhan, Tsaritsa of Siberia, Tsaritsa of Kherson-Tauride [the Crimea], Lord of Pskov and Grand Princess of Smolensk, Princess of Estonia, Livonia, Karelia, Tver, Iugra, Perm, Viatka, Bulgaria and others; Lord and Grand Princess of Nizhnyi Novgorod, Chernigov, Riazan, Polotsk, Rostov, Iaroslavl, Beloozero, Udoris, Obdoris, Kondia, Vitebsk, Mstislavl, and Commander of all the Northern countries, and Lord of Iveria, Kartalinian and Georgian Tsars and Kabardian lands, and of the Cherkassian and Mountain Princes, and by inheritance the Lord and Possessor of others."

—the opening of Catherine's Charter to the Nobility, 1785

Under Catherine, the empire rode out two major challenges. The first, from 1772 to 1774, arose from tensions created by imperial management strategies applied in the middle Volga region—playing diverse groups off against each other, trying to keep nomads from defecting to the Qing, extending Russian fortifications, using Cossack forces, encouraging settlement by Russians and by foreigners. Emelian Pugachev, a Cossack leader, put together an army of serfs, Orthodox dissenters, Cossacks, Tatars, Bashkirs, and other native groups. Promising "land, water, pastures, arms and munitions, salt, grain and lead" and claiming to be the real Peter III, Pugachev set up his own court mimicking the imperial one. Catherine's troops finally got the upper hand and Pugachev was executed gruesomely in Red Square after having been exhibited in a cage.

The second challenge was the French revolution (chapter 8). Catherine managed this threat to monarchical power by selective application of the freedoms she had earlier guaranteed to nobles. Intellectuals who got too uppity were exiled; presses were closed down; property was confiscated. Russian rights were alienable.

Catherine prided herself on being a "lawgiver." In the first half of her reign, she read European legal theory, corresponded with Voltaire, wrote plays, treatises, and legal codes, and encouraged sciences and arts. In 1767, she called a "Legislative Commission" of delegates from various ranks—nobles, townspeople, peasants, Cossacks, representatives from Ukrainian, Belarusian, and Baltic areas, Tatars, Chuvash, Mordvinians, Cheremis, Votiaks, Bashkirs, Kalmyks, and Buriats. Their charge was to consider her personally composed "Instruction" for a new law code and to submit their own recommendations for imperial legislation.

The empress's consultation with representatives from the population harked back to earlier gatherings of the land in Muscovy or the Mongol kuriltai; such a multiethnic consultation would have been unimaginable for Spanish, British, or American imperial rulers. Catherine's Instruction outlawed torture, minimized capital punishment, and discouraged slavery. The theory of a social contract was soundly rejected, and, in a twist on Montesquieu, Russia's vastness was held to require that absolute power be vested in a single person, a monarch who ruled through law, but was not a despot.

The Legislative Commission met for a year and a half, but no new code came directly from it. Most non-Russians defended the status quo—that is, their rights as guaranteed by the sovereign. It was Russian settlers who wanted change, in the direction of taking over the rights and lands of non-Russians, a direction Catherine chose not to take. Instead, she promulgated laws that shored up both regularizing and differentiating tendencies of Russian government. Continuing the compacting of social categories begun under Peter the Great, she systematized distinctions through laws

Figure 9.3
Catherine the Great in legislative regalia. Portrait from 1783 by Dmitrii
Grigorevich Levitskii. Russian Museum, St. Petersburg. Scala, ArtResource.

that grouped society into four primary estates—peasants, townspeople,
clergy, and nobles—each with its own rights. The realm was divided into
fifty provinces, each with 300,000 inhabitants, subdivided into districts of
30,000, each with its capital city. For all the artifice of these decrees, they
worked to spread an administrative net across the provinces and into the
countryside.

But uniformity was not pursued consistently by Catherine and her advisors. For one thing, provincial administration did not apply to the whole of

the empire, only to what came to be thought of "European Russia" west of the Urals, and not even all of that. In the matter of religion, Catherine's legislation moved toward regulated multiplicity. Earlier the state had pursued a typically inconsistent course with respect to the many religions of the empire, favoring compliant clerics where they could be found, supporting Orthodox campaigns and mass conversions in the east, banning the building of new mosques in areas such as the southeastern steppe, where the state wanted to encourage settlement. The Pugachev revolt pushed Catherine to make religious pluralism a legal principle and a supported practice. She closed Orthodox missionary efforts in the Volga area, encouraged the construction of mosques, and in 1773 issued a decree declaring "toleration of all confessions" in the name of the "Almighty God who tolerates all faiths, languages, and confessions."

Russia and Islam

The other side of tolerance was regulation, and this in turn required drawing religious authorities into governance and rewarding them appropriately. But applying this strategy to the numerous Muslim peoples of the empire was not self-evident. Islam, from its beginnings, had not institutionalized the clergy in a single structure. Authority rested, or rather moved about, with religious communities—the ulema of different areas—and with individual spiritual leaders, scholars, jurists, and their disciples. The fluidity of Muslims' religious leadership that fit so well with the movable politics of nomadic society was a problem for the Russian way of rule.

The answer was to create a clerical command where it did not exist. Russian officials had two models for their efforts—the governance of Islam by the Ottomans, their rivals, and the religious organization of their own Orthodox church. Administrators perceived parallels between imams and priests, muftis and bishops, "muezzin" and sacristans; some Russians pointed out that both faiths were based in monotheism and on holy writings. Peter the Great, who had broken with earlier norms by requiring Muslims who wished to retain their rights to land and serfs to convert to Christianity, had sponsored a Russian translation of the Quran, published in 1716. But it was Russian expansion into the Caucasus, the steppe regions to the north of the Black Sea, and the Crimea—conquered in 1771 and annexed in 1783—that by bringing Russians directly into contact with Muslim leaders, some of whom wanted the state to recognize their particular judicial or other authority, prompted a different approach.

Baron Osip Igelstrom, a Baltic German serving as governor-general in the steppe region, sought Catherine's support for measures designed to prop up Muslim settlements as a counter to the nomadic way of life. The government responded by printing and distributing the Quran to Muslims and setting up in 1789 an institution to control the clergy, the Muslim Ecclesiastical Assembly—located in Orenburg, the fortress town Pugachev had besieged. The assembly was headed by a "mufti," who was paid a generous state salary. Its responsibilities were supervising Muslim clerics and judges and serving as an appeals board for cases decided at lower-level Muslim instances. The "muftiate" was eventually placed under the Ministry of the Interior, where it remained until 1917.

Russian administration thus managed to institutionalize Islam under secular authority. It also encouraged the engagement of Muslim subjects in running their civic affairs, building on communities organized around their mosques. The local mullah who oversaw family matters and religious rites became a key figure in keeping order. At the same time, Muslims could complain to the tsarist authorities—through the courts, the police, provincial and military governors—about "their" mullah. Mullahs, in turn, could call upon the district courts and the Orenburg Ecclesiastical Assembly to validate their performance.

The multiple connections between parishioners, clerics, and administrative and judicial authorities engaged the Russian state with its Muslim subjects, who could use the state's institutions to pursue their own—often conflicting—ends. While Muslim scholars could differ about whether Russia was indeed a "House of Islam" (dar al-Islam), the majority of Muslim leaders accepted Russian state authority. From the late eighteenth century, prayers for the emperor and his family were an obligatory part of worship on Fridays and other holy days in mosques throughout the empire.

Educating Natives into Empire

Despite the special pleading of Orthodox prelates, Islam turned out to be a religion that could be integrated into governance. At the same time, some Russian officials felt that polytheistic people in the Volga region and further east in Siberia might be attracted to the empire's preferred kind of Christianity. Chuvash, Mari, Mordvin, Udmurt, and other "small peoples" had been the targets of a campaign of Orthodox baptism in the 1740s. By and large these mass conversions were deemed a failure; in 1764, Catherine abolished the "Office of New Converts" in Kazan.

In the nineteenth century, under Nicholas I (chapter 11), who saw Orthodoxy as a pillar of Russian rule, interest in missionary action revived. A Theological Academy was founded in Kazan to train seminary teachers for the eastern part of the empire. Students studied Tatar, Mongolian, Arabic, and Kalmyk, the major languages of the region, and the cultures associated with them, laying the foundations for Russia's outstanding institutions of

"Oriental" studies. Key Orthodox texts were translated into Tatar and published by Kazan University in 1851. Nikolai Ilminskii, an influential graduate of the Kazan Academy, pushed for religious instruction in other native languages, not just in Tatar, with the goal of training natives to do religious teaching themselves. Ilminskii's recommendations became the policy of the Ministry of Education in 1870 for the schooling of non-Russian subjects of empire, an approach that allowed such people to become Orthodox but did not make them into Russians.

Land, Law, and Rights, the Russian Way

Religion was only one perspective on the multiple populations of the empire. Another was territory and how people used it. As we have seen (chapter 7), the Russian and Chinese empires had closed up their boundaries by destroying their Mongol challengers, the Zunghars. Settlement was seen by many officials as a superior way of life to nomadism. Once again, however, Russian lawmakers did not take an absolute stand on the issue, perhaps because there were simply not enough settlers to make a homestead empire plausible. Serfdom in central Russia set a limit on who could become a settler. Where steppelands could be imagined to be "open," as in the United States, Catherine called in foreigners to take up the plow. Germans, Bulgarians, Poles, Greeks, and many other Europeans arrived in the "New Russian" area north of the Black Sea. Their numbers were augmented by Cossacks, runaways from the army and from serf owners, Old Believers, resettled peoples from the Caucasus, and escapees from prisons.

The goal, as throughout much of Russian history, was to match up land and people in productive ways, on terms that pleased the ruler. There was no homestead act, no territorial set-aside for nomads. Instead the state handed out, decree by decree, land grants, resettlement funds, relief from taxation, and, of course, obligations. Foreigners got the best deal, including transit money, exemptions from import duties, free lodging on arrival, a thirty-year tax release if they occupied "empty" lands, and the right to own serfs and to live according to their religious rules. Some Cossack groups were moved from the Dnieper and resettled north of the Black Sea or elsewhere in the steppelands; dissenters from Orthodoxy were relocated, sometimes at their own request, to different edges of the empire. Russia's "colonizers" were both foreigners and less than desirable imperial subjects. As in the Ottoman empire, moving entire groups of people was an ordinary imperial tactic.

Although Catherine regarded settled agriculture as superior to nomadism, she insisted that natives should be induced to change their ways "through demonstrations of kindness and justice." Nomads were not to be settled down by force. In 1822, the legal expert Mikhail Speranskii, then governor-general of Siberia, drew up a code of regulations addressed to the natives of Siberia, for whom he used the category "*inorodtsy*," or "people of another [not Russian] origin." Siberian natives were grouped into categories—"wandering" hunters, gatherers, and fishermen; nomads; and sedentary natives. Each category was allotted distinct rights and obligations: wanderers paid no taxes, just the fur tribute; nomads governed their own clan-based regions and paid tribute in furs and taxes; and settled natives had the same rights and duties as Russians of the equivalent estate except that they did not have to provide army recruits. Each category was to have its own institutions of self-government; elders were to be confirmed by Russian officials but could make decisions on the basis of local laws and customs.

One major difficulty was that nearly half of all Russians were left dangling from the imperial rights regime in which non-Russians participated under their different rules. Forty percent of the population of the empire were serfs who worked the lands of nobles or paid dues to them, or both. The right to own serfs was granted only to the nobility, about 1.5 percent of the population in the mid-nineteenth century. A small group of magnates held more than 40 percent of all the serfs, but serf owning was the way of life for nobles even on small estates. As we have seen (chapter 7), serfdom developed as a legal means to keep peasants from leaving their masters and fleeing to Russia's expanding spaces. When nobles acquired estates on the newly "opened" steppes, they could move their serfs with them or try to acquire new ones in the region. In either case, settlement was not carried out by families of homesteaders moving on their own volition, as in the United States.

Control over serfs' mobility was only one of many powers exercised by nobles. Nobles served as the state's administrators—validating serfs' marriages, regulating their employment on or outside estates, deciding minor judicial matters. Landlords collected taxes from their serfs, mortgaged, bequeathed, and bought and sold them. Over time, serfs lost the right that lowly subjects had in Muscovy—to complain about their treatment to the sovereign and ask for justice. Peasants' legal ties to the state had been weakened as nobles enhanced their own rights; serfs did not even swear allegiance to the emperor at the time of his accession to the throne.

Emperors varied in their views on serfdom and on their capacity to intervene. Arguments against serfdom (and for it) arose during Catherine's Legislative Commission, but Catherine was in no position to go against the nobility's most valued privilege. She confined herself to setting legal limits on how people could be made into serfs. Reforms of the serf system were proposed after the French revolution and during the wars with Napoleon. From 1816 through 1819, peasants in the Baltic provinces were freed without land. Nicholas I (1825–55) defended nobles' rights over serfs. Only two years after his death, his son Alexander, who had ended the disastrous Crimean war, established a "Secret Committee on the Peasant Question" whose goal was to "correct" the "evil" of serfdom. Four years later, after a series of commissions, inquiries, consultations, and imperial interventions, the tsar signed the emancipation into law during Lent, when it was hoped that both nobles and peasants would be abstaining from alcohol and would accept the radical legislation calmly.

Despite the fact that the emancipation of 1861 did not satisfy the expectations of either nobles or peasants, it was put into effect, apart from a few instances, without violence from either side. There was no war, civil or otherwise. The major terms of Russia's emancipation were that former serfs were granted the rights of peasants who lived on state lands, including their own administrative and judicial institutions, and that most would receive household plots and allotments of agricultural land to be held and managed collectively by their villages. Their former masters, most of whom were already in debt, were compensated for this massive reallocation of approximately half of their lands with funds from the state treasury. Ex-serfs were scheduled to reimburse the state for their newly acquired land by paying redemption dues over a forty-nine-year period. Alternatively, former serfs could take a quarter of the regular land allotment and pay nothing to the state.

"Reform from above" became a reality in Russia in part because nobles, although mostly opposed to this massive undercutting of their rights, were unable to justify serfdom any more. They were familiar with antislavery movements abroad, although many hoped that the usual gradualism of Russian politics would stave off emancipation in their case. Equality, however, was neither the goal nor the achievement of Alexander's reformers, who in accord with the imperial rights regime were once again adjusting land and people, eliminating the nobles' aberrant personal command over peasants, putting ex-serfs back into the hierarchies of imperial administration, and making them, like other subjects, the personal dependents of the tsar.

Something Other Than Freedom

In the United States, Alexander II was hailed by abolitionists as a great emancipator. After the horror of the Civil War, some American reformers regarded the Russian landed settlement as a model to be followed. But that was not to be, and the distinctive repertoires of the two empires help us understand why not. First, republican empire accorded its elites much more say in making law than did autocratic Russia. The Russian autocrat could get around his nobility by bringing them selectively into the process of reform and taking their opinions as he pleased. This manhandling of elites was not possible in the American republic, based on the legally empowered representatives of the different states.

Second, while the two empires used both law and violence, the legal process was radically different in each case. Russian empire worked through impermanent allocation of rights and resources to collectivities. There were no legal obstacles to taking land from serf owners and assigning it to ex-serfs. Americans had to work out ways to change their constitution, which had allowed slavery, guaranteed property rights, and set rules for sharing sovereignty out among the states. Part of the legal settlement of the Civil War was to void any claim made by former slave owners for compensation for their losses. The Fourteenth Amendment also denied states the power to take away a citizen's property without "due process of law."

Third, there was the matter of race. Russian serfs were mostly Slavs; the officials of the empire did not themselves belong to a single ethnic group; and the multiplicity of peoples was a given rather than a problem. American slaves were of African origin, aliens whose exclusion from the polity had been underscored at the very time when elites were claiming their own political freedom from the king of England. It took a vast war to win slaves the rights of American citizenship, but there was no consensus that they had earned a right to land. Ex-slaves struggled to enter the body politic in ex-Confederate states and to obtain a measure of economic autonomy, and for a time they got somewhere. But the violence of southern elites and their white supporters and, after a few years, the federal government's unwillingness to enforce constitutional provisions made it impossible for ex-slaves to sustain their hard-won gains.

Finally, there was capitalism and private property. Russians were ambivalent about both. The emancipation reallocated land, but not to individuals. Many officials were deeply skeptical about the consequences of "free labor." The ex-serfs were obliged to be members of the communal organizations that were second nature to Russian empire; these institutions of local government meant that village and district elders would in their own patriarchal way control young men, their families, and their collective, reallocatable property. For Americans, it was private property that was sacrosanct, at least for white men. The massive collective transfers carried out by Russian administrators would have been violations of a basic right.

Both empires extended their command across a continent; both saw settlement as a foundation of prosperity and power. But their politics of difference were not the same. Native Americans were defined first as subjects of the British king distinct from colonists, and then as "nations" to be dealt with by the government of the United States. American revolutionaries did not consider Indians to be potential citizens. In the nineteenth century, as settlers claimed more land for themselves, the state used both law and war to take over Indian territories and confine Indians to reservations. Many "others," including Indians, blacks, Mexican citizens from the conquered territories, and immigrants from parts of Europe and Asia, would have to

Figure 9.4
Allegories of freedom

"Appealing to be allowed to help fight for the Union or the Condition in 1863" and
"The Voice of the Russian People."

A freed American ex-slave volunteers before President Lincoln to fight in the battle raging in the background. Former Russian serfs sing the praises of Emperor Alexander II. The American print dates from 1892, the Russian one from 1866, both from the New York Public Library.

labor mightily over generations to squeeze into the republic on the republic's terms. Only in the late twentieth century would Americans celebrate their diversity.

For the Russians, the empire was from the start a collage of different peoples, some less advanced than others in officials' perspectives, but all adding to the grandeur of the realm. Once conquered, each tribe, each nation had to be studied, its capacities estimated, its leaders if possible brought into service at an appropriate level, its rebels punished and contained, its religion exploited or challenged with care and education. Equality had nothing to do with it, and neither did the rights of man. But men, women, and children of lesser and greater gods could be drawn under the multicolored wing of Russian empire.

IMPERIAL REPERTOIRES AND MYTHS OF MODERN COLONIALISM

The nineteenth century ushered in a new era in the politics of empire. Or did it? Historians, those who despised colonial empires as well as those who admired them, have tended to accept the empire-builders' argument that they were constructing a different sort of edifice from those made by the Caesars and Napoleons of the past. The nineteenth century certainly brought much more of the world under the power of a small number of states (table 10.1). Those states got much richer relative to other places, especially their own colonies: per capita income of western Europe went from less than three times that of Africa in 1820 to five times in 1920. The differences were of the imagination, too. European elites were confident of the superiority of their civilization and their capacity to dominate others; "Europe" was contrasted to a backward colonial world. Ottoman and Chinese empires, long obstacles to European ambitions, now presented opportunities.

The idea of a modern colonialism was set forth in its own time by publications like Paul Leroy-Beaulieu's 1874 book, *De la colonisation chez des peuples modernes* (On colonization by modern peoples); by 1908 it had gone through six editions. Modern colonialism, in such accounts, would entail the action of engineers and doctors rather than conquistadors; it would give rise to a domain of mutually beneficial progress, not of extraction. Both the possibilities and limitations of the ways European empires acted in overseas territories and in relation to each other in the nineteenth century are the subject of this chapter.

Many historians now talk of a "second" (or third) British empire in the nineteenth century, of a new French empire, of a new imperialism. Rather than affirming or denying these propositions, we use the notion of repertoires of power (chapter 1) to analyze changes in the politics of empire at this time. The increasing wealth of western European empires, particularly Britain, gave them more options: either to bring overseas territories under direct control or to exercise power less directly, counting on worldwide

10

Table 10.1
Colonizing More of the World
(colonies of Western European states, United States, and Japan)

Date	Land area colonized as % of world total	Population colonized as % of world total
1760	18	3
1830	6	18
1880	18	22
1913	39	31
1938	42	32

Source: Calculated from Bouda Etemad, *La possession du monde: Poids et mesures de la colonisation* (Brussels: Editions Complexes, 2000), 172.

economic and financial networks to ensure their influence. Technological developments—the steamboat, the telegraph, the machine gun, and anti-malaria medication—allowed Europeans to penetrate more easily, more cheaply, and more safely into territories, particularly in Africa, where they earlier had stayed mostly along the edges. But technology did not necessarily translate into systematic and efficient rule over conquered territories; it could mean that Europeans were capable of being better Mongols—moving fast, inflicting terror, claiming resources and submission, and moving onward.

Professional bureaucracies and law-bound, rule-bound forms of governance, clear administrative jurisdictions, and top-down structures of command might be installed over colonial territories, or else such institutions might be considered for "whites only," while indigenous communities were governed through understandings with local elites and demarcations of realms of "custom" in which they, not Europeans, would exercise authority. The arrogance of power could take a variety of forms—programs to transform conquered societies in the image of Europe, rigid subordination of "inferior" people, or the provision of separate—and unequal—pathways to progress for peoples regarded as distinct. All these strategies had their place in the repertoires of nineteenth-century European empires.

What is remarkable about this period is the gap between the *potential* that nineteenth-century social and technological innovations made available to imperial rulers and the limited spaces in which the new means were actually deployed. The empires that seemed, over the course of world history, to have the most resources with which to dominate their subject populations were among the shortest lived. Hitching much of the world to European ideas, European political institutions, and Europe's capitalist economies did not spin the world's peoples into a single web, as images of "globalization" imply. European empires left fragmented societies and great disparities of economic condition in their wake.

Capitalist development indeed produced the "great divergence," led by Great Britain, between the economic power of societies in western Europe and elsewhere (chapter 8), but that development was played out in the political framework of empire, in 1900 as much as in 1800. Overseas colonial empires, like those that went before them, were shaped by interempire activities and conflict. Europe's nineteenth century began with Napoleon's attempt to dominate Europe; it ended with a scramble among European empires for territories, in Africa and southeast Asian primarily, that had not yet been incorporated by rivals. "Modern" colonization was a wave of preemptive claims to territories that the claimants, for all their presumptions, were not able to fully integrate or exploit.

The colonial ventures of France, Great Britain, Belgium, and Portugal were part of a quest for imperial power within Europe itself (chapter 11). Germany incorporated non-German territories in Europe before it moved overseas, and an activist "overseas" colonizer like Britain was simultaneously competing for territory overseas and confronting Russia, Austria, the Ottomans, and on the other side of Eurasia, the Chinese empire. A small number of empires, with varying mixes of territories, colonies, protectorates, and dominions, competing and allying, would still be the units of conflict in the early twentieth century. So occupied with hegemonic struggle in western Europe were the major powers that they did not appreciate the importance of a new player—Japan—entering the game.

New ideas also flourished in the framework of empire, which they influenced but did not destroy. Two modes of classifying people became more salient among the multiple ways in which Europeans thought about themselves and others: nation and race. The salience of both had much to do with the possibility of people governing themselves and the difficulty of answering clearly, which people? Governing whom? While ideas of self-governing people raised the stakes in deciding who was "in" the polity and who was "out," imperial expansion overseas both presumed and reinforced a boundary between colonizer and colonized and kept blurring it. State and nation were not coming into alignment in the nineteenth century.

The variety of repertoires of power and the diversity of interests in distant spaces made it hard for colonial powers to develop a coherent imperial imaginary. Different colonizers wanted Africans or Asians to fill different roles: subordinate laborer, Christian convert, "traditional" chief, dutiful soldier, sturdy farmer. European discourse—scientific, administrative, popular—about race was no more an object of consensus than that about nation, and it too ran into the practical questions of running an empire. Could even the extremes of racial subordination eclipse the accommodations that empires had to make with incorporated elites? And over time, might not colonized subjects, especially those who had learned the way of the colonizers, become too useful—or too dangerous—for imperial officials to keep in a neatly bounded and subordinated category? How colonial administrators, missionaries, and employers thought of and acted toward Asians and Africans cannot be reduced to a general attribute of "modern" Europe; imperial strategies responded to the fact that people pushed back.

Empire and Emancipation

What kind of empire was imaginable in Great Britain at the beginning of the nineteenth century? When William Wilberforce denounced the slave trade before Parliament in 1789, not long after the American revolution and the scandal over the British East India Company had stirred emotions, he raised the question of whether people of Great Britain should care about the oppression of people very different from themselves living in islands few of them had ever seen. The antislavery movement's campaign drew on an inclusive conception of humanity—its propaganda featured an image of a kneeling black man asking, "Am I not a man and a brother?" Abolitionists put on the table a question that persisted into the twentieth century: how differently could different people be governed when they were all, in some sense, British?

The stakes were high, for as we argued in chapter 8, the breakthrough of the British economy in the eighteenth century grew out of a symbiotic relationship between colony and metropole, based on sugar and slavery in the former and wage labor in industry and agriculture in the latter. Some scholars thought there must be an economic explanation for Parliament's decisions in 1807 to forbid British subjects from participating in the slave trade and in 1833 to abolish slavery in British colonies: the slave trade and eventually slavery, it was argued, ceased to be economically valuable for British capitalists. But despite the theoretical arguments of Adam Smith and others for the economic superiority of wage labor, sugar was at the time still quite profitable in the British Caribbean, and after slavery was abolished in British colonies the slave plantations of Spanish Cuba became the powerhouse of world sugar production.

David Brion Davis turned to a different sort of explanation, focused on the ideological underpinnings of capitalism, not its economic imperatives. Elites in European Britain were defending the moral superiority of wage labor and the market against paternalistic protections of workers. For many capitalist farmers and industrialists, the self-imposed discipline of the marketplace was closely linked to Protestant belief in the individual's direct relation to God and the importance of disciplined conduct to salvation. The antislavery movement articulated a vision of an ordered, forward-looking society, set against "old corruption"—backward-looking elites, of whom slave owners were the most vivid example.

Like Las Casas and Burke, antislavery activists were slowly making their case against slavery within an empire, conceived of as a political and moral space. In the 1790s, the autobiography of Olaudah Equiano, an ex-slave, and his tour of Great Britain captured the imagination of many, bringing the deprivation and oppression of people who were "different" home to the British isles.

To some of its opponents, slavery was a specific practice that could be neatly excised, while to others the evils of slavery opened up a more radical critique of a society dominated by the rich and cruel. In 1833, when Parliament passed the law abolishing slavery in British colonies, a conservative version of abolition—qualified by making slaves go through a period of semi-free "apprenticeship"—triumphed. The same period witnessed increasingly harsh treatment of the English poor. The officials who presided over the emancipation in the British Caribbean brought to it a tutelary ideology. Ex-slaves had to be taught lessons in self-discipline, hard work, and proper roles for men and women. This kind of thinking assumed that the question of Africans' capacities was an open one: would slaves of African origin become "rational" economic actors, or would they exhibit what one official called "savage sloth"?

The abolition story was not written in London alone. Periodic rebellions by slaves in the Caribbean made clear that more British hands would have to get bloodier to preserve a slaveholding elite. And after abolition, ex-slaves did not always follow the script laid out for them. Rather than give themselves over to the discipline of wage labor, many sought to combine farming on the plots they had used as slaves with selling small surpluses in island markets, migration to non-plantation areas of the islands, and periods of wage labor. In British Jamaica, the output of sugar fell as had been feared. Thomas Holt and Catherine Hall have shown how the gap between expectations of "free labor" and the ways in which ex-slaves used their freedom led by the 1840s to increasing hostility toward ex-slaves. A harsher racial ideology was constructed on the ground. To many officials and missionaries, people of African descent seemed to be a racial exception to an economic rule.

This deepening of racial ideology enhanced the colonial character of the state in the West Indies. Whereas the participation of a small number of property-owning ex-slaves in the local legislature had once seemed a reasonable concomitant of abolition, after an abortive rebellion in 1865 by ex-slaves in Jamaica trying to defend their access to land, London took over direct administration. The British empire, having repudiated the status of slave for its subjects, now made clear that ex-slaves were not on a path toward full integration and equality. They were to be the subjects of a racialized system of rule and labor discipline.

The capacities of worldwide empire were used to find alternative sources of plantation labor, mainly the recruitment in India (and China to a lesser extent) of laborers under indenture. Contract laborers worked a set number of years for wages. In frank moments, British leaders called indentured labor "a new system of slavery"—new in concealing its operations behind a fetishization of the contract and in turning to Asian rather than African sources of labor, analogous to slavery in its dependence on geographical displacement and coercion to maintain discipline during the period of the contract. This system moved about 1.3 million Indians around the empire before it was ended in 1920, after decades of misgivings by British officials in India and rising protests by Indian political movements.

Meanwhile, British diplomacy and naval power pressured other European powers to act against the transatlantic slave trade, although it persisted into the 1850s. After Napoleon restored slavery in French colonies in 1802 (chapter 8), it took another revolutionary situation in Europe—in 1848—as well as an antislavery movement in France and a rebellion in the French Caribbean to bring about emancipation. Ex-slaves in the French Caribbean entered directly into the category of citizen rather than an intermediary status. Under the umbrella of French citizenship, both racial discrimination and memories of enslavement were supposed to disappear. Neither did. Although the citizens of 1848 were juridically equivalent to other citizens and participated in French elections, sending representatives to the Paris legislature, France maintained a distinctive administrative structure in its "old colonies." Emancipation, citizenship, and continued discrimination were ways for an imperial government to respond to pressures, altering the balance of inclusion and differentiation among the peoples it ruled.

The Spanish empire followed yet another path in the nineteenth century. Holding onto Cuba and Puerto Rico (as well as the Philippines) after losing most of its other colonies, Spain initially became more deeply immersed in colonial slavery. The sugar boom in Spanish Cuba contradicted claims that free labor was more effective than slave. The question of slavery became closely linked to debates over the place of Cuba and Puerto Rico in the empire. In European Spain, arguments that colonies were necessary for Spain to prosper were challenged by liberals who hoped to build a more progressive country modeled on France and Britain and saw little future in slave colonies.

Some nationalists in Cuba and Puerto Rico developed a vision of a white, civilized, independent nation in the Caribbean, endangered by the presence of so many black slaves. Their conception was simultaneously anti-imperialist, anti-slavery, and racist. The unstable relationship of "nation," "race," and "empire" fed civil wars in Cuba in the 1860s and 1880s. Both pro-imperial and pro-secession forces made use of slaves and ex-slaves as supporters and fighters, not just as laborers. The slavery question in Cuba was finally decided in 1886 with abolition, and the colonial question took a new turn with the anti-Spanish rebellions of the 1890s, leading to American intervention. Brazil at last abolished slavery in 1888, by which time extensive European immigration was providing an alternative labor source and alternative ideas of politics.

There was no single relationship of slavery to empire. The capacity of empires to defend territory, protect sea routes, and prevent slave insurrection had made the slave plantation possible, and imperial power made its abolition possible as well. In the United States, freedom *from* an empire allowed for the preservation of slavery for thirty years beyond its life span in colonies that remained British. British, French, and Spanish elites, in metropoles and colonies, had been forced by slave rebellions and ocean-crossing social movements to confront the suffering and exploitation of fellow subjects. But when they were freed, the emancipated slaves of the Caribbean faced imperial rulers with the possibility that governments' attempts to direct "progress" might not work as planned. The terms of inclusion of these ex-slaves within state institutions and an imperial economy remained a political issue during—and beyond—the life of the empires.

Free Trade, Creeping Colonization, and the Refashioning of Empire Worlds

In a famous article of 1953, Ronald Robinson and John Gallagher took issue with a common view of a pause in British empire-building between the loss of American colonies and conquests in Africa one hundred years later. They noted that this was the period when Great Britain enhanced its power to act overseas—its most menacing enemy, the Napoleonic empire, having succumbed in 1815, its navy supreme, its economy growing, its industry taking off. Robinson and Gallagher argued that imperialism—the extension of power across space—was not only a question of the formal incorporation of colonies into governing institutions. The issue was how to make people do what was in the British interest: keep tariffs low, ensure British merchants access to markets. Great Britain was able to accomplish much of this agenda without conquest or annexation in different parts of the world.

Latin America was a case in point: a series of new states, no longer part of someone else's empire, had appeared in the 1820s and their fragility gave the world's superpower room to get its way without an incorporative strategy. It might suffice to send an occasional gunboat to get a reluctant ruler to accord favorable trade treatment to British merchants; in 1850, for instance, the British government sent the navy to Rio de Janeiro to get Brazilians to stop trading in slaves. Imperialism in this sense meant de jure recognition of another state's sovereignty but de facto treatment of that state as only partially autonomous.

British bankers, railway engineers, and import-export companies had something to offer ruling elites in Latin America, China, African coastal regions, and the Ottoman empire. Capital resources, skills, and mobility gave the British more than equal power to shape the terms of interaction, with the coercive capacity of their navy in the background. Yet commerce could lead to conflict, breakdowns of the exchange system, and temptation on the part of the more powerful party to move to occupation to set things right. Such outcomes became more likely over the course of the nineteenth century thanks to Europe's vast industrial expansion, increased world trade—especially after the opening of the Suez Canal in 1869—heightened competition among industrializing powers, and hence more urgent demands for secure access to raw materials and markets. These developments could lead to creeping colonization—and to even more vigorous quests for control of territory and resources.

European Power and Empire in Asia

In the nineteenth century, the Chinese and Ottoman empires, having for centuries set constraints on where and how Europeans could exercise power, faced a British empire, and later its European rivals, able to deploy more varied and compelling repertoires of power. The Qing and the Ottomans had to buy weapons and capital goods from Europe in order to keep up, while merchants in these empires had less interest in close cooperation with their rulers as the axis of trade turned westward.

We look first at the changing relationship of European empires to China. As we have seen (chapter 7), the Qing dynasty had long dealt with European commercial enclaves along its coasts by granting trade monopolies to selected groups, restricting Europeans to port cities, controlling what came into China, and insisting that Qing law applied to foreigners. But in the nineteenth century, this variation on the tribute system was fraying as the balance of power tilted in favor of Europeans in the coastal ports. Britain's two "opium wars" with China, in 1839–42 and 1855–60, are classic cases of a state using military means to make another state engage in a form of commerce it did not want.

Opium, along with tea, coffee, tobacco, and sugar—all of which "hooked" consumers in one way or another—was a significant item in the developing worldwide consumer market. The growing opium trade expanded networks of traders linking India, China, and places in between, contributed to the development of banks and insurance companies, and fostered the concentration of capital in Calcutta, Hong Kong, Canton, and London. The British

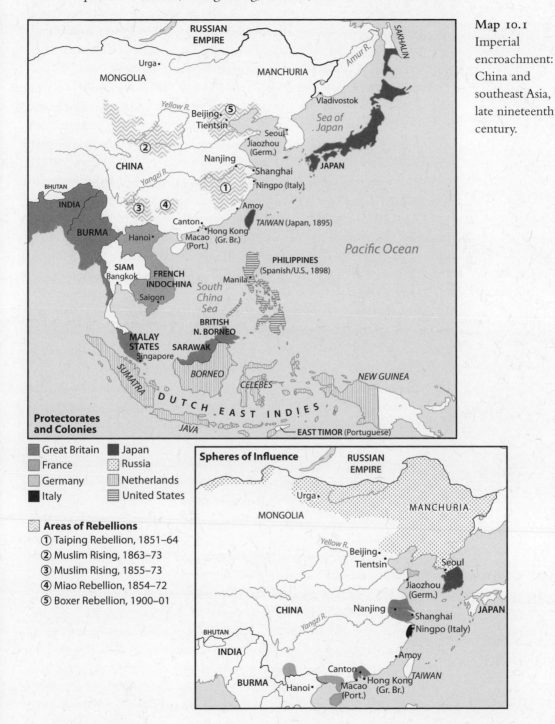

Map 10.1
Imperial
encroachment:
China and
southeast Asia,
late nineteenth
century.

Protectorates
and Colonies

- Great Britain
- France
- Germany
- Italy
- Japan
- Russia
- Netherlands
- United States

Areas of Rebellions
① Taiping Rebellion, 1851–64
② Muslim Rising, 1863–73
③ Muslim Rising, 1855–73
④ Miao Rebellion, 1854–72
⑤ Boxer Rebellion, 1900–01

East India Company was a major buyer of Chinese tea, and the EIC saw opium sales to China as the key to rescuing its commercial balance.

For the Chinese empire, opium was a risky commodity, and not just for reasons of public health. The drain on silver—used in commerce within the Chinese empire—was the major factor behind the Qing emperor's effort in the 1830s to outlaw the commercialization and use of opium. The ban—although never successful—endangered British East Asian trade. Hence the wars, through which Britain tried to force China to open its ports on British terms.

British victory in the first Anglo-Chinese war was a major shock to the Qing. The war ended with the Treaty of Nanjing (1842), for which the British set the terms—including major payments by the Qing for expenses, losses, and damages, the opening of five "treaty ports" where British subjects could reside under their own laws and carry out trade as they saw fit, and the granting of Hong Kong to the British Crown. During the second war invading British and French troops humiliated China by burning the imperial palace. The opium wars revealed that the military scales had tipped in favor of the European side: the British had machine guns, better ships, including a major breakthrough—the steam-powered military vessel—and better communications, backed by Britain's industrial production and financial institutions.

The United States and France followed the British example with their own demands. By the mid-nineteenth century, foreigners had gained "extraterritoriality"—the right to be judged by their own laws even in criminal cases occurring on Chinese territory (not just the ports).

The Qing now had to face the worst of all imperial situations—assaults from other empires at a time when their internal controls were slipping. The two dangers were connected. Over their centuries of expansion, the Qing had created (chapter 7) a country whose long land and sea borders provided opportunities for local elites to interact with the outside world. Both western regions—bordering on Islamic central Asia—and southern ones, toward Burma and Vietnam, were not fully integrated into the system of administration used in Han areas. In the west, the *beg* system left much of local administration to local Muslim leaders, with Manchu and Han soldiers concentrated in garrisons; in the south tribal leaders of various kinds still exercised authority. The multiple channels of power offered local elites and local Qing officials opportunities to make their own deals—hence a big business in smuggling, including opium. The land frontiers, not just the maritime interface with European power, became a major problem.

The Qing were playing the empire game by their old rules—focused on control of China's enormous territory and its difficult frontiers—but others were playing on a different field. Some Chinese intellectuals and activists understood this problem and sought to establish connections with like-minded people in other non-western empires—notably the Ottoman—and with others on the receiving end of European empire-building. But European powers had not only the mobility and the military capacity to fight battles where they chose but economic linkages of interest to people in China and elsewhere.

After its defeat in the opium wars, China had to trade on others' terms and try to manage Christian missionaries whose preaching challenged the empire's ideological premises. Chinese leaders also had to deal with a rise in banditry along its frontiers and revolts within them. By mid-century these threats were coming together (see map 10.1). A wave of rebellions broke out in Muslim regions of western China from the 1850s to the 1870s. Even more dangerous was the Taiping Rebellion of 1851–64, led by Hung Hsiu-chuan, a man with some mission training, embittered by his failure in the civil service examination, and virulently anti-Manchu. Hung founded a religious sect that attracted many people in a famine-stricken region of southeastern China, turned his followers into a disciplined army, and created an alternative

Figure 10.1
The European factories at Canton, China. Engraving by J. Tingle, based on drawings of Thomas Allom, 1843, published in *China, in a Series of Views* with text by G. N. Wright. The trading stations and entrepots' commercial networks intersected with European overseas commerce. New York Public Library.

state he proclaimed to be the Kingdom of Heaven on earth. Hung's forces captured Nanjing and threatened Beijing. It took many years—and millions of deaths—to defeat the rebellion, both a reflection of and a contribution to the inability of the Qing state to control its local elites.

By the end of the century, the Qing's weakness vis-à-vis foreigners helped provoke a huge anti-Christian, anti-foreign uprising. The "Boxer Rebellion," led by people connected to the martial arts and anti-bandit protection societies, was in part an expression of loyalty to the values of Chinese empire, in part a rejection of existing authority. The rebels effectively took over Beijing. In 1900, with the dowager empress Cixi favoring war against foreigners and the military and administration hesitant and ineffectual in containing the rebellion, a coalition of foreign powers took matters into their own hands. British, French, German, and—the newest empire element—Japanese forces took part in the bloody repression of the Boxers, occupying Beijing as they did so.

If the incursions of European empire-builders and the porosity of frontiers were dangers to the Chinese state, they offered opportunities to potential intermediaries. Chinese merchants in Hong Kong helped turn this once sleepy coastal town annexed by the British during the first opium war into a free port and a major entrepot of trade between China, southeast Asia, and across the Pacific and Indian oceans. British interests depended on these merchants' familiarity with Chinese commercial networks, and a number of Chinese were among the wealthiest inhabitants of Hong Kong. When Chinese emigration to the western United States began in the late 1840s, Hong Kong entrepreneurs profited from organizing the movement of people and then supplying Chinese goods to the new Chinese enclaves on American soil.

Hong Kong society was no paradise of equality, for British inhabitants insisted on living in segregated spaces and led separate social lives. But Hong Kong does not fit a model of colonialism that neatly divides resistance from collaboration. For Chinese who chose to come to Hong Kong in the nineteenth century, as for Chinese merchants who had earlier moved to Manila or Melaka, contingent accommodation to imperial power provided a chance to acquire wealth and build a social milieu using their position between empires.

China's vulnerability opened up opportunities in the wider Asian sphere where the empire had long exercised great economic and cultural influence. The kingdoms of Vietnam, Cambodia, and Laos had paid tribute to China; their ways of rule displayed Chinese influence, most visibly in the role of "mandarins"—an educated official class—in positions of authority. France, in both its Second Empire and Third Republic phases, saw its chance for an entree into this regional economy.

In contrast to Britain's "open door" policy for Hong Kong, France developed a "river policy" in what it called Indochina, seeking exclusive control over key outlets between the territory and the outside world. A gradual French conquest—from 1858 to the mid-1880s—put in place protectorates over the monarchies of Laos, Cambodia, and the northern and central parts of Vietnam and direct colonial rule over the southern part of Vietnam (Cochinchina). Behind the category of "protectorate"—applied later to Tunisia and Morocco—was the fiction that the protected state still enjoyed its sovereignty and retained its ruler, while ceding by treaty many of the prerogatives of government to the protecting power. Much of the mandarinate that had served Vietnamese rulers now served the French.

Vietnamese proprietors expanded production in the rich rice-growing area of Cochinchina, and Vietnam became one of China's main outside suppliers of rice, an exporter to Singapore, the Dutch East Indies, and Japan, and overall the second biggest world exporter of rice after Burma. Chinese and Indian merchants were major actors in the Indochinese economy, especially in finance and trade. European settlers arrived in significant numbers only in the twentieth century, drawn by the growth of rubber plantations based on cheap and exploited labor from more marginalized parts of the region. Tin, coal, and other minerals and an important banking center integrated Vietnam into French capitalism and made it the most lucrative—as well as the most populated—component of the French empire.

The ensemble of colony and protectorates in Indochina created a particular sort of colonial society. As of 1913, there were an estimated 23,700 European French people among a total population of 16 million in Vietnam. Colonial Vietnam was both hyper-French and distinctly colonial. Settlers in Hanoi and Saigon insisted on the Frenchness of their way of life, while making much of their exotic surroundings and expecting deference and service from Vietnamese. The *colons* (settlers) rarely acknowledged that the colony depended not only on the subservience of its population but also on the entrepreneurship and administrative savvy of its elite. Significant numbers of European Frenchmen, especially of lower or middle position in the colonial pecking order, made liaisons with Vietnamese women, and at times marriages. These relationships gave rise to a sizable mixed population and tensions over whether the offspring of such people should be integrated into the "French" or indigenous side of a divided society. A "middle" option often was exercised in practice but not given juridical recognition by a colonial state anxious to maintain clear boundaries between European and indigenous people.

In Hong Kong and Vietnam, then, we see versions of an enclave colony and of territorial colonization. Vietnam's export-intensive economy depended on production by indigenous proprietors, French settlers, corporate plantations, and mines; Hong Kong grew rich via networks developed by Chinese entrepreneurs. The economic interest of entrepots and territories of production lay in their linkages above all to China, but also to Japan, the Dutch East Indies, the Spanish Philippines, Portuguese enclaves in Macao, East Timor, and Goa, and, further afield, British India. Britain, over the course of the nineteenth century, also picked up key enclaves and territories in the system—Aden, Burma, the series of sultanates that eventually became Malaya. The opening of the Suez Canal in 1869 brought the Indian Ocean region and east Asia into closer connection to Europe (map 10.3).

In the territories that eventually made up Australia, the British government founded its first official colonial settlement in 1788, following a series of visits by explorers. These colonies became a place to dispose part of Britain's convict population, keeping prisoners far away, punishing them, and providing labor to build a settlement of uncertain promise. France used Guyana (in the Caribbean) and later New Caledonia (in the Pacific) for similar purposes, and Russia had its convict settlements in Siberia. Here we see another way in which territorial control at a distance could be useful.

Eventually, free settlers became more numerous in Australia than the convicts, and a unified system of administration was finally erected in the 1850s. The British Crown, and settlers themselves, paid little regard to the land needs and claims of the aboriginal population of the continent—extending to them the imperial conceit developed in Ireland that land occupied by "nomads" was there for the taking. In New Zealand, settlers had to tread more carefully, for the Maori people were more tightly settled and organized. The Waitangi treaty of 1840, although much abused by state and settlers, conceded the reality of indigenous presence and left the Maori with some land and a stronger sense of cultural integrity than their Australian counterparts were able to retain.

By mid-nineteenth century, Australia and New Zealand, like Canada, were forming communities aware of their connection through history and "kith and kin" to Britain. Some writers and politicians envisioned a "Greater Britain" of white, Protestant, consciously free, and prosperous people spread around the globe from Australia to South Africa to Scotland, their virtuous patriotism an antidote to both the crass materialism and the dangers of socialism that industrialization was generating at home. But their "white" vision of empire and of Britishness did not tell officials how they should actually govern a diverse and unequal empire.

The British government did not repeat the mistakes of the 1770s in North America in its remaining colonies of settlement; it instead allowed them to move slowly toward responsible government within the empire. It thus gave rise to another version of its composite polity, suited to an age of fledgling, if exclusionary, democracy—an amalgam of political units, each exercising sovereign functions but recognizing another layer of sovereignty at the imperial level. The use of the term "Dominion," originating in Canada and applied to New Zealand and Australia, came from the Latin "dominium" and reflected an older imperial idea of possession (chapter 6). A dominion was a component—neither fully subordinated nor entirely autonomous—in a complex repertoire of imperial power.

"There is no need for any nation, however great, leaving the Empire, because the Empire is a commonwealth of nations."

—Lord Rosebery, liberal politician (future prime minister), speaking in Australia, 1884

The Dutch empire in southeast Asia had been transformed by the bankruptcy of the VOC at the end of the eighteenth century and the formal takeover of the empire by the Dutch state. This state's attempt to tighten its grip on Indonesia gave rise to wars in the 1830s in Java and to bloody conquests and the suppression of rebellion in other islands from the 1870s through the early 1900s. From the 1830s, the Dutch state, under the "Cultivation System," distributed seeds to indigenous farmers, supervised the planting and care of crops, and took part of the harvest for itself. As of 1860, a mere 190 Dutch men—and many Indonesian intermediaries—directed the activities of some two million agricultural workers. Some entrepreneurial farmers turned this system, for all its oppressiveness, to their advantage, extending cultivation and developing a lively marketing system; others became increasingly vulnerable to the exactions of state and landlords and to the fluctuations of weather and markets; many fell into poverty. Later in the century, private mining and plantation sectors developed under direct Dutch management. A diverse archipelago acquired a degree of common experience under a heavy-handed colonial regime.

Even as European powers imposed stronger political authority on southeast and east Asia and helped themselves to lucrative economic positions, they did not extinguish the roles of indigenous elites in production and commerce—activities that had drawn European attention to Asia centuries before. At the same time, Britain, France, the Netherlands, and later Germany and Russia were circling around China—forcing themselves into its markets, colonizing nearby territories and coastal ports, profiting from the enterprise of diasporic Chinese throughout southeast Asia. There was another political regime at China's edge, also capable of action and disruption in this interempire arena—Japan.

A New Empire

In the 1870s Japan entered an imperialist game whose rules had already been set. Yet by being a different sort of player, Japan set in motion a dynamic that seventy years later took a dramatic turn.

More than European powers, Japan fits a model of imperial expansion following the consolidation of a more national regime at home. Japan's "isolation" until the American navy's incursion in 1853 is easily exaggerated, but Japan was not then engaged in foreign conquests and its population had become relatively integrated. Power under the old Tokugawa dynasty was widely diffused to local territorial lords. In the 1860s, the new Meiji dynasty proved to be a dynamic force for the political restructuring necessary for Japan to become competitive in world markets and for engineering a revolution from above in transportation, basic industry, and manufacturing.

> *"In my opinion what we must do is to transform our empire and our people, make the empire like the countries of Europe and our people like the people of Europe. To put it differently, we have to establish a new, European-style empire on the edge of Asia."*
>
> —Foreign Minister of Japan Inoue Kaoru, 1887

Japan's leaders were aware not only of American demands to "open" their economy but of the changing configuration of imperial power in east Asia. With China losing its grip on areas once within its control and France, Germany, Great Britain, and Russia extending their reach into the region, Japanese rulers feared that further European encroachment would limit their own influence. As Japanese industrialization advanced toward the end of the century, leaders worried about access to markets for the country's output and to raw materials the resource-poor islands lacked.

Japan sent its own expedition to "open" Korea in 1876. When China and Japan got into a dispute in 1894 over attempts by both to pull the strings in Korea, they went to war. The Chinese government had expected Japan to be no match but was forced to sue for peace. Japan's stunning victory in 1895 allowed it not only to exercise ever closer control over Korea but also to annex Taiwan, take over part of Manchuria, and collect a big indemnity. Japan was able for a time to practice in Korea something akin to the imperialism of free trade. Then as Korean collaborators proved unable to meet all of Japan's demands and as western empires provided alternative connections to Koreans, Japan escalated its level of intrusion and finally, in 1910, annexed Korea.

This self-conscious project of empire-building took place alongside Japan's industrialization and militarization at home. It was a vulnerable undertaking, for Japan's military ventures depended on warships bought from the west and its economic development required extensive use of foreign capital markets. Japanese leaders feared western intrusion themselves—and managed only in 1911 to free the country from the last of treaties giving western powers special rights in Japanese ports. Japan was conciliatory toward its rival empires and joined them in 1900 in putting down the Boxer Rebellion in China. It was Japan's victorious 1905 war with Russia over conflicting ambitions on the eastern mainland of Eurasia that served notice to European states that a new actor was entering an arena they thought to be their own. Japan went out of its way to let European powers know that it was following the rules of the game in its conflict with Russia—making the case that the war was just, following conventions on treatment of prisoners of war, asserting its humanitarian concerns through the Japanese Red Cross, allowing foreigners to observe its conduct, and negotiating a peace treaty, with American mediation, in Portsmouth, New Hampshire.

If Japanese leaders felt they had to establish their legitimacy as an imperial power in European eyes, they still made much of the fact that they were Asian, posing as the "big brothers" of Koreans and Taiwanese. Japan's subjects were not equals, but they were not altogether "others" either, and the government hoped that the accommodation of those subjects would produce a united Asian bloc under Japanese leadership capable of countering the west's claims on territory and resources. Some Japanese leaders aspired to lead other non-western states—including an increasingly beleaguered Ottoman empire—in an alliance against western colonialism, but in Taiwan, Korea, Manchuria, and China, Japan appeared all too similar to European and American imperialists. In images as well as practices, relationships between state power, economic exchange, and cultural and ethnic affinity were shifting and reconfiguring empire in Asia.

Ottomans and Europeans

The other great power that had proved so intractable to the imperial ambitions of Europeans was the Ottoman empire. As we will explain in chapter 11, it was far from unchanging, but, as in China, its rulers had not needed to look across oceans for sustenance and their imperial projects had not provided incentives or means for the kind of economic revolution that took place in eighteenth-century Britain. The Ottomans' close relations to merchant communities—such as those of Jews and Greeks—were no longer as effective once the axis of trade turned away from the eastern Mediterranean toward western Europe and when money could be made without the blessings of Istanbul. Ottoman vulnerability was greatest in the Balkans and in north Africa, provinces not as well integrated into routine administration as those of Anatolia and the Arab-populated eastern edge of the Mediterranean.

Let us look at two cases of European encroachment into one-time Ottoman domains, one consistent with the pattern of creeping colonization, the other a thoroughgoing conquest. In Egypt, Ottoman governors had carved out a degree of autonomy from Istanbul. With help from Britain, the Ottomans had cut short Napoleon's 1798 occupation of Egypt. Under the leadership of Mehmed Ali—a governor of Albanian origin who increasingly distanced himself from Ottoman oversight—Egypt became a dynamic place in the early nineteenth century, its army strong, its role as an entrepot between Asian and European markets still important. The completion of the Suez Canal, with considerable Egyptian input of finance and labor, raised British stakes in control of the region and worked against Egyptian and Ottoman interests. Mushrooming levels of Egyptian debt became an excuse—if not a reason—for the penetration of British agents into governance. In this case, the agents of reconfigured imperialism were the accountant and the banker—something like 1,300 of them by 1882—who ensured that state receipts would get channeled to debt repayment. That led to growing tension with Egyptians who felt they were losing control of their resources.

In 1882 a series of incidents resulted in crowds attacking Europeans and a revolt against Ottoman leadership. The rebellion was led by an officer in the Egyptian-Ottoman army. British troops intervened and a military garrison remained—occupation without full conquest. Britain put in place a "veiled protectorate" over Egypt (an overt one was only declared during World War I). The khedive—the representative of the sultan—was increasingly under the thumb of the British "resident"—a sore point among Egypt's cosmopolitan, educated elites. For many Egyptians, the issue was not so much the defense of a "national" space as a wounded Ottomanism, a belief that Istanbul should have done a better job of protecting Egypt against British interference. Egypt after 1882 was barely sovereign, but not quite conquered. De facto British control lasted into the 1920s, heavy influence until the 1950s.

France had already taken its bite out of Ottoman north Africa, a little over thirty years after Napoleon's debacle in Egypt. The incursion into Algeria (map 10.3) began while France was ruled by a monarchy and was firmed up in different ways by both republican governments (1848–52 and after 1871) and the Second Empire (1852–70).

French Algeria began less as a project to forge a new sort of colonialism than as yet another episode in the jockeying for power among European monarchs and regional potentates. But the interventionist dynamic soon changed. Under the Ottomans, Algeria had been loosely ruled. The region was a base for local trading and raiding networks, and by the early nineteenth century Ottoman control was tenuous. Accusations of piracy, conflicts over trade and debt with the governor of Algiers, alleged insults, and the French king's need to have something patriotic to show for himself led to the French assault on Algiers in 1830. With French governments hesitating over whether to go further, military men took the initiative by attacking largely autonomous leaders in the interior. Fear of losing face and creating a vacuum that the British might fill kept upping the ante of conquest, which was conducted over decades with the utmost brutality: the burning of villages, the destruction of livestock and crops, massacres of civilians and soldiers.

But what sort of colony would Algeria be? Not a destination for French settlers—there was no great desire in France for emigration. Italians, Maltese, Spaniards, and Jews were prominent among the colons who moved into commerce and farming under French eyes. To this newly remixed pan-Mediterranean population, France offered differentiated rights. Non-French settlers of Christian confession could become French citizens, but Muslims and Jews were considered to come under Islamic or Mosaic law and could only ask for French citizenship if they agreed to submit themselves to French civil law instead.

France insisted early on that it was respecting the right of Muslim Algerians to run their own legal affairs, an echo of Ottoman practices. But French citizenship was very different from the Ottomans' multiplex regime. The differential application of citizenship doctrine defined Muslim Algerians as second-order members of the French imperial community, without political rights, subject to arbitrary punishment. Elaborated in Algeria, the distinction between citizen and subject gradually became government practice in much of the empire. As a legislative enactment of 1865 made clear, Muslim Algerians were French nationals, but not French citizens unless they, as individuals, gave up their status under Islamic law and were accepted by the government as living a "French" way of life.

At this time, France was once again calling itself an empire, and its ruler, Napoleon III, set forth a classic imperial vision of rule: "Algeria is not a colony but an Arab kingdom. . . . I am as much the emperor of the Arabs as of the French." In 1870, Algeria's Jews became eligible for citizenship, consistent with a frequent imperial strategy of giving certain categories of people a stake in a system in order to enhance control over those thought to pose the greatest danger to it.

When France in 1871 again became a republic, the old conception of the polity as an assemblage of different sorts of territories and people was not lost. Algeria occupied a special place: its territory was considered integral to the French Republic, but only some of its people were integral to the republic's citizenry. The colons made full use of their political rights in metropolitan and Algerian institutions to entrench their position at the expense of the Muslim majority.

Repertoires of Empire

We thus see in the nineteenth century a wide repertoire of forms in which imperial power was exercised—from economic incentives and periodic demonstrations of coercive capacity to financial controls, treaty ports, protectorates, dominions, and colonies. Sovereignty—in practice if not in the treatises of international lawyers—was an uncertain and uneven phenomenon, not something societies either had or did not have. State forms were not equivalent. People living within composite, layered, and overlapping regimes of power could experience varying degrees of racialized subordination, rubbed in by discrimination in daily life, as well as possibilities of enhancing personal power or economic connections. A Hong Kong merchant might experience both possibilities and humiliations; in Algeria, most Muslim subjects saw only subordination, land grabbing, and exploitation; in Vietnam, impoverished workers, a vestige of the old mandarin elite, and successful planters played their unequal roles in colonial society.

The imperialism of free trade was always on the verge of becoming something else—that was why it was imperialism and not just trade. It depended on reconfigurations of interempire competitions. Great Britain, with the best cards to play, extended informal power and influence over old empires and new nations. But France in Algeria and Vietnam and the Dutch in Indonesia took on territorial colonization as well. One can exaggerate the urge to colonize that is supposed to have captured European publics by the 1870s, but there were entrepreneurs, missionaries, and military men who were active colonizers throughout the century and who proudly publicized their enterprise. Even without a concentrated and conscious effort to colonize the world, rivalries among a small number of European empire-states, the vulnerabilities of Ottoman and Chinese empires, and Japanese empire-building were changing the geopolitics of empire. We turn in the next sections to the intensification and extension of colonial rule.

Empire Intensified: British India in the Nineteenth Century

India had long held a peculiar position within the British system, and not a stable one. In the eighteenth century, the East India Company had become the de facto power over much of the subcontinent and a strong influence on the rest (chapters 6 and 8). British leaders eschewed the assertion of sovereignty over India in favor of the deliberately vague and very imperial term "paramountcy." Company rule accentuated the weakening of the Mughal emperor, giving intermediaries access to resources beyond the emperor's control. The extension of company power produced a patchwork of "princely states"—under a nominally sovereign ruler kept under British eyes—and more directly ruled territories. Dependent on indigenous intermediaries to supervise complex systems of revenue collection in the different states, company officials tried to bring more regularity to the work of numerous scribes and accountants who had been recruited via kinship, clientage, and apprenticeship. But such people were able to use their positions and the aura attached to documentary evidence to exercise a measure of power for themselves.

In the first half of the nineteenth century, company and government officials differed over the extent to which they should work through Indian intermediaries—thereby reinforcing the fiction of British rule as building upon the Mughals—or act more directly and decisively to bring India under "civilized" government. They never quite did either, and Christopher Bayly points to the irony that in converting trading enclaves into a huge territorial empire the British were creating something akin to the Ottoman empire, at the very time when the Ottomans were being held up as anachronisms. British India, like the Ottomans, depended more than anything on land revenue. The regime reinforced rather than undermined local hierarchies; it did not promote industrialization or fully open markets in land.

The East India Company in much of its early nineteenth-century domain relied on the "Residency System," on the official looking over the prince's shoulder. Princes might be deposed or their treasuries put under close observation, but they still could allocate revenue, tax subjects, maintain internal law, and patronize cultural institutions. A resident with a single European assistant might be the only non-Indian official in a princely state. In British India as late as the 1880s, the ratio of European officials to population was less than 1:250,000, although in some areas British rule was more direct and more authoritarian. Over it all presided the growing Honourable East India Company's Civil Service, which was supposed to bring bureaucracy and public service norms to a company long reputed for the venality of its officers and the personal and volatile nature of their relations with the Indian intermediaries on whom they depended.

British thinking about India at the beginning of the nineteenth century was characteristically "orientalist"—a vision of India as a once great civilization, now decadent. A lingering respect of one imperial elite for another—the maharajahs living in all their splendor—coexisted with condescension and a belief that all efforts to do anything new came from the British. Some British scholars learned Sanskrit and became students of ancient India. The orientalist conception rationalized imperial rule, but it also gave an opening to Indians, especially Brahmans, who by claiming to be repositories of ancient wisdom, law codes, and authority over lower castes could manipulate British expectations of oriental patriarchy in their own interests. This process made Indian society more patriarchal than it had been before. Some scholars today argue that the concept of caste is not an artifact of the Indian past but the product of a Brahman-British dialogue.

Over the nineteenth century, British views of Indian elites and Indian culture became harsher. Liberal opinion in England was increasingly confi-

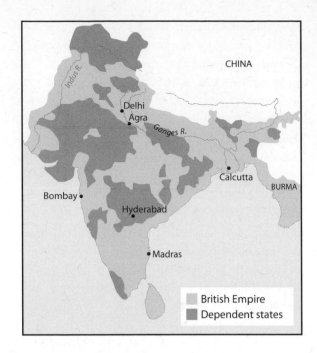

Map 10.2
British India, 1857.

dent that its ways of organizing life were superior to others. But some leaders at least entertained the possibility that people of other "races" and "cultures" could improve themselves by following a British lead. Difference, in such a view, became less a fact of life within an empire than something to be remade. A "Hindu College" was founded 1818, with English the language of instruction. The language of government had been Persian—reflecting the Mughal empire's own complex past—but it became English in 1835. Some Indians found opportunities opened up by these policies; others rejected the cultural onslaught; and still others tried to find a middle ground between two systems that were hierarchical in different ways.

Militarily, the company continued to depend on sepoys (Indian soldiers), some 155,000 of them by 1805. They were paid from local revenue and served not only in India but also in Ceylon, Java, and the Red Sea area. Within India, they were used to disarm local rulers, to punish any who rebelled, and to allow those who cooperated to maintain their status and symbolic authority.

The efforts of Protestant and some Catholic missionaries in India produced few converts. But they reflected a religious dimension of British thinking about social order and progress in the colonies. The missionaries produced a critique of Indian society analogous to the critique of slavery elsewhere in the British empire. They were particularly incensed by sati, the self-immolation of widows, and other customs held to be barbaric. British officials and businessmen developed their own codes of distinction, priding themselves on their supposedly activist masculinity as opposed to the supposedly soft and feminine nature of the Indian.

British rule did not imply a systematic attempt to bring capitalism to India. Although land-grabbing by British planters went on, both British and Indian elites were ambivalent about turning land into a fully marketable commodity. Both were dependent on the status quo, on receiving revenue from local landowners, zamindars, who had the hereditary right—made more explicit by the British in the "land settlement" of 1793—to collect revenue from peasant producers and remit part to the company. The extraction of revenue was a coercive and layered process that mirrored the layering of sovereignty under company rule. British India was acting in the manner of the eighteenth-century Ottomans, collecting most of its taxes from peasants via intermediaries. Exports also generated wealth, and over the nineteenth century the production of cotton, opium, indigo, and tea expanded. Meanwhile, the company encouraged the importation of cloth—now being mass produced in Britain at low cost—and helped destroy a once vibrant textile industry in India.

Figure 10.2
Magistrate's court in Oude, India, *Illustrated London News* 22 (May 14, 1853), 361. The engraving shows a British official (seated) with indigenous "approvers," who will assist in judging a case. The suspect appears with his hands bound in the center of the image. Falles Library, New York University.

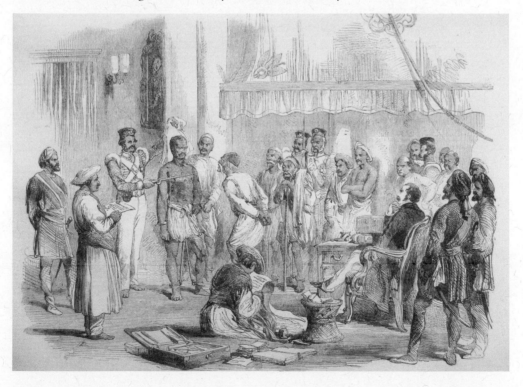

Discontent among peasants and at times local elites was rampant and sometimes flared into violence; many Indian soldiers resented being sent to distant places. Such tensions culminated in 1857 in a large-scale revolt known under the misleading name of "The Mutiny." The immediate cause was soldiers' outrage at the army's indifference to ritual taboos. There were rumors that cartridges that had to be ripped open with a soldier's teeth had been greased with animal fat forbidden to Hindus or Muslims. The Mutiny revealed the vulnerability of a system that relied for its oppressive force on people from the oppressed categories; soldiers could not be insulated from the grievances and angers of their society. Fears that the British were about to extend more direct control over princely states may have precipitated revolt in some areas. Some rulers cooperated with the rebels, as did many peasants, but others in both categories did not. Divisions within India were crucial to the ability of the British to regain control, but only after a struggle long and serious enough to force leaders to reconsider the nature of their rule.

The British response to the revolt was threefold. First, administrators decided that the East India Company had become a cumbersome anachronism, and in 1858 India at last came fully under the jurisdiction of the British state. In 1876 Queen Victoria took the title of empress of India, the first time the British monarch was formally identified as the ruler of an empire. Second, India had to be ruled more tightly, with a higher ratio of troops from the British isles to those from India and with an activist agenda of promoting progress that might ease economic tensions—more railroads, more educational facilities. Third, India had to be ruled more carefully. Land taxes were lowered, and care was taken regarding the alienation of land. The government pledged not to annex any more states, except those that had joined the Mutiny, and it eventually recognized approximately six hundred princely states within India.

During the decades after the Mutiny, Manu Goswami argues, government actions shaped India into a coherent entity and Indian political activists began to claim that very space. A British-built railroad network tied India together as never before, with middle-class Indians from all regions experiencing both the possibilities of traveling rapidly over long distances and the humiliations of segregation in the railway cars. The India Civil Service was a unified body, recruiting senior officers in England and more junior ones among British, Eurasian, and Indian candidates in India. Indians played important—but not equal—parts within it, circulating as tax collectors and census takers across India.

The unification of territory went along with the internal differentiation of its people. The British thought of India as divided, along lines of caste and religious affinity, into "communities"—as if Hindus, Sikhs, Parsis, and Muslims were neatly bounded from each other.

Indian intellectuals had as early as the 1810s been aware of constitutional developments around the world—such as the liberal Spanish constitution of 1812. In speech and writing Indians began to claim a role in legislative bodies, an end to the restrictive economic policies of the EIC, and more local administrative authority. Some promoted a progressive variant of Hinduism. Later in the century, as the public activism of Indians intensified, British ideas of the Raj—as the regime was called—ran up against an equally coherent but distinct vision of "Bharat Mata," "Mother India." For Hindu intellectuals, the notion of Bharat Mata embraced all of India, but with a Hindu slant to what constituted its core values and shared history. The large presence of Muslims, including their connection to the empire of the Mughals, was downplayed in favor of a direct link between an ancient, Sanskritic civilization and the Hindu culture of the present.

Indian activists also criticized British policy on its own terms—for failure to live up to the liberal values they had been told about in school. Some activists were sensitive to the irony that British rulers were posing as Asian overlords—paying lip service to the authority of Indian princes and rajas—while Indians were demanding the rights of Englishmen.

The political critique of colonialism went along with an economic one, for which Indian intellectuals used the term "the drain." They referred to the various means by which the fruits of Indian labor were funneled to Great Britain. "Home charges" meant that Indians paid the cost of their own repression: the salaries and pensions of officials, plus the India Office bureaucracy in London and interest on funds used for railroads and other projects. World trade, Indian critics of the economy claimed, was manipulated to serve British rather than Indian interests, leaving India overexposed to fluctuations in world markets and compelled to produce export crops even when drought conditions threatened people's livelihoods. The result was deadly famines in the late nineteenth century. Economic historians today agree with the critics that British policy in India produced little economic growth. One estimate is that per capita GDP did not grow at all between 1820 and 1870, then grew at only 0.5 percent per year until 1913, and stood below its 1913 level at the time of independence.

> *"Without India the British Empire could not exist. The possession of India is the inalienable badge of sovereignty in the eastern hemisphere. Since India was known its masters have been lords of half the world. The impulse that drew an Alexander, a Timur, and a Baber eastwards to the Indus was the same that in the sixteenth century gave the Portuguese that brief lease of sovereignty whose outward shibboleths they have ever since continued to mumble; that early in the last century made a Shah of Persia for ten years the arbiter of the east; that all but gave to France the empire which stouter hearts and a more propitious star have conferred upon our own people; that to this day stirs the ambition and quickens the pulses of the Colossus of the North [Russia]."*
>
> —George Curzon, influential colonial authority, 1892

Indian critics of empire seized upon the small spaces that colonial policy allowed, such as councils, which since 1861 had functioned with a mix of elected and appointed members. The British reserved seats for "minorities," and that term came to embrace Muslims—a sad twist for people whose religion was associated with the former empire.

Indians were thus developing a "national" conception—one that saw certain people at the core, others outside, others on the margins of their polity. This notion took on institutional form with the founding in 1885 of the Indian National Congress. Congress developed further the critiques of inadequate political representation, discrimination in the civil service, drain of wealth, and inequities of the land revenue system. Congress's sense of nation grew out of empire—from the empire's structures of rule, from Indians' service as soldiers and laborers elsewhere in the empire, from Indian merchants and financiers who contributed to and profited from imperial connections.

The layered sovereignty of the past was not entirely abandoned by the British even as the queen became empress and institutions of state were put more solidly in place. The idea that sovereignty in India should reside in the people was denied, or at least indefinitely deferred. Indian intellectuals by 1885 had grasped the significance of the new form of rule, and it was in relation to an entity called India and its British rulers that they organized politically.

Empire Expanded: The Scramble for Africa

We have been looking thus far at the ways by which empires expanded and intensified their command in the nineteenth century, asserting different degrees and forms of sovereignty. The colonization of Africa, in contrast, has seemed to many the epitome of "modern" colonialism: the imposition of a completely external power over people marked as primitive. Did imperial hierarchies turn into a colonial system split starkly in two, what Frantz Fanon labeled a "Manichean world"?

European traders and explorers had long been in contact with coastal Africa south of the Sahara (chapter 6), but with the notable exception of South Africa and areas of Portuguese settlement in what is now Angola and Mozambique, there had been little encroachment inland before the 1870s. As the slave trade waned in the first half of the nineteenth century, trade in commodities such as palm oil, coconut oil, cloves, and peanuts increased, and Africans largely kept agricultural production in their own hands. Then, in about twenty years almost all of sub-Saharan Africa was colonized, except

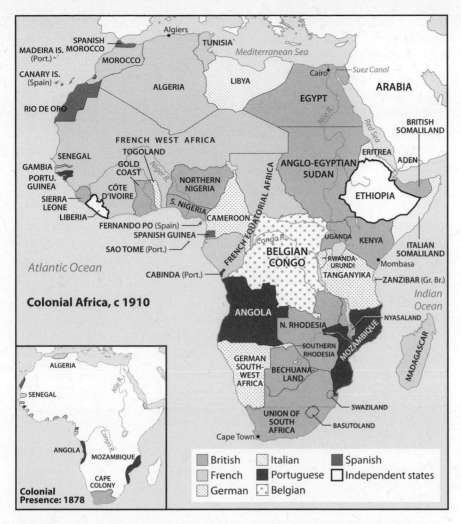

Colonial Africa, c 1910

SPANISH MOROCCO
MADEIRA IS. (Port.)
CANARY IS. (Spain)
Algiers
TUNISIA
MOROCCO
ALGERIA
LIBYA
Mediterranean Sea
Cairo
Suez Canal
EGYPT
ARABIA
RIO DE ORO
Red Sea
BRITISH SOMALILAND
FRENCH WEST AFRICA
TOGOLAND
SENEGAL
GAMBIA
PORTU. GUINEA
GOLD COAST
CÔTE D'IVOIRE
NORTHERN NIGERIA
Niger R.
S. NIGERIA
SIERRA LEONE
LIBERIA
FERNANDO PO (Spain)
SPANISH GUINEA
SAO TOME (Port.)
CAMEROON
FRENCH EQUATORIAL AFRICA
ERITREA
ADEN
ANGLO-EGYPTIAN SUDAN
Nile R.
ETHIOPIA
Congo R.
BELGIAN CONGO
UGANDA
KENYA
RWANDA-URUNDI
TANGANYIKA
ITALIAN SOMALILAND
Mombasa
ZANZIBAR (Gr. Br.)
CABINDA (Port.)
Atlantic Ocean
Indian Ocean
ANGOLA
N. RHODESIA
NYASALAND
MOZAMBIQUE
MADAGASCAR
SOUTHERN RHODESIA
GERMAN SOUTH-WEST AFRICA
BECHUANA-LAND
SWAZILAND
UNION OF SOUTH AFRICA
BASUTOLAND
Cape Town

Colonial Presence: 1878

ALGERIA
SENEGAL
Nile R.
Congo R.
ANGOLA
MOZAMBIQUE
CAPE COLONY

British	Italian	Spanish
French	Portuguese	Independent states
German	Belgian	

Map 10.3
The partition
of Africa.

for Liberia and Ethiopia. It was divided up among Britain, France, Germany, Belgium, Spain, and Portugal.

Theorists of imperialism in the twentieth century thought they saw in this burst of colonization the consequences of change in the European economy. In 1916, Lenin argued that capitalism had entered its highest stage, producing more goods more efficiently, generating more profits, but finding it hard to invest in more production because workers were being paid as little as possible and hence not consuming enough. Finance capital had become unmoored from the production of anything in particular and was searching the world for investment opportunities. But investments needed protection—from local people and European competitors—hence the need for the state to act as colonizer. There are two empirical problems with this kind of explanation of the colonization of Africa: little was actually invested in Africa, and European capitalists found many other places in which to invest, at home, in other countries, and in older colonies.

A more precise understanding of the interconnections between political and economic action is essential. Empire is not the only way to command resources, but markets do exist in a political context. In nineteenth-century Europe that context was the competitive world of empires—a small number of them—each drawing on supranational resources. By the late nineteenth century, the big players were France and Britain, as usual, and a new empire, the German Reich, which had been formed by consolidation and expansion in German-, Polish-, Danish-, and French-speaking areas of Europe (chapter 11). Belgium and Portugal were both small and for that very reason had a special interest in empire. Most frontiers of imperial expansion—across North America, between Russia and China—had been closed, and Africa was the only large and populated space that was not part of somebody's empire.

Germany was the new player in this game. The Reich's industrial capacity and military might were all too clear to its neighbors after its defeat of France in 1870. But the reference standard was still Great Britain, the first industrial power, with vast possessions and spheres of influence to defend. It was not vital to the British or the German economy that the state control Zanzibar or the Bight of Biafra—as long as no rival did. If Europe had been made up of many, smaller, more national states, no one of them would have had the resources to preempt the others, but the reality of Europe's empires meant that each sought to prevent another's monopoly over a shrinking pool of global resources.

And the African side of the encounter? The common image of an Africa of isolated tribes is false. Africa had not produced a China, but mid-nineteenth-century Africa included strong kingdoms near the coasts (Dahomey, Asante)—empires really, since they rarely assimilated populations they conquered—Islamic empires linked to the trans-Saharan trade, militaristic kingdoms like Buganda or the Zulu that prospered off expansion and redistribution of people and resources, plus a variety of smaller-scale polities. Some coastal communities had centuries of experience in trading with Europeans (west Africa) or Arabs and Indians (east Africa); there were culturally and ethnically mixed populations in coastal towns. For a time, Europeans' preference for some variant on the imperialism of free trade was compatible with leaving the interior of Africa to Africans.

The problems with such arrangements were several. First, they were unpredictable. From Europeans' perspective, African polities in conflict with each other and European polities competing with each other could lead to instability, trade monopolies, and interruptions in the flow of raw materials on which industry and social stability at home depended. Second, the technological gap between Europe and Africa had widened, and moving into Africa's vast spaces became more feasible with better weapons, communications, and medicines. Imperial advances elsewhere and improved transport lowered costs: the British used Indian troops in conquests in Africa, and all powers cultivated African allies. African kingdoms inflicted defeats on European armies—the Zulu (for a time) against the British in 1879, Ethiopia against the Italians in 1896—but the trend was in the other direction. Third, changing representations of Africa overcame much of the reluctance of European publics to get involved in what could seem too adventurous an enterprise for a bourgeois society and too vicious a one for democracies. Humanitarians, explorers, and propagandists, including the antislavery societies from the 1860s onward, publicized a picture of Africa as a place of slave trading and tyranny, in need of benevolent intervention. Finally, colonization acquired its own momentum. Outposts in Africa—the German and British trading "factories" along the coasts—had provided an imperial presence and a piece of the trading action at low cost to the state, and governments were gradually drawn into tensions emerging at the interface of African societies and the world economy. Chartered companies, like the EIC at an earlier point, were a middle step along the way to annexation. The British government authorized the Royal Niger Companies and the British South African Company to exercise administrative authority over territories, muddying the meaning of sovereignty. But companies often failed and in any case passed administrative burdens back to governments.

The leader of the imperialism of free trade, Britain, was not the first European power to escalate intervention in Africa but nonetheless ended up with the plums: Nigeria, the Gold Coast, Kenya, the Rhodesias. France got what it could—much of it arid lands on the edge of the Sahara plus choicer morsels along the coast. Germany acted aggressively and conquered some promising territories, especially Cameroon, Southwest Africa, and Tanganyika. The Congo was won by King Leopold of Belgium, in part because Belgium was small enough that others were willing to let its king, rather than a more dangerous rival, have a big, centrally located territory.

For all their rivalry, Europeans agreed to certain rules for contests among themselves. Following on a series of congresses that since 1815 had tried to regulate the political order of Europe (chapters 8 and 11), the Berlin Conference of 1884–85 set out the key principle: a power had to demonstrate effective occupation of a territory it claimed. At Brussels in 1889–90, European leaders agreed that each colonial power should assure the end of traffic in slaves, arms, and liquor. These two conferences helped define "Europe," for their premise was that one set of states set the rules for acting somewhere else. Europe announced itself as the repository of rational regulation and international law, demarcated from the uncivilized populations in Africa.

German chancellor Otto von Bismarck, the host of the Berlin Conference, did not want conflict in Africa to unleash a wider war that would interfere with the long-term process of consolidating the German empire in central Europe. He understood better than most leaders in Europe's arrogant nineteenth century the limits of empire. The conferences were attempts at making interempire competition a rule-bound exercise, but they did not end the basic, centuries-old, problem of conflict among a small number of powerful players for dominance of Europe. Not all leaders, including German ones, shared Bismarck's restraint—with disastrous consequences later on.

If the international conferences seemed to announce that the latest phase of European empire-building would be orderly, systematic, and reformist, the reality was anything but. Conquering Africa was the easy—if brutal—part, administering it the difficult one. The "modern" imperial state imposed a thin administration; advanced capitalism invested little; and a civilizing mission ended up supporting conservative chiefs and worrying that too much social change would compromise order.

After defeating kingdoms, colonizers generally tried to knock off the top layer of indigenous leadership and work with middle-level authorities. Elsewhere, they looked for cooperative chiefs, even where their authority was largely invented. Beneath the chiefs, indigenous policemen and translators acquired a measure of local power. Chiefs could be dismissed on the whim of a white official, and the colonial army stood in the background. There were revolts, some of them drawing on networks that were far more than local, but colonial strategies of divide and rule could usually contain them, with great violence. As many as one hundred thousand Africans died in the German repression of an uprising in Tanganyika in 1905; in Southwest Africa, the Herero revolt met a response close to systematic extermination; French campaigns in Sahelian west Africa went their brutal way for years. But sometimes—as the Germans found in Tanganyika—scaling back colonial ambitions for systematic exploitation was necessary in the face of African collective action.

The British later gave a name to governing through chiefs—indirect rule—but this was a version of ruling through indigenous intermediaries, practiced in one form or another in empires past and present. Chiefs were expected to collect taxes, organize labor to build roads, and sometimes round up workers for railway construction or white settlers. They maintained local order and justice under the guise of "customary" law, treated as if a timeless practice but purged of elements Europeans considered obnoxious. France made gestures toward a more assimilative policy intended to produce a small number of French-educated Africans. Belgium and colonies of white settlement policed Africans with particular vigor, but colonizing powers could only stray so far from indirect rule without encountering expenses and dangers they did not wish to entertain.

Colonial governments spent little on education. Mission societies—even under otherwise anticlerical French administrations—took up some of the slack. Missionaries often followed the flag and depended on government permission to operate, but missionaries from one country sometimes worked in the colony of another. Many saw themselves as serving a higher power than those of rival empires and defending a broader conception of humanity against the predations of exploitative settlers.

The French government considered its newly conquered populations in sub-Saharan Africa to be subjects, distinguishing them from citizens. Citizens included those of European France who settled in Africa, the people of African descent in the West Indies, and the original inhabitants of the "old" colonies of Senegal (the Four Communes), who, almost uniquely in

Figure 10.3
French officers with African soldiers in Senegal, c. 1885. Colonial armies made extensive use of African recruits in wars of conquest. Adoc-photos, ArtResource.

the French empire, had the rights of citizens without giving up Islamic civil status. Subjects, unlike citizens, came under a distinct and arbitrary system of justice, the *indigénat*, and were often made to perform forced labor; they had little political voice. The door to citizenship, as in Algeria, was opened a crack to Africans who acquired French education, served French interests, renounced their right to have personal matters judged under Islamic or customary law, and passed muster with officials. The number who squeezed in was infinitesimal, but the possibility that they might helped republican politicians in France convince themselves that their principles were compatible with colonization.

Some leaders of the Third Republic, like Jules Ferry, had a strongly "national" conception of France—a French state exercising power over backward people overseas to serve its own interests and stature and in the long run to spread French civilization. Business lobbies and imperial visionaries spun fantasies of a "Greater France" in which each part played its assigned role for the benefit of the French nation. But there was no wide consensus around such visions. Some politicians thought colonization wrong on principle or that it provided a protected hunting ground for short-term profit; many were indifferent and went along with colonial ventures only because they were cheap. Legislative efforts to allow a more inclusive concept of citizenship failed, but so too did attempts to take away the citizenship rights of Africans from the Four Communes of Senegal.

In French as well as British colonies, racial discrimination was harshest and most systematic in colonies of settlement, such as southern Rhodesia, Kenya, and Algeria. Even elsewhere, Africans who went furthest in acquiring European education, professional advancement, and higher status found discrimination grating. Empires had never treated their subjects equally, but the juxtaposition of racial divides with European rhetorics of democracy and progress was volatile.

Early colonizers were largely men, and many thought their masculine prerogatives included liaisons with African women and the right to recognize their offspring or not to do so, as they chose. Many colonial elites—and women who came to settle or were active in colonial lobbies back home—became increasingly anxious about the kind of society this version of masculine power was producing. Colonial regimes moved to curtail miscegenation and enforce segregation—as if claims to represent European civilization implied, as Ann Stoler puts it, "self-restraint, self-discipline, in a managed sexuality."

Colonial leaders worried as well about social dangers coming from the people they ruled: the young man detached from "traditional" authority, the young woman freed from patriarchal control. African men and women had their own ideas about changing gender relations, which fit neither the models of their elders nor those of colonial officials. Periods of wage labor could give young men a chance to marry and found a household outside of parental control, and cities became the sites of efforts to forge new familial forms. People experienced different kinds of social relations—in city and country, under elders' control or otherwise—over the course of a single life.

Colonial economies took different forms. In most of west Africa, British and French administrations tapped into systems of peasant production and commercial networks that had already been integrated into overseas trade. European merchant firms seized the import-export sector, but expanding exports of such crops as cocoa in the Gold Coast, Nigeria, and later the Côte d'Ivoire owed more to African initiative—planting new crops, migration to favorable agricultural zones, mobilization of labor through kinship and clientage—than colonial imposition. Some African farmers in such areas attained a moderate degree of prosperity. Mining—copper in central Africa, gold in the south—was controlled by European corporations, which created enclaves of wage labor surrounded by much larger areas where labor was recruited.

Colonial governments had mixed feelings about white settlement. Settler colonialism could be an outlet for Europeans to avoid unemployment or fulfill ambitions and fantasies, a way of ensuring predictable export production, and a bastion of European community in strategically useful lands. But settlers also demanded a European standard of living and expected colonial states to protect them from Africans' anger unleashed by land-grabbing, labor exploitation, and racial abuse. Generating labor for settlers usually meant restricting opportunities for African producers, even though the latter demanded less state expense and less fuss. In Kenya, southern Rhodesia, and for a time the Côte d'Ivoire white farmers obtained the repressive services they needed from the state, at the cost of high social tension.

A capitalist revolution took place in South Africa, in a racialized form. The possibility derived from South Africa's past. Settlement by Dutch (who later called themselves Afrikaners) dated to 1652 and produced a large and well-entrenched white population. After Europe's empire wars put South Africa under British rule, major chiefdoms were conquered and British settlers joined Afrikaners in claiming agricultural land. For a time, African peasants remained active producers, often as tenants on land seized by whites. Afrikaners formed semi-autonomous republics under British overrule. Then, with the discovery of diamonds in 1866 and gold in 1886, large-scale investment was concentrated in South African mines, and labor demands grew voracious.

The growing mine force, urbanization, and improved transport created incentives for grain farming on a capitalist basis. White farmers pushed tenants off land and relied more and more on hired labor. African loss of land contributed to a large mine and urban labor force, and that force had to be closely supervised—in large part by whites resident in South Africa, not by officials circulating around the empire. Male workers in the mines were kept in compounds apart from families and community; African men were made to carry passes and could be arrested for being in a "white" area while not at work; residential space was segregated. South Africa, alone among white-ruled states in sub-Saharan Africa, had the bureaucratic and police capacity to generalize such a system of labor and racial control.

Adapting Afrikaner republics under British overrule to the exigencies of a capitalist system led to conflict and by 1898 to war between the British government and the republics. The layered sovereignty of the nineteenth century gave way after a hard and bitter fight to an authoritarian colonial state. That the "Boer" war proved unexpectedly costly in lives and money led to doubts in some quarters about the colonizing project—eloquently expressed in J. A. Hobson's book *Imperialism* (1902). A few hundred Irish militants traveled to join Afrikaners fighting British imperialism, but these volunteers fought against a larger number of Irish who served in British forces. The Russian press, out to showcase British perfidy, supported the Afrikaners, while some Chinese intellectuals identified with their supposedly anticolonial stance.

But in South Africa, the wealth produced by the diamond and gold industries assured that ways would be found to overcome any doubts. After a short period of "reconstruction" during which the British tried to show that "modern" ways of running a state could be beneficial to Afrikaner as well as British elites, cooperation developed between rich Afrikaner farmers, British officials, and international capital, sufficient to transform South Africa into a self-governing dominion in 1910. Meanwhile, African men shuttled back and forth between places of wage labor and impoverished villages, left overpopulated with the old, the young, and women who were expected to keep alive everyone not away at work.

South Africa's capitalist transformation was at one end of the colonial economic spectrum. At the other extreme was predatory extraction. The most notorious example was the Congo of King Leopold of Belgium. Like kings of old, Leopold held the Congo as a personal fief, and he assigned companies to administer and collect products and revenue from each territory. With no long-term interest in the vitality of African society and with the temptations of a world boom in wild rubber, the companies devised a murderous system of extraction. They hired guards, including Africans from distant regions, and gave villages quotas for rubber delivery. Failure to meet quotas could result in exemplary mutilations and executions.

The result was an international scandal that helped separate what European opinion regarded as legitimate colonization from insupportable brutality. By 1908, Leopold was forced to turn the Congo from a private domain into a formal Belgian colony and make gestures to cleaning up its administration. The exhaustion of rubber supplies brought some relief to its victims. But concessionary companies also had their place in French, Portuguese, and British Africa. The results were harsh for Africans under their jurisdiction, but rarely durable as a method of colonial rule or business.

As the scramble to divide Africa closed the last frontier available for colonization, European empires seemed to have remade the world's geography. Britain alone could claim that a quarter of the world's population lived under its flag. Colonization now appeared as a truly global phenomenon, subjecting much of the world's people to alien rule, while a few cross-empire networks of Africans and Asians were beginning to mobilize against colonialism on the same worldwide scale. Both those who condemned and those who celebrated Europe's apparent subordination of the rest of the world had no way of knowing how short-lived this phase of empire-building would be.

Colonization without Colonialism?
Myths and Practices of the American Empire

In 1898, as imperialist land-grabs by European powers in Africa and Asia were at their peak, the United States went to war with Spain and with relative ease took over its colonies of Cuba, Puerto Rico, and the Philippines. We have argued (chapter 9) that the United States over the course of the nineteenth century acted within a particular imperial mode—forging a continental empire that sharply distinguished the included from the excluded, giving rise to a polity that defined itself as national. The late nineteenth century was for the United States a time of growing capacity to act imperially, but also of debate over whether to act abroad like other empires. France and Britain debated the ethics and value of taking colonies, but in Europe by century's end there was general acceptance that colonies, protectorates, and other forms of subordinated rule had a long-term place within an empire; specialized ministries supervised dependencies. The American debate was not resolved in the same way.

Cuba soon became a nominally sovereign state but with the United States retaining an extraordinary right of intervention on terms it chose. The Philippines were occupied and administered by the United States for forty-eight years, but as early as 1910 the government declared its intention to put the Philippines on the road to independence. Puerto Rico remained a dependent territory whose anomalous nature was signaled by labeling it a "Commonwealth." The strip of land needed for the Panama Canal was controlled by the United States from 1903 to 1979—it was called a "zone." Hawaii, for some time the focus of interest to planters and missionaries, was annexed, but it eventually was put on still another imperial trajectory—to full integration into the American polity as the fiftieth state. Meanwhile, the United States picked up a number of enclave colonies, like Guam, whose significance was mainly military and which were ruled accordingly. Finally, the United States practiced its own variant of the imperialism of free trade in heavy-handed fashion, via a long string of armed interventions, especially in Latin America. These actions sometimes led to occupations, more often replaced governments with more friendly or pliable variants, but did not produce colonies with a stable place in an American political order.

In Cuba in 1898, the United States cultivated a myth of benevolent intervention—an oppressive and degenerate Spain was chased from the Western Hemisphere, allowing an American people to exercise its freedom. Spain at the time was facing defeat at the hands of Cuban rebels, a tenuous combination of patriotic elites who resented rule from Madrid and ex-slaves and other laborers seeking relief from economic and social oppression. There was considerable sympathy within the American public for Cuban freedom fighters, but William McKinley's administration feared that a Cuba run by a motley mixture of Latin elites and masses of African origin would bring disorder and threaten property. The American invasion was less an attempt to support a liberation movement than to impose an alternative to both a weakened Spain and its potentially radical foes.

Although some in the United States had long desired the annexation of Cuba—whose proximity and plantation economy appealed to many southerners—this solution was harder to sell to a broad swath of American opinion. The alternative was to use American power to promote a social order dominated by rich, white Cuban property owners, who preferred a diminished sovereignty to either continued American occupation or social revolution. Diminished sovereignty was what they got: Cuba was legally prohibited from making treaties with other states, compelled to turn over land for a U.S. naval base (Guantanamo), and made to concede to the United States the right to intervene "for the protection of life, property and individual liberty." Later American officials and publicists reconstructed these events as American support for the liberation of Cuba from foreign tyranny and assistance for the development of good government. Even critics of American interventionism saw the event as misguided idealism, missing both the covetous context out of which the war emerged and the racialized conception of government that American rule supported.

In the Philippines, the United States also stepped into a revolutionary situation. Nationalists of largely Spanish descent, angered at being excluded from power and influence in the Spanish empire, sought to leave it. The

United States, having extended its influence into the Pacific via Hawaii, had economic motives, looking for a stepping-stone to trade with China, a goal it shared with European empires. The American military's quick defeat of Spanish forces in Manila in 1898 quickly proved deceptive. In 1899 a rebellion broke out against American rule, and in the bloody repression of it, American soldiers and leaders developed an increasingly racialized view of Filipinos as untrustworthy and unfit to rule themselves. Elite Filipinos were not immune from similar prejudices regarding non-Christian, sometimes Muslim inhabitants of some of the islands. Despite American claims to be exercising a benevolent imperialism, neither private investment nor congressional funding of administration (let alone economic development) was adequate, and officials were forced to rely on Filipino collaborators, largely from the preexisting elite, to ensure the functioning of government and economy. The imperial hierarchy layered in both American and Filipino conceptions of the unworthiness of people beneath them.

Filipino self-rule, despite the promises of 1910, was deferred until the unspecified time when Filipinos had proven themselves capable of exercising it. But the fact that the Philippines were, after all, *American* territory made U.S. leaders worry about having created too many Americans of the wrong sort. Filipinos' cooperation was needed in the Philippines, but the possibility that they might claim rights as Americans or move elsewhere in American territory, especially into employment on the mainland, was not considered desirable.

The politics of empire thus gave rise both to an imperialist mission of spreading the American way and to a racist anti-imperialism. There were American political leaders who thought that imperialism was corrupting and others who sought reform at home and in overseas territories. Some thought British India was a good model; others did not. Colonizing projects overseas seemed both an extension of American continental empire and a danger to the myth that continental expansion had produced. The idea that the United States was forging a homogeneous people as its territories advanced toward statehood depended on the radical exclusion of people who did not fit in. This homogenizing vision sat uneasily with the realities of ruling different sorts of societies overseas. In Cuba, behind-the-scenes rule seemed to reconcile these tensions. In the Philippines, deferred independence offered a solution. In Puerto Rico, American economic interests were more direct—particularly in the sugar industry—and Puerto Rican elites' alleged backwardness was considered more of an obstacle to economic progress; there a more durable and incorporative version of imperialism—the "Commonwealth"—was needed.

Meanwhile, the United States acknowledged the sovereignty of states in Latin America, but intervened whenever elite intransigence or the threat of revolution passed a certain danger point. This strategy led to invasions, as in Mexico in 1916, and occupations, whose explicitly temporary nature distinguished them from the colonization practiced by France or Britain. Haiti, Panama, the Dominican Republic, most of the Central American republics at one time or another—the list of American military interventions in its neighbor states is long. From the American conquests of 1898 onward, such actions contributed to a new self-image of the United States as a decisive, powerful actor overseas. But an influential segment of elite opinion in the United States was too invested in the task of turning a continental empire into a white, Christian nation to cultivate fully a self-image of itself as a ruler of colonies. The United States did not create institutions like the British Colonial Office that made explicit—and presumably durable—the practice of ruling people differently overseas.

Conclusion

France, Germany, Britain, Portugal, and Belgium brought to their colonial conquests of the late nineteenth century new technologies and a heightened sense of imperial entitlement. Their repertoires of rule were shifting. For Britain, an imperialism of free trade would have made no sense in the seventeenth century—that tactic would have been a sure loser in the violent world of maritime empire. In the early nineteenth century, with Britain's economic transformation, this strategy first became realistic, then turned increasingly problematic as other empires closed the economic gap. Slavery was an ordinary part of empire in the seventeenth century, but thanks to the actions of slaves and antislavery movements it was pushed out of the repertoire over the course of the nineteenth. New technology made the conquest of Africa easier to accomplish in the late nineteenth century than a century earlier, and at the same time industrialization raised the stakes for European powers to have secure access to raw materials and markets across much of the world. Nineteenth-century governments were developing ideas of good governance that were different from those of older, hierarchical regimes.

How did these changes relate to the imperatives of empire—to ensure the cooperation of intermediaries, to make imperial rule seem attractive or normal to political actors at home, and to compete effectively with other empires? The machine gun and the telegraph were different from the Mongol armed horseman and relays of messengers that had overwhelmed so much of Eurasia in the thirteenth century, but in the vast spaces of Africa speed and firepower did not necessarily translate into rule that was durable or transformative.

The colonial conquests of the nineteenth century, like earlier ones, were fast and bloody. In some contexts, colonial rule thickened into an effective apparatus of surveillance and punishment, but elsewhere its presence was thin, arbitrary, and episodically brutal. Colonial regimes sometimes articulated ambitious goals of transforming "traditional" societies and often retreated from these when colonized people pushed back. The great empires could afford to do so in large part because they had wider repertoires of power and could keep their rivals from monopolizing crucial resources.

But what of the sense of superiority—cultural and racial—that accompanied European assertions of their mastery of science, economy, and government? The nineteenth century is often seen as the time when empires' politics of difference took a crucial turn, when race came to be a key, if not *the* key, division among humankind, a harsh white-black dichotomy replacing less categorical, more relational forms of hierarchy and inequality, a set of practices reinforced by "scientific" arguments that races were distinct and unequal. Since the late eighteenth century, European thinkers had been fascinated with the relationship of physical and cultural distinction. Some argued that human populations reflected different "stages" of civilization. As more Europeans went to Africa or Asia to explore, exploit, and rule, the experience of conquest and domination could seem to validate theories of racial hierarchy.

It does not diminish the virulence of racist discourse and practices in colonial situations, the callous disregard of the humanity of indigenous people slaughtered in wars of conquest or exploited in mines and plantations, and the painful discrimination conquered people experienced to point out that European thinking and practices in regard to race were incoherent, inconsistent, and unstable. How race actually operated in colonial politics was subject to the contingencies and contradictory political imperatives that all empires faced. Administrators made strenuous efforts in the late nineteenth and twentieth centuries to impose segregation and to keep colonial agents from producing a mixed-race population or from "going native" precisely because racial barriers could be permeable.

Colonial rulers needed intermediaries, however much they belittled Indian princes or African kings. Only where colonization was sufficiently dense and lucrative—as in South Africa—to support a European bureaucracy, military, and police force could imperial rulers forgo the assistance of indigenous elites. Empires did not have consistent policies for acquiring intermediaries—they had to work with and reshape the structures of authority they found. Some indigenous elites defended their people, land, and way of life; many resisted the land-grabbing, labor-coercing, justice-denying side of colonization; others sought new opportunities for themselves in the imperial context, sometimes pushing to the limits of what colonial regimes could tolerate. Economic intermediaries were as essential as political ones: colonial revenue, outside zones of plantations and mines, depended on indigenous farmers and merchants—on the moderately prosperous businessman as well as the exploited worker.

Empires needed to provide a vision of their kind of power that could motivate their agents, and they had to acquire the support, or at least the acquiescence, of a public at home, one now conscious of its own political rights and caught up in ideologies of human perfection and progress. Both governments and private associations with interests in the colonies put much effort into propaganda—developing an explicit and positive image of the colonial project—but it is not clear how deeply these initiatives penetrated. Religious and humanitarian organizations, increasingly able to acquire and disseminate information, could expose abuses and present alternative versions of what a colonial society should be. Scandals in the colonies traveled wider than they did in the days of Las Casas or Burke. Even as colonial governments strove to police racial boundaries and tried to make racial distinction appear as the natural order of things, changes in society and politics both at home and abroad brought colonial endeavors into question.

But the most important impediment to putting a racial order into practice came from the people of the colonies themselves—their initiatives to make the most of the spaces that colonial regimes could not control, their ability to use, in their own ways, the possibilities that imperial connections provided. Colonial governments were challenged before they were consolidated, not just by rebellions but by the quiet actions of a schoolteacher living near an African mission station who recorded his community's traditions in a European language and thus refused the dichotomy of European modernity and African tradition, by the advocates of a reformed Hinduism or a modernizing Islam, by Christians in west Africa who founded churches of their own so they could practice the religion they had learned without the control of white missionaries. As soon as mission societies and colonial governments started to train enough Africans or Asians to serve them in junior positions, these intermediaries blurred the lines colonial regimes were trying to create. Educated indigenous elites were aware of the cultural resources of Europe and were conscious of the exclusions they faced; their presence complicated colonial dualisms, and their oral and written interventions provided critiques of colonial rule, in the colonizers' own terms as well as through the languages and networks of their own communities.

Racializing ideologies were also challenged on the empires' global scale when, for instance, the first pan-African Conference met in London in 1900, bringing together activists from Africa, Europe, the United States, and the West Indies to discuss the common experience of discrimination and oppression and to begin a struggle against them. The African American thinker and political leader W.E.B. DuBois wrote with prescience and precision in 1903, "The problem of the twentieth century is the problem of the color line." The distinction between white and black was and would continue to be not a given of modernity but a focus of questioning, of argument, of mobilization, and at times of violence.

If race was more a focus of argument than a coherent ideology of rule, Europeans' practices of governance in the nineteenth and twentieth centuries were less sharply distinguished from those of the past than contemporaries (or later scholars) wanted to admit. The problem for nineteenth-century empires was not a lack of new technologies of surveillance and supervision but the challenge of applying them to large populations over vast spaces at low cost. In much of Africa the first censuses—the most elementary form of gaining information about a population—were not conducted until the late 1940s—about two millennia after Chinese officials started to collect such data, nearly a century after the British began to do so in India. Colonial states—except where the stakes were exceptionally high—did not devote the financial means, the manpower, or the will to carry to their logical limits either crude exploitation or sophisticated social engineering. Europeans could run a mine; they could plan a city in which settlers could be at home; they could run an army and a prison. But technology and social engineering produced fragmented societies, not a grid of secure control over the bodies and minds of the "colonized."

Caught between a desire to rule and exploit "Africans" or "Indians" and the need to work through intermediaries, colonial empires produced visions of tribes and communities, each of which could be understood in its particularity and governed through vertical lines of authority converging at the top. Colonial governments did not want to admit that their subjects were capable of cooperating with each other to constitute a large-scale political body. In this way, imperial imaginations kept returning to the patrimonial strategies used by earlier empires and away from notions developing in Europe of a citizenry that would elect its representatives—and would also be the object of social programs and surveillance.

The newest factor in the constitution of empire was the way in which empires were being governed at home. It was harder in the nineteenth century than in the seventeenth to see top-down authority as natural, wherever it was exercised. Colonial rule came to be defined and defended as a distinct set of practices—and it also became an object of criticism and attack. The ideal of popular sovereignty in European countries was not applied to colonies, but it was a reference point for educated Asians and Africans— something they knew about but could not have.

To be sure, the victories of enlightened thought and democracy in Europe were incomplete. Emperors and kings, exercising real power, persisted into the twentieth century, and in republics, elites tried to make sure that peasants and workers did not influence government too much. But even the possibility of a sovereign citizenry implied a boundary problem. Just who should have the rights of a citizen—at home and overseas—was debated in France off and on from the 1790s to the 1950s. Racial exclusion could be a ground not just for taking and exploiting colonies but also—an argument frequently made in the United States—against doing so in order to avoid the danger that non-white people might enter the polity and perhaps claim the rights of citizens.

What imperial powers in the nineteenth century could hope for from their subjects, as in centuries past, was contingent accommodation. Many Europeans might have thought that their advances would allow them to do what they willed to their subjects—exploit them without restriction or remake them in a European image—but they could not.

For imperial ideologues of the late nineteenth century, the assertion that colonization was modern was a moral argument—a claim to be forging a better empire. Some scholars now make another moral argument—that the evils of colonialism can be explained by "modernity" and "Enlightenment ideas." Obviously, European colonialism existed at a particular time and drew some of its legitimacy from the ideological currents of the era. But as we have seen (and will explore further in the next chapter), modernizing and enlightened perspectives had multiple implications. They could inspire critique of colonial practices or colonization in general as well as its legitimation; they were subject to conflicting interpretations over the boundaries in which these perspectives applied. To frame the problem of colonialism as a problem of modernity is to deflect responsibility onto abstractions. The people who perpetuated bloody massacres, brutalized workers, and systematically denigrated African or Asian cultures made their choices knowingly and created the context in which such choices appeared natural. They did so in the face of other people—a principled few at times, in metropoles and colonies—who argued against them.

The smugness of European elites at the turn of the twentieth century coexisted with anxiety born of experience: at home, with the conflicts of capitalist development and political participation; overseas, with the difficulties of managing the tension between categorical distinctions and hierarchical connections. Yet the divisions that drove European competition in the nineteenth century and tore Europe apart in the twentieth were not struggles of Europeans against non-Europeans for domination or independence or between bourgeoisie and proletariat or between homogeneous ethnic or national populations. They were conflicts among empires, each with a heterogeneous population, combining in different ways the military and economic strength that came from within and beyond European spaces. In the nineteenth century as in the sixteenth century, a small number of European states drove each other to acquire more resources overseas as well as on contiguous territory, or at least to preempt others who might try to do so. For a time, Europeans managed to contain the conflicts that such competition entailed; but the basic problem remained.

Colonial rule did not and could not live up to a totalizing vision of Europeans remaking the world in their image or for their use. The compromises required by empire were stronger than the fantasies of modernizing European colonialism.

SOVEREIGNTY AND EMPIRE

Nineteenth-Century Europe and Its Near Abroad

Between the Congress of Vienna (1815) and the outbreak of World War I, Europe remained a contentious field of interempire competition. The rivalries that drove the quest for overseas colonies also transformed the map of Europe, more than once. In the nineteenth century a new empire was put together in central Europe (Germany); an empire to the east continued to expand (Russia); a long-lived empire shrank but retained and retooled its core (the Ottomans); and the complex Habsburg Monarchy reorganized itself—complexly—once again. Imperial leaders faced an array of challenges, as new ideologies and new social linkages threatened to disrupt established ways of managing subjects and elites. Great Britain, now a superpower overseas, and other empires in the capitalist vanguard applied their augmented resources to the competition for land and people in Europe and its near abroad. This chapter focuses on the dynamic interface between competitions among empires and reform within them. We highlight the Russian, Ottoman, German, and Habsburg empires, as each adjusted its politics of difference to shifts in the geography of imperial power.

War—among and within empires, in and outside Europe—played a major role in these imperial reconfigurations. Russians and Ottomans, abetted by European rivals, continued their long series of wars punctuated by inconclusive settlements. Prussians fought with Danes and Austrians, and with the French; Habsburgs fought against rebellious Italians, German rivals, and the Ottomans. Rebellions against Russian, Ottoman, and Habsburg sovereignty as well as attempted revolutions threatened the hold of rulers upon their subjects and offered opportunities for imperial rivals to exploit. The Crimean war—a major clash of Russian, Ottoman, British, and French empires at mid-century—took around four hundred thousand lives.

If war was the most visible way that empires intersected, economic power was crucial to sustaining imperial control or trying to expand it. New wealth, new production processes, and new ways of organizing labor spread unevenly over the continent, unsettling relations between imperial rulers and their subjects, among subjects, and among empires. The British empire wielded the weapon of "free trade" against vulnerable competitors on Europe's edges, and the German Reich harnessed its diverse regions into an industrial powerhouse.

New political, cultural, and intellectual possibilities traveled across imperial boundaries. Like participants in the antislavery movement, liberals, socialists, anarchists, nationalists, religious reformers, and feminists could connect to each other and promote their causes. "For your freedom and ours" was the slogan of Polish rebels against Russia in 1830. Such crosscutting mobilization was the nightmare of imperial rulers for whom vertical ties to subject populations were preferred instruments of control.

The foundations and functions of sovereignty were in question throughout the nineteenth century. The philosophical revolution of the eighteenth century had undermined traditional justifications for state power, and the French and American revolutions had widened the range of political imagination. If French citizens could kill their king and establish a Roman-like republic if only for a few years, what did this mean for emperors and sultans and their relations to real or potential subjects? Empire was not extinguished by revolution—two Napoleons called themselves emperor in nineteenth-century France and a new German ruler called himself a kaiser—but imperial rulers and their enemies knew that alternative sources of political legitimacy and rights were on many people's minds.

But whose rights counted when remaking or making states? In nineteenth-century Europe, there were several candidates for refounding the polity. Religion, history, class, ethnicity, civilization, political tradition—each provided a basis for people to make common cause and demands upon their rulers or to assert their own rights to rule. It was not just rebels or national patriots who deployed these claims. Empires asserted various notions of legitimacy against each other, as well as directing them selectively toward their own populations. The ideas of national or religious rights were used repeatedly to justify interventions in other people's empires.

Against the military and economic prowess of imperial rivals, leaders of the Russian, Habsburg, and Ottoman empires took measures to revitalize their polities—increase their revenues, shore up loyalties, and beef up their armies. Responding to new concepts of sovereignty, each empire experimented with its political institutions, including parliaments and adjustments of subjects' rights. Each empire looked with jaundiced but attentive eyes at the "colonial" policies of the British and the French; each carried out its own kind of civilizing mission; each came up with new variants on the politics of difference. Each empire encountered unexpected and destabilizing responses to its efforts to update people and resources. The combination of centralizing initiatives with liberals' advocacy of a homogeneous and empowered citizenry provoked turbulent hostilities between and within religious or ethnic groups. But contrary to the conventional read-back from the winners' side of World War I, Russian, Ottoman, German, and Habsburg empires arrived at 1914, like their competitors, with modernized armies, expecting a short conflict, counting on the patriotism of their subjects, and hoping that one more round of empire war would this time go their way.

Russia and Europe: Redesigning Empire

Let's start with the final scenes in Napoleon's empire drama. In March 1814, Alexander I, the emperor of Russia, with Frederick William III of Prussia led their armies into Paris. Napoleon, like so many others since Roman times, had been defeated by the ability of the multiple powers on the continent to reconfigure their alliances against a would-be universal emperor. This time, Russia played a pivotal role in the struggle to recast Europe.

Early in his reign (1801–25), Alexander, the grandson of Catherine the Great, had restructured Russia's central administration along the lines of Napoleon's ministries. In 1807, when a multistate alliance against France had failed, Alexander made a typically imperial peace with Napoleon, dividing Europe into Russian and French spheres. After Napoleon's attack on Russia in 1812, a new anti-French alliance took shape, led by Austria, Great Britain, Russia, and Prussia. Russia's decisive contributions to the allies' victory fulfilled Peter I's ambition: the empire was demonstrably a great power on the European scene.

At the Congress of Vienna, the victorious empires carved up Europe to protect and further their own interests, creating the Kingdom of the Netherlands, adding Prussian territories on the Rhine, extending Austrian sovereignty in northern Italy and the Alps, readjusting the Polish partitions, and restoring Prussian and Austrian sovereignty over various kingdoms, principalities, and duchies. Russia retained Finland and Bessarabia, annexed before 1814. Poland was established as a kingdom, with its own constitution and the Russian emperor as its sovereign. This was not a restoration but a typically imperial redrawing of the unruly European map. Sovereignty was subordinated where convenient; pieces of territory were exchanged; some kingdoms were merged; others divvied up.

The Congress produced two formal alliances, founded on different principles. Alexander, deeply religious after the torments of the war, pursued his salvationist agenda through the "Holy Alliance." Members were to pledge that their internal affairs and their relations with each other would be based on the "eternal religion of God our Savior" and on "the rules of Justice,

Christian Charity and Peace." This statement seemed ludicrous to some diplomats, but, apart from the Vatican, the Ottomans, and the British, most European powers signed on to Christian principles. The second agreement continued the Quadruple Alliance of Austria, Great Britain, Russia, and Prussia, formed to combat Napoleon. Representatives of these powers agreed to meet at fixed intervals to consult about their common interests and to consider measures that would enhance prosperity and peace in Europe. While its membership changed—France joined in 1818 and Britain later left—the alliance put in place what became known as the "congress system"—a commitment to meeting and mediation by Europe's great powers.

Together these agreements expressed Europe's transformation from a geographic space into a political entity and gave self-aware Europeans an ideological platform that endured long beyond the pacts themselves. The Holy Alliance asserted the Christian foundations of the new European order, and the congress system recognized the dangers of territorial politics

Map 11.1
Empires in and around Europe, 1815.

within Europe. The commitment to coordination came in handy in the 1880s when Europeans tried to regulate their competition for colonies in Africa (chapter 10).

Alexander's armies had proved Russia a great power, but was the giant empire really part of Europe? Eighteenth-century travelers and philosophers had drawn a line between Europe's presumed civilization and the half-savage societies to their east. The Russian victory over Napoleon and the tsar's lavish martial pageantry cast Russia's image in a military mode. The Romanov empire was feared, exoticized, but not welcomed in a European world.

In Russia, Alexander's adaptations of European ways were selective and constrained by the bargains of autocratic rule (chapter 7). His reign had begun in blood—nobles had assassinated his unpopular father—but also with reforms. Young noblemen of Alexander's age were familiar with western Europe's institutions and political theories, and both serf emancipation and constitutional change were proposed to the tsar. His legislation set some limits on landlords' powers over laborers; serfs were emancipated in the Baltic provinces. New universities were opened with the goal of improving administration. But on the question of the emperor's unique and unconstricted power, Alexander and many nobles and high officials drew an old line. As before, the patrimonial configuration of power—the tsar advised by his favorites—prevented the nobility from taking a unified position on devolving authority.

Divisions among the emperor's elite servitors were brutally revealed in December 1825, when a conspiracy of officers, many back from European victory and flush with constitutional projects, tried to seize power after Alexander's sudden death in 1825. Military commanders remained loyal to the tsar, and the "Decembrist" rebels were overcome in hours. Five leaders were executed, other conspirators were exiled to Siberia. This failed coup d'état was interpreted by the new tsar, Nicholas I (1825–55), as a rebellion against the principle of autocracy.

The conviction that contacts with the "west"—the word was gaining currency—were responsible for the insurrection led Nicholas to intensify surveillance through the infamous Third Department (an ancestor of the Soviet KGB). Potentially disruptive individuals were managed by arrest, internal exile, or being sent abroad. To combat subversive ideas, Nicholas launched an ideological offensive. Responding to idealist philosophies as well as myths of ancient national roots circulating in post-Napoleonic Europe, Nicholas exalted what were claimed as Russia's traditional values—virtue, obedience, and Christianity. In the 1830s, his deputy minister of education announced the slogan, "Orthodoxy, Autocracy, and Nationality." In dramatic ceremonies, the emperor led a sentimental cult of the imperial family as the model of caring patriarchy, romantic love, and filial devotion. The dynasty—for all its foreign credentials through Nicholas's Prussian mother and wife—sought to connect Russia's past, present, and future.

The imperial cult was not a substitute for reform, but Nicholas made sure that initiatives came from the emperor and his ministers, not an empowered public. In the 1830s the emperor sponsored codification and publication of Russia's laws. A school of jurisprudence was opened to train future officials. Although Nicholas did not abolish serfdom, his administration reformed governance for peasants who lived on state, not noble, lands (approximately half the peasants in the empire). The Imperial Geographical Society began systematic studies of the multiple peoples of the empire. As for religion, Nicholas pulled his punches: he allowed the Orthodox church to open new missions in Siberia and other areas, but "foreign" faiths remained protected and administered by the state.

Despite Nicholas's efforts to tamp down possible sources of subversion, intellectual life flourished at Russia's universities, salons, and academies and through the burgeoning press. Debates over Russia's destiny and its distinctive past set in motion imaginative historical reconstructions. The emperor's slogan evoked "nationality," although a more accurate translation would be "peopleness," as a principle of state. Did this mean Russian people or the peoples of Russia or something else? Scholars fought for their definitions and for imperial funds. Was Russia to "advance" toward European values— the position of the "westernizers"—or could some wellspring of community and goodness be found in traditions of the ancient Slavs—the argument of the "Slavophiles"?

Making Nations on Imperial Terrain

Heated arguments over a nation's essence and its possibilities were not unique to Russia. In this age of trans-imperial connections, people across Europe were searching for the right combination of artistic expression, historical achievement, and popular virtue to claim their places in the civilized world as it was being redefined. The pan-European interest in language, history, and practices of distinctive national groups had been inspired by the works of Herder, Fichte, and other Germans who viewed the German nation as a culture, not a polity. Europeans also strove to make connections back to earlier Christian eras and to Rome.

These quests for national cultures and for serviceable Christian genealogies became weapons in imperial competitions. The emergence of a new "Greek" state was a case in point. Both British and Russian empires claimed a glorious linkage to a Greek past: the British to what was now defined as classical Greek civilization—leading to Europe, of course; the Russians by virtue of Orthodox Christianity with its roots in Byzantium. Both empires sought to undermine their common rival—the Ottomans—by supporting nationalists calling themselves Greeks who rebelled in 1820s.

Rebellion on zero-sum European terrain rapidly drew other empires into play. In 1826, Russian and British leaders agreed to joint management of conflicts between rebels and the Ottoman sultan; a year later the French joined this version of imperial coordination, called "peaceful intervention" by Canning, the British foreign secretary. But after the three allies trapped the Ottoman fleet in the Bay of Navarino and destroyed it (1827), the British began to worry that they were assisting the wrong empire—Russia, the stronger one—and decided to let others do the fighting. French troops dislodged Egyptian forces from parts of what later became a Greek state, and Russia began a diplomatic campaign—their candidate was chosen president of Greece in 1827—and a military assault. In 1828, Russian troops were in position to march on Constantinople, but Nicholas drew back. Keeping the Ottoman empire in place, but getting pieces of it, was more to his advantage than destroying the sultan and unleashing a free-for-all in the region.

The Treaty of Andrianople (1829) gave Russia areas coveted since the seventeenth century—territories in the Caucasus, part of the Black Sea coast, and control of the mouth of the Danube. Russia occupied the principalities of Moldavia and Wallachia along the Danube, ostensibly to protect Christians, and promptly installed an administration dominated by large landowners. The Russian president of Greece was assassinated in 1831, and Greece got its king—son of the king of Bavaria and a Catholic—in 1832, but not all the territory patriots had claimed. For fear of encouraging further disruptive claims on Ottoman subjects, the great powers insisted that King Otto be designated "king of Greece," not "king of the Greeks," and thereby territorialized nationality in their own interests.

European powers remained fixated on curtailing each other's attempts at domination, but this strategy did not protect rulers from effects of political upheaval within empires. Multiple revolutions broke out in 1830: Belgian Catholics and Protestants revolted against Dutch rule; northern Italians rebelled against the Habsburgs; the French against their own king. For Russia, the problem was Poland: Polish nobles tried to lead an uprising against Russian rule in 1830. After putting down the rebellion, Nicholas canceled the Polish constitution of 1815 and made Poland part of Russia. In the Caucasus where Russians had been hard put to subdue mountain peoples, Shamil, an imam from Dagestan and Chechnya, began a long campaign against Russian aggression that lasted from the 1830s until his surrender in 1859.

After the turmoil of the 1830s, Russian, Austrian, and Prussian rulers agreed to help each other in case of "internal troubles" or "an external threat." This agreement was formalized by the Convention of Berlin in 1833. That same year, Russian troops came to the aid of the Ottoman sultan against his upstart challenger, Mehmed Ali of Egypt. The reward was the Treaty of Unkiar-Skelessi, confirming Russia's role as protector of the Christians in Ottoman lands. In return for Russian aid, the Ottomans agreed to close the Straits to armed vessels in time of war.

By the mid-1830s, Nicholas seemed to have secured the sovereignty of empires based on dynastic right, although his containment policies at home sent defeated elites—especially Poles—and disgruntled intellectuals—such as Alexander Herzen—to western Europe where they reinforced Russia's reputation for repression and joined circles of political activists. Revolutions elsewhere in Europe, not Russia, brought Nicholas back to the fray of inter-imperial politics. In 1848, when another spasm of political uprisings broke out across the continent, Nicholas volunteered his services as the "gendarme of Europe." His interventions assisted the Austrians in the Balkans and in Hungary, where two hundred thousand Russian troops intervened to shore up Habsburg control.

Imperial regimes were restored in Europe after 1848, but Nicholas feared a second round of revolutionary contagion. Russian students and exiles had participated in the upheavals, most famously the anarchist Bakunin with his arch-radical slogan, "the passion for destruction is a creative passion." In Paris, the Russian nobleman had called for an alliance of Poles and Russians against Russian "despotism." Bakunin was ultimately handed over by the Austrians; he remained in Russian prisons until Nicholas's death.

Repression of dangerous ideas became a leitmotif of Nicholas's last years. The university curriculum was altered to eliminate constitutional law and philosophy; censorship was tightened up. In a traumatizing display of the emperor's power over his subjects, members of a socialist study group, including Feodor Dostoevsky, were sentenced to execution and reprieved only minutes before the action was to take place. Cutting off connections to the west was a defensive strategy applied repeatedly in the Russian empire and later in the Soviet Union, each time impoverishing the resources—political and material—of the country.

Empire War in the Crimea

Nicholas, who had put so much effort into toning up Russian empire, then misplayed his hand abroad and landed the country in a war that it, surprisingly, could not win. Conflicts among Christian empires over their powers on Ottoman territory set the fuse. France's emperor Napoleon III, cultivating Catholic support, pronounced his right to oversee the church at Bethlehem and other holy sites in Palestine, while Nicholas saw himself as the guardian of all Christians in the sultan's realm.

The goal of this nineteenth-century imperial competition was ancient—control of the Straits (the Dardanelles and the Bosphorus) and the connections between the Mediterranean, the Black Sea, and beyond. Nicholas expected that the congress system would confirm his special rights and that the emperors whose skins he had saved after the 1848 attempts at revolution would rally to his side, but Britain, France, and Austria now shored up the Ottomans. With the Ottoman empire, nicknamed the "sickman of Europe," threatened by internal and external troubles, a basic rule of interempire competition kicked in. Weak empires were useful in containing strong rivals, especially the Russians with their territorial proximity to the crucial connections across continents and seas.

In 1853, after the Ottomans refused to acknowledge Nicholas I as the rightful protector of eastern Orthodox Christians in the empire, Nicholas ordered his troops to cross into the Balkan principalities. The Ottomans declared war on Russia. Initially things went the Russian way—they sank almost the entire Ottoman fleet at Sinope in the Black Sea. This victory in response to an act of war was publicized in Great Britain and France as "the

Figure 11.1
Sultan Abdulmecid I (left) and Tsar Nicholas I (right).
Portraits published in the *Illustrated London News* 23
(August 6, 1853): 92–93. Falles Library, New York University.

massacre of Sinope." The imperial imagination of the British public was more sympathetic to the sickman than the gendarme, no matter that the sickman was Muslim and the gendarme Christian. With an array of troops from their own empire, the British joined the war against the Russians in 1854, as did the French.

The location of the fighting was determined by the territorial insecurities of some empires and the maritime prowess of others. The Austrians, who understood the threat to their southern regions if they went to war, refused to join the coalition against Russia. The Prussians and the Swedes, also contiguous with Russia, held back. After a few skirmishes in the Baltic, the British and French navies transported troops through the contested straits to the Crimea and the Russian forts that guarded it.

The stakes in the Crimea were power over maritime and overland trade routes, civilizational primacy, and the privilege of meddling in the Ottoman economy. Rapid fire rifles and improved artillery made combat particularly murderous, and fighting at a great distance for three years proved unmanageable to all sides. Nicholas's conservatism on railroad construction proved a huge mistake: Russian supplies had to be transported by carts to the front. The British and the French, despite their technological and logistic edge, were unable to keep their armies adequately supplied with food. About two-thirds of the soldiers who died in the conflict succumbed to disease.

The war fascinated and shocked the publics of all sides, who followed it through the flourishing press. The British had thought that the war could be won right away against the retrograde Russians—this proved wrong. Russians prided themselves on the fortitude of their troops, who had defeated Napoleon. But loyalty proved insufficient against better British weapons. Leo Tolstoy, serving as an officer, sent home articles about the terrible suffering; it was in Crimea that he became a pacifist. In the British newspapers, the true hero turned out to be a nurse, Florence Nightingale. The field hospitals she organized for soldiers were models for the later establishment of the international Red Cross.

The carnage in Crimea provoked a new perspective on interimperial regulation and its uses. After the war Russian diplomats took the lead in efforts to draw up a code for warfare and for the humane treatment of enemy combatants. The St. Petersburg declaration of 1868 called on states to refrain from using weapons that caused horrendous wounds. The first Geneva Convention on the treatment of the wounded was signed in 1864 after another bloody imperial encounter—the battle of Solferino between French and Habsburg armies in northern Italy. The profession of international law emerged as a self-conscious discipline at this time. Interempire rivalries were creating the conditions not just for starting wars but for limiting and stopping them in places where empires could see the threats to their own well-being.

The Crimean war ended only after the death of the Russian emperor in 1855. Faced with the possibility that Austria at last might join the war, Nicholas's son, Alexander II, declared his willingness to go along with new conditions for dealing with the Ottomans. The Peace of Paris, signed in 1856, emerged from the first general meeting of the European imperial powers since 1815. France, Russia, Britain, Austria, Sardinia (which had joined the war at the last minute), and the Ottoman empire were represented, with the Prussians at some sessions. The result was a setback for the Russians and a demonstration of the western European states' self-confidence and might. The Black Sea was demilitarized but made open to all merchant shipping, a victory for the empires of free trade. The Russians were deprived of their special role as protectors of Ottoman Christians; instead the European powers were to assume joint responsibility for this matter and for maintaining the outlet of the Danube open to navigation. Russia lost territories that it had won from the Ottomans earlier in the century—including Bessarabia, islands in the Baltic, and forts on the Black Sea. The Declaration of Paris ordained that commercial activities were to be protected even during wars.

Although the Paris settlement was directed at Russia, whose ambitions for the eastern Mediterranean were taken seriously, the treaty laid the groundwork for France, Britain, and Austria to encroach increasingly on the Ottomans through "free trade" policies and the protection of Christians on the sultan's territory. For Russian and Ottoman leaders, the Crimean war exacerbated another competition—for control over populations in their contested spheres. Two-thirds of the Muslim Tatars in the Crimea left Russia for the Ottoman empire after the war. As migrants sought protection or advantages in the other empire, Russians and Ottomans resettled newcomers and displaced others. This process escalated with subsequent border adjustments in the Balkans and around the Black Sea. While some groups gained as each empire sought to keep or augment its human resources, the dynamic of resentment and violence escalated into the twentieth century.

Ottoman Adjustments

Ottomans shared with their Russian rivals an image problem in the west. Was the sickman of Europe to be healed or dismembered and absorbed into a healthier European body? As the two empires on the contestable edges of Europe struggled to match the strength of western armies and navies—not least to fight better against each other—and as they were pushed toward the sidelines of interempire diplomacy, they both confronted a powerful rhetoric of progress and civilization. This inspired discontented elites, including sultans, to rethink their place in the world and what to do about it.

The Ottoman empire had survived local rebellions, Janissary coups, and shrinkage of its territories since the glory days of Suleiman the Magnificent (chapter 5). Ottoman practices of tax farming, delegating authority to local notables, and devolving many legal matters to the several religious communities had functioned with ups and downs for centuries. In the eighteenth century the Ottomans, like their Russian enemy, sought European military technology. Sultan Selim III (ruled 1789–1807) opened military schools and began French-inspired reforms of weaponry and tactics. The empire ran up big debts to finance its—mostly losing—wars with Russia.

As earlier, a disruptive element was the Janissary corps. Although forcibly recruited from outside the empire's core to ensure their independence from social forces within (chapter 5), the Janissaries threatened Ottoman command in at least two ways. In distant areas, their violence and corruption could set off rebellions—as among Serbs in 1805. In the capital, they could plot against a sultan whose policies threatened their corporate interests. After his disruptive reforms, Selim III was deposed by Janissaries in 1807 and assassinated in 1808.

Selim III's successor, Mahmud II (1808–39), with the demonstrated weakness of the sultan's army as his best argument, dared to abolish the Janissaries in 1826 and to begin another round of military improvements. The reformed army was based on peasants conscripted by the central government and led by officers educated according to western European standards. It grew from 24,000 in 1837 to 120,000 in the 1880s. The public humiliation and execution of Janissaries was part of a radical shift in military organization; units mobilized by local notables were replaced by a regimental army controlled more directly by a centralized high command.

Other threats came from outside Ottoman borders—multiple assaults by the Russians, Napoleon's ambitious campaigns and occupations, and ongoing empire competitions after his defeat. In the nineteenth century, elites in various parts of the empire could envision and, with help from outsiders, pull off escapes from Ottoman control. Serbia, after decades of conflicts, became a fully autonomous principality in 1830, the year that European powers recognized an independent Greece.

Even worse for the sultan, his subordinates could, in classic imperial fashion, aspire to take over Ottoman domains for themselves. In the chaotic aftermath of Napoleon's unsuccessful occupation of Egypt, the sultan had delegated the impressive Mehmed Ali, a military man of Albanian origin, to restore Ottoman authority. After becoming governor in 1805, Mehmed Ali shaped up the army and navy in Egypt, helped put down rebellion in Greece, extended Ottoman power into the Sudan, and took over Syria in the 1830s. Eager to extend his personal command, he threatened Istanbul itself. The Russians and later other European empires pushed the sultan into a compromise that left Mehmed Ali's family with the hereditary right to govern Egypt—a big departure from Ottoman patrimonial norms.

This setback impelled Ottoman leaders into efforts to shore up central control, bypassing notables and other intermediaries. The bureaucracy was charged with managing the population more directly; ministries took over some functions that had been parceled out to religious authorities. The state became a more intrusive presence in society; its officials spied on the public and on foreigners, as did police agencies in western European states. The number of civil servants grew from about 2,000 at the end of the eighteenth century to 35,000 in 1908.

A better army and bureaucracy demanded new standards of education. Administrative training was transferred from households of the grand viziers or notables to educational institutions, intended to create a new kind of official who would more efficiently connect the population to the center. Ottoman officials acquired European languages, traveled and studied in Europe, and applied their experience and knowledge to Ottoman projects. In the 1830s, the Ottomans opened imperial military and medical schools, both with instructors from abroad. As before, the major goal was improving the quality of the military—the medical school was to train doctors for the army—but these initiatives were connected to broader shifts in Ottoman society. French was the preferred language of many higher institutions and of several of the newspapers that began publication in the 1830s.

Breaking with rules on attire designed to highlight hierarchy, Ottomans regulated dress codes in the direction of uniformity, at least for men. In 1829, a decree ordered all males, excepting clerics, to wear the same kind of headgear. The fez worn with a western-style suit became the uniform of officials. Elite Ottoman women continued to fashion their own variants on stylish dress and behavior, setting themselves apart from lower classes and provoking intermittent, and ineffective, prohibitions.

The centralizing impetus underlay a series of laws and codes, produced during the period of restructuring known as the Tanzimat (the Reorganization, 1839–71). In 1839, Sultan Abdulmecid I (1839–61) issued an edict guaranteeing the security of subjects' lives, honor, and property, declaring that they would be taxed according to their means and proclaiming all subjects, of whatever religion, legal equals. New penal and commercial codes were issued in the 1840s and new courts, based on western European practices, were set up in 1847. In 1858, the state produced a land code that declared equal rights for male citizens to hold private property. The intention was to tie land, its products, and its owners more directly to the state, cutting off intermediaries.

The Tanzimat reforms were undertaken by activist sultans and their viziers with the goal of standing up to challenges posed by Russian and European powers. It was unexceptional for the leaders of a threatened empire to adopt strategies employed by their foes, but the Ottomans faced two severe obstacles to their goal of modernized control. First, their imperial rivals tugged ever more voraciously at the empire's purse, and second, some of the enemies were already physically inside the empire—as missionaries, immigrants, practitioners of free trade—and their ideas of sovereignty intersected in volatile ways with both the Ottomans' traditional protections of difference and their newer centralizing reforms.

Economically, the Ottomans came up against a problem that confronted the Qing dynasty in China—the lock of the British and the French on capital. The eighteenth century had been a prosperous time for the Ottomans, but at its close the state was borrowing from Europeans and not able to pay back. In 1838, the British imposed a treaty that banned state monopolies and tariffs on external trade, cutting deeply into Ottoman revenues. Over time, Britain and other outside powers turned the Ottoman practice of granting legal jurisdiction to foreign authorities inside the empire (chapter 5) into commercial advantages for themselves and their clients. In 1881, the British and the French set up a highly interventionist Public Debt Administration.

Among the outsiders' other weapons were concepts disruptive of the sultan's sovereignty—liberalism, ethnic or cultural solidarity, feminism, the march of progress. Like their Russian counterparts, elite Ottomans educated in Europe or in European institutions drew upon this expanded repertoire of political ideas. By the 1860s, it was the turn of a new generation of intellectuals, who saw themselves as members of a transnational movement for equal rights and representative government, to be impatient with the pace of change and to demand radical reconfiguration of Ottoman governance. The "New Ottomans" (later known as the Young Ottomans) criticized the Tanzimat bureaucrats for not going far enough in restructuring the state along western lines. Active both in Istanbul and in Europe, they called in their London-based newspaper for a constitution and a parliament. Like many reform-minded officials, they supported the goal of political equality, guaranteed by law.

Between 1869 and 1878, the Ottoman government took its restructuring initiatives further. In 1869 a law declared all subjects Ottoman citizens, and in 1876, Sultan Abdulhamid II (1876–1909) approved a constitution and, in accordance with it, convened a parliament. Although the first parliament lasted less than two years—the sultan dismissed it, as was his right, after war with Russia broke out—it left its mark on subsequent political movements. As an imperial institution, the parliament displayed the absorptive creativity of Ottoman politics. The delegates represented administrative councils—elected bodies established earlier to reshape provincial leadership—including delegates from Arab regions. The 77 Muslim, 44 Christian, and 4 Jewish parliamentarians discussed such matters as the language of administration, taxation, and the basis of choosing the parliament's leaders. Parliamentary sessions revealed the crosscutting interests of many groups within the empire—exactly what the politics of patrimonialism had obscured. Although many representatives criticized the government, the goal was more rights and more restructuring, not outright rejection. Still, the sultan could not abide this forum for contentious politics.

Modernizing Ottomanism continued along several paths at once, trying to strengthen Islam against the inroads of Christian missionaries and at the same time bringing people of many religions and ethnicities—Albanians, Macedonians, Greeks, Armenians, Arabs, Kurds, Jews, and Turks—into governance. Challenged by Protestant missionaries from the United States and Britain, Orthodox clerics from Russia, and Catholics from France, who were successfully attracting Ottoman children to their schools, the Ottomans established a Ministry for Education in 1857. The 1869 law on general education attempted to introduce primary schools for all children—each group could run its own—while trying to ensure that Quranic studies would be part of the curriculum for Muslims. Abdulhamid II encouraged an Islamic revival movement, conspicuously attending Friday prayers as a ritual expression of his piety. A goal of the sultan and many of his advisors was to show that "Ottomanness" was its own kind of progressive culture, incorporating many peoples, but still celebrating its Islamic roots.

The sultan's Islamic strategy was a response to Young Ottomans' alternative vision of how the empire could be run—as a polity of Ottoman citizens united under a constitutional framework. Abdulhamid understood the danger: an elite whose positions were not dependent on personal ties to the sultan and his vizier would be less controllable than differentiated, communally based subordinates. The Ottoman system could bend to pressures from its young men with their educational and commercial connections to western Europe; it could give expression to a populace whose commonality was increasingly Islam; but it would not give up its patrimonial form of rule.

The Ottomans' reforms in the nineteenth century were unambiguously modernizing: the state's leaders were trying to be with the times by using European strategies to restructure their administration and to put themselves on a firmer financial ground. The problems that Charles V had faced in the sixteenth century—no place to expand and dependence on outsiders to bankroll both defense and innovation—were now in the Ottomans' court. But the ideological context had changed fundamentally. Europeans were still extending updated versions of Christian empire overseas (chapter 10), but they were also playing the Ottomans' own game of community protection to encourage fragmentation inside others' territories.

The combination of the bureaucracy's challenges to old elites with the determination of outside powers to themselves "protect" Christian or other communities against what they described as Islamic despotism unleashed threats to Ottoman control. In Lebanon, Druze and Maronite groups competed violently; in the Balkans, splits within the Orthodox clergy intersected with the interests of Greek and Russian states. European interventions plus the Ottomans' integrating reforms opened up a strident politics of sectarianism where once all had felt themselves under the sultan's protection.

Habsburg Reconfigurations

The Ottoman sultan Abdulhamid II had a good reason to be wary of his parliament. His enemy and acquisitive neighbor Austria had been a near victim of parliamentary assertiveness, during the pan-European wave of rebellions against royal authority that began in Paris and spread to cities in the Habsburg Monarchy and Prussia in 1848.

In Vienna, uprisings and protests forced the mentally challenged Emperor Ferdinand from his capital. His advisors promised the rebels a constitution, elections were held, and an Austrian parliament began deliberations on the future of the state. The surge of political activism could not be contained, and Austrian representatives were sent to another parliament in Frankfurt, where the question of uniting Habsburg, Prussian, and various German and Slavic-speaking regions into a new German-led polity was debated. In Hungary, representatives in the Diet demanded imperial consent to laws amounting to independence from Habsburg rule. The loyalty of the military, multiple fissures among the rebels, and Tsar Nicholas's help allowed the new emperor, Franz Joseph (1848–1916), to regain the initiative. In 1849, Franz Joseph dissolved the Austrian parliament and issued his own constitution, only to cancel it in 1851. The Austrian empire would once more be ruled by the monarch's will.

For centuries the Habsburg family had been a disruptive player on the European field—expanding through marriage politics, winning almost all of Hungary from the Ottomans in 1699; dividing Poland with Prussia and Russia in the last part of the eighteenth century. By that time, Habsburg control extended over many areas, with a variety of layers of sovereignty. The empire reached the Adriatic Sea through what is now northeastern Italy, Slovenia, and Croatia and came up against the Ottomans in Serbia and Transylvania.

To develop the resources of their linguistically, ethnically, and confessionally diverse territories, Habsburg rulers—most notably Empress Maria Theresa (1740–80) and her son Joseph II (1780–90)—had initiated a series of educational and economic projects. The key reform was the development of a centralized bureaucracy, with power to stand up to local nobilities and their representative institutions, the diets. Under Maria Theresa, schools were established to prepare commoners, including peasants, to become civil servants; under Joseph, serfdom was abolished and the powers of guilds were reduced.

A hallmark of Habsburg rule was its cultivation of ethnic and religious minorities. In 1781, Joseph's Edict of Toleration gave Protestants, Orthodox, and Uniates the same rights as Catholics and reduced restrictions on Jews. Like the Russians, the Habsburgs sought to control the clergy by supervising their education: seminaries for both Catholics and Uniates were opened in Galicia, as well as a university in Lemberg (now Lviv, Ukraine). German was made the official language of administration as a unifying measure, but where appropriate laws were issued in both German and local languages.

The Habsburgs emerged as victors from the Napoleonic wars, but the price for getting local nobles to fight had been high, and it had political consequences. Nobles were more intent than ever on having their say in diets, while industrialists, merchants, and professionals engaged in freewheeling debates over the sources of sovereignty and the proper conduct of government. But no horizontal alliance was possible across the empire. The uneven spread of industrialization created different discontents within each area, and segmentation of the polity allowed different nobles to claim different privileges and prior rights. In 1848 there was no agreement on issues of representation—liberals were frightened by the radicalism of urban violence and by socialists' demands. Czech and other Slav delegates to the Frankfurt National Assembly quickly drew back from any pan-Germanic polity that might undercut their various interests. The emperor was still the focus of both criticism and hope for change.

In Austria as in its neighboring empires, what counted in the long run was less 1848 than what rulers, elites old and new, and impatient intellectuals could make out of its provocations. 1848 had reconfirmed Nicholas I of Russia in his suspicions of European ideas: he refused any limits on the emperor's powers. The Ottomans' earlier efforts to upgrade and centralize their rule accelerated into a brief experiment with an advisory parliament. The Austrians after 1848 managed a middle way—preserving the emperor's supranational authority while modifying the empire's structure and institutions.

The weft of Habsburg politics in the nineteenth century was the imperial tradition—the royal family's rule of a multiplicity of units by dynastic right. Beginning in 1848, Franz Joseph, by temperament a modest, frugal person, revitalized court etiquette and made himself the central figure in ceremonies that harked back to the Habsburgs' special relationship to Christianity and highlighted the emperor's piety. This cultivated tie between the dynasty and Catholicism did not prevent Franz Joseph from making himself visible at Jewish, eastern Orthodox, Armenian, Greek, and Muslim ceremonies as well. He was conspicuously blessed by clerics of the empire's multiple faiths. At a time when popular sovereignty was in the political imagination of reformers and revolutionaries, the emperor reached out to his many peoples in his own way.

But in areas divided along class, confessional, or other lines, the emperor's gestures of support almost everywhere offended some subjects or inspired them to demand more rights. In 1851, when Franz Joseph took a triumphant imperial journey to Galicia—where the Austrian army had crushed Polish uprisings—his artfully arranged passage was greeted with enthusiasm by peasants, Greek Catholic clergy, and Jews, but not by Polish nobles. The various nobilities of the empire, deeply entrenched over centuries in their rights and claims, continued to present obstacles to imperial unifiers.

Unity—in a different mode—was the cause of Austria's liberals. During and after 1848, entrepreneurs, professionals, and women's and other associations called for representative politics, a free press, freedom of association, and citizenship based on education, culture, and property holding. The constitutional aspirations of Austrian liberals were defeated at mid-century, but within a decade the emperor established a bicameral legislature in Vienna, whose consent was needed on all domestic laws.

The impetus for this fundamental transformation of sovereignty was debt and defeat in Europe's interempire wars. After French emperor Napoleon III pledged to help Cavour, the prime minister in Piedmont-Sardinia, against Austria, Franz Joseph declared war in 1859. The war was a disaster for the Habsburgs and pushed the emperor toward reform. Franz Joseph's banker, Anselm Rothschild, is supposed to have said, "No constitution, no money." The Reichsrat, convened in 1861, was elected indirectly by provincial diets. Its sessions brought noble landlords, bankers, and professionals together and revealed the tensions between liberals' demands for centralized, equal, and uniform governance, and centrifugal claims for provincial autonomy and distinctive national and noble rights.

In 1866, another lost war—this time with Prussia—catalyzed further constitutional changes. A single imperial citizenship was created in 1867, guaranteeing the same civil rights to people of all religions. A supreme court was instituted the same year. But the centralizing fiscal measures demanded by liberals and their insistence on German as the language of administration pushed Hungarian and Czech activists into demands for more regional power. Federalism was proposed by national elites as a better way of distributing sovereignty. The Hungarians were particularly obstinate, inspiring a response that harked back to the days of composite monarchy. In 1867, the Austrian empire mutated into what became known as the Dual Monarchy—two states with one ruler, Franz Joseph, who was the emperor of Austria and the king of Hungary, joint ministries for foreign, financial, and military affairs, and separate parliaments and civil services in Austria and Hungary.

This solution to a problem of imperial governance, like the Ottomans' balancing acts, had unintended consequences. Both the Kingdom of Hungary and "Cis-Leithania," as the Austrian lands were known, were multi-national polities, composed of subunits with distinct political histories and populated by people of different ethnicities and confessions. The compromise rewarded Germans and Hungarians but did not satisfy other groups—Czechs, Slovaks, Croats, Serbs, Poles, Ukrainians, and Romanians. The demands of the discontented were not confined to national or liberal causes. Pan-Slav movements had taken various shapes over the century in central Europe, the Balkans, and in Russia; Muslim and Turkish modernizers had their own crosscutting Islamic or Turkic goals.

Both the structure of the Habsburgs' empire in the 1860s and the array of political imaginaries it nourished do not fit the conventional account of

Figure 11.2
Emperor Franz Joseph
in Hungarian uniform,
photographed around 1888.
Imagno, Hulton Archive,
GettyImages.

a nineteenth-century trend toward the unitary nation-state. The Catholic dynasty presided over an empire of two unequal units, each home to several kinds of Christians, as well as Jews and Muslims. The polity was administered centrally in the Austrian lands by a German-speaking bureaucracy, under a constitution that protected the use of other languages in schools and lower-level administration. Subjects were governed in foreign, financial, and military matters by an emperor/king who convened two cabinets—sometimes separately, sometimes jointly—and in domestic ones by parliaments that attempted in various ways to conjugate equality and difference. The constitutional transformations of the 1860s blended the aspirations of liberals for civil rights and representative democracy with the demands of activists in the empire's component parts for more autonomy, and the emperor's ceremonial outreach glossed the motley whole with grandeur.

The German Reich: New Empire and New Rules

In the 1870s, a new empire was formed in Europe, no mean feat. After the defeat of Napoleon, the kingdom of Prussia was only one of several states with a significant German-speaking population in the north of Europe. Principalities, duchies, grand duchies, free cities, and kingdoms earlier loosely connected by the Holy Roman Empire had survived centuries of religious and dynastic wars. In 1848, many German liberals had wanted the Prussian king, Frederick William IV, to grant constitutional government to Prussia and organize the units of the German Confederation into a larger German state. Contrary to their hopes, the king helped suppress the revolution. In the 1860s, the brilliant Prussian chancellor Otto von Bismarck (serving under the king) seized the initiative in the European interempire competition. In 1871, after Prussia's victories in wars against Denmark, Austria, and France persuaded smaller German states that they would be safer in a federal union, King Wilhelm I was proclaimed kaiser (Caesar) at Versailles. The formation of empire in Europe preceded Germany's interest in colonies overseas (chapter 10).

The Kaiserreich, as the empire of Wilhelm and Bismarck was known, was a latecomer to Europe's imperial competition. German leaders worried about lagging behind Great Britain's industrialization and about access to raw materials. They were influenced by the writings of Friedrich List (1789–1846), who advocated a "national" approach to economic policy, meaning that the state should make a vigorous effort to develop its internal resources and catch up with rivals. Whether German industrialization derived from Listian policies or the actions of entrepreneurs and markets

Figure 11.3
King of Prussia proclaimed German emperor at Versailles, 1871. Published in the
Illustrated London News 58 (February 4, 1871): 101. Falles Library, New York
University.

is hard to tell, but late nineteenth-century Germany became an economic
dynamo. The mobilizing of resources across the formerly divided areas was
one key to Prussia's success. Another was its technological achievement, especially the production of advanced weaponry and the creation of a dense
network of railroads.

Bismarck's social policies were also innovative. Aware after 1848 of the
dangers of social unrest, administrators tried to give part of the working
class a stake in the state by expanding suffrage and providing social insurance. The new empire, with its large population and its growing wealth,
became a major player on the European scene.

The German empire was less linguistically German than the territories
of the German Confederation in 1815. The Reich included areas formerly
ruled by France and Denmark, in addition to large Polish territories, with
their Ukrainian and Jewish populations. Bismarck was not an ethnic nationalist. After winning against the Habsburg empire in 1866, he did not try
to unite all German-speakers into a single state, and after 1871 he sought

balance among European empires. He hosted the major European powers at the Congress of Berlin of 1878 and again in 1884–85 (chapter 10) and attempted to contain imperial competition overseas. On the continent, Bismarck's major concern was France. To protect Germany in case of war, he revived the earlier alliance between Austria, Prussia, and Russia through the Three Emperors' League, signed in 1881.

Bismarck's caution overseas and within Europe was not shared by all Germans. He was challenged by political writers like Paul de Lagarde, who promoted a mystic vision of a German nation. Lagarde's mission for Germany was to spread its language and culture over Europe to people who could fit in, while excluding those, like Jews, who in his view did not. Although Lagarde imagined Germany as a colonizing power within Europe, he and others were ill at ease with Germany's new industrial order and with the cosmopolitan culture of much of its elite. In the 1890s, this anti-liberal, anti-modernizing kind of imperialism took an organized form in the Pan-German League. Industrialization produced other tensions over what a German nation should mean. Ethnic nationalists wanted the government to "Germanize" eastern regions populated by Polish-speakers and to prevent Poles from migrating into Germany. But large landlords (Junkers) in the east wanted immigrants as laborers to replace agricultural workers who were taking jobs in industry. These conflicting positions drew attention to the populations of the eastern, Slavic borderlands as an ethnically distinct labor force.

Romantic nationalism and anti-semitism were not specific to Germany. Xenophobic politicians, artists, and theorists could be found in every European state. But in the new German empire, in contrast to its imperial competitors, racializing visions—both liberal and reactionary—were untested by long-term experience of governing a multiplicity of populations.

New Politics in Old Empires

By the 1870s Germany, France, and Britain had each secured a leading place in the world of empires; their institutions seemed to define a "European" way to power. All three had parliaments, based on expanding but incomplete suffrage; all drew on the resources of capitalist enterprises supported by state action; all enjoyed the gains and suffered the consequences of expansive industrialization; all participated in the competition for more markets and resources outside Europe; and all affected the strategies of other empires. Confronted with the intrusions—cultural, economic, diplomatic—of the "western" powers, Ottomans, Russians, and Austrians did not hold still, and all were drawn more tightly into the web of European connections and conflicts.

Map 11.2
Empires in and around Europe, 1877.

Reform the Russian Way

The Crimean war had jolted Russian elites into a frenzy of initiatives, propelled by bureaucrats educated at universities and imperial schools and supported by the new tsar, Alexander II. Reformers avidly examined European institutions as they redesigned their own, selecting and transforming as they went along. In the 1860s, the emperor presided over a revolution from above, emancipating serfs as a category and managing a massive property transfer to provide them with land (chapter 9). Military service was made universal for males and its term reduced; local assemblies were set up to conduct welfare services in the countryside; a system of jury trials was put in place; and censorship of publications was relaxed in the cause of glasnost (publicity).

While conscious of the need to increase production and improve technology, Russian elites, inside and outside the administration, were cautious about European-style industrialization. The poverty and degradation of workers in European cities horrified conservatives and some reformers. Karl Marx's indictment and analysis of capitalism, *Kapital*, was translated and published legally in Russia in 1872 as a warning of what might happen if industrialists were given free rein. The state took an active role in regulating factory labor and preserved the peasant commune as the holder of agricultural land. Individual peasant ownership was rejected, for fear that peasants would sell their allotments and become a rootless, dangerous proletariat. The as ever disunited nobles were unable to prevent the emperor from reassigning the land and labor force they had enjoyed, as it turned out, at the tsar's pleasure (chapter 9).

The autocracy's sustained refusal to share the prerogatives of sovereignty corresponded to deep traditions of Russian empire, but it was not satisfying to many in the expanding public of professionals, civil servants, students, artists, and other middling groups. People who saw themselves as participants in a pan-European world of ideas and values resented being left out of governance. Feminism, socialism, and anarchism flourished among discontented youths and offended outcasts. Young men and women set up communes, experimented with free love, tried to link up with "the people," went abroad to universities, committed acts of terror, and conspired to liberate their country. Their more professionally minded peers and elders revived demands for constitutional government. These were firmly rejected.

There were no entrenched solidarities across Russian "society." When, after several unsuccessful tries, conspirators assassinated Alexander in 1881, neither the people nor any of its self-proclaimed representatives replaced the Tsar Liberator. His successor, Alexander III (1881–94), was all the more convinced that as in Catherine's day, a big polity required a strong emperor at the helm. Ambitious youths, like Vladimir Ulianov (later known as Lenin), who made the mistake of defending hopeless causes like faculty governance, were evicted from universities and professional careers. Across the huge empire, there was plenty of administrative talent to choose from, and potential rebels were deemed superfluous. Over the long term, this aspect of Russian patrimonialism—a cavalier attitude toward human resources—would, like censorship, deplete the empire's intellectual and administrative capacity.

The setback of the Crimean war propelled adjustments in strategies for expansion (see map 9.2). First, the empire shed an overseas possession. Since the early eighteenth century the Russians had dominated the fur trade in the North Pacific islands, but after depleting the Aleutians of animals Russia took its final cut by selling Alaska to the United States for $7,200,000 in 1867. Elsewhere, there were no signs of retrenchment. By the late 1850s the Russian military, armed with superior weapons, had wiped out most resistance in the Caucasus. The administration promoted settlement—sending out undesirable Old Believers among others—and commerce in this promising, if unruly, region. In central Asia ambitious Russian generals were given leave to move against the remaining khanates and into competition with the British, moving north from India. Military campaigns defeated Samarkand, Khiva, and Kokand in the 1870s. In the next decade, Russian armies dealt brutally with tribes on the Turkmen steppe.

To incorporate central Asia, Russia employed a range of administrative tactics. The emirate of Bukhara and the khanate of Khiva became "protectorates," while Turkestan—where there was no khanate to subordinate—was put under the administration of a military governor-general (see map 9.2). As elsewhere Russians adhered to their practice of co-opting the services of local elites. This meant not just tolerating Islam—or "ignoring" it, as one governor-general advocated—but allying with Muslim clerics and later Muslim modernizers against Sufi brotherhoods, perceived as threats by all of the above. Russian authorities generally stopped obstructing Muslim pilgrims who wished to go to Mecca and tried instead to regulate their travels, using the railroad designed to transport cotton across Turkestan. By the early twentieth century, there were far more Muslims in the Russian than the Ottoman empire. Russian strategy toward Muslims, as toward Jews and other groups, was containment, not expulsion. No one had a right to leave the empire.

In the 1870s, the Russian press pushed for interventions in the Balkan tinderbox, tapping into pan-Slav ideas proposed abroad. Russian volunteers set off to help the Serbian army against the Ottomans in 1876. Unable to get the European powers, especially Great Britain, to agree to Russian goals in the Balkans and the Black Sea, in 1877 Emperor Alexander II declared war on the Ottomans. After prolonged and difficult campaigns, the Russian army reached the outskirts of Constantinople in 1878.

But the European powers were still intent on not allowing a settlement helpful to Russia. At the Congress of Berlin in 1878, Bismarck saw to it that the Balkans would be divided into controllable units: Bosnia-Herzegovina occupied by Austria; Macedonia returned to the Ottomans; Bulgaria split into a Bulgarian principality and an Ottoman protectorate (eastern Rumelia); and independent Romania established on the Russian border. Russia regained Bessarabia, but otherwise the outcome of the war rubbed in the Romanovs' inability to make headway in the European empire wars.

In the last decades of the century, Russian administrators tried out—but never fully executed—a nationalist policy from above. Influenced by the civilizational and racist discourses of their European competitors, some officials seized on the rhetoric of cultural advance—their own. In this version of imperialism, Russia was bringing European values to the peoples of central Asia. Turkestan in particular was regarded as a colony that could be civilized through education and settlement of Russian and other agriculturalists.

In the western regions of the empire, where imperial administrators feared that Poles and Jews were too closely connected to Europe and its dangerous ideas, the government made attempts at "Russification," requiring the use of the Russian language in offices and schools. These linguistic policies were neither uniform nor uniformly enforced. As in Austria, the push for a single language of administration had different meanings for different groups. The government's attempt to Russify officialdom in the Baltic provinces was welcomed by Latvians and Estonians who resented Germans' monopoly on high office. Quotas on the number of Jewish students at universities (1887) and later restrictions on Jewish membership in professional groups or local councils catered to vociferous nationalists, many of them nobles demanding a return to privilege.

Some of Russia's modernizers, both liberal opponents of the autocracy and certain high officials, were drawn to the idea of what they called a "national state," although what this would mean in their differentiated empire remained difficult to define. The concept of "Greater Britain" was proposed as a model for Russia. Sergei Witte, the mastermind of Russian economic development, was attracted to the ideas of Friedrich List, the German theorist. Witte strove to make Russia an integrated economic space, while weeding out constitutional government from List's program. The state built the trans-Siberian railroad and acted aggressively to support industrial development, financed both by taxing peasant households and by funding from abroad. Foreign companies invested in the exploitation of Russia's black gold—the oil discovered near the Caspian. From the 1890s, Russia's industries grew exuberantly. Much investment came from France, although many technicians and entrepreneurs were German.

Playing the alliance game in their own way, Russian statesmen, frustrated by Germany's economic prowess and by Austria's competition in the Balkans, moved toward an alliance with France. In 1894, the two empires—one an autocracy, the other a republic—signed an agreement for military cooperation. For Russia, this shift away from alliances with the powers on its borders turned out to be a fatal misstep in empire geopolitics: the next all-European war would be fought in Russia's vulnerable western territories.

Unable to make further gains in the Balkans, Russian modernizers focused on the east, expanding cotton production in central Asia and encouraging peasant migration and resettlement across Siberia. Inspired by Europeans' colonial projects, Witte promoted Russian expansion along the far eastern railroad to the Pacific ports. This brought Russia into another arena of imperial competition—with Japan over the Pacific coasts, islands, and hinterlands, including Korea and Manchuria. In the far east Russians departed furthest from their politics of legitimated difference. Here Russians experimented with imperialism in western European style, with exploitative timber concessions, colonization along the railroad outside the Russian border, and explicitly racist rhetoric. Nicholas II (1896–1917) supported those who agitated for what was predicted to be a "little victorious war" against "the yellow peril."

The Russo-Japanese war of 1904–5 was neither little nor victorious. As in the Balkans, the European powers played their cards against the Romanovs. The French did not help out; the British were sympathetic to Japan, as were the Americans. The Russians were left to carry on the white man's mission by themselves. A shock to racists was the superior power of the Japanese on land and sea. The Russian navy was almost totally destroyed; Port Arthur, Russia's sea outpost, surrendered; and on land at the battle of Mukden, in which over two hundred fifty thousand soldiers fought on each side, Russians lost to Japanese troops.

Failure in the war combined with the autocracy's obstinate refusal to devolve power cracked open the shell of police control. With the troops away, Russia's liberals conducted a banquet campaign (imitating Parisians in 1848) to promote constitutional reform. Marxists and others tried to channel proletarian discontent into revolutionary parties. An outburst of assassinations of political figures revealed the radical rejection of the state that had festered in the underground. In January 1905, Emperor Nicholas II (1896–1917) violated the patrimonial mystique by authorizing the military to fire on a peaceful demonstration by workers petitioning him for the improvement of their lot. After strikes, pogroms, and peasant assaults on landlords' properties, Witte convinced the recalcitrant tsar to convoke an elected legislature and grant political liberties.

In 1906, the Russian emperor convened a parliament—the Duma—of representatives elected unevenly from all regions and peoples of the empire. Appalled by delegates' radical demands, the emperor dissolved the first two Dumas and manipulated the electoral rules to increase the proportion of nobles over workers and peasants, of Russians over other ethnic groups, and of Orthodox over other religions. Despite this manhandling, the last two Dumas (1907–17) offered a platform to spokesmen for a wide array of interests; politicians representing national groups demanded more cultural autonomy within the framework of empire. But cooperation between the Dumas and the administration was rarely attained, and the government issued its most important legislation—offering peasants title to their land, for example—as emergency regulations that did not need the Duma's accord.

Because world war and revolution put an end to the Duma and the dynasty, it is impossible to know whether the Russian empire could have sustained this experiment in representational politics. In the years before the war and after, a major threat to institutionalized sharing out of sovereignty was the radicalized and alienated intelligentsia, whose political imaginaries mirrored the monopolistic prerogatives of the autocracy they so hated. Still, in less than a decade, the dynasty had gradually transformed the Duma into a more compliant body, a course of action fully in accord with Russia's long history of twisting new strategies of rule—in this case representative democracy—into its own synthetic and patrimonial kind of governance.

In the first decade of the twentieth century, the most immediate danger to the autocracy was its involvement in the various imperial great games. In central Asia, the tsars knew where to stop—Afghanistan. In 1907, Russia signed a treaty with the British, who were set on controlling the routes to India. But the Balkans remained the sore spot for tsarist officials. How could Russia gain from the Ottomans' losses in the area when greater European powers—England, France, Germany—and lesser ones—Austria and Italy—were intent upon keeping Russia from attaining its long-term goal, Istanbul, control over the Straits and their hinterlands, an outlet to the sea once ruled by Rome?

Centralization and Contraction: The Ottomans' New Ways

The Congress of Berlin of 1878, while obstructing Russian aims, had sheared off a third of the Ottomans' territory and continued the disruptive process of making more or less independent states out of the former Ottoman lands. None of these states was an ethnic or religious whole, and in none of them were new "national" leaders content with their boundaries or with their Austrian, Russian, or British protectors. The Ottomans' millet system had provided each religious group with a structure of legal authority and access to the sultan's overarching power, but after Christian populations found themselves outside the empire, Orthodoxy became more localized. Without Ottoman rule, there was no incentive for dispersed Christians or their leaders to work together. Greece, Bulgaria, Macedonia, Montenegro, Serbia, and Bosnia had no naturally fixed boundaries; they provided murderous sites for the intersecting ambitions of empires and as yet undetermined states.

Sultan Abdulhamid II tried to take advantage of tensions in provinces that were slipping from his grip. He responded in 1870 to the Bulgarian clergy's desire to secede from the Patriarchate of Constantinople by recognizing a Bulgarian church with its own millet. His action, intended to fortify Bulgarian clerics against Bulgarian nationalists, did little to shore up Ottoman control but did feed conflict between Greeks and Bulgarians.

The contraction of the empire raised the stakes for the sultan's project of Islamic renewal. With the losses after 1878, the Ottoman empire became a much more Muslim place. War and the Congress of Berlin had set a wave of migrations, expulsions, and resettlements in motion. After the war, some Muslims returned to live in the reconfigured Balkan states; others moved into Anatolia, bringing with them new skills and contacts, but also resentments over displacement and political loss. They joined the empire's other large Muslim populations—Turks and Arabs—and smaller ones, such as Albanians (where local Muslims revolted against Montenegrin rule). The empire's major Christian populations were Greeks and Armenians; both had international connections. These groups were not consolidated territorially but lived as minorities in both cities and rural areas. Islamic empire could not appeal to them.

The expansion of education, the prosperity of the ethnically diverse middle classes of the cities, the ongoing agitation of reform-minded liberals, and above all the discontents of the ambitious and consciously modern officer corps prepared the ground for a different approach. In 1908, under pressure from the army, the sultan decided to restore the constitution he had revoked thirty years before.

The major force behind the constitutional revival was the Committee of Union and Progress (CUP), a successor to the Young Ottoman movement with wide appeal among students and graduates of military and other schools. Formed in 1894, the CUP included liberal centralizers, leaders of national minorities—Kurds, Greeks, Armenians, Jews, Albanians—as well as Arab and Turkic reformists within its ranks. Unity was possible in the disconnected underground; CUP members could be found in army cells, in Paris, and in London, as well as in Ottoman cities. Having won the parliamentary elections in 1908, the party pursued a centralizing agenda, undercutting local notables, attempting to replace entrenched bureaucrats with professional administrators, making electoral procedures more uniform, ending press censorship, and enforcing a state language—Ottoman Turkish—in public matters. This liberal program produced, first, an attempted counterrevolution in April 1909 and, later, diffuse but profound opposition to what appeared to many as a Turkification of government. The counterrevolution in Istanbul was put down by the army officers who had brought the CUP to power. Abdulhamid was deposed and replaced with Mehmet V, who remained sultan until 1918.

After 1909, the Unionist reformers tilted away from their earlier all-embracing liberalism to a more Turkish, more Islamic, more surveillance-based regime, and provoked more discontent. Islamic reformers tried to clean up unruly popular practices in favor of respectable behavior. The Turkish language policy was a particular irritant to Arabs; the centralizing fiscal and legal measures alienated Christians and other minority groups. The CUP lost electoral support. It was unable to prevent Italy from taking Libya. In 1913, with the empire on the verge of losing its last cities in Europe during a new round of Balkan wars and fearing a great-power partition of Anatolia, Young Turk officers grabbed the state in a military coup.

The fate of the Ottoman constitutional governments like that of the Russian Duma highlights the profound disruption that liberal democracy posed to empires based on principles of protected difference. In neither case did reform occur in a vacuum: both empires felt themselves threatened by western economic and political power. The Ottomans lost huge territories and a great deal of economic control after 1815; the Russians, able to expand their resource base eastward, were frustrated by the Europeans' multiple refusals to let them reap the rewards of defeating Ottomans. The threats to imperial control were also cultural. Both Russian and Ottoman empires produced generations of ambitious modernizers educated with what they thought of as European standards as their models. Restrictions on political life sent intellectuals from both empires to western capitals, where they participated in the heady, rebellious politics of challenge to established order. When political life at home opened up, a multiplicity of ideas about better kinds of sovereignty were available to those who wanted to remake their polity.

In both empires, some reformists sought secular, democratic alternatives to the protectionist and patrimonial rule of the sultan and the tsar. The Young Ottomans seemed to go the furthest in advocating liberal, centralizing, and democratic reform. But their insistence on Ottoman Turkish as the language of government, primary education, and the courts produced demands for the recognition of Arabic, Greek, and Armenian as equal languages. The underrepresentation of Arabs in the parliament also alienated many supporters of liberal reform.

It might seem that Ottoman liberalism had a choice between two directions—restructuring an Ottoman polity or forging a Turkish one. But after the loss of most of its Christian-majority provinces, Islam offered a third way forward. Between Turks and Arabs there could be a compromise based on religion. After 1913, the Union government opened a new Islamic university in Medina and rewarded powerful Arab leaders for their loyalty. In Syria, for example, local leaders made their arrangements with Ottoman officials, and in Istanbul they had a voice, if not in proportion to their population. Syrian Arabs as a collectivity did not form a significant "national" movement in opposition to Ottoman rule.

Islamism, like Russification, was not taken to an extreme and it did not tear the empire apart. Although both Russia and Ottoman leaders experimented with more restrictive—more Russian, more Islamic, more Turkic—cultural practices, homogeneity in a national or religious mode was untenable as a ruling premise in these empires. The association of different groups in a single polity was taken for granted even by reformers: national representatives in both parliaments did not agitate for independence but for more rights. In the early twentieth century, the Ottoman empire was as ever reliant on its military, whose officers were modernizers in a European mode, but as army leaders discovered once they entered government, an empire founded on protection of difference still depended on the contingent accommodation of diverse elites.

An Empire of Many Qualities

In 1898, Franz Joseph celebrated a half century on the Austrian throne, under the pall of the recent assassination by an Italian anarchist of the Empress Elizabeth. A daughter of Duke Maximilian of Bavaria, the empress had learned Hungarian and supported the Hungarians during the "compromise" of 1867 that created the Dual Monarchy. Both the mourning of Hungarians for their queen and sympathy for the emperor's conspicuous grief were signs that the Habsburg imperial aura still held sway.

Other aspects of the imperial jubilee displayed profound transformations in the empire's political culture. Prominent in Vienna's celebration was its mayor, Karl Lueger, head of the Christian Social Party. Lueger's political success was based on an explicit appeal to "German" progress, Christian values, and anti-semitism. The emperor regarded Lueger's anti-semitism as dangerous and refused to confirm him as mayor four times before finally, in 1897, allowing the vote of the city council to prevail. What made Lueger's politics possible in an empire that had extended its welcome and legal protections to Jews?

One answer was the Habsburgs' constitutionalism. The 1867 citizenship laws had made Jews equal with others in legal rights. As a result, Jews flocked to the capital from across the empire; many attended universities and later prospered in the expanding liberal professions—law, medicine, journalism—as well as in businesses. Austrian protection also attracted Jews fleeing pogroms that broke out in the Russian empire in 1881. In Vienna, like Berlin, Jews both had a place in a modernizing, cosmopolitan society and could envision alternatives—Zionism, for example—to it. They were also visible targets for anti-semites.

A second effect of Habsburg reform was the expansion of legal political organizations. As leaders strove for prominence within the emerging parties, they could try to mobilize their supporters according to language—the most obvious field of play in the diverse polity. In June 1885, the Vienna University branch of the liberals' School Association voted to bar Jews from membership. By the 1890s, a majority of Austrian liberals had gravitated toward "Germanness" and the defense of German language as a foundation of political mobilization. Austrian constitutionalism, representative institutions, and legal party activism had unleashed a German national movement into public life. This tendency continued after 1907, when universal male suffrage—a goal of the Social Democrats—was introduced.

The ethnicization of the empire's politics obliged Social Democrats to take seriously the question of nationality in a future socialist state. Their reflections included Otto Bauer's recognition that a multiplicity of nations, defined historically by cultural experience and not based on territory, was a positive element of human society. His program (before 1914) was to maximize national autonomy within the Austrian monarchy, to limit the powers of the central administration, and to allow individuals to choose their national status at will. Lueger's Christian Socials also developed a variant on multinational politics by defending the monarchy and Catholic universalism. Lueger's kind of empire, though, excluded Jews. The Christian Socials made this point in their 1898 extravaganza in honor of the emperor, where Lueger showcased uplifting German and Christian art, "emancipated" from Jewish corruption. The principles, if not the practices, of both the Social Democrats and Christian Socials were supranational, a logic of their political context.

As in the Ottoman empire, language policy became a disruptive element on the more open field of politics. On this issue, the Habsburg monarchy maintained its pluralism and flexibility. Responding to Czech demands for linguistic rights, Prime Minister Badeni instructed officials in Bohemia and Moravia that all correspondence on a legal issue was to be in the language of the case as originally filed. By 1901, officials in these provinces were to be competent in both Czech and German. German nationalists protested violently in many areas and the law was ultimately withdrawn.

Of the three empires entangled in southeastern Europe, Austria had the least censored press, the most active public, and the most developed party politics. Education, professional society, and technical infrastructure had been expanded, unevenly, but much further than in Russia or the Ottoman empire. A sharing out of sovereignty had been going on since the middle of the century, and new generations had grown up with the experience of contested party politics. The empire had worked a way around some of its problems by means of the Dual Monarchy, and its close relation with the Catholic church had not prevented it from conspicuous protection of other religions.

Thanks to the Congress of Berlin, Austria even had its own "colony," Bosnia-Herzegovina, a place where imperial architects exercised their talents, dotting the landscape with grand churches and refitting towns with Habsburg urban plans. Scholars relabeled Ottoman feats of engineering—such as the stone bridge at Mostar—"Roman" to consolidate the imperial lineage. Habsburg administrators consciously took up a civilizing mission directed against Serb and Croat nationalists, Orthodox and Muslim clerics, all considered as behind the secular times. But in Bosnia, as elsewhere, centralizing initiatives such as interconfessional education were costly and ran up against divisions between modernizers and traditionalists within each religious group.

In 1908 the dynasty was celebrated with a huge "Kaiser-Hommage" procession, replete with delegations of appropriately costumed peasants from various imperial territories. Conflicts arose over the symbolism of the parade—over whether the Polish king or Hungarian emperor (in effigy) would go first in a procession celebrating the 1683 siege of Vienna by the Ottomans. Was anything wrong with this picture of unruly but loyal imperial citizens?

Looking backward, historians and others have turned displays of imperial diversity into a tale of conflicting nationalisms, tearing up the polity. But in the late Habsburg empire, nationalists' efforts to mobilize people to their causes were running into obstacles—the dispersal of different "nations" across the empire's territory, the long-term hold of imperial institutions, the presence of Jews and others who did not fit into a world divided by nationality. Nationalists might advocate single-language schools, but German-speakers, Czech-speakers, Slovenes, and Germans clashed over such de-

LE REVEIL DE LA QUESTION D'ORIENT
La Bulgarie proclame son indépendance. — L'Autriche prend la Bosnie et l'Herzégovine

Figure 11.4
"The Reawakening of the Oriental Question." The subtitle reads: "Bulgaria proclaims its independence—Austria takes Bosnia and Herzegovina." In this satirical French representation, the Austro-Hungarian emperor and the king of Bulgaria, whose new crown sits uncertainly on his head, pull out pieces of the Ottoman empire as the sultan sulks. *Le Petit Journal*, October 18, 1908. Snark, ArtResource.

mands. Mass politics and institutions through which the Habsburgs allowed communities a measure of self-rule gave nationalist politicians unintended opportunities to try to turn their ideas into political reality. But this in turn led to antagonisms within regions, to more fragmentation of politics, and to divisions within groups that nationalists claimed to be united. Nationalists could only get so far in convincing people to think and act within the limits of single distinctive nation, and most political activists were striving for a better—their own—kind of empire, not for its end.

A more immediate danger came from Austria's weakness in relation to other empires. Great Britain and the congress system had helped the Habsburgs in the competitions in the Balkans. It was plausible to think that once the Ottomans had been laid low and Russia sidelined in 1905 by its failed Asian war and internal disorder, Austria was next on the great powers' buffet. In this context, the emperor's prerogative to make war and peace was the wild card, and the greatest threat to stability and imperial existence. In 1908, the Austrians annexed their colony, Bosnia-Herzegovina, with the goal of attaching Serbs and Croats in the region more securely to the empire. This infuriated leaders of independent Serbia, who wanted access to the sea. Serbs, Croats, advocates of Yugoslavia, and Russians all had ambitions for the region. After the Balkan wars of 1912 and 1913, Serbia was expanded— but still blocked from the Adriatic by a newly independent Albania—and Bosnia-Herzegovina was given an elected diet and made a component of the Austrian empire. All this inclined Russia and Serbia, both still seeking to expand on the former Ottoman territories, to pledge to support each other against Austria.

Nation and Empire

The century of imperial competitions, military and otherwise, on contiguous territory and overseas, after Napoleon's defeat created an identifiable Europe of great powers recognized as such by their neighboring empires. Becoming European became an aspiration of educated elites across the Habsburg, Russian, and Ottoman empires; defining difference from Europe or avoiding a European path were also comprehensible if problematic strategies.

But what did becoming European mean and were its consequences desirable? Did it entail reconfiguring sovereignty in more democratic ways? Or was the basic task of becoming "contemporary"—getting with the European times—economic and technological? Perhaps expanding education and updating it, while investing in railroads and communications systems would do the trick. But these strategies required resources not already in place. Getting them might mean acquiring land, people, and connections at the expense of other powers—as the new German Reich had done, with its origins in Prussia, its power extended over Polish-, Danish-, and French-speaking areas, plus colonies in Africa, east Asia, and the Pacific.

The most explicit challenge concerned military capacity, and Russian, Ottoman, and Habsburg leaders made the army and especially its officers primary targets for reform. In the Ottoman empire, these initiatives, combined with off-putting restrictions on political expression, made the officer corps into the Janissaries of the twentieth century—a group apart, convinced of their duty to intervene when the sultan had gone astray. In Russia, the extension of the draft to all males, with loopholes, in 1874 was a major break with estate-based recruitment, but here, consistent with Russian-style patrimonialism, ambitious generals cultivated individual ties to the emperor and posed no threat to him. An army open to all including Jews was key to Habsburg recovery after 1848. Recruitment from multiple nationalities and educational improvements meant that the officer corps in the twentieth century was still reliably loyal to the empire and, fatally, willing to go to war for its interests.

These military efforts were complemented with political reforms and social projects. Both the Habsburgs (1867) and the Ottomans (1869) offered their male subjects citizenship and declared them equal, although as elsewhere in the world what equality signified was unclear. Under duress, the Russian government offered its subjects an array of civil rights in 1906, but formal divisions in subjects' political status lasted until 1917. All three empires employed consultative bodies and all eventually created parliaments with elected representatives: the Habsburgs in 1861; the Ottomans in 1876–77, revived in 1908; the Russians in 1906. As in Great Britain, France, and Germany, suffrage did not include women. Habsburgs, Romanovs, and Ottomans expanded education significantly but unevenly in all three cases. Serfdom was abolished in both Habsburg and Romanov empires before slaves were emancipated in the United States. In the Ottoman empire, where slavery was regulated through Islamic law, the state applied the Tanzimat edict on legal equality and gradually emancipated agrarian slaves with compensation to their masters.

Imperial reformers also set their sights on western Europe's economic leap forward. The economies of each empire ballooned in the nineteenth century. Ottoman foreign trade increased ten times between 1820 and 1914; the Russian economy grew reliably and fast from the 1890s. Still, imperial ruling practices set limits on change. The Austrians were unable to dislodge Magyar landlords and their stifling agrarian politics; the Dual Monarchy arrangement did not solve this problem. Russian rulers for decades balked at peasant ownership of farms. Free trade under British rules choked Ottoman home production. Ottomans, Russians, and Habsburgs had huge debts—to Britain, France, and Germany. One apparent lesson was that the west was good at getting resources from colonies. This kind of thinking was on the minds of elites when they acquired new territories, such as Turkestan or Bosnia or Yemen, or built railroads like the trans-Siberian or Istanbul-Baghdad to carry the products of far-flung regions.

All three empires adapted imperial technologies from their neighbors, moving in what we might call a "Roman" direction toward more systematic government with fuller participation of the population. At the same time, as we have seen (chapter 10), the western European empires with their colonial projects were being forced to accommodate indigenous intermediaries and to shore up their control with indirect rule and other devolutions of power familiar to Russians, Ottomans, and Habsburgs. In places where empires intersected, such as Yemen where both Ottomans and British tried to co-opt ambitious imams, competition could, for a time, be exploited by local leaders.

What cut across the imperial field was the requirement of somehow making different people serve the empire's purposes and stay in it. Where ideology was concerned, empires moved in different directions, toward sharper distinctions—such as racial ones—or vaguer hegemonies—such as privileging Islam. Similarly, political restructuring could be taken on a more egalitarian course, or into realms of differentiation. There was no single way to decide questions of inclusion or exclusion.

Like race and religion, nation was a tool—a sharp one—in the imperial repertoire. Politicians and statesmen could try to manipulate national sentiment at home, in the near abroad, and overseas. Debates and contestations within European societies—Habsburg Austria as well as republican France—reflected and deepened tensions over who belonged to the polity and on what grounds. The respectable insider could be marked by language, ethnicity, appearance, religion, proper family relations, or class, or combinations of these. More was at stake in these questions of membership in a polity when citizens voted and—toward the end of the century in some cases—benefited from the beginnings of welfare services. The growth of the press combined with protections for civil rights and expanding literacy meant that activists could cultivate constituencies beyond the reach of the state or cosmopolitan elites.

The anti-semitism that developed in different parts of Europe in the nineteenth century reflected not the strength of exclusionary nationalism but its insecurities. A central trope of anti-semitic writing was that Jews had constituted solidarities that cut across states, territories, and peoples, and that these ties constituted a threat to the state's integrity. The image diffused in the *Protocols of Zion*, a forgery produced in early twentieth-century Russia, was distinctly imperial: the Jews aimed at world rule. There was nothing intrinsically German, French, or Russian about campaigns to make Jews out-siders. Anti-semitism was deployed in struggles within the polity—against the pragmatic cosmopolitanism of the Bismarckian elite, against secular and universal citizenship in France, against tavern keepers and middlemen in the central European countryside, everywhere against competitors in business, the military, or civil service.

For empires based on the recognition of difference, the move toward equal rights was risky. Making subjects into citizens in Austria seemed to provoke mobilization around anti-semitic, linguistic, ethnic, and regional issues. Interpreting liberalism in centralizing ways was also problematic in the Ottoman empire where particularity, personal ties between Istanbul and local elites, and special rights were the stuff of politics. The more open and clamorous the political system became, the more obvious were diver-gent interests. Each political initiative—a common state language or a serf emancipation—could be resented and exploited by offended groups. In Austria, where party politics was the most developed, liberals, Christians, nationalists—of many kinds—and socialists all pushed for changes, but dif-ferent ones. In Russia, where political opposition was suppressed until 1905, an explosion of violence against the state continued after the concessions of 1906, as did vicious attacks on the government in the liberated press. In Germany, a romantic pan-Germanism challenged a cosmopolitan imperial culture. Did these discontents mean that empires founded on the politics of difference had outlived their functionality, and if so, what was the better kind of polity?

The conventional answer to this question is the nation, but at the end of the nineteenth century and the beginning of the twentieth, the national was less a solution than a claim. The advocates of a truly national state—one people, one territory, one state—ran up against the difficulty that most peo-ple did not live that way and that exclusionary practices risked weakening rather than strengthening any polity. The Balkan wars of 1912 and 1913 dis-played the death-dealing volatility of trying to build states out of nations, on territories where populations had been mixed and remixed over millennia.

Bulgaria, Greece, Montenegro, and Serbia all wanted to expand at the expense of each other and the Ottomans. Egged on by Russia, they formed a league and declared war on the Ottomans in October 1912. Victories by the Balkan armies pushed Albanian elites to join the state-making game, the Young Turks in the Ottoman empire to make their coup, and the European powers to try to negotiate a peace. But by the summer of 1913, Bulgaria, Serbia, and Greece were fighting each other over Macedonia. Romania and the Ottomans then joined the fray.

All parties suffered huge losses in these wars, including large numbers of Muslim civilians driven from their homes. In some estimates, over half the Muslims who had lived in Ottoman provinces lost to Greece, Serbia, and Bulgaria either died or fled. Military casualties were high: over 66,000 Bulgarian soldiers were killed or died of disease; 37,000 died for Serbia; over 100,000 Ottoman defenders perished. The borders drawn up by European ambassadors meeting in London in 1913 were not national, not stable, not harmonious. The making of nations in other people's empires, a strategy of all powers since 1815, had produced a century of gruesome wars, enhanced weaponry across the continent, and entangled states old and new in the competition over European space.

The leaders of European empires in the nineteenth century thought about questions of belonging and difference in their polities, but not in the same way. The idea of national community appealed to many within empires, both those who saw a collective destiny in ruling over others and those who wanted to escape the fate of being ruled. No ethnicized conception of the body politic could be followed to its logical conclusion. The most powerful rulers manipulated the diverse ties of different collectivities to an imperial center, and some collectivities maneuvered among empires. The Ottoman, Romanov, and Habsburg empires were not Turkish, Russian, and Germanic peoples ruling "others," even if there were people within these empires who advocated Turkifying, Russifying, or Germanizing policies. Even the rulers of the German Reich—at this time—did not try to enfold all Germans into their empire or to exclude all non-Germans. Too much had been built on the accommodation and manipulation of difference for a homogenizing nationalist mission to seem a realizable imperial project.

WAR AND REVOLUTION IN A WORLD OF EMPIRES

1914 to 1945

12

In Berlin, Paris, and London in 1900, political leaders and intellectuals had reason to believe they were entering the European century. European empires now covered more than half the landed surface of the globe. The major powers had even managed to organize their colonial competition in Africa peacefully, thanks to the agreements reached in 1884–85 and 1889–90. The transformations of European economies had produced both immense wealth and tensions over inequality and social change, but European elites thought that well-targeted government interventions could address these challenges. The expansion of civil liberties in European states allowed critiques of bourgeois society, capitalism, and imperialism to be expressed in "modernist" art and literature, as well as in radical political movements from anarchism to communism. If the social ills of capitalist development could not be cured by reform, some felt they could be reversed by revolution. Bold blueprints for a better future expressed the sense of mastery over social processes shared by left and right, although questioned by some in the intellectual and cultural avant-garde.

The prospect of control was shattered after 1914, in a bloodbath whose point became harder to see as millions died. World War I revealed and did nothing to resolve the instability in the European system of empires. The war did not ease the burden of empire on the people who lived in European colonies. It destroyed empires on the losing side—Ottoman, Habsburg, and Romanov—and made the future of the people who lived on their territories all the more uncertain and conflict-ridden. It enhanced the leverage of another empire—Japan—whose growing power only added to the uncertainty and dangers within the international "order."

A young French officer who fought in the first world war and became a leader in the second, Charles de Gaulle, referred to "our century's Thirty Years' War." This perspective overlooks paths that were possible but not taken after 1918, but it highlights long-term continuities in imperial competition.

Repeatedly since the sixteenth century, one of a small number of empire-states centered in Europe attempted to dominate the whole, only to be countered by the others. World War I left a legacy of despair and bitterness, and the conflict of empires resumed with World War II, with more virulent hatreds, using more deadly weaponry, and involving more of the world. As before, empire-states brought both continental and overseas resources to their wars with each other.

World War II differed from the previous rounds of empire wars, and not just in the genocidal viciousness of the Nazis. First, there was a new, major actor beyond Europe and western Eurasia—Japan. Second, two new super-powers extended their imperial reach, while insisting they were different from other empires—the United States and the Union of Soviet Socialist Republics. Third, the outcome of World War II put an end, it seemed, to an unstable array of empires that had struggled repeatedly for dominance in Europe from the age of Charles V through Napoleon to Hitler. The first element was crucial to the third, for when Japan broke into French, British, and Dutch power in southeast Asia, the system of colonial empires began to unravel. World War II destroyed Germany and Japan as empires—and decisively weakened France, Great Britain, and the Netherlands.

At the end of this world war unlike the first one, victors and losers were freed from the compulsion to interact with each other as empires. Within narrower, more national, and apparently more durable borders European states prospered after 1945, in unprecedented peace among themselves. But if the new thirty years' war was the beginning of the end of the system of empires of Europe, it did not end imperial ambitions around the world—not least for the United States and the USSR, new rivals for world hegemony. The generalization of polities theoretically based on national sovereignty and the fiction that all states were juridically equivalent masked destabilizing inequalities among states and within them. We explore the making of this new world—and the question of whether it was a world after empire or a world with new forms of empire—in the next two chapters.

War of the Empires, 1914–1918

Explanations for the outbreak of World War I are numerous. Was it an internecine struggle among capitalists or the unintended consequence of treaty systems and political misunderstandings? One point is easily overlooked: the war was a struggle among empires. Although mobilization drew on and fostered nationalist sentiments and hatreds within Europe, there is little evidence that these passions pressured ruling elites into belligerency. We suggested in the last chapter how hard the entrepreneurs of national culture had to work to generalize the sentiments they claimed to represent and how unsure ruling elites were that appeals to national solidarity would eclipse sentiments of class, religion, or locality. World War I was a top-down war, developing over the summer of 1914 as ruling elites maneuvered in relation to each other. It was not a war over colonies—although taking colonies became a war aim—but a war among empires as multiplex polities. The belligerents intended to reallocate populations and resources, in Europe and overseas, from another empire into their own.

Soldiers to feed the deadly war machine came from throughout the empires. As the French state, for example, tried to foster patriotism among conscripts and volunteers in metropolitan France, it also recruited Africans and Indochinese soldiers—coercing and persuading them to be effective fighters in the imperial cause. The Habsburg empire counted on the loyalty of soldiers—Austrians, Hungarians, Czechs, Jews, and others—to the emperor-monarch; these expectations were largely fulfilled. The governments of British Canada, Australia, South Africa, and New Zealand saw war declared on their behalf by the king of England, but had options about how to participate. All chose to contribute to the cause of the empire of which they were self-governing parts. British subjects from protectorates, colonies, princely states, and other subordinated units had much less choice but were part of the war effort. That Britain, France, and Russia had significant material and human resources beyond the contested zones of western and eastern Europe shaped the course of the fighting.

A World Unbalanced: Empires, Nations, and Armies on the Road to War

Europe descended precipitously from master of others' destiny to a continent incapable of managing its own. Even before 1914 there were signs—which few at the time were able to read—that European global domination was not what it seemed to be: Japan's defeat of Russia in 1905, empires' failure to systematically administer or transform their African colonies, their inability to absorb the faltering Qing empire into the European imperial system, and the volatility of imperial aspirations in Europe itself.

The balance among empires was destabilized in the late nineteenth century by the growing economic power—and geopolitical insecurity—of the German empire. That tensions did not lead to all-out warfare after the Franco-Prussian war of 1870 owed much to Chancellor Bismarck's understanding of the limits of imperial power (chapter 10) and his ability to broker agreements over Africa and the Balkans that maintained the balance among empires. But the mix of autocratic, patrimonial, and parliamentary power in Germany that allowed Bismarck to play this game left his successors with tools to play a different one.

Shifts in relations among European empires (chapter 11) placed Germany between Russia and its new French ally. Germans were conscious that other empires had assets that they could only envy: Britain's overseas colonies and navy; Russia's vast grain production, huge labor force, and Caspian oil; France's manpower and material resources in Asia and Africa. German leaders were also conscious of the Reich's internal divisions—between Catholics, Protestants, and Jews, between an increasingly wealthy bourgeoisie eager to have a larger voice in politics and workers caught up in the tensions of industrialization, speaking through a militant socialist party and active trade unions. The strident "pan-German" nationalism voiced in some quarters—insisting on the unity of German-speakers in the Austro-Hungarian empire as well as the Kaiserreich—only confirmed that a German nation was far from a generally accepted aspiration.

The German military had its own ideas. The victory over France in 1870 sent the army mixed messages—the military had ultimately triumphed, but it suffered from manpower shortages and inflexible financing as a result of the government's reluctance to increase burdens on a demanding bourgeoisie and a restive proletariat. Unable to draw on deep reserves, planners realized that a new war would have to be brief and brutal, destroying the enemy in short order. This doctrine—elaborated in the Schlieffen plan—was tested in colonial wars and remained at the forefront of German military planning in 1914. Government leaders were pressured by pan-German organizations and the military command with its narrow vision of military and diplomatic options, but Germany as a whole was not in thrall to reactionary Prussian militarism or especially strong nationalism. Its ruling elite was conscious of vulnerability abroad and uncertain support at home.

Later it became clear that not only Germany but its multinational, multiconfessional neighbors Austria-Hungary, Russia, and the Ottomans maintained a high degree of imperial loyalty. The different "nations" within the Austro-Hungarian empire in 1914 did not take war as an opportunity to separate themselves. Jews and others who had a more secure imperial home than territorial base followed the counsel of one of their leaders: "We nationally-conscious Jews want a strong Austria." In Russia, the outbreak of the war was met with demonstrations of patriotic fervor, as well as with anti-German pogroms that shocked the imperial administration. (The empress, born in the Grand Duchy of Hesse, was a cousin of the German emperor.) To the unhappy surprise of British commanders, most Arabs remained loyal to the Ottoman empire until the end of the war.

But this is to leap ahead. From the perspective of 1914, what leaders were worrying about was each other in a world of empires where making the right alliance was a familiar tool against rivals. The Kaiserreich and Austro-Hungarian empire needed to cooperate, even if they had fought in 1866. Both feared another imperial—and industrializing—power to the east, Russia. Britain also worried about Russia—that it could take advantage of Ottoman weakness to move into a position jeopardizing India and other British interests via Afghanistan. But Britain—alarmed that Germany was beginning to match its industrial and naval strength—needed France, Russia's ally, to counter Germany.

All major powers were so anxious that they increased military spending by 50 percent between 1908 and 1913. All tried to ally with the right partners. In the summer of 1914, Germany and Austria-Hungary had agreed to support each other in the event of war. France was allied to Russia, Britain to France. The Ottomans made a secret agreement with Germany, their only plausible option as the least threatening of the powers that had been helping themselves to Ottoman territories over the past century.

What sent the inherently unstable mix of allied empires into the whirlpool of war was once again competition in the Balkans, where the Ottoman empire's losses had only heated up imperial rivalries and wars among would-be national states (chapter 11). Austria-Hungary had annexed Bosnia-

Map 12.1
Europe in
World War I.

Allies
Joined Allies during war
Central Powers
Joined Central Powers during war
Neutral

War and Revolution

Herzegovina. Serbia was independent and a wild card, with its memories of hostilities with Austria-Hungary and the Ottomans, its territorial ambitions, its connections to Russia, and its volatile mix of pan-Slavic and Serbian nationalist ideologies. Austria-Hungary wanted to tamp down Serbia, but with Russian intervention a danger, it needed more muscle than its own military could provide—this meant turning to Germany.

But the Germans also needed Austria-Hungary. Here we return to the Germans' post-1870 military doctrine—the Schlieffen plan, inherited by Chief of Staff Helmuth von Moltke—and to the combination of arrogance and anxiety that fed imperial politics in the early twentieth century. German worries now focused on Russia, an increasingly formidable foe. The arrogance was in the plan: if war in Europe started soon, before Russia became stronger, transportation and command bottlenecks would slow Russian mobilization—allowing the German army to knock off the more nimble French first, then rapidly move forces from west to east. The plan assumed that France could not by itself repel an all-out attack through its vulnerable northern frontier, via neutral Belgium. But Germany needed, for at least a time, to have its rear covered. Austria-Hungary could hold the Russians off and force them to defend a much longer frontier than the one with Germany. The plan's success depended on the German machine operating perfectly and everybody else playing according to stereotype.

On June 28, 1914, Gavrilo Princip, a twenty-year-old Serb—a resident of Bosnia, hence an Austro-Hungarian subject—carried out his plot, apparently with unofficial support inside the Serbian military, to assassinate Archduke Franz Ferdinand, heir to the Habsburg throne, and his wife, who were visiting Sarajevo. Franz Ferdinand was little liked and not much missed, least of all by his uncle the emperor. But his murder fed the intersecting strategies of war-minded empires.

Although the assassination had taken place on Austro-Hungarian territory and was not an action of the Serbian government, the Habsburgs could now launch their desired war on Serbia and enlist German help if Russia did not accept their justification. Despite the kaiser's reservations, German military leaders, especially von Moltke, saw this as an opportunity to put their plan into effect and fight the inevitable war against France and Russia under favorable circumstances. As Austria-Hungary threatened war on Serbia, Russia mobilized its army, Britain its fleet. Germany tried to persuade the British not to join France in a war against Germany, promising to seize only France's colonies. The British government did not take the bait.

In early August, Austria-Hungary declared war against Serbia, Russia against Austria-Hungary, Germany against Russia. Germany launched its surprise attack on France through Belgium. French colonies in the Caribbean, west and equatorial Africa, southeast Asia, and the Pacific islands were all pulled into the imperial clash. Britain declared war on August 4, bringing in its dominions, colonies, and India. Germany's colonies were dragged in as well, not to mention the diverse Eurasian populations of Russia and the various nationalities of Austria-Hungary.

European War, Imperial War

Mahatma Gandhi told his fellow Indians, "We are, above all, British citizens of the Great British Empire. Fighting as the British are at present in the righteous cause for the good and glory of human dignity and civilization . . . our duty is clear: to do our best to support the British, to fight with our life and property." For whose dignity and civilization? Gandhi's support for the empire implied that rights would come with duties. Indeed, the British government in 1917 promised India "the progressive realization of responsible government." This promise would be honored tardily, grudgingly, and only partially after the war.

Men and materiel from distant regions of the empires proved critical to the war effort, complements to the industrial might and human mobilization in Europe. The balance in overseas resources tipped against Germany, since its colonies were separated from each other and the British navy was between them and Europe. In the British case, approximately three million men were mobilized from India and the dominions, around a third of the empire's forces. India was the biggest contributor of all. Africans—in keeping with the racialized hierarchy of empire—played a different role. Nearly two million served, but mostly as carriers and mostly in fighting over Germany's colonies, Cameroon, Togo, Southwest Africa, and Tanganyika. Higher in the imperial hierarchy, Canada, Australia, New Zealand, and South Africa (white South Africa, that is) sent around a million men to the war the king had declared on their behalf, but not without misgivings about the way Britain made decisions and their people made sacrifices. The empire also contributed to the British war economy by supplying materials, earning foreign exchange via exports, and deferring consumers' needs.

French colonial subjects—Africans, Indochinese, north Africans, and others—fought in the trenches in large numbers, 170,000 from west Africa alone. Some 200,000 civilian workers came to France from the colonies to take up the slack when workers were called to the front (as did increasing numbers of women in France). Some soldiers and workers were exempted from the worst indignities, such as the separate judicial system, that colonial subjects ordinarily faced. The war gave substance to a sentimental imperialism that lauded the heartfelt participation of people of all races and religions in saving France. In fact, recruitment in the colonies was a mixture of conscription and enlistment under conditions that fell far short of free choice.

During the war there was a large-scale rebellion in the interior of French West Africa, exacerbated by conscription, and put down with large loss of life by troops from other regions.

Large numbers of colonial subjects—without citizenship rights—died for France. There were myths and countermyths of Africans' combat role: soldiers like any other; soldiers whose savagery was, for the moment, useful; cannon fodder in exceptionally dangerous situations. The colonial contribution exposed the core tension between incorporation and differentiation in empires. Let us take the case of Senegal.

The four leading towns of Senegal (the "Four Communes") had been French colonies since the eighteenth century, and their inhabitants had the rights of citizens even though their civil affairs came under Islamic law rather than the French civil code (chapter 10). These rights were often attacked by French traders, settlers, and officials who did not like their inconsistency with a racialized order. Still, the four towns could elect a deputy to

Figure 12.1
French soldiers from the colonies in a German prisoner-of-war camp, 1917.
The photo was used in German propaganda both to defend Germany's humane treatment of prisoners and to belittle France for claiming to defend civilization with African troops. The partially obscured text on the upper-right corner indicates that the prisoners were from Senegal, Guinea, Somalia, Tunisia, Annam (part of Vietnam), the Sudan, and Dahomey. Anonymous photograph, Musée d'Histoire Contemporaine/BDIC, Paris.

the Paris legislature, and since 1914 the deputy was a black African, Blaise Diagne. Diagne made a deal: he would assist the conscription of Senegalese citizens into the regular French army, help recruit elsewhere, and smooth problems that arose, while France affirmed the citizenship rights of his constituency in the Four Communes and agreed to treat them as they did other citizens—not like the second-tier soldiers recruited among the subjects. Diagne's role as a recruiter was a success, and a 1916 law ensured the citizenship status of the Four Communes. As in British India, the participation of colonial soldiers in the war left a major question on the table at the end of the war: would the tilt toward incorporation continue or be reversed?

The German leadership's conviction that the technological and organization skills of the German people could offset its disadvantage in colonial resources went sour when the plan for total, rapid victory turned into a seemingly endless battle. With more demands and hardships afflicting the civilian population, military leaders looked for explanations, as Michael Geyer explains, by "blaming workers, the bourgeoisie, women, intellectuals, universities, homosexuals, and youth, and . . . a 'Jewish conspiracy' eating away at the vitals of the German army." The cosmopolitan culture of prewar Germany was fraying under the horrors of war and the High Command's need for scapegoats.

If the war effort of France and Britain was maintained with the blood of people from around the empire, the war was ultimately won by grinding down German endurance. America's industrial and military power came to the aid of France and Britain at a crucial moment, when Russia's collapse in 1917 freed German troops on the eastern front. Although the war in Russia initially produced an outburst of patriotic loyalty, by 1917 it had exposed the autocracy's incompetence. Two revolutions in 1917 took Russia out of the war, and the Bolsheviks signed a separate peace with Germany in March 1918. But Germany's economy and military were already in shambles.

There was nothing inevitable about the outcome of the war. As military historian Michael Howard writes, "Let us not forget that the Schlieffen plan nearly did succeed." Had the rapid and massive assault on France been a little more effective, the configuration of postwar empires would have been quite different: Austria-Hungary, the German empire, the Ottomans, and perhaps Romanov Russia might have remained intact, France stripped of its colonies, and Britain weakened. Such a configuration might have been catastrophic in its own way, but the trajectories of empires would not have been the same.

Empire and Nation in the Wartime Middle East

The Middle East (a label which itself reflects a re-centering of imperial power) was a theater—a tragic and bloody one—of imperial conflict. The Ottomans tried to stave off entering the war, but their alliance with Germany pulled them in. Germany supplied officers and equipment to improve the quality of the Ottoman army. Ottoman forces lost ground to Russia in eastern Anatolia but contained the Russian advances. Some Germans hoped that their alliance with the Ottomans could be extended into a jihad against British rule over Muslims in Egypt, Afghanistan, parts of India, and elsewhere in the Middle East. Some British leaders thought they could pit Arabs against Ottomans in Syria-Palestine and thus threaten Germany's partner. The proximity of Ottoman territories to the Suez Canal and the importance for the British, Russians, and other allies of controlling access to the Black Sea via the Dardanelles made this region ripe for interempire war.

The results were not those predicted by the trope of Ottoman decline. When the British military, using troops from Australia, India, and other parts of the empire, attempted to drive their way into the Dardanelles at Gallipoli, they were blocked by an unexpectedly strong defense of the strategic heights by Ottoman troops with German equipment. A second assault on Ottoman territory—a British-led army with largely Indian soldiers attacking through Mesopotamia—met initial disaster and only reached its objective as the war was being won in France, after a quintessential empire-drama in which hundreds of thousands of peasants from British India and Ottoman Anatolia shot each other on behalf of London and Istanbul.

Important—but less so than the myth would have it—were British machinations to stir up the so-called Arab revolt against Ottomans, principally through T. E. Lawrence's cultivation of the sharif of Mecca, Husayn ibn Ali, his clan, and other Arab communities thought to be resentful of Ottoman rule. If this story is often told as a clash of budding Arab nationalism against declining Ottoman imperialism, it in fact followed a typical empire script: finding agents and intermediaries within rivals' camps.

Husayn, from the Hashemite clan of the same Meccan tribe as Muhammad, first helped keep order for the Ottomans. His kinship and regional support network became a basis for his own quest for imperial power. The British saw his ambitions as a means of prying Arab intermediaries away from Istanbul. British officers fantasized about installing a new caliph in Mecca, envisioning Husayn, "an Arab of true race," as a sort of spiritual leader; Husayn imagined himself at the head of a new empire. The notion of "Arab revolt" presumed a commonality that had been advocated by some pan-Arab intellectuals before the war, but most of the diverse Arab elites of the region found a way to reconcile local authority with Ottoman power. Husayn and his supporters followed the pattern of clan politics and imperial clientelism better than the story of Arab nationalism.

Ottoman power in Palestine and surrounding areas was fragile enough for the British, with some assistance from Husayn's followers, to capture Jerusalem from Ottoman forces. By the time the British got to Syria, the war was ending; British patron and Arab client continued to jockey for power in the Holy Land. We will return later to this region's fate.

The war gave some an opportunity to play a national card more strongly than they had earlier. As we have seen (chapter 11), the Young Ottomans, increasingly frustrated with the blockages to liberal reform by the sultan and the patrimonial structure of the Ottoman empire, had made themselves into Young Turks, whose sights were more focused on centralization under their own command than on an imagined community of Turkish-speakers. The loss of Ottoman provinces in the Balkans and the massacres and flight of Muslims in those areas in 1912–13 had pushed more people, aggrieved at the actions of "Christian" powers, into a space that could be considered Turkish. But the need to keep the remaining Arab provinces within the system had restrained the government's homogenizing tendency. War, and especially the fear that France and Britain wanted the dismemberment of Anatolia itself, played into the hands of the most nationalist of the CUP leaders, who sought to mobilize solidarity among Turks against enemies and traitors. Nonetheless, the alliance with Germany was an attempt to preserve an imperial structure, and the successful defense of the Dardanelles and the continued loyalty of most of Syria showed that the multiplex empire still had life in it. When Russia took itself out of the war in 1917, the Ottomans recovered their lost ground to the east and pushed into Baku, Russia's oil source.

Forging Turkish solidarity against the dangerous "other" was carried to an extreme along the Russian-Ottoman front, in regions where the two empires had courted, punished, antagonized, and moved peoples for over a century. The Ottoman military, claiming that Armenians—who had been dynamic participants in Ottoman commercial life and society—were conspiring with the enemy, engineered a mass deportation from the combat zone, under atrocious conditions. Soldiers, paramilitary groups, and some of the top leaders of the CUP turned the forced exodus into a brutal annihilation of men, women, and children. The killings, far more systematic than massacres of Armenians in eastern Anatolia in the 1890s, reflected an ethnicization of the threat to imperial integrity. The atrocities did not target all Armenians living in Istanbul and western Anatolia, but estimates of the death toll run over eight hundred thousand. A few of the Ottomans' German advisors sent appalled messages to Berlin, but German policymakers did not act—the doctrine of "military necessity" prevailed.

The Ottoman empire did not die from the exhaustion of its imperial structures or because the imperial imaginary of its leaders and subjects had lost its relevance. Ottoman rulers, Arab elites, and British and German governments operated within a framework of expectations that had evolved over many years as empires tried to line up intermediaries or to detach the intermediaries of rivals. British leaders and their Muslim allies thought that the seventh-century caliphate provided a reference point in a political conflict in the twentieth century. Ottomans hoped to reactivate at Russian expense connections of Turkish-speaking peoples across the Eurasian landmass. But the Ottoman empire was on the losing side of an interempire war.

Restructuring the World of Empires

The victorious powers' efforts to reconfigure the world order did not end empires, only the empires of the losers. The postwar peace talks introduced a portentous debate over "self-determination" that was applied selectively, not to the colonies of France, Britain, the Netherlands, Belgium, or the United States. In Europe, the "peace" turned one unstable configuration into a still more unstable one: a mix of empires and putative nation-states. The forcible breakup of some empires left many of their inhabitants resentful of the loss of imperial power, while many of their fellow nationals located in other states were expropriated and forced back to a homeland in which they had never lived. For nationalists who claimed a state to be "theirs," the millions of diverse people who had shared the same territory and might have similar aspirations stood in the way of turning exclusionary visions into reality. The idea of self-determination provided no coherent definition of who could determine themselves, no mechanism for adjudicating conflicting claims, no assurance that the nationalizing states that emerged from empires would be sustainable.

In addition to maintaining the empires of the victors, the war's end led to three new and disruptive imperial projects: Nazi Germany, Japan, and the USSR. In cutting the Reich down to size, the postwar settlement fostered Germans' embitterment, national imaginary, and imperial desires. In east Asia, the scramble for bits of Germany's Pacific empire along with growing wealth and self-confidence fostered Japan's empire-building mission, represented as both the fulfillment of national destiny and a pan-Asian project. The USSR recovered most of imperial Russia's territory, structured the first communist state as a federation of formally distinct "national" republics, and ruled these through pyramids of party loyalists, creating a template for remaking the world through revolution. In the background—deliberately so—loomed the United States, a minor player on the colonial front, but an increasingly major one when it came to other ways of deploying power across space. Woodrow Wilson was critical of the European imperialism of his day, but his vision echoed Jefferson's "Empire of Liberty." He proposed, as Thomas Bender puts it, an "an astonishingly smooth projection of historical American principles into a global future," a world of republics, open to communication and commerce. These new competitors for reconfiguring world order became entwined in a new interempire politics, as volatile as the imperial competition that had led to World War I.

Nations, Mandates, and Imperial Power

Wilson did not think Africans and Asians mature enough to participate in his worldwide republican order. The United States continued to assert its right to intervene militarily in Latin American states, and had just done so in Mexico. In the view of the victorious powers at the Paris peace conference of 1919, self-determination could be discussed in relation to the Czechs, Hungarians, Poles, Serbs, and others who had been under the domination of Germany and its allies. Yet in Europe the application of the principle of a "people" choosing its leaders was not simple. Even before the Paris meeting, declarations of independence, revolutionary actions, and wars between aspiring "national" groups had taken place. Populations in the Balkans and central Europe were so mixed that defining a nation in order for it to determine its fate was not a question of recognizing a given cultural-linguistic-geographic fact but of convincing the arbitrators—the major powers, who were not innocent of self-interest—of who belonged where. The borders contemplated for Poland—even discounting the complexities of identification that ethnic categories of the time obscure—contained a population that was 40 percent Ukrainian, Belarusian, Lithuanian, or German; Czechoslovakia was home to 2.5 million Germans, plus Hungarians, Ruthenians, and others, not to mention an arranged cohabitation of Czechs with Slovaks, whom many of the former considered backward. Claims to nationhood extinguished those of people who did not speak the right language, worship the right god, or have the right patrons.

British imperial statesman Lord Curzon referred to the pressures and violence that accompanied the new borders as the "unmixing" of people. Waves of refugees—ten million by one count—moved across east-central Europe. Jews, who had been active participants in the public life of the Austro-Hungarian empire, were often targets for xenophobic ire in its successor polities. The upshot of the tense Paris negotiations was the creation of new states—Czechoslovakia, Yugoslavia, Estonia, Latvia—the resurrection of others—Poland and Lithuania—the ratification of the national status of shrunken or divided former empires—Germany, Austria, Hungary—and changed borders of still others. In theory, minority rights were supposed to be protected, but the mechanisms for doing so were minimal, and the major powers—France and Britain among them—exempted themselves from any such obligation, which made the entire system appear hypocritical to many in eastern Europe. Self-determination was supposed to turn a central Europe of empires into nation-states, equivalent in international law. But

Map 12.2
Europe in 1924.

states were not equivalent in ability to defend themselves or in ambition to dominate others.

The carving up of the Ottoman empire took a different form. The British government's attempts to harness Husayn ibn Ali's imperial ambitions to their cause continued after the war, when they tried to use him and his sons (the Hashemites) to build a new locus of authority in the vacuum created by the defeat of the Ottomans. The French and British each sought a sphere of influence in the Middle East without letting the other one get too much, while the Hashemites tried to assert authority for "Arab"—but really their own—rule over all the Arabian peninsula and Syria–Palestine, or over whatever piece of it they could get, and whatever the mixture of Muslims, Christians, and Jews in each area's population.

Opposed by the Saudi royal family, the Hashemites did not get far in Arabia. Husayn's son Faisal proclaimed himself king of Syria in 1920, only to have the French take it away. The British then gave him a different piece of turf, Mesopotamia, plus the old Ottoman provinces of Basra, Baghdad, and Mosul, cobbled together as Iraq, of which he became king in 1921. His brother Abdullah wanted a big domain but had to settle for a smaller one, Transjordan, while the British took a more direct hold on Palestine, uneasily assuming responsibility to make good on their 1917 promise to allow Jews to make a homeland there while safeguarding the rights of Muslim inhabitants in the same space.

This maneuvering was folded into a new principle of governance that emerged at the Paris peace conference of 1919. People—such as Arabs in Syria—who were held to have the potential for national identification would be administered by a European power, experienced in such things, until such time as that people was ready to choose its own form of government and

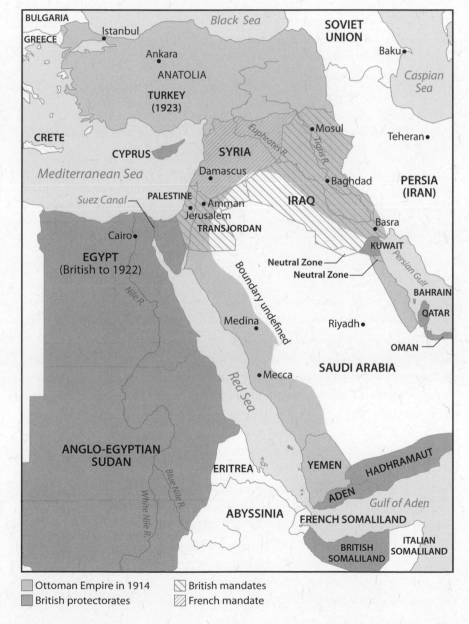

Map 12.3
Ottoman empire dismembered.

its own rulers. The "mandate" to govern such territories was to come from a vaguely conceived international community to be embodied in the new League of Nations, also a product of the peace conference. The mandate system entailed a view of global hierarchy expressed in earlier conferences at which self-defined "civilized" powers had asserted responsibilities for the uncivilized peoples in the territories they claimed (chapters 10 and 11).

The map of mandates was another imperial carve-up, corresponding neither to Ottoman provinces nor to putative ethnocultural divisions, dubious as the latter would have been. Syria was mandated to France (which later recognized Lebanon as a distinct portion of the Syrian mandate); Palestine, Jordan, and Iraq went to Britain, which remained the tutelary power as Abdullah and Faisal assumed kingships over territories whose relation to their persons was ambiguous at best. Britain and France tried to secure land rights and other assets to local leaders who were thought capable of enhancing social stability—at the risk of making those left out more vulnerable.

None of the postwar restructuring of the former Ottoman domains worked very well, even from the point of view of the mandatory powers. Rebellions against the new rulers broke out in Syria in 1920–21 and on a larger scale in 1925–26, and in Iraq starting in 1920. Palestine was tense over Jewish immigration and loss of land by Palestinians; extensive violence erupted in 1919, 1929, and especially after 1935. Crises were not limited to the mandate system. In Egypt, made a formal British protectorate in 1914, people had suffered great hardship during the war. In 1919, after the arrest of a major Egyptian political leader, a wave of strikes, peasant insurrections, and demonstrations began, involving Christians as well as Muslims, middle classes as well as the poor. British leaders feared an even wider revolt. Regaining control proved so difficult that the British decided to abandon the protectorate and exercise power from the background, as they had between 1882 and 1914.

As Britain tried to play off the rivalry between Egyptian nationalists and the Egyptian monarchy (the descendants of the khedive; see chapter 10), nationalists changed orientation. They shifted from a territorial focus—on an Egypt dating back to the pharaohs—to a supranational perspective, looking toward connections to other Arabs and other Muslims. By the 1930s, expanded education and urbanization produced a politicized population larger than the western-oriented elite that had dominated politics earlier. This public was more sensitive to the effects of colonialism in the Muslim world, more aware of anti–imperialist politics in other places, more affected by the large-scale immigration of Muslims from Palestine and Syria into Egypt, and more involved in Islamic organizations. Just how "Egyptian," "Islamic," and "Arab" the nation should be became a hotly debated question—in the context of continued British attempts to manipulate and control Egyptian governments and finances.

The toughest of negotiations at Paris and after concerned the victors' project of cutting the Ottoman heartlands down to national scale—or less. Greece and Italy wanted pieces of central Ottoman territory; there was talk of mandates—perhaps to the United States—over Armenia and of the internationalization of Istanbul. But the remnants of Ottoman military force—still a factor in Anatolia—raised the cost of such solutions higher than western Europeans wanted to pay. Turkey ended up a larger and more self-consciously national polity than its neighbors—or Britain and France—wanted it to be.

Despite the efforts of some Ottoman elites to foreground the idea of a Turkish nation before and during the war, this project did not have geographical coherence. To separate Greece and Turkey, and Greeks and Turks, required external imposition, a great deal of bloodshed, and moving people to correspond to imagined borders. Allied forces, mainly British, occupied Istanbul for a time after 1920. Greece invaded Anatolia in 1919, proclaiming not only that it acted in support of numerous Greek-speaking, Orthodox inhabitants of that region but that it stood for the "Great Idea" of a "old and advanced civilization" that could legitimately exercise authority over Turks who had proven themselves bad rulers and a "disgrace to civilization."

Led by Mustapha Kemal, the Ottoman army, now de facto Turkish, defeated the Greek invasion by 1922. Neither France nor Britain had been willing to intervene decisively, and the Russians were fighting their own civil wars. The settlement that followed defined a territory that would become the state of Turkey, but only after the coerced relocation of approximately 900,000 "Greeks" from Anatolia to Greece and of around 400,000 "Turks" to Turkey. The Armenian massacres had already made Turkey more Turkish, but the presence of a large number of Kurds inside the eventual frontiers continues to this day. In this ambiguous context Mustapha Kemal, later known as Ataturk, emerged as the maker of a Turkish nation-state, whose capital would no longer be Istanbul, the cosmopolitan center of two historic empires dating to the fourth century CE, but the Anatolian town of Ankara.

The devastation of this region was enormous, the result of ten years of fighting, before, during, and after the world war. In Anatolia, the death toll was 2.5 million Muslims, 800,000 Armenians, and 300,000 Greeks (to use conventional categories). These deaths reduced the Anatolian population by around 20 percent—more devastating losses than those of France—and the forced migrations added another layer of suffering. This vast unmixing of people was remembered long after as nation-building.

That Britain and France could not shape Turkey as they wished was part of their broader failure to provide the level of stability that the Ottoman empire had offered earlier. In the Arab provinces, the mandatory powers furnished little basis for democratic evolution, or even an order free from political violence.

In Africa and parts of Asia and the Pacific, colonies were redistributed among victorious empires, much as territories had been after the Seven Years' War of the eighteenth century and the Napoleonic wars of the early nineteenth. German colonies went to France, Britain, Belgium, Japan, and the self-governing dominions of Australia, New Zealand, and South Africa. These mandates were of a lower "class" than those of the ex–Ottoman empire, corresponding to European notions of the backwardness of Africans and Pacific Islanders. In theory, the mandatory power, rather than being sovereign in international law, was the trustee of a nationality in formation and under the supervision of the League of Nations. In practice, France, Britain, and others did what they thought they knew how to do: rule the acquired territories as colonies.

The Paris conference of 1919 (and the treaty signed in Versailles, by which it is generally known) was another episode in a sequence of interempire conferences going back to the Congress of Vienna of 1815. The 1919 conference differed in that new voices were present, even if they were not listened to—national groups within Europe, a non-European imperial power, Japan, and to a more limited extent Arabs, Jews, and others seeking political recognition. The institutions devised in Paris were too weak to enforce national borders in Europe or undertake the disinterested administration of mandated territories, but they were not entirely exercises in hypocrisy. The Treaty of Versailles posited a notion of responsibility before international bodies and provided for a—such as required reports on mandated territories and regular meetings of a mandates commission—in which the administration of "dependent people" became a subject that could be debated. People from mandates sent numerous petitions to the commission, but usually their requests were discussed in their absence.

Institutions connected to the League of Nations, like the International Labour Organisation, also provided sites to take up issues like forced labor in the colonies. The mandates and the League injected new subtleties into notions of sovereignty and expanded ideas of the responsibility of "civilized" powers developed at earlier conferences. Only in retrospect do these changes appear as steps toward the dissolution of empires: in their own time, they added to the territories of some empires—a million square miles to the British empire alone—enforced the legitimacy of administering "dependent" peoples, and reaffirmed that not all polities were equivalent in international law and practice.

Political activists in the colonies could not but notice the gap between the talk of self-determination in Paris and continued denial of political voice in the European empires overseas. They could read into Wilsonianism a universal liberating agenda Wilson never intended. Meanwhile, the racial dimension of colonialism was challenged by, among others, an imperial power, Japan, which tried to get a clause condemning racism written into the Versailles agreement. France, Britain, and the United States, whose policies at home and in colonies would hardly have met such an international standard, kept the clause out of the treaty.

After raising hopes in the colonized world, the peace process looked to many like an imperialist conspiracy: a small coterie of white men, as in the Berlin conference of 1884–85, sitting around a table, carving up the world, and keeping the lid on the aspirations of colonized people. Even before the war, imperial connections had brought African and Asian students to London and Paris; improved communications had made activists from China, the Middle East, Africa, and the West Indies aware of each other. Anger at the decisions taken in Paris—the handing over of German territories in China to Japan and the failure to apply self-determination to Korea—produced massive demonstrations in Korea and China in 1919. Pan-Africanists held a parallel meeting in Paris in 1919 that the peace conference ignored.

Rebellions in mandates like Syria and Iraq and political mobilization in India, Indonesia, and elsewhere continued into the 1920s. "Pan" movements—pan-Slavic, pan-African, pan-Arab—continued to make their voices known in the 1920s, sometimes in favor of a territorial concept of nationality, often expressing notions of affinity across space with only vague associations with state institutions. Where this ferment was leading was far from clear. Kemal's Turkey after 1924 took a strong turn toward nation-building and away from wider anti-imperial connections. The USSR tried to channel anticolonial movements into a wider communist front by sponsoring a large meeting at Baku in 1920 and then setting up a coordinating organization directed from Moscow, the Comintern. Despite agitation in Syria, Iraq, and Egypt, a coherent pan-Arab front did not emerge. Pan-Africanists found it difficult to carry their movement beyond the circuits of elites connecting London, Paris, Moscow, and colonial capitals. Colonial governments did their best to stuff politics back into ethnic containers, and they had enough resources in patronage and coercion to have some success.

Sovereignty took many forms in the twentieth-century world. The recognized sovereignty of Britain and France permitted them to enforce a much diminished sovereignty on a protectorate like Morocco or to intrude on independent Egypt or mandated Iraq, while sustaining shared sovereignty in the British Commonwealth, denying self-determination altogether in India or Africa, and maintaining that Martinique and Algeria were integral parts of France. Empires continued to govern different people differently. When in 1935 the League failed to act against the invasion of Ethiopia by Italy, it revealed that respect for the sovereignty of an aggressive European empire overrode respect for an African kingdom. That cracks in the edifice of empire would open wider was not yet evident in the decades after World War I.

Japan, China, and the Changing Imperial Order of East Asia

Japan's ambiguous position at the entrance to, but not inside, the door of the imperial club was recognized by its receiving at Versailles the modest-sized piece of China once controlled by Germany (Jiaozhou)—much to the humiliation and anger of the fledgling republican government of China and its supporters. A riot that began among students in Beijing in May 1919 and spread to other cities and social groups precipitated the radicalization of Chinese political activists in the "May Fourth Movement." But neither this protest nor the demands for self-determination coming from Korea in 1919 influenced the imperial powers. Japan responded to the massive demonstration of discontent in Korea by trying to co-opt Korean economic elites into closer relation with Japanese settler-businessmen, allowing carefully constrained Korean participation in associations, and simultaneously keeping a firm grip on its colony. The war had immensely strengthened Japan, for while formally allying with Britain and France, it had seen only minor fighting in German territory in China while supplying war materiel to the Allies. Japan boosted its industrial capacity (up 76 percent from 1913 to 1920), wiped out its foreign debt, and made itself into the economic powerhouse of eastern Asia.

All this was a sign that the imperial map—apparently centered on Europe for the past century—needed some touching up if not reorientation. China had always been too much for western imperialists to take on directly, but before the war Britain, France, Germany, and the United States had undermined the autonomy of the Chinese state and hence the legitimacy of the regime (chapter 10). Qing efforts to repress rebellions had devastated the state's finances and made it more reliant on provincial leaders who raised armies to defend the empire. Attempts at reform had offered more opportunities for autonomous action than the regime intended to governors, advisors, and political activists in provincial assemblies.

The volatility of politics in China before the world war had been affected in multiple ways by connections beyond its borders: the diaspora of Chinese merchants and workers who provided financial support to dissidents; networks established by well-traveled activists like Sun Yat-sen; grievances of Chinese in the United States against prejudices and mistreatment encountered there; awareness that the crisis in China was part of worldwide imperialist aggression; exasperation with the Qing elite for failing to protect China from foreigners. The Manchus' foreign origins became a focus of attack; activists could represent the Manchus as colonizers, the Chinese as victims of Manchu as well as European imperialism. Sun Yat-sen articulated an alternative to the Qing empire that drew on ideals of republican government and a vision of a Chinese nation—including overseas migrants—liberated from its Manchu emperors.

As Qing attempts to reform and repress failed, leaders of provincial assemblies and elements in the military increasingly supported demands for a parliament and a constitution and refused to follow orders of the Qing rulers. When a series of revolts broke out in 1911, Sun Yat-sen, with provisional support from military commanders and the provinces, was in a position to proclaim a Chinese republic on January 1, 1912. The last Qing emperor, Puyi, abdicated.

The republic was not able to become an effective national entity, either before or after World War I. It was stymied by the same kinds of problems other centralizers had faced—by the relative autonomy achieved by provincial governments, by warlords who had acquired armies and considerable power in the waning years of the Qing, and by the corruption of much of its leadership. But if uniting China after the fall of a dynasty was not an easy task, the borders and the multiethnic symbolism of the Qing empire continued to shape political imagination. The republic declared its jurisdiction over the "five peoples" of China—Manchu, Han, Mongol, Muslim, and Tibetan—and even those who contested the government's authority rarely sought the dismemberment of "China."

Alliances as usual were one strategy to keep or attain control. To subdue warlords' centrifugal powers, the nationalist party, the Guomindang, at times cooperated with a budding communist movement. (The USSR supported both nationalists and communists in its own interests.) In 1927, the nationalists broke the alliance, almost crushed the communists in the cities, but left the task of unification unfinished. The communist movement had to hunker down on the northern frontier. As in the past, this edge of China became a site where people seeking to take over the state could consolidate and mobilize.

Promises Unfulfilled

Within the European empires, the war left many claims unmet. The British dominions had seen the king declare war on their behalf in 1914, but they were now in a position to address the ambiguities of sovereignty and make explicit the extent of their autonomy. The term "commonwealth" had been around since 1868, without its meaning being specified. Wartime conferences of British and dominion governments issued documents with reference to the "autonomous nations of an Imperial Commonwealth" or more simply the "British Commonwealth of Nations." The Commonwealth was described variously as multinational, imperial, and British. Dominions were simultaneously *within* the British empire and *members* of the Commonwealth with equal status to that of Great Britain. This terminology separated the dominions from colonies while insisting that they were all part of the same polity. After another imperial conference in 1926 and a royal proclamation in 1931, the dominions established a higher degree of sovereignty without extinguishing that of Britain. But another question was left wide open: how much sovereignty would be shared when other parts of the empire, whose majority populations were not kith and kin of the people of the British isles, became self-governing?

That issue was not to be resolved any time soon. Meanwhile, the conflictual relationship of the British empire to nearby Ireland, with its Catholic majority, had entered a bloody new phase. In 1916, Irish nationalists had declared the creation of the Republic of Ireland and launched a violent revolt that turned into war with Britain and a civil war among Irish factions. British leaders thought of applying "Indian" methods to Ireland, but violent repression was not getting a good press in India. Confronting the fact that Ireland had become ungovernable, Britain negotiated. The north with its Protestant majority was partitioned off from the Catholic south, where in 1922 the Irish Free State was created. Violent disagreements in the south over the minimal trappings of sovereignty that Britain asserted were resolved—if this is the word—only in 1949 by Ireland's withdrawal from the Commonwealth and the proclamation—this time to general recognition—of the Republic of Ireland. The relationship of south to north of the island and to Britain remains to this day unsettled—a testament to how unclear and conflict-ridden territorial sovereignty can be.

Although Indians had contributed massively to the defense of the British empire in World War I, their expectations of acquiring the rights of citizens in a democratic empire were soon frustrated. Promises of a measure of self-government were stalled and diluted. The India National Congress tried to maintain pressure on the British. At a demonstration at Amritsar in 1919—illegal but peaceful—British troops shot to death at least 379 Indians, wounding 1,200 more. The massacre became a rallying point for Indian opposition and allowed Gandhi to consolidate his leadership.

Many Muslim Indians were angered by the dismemberment of the Ottoman empire, whose sultan—however remote from India—possessed the aura of a caliph and hence enjoyed a legitimacy going back to the generation after Muhammad. The "Khilfat" movement called for restoration of the caliphate, a desire that cut across different empires. Hindus cooperated with Muslims in nonviolent protest, tying specifically national goals to a critique of imperialism. Such cooperation contributed to the rise of the "All India" movement led by Gandhi. Britain was neither able to return to a politics of working through its chosen intermediaries across India nor willing to concede real power at the center. Officials and a few Indian politicians put forth proposals for variations on a federal structure, with decentralized governmental institutions, legislative seats assigned to Muslims, princes, and other categories, and a weak center, but Congress was clearly focused on India as its goal, and regional politicians, including the rulers of princely states, were too insecure in their power bases to make federalism an acceptable alternative.

In parts of Africa, an implicit imperial bargain was also broken by ruling powers. Returning soldiers did not receive the pensions, jobs, or recognition that their service alongside other imperial subjects was supposed to have earned. In Senegal, the language of citizenship expressed these claims on the state, and Blaise Diagne drew on such sentiments to build a political machine in Senegal among citizen constituents. The French government's response was on the one hand to try, with success, to co-opt Diagne, and on the other to distance itself from the citizenship ideal. Instead of celebrating its own role in "civilizing" Africans and educating an elite, France put the accent on the traditional character of African society and the central place of chiefs. In British Africa, the policy of working through chiefs and pushing for incremental change within the framework of African "tribes" was raised in the 1920s to the status of an imperial doctrine—"indirect rule."

Both the French and British governments considered economic policies that went under the name of "development" (or *mise-en-valeur*, as the French called it), but they rejected any systematic program in that direction. They refused to break with an old colonial principle that metropolitan funds should not be used to improve conditions in colonies, both because they did not want to spend the money and because they feared disrupting the delicate arrangements by which colonies functioned.

The decentralized nature of colonial rule in Africa made it difficult for political activists to transcend local idioms and local networks as they had in India, where the Indian Civil Service, the Indian railways, and other pan-Indian institutions provided unifying structures (chapter 10). There were political flare-ups in places like Kenya, Senegal, and the Gold Coast (map 13.2), but for a time, colonial regimes in Africa managed to stuff the genie of imperial citizenship—which they themselves had called up in the Great War—back into the bottle of colonial administration.

But the ferment within the world of empires did not let up. The massacre at Amritsar and its aftermath, the revolt in Ireland, and riots and rebellions in Palestine, Syria, and Iraq raised the ante. Petitions and calls for constitutional reform kept coming out of many colonies. These demands were finding receptive audiences in Europe itself, in communist parties, in religious and humanitarian circles, among intellectuals with sympathy for African or Asian cultures, and in the circuits of activists from all corners of empire who met each other in imperial capitals like London and Paris.

Some officials realized that protests, strikes, riots, and other "disturbances" during the 1930s were not just local events but signaled empire-wide problems, especially after a wave of strikes across the British West Indies in 1935–38 and in several cities and mine towns in Africa between 1935 and 1940. In 1940, the British government decided to use metropolitan funds for "development and welfare" programs intended to improve social services for colonial workers and foster long-term growth with the explicit goal of improving the standard of living of people in the colonies. The Indian National Congress pressured Britain to adopt a development policy for India. But only after World War II did significant funds to finance improvements start to flow (chapter 13).

In the two decades after World War I, rebellions and political demands in the colonies were contained. But one example from the 1920s reveals the violence and limitations of twentieth-century imperialism. Rebellious villagers and nomads in Mesopotamia, incorporated into the mandated territory of Iraq, were fought with bombs dropped from the sky, as British leaders—including future prime minister Winston Churchill—promoted a mystique of air power against colonial rebels. Air power meant, in effect, terror. Terror was the hidden face of empire, kept in the background when states were capable of providing routine administration and cultivating intermediaries, as they had tried to do for most of their histories, or when—in more recent times—they attempted to establish something like the rule of law, integrate subsistence cultivators into markets, and provide access to health care, education, and other services. The terror bombing also reflected a British presumption that Iraqi Arabs would bow to might but not to reason. Dropping bombs on Iraqi villagers was an implicit acknowledgment of the limited ability of an imperial power to govern.

If the empires of France and Britain could push their victory in World War I down the throats of Germans, Ottomans, and Austro-Hungarians, it stuck in their own. European confidence in itself as the engine of global progress came face-to-face with twenty million dead. France and Britain, among others, were in debt, worried about the increasing wealth and influence of the United States—whose insistence on full repayment of loans did not assist allies in cooperating on economic matters or Germany in reintegrating itself into Europe.

"Our government is worse than the old Turkish system. . . . We keep ninety thousand men, with aeroplanes, armoured cars, gunboats, and armoured trains. We have killed about ten thousand Arabs in this rising this summer. We cannot hope to maintain such an average; it is a poor country, sparsely peopled."

—T. E. Lawrence, *Sunday Times*, summer 1920, writing on British repression of the Iraqi revolt

Western leaders worried as well about the revolutionary alternative in the USSR. They feared that political initiatives in the colonies might resonate with an international rhetoric of self-determination—however hypocritical—or with more radical kinds of anti-imperialism. European governments had called on colonial subjects to act as if inclusion in an empire was something in which they should believe, and then refused to convey the citizenship rights that Indians and Africans felt they had earned. The war had shaken the world of empires; the peace had added new complications to the meanings of sovereignty and created even more dangerous asymmetries of power. The great war of the twentieth century was not over yet.

New Empires, Old Empires, and the Road to World War II

Three new actors asserted themselves within the rivalries and alliances that developed after World War I. The USSR defined itself against capitalism; Japan against the empires of the west; and Nazi Germany against everyone not German.

A Multinational Communist State

The appearance of a state that claimed to represent a new world order was an unexpected outcome of the war. The Bolshevik revolution in Russia was only the beginning, its leaders proclaimed, of the seizure of power around the globe by proletarians and exploited peasants. A classless society was to emerge from a class-based revolution and bring about the end of the bourgeoisie, of colonies, of empires, of all states organized in hierarchical ways.

Elements of this radical egalitarian vision had appeared during the politically turbulent nineteenth century in the writings of Marx, Engels, and other socialists and in attempted revolutions in Europe in 1848 and 1871. By the beginning of the twentieth century, many socialists were active in party politics and labor organizations, but most—including Lenin before 1917—believed that revolution lay in the distant future, after an extensive period of capitalist development and expansion of democracy. Typical of Lenin's disdain for anyone less radical than himself, he had not foreseen that his enemies, Russian liberals and other moderates, would take down the autocracy in the middle of a war.

The outbreak of World War I had not called the Russian empire into question. On the contrary, the war produced an outburst of patriotic sentiment in parades, cartoons, postcards, plays, and films. The popularity of this propaganda, much of it based on nationalized stereotypes of Germans and caricatures of enemy emperors, had a destabilizing effect on Russia's imperial inclusiveness. In Moscow in May 1915, mobs broke into enterprises owned by Germans, seized property, assaulted and even killed Germans in the street. Pogroms against Germans and Jews—at a time when the empire needed its industrialists and entrepreneurs more than ever—as well as forced sales of property held by "enemies," expulsion of people deemed unreliable from the border areas, and streams of war refugees exposed the state to attack for both injustice and incompetence. In Turkestan, attempts to conscript Kazakh and Kyrgyz men unleashed a violent rebellion. Kyrgyz nomads wanted to call a kuriltai, but before this happened they were crushed with great brutality.

In February 1917, liberals with their allies in the Russian Duma agreed that the dynasty had to go. The liberal party played the nationality card against the emperor and his German wife, the unpopular Alexandra, accusing the regime of treason. After a few days of strikes and demonstrations, the tsar was persuaded to abdicate. Liberals and moderate socialists set up a "Provisional Government." The Romanov dynasty and its kind of Russian empire were over.

The liberals now had their chance to reconstruct Russia on their principles of unitary citizenship, equal civil rights, and electoral democracy, but they were not the only people ready to replace the tsar. The abolition of the old regime opened a free-for-all—of ideas, of organizations, of force—for control of a new state and the making of its institutions. Muslims, Finns, Ukrainians, and others took the chance to demand more autonomy in the reorganized polity, while liberals remained fixated on centralized control. Germany saw an opportunity and behaved as empires had before—helping out the people whom they regarded as most likely to undermine the power of an enemy. With German aid, Lenin was able to travel in April 1917 from his exile in neutral Switzerland across Germany to neutral Sweden, then into Russia.

When Lenin arrived in Petrograd (renamed to be more Slavic than the German Petersburg), he announced his plan for taking power in the name of the "soviets"—councils of workers and socialist activists—that contested the powers of the Provisional Government. In October 1917, Lenin's Bolshevik Party overthrew the Provisional Government; in January 1918, the party dismissed the elected Constituent Assembly. The Bolsheviks withdrew from the world war in March 1918 by drawing up a separate peace (the Treaty of Brest-Litovsk) with Germany, ceding a huge terrain to the former enemy (map 12.1). In July 1918, Bolshevik leaders arranged for the execution of the entire imperial family. Both inside the much-reduced Russia and beyond its borders, the struggle for the state turned into years of war and devastation.

The imperatives of empire confronted the Bolsheviks as they strove to regain control over peoples and territories torn up by violent conflicts among communists, liberals, socialists, nationalists, conservatives, anarchists, and the armies they could muster. During the civil war, states—new, old, always with contested borders—appeared on the terrain of the former empire. Poland, Belarus, Finland, Lithuania, Latvia, Estonia, Ukraine, Armenia, Georgia, and Azerbaijan declared their independence. In Siberia and central Asia, Muslim and other activists laid claim to state power. The Bolsheviks recovered as many of these areas as they could through military campaigns and party domination of "soviet" administrations or both. To the west, the Bolsheviks fought Poland in 1920. This war had been intended to trigger revolution throughout Europe, but the Poles' victory set a western boundary to the Bolshevik state. Much of the terrain Russia had gained in the eighteenth century was lost to a reconfigured and independent Poland (see map 12.2).

The Bolshevik state that emerged from years of world war, revolution, near anarchy, civil and international war, and famine was based on a new combination of political principles. Power was to be exercised in the interests of the working class; private property was to be abolished; the state would own the means of production. Government would be a dictatorship of the proletariat. The Bolsheviks' negative experience of multiparty politics, as well as patrimonial attitudes nurtured in Russia's imperial past and the virulence of the civil war, were expressed in the new system of command, based on one-party rule, autocratic centralism, and deference to a single leader, advised by a council of loyalists.

The experience of empire and its discontents inclined Bolsheviks and their advisors to accommodate national particularities. Over several years, the Bolsheviks produced an innovative answer to the tensions between centralization and difference and to the problem of finding loyal intermediaries. Their solution was a new kind of federated state, composed of "national republics" linked to the center by a single party, whose members occupied key positions in administrative matters and who took their directions from the party leadership in the capital.

The Union of Soviet Socialist Republics was an empire by communist means. Each national republic had its own ladder of offices, but the party provided the means of climbing. But what kind of differences would constitute a nationality in a polity that, as in the past, contained so many different peoples? Ethnographers and economic specialists disagreed about how to draw the map of "nationalities" across the empire—on whether ethnicity or degree of development should matter more.

In the 1920s and 1930s, Soviet specialists and administrators continued to tinker with the problem of aligning land with people. A general principle emerged—nesting national groups inside the republics on territories in which these groups could have majorities. In 1922, the Soviet Union was

Map 12.4
The USSR in
1930 and 1945.

made up of six highly unequal "republics"—the Russian Soviet Federal Socialist Republic, the Ukrainian Soviet Socialist Republic, the Belarusian Soviet Socialist Republic, the Transcaucasian Soviet Federal Socialist Republic, the Khorezm People's Soviet Republic, and the Bukharan People's Soviet Republic. Inside the Russian Federal Republic were eight Autonomous Soviet Socialist Republics and thirteen "Autonomous Regions"; similar hierarchies were found in the other republics. The boundaries and levels of such units were adjusted many times over the next decades, but the principle of national representation remained a staple of Soviet politics and governance.

The USSR also acted in an imperial mode—a new one—in external matters. Uninvited to the peace conference in 1918—when it was not clear who was in charge in Russia—the Bolsheviks took the lead in establishing their own international alliance system based on revolutionary politics, not states. In 1919, the Communist International (Comintern) was convened in Moscow, intended to replace the Socialist International that had linked socialist parties before the war with a new alliance of communist activists and their followers. Although communist revolutions had been defeated in Germany (1918) and Hungary (1919), the Bolsheviks worked to build parties loyal to Moscow and to destroy moderate social democrats, both inside Russia and abroad. The second Comintern congress in 1920 resolved that its members should follow the Soviet position on party tactics and pronouncements.

The reconfiguration of sovereignty and world politics after the war produced a pragmatic arrangement between Germany and Bolshevik Russia—a trade agreement, mutual renunciation of debts, German technical assistance for the USSR in exchange for German use of Russian territory for military training exercises. Trade between the Soviet Union and Germany continued throughout the 1930s. In August 1939, the German-Russian relationship, to the surprise of many, took its most imperial form in the pact between Hitler and Stalin. Russia would continue to provide Germany with raw materials in return for German machines and weaponry; the two sides agreed not to attack each other; and in a secret protocol, they divided east-central Europe between themselves. Russia aimed at recovering Finland and other territories it had lost in the world war. Poland was to be split again, this time between two powers. The pact meant that when Germany invaded Poland on September 1, 1939, and Great Britain and France declared war on Germany, the USSR sided with the Nazis against the "bourgeois" empires and sent the Red Army into Poland from the other side.

What kind of empire had the Soviets introduced to the uneasy world? The one-party state would have a profound influence inside and beyond the Soviet Union. In each unit of the federation, the position of party leader at the apex of pyramids of party organizations facilitated personal and patrimonial relations between leaders and subordinates. Now that the nobility was gone, the bourgeoisie expropriated, and the professions controlled by the state, it was the party network that drew people into systems that sustained the workings of the polity. A place in the party was made available to people, not regardless of ethnicity but because of it. Educational institutions set quotas for different regions to ensure that party cadres would be trained in each of them. The party created the empire's intermediaries—giving new elites from the multiple nationalities a stake in the polity.

At the same time, the Soviet Union was dedicated to equality and civilizational uplift. In the 1920s, the Bolsheviks took up tsarist precedents of teaching people in their native languages and provided alphabets to groups who did not have them. One element of nativeness was not to be encouraged—religion. The Bolsheviks, unlike their predecessors, were determined to subvert religious authority and to treat religious belief as backward. The major enemy in this regard was Russian Orthodoxy, with its appeal to Russian peasants and converted native peoples. Bolshevik leaders in the 1920s and early 1930s encouraged the use of the Latin alphabet, instead of the Cyrillic one used by tsarist missionaries to record native languages in the far north and along the Volga. As part of a campaign against Islam, Bolsheviks tried to make Turkic peoples in the Caucasus and central Asia switch from Arabic to Latin script. Although secularism was attractive to modernizing activists, campaigns against "superstition" and practiced difference, such as veiling in some Muslim areas, alienated many who wanted to maintain their faiths.

The policy of national recognition and incorporation of "native" elites could be manipulated. Having used the Communist Party's centralizing structures and its monopoly on politics to make his way to dictatorial power, Stalin purged potentially influential national leaders in the 1930s. He forced collectivization of peasant agriculture through executions, deportations, expropriation, and starvation, conducted with particular thoroughness in Ukraine.

These brutal policies, as well as the massive use of forced labor in prison camps, were part of a campaign to promote state-managed industrialization. War, revolution, and communist control had put an end to Russia's economic expansion: Russia's foreign trade after 1932 was only one-fifth of its value in 1913.

Industrializing by command was legitimated by the state's claim to manage all property and resources, including human ones, in the interests of the working-class dictatorship, but it required ruthless control over the system's intermediaries—party bosses, prison camp directors, factory managers, army commanders, police interrogators—and cutting off the networks of international information that had proved so disruptive to Russia in the past. Stalin unleashed waves of terror—arrests, executions, spectacular show trials, destruction of families—to eradicate potential challengers in all institutions, to sever foreign ties, and to ensure that survivors knew the price of disloyalty. One casualty was the officer corps; in the 1930s over a third of Soviet military officers, including three of the five top marshals, were shot or sent to labor camps. When Hitler decided to attack the Soviet Union, the Red Army was led by subservient officers who presented no challenges to Stalin's leadership. This was patrimonialism carried to a nearly suicidal degree.

The Third Reich and the Empire of the Rising Sun

Japan and Germany were empires in both name and practice. Yet they had their own—radical—ways of configuring the relationship of empire and nation. Like the USSR, Germany and Japan both wanted to transform, if not turn upside down, the global arrangements of power.

Germany in the 1930s, vulnerable to pincer movements from all sides, faced the same geostrategic challenges that had inspired its defensive-aggressive posture in World War I. But now it had been stripped of its non-German-speaking territories in Europe and overseas colonies. Germany had no oil—found in Romania and the USSR—and lacked other essential resources. In the minds of many, it needed "Lebensraum"—space in which ambitious people could make their fortune. The numerous German-speakers now in Czechoslovakia, Poland, and other places once part of multinational empires with German-speaking emperors found themselves minorities in what they thought of as someone else's state. In a shrunken Germany, many people were susceptible to the argument that to recover its former stature Germany needed an even more thoroughgoing approach than the plan it had attempted in World War I.

The geostrategic situation of Japan was different: one neighbor, China, was a fallen empire with exploitable terrain. Here, Japan had advantages over other intruding parties through proximity and prior connections. But other nearby regions—upon which Japan depended for raw materials— were controlled by European empires. Japan worried about the imperial ambitions of the United States, whose overseas outposts in the Philippines, Hawaii, and other Pacific islands pointed directly at Japan's zone of potential expansion. Japan's imperial ventures in Korea, Taiwan, and Manchuria opened up vistas for further empire-building. Japan had the means to secure access to resources, and it would be vulnerable if it did not.

Both Germany and Japan looked back to an imperial past. The Nazis claimed to be the Third Reich (a phrase first used in the 1920s by advocates of a unified and powerful Germany), evoking a line of succession going back to the Holy Roman Empire, renewed by the Kaiserreich in the 1870s. The figure of the emperor in Japan—for all the dynastic changes and transformations of politics since the nineteenth century—also pointed to a heroic history. But Japan and Germany projected different visions of their intended polities. Nazi imperialism took the ideological distinction between Germans and others to a racist extreme; Japanese imperialism invoked Japan's role as the vanguard of a pan-Asian racial destiny. If Japan's military was nonetheless capable of treating cruelly the very people whose destiny it claimed to advance, Nazi racial logic offered Poles, Ukrainians, and Russians—let alone Jews—little more than servitude or extermination. Nazi empire left no room for advancement, assimilation, or redemption to non-German peoples.

The German military and part of its populace had begun the quest for scapegoats as expectations of triumph turned to disaster in World War I. The peace brought both humiliation and material hardship; the Depression brought more misery and a sense of powerlessness. It was in this context that advocates of a purified Germany could do their work. Striking out against the cosmopolitan culture that had flourished in prewar Germany, rejecting the balancing games by which imperial rulers of the recent past—including the German-speaking Habsburgs—had governed differentiated subjects, and heaping contempt on international law, Nazi ideologues moved toward a conception of the Reich as German domination over inferior races.

Nazi racism lies at an extreme along the spectrum of imperial politics of difference; its emergence has given rise to charged debates. Is Nazi racism colonialism come home—the dehumanization of indigenous peoples turned onto European Jews? Why was genocide a policy of Nazi Germany and not imperial France or Britain, when neither anti-semitism—think of the Dreyfus affair in France—nor colonial racism was a specifically German phenomenon? Whether the atrocities of Germans against the Herero in Southwest Africa were worse than those of Leopold of Belgium in the Congo or the murderous excesses of other colonial campaigns is a question of dubious utility. Drawing a straight line between the atrocities of Germans in Africa and those committed in Europe misses the shifting circumstances and political and moral choices made all along the way and does not answer a historical puzzle: why was genocide committed by the one European power that had once possessed but lost its extra-European colonies?

Ruling real Africans or real Asians did not make French or British rulers more sensitive or humane, but the experience of rule forced administrators to be more realistic about the limits of their own power, as had been the case with Germans in east Africa before World War I (chapter 10). Rulers of actual empires had to worry about the cooperation of intermediate authorities, about conditions conducive to production. Germans after World War I were free to develop a fantasy of a pure people exercising pure power.

Britain and France did not respond effectively to the early stages of Nazi empire-building. They had sunk in the Depression into increasingly narrow, neo-mercantilist policies, using "imperial preference" to try to insulate themselves from the crisis in world markets. This falling back upon empire—and the cost of rearmament—contributed to their immobility in the late 1930s. Some political leaders hoped to play Nazis off against communists, making mobilization against the Nazis more difficult politically. But in the end, Britain and France would find resources in their empires for the struggle with their enemies.

Japan, even more than Germany, was a late industrializer and a late imperialist. In the 1930s Japan focused on China, starting with its zone of influence in Manchuria. The army manufactured an incident in 1931 as a pretext for direct military intervention. The Japanese installed the ex-emperor Puyi—still dreaming of a Manchu restoration—and called the territory Manchukuo, "land of the Manchus." The symbols of China's imperial past were still worth using, but the reality was Japanese control.

At home, the power of the emperor and the military-minded men around him was by no means uncontested. For all of Japan's success in forging an industrial economy, an effective state bureaucracy, and a powerful military, there was much disagreement in the 1920s over how Japanese society should manage its own dynamism. Some tried to define a Marxist alternative; oth-

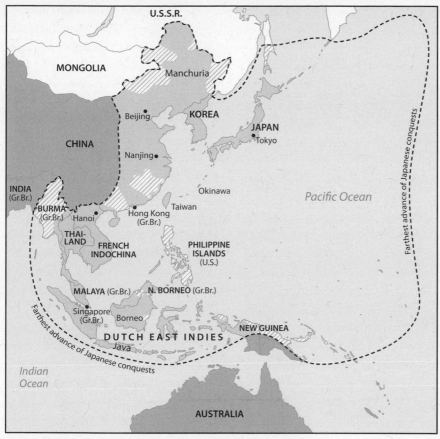

Map 12.5
East and
southeast Asia
in World War II.

ers promoted cultural projects, either aspirations to a "modern" life associated with new consumer goods and culture imported from the west or an essentialized Japanese civilization, reinforced by Japan's increasing wealth and power.

By the early 1930s—with the Depression exacerbating tension—Japan's military acquired preponderant power within the government, and the nationalist vision came to the fore. Mass media, home front support organizations, academic institutions, and economic planning units were adapted to a coherent empire-building project. Manchukuo was defined as Japan's "lifeline."

More than European colonizers in their overseas territories, Japan vigorously promoted industrialization and agricultural development in Manchukuo. Japan's developmentalist, pan-Asianist mission later took the name of the Greater East Asia Co-Prosperity Sphere. Some Chinese and Koreans found opportunities in serving the Japanese military and in Manchukuo's industrial and agricultural economy, albeit in the shadow of Japanese settlers. That colonized as well as colonizer were Asian was emphasized again and again by Japanese ethnographers and other intellectuals as well as propagandists, but the vision of racial brotherhood was a hierarchical one. Japan was the elder brother, China the younger.

If such claims had a measure of plausibility in Manchukuo, Japan's attacks on China in 1937 revealed a viciousness comparable to other colonizations: the rapid takeover of much of the seaboard, by what Japanese themselves called "annihilation campaigns," pillage of resources, and brutalization of populations. The "rape of Nanjing," a seven-week wave of looting, rape, and murder following the capture of the city, was the most notorious of such actions. Japan's invasion of China produced cries of protest from Europe and the United States, but there was little they could do to stop it. The world of empires was about to change.

Stagnation and Stirrings in the Colonial Empires

While Germany and Japan were developing their new empires in the 1930s, their eventual opponents—the Netherlands, Belgium, France, and Britain—were managing, albeit with difficulty, to maintain authority in their colonies. But colonial empire was facing new challenges.

Conventional studies of "resistance and collaboration" in colonial regimes fail to get at the variety of ways in which people tried to carve out space for maneuver within as well as against colonial regimes. The line between a subversive and a useful producer could be a fine one. Colonial economies created opportunities for some people—but not others—exacerbating generational, gender, class, and other tensions. Colonial politics, with its emphasis on working through intermediaries, encouraged regional, ethnic, and religious fragmentation.

With diminished export revenue during the Depression, governments put pressure on intermediaries to maintain tax collection and provided even fewer services than before. In Africa, much of the hardship was diffused into rural communities, but in India, decline in standard of living was experienced as a national and imperial problem.

Hardship and division fostered anger and contention, but not necessarily coherence in opposition movements. Not for want of trying. By the 1930s, a variety of political movements, not just local, not just national, had come into being. Circuits of colonial intellectuals around European capitals produced the opposite effect of policies of "native administration." Ho Chi Minh went from Vietnam to Paris, where he met up with people from all over the empire and with French communists. He moved on to Moscow and China, becoming a leading figure in a transempire movement. Many north Africans found jobs in France, joined communist unions, and took their politics back to Algeria or Morocco. West Indians and Africans met in London or in Paris and elaborated critiques of colonialism and racism, as well as ideas of racial and diasporic affinity. These interempire connections conditioned the growth of communist parties as well as other movements—such as pan-Africanism and négritude—in different colonies.

Anticolonial networks faced serious obstacles, starting with police repression and lack of funds and organizational experience. The USSR was a fickle sponsor, supporting anticolonial movements at one point, leaving them in the lurch when it backed popular fronts against fascism in European countries in the 1930s, shifting again with the Nazi-Soviet pact and once more when the Nazis invaded Russia. Some participants in communist internationalism—such as George Padmore of Trinidad—left in disgust and sought alternative forms of mobilization, such as pan-Africanism. Regardless of their relationship to the USSR, leftist movements all faced the problem of actually connecting with the "masses"; leaders' linkages were often more international than local.

National movements made the most rapid progress in south and southeast Asia. The Indian National Congress had conducted several campaigns by the 1930s and was poised to claim cabinet-level participation in the government of India. Congress was able to stitch together support across the diverse classes, regions, and religions of India through campaigns of civil disobedience, tax resistance, and boycotts of imported goods. The symbolic power of Gandhi's demonstrations of self-sacrifice captivated a national imaginary. Although Gandhi, with a strong appeal to the upper and middle classes, feared that the demands of the poor would have a divisive effect on his movement, he was able to manage such tensions. In the provincial elections of 1937—conducted under a franchise with property restrictions that still produced thirty-five million voters—Congress won a strong mandate and formed ministries in eight provinces.

With partial power, the Gandhian attempt at bridging class differences had to confront difficult choices—in economic policy, in reconciling different communities as well as dealing with the princely states that feared domination by Congress. Such problems were far from resolved when, in 1939, the British viceroy declared war against Germany on behalf of India without consulting the party or the provincial governments, leading the latter to resign and forcing the Raj into an overtly coercive posture at a delicate moment. The Quit India movement, led by Congress in 1942, was the vanguard of India-wide protests, including mass attacks on police stations and public buildings in urban areas and protests over land issues in rural villages. Tensions between Muslims and Hindus—no doubt fueled by the fact that attaining power was a real possibility—mounted.

In French Indochina, the Dutch East Indies, and other colonies of southeast Asia, nationalist movements were challenging Dutch and French authority, but here, too, it was not clear what and how inclusive the nation was. In Indonesia, one of the earliest political organizations was the Indische Partij, begun among mixed-race people; the Islamic Union expanded for a time but faltered on the divided nature of Indonesian society. Achmed Sukarno tried to forge a populist coalition through his Indonesian National Party, founded in 1927. Keeping his distance from Marxists, Sukarno tied issues of social distress and peasants' loss of control over their lives to pan-Islamic themes. He hoped to unite the divergent regional sensibilities in this multi-island colonial state, where divisions had been enhanced by Dutch strategies of cultivating local elites. The Dutch took the threat seriously enough to jail Sukarno for eight years, and others in the movement adopted a posture of greater moderation to test the boundaries of political possibility.

If some Vietnamese intellectuals, following Ho Chi Minh, were taking a radical pathway that linked them to a worldwide communist movement, others, like Phan Quyn, were willing to cooperate up to a point with the French administration while developing a form of cultural nationalism, emphasizing the uniqueness and richness of Vietnamese tradition. Directly or indirectly, both approaches challenged the French state's authority, but between the government's repressive capacity and the interest that some Indochinese elites had in the imperial system, elites' room for maneuver was limited. The war had a momentous effect on these shifting lines of political mobilization.

War of the Empires, 1939–45

World War II was a clash of different kinds of empires. It was fought differently from World War I. Technological developments—the tank and the airplane—swung the advantage to offense over defense and made the war more lethal. The total death toll came to around forty million, half of whom were civilians. The terrorizing of populations by conventional, incendiary, or nuclear bombs took place on both sides and in most theaters of the war. The systematic murder of Jews, Slavs, and other non-German civilians by the Nazis exceeded any precedent.

Germany and Japan departed from the limitations that most empire-building efforts in world history respected—and their empires proved short-lived. After their conquests, Nazis did rely on French, Danish, and Dutch bureaucrats to do routine administration, but Poland and parts of the USSR were ruled directly—and expensively—by Germans. Although many Poles and Ukrainians might before the war have seen Germans as potential liberators from the domination of the USSR, the Nazis were not looking for Slavic intermediaries or offering local elites a stake in the new order. Germany tried to expunge the very names of Poland, Yugoslavia, and Czechoslovakia because "no devolution of power to racial inferiors was permissible." Intellectuals, politicians, and professionals were slaughtered; entire villages were massacred to show the hopelessness of resistance. Some three million non-Jewish Poles were killed alongside almost all of Poland's Jewish population. Although Germany had been buying Ukrainian-grown grain from the USSR before Hitler's invasion, after the conquest the Nazis were no longer interested in Ukrainian farmers but wanted their land for settling Germans. Resettlement of Germans never got very far, but Ukrainians were killed and deported en masse—around four million civilians died. Education for Ukrainians was cut off at the fourth grade; health services were eliminated. Nazis even had doubts about using Poles and Ukrainians as slave workers in German factories. When the war turned out to be long, Germans did use Slavic labor, under the most rigid and brutal versions of their "racial laws." Extermination of the Jews was the most extreme step in a larger process of racial domination and exclusion.

Nazis were able to exploit the fragilities of a central Europe where the poor fit of state and nation after the Versailles settlement had already produced projects of ethnic cleansing. Creating a Hungary for "Hungarians" and a Romania for "Romanians" seemed compatible with Nazi racial ideas until, as the war dragged on, Hungarians and Romanians learned that German rulers did not see other nationalisms as equivalent to their own. The idea of turning eastern Europe into a breadbasket for Germany was a failure, producing massive starvation without creating a new "German" agricultural region. In France, the Netherlands, Denmark, and other countries to the west, where racially acceptable intermediaries were available, Nazis were able to obtain acceptable levels of cooperation to supply their war machine. The Nazis did not bring supposed German efficiency to European production; they deflected European production to themselves, at the expense of consumption in conquered areas.

Hitler—for ideological as well as practical reasons—did not effectively exploit the colonies of the countries Germany conquered—France, the Netherlands, Belgium. In the Middle East, with its strategic location and with all its oil, Germany failed to make a systematic effort to challenge Britain's tenuous hold on Arab territories, and Britain kept those critical resources in its own hands. Within and beyond Europe, Nazi empire declined to use many of the tools of empire that others had developed. Its approach, Mark Mazower concludes, was "not only unusual but completely counter-productive as a philosophy of rule."

Other empires—British, French, Soviet, American—cut short the Nazi attempt to remake the world, and as in World War I the victors drew on supranational resources to do so. The United States and the USSR engaged people and productive structures across two continents. The Nazi enemy drove the two unlike powers into a typically imperial alliance. The United States provided the USSR with 10 percent of its tanks, 12 percent of its combat aircraft, and massive amounts of food and technical aid.

For its part, the USSR, after terrible losses to the Nazis' assault in 1941, re-grouped its forces, partially recovered from Stalin's decapitation of the officer corps, and evacuated people and equipment far to the east. Over a million prisoners were released from labor camps to work more effectively for the state's survival. Control over information kept Soviet subjects from learning about the military's early losses, and Stalin's cult of himself provided citizens with a mobilizing ideology. Although Soviet control was weakest in Ukraine and other western regions, Nazi racism ultimately was defeated by Soviet

Figure 12.2
Soviet war poster from 1941. The text reads "Napoleon was defeated. The same will happen to the arrogant Hitler." Note that Hitler, against the background of Napoleon being stabbed with a pitchfork in 1812, is tearing up a "pact"—a reference to the 1939 agreement between Stalin and Hitler—before being bludgeoned by a rifle held in bare hands. The signature on the poster, "Kukryniksy," is the name of a team of three Soviet poster artists.

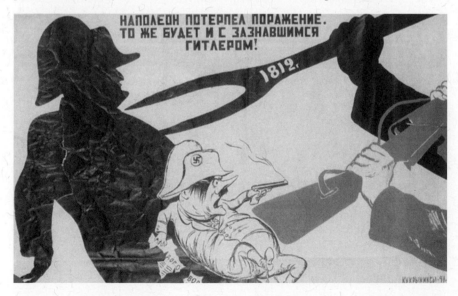

communism. The losses to the Soviet Union were staggering: 8.6 million Soviet combatants and 17 million civilians died in the war.

Approximately five million people from the colonies and dominions fought for the British empire, more than in World War I and around half of the total British forces. India's contribution to stopping and pushing back the Japanese in Burma and the rest of southeast Asia was huge. Even in the midst of anticolonial protests led by the Indian National Congress, recruitment rates remained high and desertion low. Indian troops, arguably, saved the British empire in Asia.

Unlike the first time around, European France was defeated and partially occupied at the beginning of the war. The remaining metropolitan territory was governed by a collaborationist regime based in the city of Vichy. While Vichy retained at least nominal control over most of the colonies, one set of them—French Equatorial Africa (map 10.3)—allied itself instead with the Free French of General Charles de Gaulle. French Equatorial Africa was led by Félix Eboué, a black Frenchman from Guyana whose unusual path to the top of the colonial administration helps explain the firmness of his republican convictions. Eboué's action allowed the Free French to claim continuity with an honorable France. France's north African territories were reconquered in 1942–43, with British and American help, and they provided a base (and considerable manpower) for the recovery of European France. By war's end, much of France's leadership thought that France had been saved by its overseas components.

Japan's war had begun in the 1930s with its attack on a weakened China. When France fell to the Nazis in 1940, Japan pressured the Vichy government to sign an agreement allowing use of its ports in Indochina. France became, in effect, a sub-imperial contractor for Japan. Vichy jealously guarded its nominal sovereignty while the fruits of French economic imperialism— rubber, rice, coal, and minerals—fed the Japanese war machine. But Japan's position among empires still left it in a bind, facing what it called the "ABCD encirclement"—America, Britain, China, and the Dutch. It needed oil and other resources from the region, feared boycotts by other imperial powers (the Americans embargoed oil), and realized that the United States was steadily gaining in preparedness to counter Japan's Asian ambitions.

In this context Japan decided—as Germany had in both world wars—to act preemptively against its imperial rivals. Virtually simultaneous with the attack on Pearl Harbor on December 7, 1941, came the invasions of Malaya, the Philippines, and Hong Kong. Japan hoped that after the Dutch defeat by the Nazis it could effectively take over Indonesia as it had French Indochina. It took a tough fight, but Japan gained access to all-important supplies of oil and other products. The British alone were able to deploy significant imperial forces against Japan's onslaught, but they had their hands full in Europe.

Southeast Asia from Burma to the Philippines fell under Japanese control by May 1942 (map 12.5).

For Britain, France, and the Netherlands, these losses constituted more than a military reverse. Japanese success revealed the shallowness of control over colonized territories. Japan reminded Dutch, French, and British leaders that they had achieved no more than contingent accommodation to their rule.

Whether the political activists who had begun to contest imperial domination in Indonesia, Indochina, Malaya, and Burma before the war bought into Japan's assertion of pan-Asian solidarity or whether they cooperated for other political and venal motives is controversial, but Japan too achieved no more than contingent accommodation. The Japanese ruled their rapidly conquered territories pragmatically—using European and indigenous intermediaries when possible, repressing subversive activity decisively, rounding up forced labor when useful. In some cases—Chinese in Singapore for instance—the Japanese army all but exterminated communities deemed unreliable. At their worst, conditions for coerced labor in conquered territories were deadly, paralleling Nazi use of slave labor. Forcibly recruited "comfort women" served the sexual needs of Japanese soldiers in parts of Asia. Dutch settlers who had once dominated the Indonesian economy and administrators who had run the state were interned, as were other Europeans.

Japan came closer than any invader since the Manchus in 1644 to conquering China, but it fell short. The nationalist Guomindang and its leader, Chiang Kai Shek, eventually supplied by the Americans and British over the Himalayan "Hump" from India, lost much territory while remaining undefeated. The communists under Mao Zedong, having survived their long march west in 1935, were able to reclaim their base in Manchuria at war's end. Even after decades of conflict within the republic, warlordism, foreign occupations, and invasions, the focus of struggle was still "China"—a polity brought together through empire and central to rivals' political imagination. But China was not the only empire whose existence was threatened by the processes which Japan set in motion.

Although there had been anti-Japanese guerilla movements in the conquered territories, mostly of socialist or communist inspiration, Japanese efforts to co-opt nationalists who had opposed European empires gave some political leaders room to maneuver. In Indonesia, Sukarno, earlier imprisoned by the Dutch, was able to prepare for what might come next—a claim for independence. In Vietnam, Ho Chi Minh built, village by village, an organization in rural areas where peasants were suffering greatly. He obtained arms from Chinese warlords and support from his communist connections; at one point he was held prisoner in China by the nationalists. Ho ended up in the right place, Hanoi, in northern Vietnam, to seize the

initiative when the war ended. Some Burmese and Malayan political leaders cooperated up to a point with Japan. An influential Indian nationalist,
Subhas Chandra Bose, tried to use Japan against Great Britain by recruiting
an army of Indian exiles based in Malaya and Burma to attack India, with
limited success.

With the British pushing back from India and the United States using
or capturing bases in the Pacific (demonstrating the continued usefulness of
enclave colonies), Japan tried different imperial strategies. In Indochina, it
finally kicked out the French in March 1945, giving Vietnam's nominal king,
Bao Dai, the title of "emperor" while exercising power itself. In Indonesia,
Japan promised a fuller form of independence, but did little to implement
it. But with its Asian perimeter shrinking under Allied assault and the dropping of atomic bombs on Hiroshima and Nagasaki in August 1945, Japan's
dominance gave way to a situation in which nationalist movements that had
acquired room to maneuver during the war were well placed to challenge
the return of European rule.

Sukarno and his followers declared the independence of Indonesia
within days of the war's end, and they had enough support to claim effec-

Figure 12.3
Ho Chi Minh meeting in his residence, formerly that of the French governor in
Vietnam, with French general Leclerc and commissioner Jean Sainteny, March 18,
1946. At this time, French leaders were negotiating with Ho over the terms on
which a self-governing republic in northern Vietnam could remain a part of the
French Union. LeRay, Mediathèque de la Défense, France.

tive control over part of Java. They made good use of the weeks it took the British to send troops; Dutch forces were even slower to arrive. In Vietnam, Ho Chi Minh's rural-based organization pressured the "emperor" Bao Dai to abdicate, and then set up effective government in Hanoi. Ho proclaimed the Democratic Republic of Vietnam on September 2, 1945. In his speech, he quoted to an enormous crowd from the French Declaration of Rights of Man and of the Citizen and the American Declaration of Independence, using a transempire, universalistic discourse of liberation. The French government was unpersuaded and tried to reestablish control, with some success in the southern part of Vietnam. But Ho's base in the north soon proved too strong for France to undermine. The French were willing to negotiate with Ho about a degree of autonomy within the French empire, a story we will take up in chapter 13.

The American-led victory over Japan thus left Britain, France, and the Netherlands with the task of recolonizing their lost territories, with the latter two facing nationalist governments that had implanted themselves in at least part of the territory in question. The United States would go only so far to help its allies reestablish colonial empire. U.S. leaders wavered between a preference for a more open postwar order—where American economic might, backed by military force, would have greater influence over small nation-states than on big empires—and fear that openness would benefit the expansion of communism.

Conclusion

Southeast Asia had been devastated by the violence of war, the extractive economy of the Japanese, destruction by retreating powers, and hasty attempts to fill a vacuum of power at war's end. But what had been a classic story of empires competing with each other began at the end of the war to turn into something else. Japan had reversed a trend of the previous century and shown that imperial expansion was not exclusively a European game. Germany and Japan threatened a breakout from recent imperial patterns, Germany because of what it did, Japan because of what it was. In the process, European empires, victors as well as losers, suffered enormous damage: their domestic economies were in shambles, their debts enormous, their populations eager to secure their own welfare after thirty years of preparing, prosecuting, and recovering from war. France, the Netherlands, and Britain faced an extreme problem in southeast Asia. Some of their colonies would have to be reconquered, and in 1945 it was far from clear that they could be. National movements had an opportunity to claim colonial states for themselves.

Two states emerged more powerful than ever from the war, each with a distinctive vision of itself as a world power. The USSR's victory over Hitler seemed to enhance its alternative to capitalist empire. Communist power was extended formally over much of the central European terrain that had borne the brunt of imperial contestation in the past. The Soviet version of a new world order appealed to many workers, political organizers, and intellectuals in western Europe. The future of communism seemed potentially even more promising in China, southeast Asia, and other parts of the colonial world, where rival empires had exhausted themselves.

The United States had shown the long reach of its armed forces and the power of its new military technology. But it was also positioned to think that its political repertoire included more efficient tools than colonization—a mobile military, an economy with which the commercial elites of many countries wanted to do business, a way of life that Americans believed others wanted to emulate. The United States had begun before the war devolving power to Philippine elites, drawing them effectively into its orbit; after the war, the United States made good on its promise of independence. American ambivalence about colonial empire would have an impact on the postwar world, but not entirely as the government wished or planned.

Britain and France, as we shall see, still thought that their colonial empires could be given a new lease on life. In some ways they needed empire more than ever: the sale of rubber, tin, copper, gold, oil, cocoa, coffee, and other colonial products offered perhaps the only opportunity of earning foreign exchange and reclaiming a place of influence on the world stage. They did not yet appreciate that in southeast Asia their empires had begun to come apart. They would soon learn that the thirty years' war of the twentieth century had done far more damage to the system of empires than had the great interempire wars of previous centuries.

END OF EMPIRE?

When did the world of empires come undone? Or did it? World War I had ended some empires and shaken others, but the victorious imperial powers were able to reaffirm their legitimacy and add new territories. By the 1930s, the ambitions of empire-builders were tearing up the world again. World War II resulted in the defeat of Germany and Japan and the weakening of French, British, and Dutch empires; this moment might be seen as the beginning of the end. But the leaders of the surviving empires did not think so. France and Britain began efforts at "development" to invigorate their economies and enhance imperial legitimacy. Inside empires, political activists mobilized against imperial rule, sometimes hoping to create states based on national will, sometimes trying to turn empire into another kind of supranational polity—a federation, a union, or a confederation. For some, world revolution was the goal, folding the liberation of "peoples" into the liberation of "the people" in a new international order. Most political leaders in 1945 felt that the world was changing, but few could see what direction change would take.

The mid-twentieth century was not a self-propelled movement from empire to nation-state. Ideas and practices of layered sovereignty and of varying degrees of self-rule within overarching structures were still in play. France and Britain were threatened not only by the specter of anticolonial revolution should they fail to convince their subjects of the advantages offered by imperial institutions, but also by the danger of succeeding at this goal—and thereby producing imperial citizens who would demand social and economic resources equivalent to those enjoyed by metropolitan citizens in the era of the welfare state. The colonialism that collapsed in Africa and Asia in the 1950s and 1960s was not the conservative variant of the interwar decades but a colonialism that was interventionist, reformist, and accordingly open to challenge.

13

Inside Europe, the postwar era turned into a fundamental breakout from the past. From the collapse of Rome to Hitler, the goal of resurrecting an empire of Rome's scope had haunted politics in Europe. That imagined empire vanished after World War II. Too weak to dominate each other, the states of western Europe were freed from their imperial designs and could focus on achieving prosperity and welfare within existing borders and later on constructing mechanisms for cooperation with each other. Europe was slowly reconfigured into a new sort of political entity: not an empire, not a state, a complex polity quite unlike the composite monarchies of earlier centuries. The European Union contained formally equivalent, sovereign states, each voluntarily ceding a portion of its authority to the whole, creating a confederation that could shape common institutions. But even as the Union expanded to twenty-seven member states, its capacity for generating loyalty and attachment remained unclear.

Other possibilities for a post-imperial world lived on in political imagination around the world in the second half of the twentieth century. Among these projects were an alliance of ex-colonial states in a "Third World bloc," peasant revolutions that crossed state boundaries, diasporic solidarities, and regional groupings in Asia, Africa, and elsewhere. The United Nations both reinforced the new norm of equivalence among states and led some to hope that it could institutionalize community among all the world's people.

But for the most part, by the late 1950s movements to remake or terminate colonial rule were finding that whatever new political forms they could imagine, the territorial state was what they could get. National imaginaries were as much a consequence as a prior condition of this dynamic, and they became more compelling as states proliferated and elites acquired an interest in their maintenance. Still, the picture of a world of equivalent nation-states was illusory. The military and economic power of states remained highly uneven, and the status and rights of people within each unit and across them differed enormously.

To many observers, world politics had turned bipolar, with the United States and the USSR, in international law no different from any other state, concentrating and distributing military power as they chose, acting as protectors, patrons, and policemen in theoretically sovereign states. The United States and the Soviet Union were imperial in their reach—both had the capacity and will to exercise power over great distances and many societies—but they insisted to themselves and others that they were not like previous empires. The American ideal drew on the fiction of an expanding world of nation-states, open to commerce, receptive to American culture, and united in opposition to the rival bloc. The Soviet version posited the myth of fraternal socialist states allied in the march toward world communism and the end of capitalism; this vision captured the imagination of revolutionaries, intellectuals, and their followers from Cuba to Vietnam. Both visions built on—and in different ways encouraged—the dissolution of the colonial empires.

The failure of communist variants of state power after 1989 gave rise to a new round of speculations about the future. Did this finale to a twentieth-century interempire conflict mean the "end of history," with everyone subsumed in a liberal order? The end of states, as networks and corporations extended their reach, and governments' capacity to regulate diminished? New cleavages—west-rest, rich-poor, Muslims-everyone else? A unipolar world, with only one empire—the American one—left standing? A new Asian axis of power?

Each of these speculations had its origins in the political contestations over, among, and inside empires. To illuminate them, we turn to the evolution of imperial politics in the second half of the twentieth century— the unraveling of colonial empires and the reconfiguration of Europe, the non-resolution of conflicts in the Middle East decades after the fall of the Ottoman empire, yet another transformation of Russian empire, the successful imperial reformation of China, and changes in an American state that remained imperial and national. We begin when no one could know what our present would be—with what people imagined to be possible at the end of World War II.

Empire Unraveled

Southeast and South Asia in the Aftermath of War

In December 1943, the French government-in-exile of Charles de Gaulle announced its intention to give the people of Indochina, after the war, "a new political status inside the French community." They would be part of "the framework of a federal organization," in which they would enjoy "liberties" and serve in all levels of government "without losing the original stamp of the Indo-Chinese civilization and traditions." Shortly thereafter, Free French leaders proclaimed that their policy toward the people of all the overseas territories was "the exact application of the principle of equality, that is for the suppression of the colonial concept, properly speaking."

The Dutch government-in-exile had a similar future in mind: the creation of a "Commonwealth in which the Netherlands, Indonesia, Surinam and Curaçao [the latter two possessions in the Caribbean region] will participate, with complete self-reliance and freedom of conduct for each part regarding its internal affairs but with readiness to render mutual assistance. . . . This would leave no room for discrimination according to race or nationality." Having lost control of their homelands to the Nazis and their

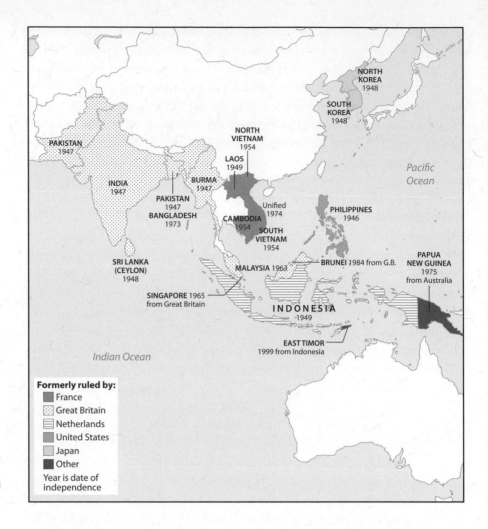

Map 13.1
Decolonization
in Asia.

Asian colonies to Japan, both French and Dutch governments realized that restoring power over Indochina and Indonesia was not assured and that they would have to find a new basis of accommodation with the people they had treated as colonial subjects.

Such proclamations were more than window dressing and less than a program. As Japan's power collapsed, nationalist leaders had proclaimed new governments in Indochina and Indonesia (chapter 12), and imperial rulers would have to either persuade independent leaders to participate in an overarching system—federation or commonwealth—or shoot their way back in. The Netherlands and France tried both approaches.

In 1945, France amalgamated its southeast Asian territories into the Indochinese Federation, Vietnam (itself an amalgam), Cambodia, and Laos. Acknowledging Ho Chi Minh's de facto control of the north, France later recognized the Democratic Republic of Vietnam as a state within the federation, while hanging onto the south and reinstalling, in 1949, the former king/emperor Bao Dai, now called "head of state." Some French leaders later regretted not having gone the extra yard to grant the Democratic Republic more autonomy and more territory, but it is hard to imagine Ho Chi Minh remaining for long as the ruler of a state within a French federation. In the event, negotiations bogged down and France bombarded the Vietnamese port of Haiphong in November 1946, starting a cascade of warfare that lasted for eight years.

The French federation appealed to some Vietnamese in cities, but Ho's base was the countryside. After the Chinese revolution of 1949, Ho had an excellent supply route, while American support of France against a communist movement was insufficient to prevent a French defeat in 1954. Cozy French relations with the kings of Cambodia and Laos came much closer to the French scheme of federation, but without Vietnam the plan for francophone federation in southeast Asia made little sense. France eventually let Laos and Cambodia march down the road from autonomy to independence, hoping to conserve influence but not sovereignty.

The Indonesian revolution was more rapid. Sukarno's cooperation with the Japanese left him well positioned at the time of their exit, and he quickly proclaimed Indonesia's independence. The Dutch needed British and American forces to reestablish themselves after the Japanese surrender, but those powers eventually convinced themselves that Sukarno was not a communist threat and that the Dutch deserved little support in trying to reestablish a colonial state, even if it went by another name. The Dutch put together enough military force to fight a short and ugly war, but they could not win on the ground or in the battle for international opinion. In 1949, the Dutch East Indies became the independent state of Indonesia. The large majority of the European Dutch population—bitter about losing country and property they considered theirs after having been interned by the Japanese throughout most of the war—were "repatriated" to a Netherlands in which many had never lived.

Sewn together out of different islands, kingdoms, languages, and religions, Indonesia joined the ranks of the world's states, proclaiming its unity under the Indonesian flag, speaking the Indonesian language (a creation of the colonial era), seeking to develop its resources and standard of living. The Netherlands had tried to make diverse kingdoms into components of the empire while playing divide-and-rule; that Indonesian nationalists could shape all this into a national whole was no foregone conclusion. Territorially based secession movements in East Timor and other parts of Indonesia and tension among communal groups—between Chinese and Javanese especially—showed that nations were no more natural units of history than heavy-handed empires.

That metropolitan Britain had not succumbed during the war left it in a better position to regain control over the strategically located, richly endowed colonies of Malaya. It, too, attempted to pull colonial provinces together in what it named the Malayan Union (later Federation), but tensions over exploitation in the rubber plantations and tin mines and conflict between ethnic Malays and Chinese, both conscious that even gradual devolution of power was raising the political stakes, soon gave rise to a bitter war. The rebellion in Malaya, led by communists, was brutally repressed. British tactics became the model for "counterinsurgency": detention without trial of alleged rebels, forced relocation of villages to isolate them from sources of supply, and efforts to win the "hearts and minds" of a population. Repression and a boom in tin and rubber exports allowed the British to regain temporary control.

But the Malayan Federation was on the road pioneered by others in Asia and Africa. What British political and military action secured was a route out of empire, not its indefinite prolongation. The Federation became the independent state of Malaysia in 1957, under a government eager for friendly relations with Britain and for vigorous participation in a capitalist world economy.

Britain had hung onto its south Asian empire throughout World War II, but its position at war's end was vulnerable. The empire had accumulated both financial and moral debts to India. Financial, because by encouraging Indians to produce while rationing consumption and collecting revenue but not spending it in India, Britain had exacerbated what Indian political activists had long called "the drain" into a large credit to the government of India held in the City of London. Moral, because Indians had again fought for the empire—with heavy losses in southeast Asia. Promises of devolving power—broken after World War I, revived with the elections of 1937, and reversed by the wartime suppression of Congress—remained unfulfilled. During the war, Gandhi, Nehru, and others had been locked up, 66,000 people convicted or detained, and 2,500 killed in putting down demonstrations. Britain was too poor to maintain a high level of repression when Congress escalated its political demands at war's end. Despite Churchill's proclaimed unwillingness to "dismantle" the British empire, more realistic voices in London accepted that a gentle letdown from imperial rule was the best they could do.

The strongest national movement within European colonial empires between the wars had been the Indian National Congress. But as power came closer to the grasp of nationalist leaders, fractures within the movement widened. Muslim activists, increasingly disenchanted with the Indian National Congress and aware that Hindus were a majority in India as a whole, had to choose between pushing for a share of power at the center of a strong all-Indian government or for a more federal solution, with a weak center and strong regions, some with a Muslim majority. That populations were mixed in most regions of India did not simplify their problem. The All-India Muslim League began to advocate a quasi-sovereign Muslim state that would be part of an Indian federation governed by an equal partnership between the Muslim League and the largely Hindu Congress. The new Muslim state would be called Pakistan.

As we have seen, federative approaches were being pushed in much of the colonial world—by imperial governments hoping that elites in different territories would be satisfied with varying degrees of autonomy, but also by politicians in colonized societies where building a nation-state would generate conflict over who constituted the nation. Federations were proposed both at the level of an entire empire—the French Union—or for portions of it, as in India, Malaya, Indochina, and parts of Africa.

In India, a federal solution ran into many Indians' ambitions not only for independence but for making the state into an agent of economic and social transformation and an actor in the world of nations. Jawaharlal Nehru, Gandhi's fellow leader in Congress, wanted a strong center, the Muslim League's leader, Mohammed Ali Jinnah, a weak one. Nehru was concerned not only with Muslim separatism but with possible claims for autonomy by India's over five hundred princely states, which he considered feudalistic. Drawing an analogy to an earlier imperial breakup, he argued against the "Balkanization" of India—a word that would later be used by African leaders worried about the consequences of turning empires into many small and weak states. Nehru thought that Congress could cut into the League's support in Muslim-majority regions by raising class issues against the property-owning League leaders, and Jinnah feared that Nehru might be right. This disagreement was played out against a background of riots in Indian cities between Hindus and Muslims, and each corpse increased polarization. By 1946, Britain was trying to get out with as little fuss as possible. Facing pressure to resolve things quickly, the competing parties could only agree on one solution: partition between India and Pakistan. Pressure from Congress and the British government combined with princes' fear of being left out of a new India with command of crucial resources led princely states to acquiesce to their inclusion within India.

The result of the India-Pakistan partition was a human tragedy at the very moment of triumph over colonialism. In August 1947, as independence loomed, an enormous unmixing of population took place, during which seventeen million people crossed the new border in both directions; hundreds of thousands on both sides were murdered. Kashmir, where partition lines could not be agreed upon, remains to this day the site of violent Indian-Pakistani conflict, while tensions between the remaining Muslim population in India and the Hindu majority continue to flare up. On August 15, 1947, India and Pakistan became independent states, each claiming to be a nation, but neither was the nation most Indian activists in the previous half century had struggled to obtain.

Empires of Development and the Development of Nations

Even the losses and ongoing struggles in Asia did not immediately or inevitably lead European powers to give up on empire. Africa loomed larger in imperial plans. Britain and France recognized that selling tropical commodities from their colonies might be the only way for countries with shattered industrial plants and huge debts to earn dollars and promote economic recovery. The complacency with which governments before the war accepted white man's rule and routine discrimination in daily life—despite considerable debate over questions of race—was badly shaken by Hitler's racist empire and the effort to mobilize colonized populations against it. The British and French governments sent directives to their colonial administrators to avoid racial insults and discrimination. Both made overtures to educated Africans, who earlier had been excluded from the politics of indirect rule on grounds of inauthenticity. Both proposed immediate reforms in how colonies were governed and invited Africans to look to a future in which, at some time and in some way, they would govern themselves.

Britain, beginning in 1940, and France in 1946 also promoted a new economic and social vision for their empires. "Development" became the new keyword. Both governments renounced the old colonial doctrine that each colony should pay for itself and proposed to spend metropolitan pounds and francs on communications, transportation, housing, schools, and health facilities, as well as industrial and agricultural projects. The goal was to raise the standard of living for colonized people, ease conditions for wage workers, and set the stage for long-term improvements in productivity. Development promised to make empires richer and more politically legitimate at the same time.

Britain and France proposed to meet their goals in contrasting ways. The British wanted each colony to evolve in its own manner and at its own pace. The government first tried to slot African activists into "local councils," which would slowly modify traditional rule into something more progressive. Only later would Africans acquire power at the center of each colony. The overall timetable was unspecified; that Africans would meanwhile sit in Parliament in London was unthinkable. But this was precisely what French leaders proposed, albeit not in proportion to population. French leaders evoked the word "federal" where the British spoke of local government. The French Union, like empires of the past, would be built out of different

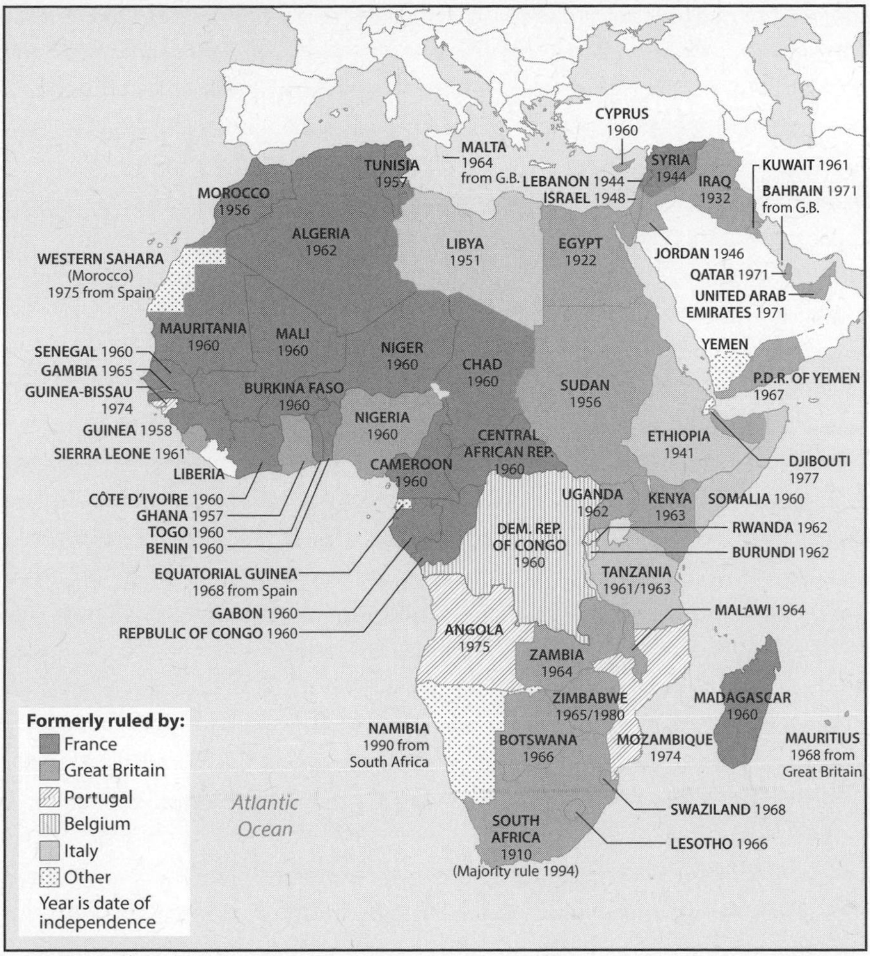

CYPRUS 1960
MALTA 1964 from G.B.
TUNISIA 1957
MOROCCO 1956
ALGERIA 1962
LIBYA 1951
EGYPT 1922
LEBANON 1944
ISRAEL 1948
SYRIA 1944
IRAQ 1932
KUWAIT 1961
BAHRAIN 1971 from G.B.
JORDAN 1946
QATAR 1971
UNITED ARAB EMIRATES 1971
WESTERN SAHARA (Morocco) 1975 from Spain
MAURITANIA 1960
MALI 1960
NIGER 1960
CHAD 1960
SUDAN 1956
YEMEN
P.D.R. OF YEMEN 1967
SENEGAL 1960
GAMBIA 1965
GUINEA-BISSAU 1974
GUINEA 1958
SIERRA LEONE 1961
LIBERIA
BURKINA FASO 1960
NIGERIA 1960
CENTRAL AFRICAN REP. 1960
ETHIOPIA 1941
DJIBOUTI 1977
CAMEROON 1960
CÔTE D'IVOIRE 1960
GHANA 1957
TOGO 1960
BENIN 1960
UGANDA 1962
KENYA 1963
SOMALIA 1960
DEM. REP. OF CONGO 1960
RWANDA 1962
BURUNDI 1962
EQUATORIAL GUINEA 1968 from Spain
TANZANIA 1961/1963
GABON 1960
REPBULIC OF CONGO 1960
MALAWI 1964
ANGOLA 1975
ZAMBIA 1964
ZIMBABWE 1965/1980
MADAGASCAR 1960
NAMIBIA 1990 from South Africa
BOTSWANA 1966
MOZAMBIQUE 1974
MAURITIUS 1968 from Great Britain
Atlantic Ocean
SWAZILAND 1968
SOUTH AFRICA 1910 (Majority rule 1994)
LESOTHO 1966
Formerly ruled by:
France
Great Britain
Portugal
Belgium
Italy
Other
Year is date of independence

Map 13.2 Decolonization in Africa.

sorts of polities connected to an imperial center in different ways: European France; Algeria, whose territory was fully integrated into France but whose population had been divided into citizens and subjects; "old colonies" like those of the Caribbean, whose inhabitants were citizens; "new colonies," such as those in Africa, whose inhabitants had mostly been subjects; protectorates, like Morocco and Tunisia, which had their own nationality and sovereignty, having ceded (under pressure) certain powers to France by treaty; and mandates, ex-German colonies that had their own potential nationality for which France was the trustee.

The 1946 constitution proclaimed that inhabitants of all these entities would now have the "qualities" of French citizens. This provision gradually expanded the participation of former subjects in elections, although it did not translate into universal suffrage for another decade. It conveyed rights and eliminated institutions that had treated imperial subjects differently:

separate judicial regimes, different standards for labor laws. The new constitution no longer made citizenship contingent on the subject's submitting to the French civil code instead of Islamic or customary law in private legal matters, such as marriage and inheritance. In principle, the new French Union would be multicultural as well as egalitarian.

Here we arrive at the basic dilemma of postwar empire: could an imperial regime adopt a more democratic form of governance, a more nuanced concept of sovereignty, and still remain imperial? Could the recognition of social and cultural difference, characteristic of the nineteenth-century Ottoman and Russian empires, be combined with an empire-wide concept of citizenship—heretofore largely reserved for the European components of western European empires? Unlike the situation in the Roman empire, which in 212 had declared all its non-slave, male subjects to be citizens—a precedent invoked by parliamentarians during the debates over the French Constitution of 1946—citizenship in Europe now entailed extensive economic and social rights as well as political ones. Norms of equivalence inside the metropolitan polity were unlike Rome's hierarchical social order. Bringing millions of impoverished subjects into citizenship in the 1940s could thus entail high costs—if claims based on contemporary standards of citizenship were made good. And it was not clear that citizens of either European or African France could quickly set aside habits and expectations of privilege and authority, of discrimination and denigration, built up over decades of colonial rule.

These dilemmas help explain the schizophrenic character of postwar French colonialism—at times integrative, capable of rational debate with African or Asian political activists, at times brutally violent against an entire category of people perceived to be a threat. Africans could sit in the French legislature, and African labor unions could organize, strike, and claim equal pay and benefits for equal work. Meanwhile, during the revolt in Madagascar in 1947, the Vietnam war of 1946–54, and the Algerian war of 1954–62, French forces used collective terror against people among whom rebels were supposed to lurk. French use of torture became a scandal during the Algerian war. But even in Algeria, French governments launched programs of *promotion sociale*—what Americans would call affirmative action—to get Muslim French citizens of Algeria to see the benefits of belonging to the French polity, including access to jobs in metropolitan and overseas France and to social services directed, in principle, toward their particular needs.

The most influential leaders of French West Africa translated France's federalizing project into claims for more vigorous development plans and fuller social equality. Léopold Senghor of Senegal sought a layered form of sovereignty: each territory would choose a government with authority over local affairs; French West Africa as a whole would constitute an African federation with a legislature and executive; and this federation would associate with other territories and federations in a reformed French Union in which all would be rights-bearing citizens. The Union would limit its actions to foreign affairs, defense, development, and other agreed-upon functions and become a confederation, recognizing the national personality of each component part. Senghor saw nationality not in terms of Senegalese or Ivoiriens but of Africans, or at least Africans who shared the French language and the experience of French institutions.

Other African leaders wanted to bypass the west African federation while favoring direct membership of each territory in a French Community. Such possibilities were being debated in Africa as the French government came to realize that it was caught in a trap between following through on the logic of citizenship—which was costly—and a cycle of rebellion and repression, now taking place under the gaze of international institutions and observers who did not see colonial rule as normal or inevitable. When the French government in 1958 offered each African territory the option of immediate independence or continued participation, with a large measure of self-government, in a French Community, only Guinea voted for complete separation. But African leaders could not agree on whether or how to federate among themselves, and France was anxious to avoid the obligations of too close a union. African politicians came to believe that bilateral relations of sovereign states with France corresponded better to the contingencies of the moment than did layered sovereignty. Still, it was only in 1960 that the dissolution of the French empire in sub-Saharan Africa into territorial nation-states became the only exit option.

The more decentralized colonial structure of Great Britain did not foster such a debate over equivalence of all subjects of the queen. But Britain could not escape the problem of preserving empire when the very terms by which the imperial state was trying to relegitimize itself—development and political participation—were producing cascades of demands for social and economic resources. Attempts to get educated Africans to focus their ambitions on local government quickly failed. Political parties in colony after colony demanded full participation in each territory's legislative and executive institutions, while social movements demanded better wages, fairer crop prices, and more educational facilities.

But when political mobilization strayed beyond certain (not entirely clear) lines, most notoriously in the so-called Mau Mau Emergency in Kenya that began in 1952, the colonial government responded with massive detentions and confinements in prison camps, interrogations under torture, capital punishment with minimal judicial oversight, and forced relocations of entire villages. Britain had by that time accepted that the Gold Coast was being governed internally by elected African politicians and that it was en

Figure 13.1
Two faces of decolonization.

Algerians wait to vote in the referendum of 1958 on a new constitution for the French Republic. Even during the war between the French army and Algeria's National Liberation Front, French officials hoped that increasing Algerian participation in French institutions—including electing representatives to the legislature in Paris—would reconcile them to continuing as citizens of France. Loomis Dean for Time Life, GettyImages.

People in Kenya are forced from their homes by the British police and military (1954) during the repression of the "Mau Mau" revolt that began in 1952. Anyone from the Kikuyu ethnic group, from which the core of the rebel movement came, was suspected of involvement and subject to arrest, investigation, and internment. George Rodger for Time Life, GettyImages.

route to independence, a status it obtained in 1957. Officials in London, like their counterparts in Paris, were by 1957 conducting cost-benefit analyses of colonial territories and concluding that while it was unclear that most colonial people were "ready" for independence, cultivating friendly post-colonial relations with African leaders would cost less than trying to hang onto the colonies.

When Kwame Nkrumah led the Gold Coast—renamed Ghana—to its pioneering independence, he called for the creation of a United States of Africa. But Africa did not go the way of the thirteen North American colonies that became independent in 1783. By the mid-1950s, older forms of pan-Africanism—whose assertion of Africa's unity with its diaspora had not been translated into political institutions—withered as activists focused on the tangible structures and rewards the slow devolution of power to individual territories was providing. The first generation of African leaders became so tied to the political apparatus and patronage opportunities in territorialized states that they could agree on only powerless forms of interstate cooperation.

The trends toward national states were softened, even in the former British empire, by efforts to maintain some sort of overarching structure. After World War II, the crucial role of colonies and dominions in saving the empire was widely recognized in Great Britain. As dominions tried to define their own national citizenships more precisely, Britain in 1948 created a kind of empire citizenship, derivative from the primary citizenship in each dominion, with colonial subjects included. Under this legislation, people from both colonies and dominions had the right to enter and live in the British isles, comparable to the right of citizens of the French Union to enter European France.

Although arrivals of non-white people from the colonies produced anxieties in both France and Britain, for a time the logic of empire trumped that of race. The right of entry of former colonial citizens into Britain and France was preserved for some years after colonies became independent. But as colonies turned into independent states and possibilities for converting empire into federation came to naught, France and Britain became more firmly centered in Europe. Over time, they drew a more starkly national line around their core populations, even as migration from the former colonies was making their residents more mixed. Imperial citizens turned into "immigrants," and by the 1970s, such immigrants were finding more and more obstacles to entering France and Britain, as both countries moved toward an exclusionary conception of the body politic.

In north Africa and the Middle East, the situation was not quite colonial, and the trajectory out of empire was not the same as in sub-Saharan Africa. The denouement of empire in Algeria—considered an integral part of France—was particularly bloody. The well-connected settlers and their allies in French military and business circles made it hard for France either to calmly calculate costs and benefits and find ways of disengaging as in west Africa or to make good on the promises of fully integrating all Algerian citizens into France. Already alienated from the French state, Algerian activists were divided over competing strategies—class struggle, Islamicist activism alongside other north African Muslims, national self-government within some sort of French federation, or total national independence. In the early 1950s, the National Liberation Front (FLN) coalesced around the goal of independence, but acute divisions within the movement remained.

The FLN's armed struggle and the counterterror of the state sparked a conflict on both sides of the Mediterranean that threatened the foundations of republican France. Charles de Gaulle had to use his status as war hero to keep government functioning in 1958. Applying terror and torture, the French military won the major combats of the war, driving the FLN to the edges of Algeria. But these were pyrrhic victories, producing neither a viable society nor a politically tenable position for the French state in a world where most colonies, including French ones, had already become independent. Although nationalist and leftist circles preserve a myth of the FLN as the model anticolonial movement, it owed much of its success in 1962 to the fact that others had paved the way—often by nonviolent means. And overcoming colonial oppression was anything but unifying: the FLN contained so many different visions of a liberated society and so many competing factions that civil war erupted within weeks after the French agreed to recognize Algerian independence.

French leaders, having insisted that Algeria was not a colony, now reconstructed what had happened as "decolonization"—France's renunciation of ruling over others. The rapid exodus—unanticipated by French leaders—of almost the entire settler population of Algeria made clear that for this element of colonial society a binary view of colonial difference had become a self-fulfilling prophecy.

If the fiction of Algeria's integration into France defined one tortuous trajectory out of empire, Egypt, nominally independent since 1922, followed another. Britain had come close to recolonizing Egypt during the war. Afterward, in 1952, a weak monarchical government, cooperating with Britain, fell to a coup d'état by young army officers, and Gamal Abdel Nasser emerged as leader. Nasser captivated the imagination of many young people in colonial and ex-colonial territories throughout the world with his decisive anti-imperial stand. In 1956, he annexed the Suez Canal. France, Great Britain, and Israel responded by invading Egyptian territory, but the United States—fearing that Egypt would be driven into the Soviet camp—pulled the rug from under them, leaving Nasser with a fait accompli and France and Britain deeply embarrassed.

The failed invasion of Nasser's Egypt began on October 29, 1956. On November 4, the Soviet army invaded Hungary to put down a widespread rebellion against Soviet domination. Within a week, the USSR had ruthlessly restored control. The coincidence in timing of the two invasions probably muted international reactions to each of them, but it revealed that the world of empires was at a crossroad. The Suez fiasco was a sign of something that had already happened—the loss of coercive capacity and political authority by the colonial powers of western Europe—while the Hungarian revolution and its repression exposed the power relations of Soviet-dominated eastern Europe, underscored later by the building of the Berlin wall in 1961 and the repression of a liberalizing movement in Czechoslovakia in 1968. The two crises of 1956 brought into view imperial power in a crude form—severely undermined in one case, harshly coercive but with diminished moral authority in the other.

The weakening of colonial empires opened the way for leaders of independent states to try to shape a new kind of international order. In 1955, President Sukarno hosted a conference in the Indonesian city of Bandung of heads of newly independent states. The conferees put forward a "third world" alternative to both American and Soviet domination. Cooperation in UN votes, in trade, and in mutual assistance against aggression all seemed on the agenda. Sovereign states working together as an anti-imperialist bloc would transform world politics.

But the horizontal unity of third world nations did not replace vertical connections between the leaders of rich states with those of poor ones. The pattern of decolonization made wide-ranging unity unlikely: the bargains exiting powers made with incoming leaders gave the latter a strictly territorial base, fragile enough that few wanted to relinquish any of the levers of national sovereignty. Ex-colonial states sought foreign aid or military assistance against internal or external enemies; their rulers often had personal ties to leaders of former colonial powers. Poor countries had an immediate need for relations of clientage with rich ones, more so than with countries with the same incapacities they faced themselves. The political deck was stacked against turning the asymmetries of empire into third world solidarity.

Nonetheless, the transformation of the normative basis of world order after World War II is visible in the paths taken by outliers to the pattern of decolonization. Although the origins of racial domination in South Africa and Rhodesia (map 10.3) lay in their colonial pasts and although their racial ideologies and forms of discrimination were well within the repertoire of colonial rule, by the 1960s the defense of a racial order had to be made in national, not imperial, terms. South Africa, self-governing since 1910, insisted on its sovereign prerogatives, denying blacks the right to vote, de-

Figure 13.2
Founding a non-aligned movement. Gamal Abdul Nasser of Egypt and Jawaharlal Nehru of India, conversing in center of photo, at Bandung, Indonesia, April 1955. Howard Sochurek for Time Life, GettyImages.

fending segregation as "separate development." It withdrew from the British Commonwealth in 1960. Rhodesian whites—who for decades had used partial self-government within the British empire to ensure that blacks would have no meaningful political role—declared unilateral independence from Great Britain in 1965, and for fifteen years defended white domination as a sovereign prerogative. Portugal remained more frankly imperial. It was not a democracy at home, and thus tension between metropolitan and colonial government was not so blatant.

None of these regimes survived the contagious nature of decolonization. Liberation movements in Portuguese Guinea–Bissau, Angola, and Mozambique found inspiration and sanctuaries in their independent neighbors and fought long and grueling guerilla campaigns. The final moment of Portuguese empire in Africa—after five hundred years—came in 1974, as the military charged with repressing the guerillas revolted against its role, liberating the motherland from fascist dictatorship and the colonies from colonialism. The majority of settlers, many of whom had never seen European

Portugal, "returned" to the motherland. Portugal, like France and Britain, became both more national and more European once it gave up an imperial conception of itself.

South Africa, with the largest white population and the strongest national traditions, held out longest of all. Despite whites' claim to represent Christianity and western civilization, it was the African National Congress (ANC) that successfully defended democratic principles before world opinion and among black South Africans. The ANC was supported by already independent African states and movements overseas, including boycotts of commercial, athletic, and cultural exchange with South Africa. Ideological and social isolation became difficult for white elites to accept; violence made South African cities increasingly unlivable. The trajectory opened by the first white settlement in 1652, developed into racialized capitalism in the late nineteenth century, and transformed into a national system of white rule in the twentieth was finally closed on April 27, 1994, when black South Africans flocked to the polls to elect leaders of their own choosing. The large majority of whites, unlike the settlers of Indonesia, Algeria, Angola, and Mozambique, remained South African citizens. But turning political equality into economic and social justice within South Africa remains as elusive as other African countries' quests for parity with the former colonizing powers.

The substance as well as the name of empire had changed. France, Britain, the Netherlands, and Belgium abandoned not only power in the present but responsibility for the past. They had "decolonized," and their former colonies were on their own. Separated states could ask for aid, but had no right to it. The United States and the USSR engaged in acts of courtship and coercion toward newly independent states, but they, too, did not accept responsibility for the consequences of their seductions, periodic invasions, and massive distribution of armaments. The United Nations became a widely accepted symbol of a world of the equivalence of sovereign states. Equivalence was a fiction, and like many political fictions it had material consequences.

The Obstructed Path to Post-Imperial Order in the Middle East

The problem of building some kind of political order to replace that maintained for centuries by the Ottoman empire over its Arabic-speaking provinces still looked intractable at the end of World War II. Rebellions had broken out in Syria, Palestine, and Iraq between the wars. British and French policy in their mandates had produced neither a viable structure of top-down control nor a path to participatory self-government.

The sons of Husayn, installed by Britain as kings, acquired de jure sovereignty in Iraq before the war and in Jordan after it. During the war, the

Vichy regime had pushed its mandates in French Syria and Lebanon toward independence, in cooperation with the Nazis, who hoped to garner support in the region against Britain (not with much success). The Free French also made promises of independence, which they did their best to break, occupying—with British help—the region to keep it out of Nazi hands. But Syrian and Lebanese elites had come too close to independence to give it up, and the postwar French government accepted the end of the mandate, hoping for cooperative relations with its former wards.

Palestine became a much thornier problem for the mandatory power as Jewish immigration escalated during and after the Holocaust. Britain was beset by claims backed by violence from both Jews and Arabs against each other and against British rule. By 1948, the British government washed its hands of the situation it had helped create, leaving two nationalist projects, with unequal resources, claiming rights to the same space.

By the 1950s, Syria and Iraq were turning from weak and clientelistic states into authoritarian ones, caught up in the machinations of major powers. Lebanon managed its communitarian divisions until the 1970s but, in part because of spillover effects from the Israel-Palestine conflict, fell into civil war, recovered, and relapsed. All competitors for leadership—Maronite Christians, Sunnis, Shi'ites, Druze, and others—operated in a post-imperial quagmire, where community and territorial boundaries did not match and power brokers feared each other's access to both the state and external support. The world is still suffering the consequences of the botched dismantling of the Ottoman empire.

Iran, the proudly independent descendant of past empires, was coveted by foreign powers for its oil. Iran's monarchs made their deals with British and American oil companies, and when an elected government tried to steer a more independent course, it fell victim in 1953 to a coup engineered by American and British intelligence services. Authoritarian kings in Saudi Arabia received considerable support from western powers. American oil companies built segregated enclaves of production within Saudi Arabia under the protective wings of the U.S. Air Force. But neither oil companies nor the United States could control what Arab leaders did with the immense "rents" that oil produced. These financed a Saudi ruling dynasty with a purist view of Islam, rejection of "western" notions of politics, and a tight hold on power. In the Muslim world, Saudis fostered Islamic education and charitable works, but also networks of Islamicists whom American and other leaders now consider a major threat to world order. For decades, the Middle East has been the site of conflict among monarchical, military, and civilian rulers, among religious groups, between partisans of democracy and defenders of authoritarian rule, between nationalist elites and outside powers and corporations. Much of the conflict in this region has been financed by the industrial states' appetite for oil.

A World Redivided? East–West, North–South, West–Rest

The end of colonial empires coincided with the remaking of power blocs, and these in turn generated new conflicts. Colonial-anticolonial and communist-anticommunist conflicts were never independent of each other, but they were not reducible to each other either. Shifts set in motion by World War I and the Bolshevik revolution, accelerated by World War II, decolonization, and the start of the cold war around 1948 seemed to turn a regime of several imperial powers into a bipolar world. But this characterization of the twentieth century needs qualification: neither superpower could remake its subordinates at will, and the bipolar world was not symmetrical.

Development and Empire, Soviet-Style

Between 1943 and 1945, Stalin, Churchill, and Roosevelt, anticipating victory, redrew the map of Europe once again. Stalin insisted on and got control over what became known as "eastern Europe." Poland, Czechoslovakia, Hungary, Romania, and states in the Balkans and the Baltic area were in the Soviet sphere. In a flagrant demonstration of the victors' power and disunity, Germany was divided into four separate zones, supervised by British, French, American, and Soviet commands. In the east, the USSR received the southern half of Sakhalin and the Kuril islands as a reward for its last-minute entry into the war against Japan.

In Europe, a new round of unmixing of people followed the imperial carve-up of territories that had been partially unmixed by the formation of nationalized states after World War I and by the murderous actions of the Nazis and their allies. Hundreds of thousands of Poles were forced out of the much-expanded Soviet Ukraine to a Poland whose borders were shifted westward. Ukrainians moved from Poland to Ukraine. Turks were again expelled from Bulgaria. German-speaking populations of eastern, central, and southeastern Europe were expelled to Germany. The creation of nominally mono-ethnic territories was not a natural evolution of nations into states but a violent, repeated, and still incomplete process of ethnic cleansing.

The Red Army's success in rolling up the Nazis in eastern Europe gave Stalin a chance to regain and go beyond tsarist territory, as well as a taste of the challenges of expanding imperial control. In places liberated—often savaged and pillaged—by the Red Army, the vitality of multiple political

Figure 13.3
Redividing Europe. Winston
Churchill, Franklin D.
Roosevelt, and Joseph Stalin,
with military advisors,
meeting at Yalta, February
1945, to discuss the future
political order of Europe.
Library of Congress.

movements, including social democratic ones, made it clear that communism would not triumph by electoral means. In areas (Estonia, Latvia, Lithuania, and western Ukraine) directly incorporated into the Soviet Union at
the end of the war, resistance movements challenged Soviet command. From
Stalin's point of view, Soviet soldiers returning home from victory were also
dangerous. They had discovered that people of capitalist Europe had homes
and possessions that were impossibly luxurious by Soviet standards.

The answer to all these threats was Stalinist discipline: establishment of
one-party rule in the new "people's democracies" of eastern Europe, containment of returning POWs in labor camps, imprisonment and execution
of potential dissenters, exile and resettlement of suspect populations, and a
shutdown of information about the other side. Inside the USSR, the traditional tool of moving people about was applied in sensitive regions: ethnic
Russians were relocated to the Baltic republics, and a quarter of the people
who had lived there before the war were moved out. Tatars and other groups
residing in the Crimea were deported to Kazakhstan and Siberia. The party
launched a campaign against "cosmopolitans" in the USSR, especially Jews.
While the war was later made into an event of mythic solidarity, Stalin made
sure that victorious officers were not too celebrated. The size of peasants'
household plots was reduced as was their pay on collective farms, contributing to a devastating famine in 1946. Forced labor remained a primary means
for reconstruction, as the gulag absorbed millions of new prisoners.

Outside the borders of the USSR, the states of Stalin's eastern European
empire maintained the pretense of formal sovereignty, with de facto subordi-

Chapter 13

nation to Soviet command. The Soviet kind of empire worked by requiring each communist leadership to establish what Tony Judt calls "replica states." Each of the people's democracies had the same formal governmental structure as the USSR; each hierarchy of officials was controlled by communists, who took orders from their party; each set of party leaders was guided by the Communist Party in Moscow. The administrations of the replica states were staffed by their own populations; this use of native intermediaries replicated the management of Soviet "peoples" in the national republics of the USSR. In eastern Europe Stalin wielded the same methods he had used at home to secure loyalty, purging communist leaders in the later 1940s and early 1950s to produce a new cohort of reliable subordinates in Czechoslovakia, Hungary, Romania, Bulgaria, and Poland. Jews were expelled or demoted in these parties as well. Three new organizations were set up to maintain the Soviet bloc: the Cominform (Communist Information Bureau) to unite the party apparatuses; Comecon (Council for Mutual Economic Assistance) for economic matters; and the Warsaw Pact, a military alliance.

On the other side of the cold war divide, NATO and international financial organizations were designed with strong American input to coordinate military policy among once-competing powers and to regulate the potentially anarchic nature of international capitalism. The economic dynamism and prosperity of industrial countries in North America and western Europe could not be matched by the communist bloc, but the threat of nuclear weapons was a new kind of equalizer, leading to a tense peace. Still, both superpowers had trouble managing weaker states emerging from former empires; the cold war was hot and violent in many of them. From the 1950s into the 1980s, the tensions between two poles of power—crosscut by the fiction of a world of sovereign nations, sustained by clientelistic politics and proxy wars—organized the field of international relations.

But one of the world's great powers came apart. The politics of empire helps us understand how the USSR unraveled and how new states took shape after 1989–91.

First, the postwar extension of Soviet power proved too much for the one-party state to control. Stalin's armies incorporated societies whose economic institutions were different and often far more productive than those on prewar Soviet territory. Many in communist Europe resented domination by what they deemed a backward country to their east. Attempts to reform communism and to break away from Soviet controls punctuated the postwar period—in Yugoslavia, Hungary, Czechoslovakia, and Poland most dramatically. It was in eastern Europe that a desire for transformation of the creaky Soviet empire into something better overwhelmed a susceptible Gorbachev. He did not call in the army when the Berlin Wall was pulled down in November 1989.

Figure 13.4
The Berlin wall being torn down, November 11, 1989. Stephen Ferry, GettyImages.

Second, state monopoly over the Soviet economic system, while useful in wartime and good at directing resources to military and scientific enterprises and the extensive Soviet educational system, proved incapable of producing in sufficient quantity and quality to satisfy people's changing needs. The "informal" economy became essential to provisioning the population and even to keeping "formal" (state) enterprises going. Moreover, the communist monopoly was corruptible. Elites within the Soviet republics, including those in the Caucasus and central Asia, turned their party and non-party pyramids into bastions of personal power.

Third, the person of the emperor counted. After Stalin's death in 1953, top party leaders gave up killing each other and agreed to keep themselves and their relatives on the ladders of management and provisioning. This stressed the system in two ways. There were more high-level consumers to support and fewer punishments available. Gradually workers learned that they, too, would usually not be sanctioned for not working. With rewards for loyal service in short supply, authorities in the late 1960s tried further restrictions on Jews' access to the elite, but that strategy deprived the system of expertise.

The party itself took the initiative—with setbacks—in opening up the flow of information that had been constricted in the past. Khrushchev's "secret" speech in 1956 denounced Stalin's crimes against the Soviet people and unleashed, for a time, the mighty forces of Soviet intellectual and creative elites upon the party's past. Ambitious leaders-in-training like Gorbachev visited Czechoslovakia as well as France and Italy. The extensive Soviet espionage network meant that many a loyal member of the KGB could appreciate the economic achievements of capitalism and the lifestyles of its managers.

Soviet leaders still felt that they had a civilizing mission in central Asia. In 1979 the Red Army went into Afghanistan—a place that empire-builders had tried repeatedly to subdue in the past—to shore up a client regime. Unable to win against a multiplicity of opponents, including Islamic militants armed by the United States, the USSR withdrew its last troops in 1989.

By the mid-1980s, the Politburo's incoming cohort of Soviet-made men were people who had seen capitalist societies, spent most of their lives in provincial Soviet postings, knew a great deal about deep flaws in the system, and were ready to change it once again. Soviet empire collapsed as the Romanov one had—from the top and center. Deep alienation from the failures and hypocrisies of Soviet claims led to an almost complete defection of elites from party rule in 1991 when conservatives tried to turn back the clock.

The Soviet repertoire of imperial strategies helped shape the way the USSR worked, the way it failed, and the way power was transfigured after 1991. The system of national republics provided a template for the formation of fifteen separate states. The top leaders of each national party believed that they had more to gain as presidents of independent countries than as subordinates of Moscow. Boris Yeltsin, who had challenged Gorbachev by

Map 13.3
Successor states
to the USSR.

turning the presidency of the Russian Republic into an office with more than symbolic power, orchestrated the impressively peaceful division of the empire along preset lines. None of the new states was nationally homogeneous, of course, but scholars within each rapidly rewrote histories to shore up their claims to sovereignty.

In eastern Europe, elites to their credit avoided yet another series of wars over boundary drawing by sticking with the postwar frontiers. The two exceptions to calm imperial collapse were Chechnya—where Yeltsin and a former general in the Red Army were unable to agree on a division of the spoils—and Yugoslavia, where Slobodan Milosevic and other nationalist politicians unleashed another murderous round of ethnic cleansing, attempting to create bigger nations on the still mixed territories that had been ruled and competed over by empires for so many centuries.

Imperial Competition during Decolonization

Let us back up in time to look at interimperial rivalry in the postwar era, specifically at how the USSR and the United States acted in relation both to western European states and to the spaces opened up by declining empires. By 1945, the United States held the fate of former western European empires in its hands—or rather in its bank vaults. Debts to the United States and American financial assistance shaped the postwar decade, although Europe's recovery was more rapid than most observers at the time expected. American leaders were well aware that too big an economic lead could be a dangerous thing and that the United States would not be able to take advantage of its productive might if nobody could afford to buy its output. The Marshall Plan was an innovative intervention, not least because it committed victorious European powers to include defeated Germany, breaking a cycle of retribution and resentment. Germany became the centerpiece of European economic revival.

The American position in regard to other people's empires was ambivalent. While planning for the future during the war, the Roosevelt administration expressed no small antagonism toward the British and French empires. But even before Roosevelt's death and well before the cold war heated up, the United States pulled its punches, favoring a slow wind-down of colonial regimes over a rapid and potentially disorderly decolonization. By refusing to support the Dutch return to Indonesia in 1945, forcing Britain and France to back down on Suez in 1956, and putting on France's mantle in Vietnam, the United States signaled that it would not unconditionally support colonial empires but that it would assume leadership against what it saw as a communist bloc.

In Japan's former colony of Korea the United States attempted to establish itself as the new protector of cooperative, dependent states and the one power still capable of drawing the line against communist expansion. But China's key role in the Korean war (as well as its support of revolution in Vietnam) and the mitigated outcomes of these bloody conflicts were signs of old limits on intrusion in the region. With a new regime in command, China was once again too strong for western powers to bend it to their will. States coming out of empires in Asia would not simply slip into clientage to the United States.

The world's most powerful state had more success in shaping a new variant on the imperialism of free trade. The United States provided incentives—including after 1949 a program of development assistance—for elites in new and old states to cooperate with transnational corporations and American policy. Washington used its economic and military muscle to prevent sovereign states from going too far against what were perceived as American interests. The managed overthrow of elected governments in Iran (1953) and Guatemala (1954) were only the most notorious of interventions to put into power elites friendly to the United States. Belgian and American secret services shared complicity in the assassination of the left-leaning leader of the former Belgian Congo, Patrice Lumumba, in 1960. Military rivalry with the USSR fostered external projection of power—networks of hundreds of American military bases placed around the globe. This was a variant on enclave imperialism with relatively weak linkages to hinterlands (the ideal base was an island), connected by airplanes and electronics to the command point, devoid of civilizing missions and of ties to local exporters that earlier enclave empires had developed.

But rulers of ex-colonial and other countries courted by the United States had other options in this version of interempire competition. The Soviet Union also had its foreign intrigues and its means of influence. The USSR's model of centralized economic planning appealed to rulers whose main political asset was control of the state. In Cuba, Vietnam, and elsewhere, the Soviet (and in some cases Chinese) models of revolutionary transformation influenced activists, both in times of armed struggle for the state and during post-revolutionary attempts to remake society. In some cases, notably India, governments refused to choose between market and planning models and between Soviet and American political camps, and sought instead to balance different economic structures and linkages.

Over the years of cold war rivalry, the United States proved a miserly patron and the Soviet Union had less to give away. European states, especially those in Scandinavia (without colonies, although with their own experiences of empire), devoted a much higher percentage of their national incomes to foreign aid. None of these initiatives got very far in addressing the vast inequalities that had emerged over the previous two hundred years. The two main rivals did, however, a great deal of harm by providing military support to repressive governments and guerilla movements thought to be on the right side.

The collapse of the Soviet Union meant for a time the end of competition between the two great powers for clients and of proxy wars in former colonial territories. Despite American triumphalism, the idea of unipolar dominance was as much an illusion as that of equivalence among nation-states with their formal sovereignty. The social and political fault lines left after the dissolution of empires were too numerous and too deep for any power to manage.

Freedom from Empire

If the liberation of colonies from empire had mixed results, some polities that failed as empires prospered as nation-states, Germany (West Germany to 1989) and Japan among them. Japan's loss of colonies after 1945 had different consequences from Germany's being stripped of its colonies after World War I, not least because of the crisis of empire that Japan's wartime victories had induced in southeast Asia.

Japan, like Germany, became an occupied country. But occupation was not colonization. It entailed no integration into an imperial, American whole. It was bounded in time and limited in ambition, even if the occupier held enormous power over humiliated, devastated, and impoverished populations. The United States and its allies decided, after hesitation, not to eliminate the Japanese emperor and to leave many of the large corporations of both Germany and Japan intact; they also tried to ensure that militarism would not return to either place. The United States wanted neither country to be a burden for long on American resources and for West Germany and Japan to be integrated into a capitalist world economy. Both defeated countries had highly educated populations and superior levels of know-how in industrial technologies. With resources developed during their previous imperial careers, Germany and Japan were quite unlike the colonized world, and their economic recoveries were rapid. For four decades, however, East Germany's absorption into the Soviet bloc put it on a different trajectory—as a replica state, much poorer than its western neighbor.

Germany and Japan were liberated in a fundamental sense: from the competition for and among empires. For the Japanese, the dismantling of Dutch, French, and British empires in southeast Asia in favor of a series of independent states removed the great fear of the 1930s—that Japan's sources of raw materials and access to markets could be undermined at the whim of European powers. Japan could now rely on world markets for supplies and outlets. Germany did not have to worry about France or Britain mobilizing their colonial resources, but could take its place as a self-consciously national state alongside an increasingly national France and an increasingly national Britain. Divided into east and west and in the shadow of the USSR's expansion into eastern Europe, Germany did have to worry about the other superpower. Fear of communism drew West Germany alongside other western European states. American military protection as well as the Marshall Plan helped make the new Europe of sovereign but collaborating states possible.

The bifurcation of Europe in 1945 had occurred with both sides in misery and insecurity; afterward the dynamism of the western European states could not be matched by those to the east. The democratic-undemocratic divide in Europe was not absolute, however. Spain and Portugal remained under fascist rule into the 1970s, and France came close to military revolt in 1958 in the midst of the Algerian crisis, emerging from this danger through procedures that were neither transparent nor in conformance with its constitution. Greece had an episode of right-wing dictatorship in the 1960s. Still the degree of interconnection—cross-border cultural contacts and migration, overlapping economic institutions and consumer cultures—within western Europe put pressure on outliers like Spain and Portugal to come into the fold. On the other side, Stalin and his successors crushed protest and revolt in Poland, Hungary, and Czechoslovakia, but the USSR lost some battles, particularly in 1948, when Tito, a war hero with geography on his side, managed to take Yugoslavia out of Soviet control.

Western Europe's freedom from empire enabled its states to contemplate cooperation on the basis of sovereign equivalence. The earliest step, the European Coal and Steel Community of 1951, was tentative and narrow in focus; the Treaty of Rome of 1957 created the European Economic Community, but it contained more promises than commitments.

Politically, national sentiments—in no small measure resulting from the loss of colonies—were stronger than ever. The European Economic Community extended its influence via administrative institutions agreed upon by elites, not via political processes in which people chose and defined a common project. The declaration of the European Union in 1993, the elimination of border formalities in part of the Union, the increasing role of Union institutions in regulating commercial and social affairs as well as a common currency after 2000, all pointed in the direction of confederation: each state retained its national identification and sovereignty but ceded some prerogatives to a common body. The idea of Europe widened when the eastern European states that had emerged from Soviet imperial power gradually became eligible for Union membership. There was no direct path from the Congress of Vienna of 1815 to the European Union of today—millions of corpses lie along the way—but thanks to the formal institutions of the Union, "Europe" is a collectivity with a range of common institu-

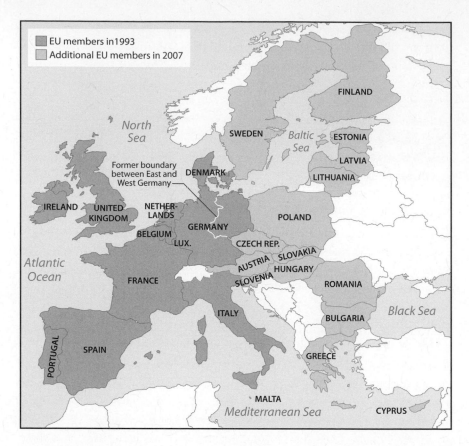

Map 13.4
The European
Union in 1993
and 2007.

EU members in1993

Additional EU members in 2007

FINLAND

North Sea

SWEDEN

Baltic Sea

ESTONIA

LATVIA

Former boundary between East and West Germany

DENMARK

LITHUANIA

IRELAND

UNITED KINGDOM

NETHER-LANDS

POLAND

BELGIUM

GERMANY

LUX.

CZECH REP.

Atlantic Ocean

AUSTRIA

SLOVAKIA

HUNGARY

FRANCE

SLOVENIA

ROMANIA

Black Sea

ITALY

BULGARIA

PORTUGAL

SPAIN

GREECE

MALTA

Mediterranean Sea

CYPRUS

tions, not a space of rivalry for imperial dominance. As Europeans acquired rights to circulate freely and to work in different parts of the Union, they marked out the limits of inclusion, keeping out children of people the colonial empires had tried to keep in.

China's New Way

Neither capitalist, anticommunist western powers nor the Soviet Union could get their way in China, with its long-lasting imperial tradition and commercial, agricultural, and political resources. For China, the years between the fall of the Qing in 1911 and the declaration of the People's Republic in 1949 turned out to be yet another interlude in a very long imperial history, not the end of a great state. Expectations of centralizing authority and familiarity with the techniques of administration were put to use by Mao Zedong and his party, this time under a worldly mandate—making China communist. Mao's aim since the 1920s had been the reconstruction of China with borders close to those established by the Qing.

The end of World War II found Mao's communist army, having fled the Guomindang and the Japanese, in the north of China, whence conquests of the Chinese state had emerged for over two thousand years. With some help from the USSR, the communists were able to regroup and hold onto cities in Manchuria. Through land reform and brutal anti-landlord campaigns, Mao's party built up support in the fragmented countryside and set out to gain control over the rest of China.

The Red Army's victory in 1949 brought in a different kind of dynasty—based on the Communist Party, its emperor-like leader, surrounded by an inner circle of advisors—focused on the reconstruction of the state and the improvement of society. As in the USSR, the party transformed older patrimonial strategies into party leaders' control over appointments to key positions in the administrative hierarchy. China was only for a brief time and never wholeheartedly a disciple of Russian communism. In the 1950s, Mao pulled away from Moscow, especially from its policy of "peaceful co-existence" with the west. At the Bandung conference, China pushed for a third—not western or Soviet—way. Chinese policy toward its near abroad expressed continuities with its imperial past—major military interventions in Korea and Vietnam, but only piecemeal efforts to aid communist movements elsewhere. China still had its imperial map in mind.

After a monumentally lethal collectivization drive (the "great leap forward" caused twenty to thirty million deaths) from 1958 to 1961, after ruthless—also deadly—purges of party cadres and other experts in the "cultural revolution" beginning in 1966, and, possibly most significantly, after Mao's death in 1976, the Chinese leadership gradually opened the way to private enterprise and investment by foreign companies. An economic boom of colossal proportions commenced. This was not a victory for "free trade" or "the west," but another transformation of the long-lived Chinese imperial tradition. In this variant, the Communist Party retains the commanding heights; peaceful demands for democracy are repressed; ethnic or other solidarities, such as those among the Muslim populations along the old frontier with central Asia or Buddhists in Tibet, are combated with the state's intrusive might. The state controls some enterprises and uses them to encourage economic growth in certain sectors or places, but—as in Chinese empires of the past—it leaves most productive activities in private hands while retaining its right to regulate all aspects of social life, including the number of children allowed to families.

In 1997 Hong Kong, one of the most visible markers of the presumptions of British empire, was returned to China. Hong Kong had been one of Britain's spoils of conquest in 1842, and its status came under treaty arrangements made with the Qing. The cession of Hong Kong back to China was hedged by negotiated qualifications, including partial administrative autonomy for the city-state. Hong Kong thus was reconfigured in British and Chinese imperial fashion, a reminder of the basic strategy of empires: governing differ-

Figure. 13.5
The retrocession of Hong Kong from Britain to China, July 1, 1997. President Jiang Zemin of China shakes hands with Prince Charles of Great Britain, as prime ministers Li Peng and Tony Blair look on. Hong Kong, ceded by the Qing empire to Britain in 1842, became a special territory under the sovereignty of the People's Republic of China. Paul Lakatos, AFP, GettyImages.

ent people differently, but not as equals or equivalents to other components of a polity. The return also underscores the volatility of imperial trajectories and their intersections. Hong Kong's British period, for all the impact of the imperial connections established then, was a short episode in the history of Chinese empire.

By the end of the twentieth century, this long-lived empire was reversing the geographies of power that had held for two hundred years, becoming the creditor of the United States, the purchaser of raw materials in the west's ex-colonies, a consumer of Europe's luxuries. Bipolar rivalry has ended, but another power on the Eurasian landmass has reemerged as a driving force in world politics, innovating and invigorating its imperial tradition once again.

EMPIRES, STATES, AND POLITICAL IMAGINATION

14

Empire has not given way to a stable, functioning world of nation-states. Many recent bloody and destabilizing conflicts—in Rwanda, Iraq, Israel/Palestine, Afghanistan, ex-Yugoslavia, Sri Lanka, the Congo, the Caucasus, and elsewhere—emerged from failures to find viable alternatives to imperial regimes. States created on the terrain of former colonies have not achieved many of the goals hoped for at the time of independence. The great powers proclaim a world of inviolable and equal nations, while deploying economic and military might to undermine other nations' sovereignty. Meanwhile, political leaders and others try to organize supranational bodies to regulate conflict and interaction among states. In Europe ideas of confederation that surfaced during debates over colonial empires in the 1950s are now being applied to bring together states on a continent that had been torn by conflict from the fall of Rome through the fall of communism.

Imperial Trajectories Revisited

The pathways taken by empires do not predict the future, but they help us understand the conditions, ideas, and actions that brought us to this uncertain present. Let us look back at how empires made history happen over a long sweep of time. We have emphasized the ways in which empires juggled strategies of likeness and difference within expanding or contracting polities. We stressed the vertical nature of power relations within empires, as leaders tried to recruit intermediaries—from their own milieu or from incorporated societies—to administer distant territories and assure contingent accommodation to imperial rule. We looked at the intersections of empires—the emergence of new empires on the edges of others, the thwarting of imperial expansion by rival empires, and the effects of imperial power and aspirations for national autonomy upon each other. Rather than classifying empires in static categories, we have seen how ruling elites combined different ways of exercising power at a distance. Varied but intertwined imperial trajectories repeatedly transformed the world over two millennia.

We began with China and Rome in the third century BCE. Both produced techniques for empire-building, including strong distinctions between those who joined the process and those who were seen as outsiders, labeled nomads and barbarians. Ever since the Qin put "China" together, the possibility of imperial command over a vast and productive space has fired political imagination, even when the space that dynasties actually governed expanded, contracted, and split. Conquerors aspired to rule, not destroy, China. The Yuan in the fourteenth century and the Manchus starting in the seventeenth used their distinctiveness to transform imperial power and expand the empire's territory.

Rule by officials helped Chinese emperors avoid dependence on local lords, making China's imperial trajectory different from that of Rome and post-Roman polities in western Europe. The Chinese imperial state controlled waterworks and granaries to reduce the risk of famine, but it did not create a singular religious edifice or attempt to homogenize the economic or cultural lives of people across the empire. China ran into trouble in the nineteenth century when much younger empires—offering new incentives, new ideas, new connections, and new threats—revealed the weaknesses of the Qing economy and suggested alternative strategies to some Chinese elites. But anti-Manchu, anti-foreigner, nationalist, and communist movements all maintained a focus on China as a unit.

Rome had a run of some six hundred years in the west and a further thousand years in the east, in Byzantium's modified, more flexible imperial style. Rome's influence as a model outlived its existence as an empire. The possibility that diverse people could become Romans by adopting its civilizational practices and accepting its authority inspired both the flexibility and the arrogance of future empires. Rome incorporated distant gods into its pantheon, recruited peripheral elites to positions of high status, and assimilated earlier cultural achievements into its idea of civilization. This enriched and unifying Roman culture attracted loyalty and emulation over an enormous space.

Of fundamental significance was Roman citizenship: once the attribute of the soldiering elite of the imperial city, citizenship was gradually extended to many in the empire and in 212 to all free males. The idea that people living in scattered places could become citizens of empire and enjoy rights throughout the polity echoed in movements for constitutional reform—in the French Caribbean in the 1790s, among Latin American creoles in 1812, Ottomans in 1869, French Africans in 1946.

A path that Rome took and China avoided was to turn from the synthesizing, polytheistic religious practices of its early centuries toward monotheism. The idea of a universal empire linked to a single universal faith— Christianity—left a lasting imprint on later empires that emulated Rome. Yet when Constantine moved his capital to Byzantium, he and his successors, while relying on the church to shore up their power, adjusted their mode of rule to the multiple peoples, cultures, and economic networks of the eastern Mediterranean. The eastern Roman empire left a different version of Christianity to empires, like Russia, that took shape at the edges of its cultural orbit.

The marriage of monotheism and empire appeared to provide coherence to imperial polities, but its effects on imperial regimes were both profound and volatile. The Islamic caliphates built empires based on a new monotheism in the southern and eastern regions of what had been the Roman empire. These empires expanded rapidly, spreading Islam to distant places, from Spain to southeast Asia. But founding empires on the all-encompassing notion of Islamic community proved easier than sustaining them. The caliphates were wracked by schisms and attacks by rival candidates for rule. These assaults pushed Islamic rulers into political innovations, as well as competitions for artistic and scholarly talent. Under protection of different Muslim rulers, classical learning was integrated into an Arabic-based high culture and preserved, even as the caliphates fragmented and were reconfigured.

In western Europe, Christianity (and in part of that region Latin-derived languages) proved a more durable Roman legacy than state institutions. A politics of landed magnates with armed retainers emerged from the collapse of the Roman center. As competing lords reclaimed and redefined Rome's legal traditions, they enforced—for themselves and upon their dependents—the idea of noble rights and status. Lords provided would-be emperors with assemblages of military followers, but they could do the same for opponents of any empire-builder. Charlemagne, crowned by the pope in 800, came closest to reestablishing a universalizing empire, but his successors soon fell victim to rivalries and aristocratic combinations. The fragmentation of power in Europe continued to stymie attempts to reconstitute a Roman empire.

Islamic empires, starting with the Umayyads, avoided the aristocratic conundrum by relying instead on an imperial household, staffed largely by outsiders—slaves, clients, and recent converts. On the Eurasian steppe, empire-builders used other tactics to secure intermediaries—blood brotherhood, marriage politics, and tribal allegiances. From ancient times, nomadic peoples had made major technological contributions to state formation across Eurasia, including the armed horseback warrior. The intersections of agrarian empire, from the Qin and Han dynasties onward, with the military and commercial talents of "barbarians" on their borders forced Chinese leaders to build a polity capable of both resisting and managing nomads. Turkic confederacies created the institution and title of the khan. Warriors brought as slaves from Eurasia—with their steppe ethos and skills at horsemanship—were crucial to several empires, including the Abbasid caliphate with its slave armies and the Mamluks, slave-warriors who had taken power into their own hands. The Seljuks who conquered Baghdad in 1055, and later the Mongols, who captured the city in 1258, were organized along Eurasian principles and brought Turkic and Mongol practices into the Mediterranean arena.

The most spectacular demonstration of nomads' capacity for imperial expansion was Chinggis Khan's thirteenth-century conquest. His campaigns across Eurasia produced the largest territorial empire of all time. The Mongols, under Chinggis and his sons and grandsons, with their cross-continental relay system and mobile armies, ruled from the Danube to the Pacific at a time when western Europeans could barely dream of reconstructing Rome. The Mongols protected trade routes and linked a variety of cultural and religions traditions. Mongol overlords taught Russian princes how to administer and make a realm, while in China, Mongols founded the Yuan dynasty and reassembled an empire that had split apart.

The Ottomans, who drew on Turkic, Arab, Persian, Mongol, and Byzantine experience to produce the most durable Islamic empire, were little concerned with doctrinal purity, avoided or managed confessional schisms, and integrated diverse communities into an imperial whole. Flexibility and recognition of difference were hallmarks of Ottoman rule, enabling them to survive multiple shifts in the world economy and politics between their initial forays in the fourteenth century and their destruction in the twentieth.

The trajectory of European empire is best understood not as a narrative of "expansion" whose dynamic lay in characteristics peculiar to Europeans but in relationships and competitions among empires. Blocked on the eastern and southern Mediterranean by the Ottomans, constrained at home by aristocratic-dynastic politics, the would-be emperors of western Europe had to look overseas. The true pioneers of an ocean-crossing economy—with specialized trading groups, linkages to markets, and tools for exchange and credit—were in Asia, from India across southeast Asia to China. It was by forcefully inserting themselves into nodal points in those commercial systems that Portuguese and Dutch empires got their start.

The rulers of Castile and Aragon were trying to break into the inter-empire game of Asia trade when Columbus happened upon the Americas. What made that event so promising was the subsequent discovery of other empires. Without the ability of Aztec and Inca empires to concentrate wealth, the new continent and nearby islands might not have been so attractive to Europeans. At the same time, the fractures within these empires allowed conquistadors to gain Indian allies and a foothold. Later, it was the connections among world regions that made the American venture worthwhile for European states and colonial settlers. American silver paid for many of Europe's empire wars and fostered its financial service business; it allowed Europeans to purchase commodities they sought in Asia. Slaves bought in Africa produced sugar on plantations in the Caribbean that fed people in Europe, including by the eighteenth century workers who were making England's industrial revolution and providing goods that people across the world wanted to buy.

The goal of individual empires was not to make the world a more interconnected space—empires tried to restrict their competitors' connections. But empire-building had effects beyond the intentions of its makers. Islamic pilgrimage to Mecca shaped a Muslim world beyond any caliphate's boundaries; Gujaratis crossed the Indian Ocean before Europeans got there, later helped make European trade routes work, and traveled across imperial boundaries after European empires were installed; Chinese traders dynamized exchange across southeast Asia—and indirectly to Europe—even when the Ming emperors did not support overseas trade. Agents of empire—traders, company officials—sometimes circumvented the very imperial channels they were meant to keep in place. The size and wealth of empires made it attractive for smugglers, pirates, and interlopers to operate on a large scale, too.

The extensions of European empires overseas took many pathways. They produced slave societies and settler colonies. In some areas, indigenous populations were decimated by disease, violence, coercive conversion, and acculturation. In other circumstances, societies retained and cultivated their integrity in the face of European interventions, more successfully in Asia than the Americas. Overseas empire lived off the organizational and managerial skills—not just the brute labor—of their subjects. In some instances, a colonial society took root, its elites modeling themselves on English gentry or Spanish aristocracy, exercising different forms of domination over descendants of Europeans, indigenous peoples, and imported slaves. Some colonials aspired to break away from one empire and build another in their own right—the "Empire of Liberty" of the American revolutionaries and the Brazilian empire that emerged when a branch of the Portuguese royal family did not go home.

The implications for empires of eighteenth-century political theories and revolutions were far from clear. If in monarchies, all subjects came under the power of the king or emperor, when "the people" ruled the question of who was inside or outside this category became crucial. The idea of popular sovereignty had explosive consequences when claimed by settlers in British North America and slaves in French Saint Domingue.

The United States became united in part out of fear of other empires. The new polity declared equality as its foundation but did not extend it to all on the territories it claimed and conquered. American empire destroyed and marginalized indigenous communities and could not resolve the tensions between "slave" and "free" states short of civil war. Well into the twentieth century, the republic kept Native Americans outside the polity and failed to establish equal rights for descendants of slaves. The strong sense of moral community in American ideology allowed a huge empire that spread across a continent and eventually overseas to play down its imperial history and conceive of itself as a single large nation, divided into federated states that had a measure of self-rule but were equivalent to one another.

The rulers of European states did not necessarily want to limit themselves to governing one people; they were familiar with the polity as a differentiated entity and could shift strategies among its components. Imperial organization persisted after revolutions, was extended by Napoleon, and restructured yet again after his defeat. For Britain, the "imperialism of free trade"—the exercise of economic power punctuated by intermittent military interventions—became as important a strategy as the various kinds of authority it exercised over Scotland, Ireland, Canada, India, and the Caribbean islands—and later over much of Africa.

The colonizations of the nineteenth century did not make entirely new empires as some historians have suggested. Instead they built upon and expanded the repertoire of imperial techniques, extended crosscutting networks and contagious ideas, and raised the stakes of interempire competition. Europeans acquired more effective means to make people in distant lands serve their interests, but they were deeply divided over treating them as exploitable objects or as junior members of an imperial community. Challenged by slave revolts and transcontinental abolition movements, Britain in 1833, France in 1848, and Brazil and Cuba in the 1880s renounced slavery. Many did not believe Africans or Asians or their descendants would ever merit equal rights and equal political voice, but the limits of colonial authority and the possible "elevation" of colonized peoples into civilization became subjects of debate.

At conferences of imperial rulers, European powers expressed their collective entitlement to rule others, reinforced by theories of social evolution and racial distinction. But within a few years of the late nineteenth-century scramble, even advocates of a vigorous transformation of Africa were backing off, faced with the intractable problems of ruling a vast space, lining up intermediaries, controlling excesses on the part of their agents and settlers, and changing habits of people who had their own networks of support and could adapt to new circumstances.

No one form of colonial rule was ever the object of a stable consensus among metropolitan publics—or broadly convincing to the people in the colonies whose contingent accommodation was needed. Using the political language of their colonizers, Asians and Africans insisted that ideas of liberty should apply to themselves. Colonial rule was also contested in other idioms and with other objectives—restoration of local forms of rule, Islamic unity, and anticolonial alliances.

Colonization occupied a particularly important place in the repertoire of economic and political power in late nineteenth-century Europe because of the competition among a small number of empires, each with supranational resources within and beyond the continent. Austria-Hungary, Russia, and the Ottomans, like Britain, France, and other European powers, aspired by whatever means they could to control territory, people, and their connections by land and sea.

Both in Europe, and on its edges, empires tried out variants on political reform and more vigorous ways to incorporate people into imperial structures. The rise of a German Reich, including non-German-speaking territories in Europe and then extending overseas, raised tensions among European powers. Empires were all looking at each other, and many used the ideas of national rights or protection of coreligionists to stir up trouble inside rivals' empires.

The nationalist sentiments on which such manipulations played were real enough, at times virulent. But nationalists had to come to grips with two problems: first, the people of Europe, as on other continents, did not live in homogeneous linguistic and cultural blocks, and second, empires were capable of both attracting loyalty and inflicting discipline.

The national idea is often linked to a particular kind of citizenship—to a united people expressing their desires through democratic means, claiming resources for well-being from "their" state, sometimes seeking redress for inequities produced by capitalism and markets. Certainly, the increasing role of states in social life encouraged people to focus on themselves as a collectivity—the better to make claims and to limit the populations to which those claims applied. But the boundaries of belonging and access to the state remained uncertain into the twenty-first century.

In the case of France, the possibility of a citizenship embracing people in the colonies was opened in the 1790s, shut down by Napoleon in 1802, reopened in 1848 when citizenship was proffered in the Caribbean and parts of Senegal, narrowed as late nineteenth-century colonization put more and more people into the category of subject, debated anew when France needed men to fight for the empire, and fulfilled, briefly, with the declaration of citizenship for all subjects in 1946. Britain, like France, saw after World War II that extending social rights and technological advances to the colonies might give empire a new legitimacy. It was the cost of this endeavor—as people in the colonies brought ever more claims against imperial resources—that gave British and French administrators second thoughts about the viability of empire.

Similarly, whether the scope of labor movements should be national, imperial, or international was debated throughout the lifetimes of these organizations. In short, the struggles for a citizenry that could choose its government and claim state resources did not coincide with national ideas or ethnic boundaries: citizenship was also a question for and about empire. Democratizing empire was a political issue from the days of Toussaint L'Ouverture to those of Léopold Senghor.

Both the extension of European empires' control to new territories overseas and the methods of their competition with each other were profoundly shaped by the development of industrial capitalism, spreading outward from eighteenth-century England. The growth of European economies broke open a technology gap with Asian powers, pushed Ottoman and Chinese empires into debt to buy arms and capital equipment, and enhanced the mobility of European armies and corporations. The competition among European empires decisively conditioned the terms under which capitalist development took place. Technologies provided by and required for industrialization combined with capital's needs for raw materials and markets pushed empires' efforts to ensure control of resources nearby and far away.

But when territories were taken over, colonized people did not simply fall into whatever role striving industrialists could imagine for them. Empires still came up against the limits of their power at the far end of lines of command, where they had to mobilize conquered communities and find reliable intermediaries—all at a cost that did not exceed the benefits. Hence the apparent paradox that late nineteenth-century empires did not go all out in areas they seemed capable of dominating; they were unable or unwilling to turn most Africans into proletarians or to transform Indian landowners into a replica of an English capitalist class. The unevenness of state power around the world accentuated the unevenness of capitalism's effects.

Nor could European capitalists keep their rivalries with each other in check. It was the evolving system of empires that twisted conflicts in Europe into the spiral of violence leading from the Crimean war to World War I. The twentieth-century empire wars were fatal to millions of people and fatal to some forms of empire. The conflicts *among* empires, not just the resistance of conquered peoples or the rebellions of settlers, weakened and challenged imperial control.

Colonial empire was an important resource for Britain and France in World War I. Afterward both powers sought to entrench their control over dependencies, while helping themselves to a share of German colonies and Ottoman provinces under League of Nations mandates. The destruction of

German, Ottoman, and Austro-Hungarian empires did not lead to a viable alternative to empire. Quite the contrary, for after waves of ethnic cleansing in central Europe after 1919, the states that emerged were weak. Their national insecurities turned into xenophobia and anti-semitism.

The Ottoman empire even before the war suffered from the disruptions unleashed by centralizing and nationalizing initiatives. While for the most part retaining the loyalty of the Arab provinces, Ottoman leaders had put a new emphasis on Turkification, particularly after the losses, violence, and expulsions Ottomans suffered in the Balkans. The war brought out the worst of these homogenizing tendencies; the massacres of Armenians took them to an extreme. After the destruction of the Ottoman empire at the end of the war, Turkish nationalists insisted on the unitary nature of the state—expelling Greeks in an enormous population "exchange," cracking down on minorities like the Kurds, and replacing religious toleration with militant secularism. Turkey is still affected by these actions that seemed to put an end to the Ottomans' earlier inclusivity.

At the beginning of the century, Japan changed the imperial game by joining it, having demonstrated its strength at the expense of the Chinese and Russian empires in 1895 and 1905. Japan's drive to make an Asian alternative to European empire put it on a collision course with European and American powers who had brought much of the resources of southeast Asia under their control.

Inside Europe, the geopolitical situation in the mid-1930s was not radically different from what it had been in 1914, but Nazi Germany was not the Kaiserreich and the USSR was not the Russia of the tsars. The imperial peace that ended World War I stripped Germany of its overseas colonies as well as cutting it down in size in Europe. Deprivation and wounded imperial entitlement intensified Nazis' chauvinistic, anti-semitic, and Slavophobic visions and culminated in the idea of a purely German empire. This unmitigated racialization broke with other empires' strategies of conjugating incorporation and differentiation in more flexible ways and made it difficult to secure intermediaries from conquered peoples. During World War II, this extreme variant of exclusionary empire failed, brought down by empires with more wide-ranging political, economic, and social resources.

One of the victors over Nazi Germany, and belatedly over Japan, was the Soviet Union. Like its competitors before and after the war, the USSR also claimed to be leading its peoples into a higher stage of civilization, in this case, into international communism. The USSR carried on a supervised affirmative action program inside its borders, trained and disciplined "national" leaders on and sometimes beyond its territories, tried to keep its satellite states fixed on the Soviet sun, and conducted a powerful ideological offensive among discontented or rebellious people in other empires. At the end of World War II, Stalin was able not only to extend the USSR beyond Russia's 1914 frontiers but also, in accord with his wartime allies, to give the Soviet state a generous buffer zone of subordinated polities in contentious central Europe where the war had begun. Victory gave the Soviet version of Russian empire a new lease on life and a new influence around the world.

Nazi Germany and especially Japan brought other empires down with them. Before World War II, anticolonial movements had spread, exposing the abuses of colonial rule and attacking its normality. But through the 1930s, colonial strategies of limiting ambition and concentrating forces to repress rebellions kept the lid on. It was during and immediately after the war that the edifice of colonial empire began to crumble, but not before both France and Britain tried to reconstitute imperial hegemony via programs of development and expanded political participation.

By the late 1940s and 1950s, the combination of revolutionary movements in some places, claim-making by trade unions and activists' associations in others, international pressures, and mobilization in colonies for equality, citizenship, economic development, and self-determination came to a head. Giving up empire was not what Britain, France, and other European powers had in mind at the war's end, nor was national independence the only direction in which social and political movements in the colonies were looking. But independence in the form of territorial states became the one alternative on which colonial powers and political movements in the colonies could agree.

The trajectory from the last round of colonization in Africa and southeast Asia to independence lasted only seventy or eighty years—not a long time by the standards of historical empires. The life span of the Soviet Union was similar, as was Japan's rule over Taiwan. These empires, communist and capitalist, claimed to be lifting societies to a higher level of economic and social life. But their goals of "development," "socialism," or an "Asian Co-Prosperity Sphere" were all variants on the civilizing projects of many empires before them.

For a long time the United States, acting in a world of empires, had insisted it was different, but it developed a repertoire of power that included familiar imperial tools, employed selectively in accord with American tastes. The imperialism of free trade and periodic occupations of countries that did not play by American rules were more evident than formal colonization. Many feared the consequences of bringing non-white aliens into the polity even as colonized subjects.

The American repertoire of power seemed to function nicely in a post–World War II world of nation-states, each open to commerce, investment, and American cultural effusions, each vulnerable to enforcement by the American military should the need arise. But the real world never fell in line. In the late twentieth century, faced with competition from the world's other remaining superpower, the United States vigorously sought client states and tried to set limits on other countries' supposed freedom of action—fomenting coups, invasions, occupations, and several wars. When bipolar rivalries ended after 1991, places like Afghanistan and Somalia, once objects of cold war intrigue by both sides, could be abandoned to their fate, and only belatedly did policymakers realize that people like the rebels who had fought the Soviets in Afghanistan were not mere puppets. They could turn from clients into enemies, as so many imperial intermediaries had done before.

The Present of the Past

Where do the intertwined trajectories of empires past leave us in the present? Certainly, with awareness that the inequalities of power and resources that led to empires and drove them on are still with us. So, too, are the disruptive effects of imperial breakdown.

Making nation conform to state was destructive in central Europe after 1919 and 1945, in the Balkans in 1878, 1912, 1919, 1945, and the 1990s, in parts of former empires in Africa and the Middle East into the twenty-first century. Yet carving out territorial boundaries gave political leaders spaces where they could make careers, acquire followers, and reach out to the world. Maintaining these boundaries or extending them, however inconsistent with the ways that people actually live, move, and associate with one another, remains a primary focus of ruling elites around the world.

Many hoped that with the end of empire, the vertical ties by which many empires exercised authority would give way to the horizontal affinity of citizens. In some post-imperial cases, these aspirations have been fulfilled, at least as fully as elsewhere in the "democratic" world. In India, for example, a politics of citizenship has defined most of its over sixty years of existence as a national state. Independent African states have experienced periodic mobilizations for citizens' rights, as well as military coups and impositions of one-man or one-party rule.

After World War II, some aspirations for horizontal affinities went beyond the nation-state, as in French West Africans' campaign for federation among their territories and in calls for "African" or "Arab" unity, or for international revolution. The Bandung idea of a third world took these hopes to a higher plane. None of these desires came to fruition, and the decolonizations that took place often did more to accentuate vertical ties than horizontal ones. Leaders governing small nation-states with few resources and uncertain hold on people's political imaginations often sought to eliminate alternatives to their rule by practicing a politics of clientelism within their territories and seeking patrons from powerful states and wealthy corporations abroad. A similar reconstruction of patrimonial power developed in many of the post-Soviet successor states. These personal connections, from leader to leader, are subject neither to the electoral will of the people involved nor to much scrutiny from interested groups in former imperial powers. European voters have now distanced themselves from responsibility; Russian ones never had it; Americans look the other way.

Pessimists have claimed that not much has changed in former colonies, that Africans now live in a "neocolonial" world. But even the disillusioning scenario described above represents a change, if not the one Africans thought they were getting in the 1960s. Sovereignty had its consequences, and for some, these were rewarding—the control of assets, like oil; the possibility of seeking patrons, especially during the cold war; and some room for maneuver in negotiating with foreign corporations, aid agencies, and international financial organizations. Sovereignty lowered a curtain behind which national rulers could conceal many actions, from corruption to ethnic cleansing.

Some ex-colonies, especially in southeast Asia where the history of integration into wider markets goes back before colonization, industrialized and dynamized their economies after independence—ex-British Malaysia and ex-Japanese South Korea, for example. But where colonial infrastructure was designed to bring a small number of primary commodities through narrow channels into markets dominated by a few transnational corporations, creating new economic structures has been an elusive goal. In much of Africa, leaders of ex-colonial states became fixated on a key achievement of their colonial predecessors—gatekeeping. The new rulers could take over as controllers of relations with the rest of the world, collecting revenue on goods (including aid) coming in and out, keeping tabs on wealthy farmers or businessmen who might develop commercial—and political—networks independent of the state elite. Just as the emancipation of slaves in the United States during the Civil War gave them "nothing but freedom," the independence of most colonial territories after World War II gave them nothing but sovereignty. Political elites made use of it—not necessarily in the interests of the people they governed and who had aspired to something more.

Transnational corporations have often profited from low wages and corrupt governments in resource-rich ex-colonial states, but they also run into limits set by insecurity, minimal infrastructure, and small or poorly organized markets. Access to vital commodities like oil—which imperial states from the British to the Nazis once sought in territories they could dominate—is now the fiercely guarded sovereign prerogative of countries whose reliability as suppliers is questionable and whose wealth might well be used against the interests of their best customers. Iran, Saudi Arabia, Iraq, the Sudan, Nigeria, Angola, Venezuela, and Russia are cases in point. Neither the development of apparently open world markets nor the periodic exercise of raw power by the United States has secured supplies of the most basic resources.

If we look at the most powerful states today, we see the present of the imperial pasts we have examined in this book. First and most obviously, China is back. The two hundred years when China could be characterized as falling "behind" western empires in their moment of economic and cultural effervescence may turn out to be comparable to the other dynastic interregnums in Chinese history. China now exports industrial commodities along with silk and takes in financial instruments rather than bullion. With more complex resource needs than in the past but no longer obliged to credit other empires' versions of free trade, China has integrated itself into markets around the world.

The leaders of China now evoke the imperial tradition to enhance state power; the Yuan and the Qing are celebrated as unifiers of Chinese terrain. China is still distinguished by its strong officialdom relatively detached from the society over which it presides. Administrators worry about desires of Tibetans for independence and secessionist politics in the largely Muslim region of Xinjiang—classic problems at the edges of this empire. Once again, Chinese rulers must control its economic barons and monitor diverse populations, but the polity can draw on its accumulated statecraft to meet these challenges and resume a prominent place in a shifting geography of power.

The rapid recovery of the Russian Federation after the communist collapse reveals another strong imperial culture at work. Like its predecessor empires, the Russian Federation is explicitly multiethnic, retaining subordinated "national" territories, some nested within each other. The Russian constitution of 1993 offered all republics the right to establish their own official languages, while defining Russian as the "state language of the Russian Federation as a whole." The constitution also guaranteed the rights of "national minorities" in accord with international principles of human rights. After a short unruly interlude, during which American advisors and missionaries had their turn at propaganda and when ambition of all kinds ran wild, Vladimir Putin revived the techniques of patrimonial power. As he and his protégés reconnect magnates to the state, tighten control over religious institutions, bring the media to heel, transform electoral process into a "sovereign democracy" supported by a single party, compel loyalty from the federation's governors, flirt with nationalism in Russian areas, reenter the competition for Russia's borderlands, and effectively wield Russia's prime weapon—energy—in the international arena, Russian empire has reappeared in yet another transmutation on its Eurasian space.

The most innovative of today's large powers is the European Union. Europe had been trapped from the fifth century to the twentieth between aspirations of some of its elites to produce a new Rome and the determination of others to prevent such an outcome. It was only in the 1950s and 1960s that Britain and France gave up their attempts to reconfigure imperial power as the British Commonwealth or French Community and accepted that their framework of operations was national—whatever their political, economic, sentimental, linguistic, and personal connections to ruling elites of the ex-empires. Between the 1960s and 1990s European states put their freedom from empire to use in working out confederal arrangements among themselves.

The confederal structure has functioned most effectively when limiting its ambitions to administration and regulation, using the well-honed skills of European planners. But anyone who passes abandoned customs houses along frontiers where millions of people have died in repeated wars can appreciate the remarkable achievement of the so-called Schengen states. One of the most basic attributes of sovereignty—control of who crosses a border—has been pushed up to a European level. The European Union has not securely captured the political loyalty of most people on its territories, but its leaders have a means to act coherently in the face of outside powers and to try to tamp down conflicts among member states. The concert of Europe plays new music, although it is not clear who is listening.

After 2001, it became fashionable among pundits to anoint the United States as an "empire," either to denounce the arrogance of its actions abroad or to celebrate its efforts to police and democratize the world. The "is it or isn't it?" question is less revealing than an examination of the American repertoire of power, based on selective use of imperial strategies. These tactics obviously include the use of force and occupation—in violation of norms of sovereignty—but even the most interventionist of American politicians do not contemplate turning Iraq or Afghanistan into Puerto Rico.

The mix of ways by which the United States tries to project authority across space reflects its own imperial trajectory—the development from the eighteenth century of a land empire, constructed on the basis of equal rights and private property for people considered citizens and the exclusion of Native Americans and slaves. Extension over a continent eventually put great resources in the hands of Euro-Americans; they thought of their conquests as the fulfillment of manifest destiny. After nearly foundering on the rock of slavery, American leaders had the strength to choose the time and terms of their interventions in the rest of the world.

Throughout the twentieth century the United States deployed an array of imperial strategies abroad: it occupied countries, dispatched troops to dislodge hostile leaders, sponsored proxy wars against foes, made use of enclave colonies and military bases on foreign soil, sent out missionaries, and, more recently, supplied development aid and expertise. But perhaps the most striking outcome of the American invasion of Iraq in 2003 is that occupying one weak, divided country has stretched the military, financial, and political capacities of the United States. In Afghanistan, Americans did not learn lessons from the earlier failures of British and Russian empires, and for that matter Tamerlane, to secure power over this region of fluid political allegiances.

None of these imperial powers links itself to a religious project, and even the secular religions of modernization and communism have lost much of their fervor. The monotheistic religions that earlier rulers thought would bring coherence and legitimacy to empire-building produced schism and dissent rather than unity; imperial regimes least demanding of religious conformity, including China and Russia, have been among the most durable. Although empires took very different approaches to cultural differences among incorporated peoples, some kind of tolerance of diversity has been essential for imperial longevity.

China, Russia, the European Union, and the United States all find themselves threatened by movements that do not line up neatly with state power. China in Xinjiang, Russia in Chechnya and other areas, and the United States and the European Union in Afghanistan seem to be battling networks often labeled "militant Islam." Muslims with no connection to militant movements are tarred with the brush of terrorism, treated as if they are unassimilable to dominant cultures inside states, transformed into the ultimate "other" a millennium after the crusades.

As we have seen, Islam spread initially as an empire-building project. But Islam's relationship to state power has been varied, from rival efforts to constitute a truly Islamic polity, to the Ottomans' cautious caliphate, to Russia's institutionalization of a Muslim hierarchy, to today's "Islamic" states, such as Iran and Saudi Arabia. But empires cannot always contain the long-distance connections they spawn, and what threatens today's governments is precisely that networks claiming the mantle of Islam—some with the goal of restoring the caliphate—are not subject to the self-interest and discipline of states. The grievances and suffering of many Muslims and the volatility of their political initiatives are part and parcel of the history of empires in the recent past—the encroachments of European empires in the nineteenth-century Middle East, the chaotic breakup of Ottoman rule, the failures of the mandate system, the interventions of world powers in vulnerable states, the poverty and hopelessness in regions where authoritarian rulers are abetted by "western" states.

A history of empires clashes with an imaginary of nations in the early twenty-first century's most notorious war so far. The space now assigned the national label "Iraq" was ruled by the ancient empires of the Fertile Crescent and much later by the Abbasids, whose empire was centered in Baghdad. It was invaded and occupied by Seljuks and Mongols; incorporated into the Ottoman empire; transferred to the British empire; administered by rulers who were clients of the British; occupied by the United States; and run by a military dictator who lived off oil sold to western states, fought a war against Iran, another against Kuwait, and brutalized Iraqis whose version of Islam, whose ethnicity, or whose politics made them suspect. Al-Qaeda is only one of the border-crossing projects that impinge on the "national" space of Iraq. Like many parts of former empires, Iraq corresponds to no indigenous society of long standing; its history has been and still is being carved at the intersections of states and networks and by changes in power relations among them.

Coming to grips in one way or another with the mixity of people across space has been a necessity for any ruler with ambitions beyond the local. Empires came up with different answers to this problem. This book has stressed the variations in the politics of difference deployed by empires. Many empires used difference as a tool of rule, making sure that the ties of elites and groups to the sovereign were stronger than linkages of imperial subjects to each other. Other empires strove for conformity among insiders and extruded or denigrated those who were unlike. Empires mixed and modified these strategies; the ability to apply different tactics to different segments of their populations may be a clue to their political endurance.

Empires, for better or worse, dealt directly with difference; nation-states had the idea—illusion perhaps—that difference could be overcome by the appeal of the national idea and of participation in state institutions, or negatively by exclusion, expulsion, and compulsory assimilation. But nation-states could never exclude, expel, and assimilate enough to produce uniform populations or erase crosscutting loyalties. Even in colonial situations, many people did not see the nation-state as the way to escape from empire. The end of colonial empires was conflictual and contingent. European empires gave up a sovereignty that was becoming costly and the new founding fathers took over sovereignties that they thought they could entrench. We live with the consequences of these uneven and broken paths out of empire, with the fiction of sovereign equivalence, and with the reality of inequality within and among states.

Thinking about empire does not mean resurrecting the British, Ottoman, or Roman empire. It allows us to consider the forms in which power is exercised across space—with their possibilities and limitations; the ways in which incorporation into polities and differentiation within them are imagined and enacted; the means by which the contingent accommodation of intermediaries to imperial power is obtained; and the alternatives to imperial power that settlers, indigenous people, officials, scholars, imported slaves, religious guides, and border-crossing traders were able to develop.

The past does not provide clear models—national or imperial—for building better polities, but exploring historical trajectories reminds us that the present has not been here forever and will not endure. As individuals and collectivities, we imagine different futures, make choices, and face their consequences. New and different forms of layered and overlapping sovereignty are possible, not just the ones we have studied in this book. People have envisioned and will create other forms of political organization. The past of empires displays the human costs of the arrogance of power—whether in the name of a great leader, a civilization, or a people—as well as the multifaceted transformations of social life that empires have produced. We have examined the wide range of ways in which empires incorporated and made distinctions among populations, the consequences of keeping people separate but unequal or trying to make them equal and alike. The challenge for the future is to imagine new polities that recognize widely held desires for political belonging, equality of opportunity, and mutual respect.

SUGGESTED READING
AND CITATIONS

Chapter 1

General Works on Empire

The Oxford and Cambridge histories of Rome, medieval Europe, China, Latin America, the British Empire, and other domains provide valuable introductions to different empires. Two excellent surveys of world history are Robert Tignor, Jeremy Adelman, Stephen Aron, and Stephen Kotkin, *Worlds Together; Worlds Apart: A History of the World from the Beginnings of Humankind to the Present*, 2nd ed. (New York: Norton, 2008), and Richard Bulliet, Pamela Crossley, Daniel Headrick, and Steven Hirsch, *The Earth and Its Peoples: A Global History*, 4th ed. (New York: Houghton Mifflin, 2007). Other works on empires across large areas and long time periods include the following:

Abernethy, David. *The Dynamics of Global Dominance: European Overseas Empires, 1415–1980*. New Haven: Yale University Press, 2000.

Cooper, Frederick. *Colonialism in Question: Theory, Knowledge, History*. Berkeley: University of California Press, 2005.

Cooper, Frederick, and Ann Laura Stoler, eds. *Tensions of Empire: Colonial Cultures in a Bourgeois World*. Berkeley: University of California Press, 1997.

Darwin, John. *After Tamerlane: The Global History of Empire since 1405*. London: Bloomsbury Press, 2008.

Findlay, Ronald, and Kevin H. O'Rourke. *Power and Plenty: Trade, Power, and the World Economy in the Second Millennium*. Princeton: Princeton University Press, 2007.

Kennedy, Paul. *The Rise and Fall of the Great Powers: Economic Change and Military Conflict from 1500 to 2000*. New York: Random House, 1987.

King, Charles. *The Black Sea: A History*. New York: Oxford University Press, 2004.

Lieven, Dominic. *Empire: The Russian Empire and Its Rivals*. London: Murray, 2001.

Pagden, Anthony. *Peoples and Empires: A Short History of European Migration, Exploration, and Conquest from Greece to the Present*. New York: Modern Library, 2001.

Pocock, J.G.A. *The Discovery of Islands: Essays in British History*. Cambridge: Cambridge University Press, 2005.

Chapter 2

Suggested Reading

Dench, Emma. *Romulus' Asylum: Roman Identities from the Age of Alexander to the Age of Hadrian*. New York: Oxford University Press, 2005.

Di Cosmo, Nicola. *Ancient China and Its Enemies: The Rise of Nomadic Power in East Asian History*. Cambridge: Cambridge University Press, 2002.

Finley, M. I. *The Ancient Economy*. Berkeley: University of California Press, 1973.

Garnsey, Peter, and Richard Saller. *The Roman Empire: Economy, Society and Culture*. Berkeley: University of California Press, 1987.

Harris, W.V., ed. *Rethinking the Mediterranean*. Oxford: Oxford University Press, 2005.

Hui, Victoria Tin-Bor. *War and State Formation in Ancient China and Early Modern Europe*. New York: Cambridge University Press, 2005.

Lewis, Mark Edward. *The Early Chinese Empires: Qin and Han*. Cambridge, MA: Harvard University Press, 2007.

Nicolet, Claude. *The World of the Citizen in Republican Rome*. Berkeley: University of California Press, 1980.

Rostovtzeff, Michael Ivanovitch. *Rome*. Translated from the Russian by J. D. Duff. New York: Oxford University Press, 1962.

Twitchett, Denis Crispin, and John King Fairbank, eds. *The Cambridge History of China*. Vol. 1. New York: Cambridge University Press, 2002.

Ward Perkins, Bryn. *The Fall of Rome and the End of Civilization*. Oxford: Oxford University Press, 2005.

Wolfram, Herwig. *The Roman Empire and Its Germanic Peoples*. Trans. Thomas Dunlap. Berkeley: University of California Press, 1997.

Woolf, Greg. *Becoming Roman: The Origins of Provincial Civilization in Gaul*. New York: Cambridge University Press, 1998.

Works Cited

30   "government without bureaucracy": Garnsey and Saller, *Roman Empire*, 20.

34–35   Figures on "feeding" from Garnsey and Saller, *Roman Empire*, 83, 88, 89.

38   "temple of the whole world": Thismistius, cited in Elizabeth Key Fowden, *The Barbarian Plain: Saint Sergius between Rome and Iran* (Berkeley: University of California Press, 1999), 46.

40   box: "An effective": cited in Michael Mann, *The Dark Side of Democracy: Explaining Ethnic Cleansing* (New York: Cambridge University Press, 2005), 35.

47   box: "If the country is strong": cited in Lewis, *Early Chinese Empires*, 50.

48   "vanquishing various states": Li Si, cited in Hui, *War and State Formation*, 101.

48	"wherever sun and moon shine": cited in Lewis, *Early Chinese Empires*, 52.
49	box: "Anciently": cited in Twitchett and Fairbank, *Cambridge History of China*, 1:75.
49	"mobilization of huge armies": figures from Hui, *War and State Formation*, 217.
52	box: "I and the chanyu": cited in Lewis, *Early Chinese Empires*, 133.

Chapter 3

Suggested Reading

Barbero, Alessandro. *Charlemagne: Father of a Continent*. Berkeley: University of California Press, 2004.

Bartlett, Robert. *The Making of Europe: Conquest, Colonization and Cultural Change, 950–1350*. Princeton: Princeton University Press, 1993.

Crone, Patricia. *God's Rule: Government and Islam*. New York: Columbia University Press, 2004.

Donner, Fred McGraw. *The Early Islamic Conquests*. Princeton: Princeton University Press, 1981.

Fowden, Garth. *Empire to Commonwealth: Consequences of Monotheism in Late Antiquity*. Princeton: Princeton University Press, 1993.

Geary, Patrick. *The Myth of Nations: The Medieval Origins of Europe*. Princeton: Princeton University Press, 2002.

Herrin, Judith. *Byzantium: The Surprising Life of a Medieval Empire*. Princeton: Princeton University Press, 2007.

Kennedy, Hugh. *The Prophet and the Age of the Caliphates: The Islamic Near East from the Sixth to the Eleventh Century*. 2nd ed. Harlow, U.K.: Pearson, 2004.

———. *When Baghdad Ruled the Muslim World: The Rise and Fall of Islam's Greatest Dynasty*. Cambridge, MA: Da Capo Press, 2005.

Ringrose, Kathryn M. *The Perfect Servant: Eunuchs and the Social Construction of Gender in Byzantium*. Chicago: University of Chicago Press, 2003.

Wickham, Chris. *Framing the Early Middle Ages: Europe and the Mediterranean, 400–800*. Oxford: Oxford University Press, 2005.

Works Cited

69	Herrin, *Byzantium*, xviii.
72	box: "human race": cited in Michael Bonner, *Jihad in Islamic History: Doctrines and Practice* (Princeton: Princeton University Press, 2006), 12.
72	"characteristics of a state": Donner, *Early Islamic Conquests*, 54.
78	"urban islands": Findlay and O'Rourke, *Power and Plenty* chapter 1, 50.
85	"no Romans": Barbero, *Charlemagne*, 109.
88	Thomas Bisson, "Medieval Lordship," *Speculum* 70 (1995): 749.
89	box: "these Christian people": quotation from Nicetia Choniates, cited in Olivier Clement, *L'Essor de Christianisme oriental* (Paris: Presses Universitaires de France, 1964), 82.
91	Bartlett, *Making of Europe*, 292.

Chapter 4

Suggested Reading

Allsen, Thomas T. *Commodity and Exchange in the Mongol Empire: A Cultural History of Islamic Textiles*. New York: Cambridge University Press, 1997.

———. *Culture and Conquest in Mongol Eurasia*. New York: Cambridge University Press, 2001.

Biran, Michal. "The Mongol Transformation: From the Steppe to Eurasian Empire." *Medieval Encounters* 10, nos. 1–3 (2004): 339–61.

Christian, David. *A History of Russia, Central Asia and Mongolia*. Vol. 1: *Inner Eurasia from Prehistory to the Mongol Empire*. Oxford: Blackwell, 1998.

Cleaves, Francis Woodman, trans. and ed. *The Secret History of the Mongols*. Cambridge, MA: Harvard University Press, 1982.

Di Cosmo, Nicola. *Ancient China and Its Enemies: The Rise of Nomadic Power in East Asian History*. New York: Cambridge University Press, 2002.

———. "State Formation and Periodization in Inner Asian History." *Journal of World History* 10, no. 1 (1999): 1–40.

Fletcher, Joseph. "The Mongols: Ecological and Social Perspectives." *Harvard Journal of Asiatic Studies* 46 (1986): 11–50.

King, Charles. *Black Sea* chapter 1.

Manz, Beatrice Forbes. *The Rise and Rule of Tamerlane*. Cambridge: Cambridge University Press, 1989.

Morgan, David. *The Mongols*. 2nd ed. Malden: Blackwell, 2007.

Ratchnevsky, Paul. *Genghis Khan: His Life and Legacy*. Trans. Thomas Nivison Haining. Cambridge, MA: Blackwell, 1992.

Roux, Jean-Paul. *Genghis Khan and the Mongol Empire*. London: Thames and Hudson, 2003.

Spuler, Bertold. *The Mongols in History*. New York: Praeger, 1971.

Works Cited

94   "terrorized both empires of the Roman world": Christian, *History of Russia, Central Asia, and Mongolia*, 1:231.

99   "130,000": figures from Christian, *History of Russia, Central Asia, and Mongolia*, 1:397.

102   "the same clothing . . . my brothers": cited in Christian, *History of Russia, Central Asia, and Mongolia*, 1:395.

103   "We should undertake": cited in Christian, *History of Russia, Central Asia, and Mongolia*, 401.

111   "a general account . . . history": cited in Allsen, *Culture and Conquest*, 83.

Chapter 5

Suggested Reading

Barkey, Karen. *Bandits and Bureaucrats: The Ottoman Route to State Centralization*. Ithaca: Cornell University Press, 1994.

———. *Empire of Difference: The Ottomans in Comparative Perspective.* Cambridge: Cambridge University Press, 2008.

Elliott, J. H. *Empires of the Atlantic World: Britain and Spain in America, 1492–1830.* New Haven: Yale University Press, 2006.

———. "A Europe of Composite Monarchies." *Past and Present* 137 (1992): 48–71.

Finkel, Caroline. *Osman's Dream: The History of the Ottoman Empire.* New York: Basic Books, 2005.

Goffman, Daniel. *The Ottoman Empire and Early Modern Europe.* Cambridge: Cambridge University Press, 2002.

Inber, Colin. *The Ottoman Empire, 1300–1650: The Structure of Power.* Houndsmills and New York: Palgrave Macmillan, 2002.

Kafadar, Cemal. *Between Two Worlds: The Construction of the Ottoman State.* Berkeley: University of California Press, 1995.

Kamen, Henry. *Empire: How Spain Became a World Power, 1492–1763.* New York: HarperCollins, 2003.

Las Casas, Bartolomé de. *History of the Indies.* Trans. and ed. Andrée Collard. New York: Harper, 1971.

Lowry, Heath W. *The Nature of the Early Ottoman State.* Albany: State University of New York Press, 2003.

Pagden, Anthony. *Spanish Imperialism and the Political Imagination.* New Haven: Yale University Press, 1990.

Parker, Geoffrey. *The Military Revolution: Military Innovation and the Rise of the West, 1500–1800.* Cambridge: Cambridge University Press, 1996.

Peirce, Leslie. *Imperial Harem: Women and Sovereignty in the Ottoman Empire.* New York: Oxford University Press, 1993.

———. *Morality Tales: Law and Gender in the Ottoman Court of Aintab.* Berkeley: University of California Press, 2003.

Subrahmanyam, Sanjay. "A Tale of Three Empires: Mughals, Ottomans, and Habsburgs in a Comparative Context." *Common Knowledge* 12, no. 1 (2006): 66–92.

Works Cited

119   box: "Charles and Suleiman": quoted in Carmen Bernand and Serge Gruzinski, *Histoire du Nouveau Monde: De la découverte à la conquête, une expérience européene, 1492–1550* (Paris: Fayard, 1991), 242.

124   "silver and gold": Carlos Marichal, "The Spanish-American Silver Peso: Export Commodity and Global Money of the Ancien Regime, 1550–1800," in Steven Topik, Carlos Marichal, and Sephyr Frank, eds., *From Silver to Cocaine: Latin American Commodity Chains and the Building of the World Economy, 1500–2000* (Durham: Duke University Press, 2006), 28.

127   box: "the cow": cited in Bernard Bailyn, *Atlantic History: Concept and Contours* (Cambridge, MA: Harvard University Press, 2005), 87–88.

134   "good order": the "Law Book" of Mehmet II: cited in Imber, *Ottoman Empire,* 109.

134   "did not sleep": Leslie Peirce, "An Imperial Caste: Inverted Racialization in the Architecture of Ottoman Sovereignty," in M. R. Greer et

al., *Rereading the Black Legend: The Discourses of Racism in the Renaissance Empires* (Chicago: University of Chicago Press, 2007), 43–44.

140   box: "this slave": cited in Barkey, *Bandits and Bureaucrats*, 189.

141   "killed everyone": cited in Imber, *Ottoman Empire*, 21.

Chapter 6

Suggested Readings

Adams, Julia. *The Familial State: Ruling Families and Merchant Capitalism in Early Modern Europe*. Ithaca: Cornell University Press, 2005.

Benton, Lauren. *Law and Colonial Cultures: Legal Regimes in World History, 1400–1900*. New York: Cambridge University Press, 2002.

Brenner, Robert. *Merchants and Revolution: Commercial Change, Political Conflict, and London's Overseas Traders, 1550–1653*. 1993. Reprint, London: Verso, 2003.

Brewer, John. *The Sinews of Power: War, Money, and the English State, 1688–1783*. New York: Knopf, 1989.

Brown, Kathleen. *Good Wives, Nasty Wenches, and Anxious Patriarchs: Gender, Race, and Power in Colonial Virginia*. Chapel Hill: University of North Carolina Press, 1996.

Elliott, J. H. *Empires of the Atlantic World* chapter 5.

Eltis, David. *The Rise of African Slavery in the Americas*. New York: Cambridge University Press, 2000.

Gruzinski, Serge. *Les quatre parties du monde: Histoire d'une mondialisation*. Paris: Editions de la Martinière, 2004.

Kupperman, Karen Ordahl. *Indians and English: Facing Off in Early America*. Ithaca: Cornell University Press, 2000.

MacCormack, Sabine. *Religion in the Andes: Vision and Imagination in Early Colonial Peru*. Princeton: Princeton University Press, 1991.

MacMillan, Ken. *Sovereignty and Possession in the English New World: The Legal Foundations of Empire, 1576–1640*. Cambridge: Cambridge University Press, 2006.

Newitt, Malyn. *A History of Portuguese Overseas Expansion, 1400–1668*. New York: Routledge, 2005.

Pagden, Anthony. *Lords of All the World: Ideologies of Empire in Spain, Britain and France c. 1500–c. 1800*. New Haven: Yale University Press, 1995.

Pearson, M. N. *The Indian Ocean*. London: Routledge, 2003.

Raudzens, George, ed. *Technology, Disease and Colonial Conquests, Sixteenth to Eighteenth Centuries: Essays Reappraising the Guns and Germs Theories*. Leiden: Brill, 2001.

Stern, Steve. *Peru's Indian Peoples and the Challenge of Spanish Conquest: Huamanga to 1640*. 2nd ed. Madison: University of Wisconsin Press, 1993.

Subrahmanyam, Sanjay. *The Portuguese Empire in Asia, 1500–1700*. London: Longman, 1993.

Taylor, Jean Gelman. *The Social World of Batavia: European and Eurasian in Dutch Asia*. Madison: University of Wisconsin Press, 1983.

Teschke, Benno. *The Myth of 1648: Class, Geopolitics and the Making of Modern International Relations*. London: Verso, 2003.

Tracy, James D., ed. *The Political Economy of Merchant Empires: State Power and World Trade, 1350–1750*. Cambridge: Cambridge University Press, 1991.

———. *The Rise of Merchant Empires: State Power and World Trade, 1350–1750*. Cambridge: Cambridge University Press, 1990.

Williams, Eric. *Capitalism and Slavery*. Chapel Hill: University of North Carolina Press, 1944.

Works Cited

149   Columbus's interpreter: from John Tolan, "The Middle Ages," in Henry Laurens, John Tolan, and Gilles Veinstein, *L'Europe et l'Islam: Quinze siècles d'histoire* (Paris: Odile Jacob, 2009), 113.

149   "commerce grew": statistics from Kennedy, *Rise and Fall* chapter 1, 27.

150   "most warlike": J. S. Levy, 1983, quoted in Parker, *Military Revolution* chapter 5, 1.

156   "King John III's revenue": figure from Tracy, *Rise of Merchant Empires*, 29.

159   "muscle and money": Jean Gelman Taylor, *Indonesia: Peoples and Histories* (New Haven: Yale University Press, 2003), 198.

161   box: "Postlethwayt": quoted in Tracy, *Rise of Merchant Empires*, 196.

163   box: "two Spanish views": quoted in John Lynch, *Spain under the Habsburgs* (New York: New York University Press, 1984), 1:158.

163   The "steel and germs" argument is made in Jared M. Diamond, *Guns, Germs, and Steel: The Fates of Human Societies* (New York: Norton, 1998).

163–64   On debates over population and conquest, see Raudzens, *Technology, Disease and Colonial Conquests*.

170   "entire of itself": phrase from Act of Restraint of Appeals, 1533, quoted in MacMillan, *Sovereignty and Possession*, 21–22.

171   Statistics on settlement from Jane H. Ohlmeyer, "'Civilizing of those rude partes': Colonization within Britain and Ireland, 1580s–1640s," in William Roger Louis, Alaine M. Low, Nicholas P. Canny, and P. J. Marshall, eds., *The Oxford History of the British Empire, Volume I* (New York: Oxford University Press, 1998–99), 137.

174   "infiltration": George Raudzens, "Outfighting or Outpopulating? Main Reasons for Early Colonial Conquests, 1493–1788," in Raudzens, *Technology, Disease and Colonial Conquests*, 39.

175   "wildernes": William Bradford, *History of Plymouth Plantation, 1620–1647, in Two Volumes* (New York: Russell and Russell, 1968), 1:156.

176   ratios from Findlay and O'Rourke, *Power and Plenty* chapter 1, 232.

176   government expenses: figures from Brewer, *Sinews of Power*, 40.

178   Slave-trade statistics from Philip Curtin, *The Atlantic Slave Trade: A Census* (Madison: University of Wisconsin Press, 1972), 7. For an update, see David Eltis and David Richardson, eds., *Extending the Frontiers: Essays on the New Transatlantic Slavetrade Database* (New Haven: Yale University Press, 2008).

179   "exit option": Albert O. Hirschman, *Exit, Voice, and Loyalty: Responses to Decline in Firms, Organizations, and States* (Cambridge, MA: Harvard University Press, 1970).

Chapter 7

Suggested Reading

Amitai, Reuvan, and Michal Biran, eds. *Mongols, Turks, and Others: Eurasian Nomads and the Sedentary World.* Boston: Brill, 2005.

Crossley, Pamela Kyle. *A Translucent Mirror: History and Identity in Qing Imperial Ideology.* Berkeley: University of California Press, 1999.

Elliott, Mark. *The Manchu Way: The Eight Banners and Ethnic Identity in Late Imperial China.* Stanford: Stanford University Press, 2001.

Kivelson, Valerie. *Cartographies of Tsardom: The Land and Its Meanings in Seventeenth-Century Russia.* Ithaca: Cornell University Press, 2006.

Kollmann, Nancy Shields. *By Honor Bound: State and Society in Early Modern Russia.* Ithaca: Cornell University Press, 1999.

———. *Kinship and Politics: The Making of the Muscovite Political System, 1345–1537.* Stanford: Stanford University Press, 1987.

Mote, F. W. *Imperial China, 900–1800.* Cambridge, MA: Harvard University Press, 1999.

Ostrowski, Donald. *Muscovy and the Mongols: Cross-Cultural Influences on the Steppe Frontier, 1304–1589.* Cambridge: Cambridge University Press, 1998.

Perdue, Peter C. *China Marches West: The Qing Conquest of Central Eurasia.* Cambridge, MA: Harvard University Press, 2005.

Rowe, William T. *Saving the World: Chen Hongmou and Elite Consciousness in Eighteenth-Century China.* Stanford: Stanford University Press, 2001.

Shin, Leo. *The Making of the Chinese State: Ethnicity and Expansion on the Ming Borderlands.* Cambridge: Cambridge University Press, 2006.

Spence, Jonathan. *The Search for Modern China.* New York: Norton, 1990.

Wakeman, Frederic E. *The Great Enterprise: The Manchu Reconstruction of Imperial Order in Seventeenth-Century China.* Berkeley: University of California Press, 1985.

Waley-Cohen, Joanna. *The Culture of War in China: Empire and the Military under the Qing Dynasty.* London: I. B. Tauris, 2006.

Wong, Roy Bin. *China Transformed: Historical Change and the Limits of European Experience.* Ithaca: Cornell University Press, 1997.

Wortman, Richard S. *Scenarios of Power: Myth and Ceremony in Russian Monarchy.* Vol. 1. Princeton: Princeton University Press, 1995.

Zitser, Ernest A. *The Transfigured Kingdom: Sacred Parody and Charismatic Authority at the Court of Peter the Great.* Ithaca: Cornell University Press, 2004.

Works Cited

194   box: "Alas, my tears": cited in Ostrowski, *Moscovy and the Mongols,* 163.
198   "order of Judas": Zitser, *Transfigured Kingdom,* 99.
208   "reaching 420 million": Mote, *Imperial China,* 905–6.

210   "Reflecting on the study": cited in Elliott, *The Manchu Way*, 292.

212   box: "The Lord of Heaven": cited in Elliott, *The Manchu Way*, 241.

Chapter 8

Suggested Readings

Adelman, Jeremy. *Sovereignty and Revolution in the Iberian Atlantic*. Princeton: Princeton University Press, 2007.

Armitage, David. *The Ideological Origins of the British Empire*. Cambridge: Cambridge University Press, 2000.

Broers, Michael. *Europe under Napoleon, 1799–1815*. London: Arnold, 1996.

Colley, Linda. *Britons: Forging the Nation, 1707–1837*. New Haven: Yale University Press, 1992.

Dubois, Laurent. *A Colony of Citizens: Revolution and Slave Emancipation in the French Caribbean, 1787–1804*. Chapel Hill: University of North Carolina Press, 2004.

Elliott, J. H. *Empires of the Atlantic World* chapter 5.

Forrest, Alan. *Napoleon's Men: The Soldiers of the Revolution and Empire*. London: Hambledon and London, 2002.

Gould, Eliga. *The Persistence of Empire: British Political Culture in the Age of the American Revolution*. Chapel Hill: University of North Carolina Press, 2000.

Hulsebosch, Daniel J. *Constituting Empire: New York and the Transformation of Constitutionalism in the Atlantic World, 1664–1830*. Chapel Hill: University of North Carolina Press, 2005.

James, C.L.R. *The Black Jacobins*. 1938. Reprint, New York: Vintage, 1963.

Marshall, P. J. *The Making and Unmaking of Empires: Britain, India, and America, c. 1750–1783*. New York: Oxford University Press, 2005.

Muthu, Sankar. *Enlightenment against Empire*. Princeton: Princeton University Press, 2003.

Pitts, Jennifer. *A Turn to Empire: The Rise of Imperial Liberalism in Britain and France*. Princeton: Princeton University Press, 2005.

Pomeranz, Kenneth. *The Great Divergence: Europe, China, and the Making of the Modern World Economy*. Princeton: Princeton University Press, 2000.

Woolf, Stuart. *Napoleon's Integration of Europe*. London: Routledge, 1991.

Works Cited

231   "imperial nobility": Woolf, *Napoleon's Integration of Europe,* 129.

232   "inner empire": Broers, *Europe under Napoleon*.

234   "damn colonies": quoted in Jon Kukla, *A Wilderness So Immense: The Louisiana Purchase and the Destiny of America* (New York: Knopf, 2003), 249.

234   "Brandenbergers, Prussians": cited in Clive Emsley, *Napoleon: Conquest, Reform and Reorganisation* (Harlow, U.K.: Pearson/Longman, 2003), 65.

236-37   Trade figure from Marshall, *Making and Unmaking*, 13.

238   "diversified mass": quoted in Marshall, *Making and Unmaking*, 204; figures from Hancock, *Citizens of the World*, 27, 29, 387; "sun never sets": Sir

George Macartney, 1773, cited in P. J. Marshall, introduction to in William Roger Louis, Alaine M. Low, Nicholas P. Canny, and P. J. Marshall, eds., *The Oxford History of the British Empire*, vol. 2 (New York: Oxford University Press, 1998–99), 7–8; Armitage, *Ideological Origins*, 9.

243   Publication statistics from Marshall, *Making and Unmaking*, 199.

243   box: "impeach him": Edmund Burke, *On Empire, Liberty, and Reform: Speeches and Letters*, ed. David Bromwich (New Haven: Yale University Press, 2000), 400.

245   Benedict Anderson, *Imagined Communities: Reflections on the Origin and Spread of Nationalism* (New York: Verso, 1991).

247   1812 constitution cited in Elliott, *Empires*, 284–85.

Chapter 9

Suggested Reading

Anderson, Fred, and Andrew R. L. Cayton. *The Dominion of War: Empire and Liberty in North America, 1500–2000*. New York: Viking, 2005.

Armitage, David, ed. *Theories of Empire, 1450–1800*. Brookfield: Ashgate, 1998.

Banner, Stuart. *How the Indians Lost Their Land: Law and Power on the Frontier*. Cambridge, MA: Harvard University Press, 2005.

Bender, Thomas. *A Nation among Nations: America's Place in World History*. New York: Hill and Wang, 2006.

Breyfogle, Nicholas B. *Heretics and Colonizers: Forging Russia's Empire in the South Caucasus*. Ithaca: Cornell University Press, 2005.

Brower, Daniel R., and Edward J. Lazzerini, eds. *Russia's Orient: Imperial Borderlands and Peoples, 1700–1917*. Bloomington: Indiana University Press, 1997.

Brown, Kathleen. *Good Wives, Nasty Wenches* chapter 6.

Burbank, Jane, Mark von Hagen, and Anatolyi Remnev. *Russian Empire: Space, People, Power, 1700–1930*. Bloomington: Indiana University Press, 2007.

Crews, Robert D. *For Prophet and Tsar: Islam and Empire in Russia and Central Asia*. Cambridge, MA: Harvard University Press, 2006.

Foner, Eric. *Nothing But Freedom: Emancipation and Its Legacy*. Baton Rouge: Louisiana State University Press, 1983.

Geraci, Robert. *Window on the East: National and Imperial Identities in Late Tsarist Russia*. Ithaca: Cornell University Press, 2001.

Hendrickson, David C. *Peace Pact: The Lost World of the American Founding*. Lawrence: University Press of Kansas, 2003.

Hinderaker, Eric. *Elusive Empires: Constructing Colonialism in the Ohio Valley, 1673–1800*. New York: Cambridge University Press, 1997.

Hoch, Steven L. *Serfdom and Social Control in Russia: Petrovskoe, a Village in Tambov*. Chicago: University of Chicago Press, 1986.

Kappeler, Andreas. *The Russian Empire: A Multi-Ethnic History*. Trans. Alfred Clayton. Harlow, U.K.: Pearson Education, 2001.

Kupperman, Karen Ordahl. *Indians and English: Facing Off in Early America*. Ithaca: Cornell University Press, 2000.

Meinig, D. W. *The Shaping of America: A Geographical Perspective on 500 Years of History.* Vol. 2: *Continental America, 1800–1867.* New Haven: Yale University Press, 1986.

Merry, Sally Engle. *Colonizing Hawai'i: The Cultural Power of Law.* Princeton: Princeton University Press, 2000.

Montoya, Maria E. *Translating Property: The Maxwell Land Grant and the Conflict over Land in the American West, 1840–1900.* Berkeley: University of California Press, 2002.

Ostler, Jeffrey. *The Plains Sioux and U.S. Colonialism from Lewis and Clark to Wounded Knee.* Cambridge: Cambridge University Press, 2004.

Richter, Daniel K. *Facing East from Indian Country: A Native History of Early America.* Cambridge, MA: Harvard University Press, 2001.

Smith, Douglas. *Love and Conquest: Personal Correspondence of Catherine the Great and Prince Grigory Potemkin.* DeKalb: Northern Illinois University Press, 2004.

Stanislawski, Michael. *Tsar Nicholas I and the Jews: The Transformation of Jewish Society in Russia, 1825–1855.* Philadelphia: Jewish Publication Society of America, 1983.

Sunderland, Willard. *Taming the Wild Field: Colonization and Empire on the Russian Steppe.* Ithaca: Cornell University Press, 2004.

Werth, Paul. *At the Margins of Orthodoxy: Mission, Governance, and Confessional Politics in Russia's Volga-Kama Region, 1827–1905.* Ithaca: Cornell University Press, 2002.

White, Richard. *It's Your Misfortune and None of My Own: A New History of the American West.* Norman: University of Oklahoma Press, 1991.

———. *The Middle Ground: Indians, Empires, and Republics in the Great Lakes Region, 1640–1815.* New York: Cambridge University Press, 1991.

Works Cited

254   "250,000 ... 1.25 million": statistics from Richter, *Facing East*, 7.

255   "negroe, mulatto": Colony of Virginia Law, 1691, cited in Brown, *Good Wives, Nasty Wenches*, 197.

257   box: "Our fathers": cited in Richter, *Facing East*, 59.

258   "Apaches killed" and "During the heyday": figures from White, *It's Your Misfortune*, 30, 33.

259   "all parts of the world" and "has excited": Thomas Paine, *Common Sense*, ed. Edward Larkin (Buffalo: Broadview Press, 2004), 219.

260   "Empire of Liberty": Robert W. Tucker and David C. Hendrickson, *Empire of Liberty: The Statecraft of Thomas Jefferson* (New York: Oxford University Press, 1990); "formation and establishment of an empire": cited in Norbert Kilian, "New Wine in Old Skins? American Definitions of Empire and the Emergence of a New Concept," in Armitage, *Theories of Empire*, 319

260   "Disunited people": cited in Hendrickson, *Peace Pact*, 4.

261   "on an equal footing": Northwest Ordinance of 1787, cited in Hinderaker, *Elusive Empires*, 231.

261   "free white person": naturalization law of 1790, quoted in Hinderaker, *Elusive Empires*, 261.

262   "subdued people": quoted in Hinderaker, *Elusive Empires*, 233; "the back country . . . now live": John Dickinson, quoted in Richter, *Facing East*, 224; Washington and Jefferson cited in Mann, *Dark Side of Democracy* chapter 2, 92.

263   "I now adopt you": cited in Meinig, *The Shaping of America*, 2:184.

263   "absurdity": Andrew Jackson quoted in Richter, *Facing East*, 234.

263   "inferior race": *Johnson v. M'Intosh*, 1823; "domestic dependent nations": *Cherokee Nations v. Georgia*, 1831.

264   "One out of eight died": figures from White, *It's Your Misfortune*, 87.

265   "We do not want": quoted in Montoya, *Translating Property*, 87.

266   box: "extermination": quoted in Mann, *Dark Side of Democracy* chapter 2, 92.

266   "hereafter no Indian nation": Indian Appropriation Act of March 3, 1871.

267   "until the Indians": Ostler, *The Plains Sioux*, 130.

268   "save the Union": Howard Zinn, *A People's History of the United States: 1492–Present* (New York: HarperCollins, 2003), 191.

269   "nothing but freedom": quoted in Foner, *Nothing But Freedom*, 55.

270   box: "growing empire": Brooks Adams, *The New Empire* (New York: Macmillan, 1902), xv.

273   "sixty and eighty nations": figures from Johann Gottlieb Georgi and Heinrich Storch, cited in Kappeler, *Russian Empire*, 8, 141.

274   "acquired privileges": cited in Kappeler, *Russian Empire*, 73.

274   "general, final, and irrevocable": treaty cited in Kappeler, *Russian Empire*, 80

275   "Polish origin": figure from Kappeler, *Russian Empire*, 83.

279   "toleration of all confessions": cited in Crews, *For Prophet and Tsar*, 45.

281   "demonstrations of kindness": cited in Sunderland, *Taming the Wild Field*, 64.

282   Statistics from Hoch, *Serfdom and Social Control*, 3.

Chapter 10

Suggested Reading

Bayly, C. A. *Imperial Meridian: The British Empire and the World, 1780–1830*. Harrow, U.K.: Longman, 1989.

Benton, Lauren. *Law and Colonial Cultures* chapter 6.

Bose, Sugata. *A Hundred Horizons: The Indian Ocean in the Age of Global Empire*. Cambridge, MA: Harvard University Press, 2006.

Chanock, Martin. *Law, Custom and Social Order: The Colonial Experience in Malawi and Zambia*. Cambridge: Cambridge University Press, 1985.

Cohn, Bernard. *Colonialism and Its Forms of Knowledge: The British in India*. Princeton: Princeton University Press, 1996.

Cole, Juan. *Colonialism and Revolution in the Middle East: Social and Cultural Origins of Egypt's 'Urabi Movement*. Cairo: American University of Cairo Press, 1999.

Conklin, Alice. *A Mission to Civilize: The Republican Idea of Empire in France and West Africa, 1895–1930*. Stanford: Stanford University Press, 1997.

Daughton, J. P. *An Empire Divided: Religion, Republicanism, and the Making of French Colonialism, 1880–1914*. Oxford: Oxford University Press, 2006.

Davis, David Brion. *The Problem of Slavery in the Age of Revolution*. Ithaca: Cornell University Press, 1975.

Ferrer, Ada. *Insurgent Cuba: Race, Nation, and Revolution, 1868–1898*. Chapel Hill: University of North Carolina Press, 1999.

Gilmartin, David. *Empire and Islam: Punjab and the Making of Pakistan*. Berkeley: University of California Press, 1988.

Goswami, Manu. *Producing India: From Colonial Economy to National Space*. Chicago: University of Chicago Press, 2004.

Hall, Catherine. *Civilising Subjects: Metropole and Colony in the English Imagination, 1830–1867*. Chicago: University of Chicago Press, 2002.

Holt, Thomas. *The Problem of Freedom: Race, Labor and Politics in Jamaica and Britain, 1832–1938*. Baltimore: Johns Hopkins University Press, 1992.

Kramer, Paul A. *The Blood of Government: Race, Empire, the United States, and the Philippines*. Chapel Hill: University of North Carolina Press, 2006.

McKittrick, Meredith. *To Dwell Secure: Generation, Christianity, and Colonialism in Ovamboland*. Portsmouth, NH: Heinemann, 2002.

Metcalf, Thomas. *Imperial Connections: India in the Indian Ocean Arena, 1860–1920*. Berkeley: University of California Press, 2007.

Robinson, Ronald, and John Gallagher. "The Imperialism of Free Trade." *Economic History Review*, 2nd ser., 6 (1953): 1–15.

Schmidt-Nowara, Christopher, and John Nieto-Phillips, eds. *Interpreting Spanish Colonialism: Empires, Nations, and Legends*. Albuquerque: University of New Mexico Press, 2005.

Stora, Benjamin. *Algeria: A Short History, 1830–2000*. Trans. Jane Marie Todd. Ithaca: Cornell University Press, 2004.

Trautmann, Thomas. *Aryans and British India*. Berkeley: University of California Press, 1997.

Wildenthal, Lora. *German Women for Empire, 1884–1945*. Durham: Duke University Press, 2001.

Works Cited

287   Income statistics from Findlay and O'Rourke, *Power and Plenty* chapter 1, 414.

291   "savage sloth": phrase from British colonial official Henry Taylor, 1833, cited in Holt, *Problem of Freedom*, 74.

292   Indentured labor statistics from Metcalf, *Imperial Connections*, 136.

299   Figures on Vietnam from Pierre Brocheux and Daniel Hémery, *Indochine, la Colonisation Ambigue, 1858–1954* (Paris: Découverte, 2001), 175.

301   box: "commonwealth of nations": quoted in W. David McIntyre, *The Commonwealth of Nations: Origins and Impact, 1869–1971* (Minneapolis: University of Minnesota Press, 1977), 4.

301   Cultivation system figures from Jean Gelman Taylor, *Indonesia: Peoples and Histories* (New Haven: Yale University Press, 2003), 240.

302   box: "European style empire": quoted in Marius Jansen, "Japanese Imperialism: Late Meiji Perspectives," in Ramon Myers and Mark Peattie, eds., *The Japanese Colonial Empire, 1895–1945* (Princeton: Princeton University Press, 1984), 64.

304   Figure on accountants from C. W. Newbury, *Patrons, Clients, and Empire: Chieftaincy and Over-Rule in Asia, Africa, and the Pacific* (New York: Oxford University Press, 2003), 84.

305   "emperor of the Arabs": quoted in Stora, *Algeria*, 5.

307   Christopher Bayly, "Distorted Development: The Ottoman Empire and British India, circa 1780–1916," *Comparative Studies of South Asia, Africa and the Middle East* 27 (2007): 332–44.

311   box: "without India": George Curzon, *Persia and the Persian Question* (1892; London: Cass, 1966), 1:4.

311   GDP figures from Angus Maddison, *The World Economy: Historical Statistics* (Washington, DC: OECD, 2003), tables 5a–5c, 180–85.

312   Frantz Fanon, *The Wretched of the Earth*, trans. Constance Farrington (New York: Grove Press, 1965).

313   V. I. Lenin, *Imperialism, the Highest Stage of Capitalism* (1916; New York: International Publishers, 1939).

318   Ann Laura Stoler, *Race and the Education of Desire: Foucault's History of Sexuality and the Colonial Order of Things* (Durham: Duke University Press, 1995), 177.

320   J. A. Hobson, *Imperialism: A Study* (1902; Ann Arbor: University of Michigan Press, 1965).

321   "quarter of the world's population": Kennedy, *Rise and Fall* chapter 1, 225–26.

327   "color-line": W.E.B. DuBois, *The Souls of Black Folk* (Chicago: A. C. McClurg, 1903), 1.

Chapter 11

Suggested Reading

Barkey, Karen, and Mark Von Hagen, eds. *After Empire: Multiethnic Societies and Nation-Building, the Soviet Union and the Russian, Ottoman, Habsburg Empires*. Boulder, CO: Westview Press, 1997.

Brower, Daniel. *Turkestan and the Fate of the Russian Empire*. New York: Routledge-Curzon, 2003.

Burbank, Jane, and David Ransel, eds. *Imperial Russia: New Histories for the Empire*. Bloomington: Indiana University Press, 1998.

Burbank, Jane, Mark von Hagen, and Anatolyi Remnev. *Russian Empire* chapter 9.

Deringil, Selim. *The Well-Protected Domains: Ideology and the Legitimation of Power in the Ottoman Empire, 1876–1909*. London: Tauris, 1999.

Field, Daniel. *The End of Serfdom: Nobility and Bureaucracy in Russia, 1855–1861*. Cambridge, MA: Harvard University Press, 1976.

Finkel, Caroline. *Osman's Dream* chapter 5.

Friedman, Rebecca. *Masculinity, Autocracy and the Russian University, 1804–1863*. New York: Palgrave Macmillan, 2005.

Hoch, Steven. *Serfdom and Social Control in Russia* chapter 9.

Judson, Pieter M. *Exclusive Revolutionaries: Liberal Politics, Social Experience, and National Identity in the Austrian Empire, 1848–1914*. Ann Arbor: University of Michigan Press, 1996.

———. *Guardians of the Nation: Activists on the Language Frontier of Imperial Austria*. Cambridge, MA: Harvard University Press, 2006.

Kayali, Hasan. *Arabs and Young Turks: Ottomanism, Arabism, and Islamism in the Ottoman Empire, 1908–1918*. Berkeley: University of California Press, 1997.

Makdisi, Ussama. *The Culture of Sectarianism: Community, History, and Violence in Nineteenth-Century Ottoman Lebanon*. Berkeley: University of California Press, 2000.

Marks, Steven G. *Road to Power: The Trans-Siberian Railroad and Colonization of Asian Russia, 1850–1917*. Ithaca: Cornell University Press, 1991.

Porter, Brian. *When Nationalism Began to Hate: Imagining Modern Politics in Nineteenth-Century Poland*. New York: Oxford University Press, 2002.

Quataert, Donald. *The Ottoman Empire, 1700–1922*. 2nd ed. Cambridge: Cambridge University Press, 2005.

Stites, Richard. *Serfdom, Society, and the Arts in Imperial Russia*. New Haven: Yale University Press, 2005.

Szporluk, Roman. *Communism and Nationalism: Karl Marx versus Friedrich List*. New York: Oxford University Press, 1988.

Unowsky, Daniel L. *The Pomp and Politics of Patriotism: Imperial Celebrations in Habsburg Austria, 1848–1916*. West Lafayette: Purdue University Press, 2005.

Whittaker, Cynthia. *The Origins of Modern Russian Education: An Intellectual Biography of Count Sergei Uvarov, 1786–1855*. De Kalb: Northern Illinois University Press, 1984.

Wolff, Larry. *Inventing Eastern Europe: The Map of Civilization on the Mind of the Enlightenment*. Stanford: Stanford University Press, 1994.

Wortman, Richard S. *Scenarios of Power: Myth and Ceremony in Russian Monarchy*. Vol. 2. Princeton: Princeton University Press, 2000.

Works Cited

332   "For your freedom and ours": Porter, *When Nationalism*, 22.

333–34   "eternal religion": Barbara Jelavich, *St. Petersburg and Moscow: Tsarist and Soviet Foreign Policy, 1814–1974* (Bloomington: Indiana University Press, 1974), 42.

342   Figures on army: Quataert, *Ottoman Empire*, 63.

343   Figures on civil servants: Quataert, *Ottoman Empire*, 62.

355   "ignoring" General Kaufman: cited in Daniel Brower, "Islam and Ethnicity: Russian Colonial Policy in Turkestan," in Brower and Lazzerini, *Russia's Orient* chapter 9, 119.

367–68   war casualties: Richard C. Hall, *The Balkan Wars, 1912–1913: Prelude to the First World War* (New York: Routledge, 2000), 135.

Chapter 12

Suggested Reading

Barkey, Karen, and Mark von Hagen, eds. *After Empire* chapter 11.

Bose, Sugata, and Ayesha Jalal. *Modern South Asia: History, Culture, Political Economy.* London: Routledge, 1998.

Fromkin, David. *Europe's Last Summer: Who Started the Great War in 1914?* New York: Knopf, 2004.

———. *A Peace to End All Peace: The Fall of the Ottoman Empire and the Creation of the Modern Middle East.* New York: Henry Holt, 1989.

Hirsch, Francine. *Empire of Nations: Ethnographic Knowledge and the Making of the Soviet Union.* Ithaca: Cornell University Press, 2005.

Hull, Isabel V. *Absolute Destruction: Military Culture and the Practices of War in Imperial Germany.* Ithaca: Cornell University Press, 2005.

Lohr, Eric J. *Nationalizing the Russian Empire: The Campaign against Enemy Aliens during World War I.* Cambridge, MA: Harvard University Press, 2003.

Lower, Wendy. *Nazi Empire-Building and the Holocaust in Ukraine.* Chapel Hill: University of North Carolina Press, 2005.

Macmillan, Margaret. *Paris 1919: Six Months That Changed the World.* New York: Random House, 2003.

Manela, Erez. *The Wilsonian Moment: Self-Determination and the International Origins of Anticolonial Nationalism.* New York: Oxford University Press, 2007.

Martin, Terry. *The Affirmative Action Empire: Nations and Nationalism in the Soviet Union, 1923–1939.* Ithaca: Cornell University Press, 2001.

Mazower, Mark. *Dark Continent: Europe's Twentieth Century.* New York: Vintage, 1999.

———. *Hitler's Empire: Nazi Rule in Occupied Europe.* London: Allen Lane, 2008.

Myers, Ramon, and Mark Peattie, eds. *The Japanese Colonial Empire, 1895–1945.* Princeton: Princeton University Press, 1984.

Sinha, Mrinalini. *Specters of Mother India: The Global Restructuring of an Empire.* Durham: Duke University Press, 2006.

Spence, Jonathan. *Search for Modern China* chapter 7.

Young, Louise. *Japan's Total Empire: Manchuria and the Culture of Wartime Imperialism.* Berkeley: University of California Press, 1998.

Zürcher, Erik J. *Turkey: A Modern History.* London: I. B. Tauris, 1993.

Works Cited

369   de Gaulle quoted in Michael Stürmer, *The German Empire, 1870–1918* (New York: Modern Library, 2000), 84.

372   "nationally-conscious Jews": quoted in Marsha Rozenblitt, "Sustaining Austrian 'National' Identity in Crisis: The Dilemma of the Jews in Habsburg Austria, 1914–1919," in Pieter M. Judson and Marsha L. Rozenblit, eds., *Constructing Nationalities in East Central Europe* (New York: Berghahn Books, 2005), 185.

375   Gandhi quoted in Niall Ferguson, *Empire: The Rise and Demise of the British World Order and the Lessons for Global Power* (New York: Basic Books, 2003), 302–3.

375   Figures on colonial soldiers from Ferguson, *Empire,* 304, and A. S. Kanya-Forstner, "The War, Imperialism, and Decolonization," in J. M. Winter, Geoffrey Parker, and Mary R. Habeck, eds., *The Great War and the Twentieth Century* (New Haven: Yale University Press, 2000), 246.

377   "blaming workers": Michael Geyer, "German Strategy in the Age of Machine Warfare, 1914–1945," in Peter Paret, ed., *Makers of Modern Strategy: From Machiavelli to the Nuclear Age* (New York: Oxford University Press, 1986), 550–51.

377   "Schlieffen plan": Michael Howard, "The First World War Reconsidered," in J. M. Winter, Geoffrey Parker, and Mary R. Habeck, eds., *The Great War and the Twentieth Century* (New Haven: Yale University Press, 2000), 26.

378   "Arab of true race": Lord Kitchner cited in Efraim Karsh and Inari Karsh, *Empires of the Sand: The Struggle for Mastery in the Middle East, 1789–1923* (Cambridge, MA: Harvard University Press, 1999), 204–5.

380   Bender, *Nation among Nations* chapter 9, 243.

381   Population figures from MacMillan, *Paris 1919,* 211–19, 241.

381   Curzon's phrase is taken up in Rogers Brubaker, *Nationalism Reframed: Nationhood and the National Question in the New Europe* (New York: Cambridge University Press, 1996), chapter 6; refugee figures from Mann, *Dark Side of Democracy* chapter 2, 67.

385   "Great Idea. . . . civilization": phrases from Greek prime minister Eleutherios Venizelos, 1919, cited in Efraim Karsh and Inare Karsh, *Empires of the Sand: The Struggle for Mastery of the Middle East, 1789–1923* (Cambridge, MA: Harvard University Press, 1999), 94, 330.

385   Relocation and mortality figures (both notoriously imprecise) from Zürcher, *Turkey,* 164, and Justin McCarthy, *Muslims and Minorities: The Population of Ottoman Anatolia and the End of Empire* (New York: New York University Press, 1983), 130–33.

386   "million square miles": John Howard Morrow, *The Great War: An Imperial History* (New York: Routledge, 2004), 308.

388   Japan's industrialization: figure from Kennedy, *Rise and Fall* chapter 1, 299.

392   box: "ten thousand Arabs": cited in Fromkin, *Peace to End All Peace,* 497.

402   "Annihilation campaigns": quoted in C. A. Bayly and T. N. Harper, *Forgotten Armies: The Fall of British Asia, 1941–1945* (Cambridge, MA: Harvard University Press, 2006), 2.

405   mortality figures from Mann, *Dark Side of Democracy* chapter 2, 186–87.

405   "racial inferiors": cited in Mazower, *Dark Continent*, 148, 212.
406   Mazower, *Hitler's Empire*, 7.

Chapter 13

Suggested Reading

Allina-Pisano, Jessica. *The Post-Soviet Potemkin Village: Politics and Property Rights in the Black Earth*. New York: Cambridge University Press, 2008.

Allman, Jean Marie. *The Quills of the Porcupine: Asante Nationalism in an Emergent Ghana*. Madison: University of Wisconsin Press, 1993.

Bayly, C. A., and T. N. Harper. *Forgotten Armies: The Fall of British Asia, 1941–1945*. Cambridge, MA: Harvard University Press, 2006.

Christie, Clive. *A Modern History of Southeast Asia: Decolonization, Nationalism and Separatism*. London: Tauris, 1996.

Connelly, Matthew. *A Diplomatic Revolution: Algeria's Fight for Independence and the Origins of the Post–Cold War Era*. New York: Oxford University Press, 2002.

Cooper, Frederick. *Decolonization and African Society: The Labor Question in French and British Africa*. Cambridge: Cambridge University Press, 1996.

Dower, John. *War without Mercy: Race and Power in the Pacific War*. New York: Pantheon, 1986.

Grant, Bruce. *In the Soviet House of Culture*. Princeton: Princeton University Press, 1995.

Guha, Ramachandra. *India after Gandhi: The History of the World's Largest Democracy*. London: Macmillan, 2007.

Hyam, Ronald. *Britain's Declining Empire: The Road to Decolonisation, 1918–1968*. Cambridge: Cambridge University Press, 2006.

Judt, Tony. *Postwar: A History of Europe since 1945*. New York: Penguin, 2005.

Kotkin, Stephen. *Armageddon Averted: The Soviet Collapse, 1970–2000*. New York: Oxford University Press, 2001.

Louis, Wm. Roger. *The British Empire in the Middle East, 1945–1951: Arab Nationalism, the United States, and Postwar Imperialism*. Oxford: Oxford University Press, 1984.

Marr, David. *Vietnam 1945: The Quest for Power*. Berkeley: University of California Press, 1995.

Shepard, Todd. *The Invention of Decolonization: The Algerian War and the Remaking of France*. Ithaca: Cornell University Press, 2006.

Stora, Benjamin. *Algeria, 1830–2000: A Short History*. Trans. Jane Marie Todd. Ithaca: Cornell University Press, 2001.

Westad, Odd Arne. *The Global Cold War: Third World Interventions and the Making of Our Times*. Cambridge: Cambridge University Press, 2005.

Works Cited

415   Proclamation of French Committee of National Liberation, December 8, 1943, and of Queen Wilhemina of the Netherlands, December

1942, quoted in Paul H. Kratoska, "Dimensions of Decolonization," in Marc Frey, Ronald W. Pruessen, and Tai Yong Tan, *The Transformation of Southeast Asia: International Perspectives on Decolonization* (Ardsley: M. E. Sharpe, 2003), 11, 13; Henri Laurentie, "Pour ou contre le colonialism? Les colonies françaises devant le monde nouveau," *Renaissances*, October 1945, 10.

418   arrest and death figures from Bayly and Harper, *Forgotten Armies*, 548.

419   death statistics from Sugata Bose and Ayesha Jalal, *Modern South Asia: History, Culture, Political Economy* (London: Routledge, 2003), 190.

433   Judt, *Postwar*, 167.

INDEX

Abbasid caliphate, 75–80, 86, 91, 105, 109, 136, 141, 446, 458. *See also* Islamic empires
Abdulhamid II, 344–46, 358
Abdullah ibn Husayn, 382, 384
Abdulmecid I, 339, 343
Abraham, 71
absolutist monarchy, 182
Abu Bakr, 74
Abu Sa'id, 112
Aceh, 156
Adams, Brooks, 270
Adams, John, 238
Aden, 300
administration: centralization of, 43, 48, 50, 54, 57, 201, 229, 270–71, 346–47, 359–60, 394; dual governance and, 114, 209; institutions of, 28–31, 49–52, 57–58, 66–68, 73, 77, 83–84, 96, 104, 107–8, 119, 125–26, 136–40, 146–48, 154, 156–57, 159–61, 167, 176–77, 190, 194–99, 201, 205, 208–9, 229–35, 238–40, 242–44, 260–61, 271–72, 276–82, 301, 306–10, 316, 342–43, 345–50, 354–55, 361–62, 390–91, 394–96, 405–6, 419–22, 432, 437, 441, 445–46, 448–49; languages of, 308, 356; and surveillance, 46–49, 56, 107, 307, 316, 325, 327, 335, 338, 343, 398; thinness of, 13, 307, 316, 325, 392.

See also bureaucracy; census; Chinese empires: officials in; intermediaries; officials; populations; taxation
Aegean, 129, 132
Aeneas, 24, 38
affirmative action, 209, 422, 451
Afghanistan, 75, 96, 103, 113, 114, 358, 373, 378, 435, 443, 453, 456, 457
Africa, 312–21, 324–28, 419–28, 448–50; Chinese (Ming) exploration of, 153, 203; colonization of, 287–90, 293–321, 324–28, 365, 388, 400; decolonization in, 419–28, 448; European trade and exploration in, 18, 150, 154–58, 160, 180, 221, 248; indigenous empires in, 10, 179, 314; Islamic empires in, 70, 74–75; maintenance of ethnic distinctions in, 316, 391, 420; Ottoman empire in, 18, 122, 132; and post–World War I restructuring, 381, 386, 391, 402–3; Roman empire in, 24, 30, 35, 38, 64; and slave trade, 5, 19, 136, 157, 164, 173, 178–79. *See also* colonial empires
African National Congress, 429
Africans: in Americas, 163–68, 176, 226, 236, 246–47, 251, 261, 284; as objects for reform, 10, 289–91, 315–16, 318, 326–28,

371, 392, 413, 420, 448, 450; in world wars, 371–77, 391, 393, 407. *See also* anticolonial movements; citizenship; slavery
Afrikaners, 319, 320
agriculture and indigenous producers, 301, 312, 319. *See also* peasants; planters and plantations; slavery
air power, 392, 430. *See also* military
Al-Queda, 458
Alaska, 254, 271, 354
Albania, Albanians, 304, 342, 345, 359, 364, 367. *See also* Balkans; Ottoman empire
Aleutians, 254, 354
Alexander I, 333
Alexander II, 283, 285, 341, 353, 355
Alexander III, 354
Alexander the Great, 23, 34, 117, 311
Alexandria, 64, 66
Alexei Mikhailovich, 196, 197
Algeria, 17, 123, 144, 304–6, 318, 387, 403, 421–22, 424–26, 429
Algiers, 132, 145, 304
Algonquin, 256
Ali (Muhammad's son-in-law), 74
Allah, 72
Almohads, 75

British empire *(continued)*
different forms of, 170, 287,
290, 293, 300, 306–8, 310, 312,
324; and ideological basis of
American revolution, 238–40,
249; and indentured labor,
292; in India, 172, 242, 306–12,
390–92, 403–4, 418–20; and
Iran, 430; and Iraq, 384, 387,
392, 458; in Ireland, 171,
244–45, 252, 390; king vs.
Parliament in, 177, 239; and
Latin America, 248, 294; as
model, 323, 332; as moral
and political community, 12,
243–44, 290–92; and Napoleonic empire, 233–34, 244; and
Native Americans, 175–76,
240, 249, 256–58, 262–63, 284;
in North America, 173–78,
220, 221, 238–40, 252–58, 260;
origins of, 170–78; and Ottoman empire, 172, 180, 303–4,
339–40, 344, 365–66, 378–79;
penal colonies of, 300; post–
World War I restructuring of,
281–87; and settlement, 171,
173–77, 238–41, 250–59, 300;
sovereignty in, 177, 240–44,
389–90, 425; in World War I,
370–78, 392; in World War
II, 397, 400, 405, 407–10, 418.
See also dominions (British);
economies, imperial: in British
empire; Great Britain; military:
in British empire; slavery
Broers, Michael, 232
bronze, 43, 102
Brussels Conference (1890–91),
315
Buda, 145
Buddhism, 13, 51, 54, 96, 100, 105,
109, 110, 112, 202, 204, 212,
273, 441
buffalo, 253, 254, 256, 265, 266
Buganda, 314
Bukhara, 100, 113, 355
Bulgaria, 129, 281, 355, 358, 363,
367, 368, 431, 433
Bulgars, 96, 100, 103
bureaucracy: and Africa, 325;
and Bureau of Indian Affairs,
267; in Byzantine empire, 66,
68, 73; in Chinese empires,
51, 204–5, 207–9, 232; and
European colonies, 288, 325;
in Habsburg empire, 346,
350; in India, 307, 310–11; and

Japanese empire, 400; and
Napoleonic reforms, 229–32;
in Ottoman empire, 136, 139,
145, 343, 345; absence of, in
Rome, 30; in South Africa,
320, 325. *See also* Chinese
empires: officials in; intermediaries; officials
Burgundy, 122
Burke, Edmund, 238, 243, 244,
291, 326
Burma, 151, 156, 296, 299, 300,
407–9
Burqan Qaldun, 97, 103
Bursa, 129, 141
Buyyids, 77
Byzantine empire, 3, 61–70,
444–46; administration of,
66–68, church and state in,
65–66; and crusades, 70, 89;
diversity of, 64; economy of,
67–69; influence of, 66, 69, 91,
139, 143, 148, 186–90, 444–46;
law in, 64; and neighboring
empires, 18, 67–72, 73, 75,
80–94, 97, 108, 118, 123, 129,
132, 134, 141, 147, 186–90; as
new Rome, 13, 40–42, 61–62,
67; and Russia, 70, 91, 186–90,
194, 199, 251, 445; ups and
downs of, 62–64, 69–70. *See
also* aristocracies; Christianity;
eunuchs; military: in Byzantine empire; monotheism;
Orthodox church

caciques, 164
Cadiz, 124, 162, 246, 247
Caesar, 31, 32, 38, 70, 143, 144,
194; as title, 350. *See also* kai-
ser; tsar
Cairo, 78, 79
Calcutta, 160, 173, 295
California, 166, 258, 259, 265, 271
caliph, 74–77, 79, 86, 91, 93, 105,
148, 378, 390
caliphates. *See* Islamic empires
Calvinists, 183
Cambodia, 298, 299, 416, 417
Cameroon, 315, 375
Camillus, 25
Canada, 11, 224, 241, 245, 254,
266, 300–301, 371, 375, 448
canals, 49, 203, 294, 300, 304, 321,
378, 426
Canary Islands, 122, 152, 154, 162
Canton, 160, 295, 297
Cape Verde, 154

capital: empires' need for, 157–59,
162, 166–67, 173, 236, 248, 290,
294–95, 302, 313–14, 344, 384
capital cities: importance of, 25,
31, 35, 45, 49, 51, 57, 70, 75, 105,
106, 112–13, 132, 186, 189, 274,
387, 392, 402; movement of,
4, 13, 25, 40, 50, 54, 56, 62, 71,
83, 105, 129, 198, 200–203, 238,
385, 495
capital punishment, 28, 142,
277, 423
capitalism: development of, 235–
37, 289, 319, 328, 352, 393, 450;
hesitations about imposing,
284, 309, 354, 450; and interempire competition, 313–14,
329; normative basis of, 222–
23, 237, 245, 290–91; regulation
of, 433, 436, 438; relationship
to empire of, 170, 221, 236–37,
245, 284, 289, 299, 309, 440,
449–50, 452; as revolution,
221–22; in South Africa,
312–20, 429; and theories of
imperialism, 20, 221, 313–14,
370; and world after empires,
418, 433, 438, 440, 449. *See also*
commercial networks; com-
munism; economies, imperial;
extraterritoriality; socialism
Caribbean, 19, 124, 149, 161–63,
168, 179, 227, 236, 240–41, 255,
290–92, 447. *See also* British
empire: in Caribbean; Cuba;
French empire: in Caribbean;
Guyana; Haiti; Jamaica; Puerto
Rico; Saint Domingue; Spanish empire: in Caribbean
Carolingian empire, 4, 10, 13, 42,
80–88, 90–91; administration
of, 83–84; and Byzantium,
82, 86; economy of, 81, 85;
influence of, 86–87, 90; and
Islamic empires, 82, 86, 91; as
model for Napoleon, 230; and
religious institutions, 84; as a
type of empire, 90, 91. *See also*
aristocracies; Catholic church;
Charlemagne; Franks; military:
in Carolingian empire; papacy
Carthage, 29, 30
Caspian, 105, 356, 372
caste, 307, 310
Castile, 113, 119–27, 143, 147,
162, 446
Catalonia, Catalans, 122, 127, 246
Cathay, 97

Christianity, Christians *(continued)*
universalism and, 38, 88, 89,
117, 145, 170, 445; and wars
in Europe, 144, 183. *See also*
Catholic church; crusades;
Latin kingdoms; missionaries; monotheism; Ortho-
dox church; pilgrimage;
Protestantism
Chu state, 46
Chu Yuan-chang, 202
Chukchis, 272
Churchill, Winston, 392, 431–32
Chuvash, 277, 280
Cicero, 37
Cis-Leithania, 349
citizenship: in British empire,
425, 449; and claims to social
services, 410, 422, 426, 449–50;
and cultural difference, 305,
366, 367, 422; and decolonization, 422–26, 449–50, 452–53;
exclusions from, 226, 260–65,
268, 275, 284–85, 305, 318,
327–28, 391, 456; extension
across empires of, 12, 29–30,
39, 57–58, 226–29, 270, 292,
420–22, 426, 444, 449; in
French empire, 19–20, 223–30,
292, 305, 317–18, 367, 376,
391, 421–22, 426, 444, 449; in
Habsburg empire, 348, 361,
365, 367; national vs. imperial,
7, 16, 20, 220–29, 249, 328, 333,
375, 391, 413, 410, 420–21, 444,
449–50; in Ottoman empire,
344, 365, 444; and political and
social equivalence, 14, 21, 245,
249, 260, 270, 410, 423, 452;
restrictive versions of, 121,
224, 305; in Roman empire, 4,
24–26, 28–36, 39–42, 56–59,
121, 444; in Russia, 394; and
slave emancipation, 19, 269–
70, 292; and subject-citizen
distinction, 19–20, 305, 317–18,
327, 391, 421–22; in United
States, 249, 251, 260–61, 265,
269–70, 284–86; and war
service, 30, 33, 39, 223–24,
232, 375–77, 391, 444. *See also*
nation, idea of
city-states, 10, 11, 16, 24, 42–43,
58, 70, 121, 151, 224, 441
Civil Rights Act, 269
Civil War (United States), 6,
229, 251, 266, 268, 270, 284,
448, 454

civil wars, 49, 74, 96, 183, 195,
235, 240, 247, 270, 283, 390,
395, 426, 430
civilization, civilizations: as claim
to superiority, 13, 14, 41, 59,
145, 198–99, 209, 253, 268, 271,
287, 293, 315–16, 325, 335, 385,
429; clash of, 70; and status
of incorporated peoples, 168,
184, 263, 311, 415
civilizing missions, 13, 42, 171,
225, 232–33, 252, 332; of European empires, 6–7, 15–16, 307,
308, 316, 318, 391, 448, 452;
in Habsburg empire, 362–63;
in Hawaii, 268; in North
America, 252, 267; in Ottoman empire, 341; in Russian
empire, 355; in USSR, 397,
435, 451. *See also* Africans: as
objects for reform; barbarians; development, economic;
humanitas; missionaries
Cixi, 298
class: in American revolution,
240; and assimilation into
imperial elites, 30; and capitalist development, 237, 351; and
French revolution, 223–24;
and hierarchy in colonized
populations, 27, 28, 47, 246,
310, 323, 384, 402–3, 419,
426, 450; in Indian politics,
403, 419; knightly, 88, 91; and
mobility in imperial societies, 30, 51–52, 171, 240; and
models of imperial hierarchy,
145–47, 199; in Napoleonic
Europe, 233; official, 4, 66, 140,
298; in Philippines, 323; popular, 171, 223, 343, 351; in post-
revolutionary Latin America,
246; and property, 166, 177,
236–37; and Soviet society,
393–95, 398; and tensions in
nineteenth century Europe,
237, 351, 359, 366; and tensions
in World War I, 371–72; working, 328, 351, 354, 357, 372, 393,
395, 450. *See also* aristocracies;
capitalism; nobility
clientage, 18, 73–76, 80, 90–91,
159, 166, 188, 306–7, 319, 378–
79, 427, 430, 433, 435, 437–38,
445, 453–54, 458
climate change, 205, 253
Clive, Robert, 242
Clovis, 82

coal, 236, 299, 407, 439
cocoa, 319, 411
code. *See* law: codes
coffee, 223, 234, 267, 294, 411
coinage, 46, 66, 69, 78
cold war, 414–15, 427, 431
Colombia, 249
colonial empires, 6, 127, 287–329,
352, 370, 389–92; and capitalist
development, 236–37; dissolution of, 7, 9–11, 121, 413–29,
452; as distinct imperial form,
6, 19–20, 203, 264, 287–90,
305, 324–29; duration of, 21,
321, 452; and European states
in fifteenth to eighteenth
centuries, 18–19, 122, 125,
127, 149–51, 156, 158, 162–66,
168, 176–68, 252–59, 447; and
European states in nineteenth
century, 12, 19–20, 220–21,
235–41, 246–50, 287–90, 299–
301, 305, 314–19, 321, 324–29,
448–51, 454; Japan as, 302–3,
388, 401–2, 407; and Napoleon, 234–45; restructuring of,
after World War I, 380, 384–87,
390–99, 402–4; restructuring
of, after World War II, 21, 411,
413, 420–21, 449–51; and revolutionary era, 220–21; United
States as, 6, 321–23, 452, 457;
and World War I, 371, 375–77,
402–4; and World War II, 405,
407–11. *See also* anticolonial
movements; colonization;
decolonization; empires
colonial social structures, 12, 14,
150, 162, 168, 174–76, 181, 220,
226, 238, 289, 291, 306, 325–27,
402–3, 447–49, 458; in Africa,
318–19, 326, 391; in Algeria,
305; in Americas, 18–19, 154–
58, 162–70, 174–76, 245–47,
252–59, 290–93; in enclave
colonies, 157, 298; in Japanese
colonies, 303, 401; and Nazi
racism, 400; and slavery question, 226–28, 238, 291–93; in
southeast Asia, 150, 298, 299–
300; and United States, 264,
284–86. *See also* class; difference; empires, incorporation
and differentiation in; Native
Americans; populations; race;
colonialism: as "modern," 6,
287, 289, 312, 316, 326–29; as
political concept, 287, 311. *See*

constitutions *(continued)*
  tional reform, 391, 444; English, 177; of French empire, 20,
  225, 227, 421–22; in Habsburg
  empire, 346, 348, 350, 361; in
  Ottoman empire, 344, 360;
  Polish, 274, 333, 337; in Russia, 335, 338, 354, 356–57, 360,
  455; Spanish (1812), 246–47,
  311; of Toussaint L'Ouverture,
  228; of United States, 251, 260,
  268–70, 284
continental empires. *See* Chinese
  empires; Mongol empires;
  Ottoman empire; Russian
  empire; United States
Convention of Berlin (1833), 338
copper, 102, 319, 411
Coptic, 64, 66, 90
Cordoba, 75, 78, 79
Cornwallis, Lord, 243
corporal punishment, 28, 51,
  212, 276
Corsica, 25, 30
Cortes (Spanish Parliament),
  246–47
Cortes, Hernando, 119, 124, 143,
  163, 164
Cossacks, 191, 192, 271, 274,
  277, 281
cotton, 78, 102, 132, 172, 201, 236,
  269, 309, 355, 356
counterinsurgency, 418
Crazy Horse, 266
creoles, 238, 240, 245–46, 444
Crimea, 20, 279, 338, 340, 341,
  432
Crimean khanate, 191
Crimean War, 283, 331, 341,
  353–54, 450
Croats, 349, 364
crusades, 18, 70, 87–91, 148, 188,
  457
Cuba, 247, 290, 292–93, 321–23,
  415, 437, 448
CUP. *See* Committee on Union
  and Progress
Curzon, Lord, 311, 381
Custer, Gen. George, 267
Cyrillic, 188, 397
Czartoryski, Adam Jerzy, 275
Czech Republic, 1
Czechoslovakia, 381, 399, 405,
  427, 431, 433, 435, 439
Czechs, 347, 348, 362, 363, 381

Dagestan, 337
Dahomey, 179, 314

Dalai Lama, 212, 215
Damascus, 74, 75, 78
Danes, Danish-speakers, 85, 123,
  215, 314, 331, 365, 405
Daniil, 190
Daniilovichi, 190, 191, 195. *See
  also* Muscovite princes
Danube, 35, 337, 341, 446
Daoism, 13, 103, 204, 212
dar al-harb, 72
dar al-Islam, 72, 280
Dardanelles, 129, 132, 339, 378,
  379
Davis, David Brion, 290
de Gaulle, Charles, 369, 407,
  415, 426
Decembrist conspiracy, 335
Declaration of Independence
  (United States), 268, 410
decolonization, 9–11, 17, 413–29,
  452–53; of Africa, 420–28, 454;
  of Algeria, 424–26; in Haiti,
  228–29; of India, 418–20; and
  Japanese conquests in southeast Asia, 15, 21, 409–11, 452;
  and liberation of European
  states, 21, 438–39; and new
  international order, 427, 429,
  431, 437–38, 452–53; and origins of United States, 240–41,
  259–60; of Philippines, 323,
  411; and postcolonial politics,
  9, 427, 437, 443, 453–54; and
  responsibility for colonialism,
  429, 454; of southeast Asia,
  415–18, 454; of Spanish America, 247–48; United States and,
  436–37. *See also* anticolonial
  movements; colonial empires:
  restructuring of, after World
  War II; nation-state
Delhi, 113, 200
democracy: in China, 441; and
  empire, 315, 350, 358, 360, 390,
  393–94, 422, 428, 450; exclusions in and restrictions on,
  248, 300, 328, 428, 439; export
  of, 21, 456; in India, 453; and
  post-colonial states, 429, 430,
  453; and types of state, 7, 11,
  221, 364. *See also* elections;
  republics
depression (1929), 399, 400,
  402–3
development, economic, 181,
  302, 323, 356, 391–92, 401,
  413, 420–23, 428, 431, 437, 438,
  452, 457. *See also* capitalism:

development of; economies,
  imperial
devshirme, 136–38
dhimma, 73
Diagne, Blaise, 377, 391
diamonds, 319
diasporas, and cross-empire
  networks, 22, 91, 133, 147, 388,
  425, 439, 458, 459
Dickinson, John, 262
dictators, 11, 25, 31, 230, 261, 395,
  398, 428, 439, 458
Diderot, Denis, 225
Diets, 346, 364
difference, 11–13, 251, 458–59;
  and classifications of peoples,
  225, 289, 310–11, 325, 327; and
  imposition of dominant culture, 12, 40, 49, 167, 232, 280–
  81, 291, 307–8, 323, 355–56,
  435, 452, 458; maintenance of,
  12, 325–26; politics of, 11, 12,
  58, 59, 61, 91, 92, 171, 181, 184,
  201, 209, 225, 251, 284, 288, 312,
  325, 331, 332, 367, 400, 458; as
  principle of rule, 208–13, 216,
  218, 271, 356–67, 361. *See also*
  civilizing missions; empires:
  incorporation and differentiation in; ethnicity; populations:
  unmixing of; race; religion
Directory, 225
disease, 157, 181, 340, 368, 447;
  and colonization of Americas, 162–64, 254; and Ming
  dynasty, 205; and Mongol
  empires, 110. *See also* plague;
  smallpox
diwani, 242
Dnieper River, 186, 188, 189,
  274, 281
Dom Pedro (Brazil), 248
Dom Pedro (Portugal), 154
domestic dependent nations, 263
Dominican Republic, 324
dominions (British), 300–301,
  306, 320, 386, 389–90, 425;
  in World War I, 371, 375; in
  World War II, 407, 425
dominium, 174, 301
Donglin Society, 205
Dorgon, 207, 211
Dostoevsky, Feodor, 338
dotations, 231
"the drain," 311, 312, 418
Dred Scott case, 265, 266
dress: in Ottoman empire, 343; in
  Qing dynasty, 210–11

"expansion of," 5, 149, 446; fragmentation of, 15, 117, 123, 144, 149–50, 153–54, 180, 196, 208, 246, 321, 333, 443, 445; as identifiable entity, 5, 87, 145, 235, 287, 315, 333–34, 364, 429, 439–40, 456; and immigration, 422, 440; impact of Napoleon on, 229, 234–35; loss of confidence by, 369, 392, 414, 427; Ottoman empire in, 129, 142–44, 359, 367–68; post-Roman political structure in, 82, 86, 90–92; and racial thinking, 289, 315, 318, 325–27, 399–400; recovery of, after World War II, 436–39; reorganization of state system of, 234–35, 333, 341, 381–87, 431–32, 439–40, 456; and Russian empire, 196–98, 277, 279, 333, 336–42, 353–56, 360, 395; sovereignty in, 1, 7, 17, 20–21, 120–21, 145, 182–83, 225, 332, 348, 362, 387, 432–33, 447, 456, 458. *See also* economies, imperial; European empires; European Union; nation, idea of; Nazi empire; religion; revolutions and rebellions

European Coal and Steel Community, 439

European Economic Community, 1, 439

European empires, 5–7, 12, 15, 17–21, 287–330, 447–48; and American federalists' arguments for union, 260; compared to Mongols, 151, 288; encroachment on Chinese empire of, 18, 294–98; encroachment on Ottoman empire of, 18, 303–6; and "epoch" of nation-states, 20–21, 219–23, 245–47, 381–82, 422, 438–39, 452–53; end of, 438–39, 452–56; on European continent, 142–45, 168, 229–35, 246, 289, 331–68; and French revolution, 224; and Japan, 303–4, 399–400, 407–8; overseas, 123–28, 145–47, 149–83, 233–34, 253–59, 331–68, 447–48; reform in, 177, 238–41, 243, 246, 331–68, 413, 420–22, 436, 449; and rules for competition in Africa, 315–16; and scramble for Africa, 312–21; world domination

by, 5–6, 19, 180–81, 287–89, 321, 352, 364–68, 447, 450. *See also* anticolonial movements; Habsburg empire; Belgian empire; British empire; colonial empires; decolonization; empires: criticism of; French empire; German empire; Nazi empire; Ottoman empire; Portuguese empire; race; Russian empire; Spanish empire; Europe: competition for dominance in

European Union, 1, 2, 414, 439–40, 443, 456–457

Europeans, as "Franks," 86, 143. *See also* settlers and settlement

exogamy, 95, 102, 108, 129, 134, 190, 211

extraterritoriality, 143, 213, 294, 296

factories, 156, 173, 237, 315, 354, 398, 405

Faisal ibn Husayn, 382, 384

family, as model for empire, 32–33, 52. *See also* patrimonialism

famines, 297, 311, 395, 432

Fanon, Frantz, 312

fascism, 403, 428, 439. *See also* Nazi empire

Fatimid dynasty, 76–78, 80

federation: as alternative to empire, 10–11, 260, 268, 348, 391, 413–17, 419–26, 453; Indochinese, 416; Malayan, 418; in post-Napoleonic Europe, 234; Russian, 1, 17, 453, 455; United States as, 260–61, 448; USSR as, 16, 380, 391, 396–97. *See also* confederation; states, types of

Fedor the Bellringer, 195

feminism, 332, 344, 354

Ferdinand (of Aragon), 120–23

Ferdinand I (Austria), 346

Ferdinand I (Holy Roman Emperor), 126, 144

Ferdinand VII (Spain), 247

Ferghana, 53

Ferry, Jules, 318

Fichte, Johann Gottlieb, 336

Finland, 94, 272, 333, 395, 397

Finns, 191, 394

Finno-Ugric speakers, 192

fiscal-military state, 176, 182, 235

fish, fishermen, 176, 238, 253, 254, 282

Fletcher, Joseph, 96

Florida, 240

foot binding, 211

Forbidden City, 203, 205

foreign aid, 427, 429, 437

Four Communes (Senegal), 317, 318, 376–77

Fourteenth Amendment, 270, 284

Franco-Prussian war, 371

Frankfurt National Assembly, 347

Franks, 16, 80, 82–88, 90, 111, 112, 143, 292

Franz Ferdinand, 374

Franz Joseph, 346–49, 361

fratricide, 96, 120, 134, 138

Frederick William III, 333

Frederick William IV, 350

free labor, 266, 284, 291, 292. *See also* labor: wage

free trade, 19, 152, 181, 293, 332, 341, 344, 365, 448, 455. *See also* imperialism: of free trade

freeborn Englishmen, 251. *See also* rights: of Englishmen

freedom of the seas, 183

French Community, 415, 423, 456

French empire, 287, 298–99, 314–17, 324, 373–77, 409–10, 415–17, 420–26, 449; and absolutist state, 182; in Africa, 314–18, 375–77, 386, 391, 403, 407, 420–23; in Algeria, 17, 304–5, 387, 421–22, 425–26, 439; and anticolonial movements, 403, 409, 410, 417, 423, 426, 450, 452; and British empire, 170–71, 183, 220, 235, 240, 244; in Caribbean, 7, 16, 170, 178, 225–29, 292, 300, 317, 421, 444, 449; and Carolingian and Merovingian polities, 82, 85; and China, 296, 298, 388; as composite polity, 305–6, 420–21; constitutions of, 227, 421–22; and decolonization, 17, 409, 410, 415–17, 420–26, 450, 452; and European alliances, 144, 174, 182, 334, 338–41, 356, 373; federal and confederal alternatives in, 9, 10–11, 416–17, 420–23, 453; and forms of state power, 8, 146, 159, 182–83, 219, 223–25, 232, 305–6; and German empire, 314, 350–52, 365, 372–77, 386, 400; and Habsburg empire, 120, 122–23, 143–44, 348; and

Great Yasa, 109
Greater Britain, 300, 356
Greater East Asia Co-Prosperity Sphere, 401, 452
Greece: and Balkan conflicts, 358, 367; and Byzantine empire, 42, 62, 64, 66; and citizenship concept, 10, 224; dictatorship in, 439; and Habsburgs, 347; independence of, 336–37, 342; and Islamic empires, 75, 79; and Ottoman empire, 129, 132–34, 140, 142, 303, 336–37, 342, 345, 358–60, 368, 385; and population exchange with Turkey, 385, 451; and Roman empire, 10, 12, 23–25, 30, 36–38, 43, 58; and Russia, 188, 196, 281; and trade and seafaring, 121, 132, 172, 181
Greek Orthodox church, 90, 140. *See also* Orthodox church
Grégoire, Abbé de, 225
Guadeloupe, 228
Guantanamo, 322
Guatemala, 437
Guinea, 423
Guinea, coast of, 155
Guinea-Bissau, 428
Gujaratis, 132, 155, 172, 181, 447
Gulf of Mexico, 234
guns: in China, 99, 102; and gunboat diplomacy, 294; machine, 288, 296, 324; as trade good, 156, 254. *See also* military; weapons
Guomindang, 389, 408, 440
Guptas, 10
Guyana, 300, 407

Habsburg empire, 6, 119, 331–34, 337–38, 346–50, 361–67, 449; alliances of, 334, 337–38, 352, 364; and Balkans, 356, 358, 364; bureaucracy in, 346; colony of, 362–64; and Crimean War, 340–41; dismemberment of, 1, 381; diversity in, 347–49, 361–64, 366–68; Dual Monarchy and, 348–50, 361; dynastic tradition in, 87, 232, 347–48, 363; education in, 346–47, 362–63, 365; and French revolution, 224; and German empire, 351; Germanness in, 361–64; and Italy, 333, 340, 346; Jews in, 361, 372, 381; liberalism in, 348–50, 361, 367; reform

in, 346–50, 361–67; rebellions against, 337–38, 346; relations with Ottoman empire of, 331, 339, 341, 346, 358, 362, 364–68; religion in, 347–50, 362–63; sovereignty in, 346–49, 362; in World War I, 369–75. *See also* citizenship; economies, imperial: in Habsburg empire; Hungary; Jews; military: in Habsburg empire; nationalism; parliaments
Habsburgs: in Americas, 123–28; as Catholic rulers, 120–28, 143, 158, 162, 167–68, 172, 347, 350; and Holy Roman Empire, 87, 117; and Hungary, 144; and Napoleon, 232; and Ottoman empire, 117–19, 121–23, 127, 133, 143–44, 147–48, 153, 346, 446; as rulers of composite polity, 120–23, 126–27, 144, 147, 346–47, 399; as rulers of Portugal, 158; and Spanish empire, 117, 119–24, 126–28, 133, 144. *See also* Habsburg empire; Hungary; Netherlands; Spanish empire
Hadiths, 71, 73
Hadramaut, 151
Hagia Sophia, 64, 90
Haiti, 228–29, 249, 324; as vanguard or pariah, 228–29. *See also* revolutions and rebellions: in Saint Domingue (Haiti); Saint Domingue
Hakluyt, 170
Hall, Catherine, 291
Hammurabi, 36
Han: as ethnic designation, 42, 59, 200–201, 208, 389; interaction with Manchus of, 209–13, 218, 296. *See also* Chinese empires
Han dynasty, 10, 43, 50–54, 97, 112, 445; and legitimacy of Qin, 48; and nomads, 52–54, 59, 94; origins of, 50; and regional elites, 43, 50, 54; upward mobility in, 51–52. *See also* Chinese empires
Hanoi, 299, 408, 410
Hanover, 220
Hanseatic League, 151
harem, 135–36. *See also* concubines; succession practices
Harun al-Rashid, 77, 79, 80, 86, 87

Hashemites, 378–79, 382–84
Hastings, Warren, 243
Hawaii, 268, 322, 323, 399
Henry the Navigator, 154
Herder, Johann Gottfried von, 336
Herero, 316, 400
Herzen, Alexander, 338
Hindu College, 308
Hinduism, 242, 311, 326
Hindus, 172, 310–11, 390, 404, 418–20
Hirschman, Albert, 179
Hitler, Adolf, 15, 370, 397, 398, 411, 414
Ho Chi Minh, 402–4, 408, 409, 417
Holt, Thomas, 291
Holy Alliance, 333–34
Holy Land, 70, 89, 379
Holy Roman Empire, 87, 117, 121–23, 126, 182–83, 230, 350, 399. *See also* Habsburgs
Holy Synod, 198
Hong Kong, 295, 296, 298–300, 306, 407; return to China of, 441–42
Hong Taiji, 207
Hongwu, 202, 203
Hormuz, 151, 156
horses: in Americas, 163, 166, 252, 255–56, 259; in Carolingian empire, 84, 86; and China-nomad connection, 43, 45–46, 53, 201, 208; and Eurasian polities, 77, 445–46; and Mongols, 94–95, 98–99, 102, 107, 109–10, 112, 259
House of Representatives (United States), 260, 269
Howard, Michael, 377
Hulegu, 93, 105, 106, 108, 109
humanitas, 37, 41, 50, 59
Hung Hsiu-chuan, 297
Hungary: and 1848 revolutions, 338, 346; communist revolution in, 396; contested by Habsburg and Ottoman empires, 123, 144, 346, 363; Mongol conquest of, 93, 105; as post–World War I state, 381; as post-Soviet state, 1; and USSR, 427, 431, 433, 439; in World War II, 405. *See also* Austria-Hungary; Dual Monarchy; Habsburg empire; revolutions and rebellions: in Hungary

Huns, 67, 94
hunting, 98, 212, 253, 254, 256, 258, 318
Hurrem (Roxelana), 135, 136
Husayn ibn Ali, 74, 378, 382, 429

icons, 66, 188
Igelstrom, Baron Osip, 279
Il-Khan empire, 105–12, 141. *See also* Mongol empires
imagination, political, 2, 3, 7, 10, 15, 16, 42, 58, 61, 71, 99, 104, 114, 128, 219, 243, 245, 289, 332, 348–49, 357, 389, 403, 408, 414, 443, 444, 457
immigration. *See* labor: and migration
imperator, 31, 32
Imperial Geographical Society, 336
Imperial Russia. *See* Russian empire
imperialism: anti-liberal, 352; as exercise of power across space, 294, 323; of free trade, 302, 306, 314, 315, 322, 324, 437, 448, 452; theories of, 313–14
imperium, 28, 32, 168, 174
imperium in imperio, 239, 270
Inca empire, 10, 18, 123–24, 152, 163–64, 167, 174, 252–53, 446. *See also* Spanish empire
independence. *See* decolonization; sovereignty
India, 171–73, 241–45, 306–12, 418–20; British views of, 244, 307–9, 327; and China, 204, 295–96; class and caste in, 244, 307, 309, 310; democracy in, 453; early empires in, 10, 23, 171, 242; Hinduism and politics in, 311, 326; independence of, 419–20, 453; and Indian Ocean and southeast Asia, 124, 132, 145, 151–52, 173, 299, 447; intensification of colonization in, 19, 241–45, 306–12; Islam in, 80, 242; local intermediaries in, 172–73, 238, 241–43, 307, 309–10; as model, 323, 390; and Mongols, 103, 113–15; Muslim-Hindu tensions in, 404, 418–20; political mobilization in, 310–12, 387, 390–92, 403–4, 418–20; political unification of, 310–12, 391; Portuguese in, 155–57; princely states in, 242–43,

306–7, 310, 419; recruitment of labor from, 292; and Russia, 271, 355; self-government in, 403; use of troops from, 308, 315; in World War I, 373, 375, 378; in World War II, 403, 407, 409, 418. *See also* British East India Company; British empire; economies, imperial: in India; Mughal empire
Indian Appropriations Act, 264
Indian Civil Service, 307, 310, 312, 391
Indian National Congress, 312, 390–92, 403, 407, 418–19
Indian Ocean, 18, 71, 132, 145, 149, 151, 152, 155, 156, 172, 181–83, 203, 300, 447
Indian Removal Act, 263
Indian title, 262
Indian Trade and Intercourse acts, 262
Indians (in Central and South America), 15, 19, 164, 166–69, 246, 247. *See also* Spanish empire
Indians (in North American). *See* Native Americans
indigénat, 318
Indochina, 299, 404, 407–9, 415–16, 419. *See also* Vietnam
Indonesia, 151, 159, 301, 306, 387, 404, 407–10, 415–17, 427, 429, 436; *See also* Dutch empire
Indus River, 103
industrial revolution, 19, 236, 447
industrialization: in China, 204–5, 236, 450, 455; and colonial products, 236, 294, 324, 447; and development, 421; in Europe, 19, 294, 350–53, 433; in Germany, 314, 332, 350, 352, 373; in Great Britain, 19, 178, 236–37, 290–93, 300, 314; in India, 172, 242, 307, 309; in Japan, 302, 388, 400–401; in postcolonial states, 454; in Russia, 356; social dangers of, 300, 314, 324, 350, 352, 354, 372; in South Africa, 320; in USSR, 398, 433. *See also* capitalism
inner Asia, 13, 77, 102, 129
Inquisition, 121, 143, 144, 167
intermediaries, 13–14, 450–51; clients as, 74, 76–77, 80, 90–91; dependent nobility as, 193–95, 199, 216; and *devshirme*, 136,

137; different systems of, 57, 90–91, 145–48, 216; dual governance and, 114; *encomenderos* as, 166; ethnic category as, 208–9, 213; and ethnic fragmentation, 402; eunuchs as, 67, 77, 135, 138, 153, 205–6; and imperial household, 91, 147–48; local elites as, 5, 14, 34, 84, 107–8, 114–15, 164, 166, 173–74, 181, 243–44, 271, 286, 306–9, 316, 323, 325–26, 343, 378, 408; local entrepreneurs as, 298, 326; metropolitan agents as, 13, 125, 156, 166, 168, 173, 232, 307, 325, 405; officeholders as, 28, 30, 43, 49–52, 66, 68, 136, 139, 142, 204–5, 210, 216–18, 229, 232, 298, 341, 343, 395, 444; party cadres as, 395, 397, 433; in post-colonial world, 427; reliance on, 13–14, 20, 28, 43, 47, 67, 82–86, 91, 156, 161, 166–67, 173, 184, 185, 208–9, 216, 316, 325–26, 329, 378, 443, 448, 450–51; risks posed by, 43, 47, 49, 54, 57, 67, 77–78, 84, 90, 123, 125–26, 157, 161, 206, 238–40, 246–47, 296, 307, 310, 326, 342, 366, 447; settlers as, 14, 126–27, 166, 177, 239–40; slaves as, 14, 75, 77–78, 91, 136–40. *See also* administration; aristocracies; bureaucracy; nobility; officials
International Labour Organisation, 386
Iran, 4, 75, 102, 103, 105, 108, 133, 141, 187, 430, 437, 454, 457, 458
Iraq, 75, 77, 78, 80, 88, 105, 382, 384, 387, 391–92, 429–30, 443, 454, 456–58
Ireland: and British rule, 171, 244–45, 390–91, 448; republic in, 390. *See also* British empire
Irene (Empress), 86
Irish: in Boer war, 320; as "nomads," 96, 174, 252, 300; movement across empire of, 176, 254
iron, 43, 95, 252
Iroquois, 256, 257, 262
Isabella, 120–22, 168
Isis, 38
Islam, 4, 13, 15, 17, 61, 70–80, 82, 88, 92, 109, 112, 133, 135–36, 141–43, 148, 149, 151, 161, 181, 326, 345, 349, 358–60,

khanates. *See* Eurasian empires; Mongol empires.

khaqan, 96, 129, 186. *See also* khan

Khazars, 96, 187

Khilfat, 390

Khitans, 97, 110

Khiva, khanate of, 355

Khubilai Khan, 93, 105–9, 112, 201, 202

Khwarezm, 100, 102–5

Kiev, 93, 103, 186–191, 196, 199, 274

Kievan Rus', 185–189; administration in, 107; and Byzantium, 186–88; census of, 107; economy of, 186, 188; and Eurasian practices, 186; and Mongols, 107, 188; religion in, 186–88. *See also* Riurikids; Rus'

kingdoms, 10, 11, 16, 151–52; in Africa, 154, 159, 179, 314–16, 387–88; in China, 43, 46, 48; under Napoleon, 232; in post-Roman Europe, 82–83, 208; reconfigurations of, 333; in Scotland, 171; of Spain, 117, 120–22, 126, 162, 168; in southeast Asia, 151, 159, 161, 298, 417

kinship, 9, 71, 95, 133, 159, 166, 179, 246, 306, 319, 378

Kipchak khanate (Golden Horde), 100, 103, 105–7, 112–13, 187, 189–92

Kipchaks, 103, 105

Kitai, 97

Kokand, 355

Kongo, 154

Korea, 110, 200, 206, 207, 302, 303, 356, 387–88, 399, 436, 437, 441, 454

Korean War, 437

kremlin, 190

Ku Klux Klan, 269

Kurdistan, 140

Kurds, 1, 77, 78, 345, 359, 385, 451

Kuril Islands, 431

kuriltai, 96, 101, 104, 106, 110, 194, 277, 394

Kyrgyz, 394

labor: agricultural, 34, 159, 166, 258, 269, 284; and compulsion, 5, 20, 49, 150, 159, 162, 164, 166, 169, 196, 199, 292, 316, 318–20, 325, 398, 406, 408, 432; dependent, 258, 265–66, 299, 319, 354; factory, 236, 354; forced, in USSR, 398, 432; "free," 266, 284; indentured, 174, 255, 292; and migration, 312, 319, 425; and strikes, 357, 384, 392, 394, 422; wage, 220, 222, 236–37, 290–92, 299, 319–20. *See also* capitalism; populations: displacement of; serfdom; slavery

labor unions, 272, 422, 450, 452

Lagarde, Paul de, 352

Lakotas, 266

lamas, 105, 202, 204, 212, 215

land: colonizers' acquisition of, 20, 157, 166, 171, 174, 238, 253, 258–59, 262–66, 300, 319, 405; and emancipation in United States, 269; and imperial control, 46, 67, 68, 81, 139, 175, 193, 199, 233, 237; and importance of landowners, 58, 223, 121, 233, 240, 250, 337; and indigenous landowners, 299, 301; and military service, 47, 67, 139; and permanent settlement in India, 309; reform of, in China, 441; revenue from, 147, 307, 309, 312; rights in, 253, 258, 262, 265–66, 354; in Russia, 193, 195, 199, 216, 353, 365. *See also* aristocracies; colonization; peasants; serfdom; settlers and settlement; slavery

language, languages: in Americas, 167, 253, 256; Arabic, 75–77, 80, 144, 149, 210, 429; in Chinese empires, 48, 202, 210; and education, 198, 280–81, 308, 343, 397; English, 308; Eurasian, 70, 76–77, 100, 105, 112, 129, 148, 191–92, 202, 206, 210, 253, 380; French, 233, 423; in German empire, 347, 350–52, 367, 372, 398–99, 449; Germanic, 41, 82, 87, 126; Greek, 42, 62, 75, 385; in Habsburg empire, 347–48, 350, 361–64; Indonesian, 417; mixity of, in Europe, 84, 89, 183, 336, 363; in Ottoman empire, 138, 148, 343, 359–60; as political issue, 344, 350, 356, 359–67, 381, 455; and propagation of orthodox Christianity, 66, 188, 280–81; in Roman and Byzantine empires, 29, 41, 61–62, 64, 82, 445; in Russian

empire, 191–92, 279–81, 354, 356; Slavic, 64; in Soviet and post-Soviet Russia, 397, 455; in Spanish empire, 145, 167–68; Turkic, 77, 210, 253, 259–60. *See also* populations

Laos, 298, 299, 416, 417

las Casas, Bartolomé de, 168, 169, 184, 243, 252, 291, 326

Latin. *See* languages: in Roman and Byzantine empires

Latin America, 248, 444; and British imperial interests, 294; and United States, 322–24, 381; *See also* Brazil; Mexico; Spanish empire

Latin kingdoms, 70, 89–90

Latins, in Roman empire, 25, 29–30, 39, 64

Latvia, 274, 356, 381, 395, 432

law: and British empire, 171, 173–74, 176–77, 255, 291, 307, 309, 316; canon, 183; Carolingian, 85; and challenges to imperial rule, 166; in Chinese empires, 46–49, 51–52, 57, 109, 204, 208, 212–13, 218, 294, 296; codes, 36, 51, 64, 109, 142, 194, 229, 232–34, 269, 277, 281–82, 307, 336, 343, 376, 422 ; in colonial Virginia, 173–74, 255; conflicting principles of, 213; customary, 273, 282, 288, 309, 316, 318, 422; and European empires, 146, 288; in French empires, 224, 229, 231–33, 305, 317–18, 376–77, 421–22; in Habsburg empire, 347–48, 361, 362; Hindu, 242; and imperial governance, 25–26, 36, 46–47, 50–51, 57, 64, 72, 109, 142, 168, 177, 283–84, 288, 305, 309, 392; international, 1, 22, 64, 143, 183–84, 213, 294, 296, 315–16, 340, 381–82, 386, 399, 414, 443; Islamic, 70–73, 76, 80, 133, 134, 136, 141–45, 148, 151, 242, 255, 272, 305, 318, 365, 376, 422; and jurists, 6, 36, 88, 109, 168, 174, 239, 279; as *kanun*, 142; and legal pluralism, 30–31, 212, 309; and legal professionals, 36; in Mongol empires, 109; Mosaic, 305; in Ottoman empire, 129, 132–34, 138, 140–45, 148, 183–84, 343–45, 365; and race, 255, 263, 269, 405; Roman, 64, 168, 174, 239; and

Roman empire, 24–28, 30–32, 36–37, 39–41, 57–58; and Russian empire, 194, 196, 199, 218, 271, 273, 277–78, 281–84, 336, 338, 357; and Spanish empire, 168–69; in United States, 260–67, 269–71, 283–85. *See also* citizenship; extraterritoriality; jury, trial by; legitimacy; rights; sovereignty

Lawrence, T. E., 378, 392

League of Nations, 384, 386, 387, 450

Lebensraum, 398

Leclerc, General, 409

legal pluralism, 31

Legislative Commission, 277, 282

legislatures and assemblies: in French empire, 224, 226–27, 377, 423; colonial participation in, 229, 291–92, 377; in Ottoman empire, 344–45, 359–60, 365; in Roman empire, 26–27, 28. *See also* Cortes; Duma; parliaments

legitimacy: assertions of, 6, 15–16, 35–37, 39, 50–51, 58, 84, 121, 166–67, 420, debates over, 6, 15–16, 20, 168–69, 184, 243–45, 332; Mandate of Heaven as, 50, 212, 218. *See also* composite monarchy; empires: criticisms of; law; rights; sovereignty

Lenin, V. I., 20, 313, 354, 393, 394

Leo III (Pope), 84

Leopold, King of Belgium, 315, 320, 321, 400

Lepanto, 127

Levant Company, 17, 172

Li Peng, 442

Liao dynasty, 97

liberalism, liberals: in British empire, 307–8, 311; as challenge to empires, 311, 332–33, 360, 367; in Europe, 332–33; and German empire, 350, 352; and Habsburg empire, 347–50, 361, 367; and Napoleon, 233; in Ottoman empire, 344, 359–60, 367, 379; in Russian empire, 356, 357; and Russian revolution, 393–95; in Spanish empire, 247, 292

Libya, 359

Lincoln, Abraham, 268, 285

Lisbon, 156–59, 221

List, Friedrich, 350, 356

literacy: and Chinese empires, 204, 207, 210; and French revolution, 223; in Habsburg empire, 366; in Rome, 41; and slave revolt, 227

Lithuania, 191, 195, 271, 381, 395, 432. *See also* Poland; Polish-Lithuanian Commonwealth

Litke, Fedor Petrovich, 272

Little Big Horn, battle of, 267

Liu Bang, 42, 50

Livonians, 191, 274

Livy, 25, 26

Lombard Kingdom, 82–85

London, 177, 219, 239, 244, 245, 291, 292, 295, 311, 326, 344, 359, 368, 369, 378, 387, 392, 403, 418, 420, 425

Louis XIV, 182

Louis XVI, 224

Louis the Pious, 86

Louisiana, 234, 258

Louisiana purchase, 252, 263

Lueger, Karl, 361, 362

Lumumba, Patrice, 437

Luoyang, 50, 54

Luther, Martin, 122

Lutherans, 183, 274

Lviv (Lemberg), 347

Macao, 156, 203, 215, 300

Macedonia, 30, 355, 358, 367

Machiavelli, 146

Madagascar, 422

Madeira, 154

Madras, 173, 243

Madrid, 169, 245, 322

Magellan, Ferdinand, 124

Mahmud II, 342

Malay Peninsula, 151, 156, 409, 418

Malaya, 300, 407–8, 419

Malayan Union/Federation, 418

Malays, 151, 155, 159–60, 418

Malaysia, 418, 454

Malians, 10

Malta, 244

Mamluk empire, 78, 90, 105, 112, 136, 446

mamluks, 76, 91

Manchukuo, 400–402

Manchuria, 45, 97, 101, 206, 212, 216, 302–3, 356, 399–400, 408, 441

Manchus, 101, 205–15, 218, 296–97, 388–89, 400, 408, 444. *See also* Jurchens; Qing dynasty

mandarins, 298, 306

Mandate of Heaven, 50, 107, 200, 207, 212, 218

mandates, of League of Nations, 383, 386–87

manifest destiny, 251, 456

Manila, 151, 153, 298, 323

Manuel II, 129

Maoris, 300

maps, map-making: and Mongol empires, 110; in Qing and Russian empires, 215

Mara, 131, 134

Maria Theresa, 346

Marie Antoinette, 224

maritime empires, 118, 149–84. *See also* economies, imperial; European empires

Marmara, Sea of, 129

Maronites, 346, 430

marriage: in Qing dynasty, 211; in Russian empire, 216; in United States, 270. *See also* polygamy

Mars, 38

Martel, Charles, 82

Martinique, 228, 387

Marx, Karl, 237, 354, 393

Marxism, 357, 400, 404. *See also* communism; socialism

Mary of Hungary, 122

Mary Tudor, 126

masculinity, 309, 318

Mau Mau, 423

mawali, 77

May Fourth Movement, 388

Maya empire, 10, 167

Mazepa, Ivan, 274

Mazower, Mark, 406

Mecca, 71–75, 78, 141, 145, 181, 355, 378, 447

medicine, 110. *See also* disease

Medina, 72–74, 78, 141, 360

Mediterranean Sea: and Algeria, 305, 426; and connections to Asia, 56, 62, 69, 92, 110–11, 136, 143–44, 148, 149, 170, 172, 339; and Ottoman-Habsburg conflict, 121–23, 127, 133, 152, 446; and Russia, 271, 341; as space of empire-building, 3, 12, 23, 24, 29–30, 35, 41–45, 56, 61, 66, 68, 70, 75, 85, 88, 89, 94, 117–18, 121, 128, 132, 143, 148, 150, 154, 244, 445–46

Mehmed Ali, 304, 338, 342

Mehmet II, 132, 134, 143

Mehmet V, 359

Meiji dynasty, 302

Melaka, 151, 153, 156, 159, 160, 298

merchants. *See* commercial networks

Merkits, 100

Merovingian dynasty, 82

Mesopotamia, 23, 154, 378, 382, 392

mestizaje, 164, 166, 246

Mexico, 19, 127, 163, 164, 166, 167, 252, 258–59, 324, 381

Mexico City, 258

Michigan, 265

Middle East, 1, 24, 108, 110, 387, 415, 425, 453, 457; and post-imperial order, 415, 429–432, 457; after fall of Ottoman empire, 430, 457; in World War I, 377–80; after World War I, 382–86; in World War II, 405

migrations. *See* labor: and migration; populations: unmixing of; settlers and settlement; slave trade

Mikhail Romanov, 196, 195

military: and air power, 392, 430; and armed commerce, 150, 154, 156–57, 161; in British empire, 162, 171, 234–35, 242, 244, 292–94, 308, 310, 340, 372–73, 375, 378, 400; in Byzantine empire, 66–70; in Carolingian empire, 81, 83–84, 91; in Chinese empires, 46–49, 53–54, 201, 205–9, 218, 450; colonial contributions to, in world wars, 375–77, 407, 418; defeats of European invasions, 315; in Dutch empire, 162; doctrines, German, 372, 374; in French empire, 224, 304–5, 317, 340, 377, 400; in German empire, 332–33, 372–74, 377; in Habsburg empire, 332–33, 346, 348–50, 365; in India, 308, 310; in Islamic empires, 73, 446; in Japanese empire, 298, 302, 357, 388, 399–402, 407–8; mobility of, 93, 99, 156, 288, 316; in Mongol empires, 97–99, 103–4, 107–8, 114, 446; in Napoleonic empire, 228, 232–33; and naval competition, 19, 30, 67, 127, 131–32, 139, 144, 152, 162, 234–35, 244, 292, 302, 337–38, 341–42, 357, 372–73, 375, and nomads, 43,

97, 445; in Ottoman empire, 127, 131–32, 138–39, 144–45, 172, 304, 337, 339–43, 359–60, 365, 378–79, 385, 450; and People's Republic of China, 440–41; in Roman empire, 28, 30, 33–34, 39, 56; in Russian empire, 186, 332–33, 353–55, 357, 365; in Spanish empire, 120–21, 127, 145–47, 163, 170; of United States, 265–66, 268, 411, 429; in USSR, 397–98, 427, 429, 433, 435; use of indigenous troops in, 163, 242, 308, 310, 315, 317, 378. *See also* conquest; guns; Janissaries; mamluks; technology: European advantage in; weapons

millet system, 358

Milosevic, Slobodan, 436

Minas Gerais, 157

Minerva, 38

Ming dynasty, 112, 150, 201–7, 209–12; anti-foreign strategy in, 202–3; cultural flourishing of, 204; economy of, 203–5; expansion of, 203; and Mongols, 206; origins of, 202; relations with nomads of, 202–6; sea voyages under, 152–53, 203, 447; vulnerability of, 205–6; and Yuan, 202–4. *See also* Chinese empires

mining: in Africa, 154, 319–20, 411; in Asia, 299–300, 407, 418; and labor, 164, 320, 325; in South America, 123–24, 163, 157; and types of empire, 150; in the United States, 265–66. *See also* copper; gold; silver; tin

missionaries, missions, 6, 12, 16; and African society, 154, 291, 315, 317, 326; American, 455, 457; in China, 297; and nineteenth-century colonization, 306; and education, 317; and emancipation, 291; in Hawaii, 268, 322; in India, 308–9; to Native Americans, 257–59, 267; in Ottoman empire, 344–45; in Russian empire, 279–281, 336, 397; in Spanish empire, 127, 166–68. *See also* Catholicism; Christianity; Protestantism

Mississippi River, 254, 258, 262, 263

mita, 164

modernity: assertions of, 287–88; and problem of colonialism, 328

Modun, 45

Mogilev, 275

Moldavia, 337

monarchy, composite, 120–22

monasteries, 64, 69, 82, 84, 86, 91

Mongke, 105–8

Mongol empires, 4, 9, 13, 90, 93–115, 172, 446; administrators in, 107–8, 115; alphabets used by, 102; and artisans, 93, 100, 103–4, 111, 115; breakdown of, 111–14; and Buddhism, 105, 109; and China, 107–8; and clergy, 103–4, 140; communications in, 109–11, 115; conflicts among, 112; and diplomacy, 102, 105–6, 115; dual governance in, 114; dynastic succession in, 105–6, 108, 114; economic expansion under, 111; expansion of, 100, 102–6, 112; and Islam, 105, 109, 115; impact of, 4, 18, 90, 93, 103–4, 111, 114–15, 446; law in, 109; and local authorities, 115; and medicine, 110; officials in, 107–8; peace in, 93, 104–6, 111, 114, 154, 185; and protection of trade, 103–4, 109–11; recognition of difference in, 4, 102, 115; registration of population in, 107; and religion, 13, 102, 108–9, 111, 114; repertoires of, 4, 104, 106–11; sovereignty in, 107, 114–15, 189; succession in, 104–6; taxation in, 107. *See also* arts and sciences: in Mongol empires; Astrakhan khanate; Chagatai khanate; Chinggis Khan; commercial networks: between Europe and Asia; Crimean khanate; Eurasia; Eurasian empires; Il-Khan empire; Kipchak khanate (Golden Horde); military: in Mongol empires; nomads; Russian empire: and Mongols; Tamerlane; trade: and Mongol empires; Yuan dynasty; Zunghar empire

Mongol khans, 13, 18, 106, 108–109, 111. *See also* Batu; Chinggis Khan; Hulegu; Khubilai Khan; Mongke; Ogodei; Oljeitu

Mongolia, 45, 49, 93, 96, 97, 99, 103, 105, 202, 206, 207

Mongols, 93–99; between China and Russia, 185, 213–18; conquests by, 78, 90, 93, 102–6, 188; food of, 94–95, 110; genetic legacy of, 103; marriage practices of, 103; merged with other peoples, 112; military organization of, 97–99, 107–8; origins of, 97; as people in Republic of China, 389; religion of, 96–97; and *Secret History of the Mongols*, 210; social organization of, 94–99; statecraft of, 13; succession practices of, 96, 104, 106, 108; and trade, 255. *See also* Chinese empires: and Mongols; Eurasia; Eurasian empires; Mongol empires

monopolies: in overseas trade, 124, 150, 156, 159–60, 172–73, 181; fear of, and preemptive colonization, 288, 314, 324; and Soviet state, 434

monotheism: as constraint on empires, 2, 12–13, 38, 40, 457; as foundational principle, 2, 4, 17–18, 40, 61–62, 65, 87–88, 90, 444–45; and politics of difference, 65, 91–92

Montenegro, 358, 367

Montesquieu, 277

Mormons, 270

Morocco, 17, 299, 387, 403, 421

Morrill Act, 270

Moscow, 105, 185, 189–91, 190–95, 197, 274, 387, 393, 396, 403, 433, 435, 441

Moses, 71, 141

Mostar, 362

Mosul, 382

Mozambique, 156, 157, 312, 428, 429

Muawiyah, 74

muftis, 142, 279, 280

Mughal empire, 4, 114, 160, 172–73, 181, 183, 200, 242–43, 306–8, 311

Muhammad, 72–73, 75, 88, 111, 141, 378, 390

Mukden, battle of, 357

mullahs, 280

Murad II, 134

Muscovite princes, 112, 190–91, 193. *See also* Riurikids

Muscovite Russia, 190–96; diversity of, 191; expansion of, 190–92; and intermediaries, 193, 196; marriage politics in, 190, 193; and Mongols, 189–96, 446; and Orthodox church, 194, 196. *See also* Kipchak khanate (Golden Horde); Russian empire

Muscovy. *See* Muscovite Russia

Muslim League, 419

Muslims: and Arab nationalism, 384; in China, 21, 201, 204, 208, 210–12, 296–97, 389, 441, 455; in contemporary political networks, 430, 457; in French empire, 305, 422, 426; in Habsburg empire, 350, 362; in India, 115, 117, 310–12, 390–91, 404, 418–19; and Mongols, 102, 109–10, 112, 113; in Philippines, 323; in Russian empire, 191, 218, 271–72, 279–80, 341, 355, 394–95, 398, 457; in southeast Asia, 159; in trade networks, 132, 154, 159; in World War I, 378. *See also* Islamic empires; Ottoman empire

Mutiny (Indian), 310

Nagasaki, 409

Nahuatl, 167

Nanjing, 203, 296, 298, 402

Naples, 120, 126, 232

Napoleon III, 235, 338, 348; as Emperor of Arabs, 305

Napoleon Bonaparte, 15, 17, 87, 220, 225, 228–35, 244, 246, 248, 272, 282, 292, 333–35, 340, 350, 370, 448, 449

Napoleonic code, 229, 232, 233. *See also* law: in French empire

Napoleonic empire, 225, 229–35, 448–49; defeat of, by other empires, 234; "Frenchness" of, 233; and Louisiana, 234; modernizing vs. restorationist tendencies in, 229–35; overseas, 228, 233–34; and restoration of slavery, 228

Narragansett Indians, 256, 257

Nasser, Gamal Abdel, 426, 428

nation, idea of, 1–11, 219–21, 245–47, 449, 458; in Austria, 361; and British Commonwealth, 389; in China, 389; and colonial empires, 21, 289, 305, 318; in Egypt, 304, 361–63; "ethnic" vs. "civic" conceptions of, 10, 20; in Europe, 219–21, 332, 336, 366–68; and European Union, 439; in France, 223–25, 228, 235, 318, 438; in German empire, 350–52, 398; in Great Britain, 177, 300, 438; in Habsburg empire, 347–50; and "horizontal" affinity, 14, 427; in India, 312; in Japan, 302; and multinational polities, 362, 365, 395, 397, 433; in Napoleonic empire, 229, 232–35; and Native Americans, 251, 263–64, 266, 284; and Nazis, 398–400; in Ottoman empire, 13, 20, 358–60, 379; relation to empire of, 7–10, 16, 19, 183, 219–21, 234, 245, 248–50, 289, 293, 305, 312, 314, 332, 348–52, 358, 360, 363–68, 387, 398–99, 413–15, 427, 450; and rights, 7, 224, 450; in Rome, 26, 31, 36, 65; in Russian empire, 20, 273, 286, 336–37; and self-determination doctrine, 380–82, 387–88; in Spanish America, 245–47, 249, 293; in Turkey, 387; in United States, 219, 249, 251, 263–64, 266–70; in USSR, 380, 395–96. *See also* difference; empires; nation-state; nationalism; populations

nation-state, 1–8, 443, 458; alternatives to, 10–11, 245, 414, 421–23, 452–53, 458; concept of, 2–3, 7, 8, 10, 20, 221, 229, 289; and cultural homogenization, 1, 8, 10, 22, 247, 267, 269, 324, 367, 380, 381, 399; equivalence of, 248–49, 382, 414, 427, 438, 443, 452; internal fragmentation of, 1, 405, 417, 431; and international bodies, 384, 386, 414, 429, 450; and mixity of populations, 368, 381, 385, 449; politicians' interest in, 425; and post–World War I restructuring, 380–88; as product of decolonization, 1, 9, 21, 414, 438; putative transition to, 2, 7, 9, 20, 183, 219, 413; recent origins of, 1–3; resources of, compared to empires, 15, 16, 22, 294, 314, 372, 453; role of empires in fostering, 9, 332, 336–37, 358, 449; and United States' diplomacy, 410, 414,

Russian empire, 280. *See also* shamanism

Pomeranz, Kenneth, 236

Pompeii, 36

population: of China, 35, 56, 97, 208; of colonies, 288, 321; decline of, in Americas, 19, 127, 150–51, 157, 162–64; decline of, in Anatolia, 385; measures of, 46, 107, 327; of Mongols, 199; of Napoleonic empire, 229; of North America, 238, 253–54, 258; of Rome 35, 56; of Russian serfs, 282; of Vietnam, 299. *See also* census

populations: diversity of, 2–3, 20–21, 23, 59, 62, 71, 115, 172, 199, 220, 251, 274, 281, 328–29, 352, 359, 381; mixing of, 20, 92, 125, 151, 161, 164, 166, 209, 211, 246, 255, 257, 273 299, 314, 322, 367, 381, 404, 419, 458; remixing of, 110, 305, 367; transfers of, 19, 54, 110, 379, 431; surveillance and regulation of, 12, 46–49, 56, 107, 271–72, 307, 316, 325, 327, 335, 338, 343, 459; unmixing of, 379, 381–82, 384–85, 399, 405, 419, 431, 451. *See also* administration; ethnicity; race

porcelain, 152, 153, 204, 205

Port Arthur, 357

Portuguese empire, 153–58, 314; in Africa, 154, 156, 157, 312, 314; and China, 203, 215; decolonization in, 428–29; and domestic weakness of, 153–54, 182, 237; and dynastic politics, 158; Dutch encroachment on, 158–60, 162; expulsion from Japan of, 156; fascist rule in, 439; and independence of Brazil, 248; and maritime exploration, 149, 154–57, 182; and Napoleon, 248; and Ottomans, 145; and slavery, 154–58, 178, 237; in southeast Asia, 155–56; and Spain, 120, 122, 124, 127–28; as territorial empire, 157–58, 168, 248; trading enclaves of, 155–57, 162, 300. *See also* Brazil; Spanish empire

postcolonial states and society, 9, 179, 426, 429, 453–54; and idea of Third World, 427

Postlethwayt, 161

Potemkin, Grigory, 276

pottery, 35, 41

Powhatan, 174, 254

praetor, 28, 30, 31

Praetorian guard, 33, 34

prefects, 17, 68, 232, 233

princely states. *See* India: princely states in

princeps, 32

Princip, Gavrilo, 374

principate, 32, 35

proletariat. *See* class: working proletariat, dictatorship of, 395

property, communal, 284, 354

property, private: abolition of, in USSR, 395; in United States, 259, 266, 268, 284, 456; in Ottoman empire, 343. *See also* land: rights in

protectorates, 7, 17, 289, 299, 304–6, 321, 355, 371, 384, 387, 421

Protestantism, Protestants: in 1830 revolts in Europe, 337; and antislavery movement, 290–91; and British empire, 170–71, 244, 300, 390; and conflict in Europe, 127, 170; conversion to, 122–23; and expansion of British empire, 170–72; in Germany, 122–23, 126, 372; and Habsburg dynasty, 126, 127, 347; and Ottoman empire, 142–43, 345; in United States, 262, 267; and uprisings, 126–27. *See also* Christianity; missionaries; religion

Protocols of Zion, 366

Provisional Government, 394

Prussia: dynastic connections to Russia of, 276, 336; and European conflicts, 220, 234, 274, 331, 333–34, 337, 340–41, 346, 348; and formation of German empire, 350–51, 365, 372; and French revolution, 224. *See also* German empire; Germany and Germanic peoples

Przhevalski horse, 95. *See also* horses

pueblos, 258

Puerto Rico, 9, 247, 292, 293, 321, 323, 456

Pufendorf, Samuel, 127

Pugachev, Emelian, 277, 279, 280

Purchas, 170

Putin, Vladimir, 455

Puyi, 389, 400

Qara Qorum, 105

Qianlong emperor, 202–3, 210, 216–17

Qin dynasty, 42–50, 52, 112, 444, 445; and militarized centralism, 43, 45–46, ; and nomads, 43, 46; origins of, 43–44; public works projects of, 46, 49; violence of, 48. *See also* Chinese empires

Qing dynasty, 185, 206–18, 444; banner system of, 208–9; borders of, 215, 440; and Boxer Rebellion, 298; criticism of foreign origins of, 388–89; and ethnic distinction, 208–9, 213; and Eurasian political practices, 216–18; expansion of, 207–8, 214–15; fall of, 388–89; and Han Chinese, 209–13, 218, 296; and languages, 210; military organization of, 206–9, 218; and Mongols, 185, 212–18; origins of, 206–7; rebellions against, 297–98; reuniting of China by, 207–8, 455; and Russian empire, 185, 213–18, 277; and Taiwan, 214–15; threats to, in nineteenth century, 296–98. *See also* Chinese empires

Quadruple Alliance, 334

Quechua, 168

Quit India Movement, 403

Quran, 71, 72, 80, 142, 279, 280

race: and American actions overseas, 322–24; in American revolution, 240, 255; and arguments against colonization, 293, 322–23, 324, 328; and colonial practices, 15–16, 255, 289–91, 325–26, 352, 427, 451; and "color line," 327; and discrimination, 292, 298, 306, 318–20, 375–76; in European thought, 289, 325, 327–29, 448; and French and Haitian revolutions, 225–26; in German empire, 352; and Japan in Asia, 303, 399, 401–2; and law, 255; and mixing, 20, 125, 161, 164, 165, 226, 246, 255, 257, 299, 322, 404; and Nazi empire, 399–400, 405–6, 451; at Paris Peace Conference, 387; and repudiation of racism by colonial empires, 415, 420, 427;

race (continued)
  in Russian empire, 284, 355,
    357; and science, 325; sharpen-
    ing distinctions of, 20, 255,
    263, 288–92, 325–26; in Span-
    ish Americas, 165; in United
    States, 262–63, 269, 270, 284,
    322–23. See also difference;
    empires: incorporation and
    differentiation in; populations;
    slavery
railroads, 364, 366; and British
    engineers, 94; in Germany,
    351; in India, 310–11; labor for,
    316; in Russia, 340, 355–57; in
    United States, 266, 270
Raj, 311, 403
rajas, 311
ramadan, 72
Rashid al-Din, 103, 111
rebellion. See revolutions and
    rebellions
reconquest, 120, 121, 208
Reconstruction, 150, 269, 432,
    440, 441, 454
Red Army (China), 441
Red Army (USSR), 397–98, 431,
    435, 436
Red Cross, 340
Red Sea, 132, 308
Reich. See German empire; Nazi
    empire
religion: and American empires,
    167, 169; and claims to sov-
    ereignty, 332, 366, 449; and
    conflict between empires, 70,
    88–90, 117, 150; in Habsburg
    empire, 362; and imperial
    practice, 4, 12–13, 15–18,
    37–40, 61–66, 69–80, 84–85,
    90–92, 102, 108–9, 111, 114–15,
    146, 166–67, 186–88, 201–2,
    212, 218, 251, 275, 286, 332,
    360, 362, 444–46, 457; imperial
    origins of, 70–71; imposition
    of, 4, 38, 166–67; and indepen-
    dent churches, 326; and Indian
    National Congress, 403; intol-
    erance of, 119, 121, 133, 143–
    44, 167; and Mongol empires,
    13, 96–97, 102, 107–10, 114–15,
    446; and North American
    colonies, 174; and Ottoman
    empire, 119, 133, 141–45, 148,
    345; and Qing dynasty, 212;
    and Roman empire, 12–13, 24,
    37–41; and Russian empire,
    251, 273, 275, 279–81, 286,

336; schisms in, 18, 61, 65–66,
  74–75, 77, 78, 88, 90, 97, 196,
  445, 446, 457; spread of, 72–74,
  79–80, 91–92, 151, 167; tolerance of, 4, 13, 38, 102, 108, 119,
  143–44, 148, 204, 212, 218, 275,
  279; and trading networks,
  79–80, 133, 181; in USSR,
  397–98; and Yuan dynasty,
  201–2. See also Buddhism;
  Catholic church; Catholic
  monarchy; Christianity;
  crusades; Hinduism; jihad;
  Judaism; Islam; monotheism;
  Muslims; Orthodox church;
  polytheism; Protestantism;
  shamanism
Renaissance, 224
repertoires of rule, 3–8, 16–17,
  184–85, 238, 283, 289, 294,
  299, 301, 305–6, 324, 362,
  400, 405–6, 435, 443–44; and
  mixes of imperial types, 4, 16,
  92, 117–18, 150, 157, 176, 180,
  185–86, 190, 196, 199, 216,
  232, 238, 251, 355–56, 362, 358,
  444, 456; reconfigurations
  of, 17–22, 39–41, 50, 61–62,
  180–82, 188, 229–35, 240 –41,
  287–89, 316, 324–29, 352–64,
  380–89, 393–402, 410–11,
  414–15, 420–23, 438–40, 443–
  53; and types of empires, 3–5,
  7, 12–13, 16, 145–48, 150–57,
  289, 305–6
Republic of Ireland, 390
República de los indios, 164,
  177, 264
republics: Baltic, 432; in China,
  388–89, 408; French, 17, 219,
  225–28, 235, 298, 304–5, 318,
  366, 426; Haitian, 183; idea
  of, in Britain, 238; Irish, 390;
  Latin American, 248, United
  States as, 261–62, 268, 271, 283,
  448; Roman, 11, 24–28, 32,
  35–36, 39, 57–58, 174; in South
  Africa, 319–20; and world
  order 380–81. See also China,
  People's Republic of; Union
  of Soviet Socialist Republics;
  Vietnam, Democratic Republic of
reservations. See Native Americans: reservations for
Residency System (India), 307
resistance, to conquest, 14, 161,
  164, 166, 315, 316, 402, 404.

  See also empires: contingent
    accommodation to; revolu-
    tions and rebellions
Revere, Paul, 239
revolutions and rebellions,
  219–23; of 1830, 337; of 1848,
  292–93, 338, 346–47, 350–51;
  of 1871, 393; in Afghanistan,
  75, 435, 443, 453; in Algeria,
  422, 424, 425–26; anticolonial,
  21, 413–14, 423, 452; and "Arab
  revolt," 378; capitalist, 19,
  221–23, 319, 447; in Chinese
  empires, 20, 42, 45, 54, 112,
  202, 207, 214, 216, 295, 297–98,
  302, 388–89, 417, 440–41; and
  communism, 357, 369, 380,
  393, 395–96, 413–14, 437; in
  communist eastern Europe,
  433, 439; in Cuba, 292–93,
  322; in Czechoslovakia, 427;
  in Egypt, 304, 384; English,
  177; fear of, in United States,
  323–24; in France, 7, 19, 219–
  29, 234, 246–49, 277, 292, 332;
  in French West Africa, 376; in
  German Africa, 316; in Greece,
  336–37; against Habsburgs,
  121, 123–24, 126–27, 331, 337,
  346; in Hungary, 427, 433, 439;
  in India, 310, 390–91; in Indonesia, 301, 415–17; in Iraq, 384,
  387, 391, 392, 429; in Ireland,
  177, 244, 390–91; in Islamic
  empires, 75, 77; in Kenya,
  424; in Madagascar, 422; in
  Middle East, 391–92, 429; in
  Netherlands, 123–24, 126–27,
  158; in North America, 6, 220,
  238–40, 251, 259–60, 447; in
  Ottoman empire, 131, 133,
  139, 144–45, 304, 336–37, 342;
  in Palestine (66 CE), 38; in
  Palestine (twentieth century),
  384, 391, 429; in Philippines,
  322–23; in Portuguese Africa,
  428–29; in Roman empire,
  29, 40; in Russia, 188, 196,
  277, 279, 332, 335, 337–38, 357,
  393–95; in Saint Domingue
  (Haiti), 223, 226–29; by slaves,
  78, 158, 179, 228, 241, 291–92;
  in Spanish America, 164, 166,
  220, 245–48; in Syria, 384,
  387, 391, 429; in Vietnam, 404,
  408–10, 415–17, 422, 437; war
  of 1756–63 and, 220, 239;
  war as catalyst of, 8, 220, 450;

within or against empires,
7, 16, 19, 221, 223, 225–28,
238–40, 245–49, 332, 448; after
World War I, 381, 384, 392. *See
also* civil wars
Rhine River, 38, 85, 232–34, 333
Rhineland, 83
Rhode Island, 268
Rhodesia, 318, 319, 427
rice, 19, 42, 53, 78, 102, 110, 176,
242, 254, 299, 407
Richardson, Robert V., 269
rights: in American revolution,
223; in British empire, 171,
174, 177, 238–39, 253, 257–58,
309, 375, 390, 425; of British
East India Company, 171–73,
242; in Byzantine empire,
67–68; in Chinese empires, 46,
210, 211, 441; claims to, within
empires, 7, 219–20, 249, 326,
332, 344–45, 360, 366, 393, 444,
448; conflicts and negotiations
over, among empires, 144,
172–73, 215, 242, 338–39, 381,
449; differentiated, 29, 142,
251, 273, 305; and empires
overseas, 156, 296, 302, 318,
328, 449–50; of Englishmen,
177, 184, 251–52, 311; equal,
251, 261, 270; in Europe, 5,
120–21, 128, 219–20, 366–67,
422, 425, 440, 445; in ex-
colonial states, 414, 425, 429,
453; in French empire, 18–19,
221, 223–29, 305, 317–18, 328,
376–77, 421–23, 425; in French
revolution, 19, 221, 223–29;
in Greek city-states, 10; in
Habsburg empire, 347–50,
361–62; of intervention,
321–22, 381; of man and of
the citizen, 221, 224, 410; in
mandates and protectorates,
383–84; of minorities, 381;
in Mongol empires, 111; and
nation-state, 10; national, 449;
natural, 7, 220, 260, 273; in
Ottoman empire, 140, 142–43,
183, 343–45, 367; in Palestine,
383, 430; in Roman empire,
12, 28–30, 36, 39, 41–42, 57,
58; in Russia, 194, 196, 199,
251, 273–79, 281–84, 355, 365,
394, 455; in South Africa,
427–29; in Spanish empire,
166; in United States, 249, 251,
260–62, 265–66, 269, 270, 284,

286, 323, 328, 448, 456. *See also*
colonial empires; extraterritoriality; land; law; legitimacy;
property, communal; property,
private; sovereignty; succession
practices; women
Rio de Janeiro, 294
rituals of imperial power, 194; in
Byzantium, 68; in China, 51,
211–12; in Habsburg empire,
361, 363; in Kipchak Khanate,
189; in Napoleonic empire,
230; in Russia, 194, 336. *See
also* legitimacy
Riurik, 186
Riurikids, 186, 188–90, 193, 195,
199. *See also* Kievan Rus'; Rus'
river policy, 299
roads, 24, 30, 45, 49, 56, 66, 81, 92,
172, 265, 316
Robinson, Ronald, 293
Roman empire, 23–42, 444;
adoption of Christianity in,
12–13, 38–42, 59, 61, 65, 445;
cities in, 36; colonies of, 29;
eastern, 62–70; economy
and culture in, 34–38; Greek
influence on, 37; and idea of
civilization, 35–36; institutions
of, 28–34, 39; as model for
empires, 3, 24, 28–29, 41–42,
61, 82, 84–85, 87, 117, 143,
173–74, 197, 362; origins of,
24–25; as republic, 24, 26–27,
31–32; slavery in, 33–35; sovereignty in, 25–33, 56–59; turn
to one-man rule in, 31–33; as
universal empire, 36–38, 40;
weakening of, 39–41, 147. *See
also* Byzantine empire; citizenship; law: in Roman empire;
military: in Roman empire;
religion: and Roman empire
Romania, 355, 367, 398, 405,
431, 433
Romanians, 349, 405
Romanov dynasty, 185, 195–96,
199, 251, 271, 335, 357, 365,
368–69, 377, 394, 435
Romulus, 24
Roosevelt, Franklin D., 431,
432, 436
Rothschild, Anselem, 348
Roxelana. *See* Hurrem
Royal Africa Company, 173
rubber, 299, 320–21, 407, 411, 418
Rus', 103, 105, 107, 185–90;
contacts with Turkic peoples

of, 186; dynastic practices of,
186, 190; princes of, 186; trade
routes of, 186. *See also* Kievan
Rus'; Riurikids
Russian empire, 3, 6, 20, 185–99,
213–18, 220, 251, 271–86,
331–41, 352–58, 449, 451–52,
455, 457; anti-German sentiment in, 393–94; autocracy
in, 335; and Boer war, 320;
and British empire, 271, 337,
358; and Central Asian khanates, 271, 355; conscription in,
323–33, 365; diversity in, 20,
191–92, 195, 201, 251, 271–86,
356–57; dynasties of, 190,
195–96, 199, 217; economy of,
353–56, 365–66; education in,
198, 280–81, 335–36, 356; end
of, 377, 393–95; and Europe,
196–99, 234, 333–41, 352–58,
360, 364–68; expansion of
191–92, 195, 197, 199, 213–24,
251, 253, 254, 271–77, 279, 337,
354–57; impact of French
revolution in, 277; ideology
of, 193–95, 335–36; and Islam,
279–80, 355, 457; Jews in,
275, 355–56; Marxism in, 353;
nationality and nationalism in,
336, 355; and Mongols, 4, 18,
186, 213–18, 281; origins of,
185–90; and Ottoman empire,
271, 337, 338, 341–46, 355, 360,
379; patrimonial principles of,
193–95, 199, 216, 218, 271, 335,
354–58; peasant commune
in, 354; political movements
in, 354, 357; as protector of
Christians, 338–39, 341; and
Qing empire, 214–28, 301;
reform in, 13, 275, 282–84,
335–36, 353–58, 364–67, 394;
religion in, 186–88, 193–94,
196, 198, 275–76, 279–81; and
regulation by groups, 275,
278, 281–82, 284; repertoire of
rule of, 6, 185, 196, 276; rights
in, 251, 273–79, 281–84, 365,
379; Russification in, 356, 360;
sovereignty in, 218, 251, 273,
284, 354, 357; succession in,
210; surveillance and policing
in, 335, 338; in World War I,
371–80, 393–94. *See also* autocracy; Catherine II (the Great);
Crimean war; Daniilovichi;
Duma; emancipation; Kievan

in colonial Americas, 19, 122, 157–58, 164–68, 174, 176, 178–79, 184, 226–29, 237–38, 241, 245–48, 254–55, 258, 268, 290, 292–93, 447–48; debates over, 6, 19, 168–69, 181, 225–26, 229, 241, 244, 249–50, 265, 268, 283, 290–94; and emperor's household, 136–38; empires' importance for, 178–79, 238, 247–48, 290–94, 447; empires' repudiation of, 290–93, 324; and exclusion, 6, 10, 12, 26, 39, 260–61, 265, 270, 284, 456; and Haitian revolution, 225–29, 234, 268; importance to empires of, 178–79, 236–37, 324; in Islamic empires, 75, 77, 78, 91, 445–46; and military and administrative service, 14, 33, 75, 77–78, 80, 90–91, 136–38, 142, 227, 445–46; and Mongols, 103; in Nazi empire, 405, 408; "new system of," 292; in Ottoman empire, 134–38, 140–41, 365; and power of kings, 9, 179; restoration of, by Napoleon, 228; in Roman empire, 33–35, 179; in Russia, 186, 189, 277; and slave revolts, 78, 226, 238, 247–48, 291–93, 448; in southeast Asia, 160; and sultanic concubinage, 134–36, 147; in United States, 236, 249, 251, 255, 260, 266, 268–69, 284, 293, 448. *See also* emancipation; mamluks; serfdom; slave trade

Slavs, 64, 67, 136, 186, 191, 284, 336, 404; and Frankfurt parliament, 346; and German empire, 352; and Nazi empire, 405; religion of, 187, 188. *See also* pan-Slavism

Slovaks, 349, 381

smallpox, 163, 181, 214

Smith, Adam, 244, 290

Smith, John, 254

social contract, 220, 277

Social Democrats, 361, 362, 396

Social Democrats (Habsburg empire), 361–62

social policy: in colonies, 21, 420–22, 449–50; in German empire, 351; in Habsburg empire, 366. *See also* development, economic; states: welfare

socialism, socialists: and British empire, 300; as civilizing project, 452; in Europe, 332, 393, 396; in German empire, 372; in Habsburg empire, 347, 362, 367; and anti-Japanese movements, 408; in Russian empire, 338, 354, 393; in Russian revolution, 394, 395. *See also* communism; Marxism; Union of Soviet Socialist Republics

Socialist International, 396

Société des Amis des Noirs, 225

Solferino, battle of, 340

son of heaven. *See* Mandate of Heaven

Song dynasty, 55, 93, 97, 100, 102, 105, 201, 202, 204

Songhai empire, 10

Sorhokhtani, 108

South America, 7, 10, 117, 164, 245, 249. *See also* Brazil; Portuguese empire; Spanish empire

South Africa, 11, 244, 300, 312, 315, 319–20, 325, 371, 375, 386, 427–29

South Asia, 10, 114, 224, 241, 415, 418. *See also* India; Pakistan

South African Company, 315

South Carolina, 176

South Korea, 454

southeast Asia: and Chinese empires, 203, 205, 298; colonization of, 298–301, 416, 452; commerce in, 5, 71, 97, 149, 161–63, 173, 205, 241, 298, 447; decolonization of, 415–18; European merchant empire and, 155, 159–62, 172; Islam in, 79, 445; Japanese conquest of, 21, 407–10, 438; post-colonial prosperity of, 454; United States in, 321–23, 399, 407–8, 436. *See also* Burma; Cambodia; Indochina; Laos; Malaya; Philippines; Thailand; Vietnam

Southwest Africa, 315, 316, 375, 400

sovereignty: changing nature of, 1, 7, 10–11, 16, 22, 145, 180–84, 219–20, 225, 240, 249–50, 306, 320, 332, 344, 347–48, 360, 364, 386–87, 393, 422–23, 435–36, 439, 443, 456, 458–59; and company government, 17, 160–62, 172, 241–43, 309, 315, 320–21; dynastic, 108, 114, 189–90, 193, 338, 347; in ex-

colonial states, 21, 427–28, 454, 458; fictions of, 17, 299, 370, 407, 414, 426, 429, 432–33, 458; intrusions upon, 294, 323–24, 443, 456; and juridical equivalence, 370, 429; layered, shared, partial, and overlapping, 1–2, 10–11, 16–17, 22, 87, 120–21, 172, 177, 181–84, 300–301, 305–6, 309, 312, 322, 332–33, 346, 387–90, 393, 413, 420–23, 439–40, 456, 459; and mandates, 386–87; and nation-state, 1–2, 7, 20, 454, 458; national vs. imperial, 220, 225–29, 234–35, 249–50; of Native Americans, 262; opposed claims to, in Americas, 174; overlordship and, 189, 207; and overseas settlers, 177; personalization of, 114; popular, 6, 7, 20, 28, 57, 177, 219–20, 225, 249–50, 312, 327, 348, 447; of protectorates, 299, 387, 421; of seas, 156; and Westphalia, Treaty of, 7, 182–83; universal, 212. *See also* emperor; European Union; khan; legitimacy; nation, idea of; succession practices

Soviet Union. *See* Union of Soviet Socialist Republics

Spain, fascism in, 439; Islamic polities in, 74–75, 83

Spanish empire, 117–28, 143–48, 162–70, 245–48; administrative practices of, 125–26, 164, 166, 168; in Caribbean, 155, 247, 290, 292–93, 321–23; as Catholic monarchy, 15, 121, 123, 162, 166–70; central control in, 124, 126–27, 145, 168, 258; compared with Ottoman empire, 117–19, 145–48; constitution of (1812), 247, 311; debates over, 19, 168, 247–49, 292–93; dynastic shifts in, 122, 245; emancipation in, 292–93; extension of, 118, 124, 128, 145; finances of, 122–24, 127, 162, 246; and indigenous peoples of Americas, 162–70, 247, 258, 265–66; and intolerance of religious difference, 119, 121, 144–45; loss of colonies of, 245–48, 322–23; and Napoleonic empire, 246; national ideas in, 245–47, 249, 322; in North America, 175,

Spanish empire *(continued)*
258, 265–66; origins of, 5,
117, 120–23, 145; and Ottoman empire, 117, 123, 127,
144–45; in Philippines, 127,
128, 292, 321–23; race mixing in, 164–65; reforms in,
246; repertoires of, 145–47;
and settlers, 126, 162–70, 174;
and slave trade, 155, 168, 181;
and slavery, 164, 166–68, 178,
247–48, 290, 292–93; in South
and Central America, 124–26,
162–70, 174, 245–48; and wars
with England, 127, 170; and
United States, 322–23. *See also*
Habsburg empire; economies,
imperial; military: in Spanish empire; revolutions and
rebellions: against Habsburgs;
revolutions and rebellions: in
Spanish America
Speranskii, Mikhail, 281
spices, 5, 110, 124, 152, 154, 155,
157, 159, 181
Sri Lanka, 443. *See also* Ceylon
St. Petersburg, 340, 394
Stalin, Joseph, 397, 398, 431–33,
439, 452
states: and chartered companies,
161–62, 174, 176–77; consolidation of, 7–8, 237; fiscal-military, 176, 235; imperial roots
of, 176–77; multinational, 1;
and territoriality, 182, 414;
types of, 8–11, 180, 182–83,
305–6, 397; in United States,
261; welfare, 351, 413, 420–22.
See also empires; nation-state;
postcolonial states and society
steppe, 94, 257; communications and trade across, 43, 110,
192; empires formed on, 9,
13, 45, 77, 94, 445–46; leaders
on, 96–97, 104; migrations
from, 39; Russian conquest
and settlement of, 218, 276,
279, 281–82. *See also* Eurasia;
Eurasian empires; Mongol
empires; nomads
Stoler, Ann Laura, 318
strikes. *See* labor: and strikes
succession practices: in Byzantine empire, 68, 69; in
Carolingian empire, 82, 85–87;
of Chinese empires, 210; compared, 91; dynastic, 74, 105–6,
108, 114, 122, 126–27, 134,

189; Eurasian, 186; in Islamic
empires, 74–75, 78; in Mongol
empires, 96, 106, 114, 188–89;
Mongol-Turkic, 133–34; in
Ottoman empire, 133–36; in
Portuguese empire, 127; in
Roman empire, 33–34; of Rus'
princes, 186,-188; in Russian
empire, 193, 199, 210; in Spanish empire, 120, 122, 126–27.
See also Chinese empires:
dynastic cycles in
Sudan, 342, 455
Suez Canal, 294, 300, 304, 378,
426
Suez crisis, 426–27, 436
suffrage, 225, 351–52, 361, 365,
421. *See also* elections
sugar: in Atlantic empires, 19,
122, 124, 155, 157, 158, 162, 176,
178, 179, 182, 219, 223, 224,
228, 234, 236–39, 248, 254,
267, 290–92, 294, 323, 447;
consumption of, 236, 294; and
empire connections, 7, 154.
See also economies, imperial; planters and plantations;
slavery
Sugar and Stamp Acts, 239
Sui dynasty, 54, 97
Sukarno, Achmed, 404, 408, 409,
417, 427
Suleiman the Magnificent, 15,
117–19, 135, 136, 138, 143–46,
193–94, 342
sultan, sultans: Mamluk, 105, 141;
Seljuk, 77; in southeast Asia,
151, 159, 300
sultan, Ottoman, 132–48, 172,
304, 337–38, 358–60; deposi-
tion of, 342, 359, 365; as guardian of Islam, 141–42, 148, 345,
358, 390; harem of, 134–36,
147; household and officials
of, 119, 132–39, 142, 145,147 ;
and reform, 343–45, 359–60.
See also succession practices: in
Ottoman empire
Sumatra, 161, 162
Sun Yat-sen, 388, 389
Sunnis, 1, 74, 75, 77, 78, 90, 109,
142, 430. *See also* Islam
Supreme Court (United States),
263, 265, 348
Suzdal, 188
Sweden, 182, 183, 191, 195,197,
220, 274, 340, 394
Switzerland, 10, 232, 394

Syria, 38, 68, 69, 73–75, 78, 80,
88, 91, 133, 141, 143, 342, 360,
378–79, 382–84, 387, 391,
429–30

Taiping rebellion, 295, 297
Taiwan, 160, 200, 207, 214, 302–3,
399, 452
Tamerlane, 113–14, 129, 172, 191,
311, 457
Tang dynasty, 54, 97, 204
Tanganyika, 315, 316, 375
Tangut empire, 100, 102, 103, 201
tanistry, 96, 104, 106, 135, 193, 210
Tanzimat, 343, 344, 365
Tatar yoke, 194
Tatars, 99, 100, 136, 191, 194, 216,
274, 277, 280, 281, 341, 432
taxation: collectors of, 30, 33,
39, 50, 133, 136, 138–39, 243,
310, 316; on commerce, 110,
215; and company rule, 161,
242; and dangers of declining
revenue, 41, 69; and depression
of 1930s, 342; differential, 73,
76–77, 91, 142, 275, 281–82;
and fiscal-military state, 176;
as imperial necessity, 12–13,
34–35, 41, 46, 49, 56, 66–67,
84–85, 104, 107–8, 133, 136,
140, 152, 189–91, 193, 198, 215;
and "Indians not taxed," 270;
and labor or military service,
46, 49; and land revenue state,
242, 309; and peasantry, 152,
205; and political rights, 27,
239; regularizing collection
of, 229, 270, 343; resistance to,
239, 403; and revolutions, 224,
239, 259; and tax farming, 139,
342. *See also* administration;
tribute
tea, 95, 153, 172, 178, 204, 236,
239, 294, 296, 309
technology: and British empire,
236, 296; in Chinese empires,
46, 201, 203–4, 214, 246; European advantage in, 6, 145, 180,
252, 259, 288, 296, 315, 324–25,
327, 340, 351, 449, 450; and
German empire, 351, 377, 438;
maritime, 132, 139, 145, 151,
154, 162, 180; of Mongols, 4,
18, 93, 95, 216, 259, 445; Russian acquisition of, 196–97,
342, 353; of United States,
411. *See also* industrialization;
weapons

508   Index

Temujin, 99–101. *See also* Chinggis Khan

Tengri, 96, 101

terror: and antistate movements,
354, 457; as imperial practice,
13, 105, 156, 288, 392, 398, 418,
422, 426

Texas, 252, 258, 265

Thailand, 151, 156, 160

themata, 67

Theodora, 62, 64

Theodosius, 64

Thessalonica, 64

Third Reich, 398, 399. *See also*
Nazi empire

Third Republic, 298, 318. *See also*
French empire

Third World, 414, 427, 453

thirteen colonies, 220, 221, 238,
240, 245

Thirteenth Amendment, 269,
270

Thirty years' war, 182; of twentieth century, 369

Thrace, 129, 132

Three Emperors' League, 352

Tiberius, 32

Tiberius Gracchus, 31

Tibet, 21, 105, 107, 185, 200–202,
204, 207, 212, 215, 441, 455

timar, 139

Time of Troubles, 195, 196

Timor, 300, 417

tin, 172, 299, 411, 418

Tippu Sultan, 243

Tito, Josip Broz, 439

tobacco, 174, 176, 254, 255, 294

Togo, 375

Togrul, 99–101

Tolstoy, Leo, 340

Tolui, 105, 106, 108

torture, 277, 422, 423, 426

Toulon, 144

Toussaint L'Ouverture, 227,
228, 450

trade: and British empire,
170–73, 176–77, 237, 240,
294–96, 315, 324; and Carolingian empire, 85; and Chinese
empires, 43, 97, 152–53, 203,
206, 294–98, 303, 447, 455;
and creeping colonization,
241, 306; and Dutch empire,
159–61; and contestation over
Indian Ocean, 156, 159–60,
162, 181; and industrial revolution, 236–37, 294; and Islamic
empires, 71, 78–79, 92; and

Mongol empires, 95, 103–4,
109, 111, 115; and Native
Americans, 254–55, 258, 262;
and Ottoman empire, 128,
132–33, 152, 172, 303, 341,
365; and Roman empire, 35;
and Russian empire, 189–91,
354; and scramble for Africa,
314–15; Soviet-German, 397;
and southeast Asian societies, 151–52, 159, 299–300; and
Spanish empire, 124–27, 182,
246; and state formation, 9–10,
124–27, 132–33, 159–60, 182,
189–91, 446–47; United States
and, 323, 437, 452; and USSR,
398. *See also* British East India
Company; cocoa; commercial
networks; cotton; Dutch East
India Company; economies,
imperial; fur; gold; monopolies; opium; palm oil; silver;
slave trade; spices; sugar; tea

Transjordan, 383

treaties: of Adrianople, 337;
of Brest-Litovsk, 394; of
Guadalupe Hidalgo, 265; of
Greenville, 262–63; Horse
Creek, 265; of Kiakhta, 216;
of Nerchinsk, 215–16; of
Paris, 262; of Rome, 439; of
Waitangi, 300; of Westphalia,
7, 182–83; of Unkiar-Skelessi,
338; of Versailles, 386

Trebizond, 93

tribe: definitions of, 9, 95; and
empire formation, 9; leaders
of, 93. *See also* Eurasia; Eurasian empires; nomads

tribute, 12, 94, 59, 102, 104, 144,
156, 164, 191, 201–3, 206, 216,
273, 282, 294

Trojans, 24

tsar, tsars, 129, 194–98, 258, 274,
275, 283, 335, 346, 353–58, 360,
394, 451; as title, 194. *See also*
Caesar; Russian empire

Tunisia, 17, 30, 299, 421

Turkestan, 355, 366, 394

Turkey: formation of, 385–86,
451; and nation-building, 387,
451; *See also* Ottoman empire

Turkic empires, 10, 18, 96–97,
445–46. *See also* Eurasia; Eurasian empires; khaqan; Seljuk
empire

Turkic speakers: in Anatolia,
129; and Byzantine empire,

67, 97; conversion to Islam of,
76; Eurasian origins of, 94; in
Il-Khans' areas, 112; in Islamic
empires, 77; marriage practices
of, 134; under Mongol rule,
111; and origins of Mamluk
empire, 78; and Ottoman
empire, 118, 119, 129, 138,
147–48, 345, 349, 359–60, 368,
379, 446; and Qing dynasty,
213–15; and Russian empire,
186, 191–92, 213–14, 355, 397;
and Tang dynasty, 54. *See also*
Eurasia; Eurasian empires;
Keriats; Kipchaks; Mongol
empires; Ottoman empire;
Seljuk empire; Tamerlane;
Turkestan; Turkic empires;
Turks; Uighurs

Turkification, 359, 451

Turkmenistan, 1

Turks: forced relocations of,
379, 385, 431; in World War I,
379–80. *See also* Balkans: wars
in; Committee of Union and
Progress; Ottoman empire;
Turkey; Turkic speakers; Young
Turks

Uighurs, 96, 97, 100, 102, 107,
108, 210

Ukraine, 103, 105, 135, 191, 196,
234, 271, 273–75, 347, 395–96,
398, 406, 432; and Orthodox
clergy, 274–75; and Russian
empire, 191, 196, 273–75,
277; in Russian revolution,
394–95; in USSR, 396, 398,
406, 431–32

Ukrainians: in Polish-Lithuanian
Commonwealth, 274; in
Habsburg empire, 349; in German empire, 351; in Poland,
381, 431; in Russian revolution, 394; and Nazi empire,
399, 405–6; in USSR, 431

ulus, 104–6, 113, 114, 189

Umayyad caliphate, 74–75,
78–79, 82, 91, 445

umma, 72, 75–77, 80, 88, 92

Uniate church, Uniates, 274–75,
347

Union Act, 244

Union of Soviet Socialist
Republics (USSR), 393–98,
406, 431–36, 451–52; breakdown of, 1, 415, 433–36; and
central and eastern Europe,